JONATHAN EDWARDS

Jonathan Edwards

REPRESENTATIVE SELECTIONS, WITH
INTRODUCTION, BIBLIOGRAPHY, AND NOTES

BY

CLARENCE H. FAUST

AND

THOMAS H. JOHNSON

Revised Edition

American Century Series

HILL AND WANG — NEW YORK

Standard Book Number: 8090–0047–4
Library of Congress Catalog Card Number: 62–9490

FIRST AMERICAN CENTURY SERIES EDITION FEBRUARY 1962
SECOND PRINTING NOVEMBER 1963
THIRD PRINTING FEBRUARY 1965
FOURTH PRINTING JANUARY 1966
FIFTH PRINTING DECEMBER 1966
SIXTH PRINTING AUGUST 1967
SEVENTH PRINTING JUNE 1968
EIGHTH PRINTING FEBRUARY 1969

The bibliography in this American Century Series edition of
Jonathan Edwards has been revised and brought up to date.
The original edition was published in the American Writers
Series, under the general editorship of Harry Hayden Clark.

Manufactured in the United States of America

PREFACE

The editors of this volume have attempted in their introduction, selections, and notes to present all the important aspects of Edwards as a man, writer, and thinker. Modern readers will find ample evidence here, not only of Edwards's literary power, but of his gentleness of spirit—a quality too often concealed by the popular notion that he was foremost a preacher of hell-fire sermons. The dignified humility of Edwards as a man stirs our admiration, but the robustness of his mind challenges an equally vigorous response. The philosophical system to which Edwards devoted his large powers for a period of almost forty years is one of great depth and complexity, therefore *caveat lector:*—he must not expect an analysis of Edwards's views to be easy reading, but he may be certain that a study of them will enrich the spirit.

Section II of the Introduction, "Jonathan Edwards as a Thinker," is the work of Clarence H. Faust, and Sections I and III, "Jonathan Edwards, the Man" and "Edwards as a Man of Letters," as well as the Notes at the end of the volume, are the work of Thomas H. Johnson.

Acknowledgments are gratefully made to Andover Theological Library, to the New York Public Library, and to the libraries of Princeton University and Yale University for their gracious permission to examine manuscript material, some of which is now published for the first time.

To Professor Kenneth B. Murdock and Dr. Perry Miller of Harvard University go our thanks for reading the introduction. Indebtedness is gratefully acknowledged also to Dr. R. S. Crane of the University of Chicago, under whose guidance and encouragement the study which furnished the basis for the part of the introduction on "Edwards as a Thinker" was undertaken; and to Professor Percy H. Boynton, Dr. Napier Wilt, and Dr. Walter Blair of the University of Chicago for reading that section of the manuscript. Likewise the editor responsible for the section of the introduction on "Edwards as a Man of Letters" wishes to acknowledge the thoughtful attention which Professor F. O. Matthiessen of Harvard University gave to his doctoral dissertation—a thesis that furnished much of the substance imbedded in that section.

In conclusion, it is apposite for the editors to recall Falstaff's injunction to the Lord Chief Justice that "it was always yet the trick of our English nation, if they have a good thing, to make it too common." So much have they depended for helpful suggestion and ready assistance upon the scholarship of the general editor of this series, Professor Harry H. Clark of the University of Wisconsin, that they have all but taken his generosity for granted.

C. H. F.
T. H. J.

CONTENTS

Letters

INTRODUCTION

I. JONATHAN EDWARDS, THE MAN

Jonathan Edwards died in Princeton, New Jersey, on March 22, 1758, at the age of fifty-four. During the following week newspapers from Boston to Williamsburg printed notices of his death and eulogized the theologian whose writings were admired both here and abroad wherever the doctrines of Calvin found adherents. At the apex of his career, with increasing rather than diminishing productivity—(he was planning *A History of the Work of Redemption* on epic lines)—he had submitted to smallpox vaccination and had thereby been fatally stricken by the disease. He had served as president of Princeton but five weeks.

What manner of being was he, who today is remembered—if at all—as a preacher of the imminence of hell-fire? How can we, to whom in general theology is a very special field, understand that two hundred years ago religion in many of the American colonies was a subject so enthralling and vital that it occupied a conspicuous section of men's daily lives? Perhaps a solution of the second question will be evident as soon as the answer to the first has been revealed, for Edwards was a representative product, both in background and temperament, of the very elements of spiritual enlightenment for which all good Puritans yearned with a consuming ardor.

Yet however zealously the upright New Englander might center his heart upon "otherworldliness," he never forgot that for the present his path led through the pleasant and really joyous valleys of this world. The New England colonies had been founded and were controlled for several generations by a theocratic group—by men who believed that the Word of God was sufficient for all governance, that the Bible was the law of

the land, and the clergy its sole interpreters. Such a tenet was
not new. It was but another manifestation, modified to its own
faith, of various earlier church empires. Indeed, the priestly
kings of Lake Nemi and the Golden Bough had but moved to
a new wilderness. Yet New England theocracy was advanced
far beyond mere animism, and it was well aware that it could
thrive at its best only when the laity as well as the clergy were
educated and enlightened. Hence we find a support of both
secondary and higher education rarely known to groups of
colonizers, and congregations, therefore, that were able from
the start to give intelligent ear to theological discussions. Their
conception of religion, though profoundly serious, was not
lugubrious. It was exciting because it was vital, and vital
because those who professed it understood it and drew from it
spiritual aid that enlivened and directed the affairs of life.
Edwards himself gave expression to theocratic principles so
ardently that to see him clearly as a man, a thinker, and a writer,
is to envisage much that was at the heart of Colonial *kultur*.

We see, however, but one figure on the coin, if we look only
at the obverse side. New and revolutionary features were being
stamped on the reverse, very opposite in character:—humanitarian, they are called, and they emphasize the belief that man
in the savage or "natural" state is a better creature than when
he has been educated. Under theocracy sound learning was
assumed the root of true religion, but for the humanitarians too
much learning was a dangerous thing; for them the inner light
needed not training but release, that the splendor might escape.
These doctrines, taught later in various forms by Rousseau and
the French Revolutionists, had earlier found expression in the
philosophy of the deists and the Quakers, and indeed by such
leaders as John Wesley and George Whitefield—itinerant
exhorters whose stress upon their faith that conversion, or the
conviction that a "new light" had shone upon them, gave rise to
a tide of revival meetings which Edwards supported.

Incompatible as these philosophies are, we see Edwards trying to reconcile them as their vectors cut through his career, and the tragedy that overtook him may be perceived more clearly if the student watches their intersections without losing sight of their direction. It is in moments when Edwards attempted to bring his theocratic and humanitarian principles together, when he sought to establish in logical relationship the intellectual love of God with human emotions, that his mysticism is most evident—as, for example, in the *Treatise concerning Religious Affections*. The tragedy inherent in the *Farewell Sermon* is that Edwards's earlier support of emotional release, his devotion to "New Lightism," had been lessons too well learned by his congregation. His effort to re-assert theocratic government came tardily, and the casuistry to which he resorted in an attempt to reconcile the eternal antinomies passed over the heads of his pastoral children. Thus he was compelled to abandon his pulpit.

Lest we lose sight of the individual for the sake of comprehending abstract ideas, we must look at the man. Established as minister of the most prosperous inland community in Massachusetts at the age of twenty-three, married to the daughter of James Pierrepont, of New Haven, Edwards had reason to be happy in his Northampton surroundings. His portraits reveal him as he doubtless appeared to his fellow townsmen: spare of limb, with oval face, delicate features, thin lips, and the quiet eyes of Man Thinking. Lost in contemplation as he walked across the common of the elm-shaded village, or riding on horseback through wooded uplands and cultivated meadows, he might have appeared indeed to those who regarded him with awe as a Gray Champion. But to us who see him as his personal charm is unfolded by his letters and recorded conversation, he appears as an affectionate husband and father, and a devoted friend:—now buying two pounds worth of jewelry for his wife, together with a negro slave, Pompey, and

tobacco and pipes for himself; now helping his daughters to
earn pin money by selling in Boston the fans they made; or
again discussing sheep-raising with a neighboring friend, or
measuring the height of Mt. Tom with his son, Timmy.
Tradition has it that Mrs. Edwards assumed control of the more
practical affairs of living, and indeed we can but smile to
visualize the figure of the stately Mr. Edwards returned from a
ride, his coat dotted with paper slips pinned here and there—
jottings set down immediately lest he should forget them.

Most touching of all, perhaps, is the pathos of that moment
when Edwards faced his congregation on Sunday, July 1, 1750,
to deliver his *Farewell Sermon.* There he stood at the fulness of
his spiritual and intellectual power, already dismissed from the
church over which he had been settled twenty-five years before,
knowing that no immediate future lay ahead of him, soon to be
compelled to move westward with his large family into the
wilderness settlement of Stockbridge as pastor of the small
group of whites and as missionary to the Indians. The courage
required for such an undertaking can be appreciated fully only
when we realize that this task was made more uncongenial still
by local venality and petty cavilling. But his duties gave him
leisure to write, and the greatest of his treatises were executed
during his residence as missionary. Plain living and high
thinking have never been more surely paired, and as one reads
the *Freedom of the Will,* one should remember that many a
chapter must have been temporarily laid aside while the great
theologian paused to catechise the Indian boys or to set them a
spelling lesson.

II. Jonathan Edwards as a Thinker

"He that would know the workings of the New England
mind in the middle of the last century, and the throbbings of its
heart," wrote the historian Bancroft almost a hundred years ago,

"must give his days and nights to the study of Jonathan Edwards." [1]

The chief reason why studying Edwards is important to one who wishes to understand eighteenth-century New England is that he played a very prominent part in many of the major philosophical and theological controversies of the time. Between 1736 and 1746, he led one party in the heated debate over the religious upheaval known as the Great Awakening. In the middle of the century, he fought staunchly for the Calvinistic theory of the freedom of the will. A little later, he was the recognized champion of the Calvinistic forces in the bitter conflict over the doctrine of the total depravity of man. Finally, he plunged into the controversy over the nature of virtue and put on the Calvinistic armor in defense of the doctrine of election.

In the midst of these controversies, Edwards erected a stately and well buttressed theological and philosophical system, a system built both of materials inherited from his Calvinistic forebears[2]

[1] Quoted approvingly by one of Edwards's most careful biographers, A. V. G. Allen, *Jonathan Edwards* (Boston, 1889), p. vi. See in this connection Oliver Wendell Holmes's essay on Jonathan Edwards, *Works* (1892), VIII, 361 ff. Here Holmes declares that Edwards "stamped his personality and his doctrines on the New England theology of the last century" (p. 389). Another interesting recognition by an unsympathetic although understanding critic is that by Harriet Beecher Stowe. See *The Minister's Wooing*, where Edwards's disciple Samuel Hopkins is the central figure, and *Old Town Folks*, a whole chapter of which ("My Grandmother's Blue Book") is devoted to a criticism of Joseph Bellamy's *True Religion Delineated* (1750), one of the earliest and most influential statements of the Edwardean doctrines.

[2] For a summary statement of the Calvinism of the founders of New England see Ezra Byington, *The Puritan in England and New England* (Boston, 1896), pp. 284 ff. The New England churches accepted the Calvinistic statement of faith of the Westminster Assembly as their standard (see Williston Walker, *The Creeds and Platforms of Congregationalism*, New York, 1893), although their theories of church polity were probably not rooted in Calvinism (see Herbert Schneider, *The Puritan Mind*, New York, 1930, p. 18). Compare Thomas Cuming Hall, *The Religious Background of American Culture* (Boston, 1930), pp. 83–109. For formulations of the Calvinistic theology in New England see Thomas Shepard, *The Sincere Convert* (1664) and *The Sound Believer* (1659); Thomas

and of materials boldly seized from the philosophical schools of his time.[3]

One of the most important aspects of this system is Edwards's view of human nature, a view enormously significant not only because of its wide acceptance in Edwards's day but also because of the violent reaction to it in the following century. An understanding of it involves a comprehension of Edwards's psychological notions, particularly of the conception of the place of the affections or emotions in human nature presented in his writings on the Great Awakening, and of the theory of the freedom of the will set forth in his polemical work on that subject. It involves, too, the grasping, with its ramifications and implications, of Edwards's doctrine of the depravity of man. It must include, also, a comprehension of his theory concerning the nature of virtue, and, finally, an understanding of his doctrine of grace, a doctrine which, standing at the apex of his system, gives unity to the whole.

THE GREAT AWAKENING

Edwards's view of human nature was based on his psychological theories. These were first presented in his writings in defense of the Great Awakening, and were, no doubt, somewhat colored by his desire to justify that highly emotional religious movement.

Hooker, *The Soul's Vocation or Effectual Calling* (London, 1638); John Norton, *The Orthodox Evangelist* (1654); Samuel Willard, *A Compleat Body of Divinity in Two Hundred and Fifty Expository Lectures on the Assembly's Shorter Catechism* (1726).

[3] That Edwards's reading had made him widely aware of the chief philosophical movements of his time is attested not only by the numerous references to contemporary philosophical works in his writings but by the so-called "Catalogue of Books," a private record apparently of works he planned to read, which contains some seven hundred entries. The manuscript is at Yale. A transcription and interpretation of it in type-written form is available in the Hammond Library of the Chicago Theological Seminary (James A. Caskey, *Jonathan Edwards' "Catalogue of Books"*). See also Thomas H. Johnson, "Jonathan Edwards' Background of Reading," *Publications of the Colonial Society of Massachusetts*, XXVIII, 193–222 (December, 1931).

The Great Awakening began in Edwards's own Connecticut river village, Northampton, Massachusetts, in 1734, and spread finally "over the whole eastern seacoast from Maine to Georgia."[4] For fifteen years after 1734, waves of religious enthusiasm deluged New England, one of the most notable of these storms coming in 1740 when George Whitefield visited the colonies.[5]

During these years large numbers of New Englanders were enormously stirred. An eyewitness reports that when Edwards preached at Enfield in 1741 his famous, not to say notorious, sermon on "Sinners in the Hands of an Angry God"—a sermon on the painfully suggestive text "Their foot shall slide in due time"—"the assembly appeared deeply impressed and bowed down with an awful conviction of their sin and danger. There was such a breathing of distress and weeping, that the preacher was obliged to speak to the people and desire silence, that he might be heard." [6] Throughout the Connecticut valley and the surrounding territory touched by the Great Awakening, "outcries, faintings, and fits" were apparently common, and were, in fact, often welcomed as gracious signs of divine favor. [7]

Many of the revivalists tried deliberately to induce these emotional upheavals in their hearers. One witness of the

[4] Frederick Morgan Davenport, *Primitive Traits in American Revivals* (New York, 1905), pp. 94–132; Joseph Tracy, *The Great Awakening* (Boston, 1841); Thomas Henry Billings, "The Great Awakening," *Essex Institute Historical Collections*, LXV, 89–104 (1929); W. M. Gewehr, *The Great Awakening in Virginia, 1740–1790* (Durham, N. C., 1930). On the important political and economic connections of the Revival see J. C. Miller, "Religion, Finance, and Democracy," *New England Quarterly*, VI, 28–58 (1933).

[5] Whitefield visited Edwards. See an interesting account in Albert Dunning, *Congregationalists in America* (New York, 1894), pp. 236–237. For the significant connection between the Edwardean revival in America and the Wesleyan revival in England, see A. V. G. Allen, *Jonathan Edwards*, pp. 134 n. and 203 n., and Davenport, *Primitive Traits in American Revivals*, p. 133.

[6] Tracy, *The Great Awakening*, p. 216.

[7] See Tracy, *The Great Awakening*, pp. 150–151, 201–203, and chap. xiii, "Edwards—the Revival at Enfield—Outcries, Faintings, and Convulsions." See also Davenport, *Primitive Traits in American Revivals*, pp. 108–126.

emotional extravagance of the movement describes thus the
terrifying preaching of eternal damnation by one of the revivalists of the time, the Reverend James Davenport:

At length, he turn'd his Discourse to others, and with the *utmost Strength* of his Lungs addrest himself to the Congregation,
under these and such-like Expressions; viz. You poor unconverted Creatures, in the Seats, in the Pews, in the Galleries, I
wonder you don't drop into Hell! It would not surprise me,
I should not wonder at it, if I should see you drop down *now,
this Minute* into Hell. You Pharisees, Hypocrites, *now, now,
now*, you are going right into the Bottom of Hell. I wonder
you don't drop into Hell by *Scores*, and *Hundreds*, etc. . . .
Then he came out of the Pulpit, and stripped off his upper
Garments, and got into the Seats, and leapt up and down some
time, and clapt his Hands, and *cried out* in those Words, the
War goes on, the Fight goes on, the Devil goes down, the
Devil goes down; and then betook himself to *stamping* and
screaming most dreadfully.[8]

It is small wonder that under such preaching there was
"*swooning away* and *falling to the Ground* . . . bitter *Shriekings*
and *Screamings; Convulsion-like Tremblings* and *Agitations,
Strugglings* and *Tumblings*."[9]

It must of course be said that men like Edwards were not
guilty of the kind of sensationalism just described, and yet some
of the most startling psychological disturbances recorded of the
Great Awakening took place in Edwards's own congregation
and were piously reported by him in his first work dealing with
the Revival—*A Faithful Narrative of the Surprising Work of
God* (1736). This account includes the story of a young woman
who declared that "it was pleasant to think of lying in the dust

[8] Charles Chauncy, *Seasonable Thoughts on the State of Religion in
New England* (Boston, 1743), pp. 98–99. For a description of the character of the half-mad Davenport see *ibid.*, pp. 183–200, and Tracy, *The Great
Awakening*, pp. 230–255.
[9] Chauncy, *op. cit.*, p. 77.

all the days of her life, mourning for sin," who furthermore
"had great longings to die," and who, when her brother had
read from the book of Job "concerning worms feeding on the
dead body," said "with a pleasant smile" that "it was sweet to
her to think of being in such circumstances." [10] It includes, too,
the story of four-year-old Phebe Bartlet who retired to her closet
at midday to weep and pray for her sins, and who was observed
"exceedingly crying and wreathing her body to and fro, like
one in anguish of spirit" for fear of going to hell.[11] It contained,
finally, the tale of the melancholy man who "was hurried with
violent temptations to cut his own throat, and made an attempt, but did not do it effectually." [12] Edwards's own report
of the Revival, then, supports the testimony of other witnesses
and makes it sufficiently clear that at the time, in many parts of
New England at least, the "passions" were in the saddle.[13]

The Congregational and Presbyterian ministry of Massachusetts and Connecticut were sharply divided in their attitude
toward this phenomenon.[14] The "opposers" were led by
Charles Chauncy, pastor of the old First Church in Boston.
He objected strenuously to the "preaching of terror" with its
attendant "bodily effects," to use a phrase common in the
controversial literature of the time.[15] " 'Tis too well known
to need much to be said upon it," wrote Chauncy, "that
the *Gentlemen*, whose preaching has been *most remarkably*
accompanied with these *Extraordinaries*, not only use, in their

[10] *Works* (New York, 1858), III, 260–265. Except where otherwise
noted, references to Edwards's works are to this edition, which is a reprint
of the Worcester edition (see Bibliography).
[11] *Ibid.*, III, 265–269.   [12] *Ibid.*, III, 269.
[13] The word *passions* had in the eighteenth century about the signification of our word *emotions*. "Any kind of feeling by which the mind is
powerfully affected or moved" (*New English Dictionary*).
[14] See Tracy, *The Great Awakening*, pp. 286–372, for an account of this
bitter controversy. Dexter's bibliography, *The Congregationalism of the
Last Three Hundred Years as Seen in its Literature*, (New York, 1880),
lists 59 books, most of them plainly controversial, on the Revival between
1742 and 1745 alone.
[15] *Seasonable Thoughts*, pp. 76–108.

Addresses to the People, all the *terrible Words* they can get to-gether, but in such a Manner, as *naturally* tends to put *weaker* Minds out of the Possession of themselves." [16]

Chauncy's objection to the preaching of terror was part of a more sweeping condemnation of the Revival. He felt that the religious enthusiasts of the Awakening appealed merely to men's passions. He was disgusted by the irrational extravagance of the movement. It was, he charged, "a *plain stubborn Fact*, that the *Passions* have, *generally*, in *these Times*, been apply'd to, as though the *main* Thing in Religion was to throw them into Disturbance." [17] Violently he attacked the whole move-ment as a vain and dangerous explosion of emotion. "Nor unless some Persons are made sensible" of this fact, he wrote, "and take Care to keep their Passions within the Restraints of Reason, may it be expected that Things should be reduced to a State of Order." [18]

The phrase "Passions within the Restraints of Reason" indicates the fundamental principle upon which Chauncy based his condemnation of the Awakening. He believed that in all things reason should govern. "The plain Truth," he insisted, is that "an *enlightened Mind*, and not *raised Affections*, ought always to be the Guide of those who call themselves Men; and this, in the Affairs of Religion, as well as other Things." [19] "*Reasonable* Beings," he declared, "are not to be guided by

---

[16] *Seasonable Thoughts*, pp. 94, 311.

[17] *Ibid.*, p. 302. The *Dictionary of American Biography* contains, in an excellent sketch of Chauncy, the statement that "He was undoubtedly the most influential clergyman of his time in Boston, and, with the exception of Jonathan Edwards, in all New England, becoming the acknowledged leader of the liberals of his generation." For an analysis of Chauncy's rationalism see G. A. Koch, *Republican Religion* (New York, 1933), pp. 191–195. See also Williston Walker, *Ten New England Leaders* (New York, 1901), pp. 267–310; W. C. Fowler, *Memorials of the Chaunceys* (1858), pp. 49–70.

[18] *Seasonable Thoughts*, p. 422.

[19] *Ibid.*, p. 327. In this connection, Chauncy quotes Isaac Watts's *Discourse on the Use and Abuse of the Passions* (p. 420).

Passion or *Affection*, though the Object of it should be GOD, and the Things of another World." [20]

Chauncy realized that his most noteworthy opponent in the controversy over the merits of the Great Awakening was Jonathan Edwards. He did not mince matters in meeting the challenge that Edwards presented. Although he referred only casually to Edwards's "Wonderful Narrative," [21] he devoted whole sections of his *Seasonable Thoughts on the State of Religion in New England* to a destructive analysis of "Mr. Edwards' . . . late Book, *Some Tho'ts on the Revival of Religion in New-England*." [22] He did not hesitate in analyzing Edwards's position to cast some slurs upon the man himself, suggesting in one place that Edwards might "not be suppos'd to be in a proper Temper of Mind to receive the Truth," [23] and declaring boldly in another connection that Edwards had defended the Revival "with such Arguments, as I can't suppose will be thought to carry in them much Weight." [24]

Against the charges which the "opposers" of the Great Awakening under the leadership of Chauncy were making, Edwards strenuously defended the movement. He was, on the whole,[25] heartily convinced that it was "a surprising work of

[20] *Seasonable Thoughts*, p. 324. See also *ibid.*, pp. 310–313.
[21] *Ibid.*, p. 92.   [22] *Ibid.*, pp. 81–93, 301–332.
[23] *Ibid.*, p. 294.   [24] *Ibid.*, p. 307; see also p. 385.
[25] Edwards did not approve of the "censoriousness" of some of the revivalists, particularly their habit of attacking as "unconverted" preachers who did not welcome the revival (*Works*, I, 559 ff., and III, 391 ff.). He objected, also, to lay preaching (*Works*, III, 397 ff.). And he condemned the following of "impulses and impressions" as though they were immediate revelations from God (*Works*, I, 556 ff. and III, 364 ff.). Allen observes that Edwards was objecting to what "the early Puritans themselves had dreaded as the necessary outcome of Quaker preaching" (*Life*, p. 178). Edwards was faithful to the Puritan tradition in condemning "enthusiasm" like that of Anne Hutchinson and her followers (*Works*, III, 122). His tests for true religious experience were so stringent that he cannot be classed with the unthinking enthusiasts for the Revival. He warns his readers that a great stirring of the affections, marked "bodily effects," a great deal of noise, "fluent, fervent, and abundant" talking about religion, vivid imaginings, even a feeling of assurance of salvation

God," and that it was therefore wicked to oppose it. So certain
was he that the Awakening was a gloriously divine event that
he was ready to defend what Chauncy considered one of its
least defensible aspects—the preaching of terror. He brushed
aside the objection to throwing people into a state of fear with
the observation that since there is a hell men must be frightened
into keeping out of it. "Some talk of it as an unreasonable thing
to fright persons to heaven," he wrote, "but I think it is a
reasonable thing to endeavor to fright persons away from hell.
They stand upon its brink, and are just ready to fall into it, and
are senseless of their danger. Is it not a reasonable thing to
fright a person out of a house on fire?" [26]

There is ample evidence that Edwards was not guilty
of any mistaken softheartedness in the matter.[27] He did
not hesitate to terrify his listeners into fleeing the wrath to
come. In a sermon entitled *The Fearfulness which Will
Hereafter Surprise Sinners in Zion, Represented and Improved,*
he pictured the devils snatching the damned soul as it forsakes
the body and plunging it into the ocean of fire, the billows of
which, "greater than the greatest mountains, will never cease to
roll over them . . . following one another forever and ever." [28]
Plainly, Edwards was defending his own practice when he insisted upon the necessity of terrifying unregenerate men with
pictures of their future torments. The famous *Sinners in the
Hands of an Angry God* with its fearful pronouncement that
the "God that holds you over the pit of hell, much as one holds
a spider, or some loathsome insect over the fire, abhors you, and

are not certain marks of a truly religious state (*Works*, III, 22 ff., 530 ff.).
The chief evidence of "gracious affections," he declared, was good fruit
in a Christian life (III, 60, 155 ff.).

[26] *Works*, I, 538.

[27] It may be worth noting that the belief in the wisdom of making
men vividly aware of the terrors of damnation was not peculiar to the
Puritans. Augustine, Dante, and Donne, to cite notable examples, plainly
had the same attitude as Edwards toward the matter.

[28] *Works*, IV, 492–496.

is dreadfully provoked," [29] is representative of an important element in Edwards's preaching. It is true that Edwards was much more than a sensational preacher of hell-fire sermons, but no fully rounded picture of the man can disregard that aspect of his work.

Completely in agreement at this point both in theory and in practice with the "New Lights," as the ministers who participated in the Great Awakening were called, he stood at all major points in the controversy squarely with them and squarely in opposition to Chauncy and to the group of which Chauncy was the acknowledged spokesman. Chauncy bewailed the overemphasis upon the affections and the passions in the Revival. Edwards complained that they were not played upon enough. "Our people," he wrote, "do not so much need to have their heads stored, as to have their hearts touched." [30] Chauncy declared that religion ought to be primarily a matter of reason, that "an *enlightened Mind,* and not *raised Affections*" ought to be the guide in religion as in all other things. Edwards asserted that religion is primarily a matter of the affections, and devoted *A Treatise concerning Religious Affections* (1746) to proving the point. In an earlier pronouncement he had replied to those who had objected to the attempts of revivalists to stimulate the emotions of their hearers: "I should think myself in the way of my duty, to raise the affections of my hearers as high as I possibly can, provided they are affected with nothing but truth, and with affections that are not disagreeable to the nature of what they are affected with." [31] It is plain that the core of their differences was the question of the place of emotion, of the passions or the affections, in religion.

It is against this background of controversy that Edwards's psychological theories must be seen, theories that are fundamental in his view of human nature. The fact is that Edwards could not be content with an unreasoned statement of his belief

[29] *Ibid.,* IV, 318.   [30] *Ibid.,* III, 336.   [31] *Idem.*

in the kind of religion which the Great Awakening produced and encouraged. He had to justify his position, not merely on Scriptural grounds, but on philosophical grounds as well. During the course of the controversy, he seems to have become increasingly aware of the need for placing his defense of the emotionalism of the Revival on a sound basis psychologically. His last work in vindication of the movement, *A Treatise concerning Religious Affections*, begins with a careful analysis of the operations of the human mind, an analysis which, while resting firmly on Christian tradition, obviously reflects contemporary notions of psychology, and which can only be fully appreciated in the light of them.

EDWARDS'S ANALYSIS OF THE HUMAN MIND

Edwards began this analysis by asserting that the human mind has two faculties—understanding and will.[32] This division of the mind was, of course, perfectly conventional.[33] It went back to the Middle Ages and had been employed with full recognition of its commonness by Locke in *An Essay concerning Human Understanding* (1690), which Edwards had greedily devoured while in college.[34]

[32] *Works*, III, 3. See also the sermon, *Reality of Spiritual Light* (IV, 442), and *The Medium of Moral Government* (*Works*, 1817 edition, VIII, 236).

[33] The wide general acceptance of this classification of the faculties of the mind may be seen in the following references: John Calvin, *Institutes* (1813), I, 180; Thomas Shepard, *The Sound Believer* (London, 1659), p. 183; Thomas Hobbes, *Human Nature*, in *Works* (London, 1840), IV, 2; Malebranche, *De la recherche de la vérité* . . . (1674; Paris, 1893), I, 20; Richard Cumberland, *A Treatise of the Laws of Nature* (London, 1727), p. 94; Isaac Watts, *Works* (London, 1811), VI, 250.

[34] According to the psychology current in the Middle Ages and generally accepted during the Renaissance, man possessed three souls, or as it was sometimes put, the soul of man had three sets of powers—vegetable, sensible, and rational. The rational soul had two powers, understanding and will. See Robert Burton, *The Anatomy of Melancholy* (1621), Pt. I, sec. 1, mem. 2, subsect. 9; Edward Dowden, "Elizabethan Psychology," in

The understanding, wrote Edwards, is that faculty of the soul "by which it is capable of perception and speculation, or by which it discerns, and views, and judges of things." As he employed the term, it included four important operations of the mind—sensation, imagination, memory, and judgment.

Edwards had apparently come very early to the conclusion that all the activities of the mind designated by the term *understanding* depended upon sensation. In the projected "Treatise on the Mind," planned while he was a student at Yale, he hoped, according to his notebook, to show "how the mind would be without ideas, except as suggested by the Senses" and how "Reasoning, Contemplation, etc. depend on this." [35] Even the devil, he pointed out in *A Treatise concerning Religious Affections*, could insinuate ideas into a man's mind only by exciting in it impressions of external objects or by awakening in it recollections of sensations once experienced.[36] This notion of the dependence of the understanding upon sensation may have come from Locke, who had declared in the *Essay* that even the most abstruse ideas had their origin in the senses.[37]

A psychologist who believed that all thought was dependent upon sensation could not long avoid the problem of the correspondence of sense impressions with the stimulating objects of these impressions. Locke warned his readers against assuming that perceptions or ideas in the mind were "exactly the images and

---

Essays Modern and Elizabethan (London, 1910); Lily B. Campbell, *Shakespeare's Tragic Heroes* (Cambridge, England, 1930).

On the influence of Locke in America see P. Emory Aldrich, *Proceedings of the American Antiquarian Society*, April, 1879, pp. 31 ff. "Locke's essay was introduced as a text-book in Yale College as early as 1717 and continued to be used there till 1825. . . ." Edwards read Locke while in college, getting, he wrote, more pleasure from it "than the most greedy miser finds, when gathering up handfuls of silver and gold, from some newly discovered treasure" (Sereno E. Dwight, *The Life of President Edwards*, in Edwards's *Works* [New York, 1829], p. 30). It was probably under the stimulation of this experience that he set down, while still in college, notes for a "Treatise on the Mind."

[35] Dwight, *Life*, p. 667; see also p. 666.
[36] *Works*, III, 123–124.   [37] Bk. II, chap. xii, sec. 8.

resemblances of something inherent in the subject; most of those of sensation being in the mind no more the likeness of something existing without us than the names that stand for them are the likeness of our ideas, which yet upon hearing they are apt to excite in us." [38] He went on to distinguish between "three sorts of qualities in bodies." First, some qualities (solidity, extension, figure, number, and motion or rest) are "real qualities of bodies." They exist whether we observe them or not, and perception of these qualities gives us an idea "of the thing as it is in itself." Other qualities (colors, sounds, smells, tastes, etc.) are merely powers to produce certain sensations in us. These qualities, although they give rise to what seem to be images of themselves, are only the capacity of the exciting object to occasion certain impressions, and they have no resemblance to the effects they generate. From these two sorts of qualities in objects, he distinguished a third, which is the power in a body to effect changes in another body so as to make it "operate on our senses differently from what it did before." So, for instance, the sun has the power to melt wax. In this case, he pointed out, we never make the mistake of regarding the softness of the wax as a quality of the sun. No more should we, he added, consider the light and warmth we perceive when the sun shines upon us as qualities in the sun itself. [39]

This point, which others besides Locke had made, [40] became the basis of Edwards's idealism. His argument from it was carefully elaborated in the youthful *Notes on the Mind*. [41] He began by insisting that our impressions of color are not exact resemblances to something inherent in the thing perceived. "Every knowing philosopher" now grants, he wrote, that colors are

---

[38] *An Essay concerning Human Understanding*, Bk. II, chap. viii, sec. 7.
[39] *Ibid.*, sec. 23.
[40] See Hobbes, *Human Nature*, in *Works*, IV 4–9, and *Leviathan*, chap. i; Isaac Watts, *Philosophical Essays on Various Subjects* (London, 1732), p. 277; Hume, *A Treatise of Human Nature*, Bk. I, pt. IV, sec. 2.
[41] Dwight, *Life*, pp. 668–669.

not really in things any more than pain is in a needle. He followed up this statement with the declaration that nothing else exists out of the mind any more than color does unless it be "the very substance" of bodies themselves. The ideas that make up what we call body or substance are built upon impressions of color and resistance. If we disregard color, we find that solidity is resistance; that figure is the termination of resistance; that motion is the communication of resistance from space to space. Since it is granted that color has "merely mental existence," "there is nothing out of the mind but Resistance." Now resistance cannot exist outside the mind "when nothing is actually resisted. Then, there is nothing but the Power of Resistance." This Power must depend upon a constant law or establishment. To account for such a law or establishment one must assume the existence of a universal mind. "The world is therefore," Edwards concludes, "an ideal one."[42] A little later he sums up his position by saying: "Indeed the secret lies here: That, which truly is the Substance of all Bodies, is *the infinitely exact, and precise, and perfectly stable Idea, in God's mind, together with his stable Will, that the same shall gradually be communicated to us, and to other minds, according to certain fixed and exact established Methods and Laws.*"[43]

The problem of the source of this idealism is, according to I. Woodbridge Riley, "the most difficult in the history of American philosophy." "Was it the product of precocious genius, or an adaptation of the Berkeleian system, or a blending of the idealistic hints and suggestions then in the air?"[44]

[42] *Ibid.*, p. 669.   [43] *Ibid.*, p. 674.
[44] *American Philosophy: The Early Schools* (New York, 1907), p. 129. See here also an excellent summary of the problem. See, too, H. N. Gardiner, "The Early Idealism of Jonathan Edwards," *Philosophical Review*, IX, 573–596 (Nov., 1900); Clarence Gohdes, "Aspects of Idealism in Early New England," *Philosophical Review*, XXXIX, 537–555 (Nov., 1930); Georges Lyon, *L'Idéalisme en Angleterre au XVIIIᵉ siècle* (Paris, 1888); John H. MacCracken, *Jonathan Edwards Idealismus* (Halle, 1899) and his "The Sources of Jonathan Edwards' Idealism," *Philosophical Review*, XI, 26–42 (Jan., 1902); Egbert C. Smyth, "Jonathan Edwards' Idealism,"

Although in the first flush of his enthusiasm for the theory Edwards plainly intended to publish the doctrine and to fight for its acceptance, [45] it is not formally presented in Edwards's later work. There is no reason for thinking that he abandoned it; indeed it is implicit in much of what he wrote. But his early intention to force it upon the attention of the world was given up. Perhaps he felt it unnecessary to complicate the various controversies in which he was engaged by insistence upon it. Furthermore, he had even in the beginning felt that it was of no practical importance, for in the "Notes on Mind" he wrote that even if one accepted the notion that the material universe existed only mentally, one might still "speak in the old way, and as properly and truly as ever." [46]

Sensation, which, according to his theory of idealism, is the apprehension of the ideas which God has willed to communicate to us, furnishes the material for two other functions of the understanding—imagination and memory. The term *imagination* plays so important a part in the *Treatise concerning Religious Affections* that Edwards took time to define it carefully for his readers. It is, he said, that power of the mind by which one has an image of the things which are the objects of sense when those things are not actually present to be perceived by the senses. So one has a lively idea of a shape, or of a color, or of marks on paper, or of a voice when one "does not really see, hear, smell, taste, nor feel." [47] Memory, which like imagination depends upon sensation, differs from it only in being accompanied by a consciousness that the idea has been entertained formerly and that its presence in the mind formerly is the

---

American Journal of Theology, I, 950–964 (Oct., 1897), and his "Some Early Writings of Jonathan Edwards," *Proceedings of the American Antiquarian Society,* N.S. X, 212–247 (Oct., 1896). See Bibliography for statements of the positions of these writers.

[45] Dwight, *Life,* p. 671.

[46] *Ibid.,* p. 669.

[47] *Works,* III, 74–75.

cause of its reappearance.[48] These notions concerning imagination and memory were commonplaces in Edwards's time.[49]

The fourth of the powers of the mind which Edwards included in the term *understanding* is reason or judgment. He defined reason as "that power or faculty an intelligent being has to judge of the truth of propositions; either immediately, by looking on the propositions, which is judging by intuition and self-evidence; or by putting together several propositions, which are already evident by intuition, or at least whose evidence is originally derived from intuition."[50]

A great deal of light is thrown upon Edwards's opinions concerning two of these four operations of the mind designated by the term *understanding*, from an examination of his beliefs about the physiology of sensation and imagination. The sensations upon which all thinking was dependent were, according to Edwards, conveyed from the organs of sense to the brain by the animal spirits. External ideas, he said, "may be raised only by impressions made on the body, by moving the animal spirits, and impressing the brain."[51] These spirits were subtle fluids or vapors filling the nerves as water fills a pipe. They carried impressions from the organs of sense along the nerves to the brain and also conveyed impulses of the will from the brain to the muscles, stimulating them to movement.

In its broad outlines, the theory current in Edwards's day was as follows.[52] In the brain, which was the fountain of the

[48] Dwight, *Life*, p. 680.
[49] Watts, *Philosophical Essays*, pp. 91–92; Hobbes, *Elements of Philosophy*, in *Works*, I, 396, and *Leviathan*, chap. ii; Hume, *Treatise of Human Nature*, Bk. I, Pt. I, sec. 3; Locke, *Essay*, Bk. II, chap. x, sec. 2.
[50] *Miscellaneous Observations*, in *Works* (London, 1817), VIII, 216. See *Religious Affections*, in *Works* (New York, 1858), III, 119, and *Reality of Spiritual Light*, in *Works*, IV, 448. See Locke, *Essay*, Bk. IV, chap. xiv.
[51] *Works*, III, 78, 122–123.
[52] The theory concerning the animal spirits in the eighteenth century must not be confused with that current in the Middle Ages and the Renaissance. For the former see a succinct statement by Robert Burton, *Anatomy of Melancholy*, Pt. I, sec. 1, mem. 2, subsect. 2; Dowden, "Eliza-

animal spirits, certain subtle, airy substances were supposed to be separated from the coarser elements of the blood. These spirits filled the brain and the nerves, which were thought of as hollow tubes stretching from it to all parts of the body. Any stimulation of the organs of sense set them into motion, and so sense impressions were carried through the nerves to the brain. In the same fashion, mental impulses were supposed to agitate the spirits in the brain and so to be carried by the proper nerves to the organs of motion, where they stimulated to action the appropriate muscles. It is important to observe, in this connection, that abnormal disturbances of the animal spirits, such as could be induced by drink, or by the disease of melancholy, or by great mental excitement, might, by setting the spirits into a ferment, bring about illusions of the senses and involuntary movements of the muscles.[53]

It is plain, then, that as agents of sensation the animal spirits played an important part in the functioning of that faculty of the mind which Edwards labeled the understanding, and that as messengers of volition they were important in the activity of the other faculty of the mind—the inclination or will.

Edwards defined the inclination as the faculty "by which the soul does not merely perceive and view things, but is some way inclined with respect to the things it views or considers." [54]

bethan Psychology"; and Campbell, *Shakespeare's Tragic Heroes*. For the changes in the theory as a result of Harvey's discovery of the circulation of the blood see Sir Michael Foster, *Lectures on the History of Physiology during the Sixteenth, Seventeenth, and Eighteenth Centuries* (Cambridge, England, 1901), pp. 12 ff.

[53] For an exposition of the theory of the spirits see Foster, *Lectures on the History of Physiology*, pp. 275–276. See also *The Tract on Man*, in *The Philosophy of Descartes in Extracts from his Writings*, trans. by Henry P. Torrey (New York), pp. 276–279; Hobbes, *Elements of Philosophy*, in *Works*, I, 403, 391, 392, 397; Henry More, *An Account of Virtue* (London, 1690), p. 43; Cumberland, *A Treatise of the Laws of Nature* (London, 1727), pp. 144 ff.; John Mayhew, *On Muscular Motion and Animal Spirits* in *Medico-Physical Works* (Chicago, 1908), pp. 229–302 (the work was first published in 1674); Hume, *A Treatise of Human Nature*, Bk. I, Pt. IV, sec. 2.

[54] *Works*, III, 3.

The term *heart*, he said, is sometimes used in speaking of this faculty, for strong inclinations disturb the motion of the blood and the animal spirits and so give rise to sensations "especially about the heart and vitals, that are the fountain of the fluids of the body: from whence it comes to pass, that the mind, with regard to the exercises of this faculty, perhaps in all nations and ages, is called the *heart*." [55]

The exercises of the inclination are of two kinds—liking and disliking, that is, inclination toward and aversion from the things perceived by the understanding. In *A Treatise concerning Religious Affections*, Edwards wrote, in terms very close to those employed by Locke and Hutcheson, "The exercises of this faculty are of two sorts; either those by which the soul is carried out towards the things that are in view, in approving of them, being pleased with them, and inclined to them; or those in which the soul opposes the things that are in view, in disapproving of them, and in being displeased with them, averse from them, and rejecting them." [56]

These two sorts of passions or affections [57] do not, according to Edwards, occupy equal positions. Love, he said, is the chief of the affections and the fountain of all others. Out of love for a thing flows hatred for its opposite or for whatever opposes it, and out of love and hatred come all the other affections—desire, hope, joy, gratitude, complacence, on the one hand; fear, anger, grief, and the like, on the other. [58] In some affections there is a mixture of the two sorts. In pity, for example, there is love toward the person suffering and hatred toward what he suffers.

[55] *Ibid.*

[56] *Ibid.* Cf. Locke's *Essay*, Bk. II, chap. xx, and Francis Hutcheson, *A System of Moral Philosophy* (London, 1755), I, 7. See also Hobbes, *Works*, IV, 31 ff.

[57] The terms passion, affection, inclination, and will are all used by Edwards in referring to the second faculty of the mind. His identification of will and inclination is an important point in his philosophy (*Works*, III, 3–4, 279).

[58] *Works*, III, 5.

THE PSYCHOLOGICAL ANALYSIS OF THE
GREAT AWAKENING

The point about the affections which Edwards was chiefly concerned with making in the *Treatise* was that they were the "spring of men's actions." They, he said, make the world go around, for unless a man is moved by some affection, he is by nature inactive. Take away affection and human activity ceases. "Take away all love and hatred, all hope and fear, all anger, zeal, and affectionate desire, and the world would be, in a great measure motionless and dead; there would be no such thing as activity amongst mankind, or any earnest pursuit whatsoever."[59]

Now what is true in worldly things, argued Edwards, is also true in religious matters. There, too, the affections are the springs of action.[60] They are, he declared, "the very life and soul of all true religion."[61] In fact, "there can be no true religion without them."[62] And since love is the chief of the affections, "the essence of all true religion lies in holy love."[63]

For this position it seemed to Edwards that he had ample Biblical authority. "The scriptures," he wrote, "represent true religion, as being summarily comprehended in *love*, the chief of the affections, and the fountain of all other affections." Among the "innumerable texts" which, he said, might be quoted in support of this assertion he placed Jesus's saying: *"Thou shalt love the Lord thy God with all thy heart, and with all thy soul, and with all thy mind. This is the first and great commandment. And the second is like unto it, Thou shalt love thy neighbor as thyself. On these two commandments hang all the law and the prophets."*[64]

If the affections as the spring of conduct are essential to all

---

[59] *Works*, III, 6.   [60] *Ibid.*   [61] *Ibid.*, III, 279.
[62] *Ibid.*, III, 19–20.   [63] *Ibid.*, III, 10.
[64] *Ibid.* The importance of Edwards's lifelong immersion in the Christian tradition must not be lost sight of in analyzing his indebtedness to contemporary philosophy.

true religion, Edwards pushed on to say, then men like Charles Chauncy of Boston who criticized the Great Awakening, that "late extraordinary season," because during that time the affections were greatly raised in religion were plainly wrong.[65] Edwards felt sure that "the prevailing prejudice against religious affections at this day, in the land" was the work of that shrewd enemy of all good, Satan.[66] Solemnly he warned the critics of the Revival that "for persons to despise and cry down all religious affections, is the way to shut all religion out of their own hearts, and to make thorough work in ruining their souls."[67]

Edwards was not satisfied, however, to let the matter of the Revival rest upon the assertion that since the passions were the springs of conduct, religion must consist primarily in gracious affections. One of his prime interests in *A Treatise concerning Religious Affections* was the distinction between true religion and false religion. He was as ready to condemn much of the religious enthusiasm of the Great Awakening as were its bitterest opponents. How was the good to be distinguished from the bad? His answer was an elaborate attempt to indicate the differences between a purely natural religion and one that is supernatural.

In making this distinction, he first of all introduced the notion that to the natural faculties of men, the understanding and the will, there is added in the regenerate man a new sense, which he called the "supernatural sense," a new power that can come to man only by an act of divine grace. He insisted emphatically that "those gracious influences which the saints are subjects of, and the effects of God's Spirit which they experience, are entirely above nature, altogether of a different kind from anything that men find within themselves by nature, or only in the exercise of natural principles; and are things which no

[65] *Ibid.*, III, 18–20; see also III, 334–336, 279–288.
[66] *Ibid.*, III, 18.   [67] *Ibid.*, III, 19–20.

improvement of those qualifications, or principles that are natural, no advancing or exalting of them to higher degrees, and no kind of composition of them, will ever bring men to; because they not only differ from what is natural, and from everything that natural men experience, in degree and circumstances, but also kind; and are of a nature vastly more excellent." "And this," he added, "is what I mean, by supernatural, when I say that gracious affections are from those influences that are supernatural." [68]

The supernatural sense, for one thing, gives to regenerate men a "new kind of perception or sensation." [69] This "apprehension, idea, or sensation of mind . . . the natural man discerns nothing of, and has no manner of idea of (agreeable to 1 Cor. 2. 14), and conceives of no more than a man without the sense of tasting can conceive of the sweet taste of honey, or a man without the sense of hearing can conceive of the melody of a tune, or a man born blind can have a notion of the beauty of the rainbow." [70] This new apprehension of spiritual values does not consist in the "compounding of that kind of perceptions or sensations which the mind had before." In short, it is "what some metaphysicians call a new simple idea." [71]

Here he is obviously thinking of the distinctions among ideas made by such men as Locke, who used the term *simple idea* to describe an idea which "contains in it nothing but one uniform appearance or conception of the mind, and is not distinguishable into different ideas," while he employed the term *complex idea* for an idea compounded from simple ones. In receiving simple ideas the mind, he said, is "wholly passive"; whereas in forming complex ones it is active. So the mind combines the simple

[68] *Works*, III, 70–71. See also important sermon on *A Divine and Supernatural Light, Immediately Imparted to the Soul by the Spirit of God, ibid.,* IV, 438–450.
[69] *Ibid.,* III, 71.
[70] *Religious Affections, ibid.,* III, 72. Note here the fusion of scriptural teaching with contemporary psychological doctrine.
[71] *Ibid.,* p. 71.

ideas of coldness and hardness, which it has passively received, into the complex idea of ice.[72]

It is easy to see, then, why Edwards, accepting as we have noted the sensationalism of Locke, should attempt to account for the difference between the natural man and one supernaturally regenerate by devising the notion of a new sense, a sense which the unregenerate man does not possess, a sense by which the elect passively receive simple, uncompounded impressions as the basis for spiritual knowledge in a way by which the non-elect cannot possibly acquire them.

This doctrine is the rational basis of Edwards's mysticism. "The inward principle from whence they [the gracious affections] flow, is something divine, a communication of God, a participation of the divine nature, Christ living in the heart, the Holy Spirit dwelling there, in union with the faculties of the soul, as an internal vital principle, exerting his own proper nature, in the exercise of those faculties."[73] It is true of course that Edwards saw all mental activity as finally dependent upon God. In his view the sensations upon which all thinking was based were simply, as we have seen, perceptions of God's ideas; imagination and memory were the reappearance of these ideas when the exciting cause was not operating to present them; judgment was the discovery of agreement or disagreement among these ideas, and was tested by the fixed connection between them in the mind of God. But the supernatural principle operated in men in a way different from and above all this. The difference, said Edwards, was that God "acts upon the mind of a natural man, but he acts in the mind of a saint as an indwelling vital principle . . . he doth unite himself to them."

For instance, he may excite thoughts in them, may assist their

---

[72] *Essay*, Bk. II, chaps. ii and xii.
[73] *Works*, III, 186. Again he says: "This light is such as effectually influences the inclination, and changes the nature of the soul. It assimilates the nature to the divine nature, and changes the soul into an image of the same glory that is beheld" (IV, 449).

natural reason and understanding, or may assist other natural principles, and this without any union with the soul, but may act, as it were, as upon an external object. But as he acts in his holy influences and spiritual operations, he acts in a way of peculiar communication of himself; so that the subject is thence denominated spiritual.[74]

Having expounded his theory of the supernatural sense, Edwards addressed himself to the problem of distinguishing between the emotionalism of the Revival that was spurious and the true religion, which the gift of this supernatural sense induced. Many people have had experiences, he said, which they have taken to be "spiritual discoveries." They have seen visions; they have heard voices; they have had sudden, amazing revelations of truth and impulses to action.[75] Like Chauncy,[76] Edwards condemned these impulses and impressions. He regarded them as "enthusiastic delusions."[77] He saw nothing in such experiences which could be ascribed to the possession of the supernatural sense. They were merely "impressions upon the imagination." In fact, they were exactly the sort of thing he expected the overheated imagination to bring.[78]

Edwards felt the grave necessity of warning people that impressions on the imagination might easily be mistaken for supernatural inspirations. He had the authority of Locke for the assertion that enthusiasm had its roots in the imagination, that it consisted in the illusion that what had "settled itself strongly" upon the imagination was "an illumination from the spirit of God."[79] In his earliest writing concerning the Revival,

---

[74] *A Divine and Supernatural Light, Immediately Imparted to the Soul by the Spirit of God, Works*, IV, 440. See also *Religious Affections, ibid.*, III, 67 ff.

[75] *Ibid.*, III, 75.

[76] Chauncy gives a great deal of space (*Seasonable Thoughts*, pp. 178 ff.) to warning his readers that the regard for "*Impulses and Impressions*" is highly dangerous.

[77] *Religious Affections, Works*, III, 74.

[78] *Ibid.*, III, 259; see also III, 74–76.

[79] *Essay*, Bk. IV, chap. xix, secs. 5–7.

A Faithful Narrative of the Surprising Work of God, he declared that he had used the "utmost Caution" in directing people to distinguish "between what is spiritual, and what is merely imaginary." [80] The difference between spiritual understanding and all kinds of enthusiastical delusions, as he pointed out at length in *Religious Affections,* is that the former is based upon the supernatural sense; the latter, upon mere natural imagination. [81] "And a very great part of the false religion that has been in the world, from one age to another," has grown out of the sad error of mistaking the impressions of the imagination for supernatural revelations. [82] He felt about the dangers of the imagination in religion as did Bishop Butler, who said, "Indeed amongst creatures naturally formed for religion, yet so much under the powers of imagination, so apt to deceive themselves, and so liable to be deceived by others as men are; superstition is an evil, which can never be out of sight." [83]

Edwards believed that the imagination was the "devil's grand lurking place, the very nest of foul and delusive spirits." [84] It was, according to his psychology, the devil's best door to the soul. As we have seen, the only way that ideas could be excited in the mind either as sensations or as imaginations was by the motion of the animal spirits. The agitation of the spirits so as to excite the fancy was, then, the devil's only way of attacking the human soul. "But if it be so," he wrote, "that the devil cannot produce thoughts in the soul immediately, or in any other way

---

[80] *Works,* II, 259. See "Directions for Judging of Persons' Experiences," *Selections from the Unpublished Writings of Jonathan Edwards* (1865), p. 183.

[81] *Works,* III, 74–79, 121–124.

[82] *Ibid.,* III, 123. See also III, 77–78 and IV, 440.

[83] *Works* (1900), I, 213. See also the *Analogy* (Pt. I, chap. i). On imagination as a cause of religious enthusiasm see Glanvil, *The Vanity of Dogmatizing* (1661), p. 99, and Hobbes's *Leviathan* (*Works,* III, 9). For a discussion of the notion that the errors of religious enthusiasm had their roots in the imagination, see Umphrey Lee, *The Historical Backgrounds of Early Methodist Enthusiasm* (New York, 1931).

[84] *Works,* III, 122.

than by the animal spirits, or by the body, then it follows, that
he never brings to pass any thing in the soul, but by the imagination or phantasy, or by exciting external ideas." [85]   At this
point, Edwards agreed with his opponent Charles Chauncy,
who quoted Charnock's statement that Satan works upon the
soul by means of the humours of the body, particularly by the
animal spirits.[86]

Not all imagination, said Edwards, is, however, of so fearful
an origin as this. While what appears to be a supernatural
revelation may be only the devil's work in the imagination by
way of the animal spirits, not all imagination is demoniacal. The
animal spirits may be set into commotion by the passions,[87] even
by the "gracious affections" properly stimulated in the Revival.
Indeed, "gracious affections which are very strong, do excite
lively ideas in the imagination." [88]   Such effects need not be
looked upon as the malicious work of the Evil One, nor, of
course, as supernatural inspirations. They should be regarded
as simply "the accidental effect, or consequences of the affections, through the infirmity of human nature." [89] Although they
are not in themselves admirable, they do indicate an admirable
response of the heart to religious truth. So he answered the
critics of the Revival who condemned the whole movement as
merely an orgy of emotionalism generated in the overheated
imaginations of the populace.

[85] *Works*, III, 122. See also III, 77–78. "If the revival of religion be very
great in its beginning, yet if this bastard comes in [that is, imagination
comes in], there is danger of its doing as Gideon's bastard Abimilech did,
who never left until he had slain all his threescore and ten true-born sons,
excepting one, that was forced to fly."

[86] *Seasonable Thoughts*, pp. 111–112; also pp. 310–313.

[87] "Such seems to be our nature, and such the laws of union of soul
and body, that there never is in any case whatsoever, any lively and vigorous exercise of the will or inclination of the soul, without some effect
upon the body, in some alteration of the motion of its fluids, and especially
of the animal spirits" (*Works*, III, 4). See Cumberland, *A Treatise of the
Laws of Nature*, p. 127.

[88] *Works*, III, 124.

[89] *Ibid.*, I, 530–532, and III, 124.

Edwards's defense of the Great Awakening against its critics, it may then be said in conclusion, consisted in large part of a careful presentation of psychological principles quite in harmony with the best thought of his time for the purpose of proving that since the passions are the springs of conduct, vital religion must consist chiefly in a holy exercise of them, and that, therefore, the Revival could not be justly condemned because it stimulated men's emotions. He furthermore insisted that the kind of religion which the Revival produced was exactly the kind of religious expression which the supernatural sense bestowed by God's grace on the elect might be expected to bring forth.

THE ATTACK ON ARMINIANISM

Edwards's attack on the "opposers" of the Great Awakening was, in his view, but a campaign on one front against a lifelong enemy. Again and again in his writings he referred to this dreaded and powerful foe—Arminianism. In the early *A Faithful Narrative of the Surprising Work of God*, he said that in 1734 Arminian doctrines began to make a "great noise" in the country. The danger at that time was so threatening, he declared, that the "friends of vital piety trembled for fear of the issue," and even unregenerate men became apprehensive that "God was about to withdraw from the land, and that we should be given up to heterodoxy, and corrupt principles." [90] The extravagant fears of Calvinists during this time were strikingly revealed in the famous Breck case. Late in 1734 Edwards with five other ministers signed a paper advising the church in Springfield, Massachusetts, to discontinue its efforts to secure as its pastor the Rev. Robert Breck, who was suspected of holding Arminian views. The church's disregard of their protest was the signal for a resounding battle, which was featured by numerous pamphlets, special meetings of ecclesiastical bodies,

[90] *Works*, III, 233–234.

and even the arrest and imprisonment of Breck himself, the whole matter finally going before the General Assembly of Massachusetts for review.[91] Throughout the remainder of Edwards's life, he was deeply concerned with checking the spread of what he called "this fashionable new divinity."

His hatred of Arminianism and his fear of it are easily understandable, for at most important points Arminians stood diametrically opposed to Calvinists.[92] The followers of the Dutch theologian denied, for example, that some men were absolutely predestined for heaven while others were absolutely doomed to hell, laying down as one of the chief foundations of their argument the principle of the freedom of man's will. Furthermore, although Arminianism had been condemned by the Synod of Dort in 1619, it had spread greatly by the middle of the eighteenth century, being advocated at that time by many English writers of widely separated theological opinions—men who had, however, this much in common: they had no stomach for Calvinism.[93] Naturally, then, the movement to which these

[91] Ezra Hoyt Byington, *The Puritan in England and New England* (Boston, 1896), pp. 335–368; and Mason A. Green, *Springfield 1636–1886* (Boston, 1882), pp. 228–258. Francis Albert Christie believes that there were few ministers in New England who held Arminian beliefs before 1734. See "The Beginnings of Arminianism in New England," *Papers of the American Society of Church History* (second series), III, 151–172. Cotton Mather wrote in 1726: "I cannot learn, That among all the Pastors of Two Hundred Churches [in New England], there is one Arminian" (quoted by Walker, *A History of the Congregational Churches in the United States*, p. 216).

[92] Although Edwards denied complete dependence upon Calvin and complete acceptance of all his doctrines, he declared that he "should not take it at all amiss, to be called a *Calvinist*" (Preface to *Freedom of the Will*, 1754).

[93] In his *History of the Work of Redemption*, Edwards says that Arminians "first appeared in Holland about 130 years ago. They take their name from a Dutchman, whose name was *Jacobus Van Harmin*, which, turned into Latin is called *Jacobus Arminius;* and from his name the whole sect are called *Arminians*. This Jacobus Arminius was first a minister at Amsterdam, and then a professor of divinity in the University of Leyden. He had many followers in Holland. There was upon this a synod of all the Reformed Churches called together, who met at Dort, in Holland. The synod of Dort condemned them; but yet they spread and prevailed. They

men belonged seemed to Edwards dangerous—subversive. It had to be crushed.

He was plainly convinced that the crucial point in the controversy between Arminians and Calvinists was the doctrine of the will. In the conclusion to the *Freedom of the Will* (1754) he pointed out that the beliefs which Calvinists most cherished, the beliefs which they thought essential to true Christianity, depended upon the conviction that men did not have the freedom which Arminians ascribed to them; and that, furthermore, all the chief objections to Calvinistic doctrines could be invalidated by establishing the principle of necessity.[94] Edwards felt, on the other hand, that until the doctrine of necessity was uncontrovertibly proved, the Calvinistic position would be difficult to maintain against the attacks of Arminians. Until this truth was established, he wrote, "it is, to me, beyond doubt, that the friends of those great gospel truths will but poorly maintain their controversy with the adversaries of those truths. They will be obliged often to dodge, shuffle, hide, and turn their backs: and the latter will have a strong fort, from whence they never can be driven, and weapons to use, which those whom they oppose will find no shield to screen themselves from; and they will always puzzle, confound, and keep under

---

began to prevail in England in the reign of Charles I., especially in the church of England. The church of England divines before that, were almost universally Calvinists; but since that, Arminianism has gradually more and more prevailed, till they are become almost universally Arminians. And not only so, but Arminianism has greatly prevailed among the Dissenters, and has spread greatly in New England, as well as Old" (*Works*, I, 467).

See *Schaff-Herzog Encyclopedia of Religious Knowledge*, "Arminianism." For a discussion of early Arminianism in England see Perry Miller, *Orthodoxy in Massachusetts* (Cambridge, 1933), pp. 42–45. See also Godfrey Davies, "Arminian versus Puritan in England, *ca.* 1620–1640," *Huntington Library Bulletin*, No. 5, pp. 157–179 (April, 1934).

[94] *Freedom of the Will, Works*, II, 176–178. Edwards adds that the Calvinistic belief in "efficacious" and "irresistible" grace, the theory of the limited atonement, and the doctrine of the "infallible perseverance of the saints" all depend upon the doctrine of necessity.

the friends of sound doctrine, and glory and vaunt themselves in their advantage over them; and carry their affairs with a high hand, as they have done already for a long time past." [95] Edwards was in fact quite ready to admit that if his adversaries could prove the freedom of the will in the sense in which they understood it, their whole position would have to be accepted. It is small wonder, then, that he believed that the doctrine of necessity was "one of the most important truths of moral philosophy that ever was discussed, and most necessary to be known."

The men whom he attacked were as much convinced as he of the overwhelming importance of the issue. Samuel Clarke, one of the chief exponents of the doctrine of freedom of the will, had declared, for example, that the problem of the will was "the Question of the greatest Concern of all, in Matters both of Religion and Human Life." [96]

Firmly persuaded that if Arminianism were to be crushed, that highly desirable end could be achieved only by demolishing its theory concerning the will, Edwards planned a treatise on the subject. Writing to his friend Joseph Bellamy in 1741, he said that he had been engaged "pretty thoroughly in the study of the Arminian Controversy," and that he had "writ^{n} considerably upon it" in his private papers. He asked, furthermore, that Bellamy attempt to discover for him the "best Book on the Arminian side, for the defense of their notion of Free Will." [97] Six years later he wrote to his Scottish correspondent Dr. Erskine: "I have thought of writing something particularly and largely on the Arminian controversy . . . beginning first with a discourse concerning the Freedom of the Will and Moral Agency." [98] Apparently the plan was laid aside during the

[95] *Works*, II, 190.

[96] *Discourse concerning the Being and Attributes of God* (London, 1738), p. 86.

[97] "Six Letters of Jonathan Edwards to Joseph Bellamy," *New England Quarterly*, April, 1928, pp. 230–231.

[98] Dwight, *Life*, p. 250.

painful period of his difficulties with the church at Northampton. But in 1752, two years after his dismissal from that place, he said in a letter to Erskine that he had begun "to write a little on the Arminian controversy," and that while he had been forced to break off, he hoped yet to carry out his design.[99] Finally in 1754, the *Freedom of the Will* appeared.

The controversy into which Edwards hurled himself with the publication of this book had been raging long and bitterly in the English intellectual world. Exactly one hundred years before, Hobbes in writing *Of Liberty and Necessity* had spoken of "those vast and involuble volumes concerning *predestination, free-will, free-grace, election, reprobation, etc.*, which fill not only our libraries, but the whole world with their noise and disturbance."[100] In New England, according to President Samuel Johnson of King's College, the controversy, in which he himself had taken a part in opposition to the Calvinists, had been fought with particular violence between the years 1736 and 1744.[101]

That Edwards had read widely on the subject, as well as thought deeply about it, is revealed not only in his letters and in the references to the work of other men in his own treatise, but by his obvious familiarity with all aspects of the problem as they had been presented in this long controversy.

POSITIVE ARGUMENT IN "FREEDOM OF THE WILL"

Edwards's treatment of the subject which seemed to him of basic importance in the controversy between Calvinists and

---

[99] In 1748 Edwards wrote Erskine that he had been diverted from the task of writing against some of the tenets of Arminianism by the unexpected task of preparing a life of Brainerd (*ibid.*, pp. 251, 511).

[100] *Works* (London, 1839), V, 234. See also Anthony Collins, *A Philosophic Inquiry concerning Human Liberty* (London, 1717), pp. 106 ff. A summary of the debate in England may be seen in Archibald Alexander, *Theories of the Will in the History of Philosophy* (1898), pp. 158 ff.

[101] *Autobiography, Works*, I, 26, 29. See Johnson's *Letters concerning the Sovereignty of God, Works*, III, 159 ff., and Dexter's list of books centering around these letters.

Arminians and which had for years assumed a large place in his reading and thinking falls conveniently into two major divisions: first, Edwards's positive argument for the necessitarian position and his definition of the term liberty; second, his answers to the chief objections raised against this doctrine by Arminians.[102]

Both of these divisions of his work rest upon one fundamental postulate—the postulate, namely, that every event must have a cause. "I assert," he wrote, "that nothing ever comes to pass without a Cause. . . . That whatsoever begins to be which before was not, must have a Cause why it then begins to exist, seems to be the first dictate of the common and natural sense which God hath implanted in the minds of all mankind, and the main foundation of all our reasonings about the existence of things, past, present, or to come."[103]

This postulate had been basic in the arguments of such important necessitarians as Hobbes and Collins. "I conceive," wrote Hobbes in *Liberty, Necessity, and Chance,* that "nothing taketh beginning from itself, but from the action of some other immediate agent without itself."[104] And Anthony Collins had argued that man must be a necessary agent, "because all his actions have a beginning. For whatever has a beginning must have a cause."[105]

[102] It should probably be noted that not all the men whom Edwards labels Arminians would have accepted the title. President Samuel Johnson, for example, although he plainly held Arminian views, objected to that "odious name" (*Works,* II, 26, 50, 161). In the preface to *Freedom of the Will,* Edwards admits that not all the men he attacks can strictly speaking be called Arminians but defends the use of the word as a means of avoiding awkward circumlocutions.

[103] *Freedom of the Will, Works,* II, 26–27. For Edwards's definition of the term *cause* see II, 26 and Dwight, *Life,* pp. 668, 681.

[104] *Works,* V, 372–378. See also *Of Liberty and Necessity, Works,* IV, 276. For evidence of Edwards's acquaintance with Hobbes's position, see note 208 below.

[105] *A Philosophical Inquiry concerning Human Liberty* (1717), pp. 57, 49. There is no evidence that Edwards had read Collins, to whose work his own has interesting resemblances. The ideas Collins expressed were, however, obviously current, for the many attacks on his book had given them a wide dissemination.

The particular application of this principle in the *Freedom of the Will* is that volitions cannot arise without causes. There is, Edwards insisted, nothing in the nature of volitional events to exempt them from the law of causation. "It is indeed as repugnant to reason, to suppose that an act of the Will should come into existence without a Cause, as to suppose the human soul, or an angel, or the globe of the earth, or the whole universe, should come into existence without a Cause." [106]

Edwards raised then what he called the "grand inquiry," namely, "What determines the Will?" It would be, he remarked, "very tedious and unnecessary at present to enumerate and examine all the various opinions which have been advanced concerning this matter. . . . It is sufficient to my present purpose to say, it is that motive, which, as it stands in the view of the mind, is the strongest, that determines the Will." [107]

That volitional impulses must unfailingly be the result of motives had naturally been assumed by many earlier writers on the subject. Locke had taken the point for granted, [108] and Leibnitz in his debate with Clarke had declared the assertion that "the *Mind may have good Reasons to act when it has no Motives*," a "Manifest Contradiction." [109]

There was nothing new, then, in Edwards's argument that the will is determined by motives. There was nothing new, either, in his corollary statement that it is the strongest motive

---

[106] *Works*, II, 29. See also section entitled "Whether Volition can Arise without a Cause through the Activity of the Nature of the Soul" (II, 30–32). See Hobbes, *Works*, IV, 274 and V, 372–373.

[107] *Works*, II, 3–4.

[108] *Essay*, Bk. II, chap. xxi, sec. 29.

[109] *A Collection of Papers which passed between the late Learned Mr. Leibnitz and Dr. Clarke*, p. 169. See also *Works*, trans. by George Martin Duncan (New Haven, 1890), p. 172. This assumption was in fact so basic in the arguments of necessitarians that their opponents felt called upon to deny its validity. See Clarke's denial in *Remarks upon a Book Entitled A Philosophical Enquiry concerning Human Liberty* (London, 1717), pp. 26, 43. See also Thomas Chubb, *A Collection of Tracts* (London, 1730), p. 257, and Archbishop King, *Essay on the Origin of Evil* (London, 1731), pp. 258, 247 ff.

which moves the will.[110] Locke had made the point in *An Essay concerning Human Understanding*,[111] and Leibnitz had ridiculed the notion that the mind could be moved by anything but the strongest motive.[112]

Now the strength of a motive depended, in Edwards's view, upon the degree of "apparent good" presented to the mind in connection with any possible action.[113] The term *good*, he used "as of the same import with *agreeable*."[114] Man is moved, then, in the direction of what seems to him most agreeable.[115] Edwards was here obviously anxious to exclude any notion of independent activity on the part of the will. As he saw it, the will was purely passive.

This desire to prove the will a merely passive mechanism is evident in the way in which he took pains to make clear at this point a divergence in belief from his admired author Locke. Locke had insisted that will and desire must not be confounded, arguing that the two often run counter to each other. "A man, whom I cannot deny," he said by way of illustration, "may oblige me to use persuasions to another, which, at the same time I am speaking, I may wish may not prevail on him."[116] In the same way, will and preference are distinct, "for though a man would prefer flying to walking, yet who can say he ever wills it?"[117] To this argument Edwards replied that if a man wills to walk he does not actually prefer flying, that as a matter of fact the immediate object of the will in this case is an external action, the moving of his legs and feet, and that "his willing such an alteration in his body in the present moment, is nothing else but his choosing or preferring such an alteration in his body at such a moment, or his liking it better than the forbearance of it."[118] If we carefully distinguish between the

[110] *Works*, II, 4.   [111] Bk. II, chap. xxi, sec. 40.
[112] *Works*, p. 167.   [113] *Works*, II, 4.
[114] *Ibid.*   [115] *Ibid.*, II, 5.
[116] *Essay*, Bk. II, chap. xxi, sec. 30.   [117] *Ibid.*, sec. 15.
[118] *Works*, II, 1–2.

real objects of the will, said he, we see that there is no difference between will and preference.

Nor is there any difference, he went on, between will and desire. The "instance which Mr. Locke produces" does not, he said, prove his point. The thing willed in the case of a man's being obliged against his desire to use persuasions upon another is the uttering of certain words. These words the man chooses to utter, and he "does not desire not to utter them." His wishing them not to be effectual is connected with another object than the speaking of them. In short, will and desire may be different for different objects, but they can never be opposed with reference to the same object.[119]

This insistence that will, preference, desire (Edwards adds choosing, refusing, approving, disapproving, liking, disliking, embracing, rejecting, determining, directing, commanding, forbidding, inclining or being averse, being pleased or displeased) are all merely different names for the act of the will, closed, so Edwards hoped, all the loopholes by which his opponents might drag in some notion of freedom under the guise of opposition among the affections. It was Edwards's eagerness to preclude the possibility of this answer to the argument for necessity that led him to declare over and over again that "the affections of the soul are not properly distinguished from the will."[120] The point which obviously he was anxious to establish is just this, that the will is always and of necessity drawn in the direction of the greatest apparent good, that man prefers, desires, chooses, and wills it, and that there is in the mind no power to resist the motion toward it.[121]

Edwards was anxious to establish this point because he felt that it led inevitably to the conclusion which he wanted to make irrefutable, namely, that the actions of the will are necessarily

[119] *Ibid.*, II, 2–3.
[120] *Ibid.*, III, 3, 280; II, 104; and Dwight, *Life*, pp. 665, 667.
[121] *Works*, II, 5, 7–8.

determined by something outside itself. His argument hangs together beautifully. An act of the will must, like every other event, have a cause. The cause of a volitional act is the motive to that act, that is, what in the mind's view is the greatest apparent good. The will must then always and of necessity be determined by the dictate of the understanding concerning the goodness, that is, the agreeableness, of the objects proposed for election.

For if the determination of the Will, evermore, in this manner, follows the light, conviction and view of the Understanding, concerning the greatest good and evil, and this be that alone which moves the Will, and it be a contradiction to suppose otherwise; then it is necessarily so, the Will necessarily follows this light or view of the Understanding, and not only in some of its acts, but in every act of choosing and refusing. So that the Will does not determine itself in any one of its own acts; but all its acts, every act of choice and refusal depends on, and is necessarily connected with some antecedent cause; which cause is not the Will itself, nor any act of its own, nor any thing pertaining to that faculty, but something belonging to another faculty, whose acts go before the Will, in all its acts, and govern and determine them.[122]

This passage is, indeed, not a bad summary statement of Edwards's position with respect to the freedom of the will.[123]

That position he attempted to make perfectly clear by defining carefully the term *freedom* or *liberty* as he employed it. In a very important passage, he explained that by liberty he meant "*the power, opportunity, or advantage, that any one has to do as he pleases, or conducting in any respect, according to his*

---

[122] *Works*, II, 49–50. In interpreting this passage it is necessary to remember that in Edwards's view the understanding, dependent as it was upon the senses—natural and supernatural—, was purely passive.

[123] Edwards, it should be added, made a great deal of the argument that God's foreknowledge of events, a foreknowledge he thought amply evidenced in scripture, was uncontrovertable proof that men's wills are not free in the way in which Arminians defined freedom (see *Works*, II, 61 ff.).

pleasure; without considering how his pleasure comes to be as it is."[124] The question, as he saw it, was can a man do what he wills, not can he will as he wills. As long as he is able to *do* what he chooses, he is free, although he may not be able to choose his choices. Here again Edwards is in the tradition established by Hobbes, Locke, Collins, and others. Hobbes had defined liberty as "*the absence of all the impediments to action that are not contained in the nature and intrinsic quality of the agent.*"[125] "I acknowledge," he said, "this *liberty*, that I *can* do if I *will*."[126]

The definition of liberty was in fact the core of the controversy over the freedom of the will. Archbishop William King stated the point very clearly in *An Essay on the Origin of Evil.* Philosophers, he wrote, "may be distinguished into two Sects, both admitting of Liberty, the one from external *Compulsion*, but not from internal *Necessity;* the other from both."[127] Over this ground, Hobbes and Bishop Bramhall had fought with characteristic acrimony in their debate concerning the freedom of the will. Hobbes had, in fact, declared that the chief ground of difference between them was the question whether it were "in a man's power now to choose the will he shall have anon," the notion that men were "free to *do* as they *will* and to *forbear* as they *will*" being accepted by both of them.[128] The Bishop asserted the distinction here to be one without a difference, to which Hobbes replied that if the Bishop "cannot understand the difference between *free to do if he will*, and *free to will* [he] is not fit, as I have said in the stating of the question, to hear this controversy disputed, much less to be a Writer in it." [129]   The distinction seemed so important to the younger Edwards that in reviewing his father's contribution to the free-

---

[124] *Ibid.,* II, 183. See also II, 17, 18, 40.

[125] *Works,* IV, 273.

[126] *Ibid.,* IV, 240.

[127] 3rd edition (1739), p. 227. Published in Dublin and London in 1702 as *De Origine Mali.* English translation by Edmund Law in 1729.

[128] *Works,* V, preface "To the Reader," and pp. 5, 38–39, 189.

[129] *Ibid.,* pp. 43, 51.

will controversy he declared that "the whole controversy concerning liberty and necessity, depends on the explanation of the word *liberty*, or the sense in which that word is used." [130]

Having defined liberty as the ability of a man to do as he wills, Edwards asserted that no higher liberty than this could be conceived of. No one, said he with characteristic dogmatism, "can rise higher in his conceptions of liberty, than the notion of it which I have explained: which notion is apparently, perfectly consistent with the whole of that necessity of men's actions, which I suppose takes place. And I scruple not to say, it is beyond all their wits to invent a higher notion, or form a higher imagination of liberty." [131] Even that staunch necessitarian Calvin had asked, after presenting the grounds for his belief that man's will was wholly under the power of forces outside himself: "What end could it answer to decorate a thing so diminutive with a title so superb" as *free?*[132] But Edwards insisted that the freedom he ascribed to the will was the highest "that ever could possibly enter into the heart of any man to conceive." [133] Here again he was in agreement with Locke, who asked, "How can we think any one freer than to have the power to do what he will?" [134]

Strictly speaking, then, Edwards did not deny the freedom of the will. He merely defined it so as to limit it to the power of acting upon impulses in the generation of which the mind was wholly passive.

EDWARDS'S ANSWER TO OBJECTIONS

Besides elaborating the argument for necessity and defining carefully just what, in his view, liberty meant, Edwards devoted a great deal of space in the *Freedom of the Will* to a detailed consideration of the chief arguments for what he called "the

[130] *Works* (Boston, 1854), I, 484.
[131] *Works*, II, 184.
[132] *Institutes*, Bk. II, chap. ii, sec. 7.
[133] *Works*, II, 185.
[134] *Essay*, Bk. II, chap. xxi, sec. 21.

Arminian notion of Liberty of Will," exposing, so he thought, the fallacies inherent in them.

One of the most important of these was that man as an agent had the power of initiating action, a self-moving and self-determining power; that, in short, he was more than a merely passive creature. The argument for this position rested upon two chief bases and was formulated most convincingly perhaps by Samuel Clarke.

The first of these was an interpretation of the meaning of the terms *agent* and *action*. "To be an *Agent*," said Clarke in his attack on the necessitarian Collins, "signifies, to have a *Power of beginning Motion*," and "*a Necessary Agent or Necessary Action is a Contradiction in Terms*." [135]

A second argument to prove that men as agents have a self-determining power was based upon that fundamental contention of the necessitarians themselves, namely, that every event must have a cause. There must be somewhere in nature, argued Clarke, a "*Self-moving* or *Active Power* or *Principle of beginning Motion*," for to suppose otherwise is to suppose "an infinite progression of *dependent Effects without any Cause at all;* an infinite progression of *passive Communications*, without *any Agent*, without *any thing Active at all* in Nature." [136] Since this supposition is manifestly absurd, it is necessary to assume an independent being behind all the phenomena of nature, a being with the power of beginning motion. The question is whether this being has communicated the power of self-motion to any of his creatures. To this question Clarke replied that since logically any power except that of self-existence can be communicated by a creator, it is possible that men have been

---

[135] *Remarks upon a Book Entitled a Philosophical Enquiry*, pp. 5–6. See also Clarke, *A Collection of Papers which passed between the late Learned Mr. Leibnitz and Dr. Clarke*, pp. 405, 285; King, *Origin of Evil*, p. 234 n.; and Chubb, *A Collection of Tracts*, p. 311, for further discussion of this argument for freedom.

[136] *Remarks*, p. 30. See also his *Being and Attributes of God*, pp. 11–15.

endowed with the power of initiating motion. Experience and observation were, he felt, enough to prove that they do possess it.[137]

In the possession of such a power the "Essence of Liberty consists," according to Clarke. This chain of reasoning in the view of its sponsors invalidated the contention of their opponents that since determinations of the will must have causes, the will is necessarily moved by what to the mind is the greatest apparent good. Man as an agent, said they, is a real cause. It is not necessary to look for causes outside the will.[138]

To this whole argument Edwards made specific answer. One of the most devastatingly logical passages in the *Freedom of the Will* deals with the interpretation of the terms *agent* and *action*.

"The word *action*, as Mr. Chubb and many others use it, is," he said, "utterly unintelligible and inconsistent." First they say that word cannot properly be used to signify something that is passive, that is to say, according to their own definition of passiveness, action cannot be an effect. And yet they say that the mind's action is self-determined, that is, the effect of its own determination. "So that here we have this contradiction, that action is always the effect of foregoing choice; and therefore cannot be action."

In the second place, said he, these men declare that necessity is inconsistent with action, that "a necessary action is a contradiction," but they also say that actions "must be determined by the Will and free choice." In short, they make action necessarily the result of choice while declaring that a necessary action is a contradiction in terms.

Furthermore, added Edwards, they speak of action as the beginning of motion, but "they say there is no proper action

[137] *Being and Attributes of God*, pp. 83 ff.
[138] Archbishop William King's *Origin of Evil* contains a brilliant statement of the argument. See pp. 264–282 and the notes of Edmund Law, the translator, on pp. 234–239, 246, 258, 351–352.

but what is freely chosen; or, which is the same thing, determined by a foregoing act of free choice." In other words, they assert that action is the beginning of motion and then say that it must be the consequence of a preceding exertion of volitional power.

This analysis is concluded by one of Edwards's most slashing attacks on his opponents, an attack in his very best controversial manner. It reveals how relentlessly he hunted down his antagonists in the thorny thickets of the free-will controversy:

So that, according to their notion of an act, considered with regard to its consequences, these following things are all essential to it, viz., that it should be necessary, and not necessary; that it should be from a cause, and no cause; that it should be the fruit of choice and design, and not the fruit of choice and design; that it should be the beginning of motion or exertion, and yet consequent on previous exertion; that it should be before it is; . . . that it should be self-originated, and also have its original from something else; that it is what the mind causes itself, of its own Will, and can produce or prevent, according to its choice or pleasure, and yet what the mind has no power to prevent, it precluding all previous choice in the affair.

So that an act, according to their metaphysical notion of it, is something of which there is no idea: it is nothing but a confusion of the mind, excited by words without any distinct meaning, and is an absolute nonentity. . . . But it is impossible any idea or notion should subsist in the mind, whose very nature and essence, which constitutes it, destroys it. If some learned philosopher, who had been abroad, in giving an account of the curious observations he had made in his travels, should say, "He had been in *Terra del Fuego*, and there had seen an animal, which he calls by a certain name, that begat and brought forth itself, and yet had a sire and dam distinct from itself; that it had an appetite, and was hungry before it had a being; that his master, who led him, and governed him at his pleasure, was always governed by him, and driven by him where he pleased; that when he moved, he always took a step before the

first step; that he went with his head first, and yet always went
tail foremost; and this, though he had neither head nor tail:"
it would be no imprudence at all, to tell such a traveller, though
a learned man, that he himself had no notion or idea of such
an animal, as he gave an account of, and never had, nor ever
would have.[139]

Thus did Edwards in a burst of contempt dismiss the argument from the definition of the terms *action* and *agent* upon
which believers in the freedom of the will had based in great
part their contention for a self-moving power in man. With
equal assurance and severity he attacked the notion from other
points of view. Arminians contend, he said, in exactly the words
used by Clarke, that the liberty of the will most essentially
consists in a self-moving power.[140] The belief in such a power,
about which he said there has been "a great noise made,"[141] was
in his view really a rejection of the principle of causation. What
it amounted to was a notion that acts of the will "arise from
nothing; no cause, no power, no influence being at all concerned
in the matter."[142] The argument from the necessity and nature
of causation he then applied in analyzing destructively the contention that since the will is self-determined, motives are not
real causes of its action.[143]

But his chief objection to the notion of a self-determining
power in man was that it led to the following dilemma. If the
will in all of its free acts is freely self-determined, then each of
them must be preceded by a free act of the will, and that in turn
by another, and so on until one comes to a first act of the will.
Now if this first act be determined by a previous one, it is not
the first act. If, on the other hand, it is not determined by a
previous volition, it must, according to the Arminian definition
of freedom, not be free, since it is not self-determined. In

[139] *Works*, II, 123–124.
[140] *Freedom of the Will, Works*, II, 20.
[141] *Ibid.*, II, 25.   [142] *Ibid.*, II, 25.   [143] *Ibid.*, II, 26 ff.

short, it is "plainly absurd, and a manifest inconsistence, to suppose that the Will itself determines all the free acts of the Will."[144] This chain of reasoning, his famous *reductio ad absurdum*, Edwards employed over and over again. A typical passage follows:

If the Will determines the Will, then choice orders and determines the choice; and acts of choice are subject to the decision, and follow the conduct of other acts of choice. And therefore if the Will determines all its own free acts, then every free act of choice is determined by a preceding act of choice, choosing that act. And if that preceding act of Will or choice be also a free act, then by these principles, in this act too, the Will is self-determined; that is, this, in like manner, is an act that the soul voluntarily chooses; or, which is the same thing, it is an act determined still by a preceding act of the Will, choosing that. And the like may again be observed of the last mentioned act, which brings us directly to a contradiction; for it supposes an act of the Will preceding the first act in the whole train, directing and determining the rest; or a free act of the Will, before the first free act of the Will. Or else we must come at last to an act of the Will, determining the consequent acts, wherein the Will is not self-determined, and so is not a free act, in this notion of freedom; but if the first act in the train, determining and fixing the rest, be not free, none of them all can be free; as is manifest at first view, but shall be demonstrated presently.[145]

This argument resembles closely that employed by Locke to prove that it is ridiculous to ask whether a man can will what he will, that is, whether the will can determine itself. "They who can make a question of it," said Locke, "must suppose one will to determine the acts of another, and another to determine that; and so on in infinitum."[146]

Edwards likewise rejected another common argument for

[144] *Ibid.*, II, 20.   [145] *Ibid.*, II, 21.
[146] *Essay*, Bk. II, chap. xxi, sec. 25.

freedom of the will, the argument from experience.[147] Wollaston in *The Religion of Nature Delineated* (1722) had rested his case for liberty upon this contention alone. It seemed to him that all the disputes about human liberty "with which men have tired themselves and the world" were needless. "The short way of knowing," he said, whether we can act freely or not is to try.

And I am persuaded, if men would be serious, and put forth themselves, they would find by experience, that their wills are not so universally and peremptorily determined by what occurs, nor predestination and fate so rigid, but that *much* is left to their own conduct. Up and try.[148]

Dr. Samuel Johnson, when Boswell reported to him that Edwards "puzzled" him "so much as to freedom of the human will, by stating with wonderful acute ingenuity, our being actuated by a series of motives which we cannot resist, that the only relief I had was to forget it," dismissed the matter with the remark: "All theory is against the freedom of the will; all experience for it." [149]

Anthony Collins had in *A Philosophical Inquiry* made an elaborate refutation of the argument from experience. He admitted that the vulgar believe themselves to experience freedom. Since they repent some of their actions, they feel that they

---

[147] Two other arguments of lesser importance might be here noticed. One was the so-called argument from indifference. Defenders of liberty sometimes insisted that since the objects proposed for election were often either alike in themselves or alike in the view of the mind, the choice of one of them could not be the result of the apparent goodness of the object but must be determined by a free power within man (see Isaac Watts, *Works*, VI, 241 ff., and compare the answers of Collins, *A Philosophical Inquiry concerning Human Liberty*, pp. 46–52, and Edwards, *Works*, II, 35 ff.). Another argument was that men have at least the power to suspend action long enough to view carefully the paths before them. Locke used this argument to prove that men had freedom of a sort (*Essay*, Bk. II, chap. xxi, sec. 46 ff.). Here again compare Collins (pp. 38–40) with Edwards (*Works*, II, 44–45).

[148] London, 1726, pp. 63–64. Edwards refers to Wollaston in *The Nature of True Virtue* (*Works*, II, 276).

[149] *Life of Johnson* (London, 1927), II, 220–221.

could have acted otherwise than they did, a notion which is strengthened by their experience of changing their minds. Since they deliberate over some matters, they assume that their minds are often balanced in a state of indifference so that they are free to make a choice. They entertain these beliefs, however, only because they do not attend to or do not see the causes of their actions. Furthermore, they believe themselves free because they feel that they can *do* what they will, although ability to act as they will is not inconsistent with necessity. In support of his position, Collins quoted Bayle and Leibnitz.[150]

Like Collins, Edwards rejected the argument from experience. He pointed out, to begin with, that since we experience directly only what goes on in our own minds, we can reason only from our own experience. I am conscious, he said, that I can act as I please. What causes my pleasure to be as it is I do not perceive. But it would be as foolish for me to believe that because I do not see the forces which determine my will, it determines itself as it would be to believe that since "I first found myself possessed of being, before I had knowledge of a cause of my being," I either produced myself or was created by chance.[151]

One of the most important arguments for the freedom of the

[150] Pp. 12–57.

[151] *Freedom of the Will, Works*, II, 173, note. Defenders of liberty sometimes raised another point, closely related to the argument from experience. They claimed, Edwards said, that common sense supported their contentions, while necessitarians were forced to "nice, scholastic distinctions, and abstruse, metaphysical subtilties, and set those in opposition to common sense." Edwards observes that if reasoning is sound it is no confutation of it to call it metaphysical. "The question is not, whether what is said be metaphysic, logic, or mathematics, Latin, French, English or *Mohawk?* But whether the reasoning be good, and the arguments truly conclusive?" (*ibid.*, II, 171). His own exposition he insists does not depend upon "abstruse definitions or distinctions, or terms without a meaning, or of very ambiguous and undetermined signification, or any points of such abstraction and subtilty as tends to involve the attentive understanding in clouds and darkness" (*ibid.*, II, 172). The pretended demonstrations of Arminians are, however, according to him, full of "unintelligible, metaphysical phrases" (*ibid.*, II, 174). In particular he accuses Arminians of employing arguments from common sense by distorting words from their original and common use (*ibid.*, p. 135).

will, in the eyes of those who rejected the notion of necessity, was the contention that freedom was essential for morality since without it rewards and punishments were unjust. How, they asked, can a man be rightfully punished for doing what he cannot help doing? Bayle granted that this was "one of the strongest arguments alleged for the liberty of man." [152] Hobbes had admitted that the objection "of greatest consequence" offered by Bramhall was that "if there be a necessity of all events . . . it will follow, that praise and reprehension, and reward and punishment, are all vain and unjust." [153] Collins, too, had noted that these "supposed inconveniencies attending the doctrine of *necessity*" were among the chief weapons in the hands of its opponents, adding that the "great EPISCOPIUS," although he had admitted that experience supported the doctrine of necessity, had rejected that doctrine because it had seemed to him subversive of "*all religion, laws, rewards, and punishments.*"[154] Bishop Butler seems to have expressed, then, a widespread opinion when he declared that even if the doctrine of necessity were speculatively true, practice proved it false and misleading, for it would not do to teach men that they did not deserve to be rewarded or punished.[155]

That men will lose all sense of guilt if they are once convinced that they act as they do by necessity was emphatically asserted by those who believed that men were free. If a man commits a crime by necessity, said Samuel Fancourt, the fault

[152] *Dictionary Historical and Critical of Mr. Peter Bayle* (second ed., London, 1737), IV, 908.

[153] *Works*, IV, 248.

[154] *A Philosophical Inquiry*, pp. 22–24. Episcopius (1583–1643) was the leader of the Arminian party in Holland after the death of Arminius and was one of its most influential writers.

[155] A youth educated in fatalistic principles would be "insupportable to society." "Practical application" of the scheme of fatality is "absurd." "And therefore, though it were admitted that this opinion of necessity were speculatively true; yet, with regard to practice, it is as if it were false, so far as our experience reaches." (*The Analogy of Religion* [1736], Pt. I, chap. vi, secs. 5–6.)

is not his own but should be ascribed to the agent that moved him.[156] "No man," said Bishop Bramhall in attacking Hobbes, "blameth a fire for burning whole cities; no man taxeth poison for destroying men. . . . If the will of man be not in his own disposition, he is no more a free agent than the fire or the poison."[157] This contention seemed to many defenders of liberty quite unanswerable.

In meeting it, the exponents of necessity in the eighteenth century had little to say beyond what Hobbes had said in reply to it. He had argued, in the first place, that for what a man does willingly he is reasonably held blameworthy even when he acts from necessity. Since in his "scheme of fatalism" men were granted power to *do* what they will, he saw no reason why they should not be held blameworthy for evil acts. "It is enough to the judge, that the act he condemneth be voluntary."[158] So, too, Calvin had taught. "I deny," he wrote, "that sin is the less criminal, because it is necessary."[159] Sinful men find the source of evil in themselves. They sin willingly even if necessarily. They may, therefore, be justly punished.[160] This conclusion had been accepted by that good Calvinist, Solomon Stoddard, Edwards's grandfather and his predecessor at Northampton.[161]

A second answer offered by Hobbes to the contention that men cannot be justly punished for the things they must of

---

[156] *An Essay concerning Liberty, Grace, and Prescience* (London, 1729), p. 12.

[157] King, *Origin of Evil*, p. 328 n. The passage from which Bramhall's statement is taken is in Hobbes, *Works*, V, 45.

[158] *Liberty, Necessity, and Chance, Works*, V, 181. See also V, 151; IV, 252, 260.

[159] *Institutes*, Bk. II, chap. v, sec. 1.

[160] *Ibid.*, sec. 11.

[161] *The Safety of Appearing at the Day of Judgment* (Northampton, 1804), p. 238. See also Collins, *A Philosophical Inquiry*, pp. 93–94.

Both Calvin and Hobbes declare that man has no right to question the justice of God in punishing men who act only as he has determined them to. "Who art thou, O man, that wouldest impose laws upon God," asked Calvin (*Institutes*, Bk. II, chap. v, sec. 5). Cf. Hobbes, *Works*, IV, 249, 257, and V, 199.

necessity do was that punishment acts as a deterrent to crime. It "may, if not capital, reform the will of the offender; if capital, the will of others by example."[162] Many necessitarians felt, like Bayle, that the argument that freedom was necessary to justify punishment was inconclusive, because it did not take into account the use of punishment as a corrective.

> This argument for a free-will is not so strong, as it seems to be; for though men are persuaded that machines have no feeling, they will nevertheless give them a hundred blows with a hammer, when they are out of order, if they think that they may be set right by flatting a wheel, or another piece of iron. They would therefore cause a pick-pocket to be whipped, though they knew that he had no free-will, if experience had taught them that the whipping of people keeps them from committing certain actions.[163]

Collins argued the point at length, citing the treatment of animals and madmen as proof that punishment is often justly employed in handling beings admittedly without free-will.[164]

Edwards's answer to the argument that the doctrine of necessity undercut the foundations of morality was carefully elaborated. He had been considering the problem at least as early as his college days, for he had set down among the subjects to be handled in his projected "Treatise on the Mind" this one: "Concerning the prime and proper foundation of Blame."[165] The seriousness with which he regarded the matter is indicated by the title of his book, *A Careful and Strict Enquiry into the Modern Prevailing Notions of that Freedom of Will which is supposed to be Essential to Moral Agency, Virtue and Vice, Reward and Punishment, Praise and Blame.*

His first reason for thinking that necessity was not incompatible with praise and blame was that God and Christ were

---

[162] *Liberty, Necessity, and Chance, Works,* V, 181.
[163] *Dictionary,* IV, 908.
[164] *A Philosophical Inquiry,* pp. 91–92.
[165] Dwight, *Life,* p. 665.

generally considered to be necessarily good and yet deserving of praise. The argument is driven home with great vigor in the sections of his work entitled "God's Moral Excellency necessary, yet virtuous and praiseworthy" and "The Acts of the Will of the human Soul of Jesus Christ, necessarily holy, yet truly virtuous, praiseworthy, rewardable, etc."[166] On the other hand, according to Scripture, men whom God had determined to do evil were held blameworthy. If necessity "will prove men blameless, then Judas was blameless, after Christ had given him over, and had already declared his certain damnation."[167]

Edwards did more, however, than merely rely on Scriptural proof. He resorted in this connection to the distinction between natural and moral necessity. He admitted that conduct resulting from natural necessity is neither praiseworthy or blameworthy, because in such conduct the motivation is from without.[168] But he asserted, like Calvin, Hobbes, and Collins, man's guiltiness in connection with evil acts performed by moral necessity,[169] on the ground that in such acts the motivation is from within; a man is doing what he wills.[170] In fact he contended that if the moral inability to fulfill an obligation excuses an evil act, "then wickedness always carries that in it which excuses it."[171] According to this principle, the more wicked a man's heart is, the stronger his inclinations to evil are, the less blameworthy he is, for the less able is he to do right. Moreover, if a strong inclination to

---

[166] Pt. III, secs. 1–2.

[167] *Freedom of the Will, Works*, II, 95. See Pt. III, sec. 3: "The Case of such as are given up of God to Sin, and of fallen Man in general, proves moral Necessity and Inability to be consistent with blameworthiness."

[168] *Ibid.*, II, 95–96, 99 ff., 127 ff.

[169] Edwards made the conventional distinction between natural and moral necessity, the former being the result of purely physical causes, the latter, of moral causes, such as disposition and habit. (II, 13 ff.)

[170] *Freedom of the Will, Works*, II, 99. See *The Justice of God in the Damnation of Sinners, Works*, IV, 229.

[171] *Freedom of the Will, Works*, II, 103.

virtue lessens a man's right to praise, then the more indifferent to good a man is, the more praiseworthy are his good actions.[172] This conclusion, is, however, manifestly absurd, for "men do not think a good act to be less praiseworthy, for the agent's being much determined in it by a good inclination or a good motive, but the more."[173] The reasoning of Arminians, Edwards concluded, leads them, then, into the ridiculous position of asserting that indifference to good or evil is essential to virtue, while all good habits and inclinations are contrary to it.[174] He plainly had little respect for the Arminian argument that the doctrine of necessity was subversive of morality because it made punishment unjust.

It is clear that Edwards felt that he had said the last word concerning the freedom of the will. He was confident that he had set the Calvinistic theory of the will in an impregnable position, and that he had made untenable the position of Arminians on the subject. With ruthless logic he triumphantly reduced the arguments of his opponents to absurdity, remarking on one occasion, after blocking as it seemed to him all the possible avenues for eluding his conclusion, "and so the race is at an end, but the evader is taken in his flight,"[175] and declaring on another occasion that all the objections of Arminians to his theory were "vain and frivolous." The strength of his assurance that he had answered all possible objections to the Calvinistic theory is amusingly revealed in a statement regarding a possible "evasion" of his argument. "I confess," he wrote, "it is an evasion of my own inventing; and I do not know but I should wrong *Arminians*, in supposing that any of them should make use of it. But it being as good a one as I could invent, I would observe upon it a few things."[176] He believed that he had undermined the position of his foes by proving their arguments to be full of inconsistencies. Concerning what he regarded as a damaging contradiction

[172] *Freedom of the Will, Works,* II, 132.   [173] *Ibid.,* II, 133.
[174] *Ibid.,* II, 110 ff.   [175] *Ibid.,* II, 120.   [176] *Ibid.,* II, 51.

in the writings of Dr. Chubb, he said that it "at once utterly abolishes the Doctor's whole scheme of liberty of the will ... at one stroke, has cut the sinews of his arguments ... enervated and made vain all those exclamations against the doctrine of the *Calvinists*." [177] He could not resist declaring his triumph at the end of his work:

And really all the *Arminians* on earth might be challenged, without arrogance or vanity, to make these principles of theirs, wherein they mainly differ from their fathers, whom they so much despise, consistent with common sense; yea, and perhaps to produce any doctrine ever embraced by the blindest bigot of the church of Rome, or the most ignorant Mussulman or extravagant enthusiast, that might be reduced to more demonstrable inconsistencies, and repugnancies to common sense, and to themselves.[178]

There were and have been many ready to agree with Edwards in his confidence that on the question of the freedom of the will he had once and for all established the Calvinistic position and destroyed that of Arminians. The younger Edwards expressed the exultant confidence of the adherents of the New Theology in the unanswerableness of his father's work:

On the great subject of *Liberty* and *Necessity*, Mr. Edwards made very important improvements. Before him, the *Calvinists* were nearly driven out of the field, by *Arminians*, *Pelagians*, and *Socinians*. . . . The Calvinists themselves began to be ashamed of their own cause and to give it up, so far at least as relates to liberty and necessity. . . . But Mr. Edwards put an end to this seeming triumph of those, who were thus hostile to that system of doctrines. . . . Now, therefore, the Calvinists find themselves placed upon firm and high ground. They fear not the attacks of their opponents. They face them on the ground of reason, as well as of Scripture. They act not merely on the defensive. Rather they have carried the war into Italy, and to the very gates of Rome.[179]

[177] *Ibid.*   [178] *Works*, II, 181.   [179] *Works* (Boston, 1854), I, 481–484.

Foster, who probably understood the Edwardean movement better than any other historian of it, thought it not too much to say that Edwards by his work on the will had brought New England theology back to Calvinism.[180] The importance of Edwards's book in the eyes of Calvinists may be judged from the fact that it was used as the text in moral philosophy at that Calvinistic stronghold, Yale, until 1775.[181]

THE TOTAL DEPRAVITY OF MAN

At the conclusion of the *Freedom of the Will*, Edwards confidently declared his belief that by "clearing and establishing the Calvinistic *doctrine* in this point" he had knocked out the supports upon which the Arminian theology rested and had invalidated the most important objections urged by Arminians against the Calvinistic system. Among the doctrines which were, as he saw it, bolstered by his argument for necessity was the doctrine of "the *total depravity and corruption of man's nature*," the doctrine that man "is wholly under the power of sin, and . . . utterly unable, without the interposition of sovereign grace . . . to do any thing that is truly good."[182]

Edwards's argument in the *Freedom of the Will* furnished support for this doctrine in two ways. In the first place, it answered the chief objection to it. Those who opposed the theory of total depravity were wont to say that if, as Calvinists insisted, man were so corrupt by nature that he was utterly unable to do anything but evil, he could not be held responsible for his wickedness. No one, they said, can be blamed for doing what he cannot help doing. They pointed out, in short, that in preaching the doctrine of total depravity Cal-

[180] *A Genetic History of the New England Theology* (Chicago, 1907), p. 77.
[181] *The Literary Diary of Ezra Stiles*, ed. by Franklin Bowditch Dexter (New York, 1901), II, 349, and III, 361.
[182] *Works*, II, 177

vinists were overreaching themselves: instead of establishing man's sinfulness, they established his guiltlessness.[183] Edwards felt that his argument in the *Freedom of the Will* for the blameworthiness of necessary acts on the ground that such acts were voluntary relieved the doctrine of total depravity of the weight of this objection.[184]

But the *Freedom of the Will* did more in support of the doctrine than clear away objections to it. It provided, in the second place, a solid base upon which positive argument for the corruption of human nature might be built. Nothing was insisted upon more strongly in that book than that volitional acts must have causes. According to Edwards, it would not do to say merely that the cause of an act of the will was a previous determination of the will, for this would involve the assumption that each decision of the mind was the result of an antecedent choice, an assumption manifestly absurd since somewhere there must have been a first act of the will. This first act, and all succeeding acts, must be, he argued further, determined by the natural disposition of the agent to find some things agreeable and others disagreeable. This disposition cannot be the result of choice. It must be inborn. To suppose it the result of choice would be to posit another chain of volitional cause and effect, which would logically have to be carried back at last to a decision dependent upon the inborn temper of the agent.

Thus the question arose: with what dispositions do men come into the world? Edwards's answer was unequivocal. On the basis of his argument against the freedom of the will, he affirmed uncompromisingly the Calvinistic belief that men enter this life totally depraved—enter it with dispositions that make them wholly unable of themselves either to do good or to avoid evil.

---

[183] See for example, Samuel Webster, *The Winter Evening's Conversation Vindicated* (Boston, 1758), p. 13: "Such a *Fountain of Sin* in us, as *necessarily*, or as *wholly disinclines* and *disables to all good*, I do not hold. . . . For what is *necessary* can't be *sinful*."

[184] *Works*, II, 177–178.

There were many, of course, who found this harsh view of human nature too bitter a pill to swallow. One of the most influential spokesmen of this group in Edwards's days was the English divine John Taylor, whose book, *The Scripture-Doctrine of Original Sin Proposed to a Free and Candid Examination*, created at its publication in 1738 a great stir in religious circles. It furnished objectors to the doctrine of total depravity with what seemed to them quite unanswerable arguments against it and aroused its defenders to battle. Taylor contended that as a result of Adam's sin men were subject to sorrow, labor, and physical death, but that they were not thereby made guilty of sin, not totally corrupted.[185] "We may *suffer* by their Sin [that is, the sin of Adam and Eve], and actually do *suffer* by it; but we are not *punished* for their Sin, because we are not *guilty* of it." [186] Taylor examined in detail the proofs offered in the Larger Catechism for the proposition that the Fall resulted in "the corruption of his [man's] Nature, whereby he is utterly indisposed, disabled, and made opposite unto all Evil, and that continually," and he declared, "I shall not scruple to say, this Proposition in the *Assembly's Catechism* is false." [187] In fact, he asserted that men were in no worse a moral state than Adam was at his creation.[188] Like Adam, they had no "natural propensity," no "necessary inclination" to sin.[189]

To this frank and vigorous attack on the doctrine of total depravity several important English divines replied. One of them was the mild Calvinist Isaac Watts. Watts believed that "we have just reason to conclude, there is some original and universal degeneracy spread over the whole race of men from their birth" so that "though by reason of his natural faculties [man] may have a remote and speculative sufficiency of natural power to obey his Maker's law, yet he has no proximate and practical, or moral sufficiency to perform it, by reason of the

[185] P. 25.   [186] P. 21.
[187] Pp. 100–125.   [188] Pp. 184 ff.   [189] Pp. 186 ff.

perverse and sinful bias of his will and affections, and the weak
influences of understanding, reason, and conscience. . . ."[190]
Watts published his views in *The Ruin and Recovery of Mankind* (1740), to which Taylor replied in great detail in 1746.

At this point John Wesley entered the controversy. He
wrote partly in defense of Watts, but chiefly in opposition to
Taylor. As an Arminian he believed in the freedom of the will,
but he considered Taylor's doctrine dangerously subversive of
evangelical faith because it gave too small a place to God's grace
in the regeneration of men.[191]

Some time before Wesley's reply to Taylor was published,
the controversy over the doctrine of original sin had spread to
New England. In 1757 Samuel Webster, pastor at Salisbury,
Massachusetts, published anonymously a tract entitled *A Winter
Evening's Conversation upon the Doctrine of Original Sin*, which
became the center of an exciting controversy. Webster, who,
it is plain, was deeply indebted to Taylor, did not believe that
men are born depraved. Infants, he said, are "as blameless as
helpless."[192] Webster's book called forth a reply from the
Reverend Peter Clark, pastor at Salem Village, now Danvers,
Massachusetts. Clark called his work *A Summer Morning's
Conversation* (1758).[193] Webster defended himself in *The Winter
Evening's Conversation Vindicated* (1758). Clark thought it
necessary to write *A Defense of the Principles of the Summer
Morning's Conversation* (1760) and took the offensive again
in his *Answer to the Winter Evening's Conversation Vindicated*.
Meanwhile other writers came into the fray. Charles Chauncy
took Webster's side in *The Opinion of One that Has Perused the
Summer Morning's Conversation* (1758). Whereupon Clark

---

[190] *Works* (London, 1811), VI, 74–75.
[191] *The Doctrine of Original Sin*, *Works* (ed. John Emory), V, 492.
[192] Quoted by Walker, *A History of the Congregational Churches in the
United States*, p. 274.
[193] The full title was *Scripture-Doctrine of Original Sin Stated and Defended. A Summer Morning's Conversation between a Minister and a
Neighbor. A Reply to a Winter Evening's Conversation.*

paused long enough in his thumping of Webster to attack
Chauncy in *Remarks on a Late Pamphlet, entitled the Opinion*
(1758).

Among the replies provoked by Webster's book was an
anonymous dialogue by Edwards's friend and disciple Joseph
Bellamy. Writing in 1758, the stormiest year of the controversy,
Bellamy announced that Edwards was soon to publish a defense
of the doctrine of original sin. [194]

The work to which Bellamy referred appeared in the same
year with the title: *The Great Christian Doctrine of Original Sin
Defended; Evidences of its Truth Produced, and Arguments to the
Contrary Answered, containing in Particular, A Reply to the
Objections and Arguings of Dr. John Taylor, in his Book, entitled, "The Scripture-Doctrine of Original Sin Proposed to Free
and Candid Examination, etc."* Although Edwards published
in the midst of the debate over Webster's book, he made no
reference to it, unless the phrase in the preface, "Dr. Taylor,
and other opposers of the Doctrine of Original Sin," be assumed
to include him. It is likely that Edwards had finished his work
before Webster's appeared. [195]   It may be, on the other hand,
that he thought it useless to attack Webster since the latter had
obviously done little more than parrot Taylor. It was to Taylor
that Edwards turned his attention. Taylor's book, said Edwards,
had "made a great noise." He wrote, "I have closely attended to
Dr. Taylor's *Piece on Original Sin*, in all its Parts, and have
endeavored that no one thing there said, of any consequence in
this Controversy, should pass unnoticed, or that any thing
which has the appearance of an Argument, in opposition to this
Doctrine, should be left unanswered." At the same time he
revealed his intention of making his work "a *general* Defense of
that great important Doctrine"—original sin. [196]

---

[194] See Walker, *op. cit.*, p. 274.
[195] The preface to Edwards's work bears the date May 26, 1757.
[196] *Works*, II, 307.

In most respects the book was a lucid and emphatic statement of the conventional arguments for the doctrine of total depravity. Edwards began, as Wesley did a bit later, by asserting that the universal and complete corruption of human nature was a fact easily demonstrated from history and observation. "All Mankind," he wrote, "do constantly, in all Ages, without Fail in any one Instance, run into that moral Evil, which is, in Effect, their own utter and eternal Perdition, in a total Privation of God's Favor, and Suffering of his Vengeance and Wrath." [197] From this fact he drew the conclusion that men are born with an irresistible tendency toward sin. Only in this way can universal sinfulness be accounted for. [198] Now this complete depravity of the race must have a cause. It can be explained satisfactorily only by assuming it to be the result of Adam's transgression.

But Edwards did more than brilliantly elaborate the usual Calvinistic position. He could not consider a subject deeply without contributing something to the discussion of it. At two points he made contributions to the debate concerning original sin, one of them being among his most important legacies to New England theology.

The first was a bold reinterpretation of the doctrine of the "imputation" of Adam's sin and guilt to his posterity. "All mankind," reads the Larger Catechism, "descending from him [Adam] by ordinary generation, sinned in him, and fell with him in that first transgression." Objectors to this doctrine declared that sin was a personal matter, that Adam therefore could not have contracted it for us. [199] Webster, in his vindica-

[197] *Ibid.*, II, 309. Cf. Calvin's statement: "Let us hold this, then, as an undoubted truth, which no opposition can ever shake—that the mind of man is so completely alienated from the righteousness of God, that it conceives, desires, and undertakes every thing that is impious, perverse, base, impure, and flagitious; that his heart is so thoroughly infected by the poison of sin, that it cannot produce any thing but what is corrupt. . . ." (*Institutes*, Bk. II, chap. v, sec. 19.) [198] *Works*, II, 317 ff.
[199] *The Scripture-Doctrine of Original Sin* (third ed., Belfast, 1746), p. 288.

tion of *A Winter Evening's Conversation* (1758) summarized the objection tartly. According to Calvinists, said he, "we were all made in Adam, five thousand Years before we were made at all." [200]

Edwards realized, of course, the force of this objection, and countered it by a daring theory of identity according to which it was possible to regard the human race as so much a unit that Adam's sin was literally the sin of all his descendants.

He began by observing that the objection against the theory of the imputation of Adam's sin to his posterity was founded "on a false hypothesis, and wrong notion of what we call *sameness* or *oneness*, among created things." [201] Some things which on first consideration appear entirely distinct are seen upon more careful observation to be united according to an established law of nature in such a way that together they form a single whole. [202]

Edwards moved on then to the assertion that the established law of nature which was the basis of identity through successive moments of time depended wholly upon the "sovereign will and agency of God." He argued that the present existence of a created substance must be the result of the immediate exercise of a divine creative power, for it can not be the effect of its existence in the past, the latter being "no active cause, but wholly a passive thing." The continuous existence of a created substance is, then, in each successive moment, a new effect of God's power. The sameness of created things must, it follows, depend wholly upon the "*arbitrary* constitution of the Creator." Thus man's personal identity, his sameness through successive moments of time, depends wholly on the will of God.[203]

Edwards concluded that there was no reason in the nature of things why God should not have determined arbitrarily that the

[200] P. 27.   [201] *Works*, II, 486.
[202] *Ibid.* Edwards was here no doubt indebted to Locke, to whom he refers a little later in the passage. See Locke's *Essay*, Bk. II, chap. xxvii, secs. 3–5.
[203] *Works*, II, 487 ff.

human race should be one (even as he determines that individuals shall preserve their identity through successive moments of time), should have, indeed, such a oneness that Adam's fall involved all of his posterity in sin and guilt, even as a man's sinning today involves his guilt tomorrow.[204]

If this notion be granted, he wrote, the Arminian objection to the doctrine of original sin on the ground that men could not reasonably be held responsible for a sin committed five thousand years before they lived, that they could not be corrupted by a sin which they did not themselves commit, falls to the ground.[205]

Edwards's second contribution to the discussion concerning original sin grew out of facing another objection to the doctrine of the imputation of Adam's sin to his descendents. The objection was that this theory made God the author of sin. One argument which Dr. Taylor "greatly insists upon," wrote Edwards, "is, 'That this does in effect charge him, who is *the author of our nature, who formed us in the womb,* with being the *author of a sinful corruption of nature.*'"[206]

In answering this exception to his doctrine, Edwards proposed an explanation of what happened to man at the Fall which made it possible to avoid the inconvenience of implying any exertion on God's part of a positive corrupting influence on men. God created Adam, said Edwards, with two sets of principles: a natural principle of self-love and a supernatural principle of benevolence. When Adam fell, God withdrew the supernatural impulse toward benevolence and left man given over wholly to those principles inherent in mere human nature, that is, the impulses growing out of self-love. Thus God, he said, did not "infuse" or "implant" any sin in human nature. He merely withdrew the gracious influences that prevented it.[207]

The feature of chief interest perhaps in this position was the implication that the depravity of man consisted in his being

[204] *Ibid.,* II, 490–491.
[206] *Ibid.,* II, 476.
[205] *Ibid.,* II, 490–493.
[207] *Ibid.,* II, 476–478.

moved after the Fall wholly by motives of self-interest. To put it another way, Edwards was asserting that man is wholly selfish. In proposing this notion Edwards involved himself in one of the most exciting controversies of his time. Of the making of books on the subject there had been since the time of Hobbes almost no end.

"I put for a general inclination of all mankind," said Hobbes in the *Leviathan*, "a perpetual and restless desire of power after power, that ceaseth only in death." [208] "Every man," he wrote in a passage to which Cumberland strenuously objected, "is desirous of what is good for him, and shuns what is evil ... and this he doth by a certain impulsion of nature, no less than that whereby a stone moves downward." [209] He insisted that men are not naturally social. They do not seek society for its own sake, but only to "receive some honour or profit from it." "All society therefore is either for gain, or for glory; that is, not so much for love of our fellows, as for the love of ourselves." [210]

Another striking champion of the notion that men are naturally governed wholly by self-love was Mandeville. Like Hobbes he reduced all social impulses to selfishness. "Generous Notions concerning the natural Goodness of Man are hurtful as they tend to mislead, and are merely Chimerical: The truth of this latter I have illustrated by the most obvious Examples in History. I have spoken of our Love of Company and Aversion to Solitude, examin'd thoroughly the various Motives of them, and made it appear that they all center in Self-Love." [211] If, said

---

[208] *Works*, III, 85–86. In the *Freedom of the Will* (1754), *Works*, II, 142, Edwards says that he had not read Hobbes. Familiar as he was with the work of men like Hutcheson, Bishop Butler, Samuel Clarke, and Shaftesbury, not to mention others, he must have known Hobbes's position. In fact he refers to Hobbes in the notes on "The Mind," written while he was still at Yale (Dwight, *Life*, p. 724).

[209] *Philosophical Rudiments concerning Government and Society*, *Works*, II, 8. (This work was a translation made by Hobbes in 1651 of his *Elementa Philosophica de Cive*, 1641.)

[210] *Ibid.*, II, 3–5.

[211] *The Fable of the Bees* (ed. F. B. Kaye, Oxford, 1924), I, 343–344.

Mandeville, "it be urg'd, that if there are not, it is possible that there might be" people not moved by self-love, "I answer that it is as possible that Cats, instead of killing Rats and Mice, should feed them, and go about the House to suckle and nurse their young ones; or that a Kite should call the Hens to their Meat, as the Cock does, and sit brooding over their Chickens instead of devouring 'em; but if they should all do so, they would cease to be Cats and Kites; it is inconsistent with their Natures, and the Species of Creatures which we now mean, when we name Cats and Kites, would be extinct as soon as that could come to pass." [212]

At one point in his thinking, then, Edwards fits into the tradition of which Hobbes and Mandeville are the most significant representatives. Like them, he believed that all men are naturally motivated only by self-love.

His affinity with Mandeville in this respect is, however, much more striking than his agreement with Hobbes. Hobbes had concluded that since by nature men were wholly selfish, their endeavors to preserve themselves were just and right. Furthermore, "because it is vain for a man to have a right to the end, if the right to the necessary means be denied him," he must be allowed the right to do what is necessary for his own preservation. But who is to decide what is necessary for each individual's preservation? Hobbes answered that "by right of nature" each man must be allowed to be his own judge in this respect. Consequently, he concluded, every man in "the bare

---

Mandeville's *Fable* was first published as an octosyllabic verse satire in 1705, entitled *The Grumbling Hive; or, Knaves Turned Honest.* In 1714 it was reissued with a prose commentary as *The Fable of the Bees; or, Private Vices, Public Benefits.* Although there is no evidence that Edwards read Mandeville, he could not have been unaware of Mandeville's theories. He knew well Hutcheson's *Inquiry into the Original of our Ideas of Beauty and Virtue. . . . In which the Principles of Shaftesbury are . . . defended against . . . the Fable of the Bees* (1725). He read, no doubt soon after its publication, Berkeley's *Alciphron* (1732), with its withering attack on Mandeville in the second dialogue (see "Catalogue of Books").

[212] *Fable*, I, 134.

state of nature," that is, before men are united by compacts in society, has a right to do what he thinks fit and to possess himself of what he can.[213]   The state of war which such a system would produce would, however, defeat the desires of men for self-preservation. Moved, therefore, by fear for their own safety, men make contracts which involve giving up some of their rights for the sake of securing peace.[214]   It is plain that to Hobbes acting from self-interest was no sin. That men are moved wholly by self-love seemed to him no reproach upon human nature. In this respect, Edwards differed radically from him. Like Hobbes, he believed that men naturally act only from motives of self-interest; but unlike him, he saw in this fact an overwhelming evidence of men's depravity.

For this reason, Edwards was in closer agreement with Mandeville than with Hobbes. Mandeville did see in men's complete selfishness an evidence of their natural viciousness. He assumed, to begin with, that self-denial was essential to virtue, and applying this standard he found no virtue in the world. All human actions, he discovered, sprang from self-love. As Professor Kaye puts it: "From the standpoint, therefore, of his rigoristic formula, everything was vicious."[215]   Here he and Edwards were in complete agreement.

But it will not do to assume that this agreement reveals any real spiritual affinity between the two men. Temperamentally they were poles apart. To Mandeville, says Professor Kaye, "Wicked or not, the world was a good place."[216]   To Edwards, on the other hand, the world was the gloomy ruins of paradise, and man who inhabited it "a little wretched, despicable creature; a worm, a mere nothing, and less than nothing."[217]   Mandeville accepted mankind as he found it gladly; Edwards regarded a depraved humanity with loathing.

[213] *Philosophical Rudiments*, *Works*, II, 8–10.
[214] *Ibid.*, II, 11 ff.
[215] Bernard Mandeville, *Fable* (ed. F. B. Kaye), I, xlviii.
[216] *Ibid.*, II, 405.   [217] *Works*, IV, 236.

THE NATURE OF TRUE VIRTUE

Edwards's depressing picture of a totally corrupt, because completely selfish, mankind becomes even more gloomy when viewed against the background of his theory of virtue, for after declaring that men act by nature only from motives of self-love, he announced that virtue must be defined as disinterested benevolence, a doctrine he elaborated in the posthumously published *Nature of True Virtue*.

This definition of virtue, said Edwards, is "generally allowed, not only by Christian divines, but by the more considerable deists."[218] No intelligent reader in Edwards's day who was at all familiar with English sermonic literature since the time of the Restoration and with the moralists of the period would have challenged this assertion. The notion had been strongly urged in Cumberland's *De Legibus Naturae* (1672).[219] Hutcheson, writing a half century later, had felt it not too much to say that "*All mankind* agree" that virtue consists in disinterested benevolence.[220] In Edwards's day even writers whom he had strenuously opposed in the *Freedom of the Will* and in *Original Sin*, Taylor and Chubb, divine and deist, were at this point in agreement with him.[221]

The assumption that benevolence was the foundation of virtue was consistent with Edwards's view of the place of the affections as compared with reason in human economy. He had defended the emotionalism of the Great Awakening on the ground that the affections as the springs of action were the

[218] *Works*, II, 262.

[219] Trans. by John Maxwell (London, 1727), pp. 16, 20, 41, 47, 345.

[220] *Inquiry into the Original of our Ideas of Beauty and Virtue* (London, 1725), p. 179. See also pp. 150, 153.

[221] Edwards quoted Taylor on the point in *Original Sin*, *Works*, II, 383. See Chubb, *Tracts*, pp. 440–444. For evidence of the commonness of the doctrine among English latitudinarian divines long before its announcement by Shaftesbury or his follower Hutcheson, see R. S. Crane, "Suggestions toward a Genealogy of the 'Man of Feeling,'" *Journal of English Literary History*, I, 208–213 (1934).

Reference is:

essential elements of true religion. He had presented as a
prominent postulate in the *Freedom of the Will* the statement
that the will could not be distinguished from the affections. He
had laid down as a principal argument for the depravity of man
the proposition that natural man was completely under the
control of the self-regarding affections. He was, then, perfectly
consistent when he declared that virtue was a matter of the
affections and that the virtuous man was one dominated by the
good passion—benevolence.

There were those in his day who saw reason as the foundation
of virtue and as its proper measure. "The height of Virtue,"
Henry More had said, "is this, constantly to pursue that which
to Right Reason seems best." [222] "I proceed, every where, upon
this Principle," wrote Richard Fiddes in 1724, "that Reason is
the proper Rule of human Judgement, and Action." [223] This,
too, was the principle assumed as basic by Wollaston in *The
Religion of Nature Delineated* (1726). [224] And Isaac Watts declared in 1730 that "it is still Reason exercising itself, and judging of the Fitness and Unfitness of Things, by and according to
these native and essential Principles of Reasoning which I have
spoke of, that is the only Rule or Test of *what is Vice* and *what
is Virtue*." [225]

Such a position was wholly uncongenial to Edwards. Virtue,
he said, was founded not upon reason but upon a spiritual sense,
that is, upon affection. [226] This position is made clear in the
beginning of *The Nature of True Virtue*, where he laid down the
principle that virtue is a kind of beauty, not the "beauty of
understanding and speculation" but of "the *disposition and
will*." [227] Virtue, according to Edwards, is not the triumph of

[222] *An Account of Virtue*, p. 15.
[223] *A General Treatise of Morality* (London, 1724), p. 398.
[224] "To be governed by reason is the general law imposed by the Author
of nature upon them, whose uppermost faculty is reason . . ." (p. 51).
[225] *Philosophical Essays on Various Subjects*, fourth edition (London,
1732), pp. 111 f.
[226] *Works*, II, 301.   [227] *Ibid.*, II, 383.

reason over the passions, but of the good passions over the evil ones, or, to speak more specifically, of benevolence over self-love. Sin is the ascendency of the evil passion, self-love, over the good passion, benevolence.

Now the moralists who, like Edwards, upheld the exalted standard of virtue implied in defining it as disinterested benevolence were likely to find themselves confronted by an embarrassing problem. On what grounds could they urge men to be virtuous? If they pointed out as motives to benevolence the usefulness to society and so indirectly to the individual himself of benevolent acts, they could be accused of placing themselves in the slippery position of attempting to persuade men to be unselfish for selfish reasons. And if they succeeded in this attempt, they could be charged with having really failed. It could be said, in short, that in trying to make men benevolent, they had really made them selfish, because they had made benevolence issue out of a fundamental selfishness. This was in fact the charge advanced against Cumberland. Such a scheme as his, said his translator, lies open to the criticism that virtue has been degraded to a profitable good.[228]

Many moralists of the time did not hesitate from practical considerations to make this appeal. Gay, in the "Preliminary Dissertation concerning the Fundamental Principles of Virtue and Morality," stated quite frankly that the motive of self-love is the proper impulse toward virtue. *"Obligation,"* he declared, *"is the necessity of doing or omitting any Action in order to be happy."*[229] Edmund Law in his attack on Mandeville, *Remarks upon a Late Book Entitled the Fable of the Bees* (1724),[230] said that the pleasure which accompanied a good act did not make it less virtuous than it would otherwise have been—that, in brief, self-

---

[228] *A Treatise of the Laws of Nature* (1727), Appendix, pp. 46 ff. English translation by John Maxwell of Cumberland's *De Legibus Naturae Disquisitio Philosophica* (1672).

[229] *Essay concerning the Origin of Evil* (1732), p. xxxvi.

[230] Ed. by F. D. Maurice (Cambridge, 1894), pp. 32–35.

denial (which Mandeville had assumed to be essential to virtue) was not really a necessary ingredient of it. He went on to explain that in the creation of man there was such a wise union of body and soul that when the mind is delighted, the individual experiences a pleasant agitation of the spirits and the blood. The pleasure of virtue is thus justified by nature.

Such an attitude could not, however, satisfy the more idealistic moralists. Yet how were they to avoid basing unselfishness upon self-love? Maxwell in his appendix to the translation (1727) of Cumberland's *Laws of Nature* revealed a way that had been found out of the difficulty. Virtue, he said, may be presented either as beneficial or as beautiful, that is, either as a means or as an end. With great shrewdness, he analyzed the difficulties involved in each position. Those who appeal to self-love by presenting the hope of reward and the fear of punishment are accused of revealing a despicably mercenary spirit. Those who, on the other hand, insist upon a disinterested love are called enthusiasts. His own opinion was that the second position is more admirable, but that the first must often be employed because of the baseness of human nature.[231]

Maxwell named Hutcheson and Shaftesbury as proponents of the nobler view. Hutcheson, to whom Edwards often refers and who plainly influenced him profoundly, set forth sharply in *An Inquiry into the Original of Our Ideas of Beauty and Virtue* (1725) these two contrasting views of the motives to virtue. He admitted that "the greatest part of our later Moralists" hold it undeniable that morality is established by the law of a superior power, and is supported by sanctions of reward and punishment, which determine men to obedience from motives of self-interest.[232] Some other moralists, Hutcheson added, suppose an "*immediate natural Good* in the Actions call'd *Virtuous;* that is, 'That we are determin'd to perceive some

[231] Pp. 66–68.   [232] This is Cumberland's position.

Beauty in the Actions of others, and to love the Agent, even without reflecting upon any *Advantage* which can any way redound to us from the Action; that we have also a secret sense of Pleasure accompanying such of our Actions as we call *Virtuous*, even when we expect no other *Advantage* from them.' " [233]

The chief purpose of *An Inquiry* was to state the latter position convincingly. In attempting to do this, Hutcheson tried to prove that men have a moral sense, sense being defined as a "Determination of our Minds to receive Ideas independently on our Will, and to have Perceptions of Pleasure and Pain." [234] By this sense men perceive the excellence of a virtuous act even when the act offers no advantage to them. In establishing this point, Hutcheson took two steps. First he proved that men have a sense, the internal sense he called it, by which they find pleasure in the contemplation of forms having regularity and order and harmony. Now, he argued, if the existence of this sense be granted, as he thought it must be, it should not be difficult to admit the existence of another, superior sense consisting in a determination to be pleased in the presence of moral beauty— the beauty not of inanimate things harmoniously arranged, but of actions, characters, affections in which regularity and order are observable. This second sense he called the moral sense. Thus did Hutcheson avoid the embarrassing position of those who urged men to be unselfish for selfish reasons. Virtue is to be pursued not because it is useful, but because it is beautiful, not as a means but as an end. Furthermore, the moral sense may be the basis by which men come to approve and to embrace virtue; there is, therefore, no need to believe that self-love is the only possible drive to virtuous action. The moral

[233] P. 105. For references by Edwards to Hutcheson see Edwards's *Works*, II, 292, 304, 382–383. The "Catalogue of Books" contains four references to Hutcheson.

[234] This definition is taken from *An Essay on the Nature and Conduct of the Passions and Affections* ... (1728), p. 4, but it fits exactly the discussion of the internal sense and the moral sense in *An Inquiry*.

sense, like all other senses, is wholly beyond the influence of self-interest. Perception is independent of the will and the affections.

Much the same high tone had been taken earlier by Shaftesbury, to whom Maxwell had also referred in his criticism of Cumberland's employment of the profit motive in ethics.[235] In setting forth the necessity for appealing to the nobler motives to virtue, that is, the motives above self-love, Shaftesbury attempted, as Hutcheson was to do more systematically later, to establish the intrinsic value of virtue as a kind of beauty. He believed that there was a beauty in moral matters paralleling the beauty of physical forms but superior to it. Virtue, then, according to Shaftesbury, "is it-self no other than the Love of Order and Beauty in Society."[236] The convincing presentation of this proposition that virtue appealed to men by its inherent loveliness, a loveliness analogous in character and effect to that of the physical forms which we call beautiful, was, Shaftesbury said, the chief purpose of the *Characteristics*.[237]

It is against this background of discussion that Edwards's opening statement in *The Nature of True Virtue* must be seen: "Whatever controversies and variety of opinions there are about the nature of virtue, yet all (excepting some skeptics, who deny any real difference between virtue and vice) mean by it, something *beautiful*, or rather some kind of *beauty*, or excellency."[238] Like Shaftesbury and Hutcheson, he was anxious to raise virtue above the level of self-love, to place it beyond the point where it depended upon self-love. It was

[235] *Characteristics of Men, Manners, Opinions, Times* (1773), II, 272. See also II, 57–58. The first edition of the *Characteristics* was in 1711. For evidence of Edwards's acquaintance with Shaftesbury, see note 236 below.

[236] *Characteristics*, II, 75. See also *ibid.*, pp. 28–29.

[237] *Characteristics*, III, 303. Shaftesbury does point out that virtue is useful (II, 175–176, 81 ff.), but he decries pursuit of it on this ground only. For an exposition of Hutcheson's philosophy and a discussion of his relationship to Shaftesbury, see William Robert Scott, *Francis Hutcheson* (Cambridge, England, 1900).

[238] *Works*, II, 261.

to be something lovely, not merely something useful. It was to be an end in itself, not a mere means of satisfying selfish desires.

> That which is called *virtue*, is a certain kind of beautiful nature, form or quality that is observed in things. That form or quality is called beautiful to any one beholding it to whom it is beautiful, which appears in itself agreeable or comely to him, or the view or idea of which is immediately pleasant to the mind. I say agreeable *in itself*, and *immediately* pleasant, to distinguish it from things which in themselves are not agreeable nor pleasant, but either indifferent or disagreeable, which yet appear eligible and agreeable indirectly for something else that is the consequence of them, or with which they are connected. Such a kind of indirect agreeableness or eligibleness in things, not for themselves, but for something else, is not what is called beauty.[239]

Edwards, then, accepted the theory which Shaftesbury and Hutcheson had persuasively presented, namely, that the amiableness of virtue lay in its beauty rather than in its benefits.[240]

[239] *Ibid.*, II, 300.

[240] It must not be assumed that Edwards merely became a convert to the views of Hutcheson and of his group. Not only did he differ from these men at points so important that he can hardly be regarded as a follower of the group, but he was no doubt influenced also by the Cambridge Platonists in formulating his theory of virtue. See Rufus Orlando Suter, *The Philosophy of Jonathan Edwards* (manuscript dissertation in Harvard College Library, 1932), summarized in *Harvard University Summaries of Theses* (1933), pp. 351–353. See also, in note 44 above, references to discussions of the possible influence of the Cambridge Platonists on Edwards in connection with his early idealism. It is likely, too, that beside the influences mentioned ought to be laid that of Newtonianism, with which Edwards was familiar. (The "Catalogue of Books" contains five references to Newton's work. See also reference to Newton in the early notebooks, Dwight, *Life*, p. 678.) Edwards's mathematical calculations concerning the relative claims of God and humanity to benevolence (*Works*, II, 265–266) and his argument for a virtuous kind of self-love by analogy with the phenomena of gravitation (II, 279–280) are evidence of the influence of Newtonianism in his thinking. For a discussion of the relationship of Newtonianism and ethical theory in the eighteenth century see Herbert Drennon, *James Thomson and Newtonianism* (manuscript dissertation, University of Chicago Library, 1928), pp. 137–176.

In one respect, however, this notion failed to achieve the chief purpose for its adoption. It had been urged as proof that men may be and ought to be moved to benevolence without an appeal to self-love. And yet in stressing the beauty of virtue, its supreme loveliness, its proponents laid themselves open to attack from cynical moralists on the ground that according to this theory virtue was made to appear so attractive that men followed it to please themselves. In short, that, far from removing virtue beyond the limits of self-love, it merely stimulated a refined and subtle kind of selfishness—a selfishness rising out of the pleasures of benevolence. It was with these critics in mind, no doubt, that Hutcheson wrote with irritation: "Some *Moralists* . . . will rather twist *Self-Love* into a thousand Shapes, than allow any other Principle of Approbation than *Interest*." [241]

To this criticism, Hutcheson offered several replies. He answered, for one thing, that self-interest could not affect the operation of any sense. If then there be, as he felt he had proved beyond question, a moral *sense*, its exercises must be as unaffected as are the exercises of the other senses by selfish impulses.[242] A more important rejoinder, however, rested upon an analysis of the meaning of the term *self-love*. From one point of view, said Hutcheson, it is true that men pursue beauty from self-love, that is, for the pleasures they find in it, but it must be observed that in such cases a sense of moral beauty must exist antecedent to any prospect of pleasure. Unless a man first loves virtue, perceives a prospect of pleasure in the practice of it, he cannot be moved by self-love to pursue it. Thus it is wrong to assume that the pleasure of a virtuous act is the real cause of the act, and wrong to announce that because virtue gives pleasure, it is sought only from self-love.[243] Men always act of course as they are pleased to act. This is merely to say that men are pleased with that which pleases them. The important question about a moral agent is *what* pleases him?

[241] *Inquiry*, p. 114.   [242] *Ibid.*, p. 10.   [243] *Ibid.*, pp. 140–143.

Is it his own private good? Then he may properly be said to be moved by self-love. Is it the public good? In that case, he may justly be regarded as benevolent.[244]

Edwards felt it necessary to consider this matter in *The Nature of True Virtue*. "Many," he said, "assert that all love arises from self-love. In order to determine this point, it should be clearly ascertained what is meant by self-love."[245] He rejected as ambiguous the apparently plain definition that self-love "is a man's love of his own happiness." The term may, he went on, be taken in two very different senses. It may be used to designate a man's love for his own private, separate happiness. In this sense the term is properly employed. But it is often used to denote man's general capacity for happiness, that is, his liking what he likes and being pleased with what pleases him. In this sense, of course, all love may be resolved into self-love, "for it is undoubtedly true, that whatever a man loves, his love may be resolved into his loving what he loves—if that be proper speaking"—whether he loves his own private good or that of his neighbor. Men who love the good of humanity love what affords them pleasure, but such love cannot be called selfish. Only the pleasure arising from the pursuit of private good can justly be so designated. Furthermore, said Edwards in a passage reminiscent of Hutcheson, it must be noted that when a man finds pleasure in "the good of his neighbor," the disposition to be pleased by his neighbor's happiness was prior to the pleasure derived from gratifying it. To call such affection selfish is to confuse the effect with the cause.

Up to this point Edwards's theory of virtue was, it is plain, closely akin to that of Hutcheson. At two points, however, Edwards found objections to Hutcheson's scheme. In the first place, he felt that Hutcheson and others near him in theory were

[244] See Thomas Chubb, *A Collection of Tracts*, p. 439; Bishop Joseph Butler, *Works*, I, 16–17, and 139–140.
[245] *Works*, II, 277.

guilty of giving too little place in their systems to man's obligations to the Deity. "There seems to be an inconsistence in some
writers on morality, in this respect, that they do not wholly
exclude a regard to the *Deity* out of their schemes of morality,
but yet mention it so slightly, that they leave me room and
reason to suspect they esteem it a less important and a subordinate part of true morality. . . . "[246]

In support of his assertion that the supreme concern of the
virtuous man is the Deity, that to the Deity should the greatest

[246] *Nature of Virtue, Works,* II, 267, 271. Hutcheson does say that love
to God is the highest obligation of man (*Inquiry,* pp. 24, 64, 77) but there
is no doubt that he tended toward a secular ethics. The same might be
said of Cumberland. See *Laws of Nature,* pp. 16–21. It should be observed
that Edwards resisted the drift of eighteenth-century ethics toward Utilitarianism, a drift to which Cumberland and Hutcheson gave impulse and
which eventuated in the system of J. S. Mill. As Rufus Suter puts it,
Edwards's theories stand opposed to the belief that "mistakes the material
welfare of the people as a whole for the highest moral good; and mistakes
the proclivity of an act to beget this universal welfare for true virtue"
("The Conception of Morality in the Philosophy of Jonathan Edwards,"
Journal of Religion, XIV, 266–267, July, 1934). Approaching the question
from another point of view, Joseph Haroutunian declares that "as seen from
the perspective of the theology of Edwards, the history of the New England
Theology is the history of a degradation. It declined because its theocentric character, its supreme regard for the glory of God and His sovereignty over man, made it ill-fitted to give expression to the ideals of
the eighteenth century New England and to meet its immediate social
needs. The social and political forces of the time gave rise to principles
which were either inimical or irrelevant to the spirit of the Edwardean
theology" (*Piety Versus Moralism,* New York, 1932, p. xxii). Over
against this belief may be set that of Williston Walker, who says that
Edwards's doctrines were "effective in giving a basis for philanthropy"
(*Ten New England Leaders,* New York, 1901, p. 256).
    Edwards does make the "beauty of order in society, besides what con-
sists in benevolence," a beauty of a "secondary kind" (II, 275), and he
puts benevolence toward men below love of God (II, 266 ff.), but he certainly had no desire to cause men to slight their duty toward their fellows.
In fact, he asserts emphatically that "Christian practice" is "the chief of
all signs" of a true religion (II, 182–228, and note 25 above). He felt,
no doubt, that by attaching the obligations of men to exercise good will
toward humanity, even as a secondary matter, to their obligations to love
God, he had exalted the virtue of interest in the common good far above
its position at the head of any secular ethics. His series of sermons on
Charity and its Fruits (ed. T. Edwards, 1851) is evidence of his interest in
man's obligation to man. Our age is perhaps too ready to condemn the
Puritans as indifferent to humanitarian concerns.

share of a good man's benevolence be directed, Edwards laid down two principles for determining the degree of benevolence that men are obliged to exercise toward any being. The first rule is that benevolence should be proportioned to the extent or amount of a being's existence. He thought it proper that the "Being who has the *most* of Being, or has the greatest share of existence, other things being equal, so far as such a Being is exhibited to our faculties or set in our view, will have the *greatest* share of the propensity and benevolent affection of the heart."[247] The second rule governing the degree of benevolence due to any being is that the greater the degree of that being's benevolence to others, the more benevolent affection he deserves. In support of this principle, Edwards said that "so far as the Being beloved has love to Being in general, so far his own Being is, as it were, enlarged, extends to, and in some sense comprehends, Being in general," so that the greater a Being's benevolence, the greater his existence and therefore, according to the first principle of benevolence, the greater his claim as a recipient of affection.[248]

It is clear on the basis of these two principles that of all beings, God is most worthy of being loved, for he has infinitely the greatest degree of existence and infinitely the most benevolence.[249] Proceeding from this conclusion, Edwards contended that the obligation under which moral agents lie to exercise love to God had been too little stressed in the chief ethical systems of his day.[250]

There was another and much more important point at which Edwards diverged from Hutcheson and his school. This was over the question whether there was in mankind any natural

[247] *The Nature of True Virtue, Works*, II, 264. See *Notes on the Mind, Works* (ed. Dwight), I, 698–699.
[248] *Works*, II, 265. Cf. Hutcheson, *Inquiry*, pp. 162 ff., and Cumberland, *Laws of Nature*, p. 169 n.
[249] *Works*, II, 265.
[250] *Works* (New York, 1808), VIII, 281; *Works* (1858), III, 542.

impulse toward virtue.[251] Edwards's answer to this question was an unqualified denial that there was any natural disposition to benevolence in man. "Natural men," he told his congregation at Northampton, in a sermon with the significant title "Natural Men in a Dreadful Condition," "have no higher principle in their hearts than self-love." [252]

It is at this point that his theory of virtue and his doctrine of depravity unite to form a dreadful view of human nature. Virtue, he asserted with all the dialectical skill at his command, consists in disinterested benevolence toward Being in general; nothing rising out of self-love can by any stretch be called virtuous. Men, he declared with unhesitating assurance, are, on the other hand, given over wholly to self-love; nothing they do can have any higher origin than self-interest.[253]

The full force of Edwards's teaching concerning the depravity of man is felt only when that teaching is presented against the background of his exalted theory of virtue. The full enormity of that depravity in Edwards's view can be realized only by comparing man as he is, a slave to self-love, with man as he ought to be, disinterestedly benevolent.

The larger part of *The Nature of True Virtue* is taken up with the enforcing of this contrast. More than half of its eight sections are designed directly and indirectly to show that there is no virtue in natural man. After two opening chapters presenting his lofty standard of virtue, Edwards proceeds to the proof of the fact that everything in natural man having the appearance of virtue is really infinitely below it.

Now the writers who accepted the high view of moral good-

[251] By the word *natural*, Edwards meant without grace. Natural man is man as he is since the Fall when all supernatural impulses were withdrawn, leaving him with the qualities which as mere man he possesses. Cf. Hume's analysis of the various meanings of natural: 1) as opposed to miraculous, 2) as rare, 3) as opposed to artificial (*Treatise of Human Nature*, Bk. III, Pt. I, sec. 2).

[252] *Works* (London, 1865), II, 818. See also *Works* (ed. Dwight), I, 665, 667.

[253] *Christian Love*, p. 235.

ness which made benevolence the criterion of virtue generally protested stoutly against the low view of human nature as moved only by self-love. The antagonism of these moralists to the notion that men are wholly selfish is clearly seen in the attack of one of the earliest of them, Cumberland, upon Hobbes. Hobbes, said Cumberland, asserts the monstrous doctrine that "Men are so fram'd, that it is contrary to their Nature, and, consequently, plainly *impossible, that they should desire anything but their own Advantage and their own Glory*." [254] Hobbes, he said, declares that men are less benevolent than animals, that they are in fact "*fiercer than Bears, Wolves, and Serpents*." [255] To this disparagement of human nature, he objected bitterly. Men are, he argued, physiologically fitted for benevolence, because love induces "better and more flowing Juices, brisker Spirits" in human veins, while hatred and its kindred passions clog the blood. [256] Indeed, the "more powerful inclinations of all Mankind" carry them toward the common good. [257] In fact, said Cumberland, nothing but madness or passion, that is, some disease of the mind, ever thwarts this natural inclination. [258] In enforcing this point, he did not hesitate to attack Hobbes personally. I grant, he wrote, that man by abuse of his free will and by narrowness of soul may consider only himself and desire only what seems profitable to himself; but, he concluded tartly, "I could never observe any Symptoms of *such* a Will, in any Man, except in *Hobbes* only." [259]

This notion that men have powerful, although sometimes thwarted, natural impulses toward benevolence was strongly maintained by writers like Hutcheson. To many of them, as to Cumberland, the denial of this assertion seemed a monstrous injustice to the human race. [260]

Edwards, then, is in this interesting position. He combined

[254] *Law of Nature*, p. 171. [255] *Ibid.*, p. 136.
[256] *Ibid.*, pp. 126–127. [257] *Ibid.*, p. 28.
[258] *Ibid.*, p. 125. [259] *Ibid.*, p. 172.
[260] See Shaftesbury, *Characteristics*, I, 115 ff., II, 310 ff.; Hutcheson,

in one coherent system elements from two very diverse schools of thought. Like one group, of which Hutcheson is a good representative, he made virtue wholly a matter of disinterested benevolence; like another, the group in fact that men like Hutcheson most cordially disliked, he asserted that natural man is always and of necessity moved by an overwhelming contrary principle of self-love. His position is in this respect much like that of Mandeville, who insisted that self-denial was necessary to virtue but that men never naturally behave according to any other principle than self-interest.

In supporting this belief, Edwards devoted a great part of *The Nature of True Virtue* to proving that all the seemingly virtuous acts and impulses of natural man, all those that have the appearance of benevolence, lack the essential quality of this virtue. Moralists like Hutcheson had offered men's natural impulses to pity and gratitude, the love between the sexes and that between parents and children, men's sense of justice and their approbation of virtue as evidences of a disinterested love for others in mankind. Edwards accounts for all these impulses which seem to reveal a virtuous benevolence in natural man by reference to three psychological factors, none of which, he claims, has any element of true virtue.

The first of these is natural instinct. There are, argued Edwards, certain particular laws of nature which drive men to love those of the other sex, to care for their children, and to pity those in distress. These have been generously planted in men by a wise creator for the sake of their preservation and comfort in a world which since the fall of Adam is full of suffering and danger. They have in them nothing of a truly virtuous, that is, truly benevolent, quality.[261] Thus he rejected the love

---

Nature and Conduct of the Passions, p. 13, and *Inquiry*, pp. vii, 132, 156, 173, 195, 205, 221, 252–253. These men did not, of course, insist that men are never moved by self-love or that self-love never overcomes benevolence. They did insist, however, that men have natural impulses toward benevolence.   [261] *The Nature of True Virtue, Works*, II, 291 ff.

between men and women, the affection between parents and children, and pity—of which Cumberland, Shaftesbury, and Hutcheson had made much—as evidence of natural benevolence.[262]

A second tendency in human nature which sometimes results
in attitudes and behavior which seem virtuous but are not is,
according to Edwards, the association of ideas. It is by reference to this that Edwards explained in large part the approbation
of virtue which Hutcheson had held before his readers as evidence of a benevolent temper natural to man. Hutcheson had
contended that an appreciation for the moral goodness of men
not rising out of self-love was proved by our approval of and
admiration for the good deeds of people in distant countries and
ages, good deeds from which we could not hope to receive any
benefit. We find ourselves, he said, approving of good deeds
and disapproving of evil ones when there is no possibility of
advantage to us or harm to us in them.

Edwards attempted to demolish this argument by an analysis
of such approbation and disapprobation, designed to prove
that they are simply the effect of self-love directed by the
association of ideas. Things may, by the association of ideas,
arouse in us a feeling of aversion or of liking, he said, even
when we have no immediate prospect of pleasure or fear of
pain. A child, for example, may have so strongly fixed a fear
of rattlesnakes as the result of associating the idea of danger
with the idea of snakes that even the picture of a snake is sufficient to arouse disgust.[263] In this way, Edwards went on to
say, "some vices may become in a degree odious" and some
virtues may awaken admiration "by the influence of self-love,
through an habitual connection of ideas of contempt" or of
approval with them.[264]

[262] Cumberland, *Laws of Nature*, pp. 128–129; Shaftesbury, *Characteristics*, II, 78, and I, 118. Hutcheson, *Inquiry*, pp. 144, 195, 215; Cf. Hume,
Treatise, pp. 394, 481; Hobbes, *Works*, IV, 44, 49; Mandeville, *Fable*
(ed. Kaye), I, 255, 259.
[263] *Works*, II, 283.
[264] *The Nature of True Virtue*, *Works*, II, 284.

A third natural disposition of men which sometimes creates feelings or behavior which have the appearance although not the quality of true virtue is an appreciation for what Edwards called the secondary kind of beauty. His argument here is a neat turning of Hutcheson's dialectic guns back upon himself. Hutcheson in attempting to establish the existence of a moral sense had, as has been pointed out, distinguished between the perception of that harmony which constitutes beauty in animate things and the appreciation of that harmony which is the essential element of beauty in inanimate objects. The perception of symmetry in inanimate things he referred to an internal sense, that of proportion in animate things to a moral sense. Seizing upon this distinction, Edwards posited a primary and a secondary kind of beauty—the primary beauty being the harmony of spiritual beings, the secondary and inferior beauty being the agreement, the proportion, the symmetry found in inanimate objects.[265]

This secondary beauty, he went on to say, appears not only in material things but in immaterial things as well. There is, for instance, a beauty in a well-ordered society that is of this sort.[266] Now this kind of beauty is utterly different from the beauty of benevolence. A relish for it may exist without there being any real taste for the loveliness of true virtue.[267]

Furthermore, the disposition to be pleased by this secondary kind of beauty which has nothing of benevolence in it, is the basis for that natural approbation of justice, which has been used by some moralists to prove a natural benevolence in men. Justice, said Edwards, is merely the pleasing harmony between an act and its consequences.[268] It is also, together with self-love, the ground of a seemingly virtuous gratitude, for gratitude is the just return of affection in exchange for a favor.[269] Finally, it combines with self-love to form the basis for natural con-

[265] *Works*, II, 271–272.   [266] *Ibid.*, II, 274–275.
[267] *Ibid.*, II, 277.   [268] *Ibid.*, II, 275.   [269] *Ibid.*, II, 281.

science. Conscience, said Edwards, is not, as Hutcheson and
Butler had declared, a true virtue or a revelation of a truly
virtuous disposition. We feel pleased in the consciousness of
having treated someone in a way which were we in his place we
should like to have him treat us, and we are uneasy in the
consciousness of not having so treated him. In this sense,
natural conscience is rooted in self-love, that is, our affection
for ourselves is the basis of it. To this sense of the effect of
our actions with respect to others in the awareness of our feeling
about those actions if others performed them with respect to
ourselves must be added in accounting for natural conscience
another sense, that of desert. The last plainly consists in an
appreciation for the secondary kind of beauty.[270]

In natural conscience, then, there is, as in love for those of
the opposite sex, in affection between parents and children, in
pity, in the natural approbation of virtue, in justice, no necessary
element of virtue. A virtuous man may have these dispositions,[271] but they are no evidence in themselves that a man is
virtuous. Above all they are no evidence of any natural inclination toward benevolence in men. They do not make it necessary
to deny the doctrine of total depravity.

Of charity, or Christian love, it is peculiarly true, that it is above
the selfish principle. Though all real love to others seeks the
good, and espouses the interests of those who are beloved, yet
all other love, excepting this, has its foundation, in one sense,
in the selfish principle.

So it is with the natural affection which parents feel for their
children, and with the love which relatives have one to another.
If we except the impulses of instinct, self-love is the main spirit
of it. It is because men love themselves, that they love those

[270] *Ibid.*, II, 287. See also Dwight, *Life*, I, 701. Cf. Hutcheson,
Inquiry, pp. 18, 26, 40. An interesting comparison may be made between
Edwards and Bishop Butler concerning natural conscience. Butler makes
it the "capital part" of his ethical system (*Works*, I, 58).
[271] *Works*, II, 295 ff.

persons and things that are their own, or that they are nearly related to, and which they look upon as belonging to themselves, and which, by the constitution of society, have their interest and honor linked with their own. And so it is in the closest friendships that exist among men. Self-love is the spring whence they proceed. Sometimes natural gratitude, for good turns that have been done them by others, or for benefits received from them, disposes men, through self-love, to a similar respect to those that have shown them kindness, or by whom their self-interest has been promoted. And sometimes natural men are led into a friendship to others, from qualifications that they see or find in them, whence they hope for the promotion of their own temporal good. . . . And so there are many other ways, in which self-love is the source of that love and friendship that often arises between natural men. Most of the love that there is in the world, arises from this principle, and therefore it does not go beyond nature. And nature cannot go beyond self-love, but all that men do, is, some way or other, from this root.[272]

Now one objection to the Calvinistic belief in the depravity of man which these theories of Edwards's were designed to support inevitably suggests itself. Did they not by completely discrediting human nature present to men an outlook so desperately hopeless as to discourage them from all attempts at virtue? Taylor in attacking Watts's doctrine of original sin hurled against him this accusation: "He villifies and pours great Contempt upon the human Nature."[273]   And Taylor added that the Calvinistic doctrine by defaming human nature enfeebled men's hope and cut the nerve of ethical endeavor.[274]   When men, he declared, believe that they are worse than brutes, it is small wonder that they behave worse than brutes.[275]

And what Wonder if the Generality of Christians have been the

[272] *Charity and its Fruits*, a series of sermons on Christian Love delivered in Northampton, 1739, p. 226.
[273] *The Scripture-Doctrine of Original Sin*, p. 350.
[274] *Ibid.*, pp. 230–231, 257.   [275] *Ibid.*, p. 259.

most wicked, lewd, bloody, and treacherous of all Mankind? Certainly nothing generous, great, good, pure can spring from Principles, to say the least, so low and groveling.[276]

This charge Edwards faced squarely in *Original Sin*. Referring specifically to Taylor, he argued, for one thing, that if we are actually depraved, "he acts but a *friendly* part to us, who endeavors fully to discover and manifest our disease." [277] A second part of Edwards's reply to Taylor's criticism of the doctrine of original sin was much more significant. No contempt is cast by the doctrine of the total depravity of man, said Edwards, upon the noble possibilities of man.[278] Just what noble possibilities remained to men who since the Fall are given over wholly to self-love in a world where the only virtue is disinterested benevolence Edwards made abundantly clear. Again and again he declared that although men are wholly corrupt and wholly unable of themselves to become virtuous, some of them are by the atonement of Christ and the consequent operation of supernatural and irresistible grace lifted out of their depravity.

THE DOCTRINE OF GRACE

The doctrine of grace rounds out and completes Edwards's ethical system. In the light of it, all the elements of that system fall into their proper places and reveal themselves in their just proportions. God has "absolutely determined," said Edwards in *Decrees and Elections*, that a certain number of men completely helpless of themselves to achieve virtue shall by the irresistible operation of his grace become truly good. Thus does he resolve for men the dreadful dilemma presented to them by his doctrines of depravity and virtue, doctrines that seemed to hold out no hope. Man is, it is true, given over wholly to self-love. Virtue, it is true, consists wholly in benevolence. Grace bridges the gap.

[276] *Ibid.*   [277] *Works*, II, 503.   [278] *Ibid.*, II, 502.

And it is grace alone that bridges it. Nothing that men can do is of any use in making the leap from self-love to disinterested benevolence. Against such men as Taylor, Whitby, Chubb, and Watts, some of whom asserted man's ability to raise himself to virtue and some of whom asserted man's power to place himself in a position where divine grace must raise him,[279] Edwards declared uncompromisingly that when men become virtuous God does all, that men do nothing.[280]

According to Edwards, virtue cannot be cultivated. It cannot be developed by repeated good choices. Here again he falls back upon his favorite argument in the *Freedom of the Will*. Each virtuous volition of an agent must proceed either from a preceding virtuous choice or be immediately imparted to the agent. Now every good choice cannot have its origin in an antecedent act of the will, for there must somewhere be a first act from which all others spring. This first act, which by definition cannot spring from a previous choice, must result from impulses external to the agent's will. Edwards concluded, then, that virtue could not be cultivated by repeated acts of choice. It must "take its rise from creation or infusion by God." [281] No truly virtuous acts are begotten, said Edwards, before the marriage of God and the soul. "Seeming virtues and good works before, are not so indeed. They are a spurious brood, being bastards, and not children." [282] "All moral good is from God." [283]

In Edwards's view of human nature, then, God's "efficacious, determining grace" in the lives of those whom he has from all

<hr/>

[279] Whitby, *A Discourse*, p. 26; Watts, *The Ruin and Recovery of Mankind*, pp. 148 ff. (Watts presents very clearly—pp. 165 ff.—the Arminian, the Calvinistic, and his own compromise view, labeling them A, C, and R); for a discussion of the controversy over the matter in New England, see Walker, *Ten New England Leaders*, pp. 303 ff.

[280] See Edwards's attack on Taylor at this point (*Works*, II, 463) and on Whitby (*ibid.*, II, 534 ff.); also II, 549.

[281] *Efficacious Grace, Works*, II, 569.

[282] *Ibid.*, II, 597.   [283] *Ibid.*, II, 578.

eternity decreed shall receive it, is the cause, the only possible
cause, of virtue.[284]

This doctrine forms the pinnacle of the philosophical and
theological system which Edwards skillfully and patiently built.
With great architectural skill, he reared a carefully proportioned
and buttressed, if not completely consistent, structure composed
both of notions inherited from the Calvinistic tradition and of
materials boldly seized from the philosophical systems current
in his day. At its base he laid the psychological theories announced at the time of the Great Awakening and proclaimed
in his controversies over the freedom of the will. Upon these
he erected solidly his doctrine of depravity and his doctrine of
virtue, enunciated in his controversies over these subjects. At
the apex of the whole he set his doctrine of grace.

The whole edifice was designed to make evident the majestic
power of God. "It is manifest," wrote Edwards in the opening
sentence of *Efficacious Grace*, "that if ever men are turned from
sin, God must undertake it, and he must be the doer of it; that
it is his doing that must determine the matter; that all that
others can do, will avail nothing, without his agency." [285] The
key to Edwards's work and, for that matter, to his life as well,
lies in his own account of his early religious experiences. That
account makes it plain that Edwards in his youth surmounted
his logical objections to the doctrine of God's sovereignty and
rose above a mere acceptance of the doctrine to an ecstatic
delight in it.

From my childhood up, my mind had been full of objections
against the doctrine of God's sovereignty, in choosing whom
he would to eternal life, and rejecting whom he pleased; leaving
them eternally to perish, and be everlastingly tormented in
hell. It used to appear like a horrible doctrine to me. But I
remember the time very well, when I seemed to be convinced,
and fully satisfied, as to this sovereignty of God, and his justice

in thus eternally disposing of men, according to his sovereign pleasure. . . . But I have often, since that first conviction, had quite another kind of sense of God's sovereignty than I had then. I have often since had not only a conviction, but a *delightful* conviction. The doctrine has very often appeared exceedingly pleasant, bright, and sweet. Absolute sovereignty is what I love to ascribe to God. . . .

The first instance, that I remember, of that sort of inward, sweet delight in God and divine things, that I have lived much in since, was on reading these words, I Tim. i. 17. *Now unto the King eternal, immortal, invisible, the only wise God, be honour and glory for ever and ever, Amen.* As I read the words, there came into my soul, and was as it were diffused through it, a sense of the glory of the divine Being; a new sense, quite different from anything I ever experienced before. Never any words of Scripture seemed to me as these words did. I thought with myself, how excellent a Being that was, and how happy I should be, if I might enjoy that God, and be rapt up to him in heaven, and be as it were swallowed up in him forever! I kept saying, and as it were singing, over these words of scripture to myself.[286]

It is in this exalted and mystical worship of the divine that Edwards's views of human nature have their roots.

CONCLUSION AND SUMMARY

Edwards's whole thought life, it may be fairly said, was centered about the deep conviction of the all-sufficient, all-encompassing power of God which had mastered him as a young man. This power he delighted to contemplate and made it his chief purpose in life to proclaim. The conception of it was basic in all his theorizing, much as that theorizing was influenced by the psychological and philosophical beliefs current in his day. It underlay his attitudes toward human nature as they are revealed in his contributions to the controversies in which he engaged.

[286] Dwight, *Life*, p. 60.

He defended the outburst of emotionalism known as the Great Awakening because it seemed to him to be an expression of the kind of religion toward which a recognition of the sovereignty of God would lead. That defense rested upon a psychology derived from the leading thinkers of his time, a psychology in which the passions were regarded as the prime movers in human life, and it included the positing of a supernatural sense granted arbitrarily by an all-powerful God to those men whom He had elected for salvation.

In the controversy over the freedom of the will, where Edwards revealed a wide acquaintance with the aspects of the problem that had been violently debated in the English intellectual world for generations, his chief interest was in establishing the principle that men's behavior is directed by a divine power outside themselves. He was anxious, in short, to lay a solid foundation for the Calvinistic doctrine of the sovereignty of God.

In arguing for another Calvinistic doctrine, the total depravity of man, against writers like John Taylor, Edwards was aiming at proving a principle closely related to his basic belief in the absolute authority of God. He was eager to make men recognize their utter helplessness by convincing them that because of Adam's sin they were, as men like Hobbes and Mandeville had taken delight in pointing out, completely under the domination of self-love and, since they lacked freedom of will, wholly unable of themselves to achieve virtue.

To make this helplessness more emphatically clear, he defined virtue as disinterested benevolence, endorsing a concept in accord with the views of morality held by writers like Cumberland, Shaftesbury, and Hutcheson, with whom, understandably enough, he disagreed concerning men's possessing any natural impulses toward virtue.

All of these theories pointed toward and supported the conclusion dear to Edwards as a Calvinist that only divine grace could make men truly good. Since men's characters are determined by the nature of their passions, which after the Fall of Adam are completely selfish, since men have no freedom of will by which they can reform their selfish natures, they can hope to achieve virtue only as God may according to his own good pleasure grant to them the supernatural sense by which they may be completely remolded in disposition. "All moral good," he concluded, "is from God."

III. Edwards as a Man of Letters

LITERARY THEORY IN ENGLAND AND AMERICA

Modern prose style is commonly said to begin with the Restoration; it was a product suited to the age of reason: simple, lucid, precise, and correct—and remains in structure essentially the same today.[287] The superfluities of ornament, to be sure, had long since been disdained by Jonson and Bacon; but Sprat and Hobbes perhaps stated as clearly as any the principles which came into general acceptance during the seventeenth century and helped establish the structure of prose style,[288] for both attempted by precept and example to purge English prose of rhetorical and decorative encumbrances. Form, it was thought, was not a paramount requisite for writing wherein the thought concentrated upon discussion and solution.

[287] For general discussion, see *The Cambridge History of English Literature*, VII, chap. xvi: "The Essay and the Beginning of Modern English Prose" (and bibliography).

[288] See Thomas Sprat, *The History of the Royal Society of London* (1667), in which he states that the Society was founded with the idea (among many) of correcting excesses of extravagance in writing. See Bishop John Wilkins, *Ecclesiastes; or, A Discourse concerning the Gift of Preaching* (1646), against rhetorical flourishes. See Hobbes's preface to Sir William D'Avenant's *Gondibert*, where he states a theory of writing that is a logical result of his philosophy: his distinction between *fancy* and *judgment* became a commonplace of criticism, adopted by Boyle, Locke, Temple, Addison, and others. For a discussion of the problems, see J. E. Spingarn, introd. to *Critical Essays of the Seventeenth Century* (Oxford, 1908–1909, 3 vols.).

Reasoning was to be just and forceful, vigorous and intelligent, but not clothed in figurative splendors.[289]

The first half of the eighteenth century was a period of vehement discussion of problems religious, ethical, and aesthetic.[290] Polemical works dominated the field, and the prose vehicle for such controversies, excepting perhaps Swift's, remained pedestrian, unimaginative, and neutral.[291] Locke's *An Essay concerning Human Understanding* (1690), though more influential on ideas than any work of its time,[292] made no effort by precept of style to rise above a dead level of mediocrity; and his *Some Thoughts concerning Education* (1693), even while pleading for a more accurate training of the young in intellectual precision, asks what is possibly to be gained by teaching them poetry. "Poetry and Gaming, which usually go together, are alike in this too, that they seldom bring any advantage, but to those who have nothing else to live on." [293] Toward style, as toward ideas, Locke's attitude—purely common-sense—eschewed florid declamation. In this he was later supported by Lord Kames.[294]

William Law, the most eminent of the fervid religious thinkers, was a clear reasoner whose scorn of finished style was less to belittle style itself than to make it subservient to the matter;[295]

[289] See J. G. Robertson, *Studies in the Genesis of Romantic Theory in the Eighteenth Century* (Cambridge, Mass., 1923), chap. i; W. H. Durham, Introd. to *Critical Essays of the Eighteenth Century, 1700–1725* (New Haven, 1915); and John W. Draper, *Eighteenth Century English Aesthetics, A Bibliography* (including a list of commentaries and interpretations) (Heidelberg, 1931), supplemented by W. D. Templeman, *Modern Philology*, XXX, 309–316 (1933), R. S. Crane, *Modern Philology*, XXIX, 251 f. (1931), and R. D. Havens, *Modern Language Notes*, XLVII, 118–120 (1932).

[290] See Leslie Stephen, *History of English Thought in the Eighteenth Century* (3rd ed., London, 1902), II, 368.

[291] See E. Gosse, *A History of Eighteenth Century Literature* (London, 1901).

[292] Thomas Fowler, *Locke* (English Men of Letters, New York, 1902), p. 150.

[293] Pp. 207 f.

[294] See Henry Home (Lord Kames), *Elements of Criticism* (1762).

[295] See Law, *The Way to Divine Knowledge* (*Works*, 1753–1776), VII, 93.

his own style is precise, explicit, repetitious, and stiff,[296]—
qualities that adequately describe the rhetoric of a very great
number of the writers of the period, especially of those for whom
Reason was the final criterion of literary judgment;[297] and the
writings of Isaac Barrow (which he very carefully revised)
demonstrate how prose that appeals to reason can be direct
and strong without conceits and flourishes.[298] Finally, it is
well to note that those who did consider literary theories—
Swift, Boyle, Dryden, Atterbury, Addison, Steele, Hume,
Chesterfield, and Johnson—stoutly urged a purification of the
tongue from obscurity, conceits, fanciful figures, and ped-
antry.[299]

Since American culture was founded upon English models,
it might be expected that the general trend of conscious literary
style would follow English fashions.[300] Thomas Hooker in his
preface to *A Survey of the Summe of Church Discipline* (London,
1648) demands, among other straightforward qualities, "plain-
esse and perspicuity." [301] Cotton Mather—excepting his father,
the most learned man in America—has really trenchant advice
to give on studies to pursue, books to read, and the use of
judicious quotation. "After all, Every Man will have his own

[296] E.g., *A Serious Call to a Devout and Holy Life* (1729).
[297] See A. Bosker, *Literary Criticism in the Age of Johnson* (The Hague,
1930), especially chap. i, pp. 6–42, on "Rationalism." See G. Saintsbury,
A History of English Prose (1908), II, Bk. V, chaps. ii–v; Bk. VI. For important qualifications of Bosker's conventional view, see D. F. Bond,
"'Distrust' of Imagination in English Neo-Classicism," *Philological
Quarterly*, XIV, 54–59 (Jan., 1935).
[298] E.g., see his sermon on the Beauty of Thankfulness, *Works* (1859),
I, 390.
[299] See Bosker, *op. cit.*
[300] See E. F. Bradford, "Conscious Art in Bradford's *History of the
Plymouth Plantation*," *New England Quarterly*, I, 133–157 (1928). See
also F. O. Matthiessen, "Michael Wigglesworth, A Puritan Artist," *ibid.*,
pp. 491–504. For a brilliant general survey, see Thomas G. Wright,
Literary Culture in Early New England, 1620–1720 (New Haven, 1920).
See also E. C. Cook, *Literary Influences in Colonial Newspapers, 1704–1750*
(New York, 1912), and M. C. Tyler's comprehensive *History of American
Literature, 1607–1765* (New York, 1878).
[301] *The Way of the Churches . . .* , in *Old South Leaflets*, III, No. 55, p. 11.

Style." [302] Elsewhere he urges the young to read Blackmore, Homer, and Vergil; they should primarily seek instruction and reproduce their thoughts emphatically and easily,—"closely couched." [303]

But Cotton Mather's prose was fantastic by comparison with the writings of Thomas Prince, Benjamin Colman, Charles Chauncy, John Barnard, and Mather Byles. Prince pleaded for accuracy of thought and judiciously applied citation;[304] Colman said that he formed his literary manner by a study of such masters of English pulpit oratory as Bishop Pearson, John Howe, and Archbishop Tillotson;[305] Chauncy condemned the slipshod utterances of Whitefield;[306] Barnard's models, he proudly divulges, were Stillingfleet, More, and Tillotson;[307] and Byles, eschewing the oratory of Samuel Davies's *The Great Resurrection*, remarked: "[The preacher] must study an easy style, expressive diction, and tuneful cadences. . . . Rattling periods, uncouth jargon, affected phrases, and finical jingles— let them be condemned; let them be hissed from the desk and blotted from the page." [308]

EDWARDS'S LITERARY MODELS

Edwards fortunately left an early record of his theory of style in a series of twenty rules which he laid down for himself on

---

[302] *Manuductio ad Ministerium* (Boston, 1726), pp. 44–46.

[303] *Magnalia Christi Americana* [1702] (ed. 1853), I, 31.

[304] *A Chronological History of New England* (1736), pref. iv, ix, xi.

[305] *Practical Discourses upon the Parable of the Ten Virgins* (London, 1707), p. 57. For a detailed discussion of the literary training, theory and practice of the English divines, see W. F. Mitchell, *English Pulpit Oratory from Andrewes to Tillotson* (London, 1932).

[306] *Memorials of the Chaunceys* . . . (1858), p. 65.

[307] *Sermons on Several Subjects* (Boston, 1727), pp. 11, 38, 40–42, 120.

[308] Sermon at the Ordination of his son [Mather Byles, jr.] (New London, 1758), pp. 11, 12. For a general survey of the period, see M. C. Tyler, *A History of American Literature, 1607–1765* (New York, 1878); still the best authority on the period.

the cover to his *Notes on Natural Science*.[309] The more pertinent of them deserve quotation:

2. To give but few prefatorial admonitions about the style and method. It doth an author much hurt to show his concern in those things . . .

4. Let much modesty be seen in the style . . .

6. [In shorthand.][310] The world will expect more modesty [because] of my circumstances in America young &c . . . Yet the models ought not to be affected and foolish but decent and natural . . .

9. To be very moderate in the use of terms of art. Let it not look as if I was much *read*, or was conversant with books, or with the learned world . . .

12. In writing, let there be much compliance with the reader's weakness, and according to the rules in the Ladies Library Vol. 1 p. 340, and sequel . . . [311]

17. [In shorthand.][312] Before I venture to publish in London to make some experiment in my own country to play at small games first. That I may gain some experience in writing first to write letters to some in England and to try my [hand in] lesser matters before I venture in great.

Some years later he wrote in his preface to *Five Discourses* . . . (1738):

And have we not reason to think, that it ever has been, and ever will be God's manner, to bless the foolishness of preaching to save them that believe, let the elegance of language and excellency of style be carried to never so great a height, by the learning and wit of the present and future ages?" [313]

---

[309] S. E. Dwight, *The Life of President Edwards* (1829), pp. 702, 703. The MS of the cover is in the Edwards Collection at Yale University. Edwards was about sixteen years old at the time he wrote the rules.

[310] Deciphered by Upham, *Massachusetts Historical Society Proceedings* (second series), XV, 515.

[311] The reference is to modesty in writing. *The Ladies' Library* was "written by a lady" [Mary Wray, granddaughter of Jeremy Taylor and wife of Sir Cecil Wray?], and published by Sir Richard Steele in three volumes (1714).

[312] Deciphered by Upham, *loc. cit.*, p. 517.   [313] *Works* (1829), V, 349.

It was not until late in his life that he ceased to scorn rhetoric, and Richardson evidently was the author who stimulated his interest in the art of writing, for Dwight says:

About the time of his leaving Northampton, he received one of the works of Richardson, [Note: *Sir Charles Grandison.* I had this anecdote through his eldest son (Timothy Edwards)] which he read with deep interest, and regarded as wholly favourable to good morals and purity of character. The perusal of it led him to attempt the formation of a more correct style, his previous inattention to which, he then deeply regretted.[314]

In the conclusion to *Qualifications . . .* (1749) he pleads for "close reasoning" as against "dogmatical assertion" and "passionate reflection";[315] and in the preface to *Misrepresentations Corrected . . .* (1752) he states that he has sought "to avoid pointed and exaggerated expressions." Taken all together, Edwards's statements on style furnish ample proof that he gave the subject careful thought.[316]

Thus we see that in his concern for modest, unadorned, cogent logic, Edwards was closely following the prevailing theories of literary art as they were expressed both here and in England. The rules for writing laid down in *The Ladies' Library* were but the commonplaces adopted by all grammarians,[317] and his theories of "close reasoning" are to be found repeatedly stated by *The Guardian*,[318] *The Tatler*,[319] and *The Spectator*.[320]

[314] *Life*, p. 601.
[315] *Works*, IV, 433.
[316] *Ibid.*, IV, 455. For further comments made by Edwards on the proper use of logic and on the value of unadorned language as a medium for argument, see *Miscellaneous Remarks, ibid.*, VII, 570; see further, *ibid.*, II, 12, 581.
[317] See *The Cambridge History of English Literature*, IX, 425–462 (chapter on "Education"), and the bibliography of "Writings on Education" and "Courtesy Books," *ibid.*, pp. 620–622.
[318] Nos. 62, 72, 94, 105, 155.
[319] Nos. 63, 173, 234, 252, 253.
[320] Nos. 157, 168, 230, 294, 307, 313, 330, 337, 353, 430. That Edwards had access to all three of these magazines is clear from his references to them in his "Catalogue" (Edwards Collection, Yale University), a note-

Edwards's theories of beauty are set forth in *The Nature of True Virtue* (1765). That highly important essay[321] inquires into the nature of harmony and proportion (which he regarded as constituting the essence of beauty) and by analogies drawn from the beauty of nature, of the phenomenal world, he applied them to the world of the spirit. "Such is, as it were, the mutual consent of the different parts of the periphery of a circle, or surface of a sphere, and of the corresponding parts of an ellipsis."[322] Thence he proceeds to a discussion of the beauty of holiness and of heaven.[323] His theory is directly built upon Francis Hutcheson's *An Inquiry into the Original of our Ideas of Beauty and Virtue* (1725), for he not only acknowledges the debt, but directly paraphrases.[324] Hutcheson's famous analogy between beauty and virtue had already been postulated by Shaftesbury,[325] with whom Edwards was early acquainted.[326]

Edwards was concerned with theories of beauty only in so far as he might find analogies between nature and the divine excellence, but in his treatment of nature Edwards anticipated the romantics of the later eighteenth century.[327] The following

---

book in which Edwards set down, with comments, the titles of books which interested him. A valuable transcription and interpretation of the "Catalogue" by James A. Caskey (MS dissertation, 1931) is in the Hammond Library of the Chicago Theological Seminary.

[321] *Works* (1829), III, 94.

[322] *Ibid.*, pp. 110, 111.

[323] Cf. also *Miscellaneous Observations, Works* (1829), VIII, 531.

[324] Cf. Edwards, *Works* (1829), III, 110, 111, with Hutcheson, *op. cit.*, pp. 16–20.

[325] *Characteristics* . . . (1711), especially in "Soliloquy" and "Wit and Humor."

[326] "Notes on Natural Science": "Oftentimes it suits the subject and Reasoning best to Explain by way of objection and answer after the manner of Dialogue like the Earl of Shaftesbury." (From Edwards's MSS, Andover Theological Seminary.) For suggestive ideas of the aesthetic opinions of the time and earlier, see Ida Langdon, *Milton's Theory of Poetry and Fine Arts* (New Haven, 1924). For a good discussion of Edwards's aesthetic theories, see A. C. McGiffert, *Jonathan Edwards* (New York, 1932), pp. 186–200.

[327] See Myra Reynolds, *The Treatment of Nature in English Poetry between Pope and Wordsworth* (Chicago, 1896), chapter ii, "Indications of

passage, from the *Narrative of His Conversion*, written probably
between 1735 and 1745, is more pantheistic than its author was
perhaps consciously aware, and points ahead to the Wordsworth
who wrote "Of splendour in the grass, of glory in the flower":

After this [experience of conversion] my sense of divine
things gradually increased, and became more and more lively,
and had more of that inward sweetness. The appearance of
every thing was altered; there seemed to be, as it were, a calm,
sweet cast, or appearance of divine glory, in almost every thing.
God's excellency, his wisdom, his purity and love, seemed to
appear in every thing; in the sun, moon, and stars; in the clouds,
and blue sky; in the grass, flowers, trees; in the water, and all
nature; which used greatly to fix my mind. I often used to sit
and view the moon for continuance; and in the day, spent much
time in viewing the clouds and sky, to behold the sweet glory
of God in these things; in the mean time singing forth, with a
low voice, my contemplations of the Creator and Redeemer
. . . I felt God, so to speak, at the first appearance of a thunder
storm . . ."[328]

In passing, one should not neglect Edwards's theories of

a New Attitude towards Nature in the Poetry of the Eighteenth Century,"
in which she remarks that "During the period from Waller to Pope the
general feeling towards nature was one of indifference" (p. 242). Cicely
Davies, "Ut Pictura Poesis," *Modern Language Review*, XXX, 159–169
(April, 1935), points out that until the latter half of the eighteenth century,
color in both painting and writing was considered a mere appendage to
linear design, and that the traditional Renaissance concept of the value of
words as poetic ornament prevailed, wherein they were to be treated apart
from subject and design. Hogarth's explanation of his "Line of Beauty"
(*Analysis of Beauty*, 1753), which added strangeness and irregularity to an
otherwise conventional neo-classical line, only added to the confusion of
the arts. There is no adequate study of nature-description as employed by
early American writers, but for suggestive ideas see Selden L. Whitcomb,
"Nature in Early American Literature," *Sewanee Review*, II, 159–179
(February, 1894); and Mary E. Woolley, "The Development of the Love
of Romantic Scenery in America," *American Historical Review*, III, 56–66
(October, 1897).
[328] *Works* (ed. Austin, 1808), I, 34. For a similar passage see the selection "Excellency of Christ," in *Observations Concerning the Scripture
Economy of the Trinity and Covenant of Redemption* (ed. Smyth, New
York, 1880), pp. 92–97.

education, for he has succinctly stated them in a letter to Erskine, scoring the "gross defects of the ordinary method of teaching among the English," of "learning without understanding,"[329] and pleading for education of "girls as well as boys."[330]   Edwards's early enthusiasm for Locke is well known, and on the first page of the "Catalogue" he has entered, as undoubtedly read, Locke's *Thoughts concerning Education* (1693), and his ideas on the subject bear marked resemblances to Locke's.[331] Likewise he seems to have adopted advice that Halifax offered his daughter in *A Lady's Gift; or, Advice to a Daughter* (1688),[332] for Edwards has quoted from it in his "Catalogue."[333]

"Preaching should be Methodical," says Joseph Glanvill in *An Essay concerning Preaching* (1678); "Method is necessary both for the understanding, and memories of the hearers ..."[334] —and Edwards's sermons closely followed the sermon-type of the day.   The text, whose Doctrine is expounded under various Propositions, is followed by the Application (Improvement, Use, or Exhortation), and that in turn is divided into Inferences. Ministers seldom departed from the established norm,[335] and Edwards is no exception to the rule.   The rhythmic, musical sentences, packed with fanciful figures and bookish affectations employed by an earlier generation [336] have been abandoned.

On whom did Edwards directly model his sermon style?

[329] Dwight, *Life*, p. 475.   [330] *Ibid.*, p. 478.
[331] *Ibid.*, pp. 516–518; 533, 534 (letters to McCulloch and Erskine); and letter to Bellamy in *New England Quarterly*, I, 242 (1928).
[332] Cf. Edwards's letter to his daughter, Esther Burr, November 20, 1757, Selections following, p. 414.
[333] P. 35. For further suggestions of sources from which Edwards might well have formed various literary, aesthetic, and philosophic theories, see T. H. Johnson, "Jonathan Edwards' Background of Reading," *Publications of the Colonial Society of Massachusetts*, XXVIII, 193–222 (1931).
[334] P. 38.
[335] C. F. Richardson, *English Preachers and Preaching, 1640–1670* (New York, 1928), pp. 115–118.
[336] See, e.g., Jeremy Taylor's *The Golden Grove* (1655).   On the other hand, Tillotson's sermons rarely contain rhetorical flights, and Edwards follows them much more closely.

The answer is in part to be sought, no doubt, in the sermons with which Edwards must early have been familiar—those of his father, Timothy Edwards, and of his grandfather, Solomon Stoddard.[337] The emphasis on one idea, and the repetition of the main theme, so common in all of Edwards's sermons, is a characteristic noted also in the sermons of Increase Mather;[338] and though Cotton Mather's sermons are often prolix, they are also, as are Edwards's, lucid.[339]

But Edwards shows a greater sensitivity than those already discussed to the style of the King James version of the Bible,[340] —by far the most important model on which he framed his own, consciously and unconsciously.[341] It is clear from an examination of his sermons, both published and unpublished,[342] that Edwards chose his texts from every book of the Bible, but predominantly from the more poetical chapters—Psalms, Proverbs, Ecclesiastes, Solomon, and the Gospels;[343] and it

[337] See J. A. Stoughton, *Windsor Farmes* (Hartford, 1883), pp. 121–142, where a few of Timothy Edwards's sermons are transcribed. The manner of their composition closely resembles the manner adopted by his son. See also, e.g., Solomon Stoddard's *Some Cases of Conscience respecting the Country* (1722), especially pp. 4–7, where there is close parallelism to Edwards's sermon *Joseph's Great Temptation* (S. Hopkins, *Life . . . of . . . Edwards*, Boston, 1765). Both sermons are warnings to the congregation against lust.

[338] K. B. Murdock, *Increase Mather* (Cambridge, Mass., 1925), pp. 130, 131.

[339] B. Wendell, *Cotton Mather, the Puritan Priest* (New York, 1891), p. 160.

[340] Edwards's own annotated copy (edition 1653) is in the Edwards Collection, Yale University.

[341] The influence of the Bible on English literature is a very important subject: see J. M. MacCulloch, *Literary Characteristics of the Holy Scripture*, 1845; L. J. Halsey, *The Literary Attraction of the Bible*, 1889; A. S. Cook, *The Bible and English Prose Style*, 1892; R. G. Moulton, *The Literary Study of the Bible*, 1899; J. H. Gardiner, *The Bible as English Literature*, 1906.

[342] The latter—nearly 1100—are mostly in the Edwards Collection, Yale University.

[343] This helps substantiate the conclusions of K. B. Murdock, "The Puritans and the New Testament," *Publications of the Colonial Society of Massachusetts*, XXV, 239–243 (1923), that the idea of the "fiery puritan" must be re-examined.

is quite plain that Edwards's sensitive nature was so inspired
by the beauty of text in Psalms, Solomon, St. John, and
especially in Revelation, that a very direct modeling upon
their phrasing can be established.[344] Edwards was steeped in
scriptural literature; all else was ancillary to it, and his sermon
imagery and rhetoric show a heavy, direct, and almost exclusive
debt to it. His very animal figures are biblical: "angry wild
beasts," "lions of the forests," "like a moth," "worm," "spider,"
"the old serpent";[345] and in the imprecatory sermons, where
images are most frequent, he depends entirely upon biblical
figures.[346] The wrath of God is described thus: "He will crush
out your blood, and make it fly, and it shall be sprinkled on his
garments, so as to stain all his raiment." [347]

The models adopted by Edwards for his treatises conformed
very closely to those rules which he had set for himself in his
youth;[348] that is, he followed the method of the controversial-
ists: men of learning and common sense, who lacked originality
and fire, and were without contemporary literary merit—Isaac

---

[344] Compare Edwards's letter to Bellamy, *New England Quarterly*, I,
239–240 (1928), with the third Psalm; *Observations on the Trinity* (ed.
Smyth, 1880), pp. 92–97, with Canticles; *Treatise on Grace* (ed. Grosart,
1865), pp. 38, 45, 46, 56 (written after 1752), with St. John passages on love.
Passages echoing Revelation are many, but see *Miscellaneous Observations*,
Works (ed. Dwight, 1829), VIII, 577 (section on "Angels or Heaven");
Peace which Christ Gives, ibid., VI, 134, 135; *Thanksgiving Sermon, Nov.
7, 1734, ibid.*, VIII, 311 (with which cf. Rev. 14); *Charity and its Fruits*
(ed. T. Edwards, 1851), pp. 506, 510, 512, and especially p. 530, which
reads: "There they shall hunger no more, neither thirst any more; neither
shall the sun light on them, nor any heat, for the Lamb which is in the
midst of the throne, shall feed them, and lead them to fountains of living
waters, and God shall wipe away all tears from their eyes." This should
be compared with Rev. 7:16. For further but less tangible influence of the
Anglo-Saxon monosyllable, and the very repetitious character of such
words as *kingdom, possess, inherit, blessed, love, sweet*, see *Works* (1829),
VIII, 250, 280, 285, 311.

[345] *Works* (1829), VI, 103 (cf. Revelation 20:2), 165.

[346] See, especially, *Sinners* (*Works*, 1829, VII), and *Future Punishment,
ibid.*, VI, for innumerable use of *loathsome, vile, lake of fire*.

[347] *Sinners, ibid.*, p. 173. See Isaiah 63:3 for identical image—though
possibly used more powerfully by Edwards.

[348] See *ante*, p. cii.

Barrow, George Bull, John Beach, Thomas Chubb, Samuel
Clarke, Ralph Cudworth, Theophilus Gale, John Taylor, and
George Turnbull.[349]

EDWARDS'S STYLE

During the first one hundred and sixty years of American
letters no writer achieved the eminence or popularity of Edwards—with the possible exception of Franklin—if the fre-
quency with which his works were published in Europe and
America between 1731 and 1800 is a criterion. The total
quantity of his published writing was not great, for he gave to
the press during his life not above thirty items,[350] but his life
was cut in its prime at the moment of his greatest productivity.
It was not until 1737 that the works intended for publication
began to appear, nor until 1754 that *Freedom of the Will*, his
greatest work, was issued.[351] It is estimated that 1074 of his
sermons exist;[352] but not more than half were written out fully,

[349] Partly because Edwards was in haste while writing his later treatises,
and did not revise them for publication, and partly because his method and
manner are very reminiscent of those of his opponents, his treatises do not
excel in grace of phrase. Gale's *The Court of the Gentiles* (1669–1676), to
which Edwards is said to be strongly indebted (C. Gohdes, "Aspects of
Idealism in Early New England," *Philosophical Review*, XXXIX, 537–555,
1930), like Cudworth's *Intellectual System* (1678), is a storehouse of
chaotic and unsystematic knowledge; and much of Edwards's carelessness
is perhaps chargeable to their own.

[350] Compare Samuel Willard's forty-eight; Gilbert Tennent's fifty-three;
Benjamin Wadsworth's fifty-five; Charles Chauncy's fifty-six; George
Whitefield's sixty-five; Benjamin Colman's ninety; Increase Mather's one
hundred and eight; Cotton Mather's four hundred and nine. But all these
men lived longer than Edwards, and with the exception of Cotton Mather
and Whitefield, the works of none were republished more than once or
twice posthumously. In the case of Edwards, twelve new items appeared
after his death, and the total of new editions and reprints from 1731 to the
present, here and abroad, is not less than two hundred and fifty. (These
data are based on a comparison and analysis of the works of all writers,
especially American, whose books were issued from American presses, as
they are named in the twelve volumes of Charles Evans's *American Bibliography 1639–1797* [1903–1931]; and on an inquiry into Edwards's works
published abroad.)

[351] See rule No. 17, from his *Notes on Natural Science*, quoted p. cii, *ante.*

[352] See inventory of his estate, *Bibliotheca Sacra*, XXXIII, 438 ff.

and since but a fraction have been published, and since so large
a number—especially the later sermons—are scarcely more than
sermon notes, it is impossible to discover in them any develop-
ing literary style.

It is plain that Edwards followed in general the sermon style
of Chillingworth, Baxter, Robertson, and Tillotson—precise,
correct, clear, dignified, and obvious. But many sermon faults
are not his: verbosity, affected and paraded learning, strained
metaphors, startling similes, long sentences, complicated clauses,
entangled parentheses, puns, rhetorical questions, verbal antith-
eses. He makes little use of *exempla*, and no use of quotation
from classical authority; he seldom tells "good stories" of timely
or personal interest; in short, he lacks "literary dress."

To aid in classifying Edwards's sermons, one might list them
in four general categories: disciplinary, pastoral, doctrinal, and
occasional—though, of course, the categories overlap. The
disciplinary sermons form about one third of his total published
number, and can be subdivided into three types: the imprecatory[353]—those in which he emphasizes the principles of total
depravity and pictures the horrors that will overwhelm the
unconverted; the corrective[354]—those in which he draws attention to the backslidings of his parishioners; and the hortatory[355]
—those that urge repentance and conversion after conviction
of sin.

The sermons of the pastoral group—by far the largest, for it
comprises fully one half of all he wrote—differ from those of the
disciplinary essentially in that they do not imply a sense of guilt
when they discuss the duties and privileges of religion.[356] They

[353] For example, *The Punishment of the Wicked*, *Justice of God in the
Damnation of Sinners*, *Eternity of Hell Torments*, and *Sinners in the Hands
of an Angry God*.
[354] For example, *Joseph's Great Temptation*, and *The Nature and End
of Excommunication*.
[355] For example, *Exhortation to Gain Christian Knowledge*, *The Un-
reasonableness of Indeterminateness in Religion*, and *Christian Cautions*.
[356] For example, *The Duty of Charity to the Poor*, *The Preciousness of
Time*, and *The Portion of the Righteous*.

set forth in positive, joyous, tender, rhapsodic, and even rapt language the beauty of religious contemplation.

But the more perfect view which the saints have of God's glory and love in another world, is what is especially called the seeing of God. Then they shall see him as he is. That light which now is but a glimmering, will be brought to clear sunshine; that which is here but the dawning, will be perfect day.

Those intellectual views which will be granted in another world are called seeing God.[357]

In the doctrinal sermons Edwards interprets his faith and concentrates on Bible exegesis; and such sermons, more often reserved for occasions when he preached outside his own pulpit, established his reputation as a leading theologian.[358] The final division of occasional sermons—those prepared for special events—form but a small fraction of the total; such are his Thanksgiving and Christmas sermons, and those written for baptisms, ordinations, installations, and funerals.[359]

The imagery in Edwards's sermons is sparse and conventional; the rhetoric is seldom heightened except when Edwards is trying to arouse an emotion of powerful yearning or revulsion.[360] The restrained, dramatic power of the rhetorical question: ". . . How many is it likely will remember this discourse in hell?" is unusual.[361] Far more often his sermons were

[357] *The Pure in Heart, Works* (1829), VIII, 280.

[358] *God Glorified in Man's Dependence* (1731), *A Divine and Supernatural Light* (1734).

[359] For a general discussion of the occasional sermon, see C. F. Richardson, *English Preachers . . .* (1928), pp. 88 ff. Installation sermon: *The Church's Marriage;* funeral sermon: *True Saints;* to this category, *Farewell Sermon.*

[360] O. W. Holmes, *Pages from an Old Volume of Life* (1889), p. 386, calls attention to the possibility that Edwards's imprecatory flights may be traced to the writings of the elder Thomas Boston, but examination does not substantiate Holmes's theory. The imagery in both can be traced to the Bible.

[361] *Sinners, Works* (1829), VII, 175. For other examples, see *Thoughts on Revival (ibid.,* IV, 164 f.), the *locus classicus* in which he compares children to vipers; and also *Procrastination; or, The Sin and Folly of Depending on Future Time (ibid.,* VI, 503), in which he contrasts our physical beauty with the decay of a corpse.

tender, fervid, fresh, seldom controversial, and never contentious. They are very frequently held together by a thread of
such recurrent words as *delightful, pleasant, bright, lovely,* and
sweet.[362]

Taste and see; never was any disappointed that made a trial.
You will not only find those spiritual comforts that Christ
offers you to be of a surpassing sweetness for the present, but
they will be to your soul as the dawning light that shines more
and more to the perfect day; and the issue of all will be your
arrival in heaven, that land of rest, those regions of everlasting
joy, where your peace and happiness will be perfect, without
the least mixture of trouble or affliction, and never be interrupted nor have an end.[363]

He employs word-pairs until the mind of the reader is lulled
into forgetfulness, but they are less frequently mere ornamental
alliterative pleonasms—"search and seek," "mildness and mercy"
—than supplementary groups: "Labors and sufferings,"[364]
"prepossession and desire,"[365] "congruous and fit,"[366] "remembered and commemorated."[367] His sentence rhythms are
a unit, sensitively built—the word-pairs, even when conventional and redundant, are not forced. Repetition of words and
constructions is the essence of his style. He is notably free
from clichés and jargon, and though the thought as expressed
in the sermons is conventional, it is vigorous and never trite.[368]

[362] See especially, *Observations on the Trinity* (ed. Smyth, 1880), "Excellency of Christ," pp. 92–97. See also *Twenty Sermons* (1789), p. 197
(cf. Psalms 34:8) and p. 313. See *Thanksgiving Sermon* (*Works*, 1829),
VIII, 311.
[363] *Peace I Leave with You* (*Twenty Sermons*, 1789), p. 197; cf. Psalms
34:8.
[364] *Works* (1808), VIII, 238.
[365] *Ibid.*, p. 119.
[366] *Ibid.*, p. 399.
[367] *Ibid.*, p. 268. For the wide use made of these word-pairs, see G. P.
Krapp, *Modern English: Its Growth and Present Use* (New York, 1910),
pp. 250, 252.
[368] Compare Edwards's *A Divine and Supernatural Light* (1734) with
Tillotson's *The Reasonableness of a Resurrection*. Tillotson is more ample
and flowing, but his prose is less alive.

Edwards's ear for a prose cadence, for rise and fall and well matched vowel sounds, is best seen in the sermons.

This light, and this only, has its fruit in an universal holiness of life. No merely notional or speculative understanding of the doctrines of religion will ever bring to this. But this light, as it reaches the bottom of the heart, and changes the nature, so it will effectually dispose to an universal obedience. It shows God's worthiness to be obeyed and served. It draws forth the heart in a sincere love to God, which is the only principle of a true, gracious, and universal obedience; and it convinces of the reality of those glorious rewards that God has promised to them that obey him.[369]

The ebb and flow of the quiet, unostentatious thought shows Edwards at his best—a level which he achieved without effort and maintained whenever he avoided the passions of controversy. In his sermons his oratorical heights are infrequent, his rhetorical effects are limited, and his vocabulary is shaped to the comprehension of his listeners, but his clarity, freedom from eccentricity, and easy straightforwardness are virtues that go far to supplement any want of a more conscious artistry of style.

The treatises differ in style from the sermons essentially in that they depend upon severe, undilated exposition and precise, subtle distinction for the force of their argument. In them Edwards becomes the debater. He holds to the integrity of the syllogistic method: stating his proposition, defining his terms, establishing a connection between antecedent and consequent, after which he proceeds to a clear and logical conclusion by justly locating the burden of proof, conceding where he can, and waiving irrelevance. He meets his opponents fairly and

[369] *A Divine and Supernatural Light* (*Twenty Sermons*, 1789), p. 273.* For a discussion of revisions of his published writings made by Edwards himself or by his editors, see T. H. Johnson, *Jonathan Edwards as a Man of Letters* (MS thesis, Harvard College Library), pp. 180–185, 236–238.

honestly by all forms of argument: direct evidence of fact,[370] presumption of fact,[371] testimony,[372] appeal to authority,[373] analogy,[374] appeal to common rationality,[375] and statement of cause and effect;[376] and he is righteously angry when he feels opponents have not treated him with the same fairness.[377]

The style of the treatises was seriously condemned by Henry Rogers[378] a century ago, and Thomas Huxley called them "lumbering and awkward." [379]   But let Edwards's works be judged by a careful reading in the light of their virtues, not their defects.   S. E. Dwight said of *Religious Affections* that it was ". . . the most incorrect of all his works, published by himself." [380] The following passage from *Religious Affections* is chosen for quotation, not because its style rises above that of other selections, but because it seems typical of the whole; and the reader may judge for himself if Dwight is to be credited.

And so a spiritual application of the promises of scripture, for the comfort of the saints, consists in enlightening their minds to see the holy excellency and sweetness of the blessings promised, and also the holy excellency of the promiser, and his faithfulness and sufficiency; thus drawing forth their hearts to embrace the promiser, and thing promised; and by this means, giving the sensible actings of grace, enabling them to see their grace, and so their title to the promise.[381]

The style of the later treatises must be judged by their success

[370] *Narrative of Conversion* (very frequently).
[371] *Freedom of the Will* (opening chapters).
[372] *Narrative of Conversion* (concluding chapters).
[373] *Original Sin* (very frequently).
[374] *Nature of Virtue* (see especially *Works*, 1808, VI, 39).
[375] *An Humble Inquiry* (see especially *Works*, 1808, I, 334, 335).
[376] *God's Chief End* (*ibid.*, VI, 39).
[377] *An Humble Inquiry* (*ibid.*, I, 334, 335).
[378] Preface to his edition of Edwards, *Works* (2 vols., London, 1839), p. xv.
[379] Article on Edwards in the ninth edition of the *Encyclopædia Britannica* (1878).
[380] *Life* (1829), p. 602.
[381] *Works* (1808), IV, 156, 157.

as polemical literature, and on that basis their merit is high. In *Freedom of the Will* and *Original Sin* the attack is bold and original, with occasional flashes of ready wit that served him well as strategy in controversy, to be seen in craft and maneuver rather than in sparkling sally. And finally, in those moments when he set controversy aside to describe with rapt love his visions of heavenly joy, his prose communicates such a tender and idyllic glow, that the reader must be insensitive who is not warmed by it.[382]

[382] See *Observations* (ed. Smyth, 1880), pp. 92–97, for an especially fine example.

CHRONOLOGICAL TABLE

1703. Jonathan Edwards born, at East Windsor, Connecticut, October 5.
1715. Wrote "Of insects."
1716. Entered Yale College.
1720. Graduated from Yale College.
1720–22. Studied theology in New Haven.
1721. Beginning of his conversion.
1722. August, went as minister to a Presbyterian church in New York City.
1723. May, left the New York church.
1724. Elected to office of tutor at Yale.
1725. Teaching career interrupted by illness.
1726. Resigned tutorship; became colleague of his grandfather, Rev. Solomon Stoddard, in Northampton, Massachusetts.
1727. July, married Sarah Pierrepont.
1731. *God Glorified in the Work of Redemption by the Greatness of Man's Dependence upon Him in the Whole of It.*
1734. *A Divine and Supernatural Light, Immediately Imparted to the Soul by the Spirit of God, Shown to be both a Scriptural, and Rational Doctrine.*
1737. *A Faithful Narrative of the Surprising Work of God in the Conversion of Many Hundred Souls in Northampton, and the Neighboring Towns and Villages.*
1738. *Charity and its Fruits* (preached 1738, pub. 1851); *Discourses on Various Important Subjects* (preached 1734).
1739. *Narrative of His Conversion* written.
1741. *The Distinguishing Marks of a Work of the Spirit of God* and *Sinners in the Hands of an Angry God* (preached at Enfield, Connecticut).
1742. *Some Thoughts concerning the Present Revival of Religion in New England.*

1746. *A Treatise concerning Religious Affections* (preached 1742–43).

1747. *An Humble Attempt to Promote Visible Union of God's People in Extraordinary Prayer for the Revival of Religion;* announced to the Rev. Mr. John Erskine his projected attack on Arminianism.

1748. Beginning of dissension in his Northampton parish.

1749. *An Account of the Life of the Late Reverend Mr. David Brainerd* and *An Humble Inquiry into the Rules of the Word of God, concerning the Qualifications Requisite to a Complete Standing and Full Communion with the Visible Christian Church.*

1750. July 1, preached *Farewell Sermon* at Northampton church.

1751. Settled in Stockbridge, Massachusetts, as pastor of the local church and missionary to the Indians.

1752. *Misrepresentations Corrected, and Truth Vindicated.*

1754. *A Careful and Strict Enquiry into the Modern Prevailing Notions of that Freedom of Will which is supposed to be Essential to Moral Agency, Virtue and Vice, Reward and Punishment, Praise and Blame.*

1755. Wrote "The Nature of True Virtue" and "Concerning the End for which God Created the World" (pub. 1765 as *Two Dissertations*).

1757. Chosen president of the College of New Jersey (now Princeton) as successor to his son-in-law, Aaron Burr.

1758. January, assumed office; *The Great Christian Doctrine of Original Sin Defended;* March 22, died of smallpox in Princeton.

The bibliography for this edition has been revised and brought up to date by Stephen S. Webb.

I. TEXT

Works. Ed. by E. Williams and E. Parsons. 8 vols. Leeds: 1806–11. New edition, 8 vols. London: 1817. A two-volume supplement to the London edition was edited by R. Ogle. Edinburgh: 1847.

Works. Ed. by S. Austin. 8 vols. Worcester: 1808. Reprint with additions, volumes 5–6 being the supplementary volumes edited by R. Ogle, and an index. New York: 1847. Volumes 1–4, New York: 1844, and often thereafter. (Best edition until superseded by completion of the Yale edition now in process under the general editorship of Perry Miller, below.)

Works. Ed. by Sereno E. Dwight. 10 vols. New York: 1829–30. (First volume contains *Life* by Dwight.)

Works. Ed. by E. Hickman. 2 vols. London: 1833. Reprinted with essay on genius and writings of Edwards by H. Rogers and memoir by Sereno Dwight. London: 1834, and several times thereafter. Reprinted in one volume with essay by H. Rogers. London: 1835. 10 vols. Edinburgh: 1847. 4 vols. New York: 1843.

Works. Ed. by Perry Miller. In process, New Haven: 1957 *et seq.* Volume One, *The Freedom Of The Will.* Ed. by Paul Ramsey. Volume Two, *Religious Affections.* Ed. by John E. Smith. (With extensive scholarly introductions and the utmost attention to textual accuracy, upon completion this will become the standard edition of Edwards' *Works.* See the essay review of the first volume: William S. Morris. "The Reappraisal of Edwards," *New England Quarterly,* XXX, pp. 515–25 [Dec., 1957], and Murphy, below.)

Select Works. In process, London: 1958 *et seq.* (Volume One contains *A Narrative Of Surprising Conversions,* four supplementary sermons, and a memoir and bibliography by Ian H. Murray based on the Dwight *Life.* Volume Two contains ten representative sermons. Volume Three consists of *The Religious Affections,* reprinted from the Worcester Edition, with expanded contractions, altered footnotes, and revised punctuation.)

Images or Shadows of Divine Things. Ed. by Perry Miller. New Haven, London: 1948. (A volume in the Yale University Edwards manuscripts, these two hundred and twelve notations show their author trying to "work out a new sense of the divinity of nature and the naturalness of divinity," according to Mr. Miller. The editor remarks on Edwards' debt to Newton and Locke and characterizes Edwards as "the first American empiricist." For criticism of these emphases see the review by H. Shelton Smith, *American Literature,* XXII, pp. 192–94 [May, 1950].)

"Jonathan Edwards on the Sense of the Heart," ed. by Perry Miller. *Harvard Theological Review,* XLI, pp. 123–45 (April, 1948). (Number 782 of the "Miscellanies" from the manuscript in the Yale University Library, "the entry most pertinent to the rhetorical theory" of Edwards.)

"Jonathan Edwards' sociology of the Great Awakening," ed. by Perry Miller. *New England Quarterly,* XXI, pp. 50–77 (March, 1948). (Excerpts from three manuscript sermons.)

The Life and Diary of David Brainerd. Ed. by Jonathan Edwards. Newly edited and with a biographical sketch of President Edwards by Philip E. Howard, Jr. Chicago: 1949. (A condensed and modernized text with a jejune biographical sketch of Edwards.)

The Nature of True Virtue. Foreword by William K. Frankena. Ann Arbor: 1960. (Somewhat superficial introduction discusses Edwards' current status and relates him to the modern theologians Niebuhr and Barth.)

The Philosophy of Jonathan Edwards From His Private Notebooks. Ed. by Harvey G. Townsend. Eugene, Oregon: 1955. (Includes "On Being," "The Mind," and selections from the philosophical sections of Edwards' massive "Miscellanies." The editor stresses the influence of Locke.)

Puritan Sage: Collected Writings of Jonathan Edwards. Ed. by Vergilius Ferm. New York: 1953. (Includes material heretofore unpublished but its usefulness is limited by the silent modernization of the texts and the lack of identification and dating of their sources.)

"An Unpublished Letter by Jonathan Edwards," ed. by George Peirce Clark. *New England Quarterly,* XXIX, pp. 228–33 (June, 1956). (Letter of May 7, 1750 to the Reverend Peter Clark of Salem Village. Important in relation to Edwards' dismissal from Northampton.)

Johnson, Thomas H. "Jonathan Edwards," *Princeton University Library Chronicle,* XII, pp. 159–60 (Spring, 1951). (Notes the acquisition by the library of a 1743 sermon of Edwards and a 1738 German translation of *A Faithful Narrative,* the latter indicative of his Continental reputation.)

Rice, Howard C., Jr. "Jonathan Edwards at Princeton: With a Survey of Edwards Material in the Princeton University Library," *Princeton University Library Chronicle,* XV, pp. 69–89 (Winter, 1954). (Prints eight Edwards letters and sermon notes dated 1744.)

For descriptions of the mine of manuscript left by Edwards see *The Cambridge History of American Literature,* I, pp. 426–27, and Dexter, Upham, Winslow, and article on "The Manuscripts of President Edwards," below.

For all other text items published prior to 1940 see: Thomas H. Johnson. *The Printed Writings Of Jonathan Edwards 1703–1758: A Bibliography.* Princeton: 1940. (Gives complete bibliographical information for Edwards' sermons, treatises, biography, narrative essays, and letters, but does not include anthologies. Provides evidence of Edwards' European reputation and his great popularity in nineteenth-century America.)

II. BIOGRAPHY AND CRITICISM

Aldridge, Alfred Owen. "Jonathan Edwards and William Godwin on Virtue," *American Literature,* XVIII, pp. 308–18 (Jan., 1947). (An account of the three-cornered dispute between William Godwin, Samuel Parr, and Robert Hall on Edwards' recognition of two levels of virtue. Illustrative of Edwards' influence in England.)

———. "Benjamin Franklin and Jonathan Edwards on Lightning and Earthquakes," *Isis,* XLI, pp. 162–64 (Fall, 1950). (Use of a mutual source.)

———. "Edwards and Hutcheson," *Harvard Theological Review,* XLIV, pp. 35–53 (Jan., 1951). (Influence of Hutcheson's philosophy upon Edwards' *The Nature of True Virtue.*)

Allen, Alexander V. G. *Jonathan Edwards.* Boston: 1889. (Long the standard biography, this work is sound and authoritative. The presentation of Edwards' theological position is admirable, but the more purely philosophical aspects of Edwards' work are slighted. The book fails to evoke a convincing and lively impression of Edwards the man.)

Anderson, Wilbert L. "The Preaching Power of Jonathan Edwards," *Congregationalist and Christian World,* LXXXVIII, pp. 463–66 (Oct. 3, 1903). (The interest of this rather uncritical analysis of Edwards' effectiveness as a preacher is enhanced by numerous illustrations—portraits of Mrs. Edwards, Jonathan Edwards the younger, pictures of Edwards' birthplace, his tankard, the memorial window in Yale College chapel, a desk used by him, and so on. This number of the *Congregationalist* is devoted to Edwards.)

Blau, Joseph L. *Men and Movements in American Philosophy.* New York: 1952. (Sees Edwards' idealism setting a pattern for more than a century of American thought but concludes that, "there is little vitality left in Edwards' thought.")

Bledsoe, Albert T. *An Examination of President Edwards' Inquiry into the Freedom of the Will.* Philadelphia: 1845.

Boardman, George Nye. *A History of New England Theology.* New York: 1899. (A very good analysis of the Edwardean theology and of the systems to which it gave birth, but unfortunately with almost no attention to the historical setting of the New England doctrines, there being little reference to the influence of contemporary philosophical notions upon Edwards and his followers.)

Buranelli, Vincent. "Colonial Philosophy," *William And Mary Quarterly* (third series), XVI, pp. 343–62 (July, 1959). (An excellent review of the history of colonial philosophy which includes an extensive critique of Edwards scholarship.)

Byington, Ezra Hoyt. "Jonathan Edwards and the Great Awakening," *Bibliotheca Sacra,* LV, pp. 114–27 (Jan., 1898). (Presents the important aspects of the Revival in as favorable a light as possible.)

Cady, Edwin H. "The Artistry of Jonathan Edwards," *New England Quarterly,* XXII, pp. 61–72 (March, 1949). (An analysis of "Sinners in the Hands of an Angry God" as "a work of literary art," stressing its imagery as the source of its emotional power.)

Carpenter, Frederic Ives. "The Radicalism of Jonathan Edwards," *New England Quarterly,* IV, pp. 629–44 (Oct., 1931). (Believes that "essentially Edwards was a free spirit—perhaps freer in his old Calvinistic cloak than was Franklin in the jacket of the new utilitarianism." Sees parallels, which he admits are "perhaps accidental," between Edwards and Robinson Jeffers and James Branch Cabell, and other parallels which are "indubitable" between Edwards and William James.)

[Cattell, J. McKeen.] "Jonathan Edwards on Multidimensional Space and the Mechanistic Conception of Life," *Science,* N. s. LII, pp. 409–10 (Oct. 29, 1920). ("Einstein, Conklin; Behold your King!")

Channing, W. H. "Jonathan Edwards and the Revivalists," *Christian Examiner,* XLIII (4th ser., VIII), pp. 374–94 (Nov., 1857).

Christie, Francis A. "Jonathan Edwards," in *Dictionary of American Biography,* VI, pp. 30–37. (Sound, authoritative, compact, the best thing of its kind about Edwards.)

Clark, Irene Woodbridge. "A Wifely Estimate of Edwards," *Congregationalist and Christian World,* LXXXVIII, pp. 472–73 (Oct. 3, 1903). (Presents a letter written by Mrs. Edwards and given to the council which met at Northampton on June 22, 1750, for the purpose of examining the difficulties between Edwards and his congregation.)

"A Contemporaneous Account of Jonathan Edwards," *Journal of the Presbyterian Historical Society,* II, pp. 125–35 (Dec., 1903). (Includes facsimile of title page of the first edition of *Original Sin* and reprints the interesting account of Edwards which was prefixed to the work.)

Crabtree, Arthur B. *Jonathan Edwards' View of Man; a Study in Eighteenth Century Calvinism.* Wallington, England: 1948.

Crooker, Joseph H. "Jonathan Edwards: A Psychological Study," *New England Magazine,* N. S. II, pp. 159–72 (April, 1890). (Analysis of Edwards' home training and beliefs to explain and support the contention that Edwards was "a theological monomaniac, a man who thought in a trance and lived in an unreal world of his own making . . . a melancholy example of a saintly character wasted by false dogma.")

Curti, Merle. *The Growth of American Thought.* New York: 1943. (This standard work offers brief but illuminating comments on Edwards and is especially valuable in placing him in an American religious context. Little attention to his philosophy.)

Curtis, Mattoon Munroe. "Kantian Elements in Jonathan Edwards," in *Festschrift für Heinze.* Berlin: 1906. (Attempts to prove that Edwards anticipated Kant at several points.)

——. *An Outline of Philosophy in America* (reprinted from *Western Reserve Bulletin,* March, 1896). (Includes sketch of Edwards' philosophical views and suggests many possible influences.)

Dana, James. *An Examination of the Late Reverend President Edwards' "Enquiry on Freedom of Will": More Especially the Foundation Principles of his Book, with the Tendency and Consequences of the Reasoning therein Contained.* Boston: 1770. (Has "no manner of doubt but the foundation principles of [Edwards'] book are false," and have a "most dangerous tendency," a conclusion he buttresses by a detailed criticism of Edwards' argument.)

——. *The Examination of the Late Rev'd President Edwards' Enquiry on Freedom of Will, continued.* New Haven: 1773.

Darrow, Clarence. "The Edwardses and the Jukeses," *American Mercury,* VI, pp. 147–57 (Oct., 1925). (Hoots at the easy generalizations of some students of eugenics concerning the importance of heredity as revealed in the descendants of Edwards and Jukes.)

Davidson, Frank. "Three Patterns of Living," *Bulletin of the American Association of University Professors,* XXXIV, pp. 364–74 (Summer, 1948). (On Edwards', Benjamin Franklin's and John Woolman's approaches to life as adaptable to today.)

Day, Jeremiah. *An Examination of President Edwards's Inquiry on the Freedom of the Will.* New Haven: 1841. (In an elaborate exposition of Edwards' work, Day attempts by restating Edwards' argument to make it clear and convincing.)

De Normandie, James. "Jonathan Edwards at Portsmouth, New Hampshire," *Massachusetts Historical Society Proceedings* (second series), XV, pp. 16–20 (1902). (An interesting account of the events surrounding Edwards' preaching of a sermon at Portsmouth on

June 28, 1749. Includes a letter from Edwards to his daughter
Mary.)

Dewey, Edward Hooker. "Jonathan Edwards," in *American Writers
on American Literature*. Ed. by John Macy. New York: 1931. (A
stimulating essay, but often vague and loose. Suggests a conflict
between the preacher and the thinker, for the existence of which
there is certainly little evidence.)

De Witt, John. "Jonathan Edwards: A Study," *Princeton Theological
Review*, II, pp. 88–109 (Jan., 1904). (A sympathetic analysis of
Edwards' theology.)

Dexter, Franklin B. "On the Manuscripts of Jonathan Edwards,"
Massachusetts Historical Society Proceedings (second series), XV,
pp. 2–16 (1902). (Discusses the extent and character of the manuscript legacies of Edwards and contains some interesting references
to details of Edwards' personal life.)

Dwight, Sereno E. *The Life of President Edwards*. Volume I of
Works, ed. by Dwight. New York: 1829. (Still invaluable because
of its extensive quotations and mass of biographical detail.)

The Edwardean, Devoted to the History of Thought in America. Ed.
by William H. Squires. Clinton, New York: 1903–1904. (A
quarterly devoted to articles on Edwards, the most valuable of
these rather sketchy discussions being "Some Estimates of President
Edwards" [I, 32–50], "Edwards's Metaphysical Foundations" [I, 51–
64], and "Edwards's Psychology of the Will" [II, 84–108].)

"The Edwards Bicentennial," *Journal of the Presbyterian Historical
Society*, II, pp. 166–69 (Dec., 1903). (Contains brief account of
the memorial services held at Stockbridge, New Haven, Hartford,
Andover, and other places on the two-hundredth anniversary of
the birth of Edwards, and a list of articles in periodicals commemorating the event.)

Edwards, Jonathan (the younger). "Remarks on the Improvements
Made in Theology by His Father," in *Works*, ed. by Tryon Edwards.
Boston: 1854. I, pp. 481 ff. (Significant for its indication of what
in the eyes of his followers were Edwards' contributions to
theology.)

Elwood, Douglas J. *The Philosophical Theology of Jonathan Edwards*.
New York: 1960. (Depicts Edwards as a great religious thinker
whose system of thought is particularly relevant to the philosophical
crisis of the present, admitting the synthesis of science, philosophy,
and theology, while stressing the "immediacy of the divine Presence.")

*Exercises Commemorating the Two-Hundredth Anniversary of the
Birth of Jonathan Edwards, held at Andover Theological Seminary,
October 4 and 5, 1903*. Andover: 1904. (Interesting for the light
thrown on the vitality of Edwardeanism.)

Faust, Clarence H. "Jonathan Edwards as a Scientist," *American*

Literature, I, pp. 393–404 (Jan., 1930). (Attempts to show that in spite of a thin vein of scientific interest and of some powers of observation, Edwards' early dedication to theology makes untenable the oft-repeated belief that he might have been "a remarkable scientific observer.")

————. "The Decline of Puritanism," in *Transitions in American Literary History,* ed. by Harry H. Clark. Durham, N. C.: 1953. (Includes an analysis of Edwards as a spokesman of Puritanism attempting to arrest its gradual decay "by reinterpreting Calvinistic theology in the terms current in late seventeenth and early eighteenth century philosophy.")

————. *Ideological Conflicts in Early American Books.* Syracuse, New York: 1958. (Points to Edwards' dependence on the emotion as prefacing modern obscurantism.)

Fay, Jay Wharton. *American Psychology before William James.* New Brunswick, N. J.: 1939. (Extensive discussion of Edwards includes his use of Locke to arrive at a Berkeleian idealism, high praise for his independent investigation of the will and his scholastic psychological argument therein, and his anticipation of William James in the study of the varieties of religious experience. Study lacks originality and penetration but together text and notes constitute a good summary of the discussion of Edwards' role in psychology. Author concludes that Edwards "illustrates the conclusions a rigorous logic can reach from data supplied by imperfect observation and inadequate analysis.")

Fisher, George P. "The Philosophy of Jonathan Edwards," *North American Review,* CXXVIII, pp. 284–303 (March, 1879). Reprinted in *Discussions in History and Theology.* New York: 1880. (An excellent analysis of Edwards' philosophy.)

————. *History of Christian Doctrine.* New York: 1896. (Includes, pp. 395 ff., a very able and compact sketch of Edwards' theological opinions with valuable references to their position in the development of Christian doctrine.)

————. "The Value of Edwards for Today," *Congregationalist and Christian World,* LXXXVIII, pp. 469–72 (Oct. 3, 1903). (Fisher sees Edwards as not only the pre-eminent theological figure of New England but as the source of subsequent New England theology. Illustrated.)

Foster, Frank Hugh. "The Eschatology of the New England Divines," *Bibliotheca Sacra,* XLIII, pp. 6–19 (Jan., 1886). (The part of the article dealing with Edwards is important as a clear and sympathetic explanation of Edwards' notions concerning the eternal punishment of the wicked, notions which have earned for him an unfortunate reputation as a preacher of hell-fire sermons.)

————. *A Genetic History of the New England Theology.* Chicago

1907. (One of the most valuable studies of Edwards' work—a presentation of Edwards' views with some attention to their historical roots and an analysis of the career of Edwards' doctrines during the century after his death.)

Gardiner, H. N. "The Early Idealism of Jonathan Edwards," *Philosophical Review*, IX, pp. 573–96 (Nov., 1900). (Good analysis of Edwards' youthful notes on "The Mind" and on "Natural Science." Gardiner concludes that Berkeley did not influence Edwards, that Locke, Newton, and Cudworth did.)

Gardiner, H. N., and Webster, Richard. "Jonathan Edwards," in *Encyclopædia Britannica* (11th ed.). (Good brief sketch of "Edwardean System.")

[Gardiner, H. N., ed.] *Jonathan Edwards, a Retrospect; Being the Addresses Delivered in connection with the Unveiling of a Memorial in the First Church of Christ in Northampton, Massachusetts, on the One Hundred and Fiftieth Anniversary of his Dismissal from the Pastorate of that Church. . . .* Boston: 1901. (The most interesting addresses are A. V. G. Allen's "The Place of Edwards in History," E. C. Smyth's "The Influence of Edwards on the Spiritual Life of New England," and H. N. Gardiner's "The Early Idealism of Edwards.")

Gaustad, Edwin Scott. *The Great Awakening in New England.* New York: 1957. (Interested in "religious effects, institutional and theological" of the Great Awakening, Gaustad de-emphasizes the social and cultural aspects. He notes in Edwards the Augustinian tradition of evangelical piety and sees him "less a harbinger of Channing than a reminiscence of Aquinas." He insists that the Awakening was general in scope, not urban or rural, upper or lower class, seaboard or backcountry. See J. C. and P. Miller, White, and Mosier, below.)

Jerstner, John H. "American Calvinism Until the Twentieth Century," in *American Calvinism A Survey.* Ed. by Jacob Tunis Hoogstra. Grand Rapids, Mich.: 1957. (Contextually useful, if sectarian, view of Edwards' position in the Calvinistic tradition.)

———. *Steps to Salvation; the Evangelistic Message of Jonathan Edwards.* Philadelphia: 1960. (A severely restricted study dealing only with Edwards' theory of evangelism as derived from his manuscript sermons.)

Gillett, E. H. "Jonathan Edwards, and the Occasion and Result of his Dismission from Northampton," *Historical Magazine* (second series), I, pp. 333–38 (June, 1867). (Detailed statement of Edwards' difficulties with the church at Northampton over the Half-Way Covenant.)

Goen, C. C. "Jonathan Edwards: A New Departure in Eschatology," *Church History*, XXVIII, pp. 25–40 (March, 1959). (A somewhat inconclusive study of Edwards' chiliasm seen as a "factor in the religious background of the idea of progress.")

Gohdes, Clarence. "Aspects of Idealism in Early New England," *Philosophical Review*, XXXIX, pp. 537–55 (Nov., 1930). (Points out the influence of the Cambridge Platonists on the clergy of colonial New England, particularly that of Theophilus Gale, who is suggested as a possible source of Edwards' early idealism.)

Haroutunian, Joseph. "Jonathan Edwards: a Study in Godliness," *Journal of Religion*, XI, pp. 400–19 (July, 1931). (A very valuable article. Remarkably successful in achieving its purpose, the presenting of "a fairly accurate statement of the essentials of Edwards' character and thought.")

———. "Jonathan Edwards: Theologian of the Great Commandment," *Theology Today*, I, pp. 361–77 (Oct., 1944). (Edwards as "possibly the greatest of Protestant philosophers" and interpreter of the nature of true virtue.)

Harper, William Hudson. "Edwards: Devotee, Theologian, Preacher," *Interior*, XXXIV, pp. 1272–74 (Oct. 1, 1903). ("We in this latter day can but faintly imagine the compelling power of the words of a man of Edwards' systematic and precise mental habits, speaking on the most vital of themes with authority fiercely assertive and almost superhuman.")

Hayes, Samuel Perkins. "An Historical Study of the Edwardean Revivals," *American Journal of Psychology*, XIII, pp. 550–74 (Oct., 1902). (A fairly elaborate point by point outline [1] of Edwards' defense of the Great Awakening and [2] of Charles Chauncy's attacks on it. Despite the title, there is no attention to the background of Edwards' theories concerning the place of emotion in religion.)

Hazard, Rowland G. *Freedom of the Mind in Willing; or, Every Being that Wills a Creative Cause.* New York: 1866. (Contains, pp. 173–415, an elaborate refutation of Edwards' *Freedom of the Will*.)

Hodge, Charles. "Jonathan Edwards and the Successive Forms of the New Divinity," *Biblical Repertory and Princeton Review*, XXX, pp. 585–620 (Oct., 1858). (A painstaking attempt to prove that "Edwards' theology was, with scarcely a variation, one with Old Calvinism, and at war with all those successive forms of New Divinity which have been so industriously and adroitly linked with his name." See Porter, below.)

Holbrook, Clyde A. "Jonathan Edwards and His Detractors," *Theology Today*, X, pp. 384–96 (Oct., 1953). (A good review of two general lines of criticism regarding Edwards: as a negative force opposing the development of man; as a "tragic" figure whose remarkable powers were stifled by his devotion to theological dogma.)

Holmes, Oliver Wendell. "Jonathan Edwards," *International Review*,
    IX, pp. 1–28 (July, 1880). Reprinted in *Pages from an Old Volume
    of Life (Works*. Boston: 1892, Vol. VIII). (Almost worthless as an
    exposition of Edwards' views but valuable as a revelation of the
    grounds for the severe antipathy to Edwardean doctrines in nine-
    teenth-century New England. Holmes recognizes Edwards' genius
    but cleverly and acidly attacks his fundamental beliefs.)

Hopkins, Samuel. *The Life and Character of the Late Reverend Mr.
    Jonathan Edwards, President of the College of New Jersey: Together
    with a Number of his Sermons on Various Important Subjects.*
    Boston: 1765. (This biographical sketch by one of Edwards' close
    friends and one of his most important disciples has been justly
    declared by Allen to have "the quaint charm of Walton's lives.")

Hornberger, Theodore. "The Effect of the New Science upon the
    Thought of Jonathan Edwards," *American Literature*, IX, pp. 196–
    207 (Nov., 1937). (Demonstrates that Edwards' metaphysics were
    strongly influenced by the new science, thus influencing his theology
    despite his subordination of science to theology.)

Johnson, Thomas H. "Jonathan Edwards and the 'Young Folks'
    Bible,' " *New England Quarterly*, V, pp. 37–54 (Jan., 1932). (Im-
    portant new light on the reason for Edwards' dismissal from
    Northampton.)

———. "Jonathan Edwards' Background of Reading," *Publications of
    the Colonial Society of Massachusetts*, XXVIII, pp. 193–222 (Dec.,
    1931). (An examination of the sources, with conclusions upon
    Edwards' interest in the world of letters.)

"Jonathan Edwards' Last Will, and the Inventory of his Estate,"
    Bibliotheca Sacra, XXXIII, pp. 438–47 (July, 1876). (The long
    inventory is exceedingly interesting, including as it does references
    to Edwards' library, his manuscripts, and "a negro Boy named Titus"
    valued at £30.)

Jones, Adam Leroy. *Early American Philosophers*. New York: 1898.
    (Valuable exposition of Edwards' psychological notions.)

King, Henry Churchill. "Jonathan Edwards as Philosopher and
    Theologian," *Hartford Seminary Record*, XIV, pp. 23–57 (Nov.,
    1903). (A brief, critical statement of Edwards' psychological theories,
    of his idealism, of his doctrine of the will, of his position con-
    cerning the transcendency of God, and of his theory of virtue.)

Knox, Ronald Arbuthnott. *Enthusiasm.* . . . New York: 1950. (An
    analysis of the "ultrasupernatural," personal, inward, and chiliastic
    character of enthusiasm which is very provocative even if more
    applicable to Edwards' followers than to himself.)

Lyon, Georges. *L'Idéalisme en Angleterre au XVIIIᵉ Siècle*. Paris:
    1888. (Sets Edwards' idealism against the background of thought in

the period. Lyon's arguments for Edwards' indebtedness to Berkeley have not generally been accepted by scholars.)

McCook, Henry C. "Jonathan Edwards as a Naturalist," *Presbyterian and Reformed Review*, I, pp. 393–402 (July, 1890). (A scientist speaks very highly of Edwards' powers of observation and expresses the belief that had he devoted himself to science he might have become another Newton.)

MacCracken, John Henry. *Jonathan Edwards Idealismus*. Halle: 1899. (Believes that Berkeley was unknown to Edwards and thinks that to the impulse derived from the theories of Locke and Newton must be added as the really decisive factor the influence of Arthur Collier's *Clavis Universalis* [1713]. The argument rests upon rather tenuous evidence.)

Macphail, Andrew. *Essays in Puritanism*. Boston: 1905. (Essay on Edwards, pp. 3–67, is readable and often enlightening, but also often unjust and untrustworthy. Macphail has not escaped the error with which he charges writers on American literary history—that of distorting their work by delivering judgments based "largely upon purely idiosyncratic grounds.")

McGiffert, Arthur Cushman. *Jonathan Edwards*. New York: 1932. (Makes no startling contributions to our knowledge of the facts of Edwards' life or to our understanding of his thought, but evokes sympathetically and convincingly the personality of Edwards. A splendid picture of the man.)

Magoun, G. F. "President Edwards as a Reformer," *Congregational Quarterly*, N. s. I, pp. 259–74 (April, 1869). (Disappointing treatment of an interesting subject. Attempts to show that Edwards was "an eminent practical reformer.")

"The Manuscripts of President Edwards," *Littell's Living Age*, XXXVI, pp. 181–82 (Jan. 21, 1853). (Report of one who had examined the mine of unpublished manuscripts.)

Miller, Edward Waite. "The Great Awakening," *Princeton Theological Review*, II, pp. 545–62 (Oct., 1904). (Sympathetic study of Edwards' relation to the Revival.)

Miller, Perry. *Jonathan Edwards*. New York: 1949. (This biography of Edwards' mind is perhaps the outstanding single volume in the renaissance of Edwards' scholarship which began some twenty-five years ago. Finding the key to Edwards' thought in his naturalistic use of Locke and Newton, Miller's work has been criticized for slighting Edwards' relationship to the Bible, to Augustinian roots of piety and the concept of grace, and to Christianity in general. Critics of the volume see Edwards as an empiricist rather than a naturalist or as medieval rather than modern, and the book has been recommended as much for its demonstration of Miller's mind as for its analysis of Edwards'. See especially the reviews by Joseph Haroutunian, *Theology Today*, VII, pp. 554–56 (Jan., 1951); Reinhold Niebuhr, *Nation*, CLXIX, p. 648 (Dec. 31, 1949); and on Edwards as an "artist in ideals" by Thomas H. Johnson, *Saturday Review,* Jan. 7, 1950, p. 17. See also Tomas, below.)

————. *Errand Into the Wilderness.* Cambridge: 1956. (A collection of Miller's articles with new prefaces. Of primary importance to the student of Edwards are: "The Marrow of Puritan Divinity" in which Edwards is termed "the first consistent and authentic Calvinist in New England"; "From Edwards to Emerson," a controversial study tracing the continuum of ideas; "Edwards–Locke—and the Rhetoric of Sensation," which one critic calls "the best article ever written on Edwards" but in which Miller was unable to resist the temptation to point out "a corollary of Edwards' thinking, though I do not for a moment suppose that he . . . would agree"; and "Edwards and the Great Awakening.")

Minton, Henry Collin. "President Jonathan Edwards," *Presbyterian Quarterly,* XIII, pp. 68–94 (Jan., 1899). (Critical sketch of theological position.)

More, Paul Elmer. "Edwards," in *Cambridge History of American Literature.* New York: 1917. I, pp. 57–71. (A brilliant essay but not very informative. An exceedingly valuable bibliography by John J. Coss, I, pp. 426–38.)

Murphy, Arthur E. "Jonathan Edwards on Free Will and Moral Agency," *Philosophical Review,* LXVIII, pp. 181–202 (May, 1959). (Insists that Edwards "was a theologian first and last and a philosopher only in between . . ." and takes issue with Paul Ramsey's position on Edwards' argument against the Arminians as applied to his own position on moral agency.)

Niebuhr, H. Richard. *The Kingdom of God in America.* Chicago: 1937. (Fruitful discussion of Edwards in relation to his conception of the end of religion and suggestive in its relation of this conception to those of other religious figures.)

Nordell, Phillip Gregory. "Jonathan Edwards and Hell Fire," *Forum,* LXXV, pp. 860–69 (June, 1926). (Nordell is certainly wrong when he asserts that "one finds in a survey of his [Edwards'] religious writings that they simply reek and seethe with implacable arguments proving the horrible reality of God's wrath upon the wicked.")

Orr, James, "Jonathan Edwards; His Influence in Scotland," *Congregationalist and Christian World,* LXXXVIII, pp. 467–69 (Oct. 3, 1903). (The great Scotch clergyman sees a profound effect from Edwards' teaching in Scotland. Illustrated with pictures of Northampton.)

Park, Edwards A. "Remarks of Jonathan Edwards on the Trinity," *Bibliotheca Sacra,* XXXVIII, pp. 147–87, 333–69 (Jan. and April

1881). (Defends Edwards against the charge of having held in his late years unorthodox views concerning the Trinity. See Fisher, Smyth, and Holmes.)

Parkes, Henry Bamford. *Jonathan Edwards: the Fiery Puritan*. New York: 1930. (Superficial and prejudiced with respect to Edwards, but very valuable for its presentation of the social background and for its bibliographies. See excellent review by Herbert W. Schneider, *Nation*, CXXXI, p. 584 [Nov. 26, 1930].)

Parrington, Vernon Louis. *The Colonial Mind, 1620–1800*. New York: 1927. (One of the least valuable sections of Parrington's book— untrustworthy and unfair. Parrington sees inconsistencies and changes of front where there are none. Title reveals his prejudice—"The Anachronism of Jonathan Edwards.")

Patterson, Robert Leet. *The Philosophy of William Ellery Channing*. New York: 1952. (Illustrative of the vitality and power of Edwards' thought in its influence on Channing.)

Perry, Ralph Barton. *Puritanism and Democracy*. New York: 1944. (Incisive and insightful statements of Edwards' position and doctrines, although on such topics as Arminianism more recent scholarship should be consulted.)

Phelps, William Lyon. "Makers of American Literature. Edwards and Franklin—the Man of God and the Man of the World: a Dramatic Contrast," *Ladies' Home Journal*, XXXIX, p. 16 ff. (Nov., 1922). (Points up cleverly and with a good deal of quotation the often-noted contrast between Edwards and Franklin. Portrait.)

Porter, Noah. "Jonathan Edwards," in the appendix to Ueberweg's *History of Philosophy from Thales to the Present Time*, trans. by George S. Morris. New York: 1875. (Highly condensed statement [II, pp. 442–48] of Edwards' philosophical position.)

————. "The Princeton Review on Dr. Taylor and the Edwardean Theology," *New Englander*, XVIII, pp. 726–73 (Aug., 1860). (Attacks articles in *Princeton Review*, XXXI, pp. 489–538 [July, 1858] and pp. 585–620 [Oct., 1858]. Attempts to show that Edwards was not merely an old-line Calvinist but that he made "improvements" on Calvin and founded a new school. See Hodge, above.)

"President Edwards on Charity and its Fruits," *New Englander*, X, pp. 222–36 (May, 1852). (Review of Edwards' *Charity and its Fruits*, ed. by Tryon Edwards [1851]. Interesting statement concerning the extent of Edwards' manuscripts and an analysis of the book, with copious extracts.)

"President Edwards' Dissertation on the Nature of True Virtue," *Bibliotheca Sacra*, X, pp. 705–38 (Oct., 1853). (An elaborate defense of Edwards' doctrine and an answer to the charge that he was inconsistent.)

Rhoades, Donald H. "Jonathan Edwards: America's First Philosopher," *Personalist*, XXXIII, pp. 135–47 (Summer, 1952). (Shallow review of major scholarly studies of Edwards; relates his thought to various religious and philosophical concepts and controversies, some of them contemporary.)

Ridderbos, Jan. *De Theologie van Jonathan Edwards*. The Hague: 1907. (The *Encyclopaedia of Religion and Ethics* calls this "the most comprehensive survey of Edwards' theological teaching.")

Riley, I. Woodbridge. *American Philosophy: The Early Schools*. New York: 1907. (Still the only systematic study of colonial philosophy as a whole. Interesting analysis and valuable summary of Edwards' philosophy.)

————. *American Thought from Puritanism to Pragmatism*. New York: 1915. ("Jonathan Edwards, Mystic," pp. 28–36, is a brilliant exposition of one side of Edwards.)

Roback, Abraham Aaron. *History of American Psychology*. New York: 1952. (Mentions Edwards' religious psychology and his exploration of the will. Very sketchy.)

Sanborn, F. B. "The Puritanic Philosophy of Jonathan Edwards," *Journal of Speculative Philosophy*, XVII, pp. 401–21 (Oct., 1883). (Interesting as analysis by one who is committed to transcendentalism. Sees Edwards' philosophical power but rejects his system.)

Savelle, Max. *Seeds of Liberty: The Genesis of the American Mind*. New York: 1948. (This brief treatment of Edwards in a general history of American colonial ideas terms him "reactionary" but still the greatest theologian and philosopher of colonial America. His idealism viewed as part of a "colonial revival of Augustinian Platonism.")

Schafer, Charles H. "Jonathan Edwards and the Principle of Self-Love," *Papers of the Michigan Academy of Science*, XXXV, pp. 341–48 (1951).

Schafer, Thomas A. "Jonathan Edwards' Conception of the Church," *Church History*, XXIV, pp. 51–66 (March, 1955). (A narrow theological, particularized, solid study.)

————. "Jonathan Edwards and Justification by Faith," *Church History*, XX, pp. 55–67 (Dec., 1951). (A clarification of one of Edwards' basic doctrinal views.)

Schneider, Herbert Wallace. *A History of American Philosophy*. New York: 1946. (Large amount of relevant information on Edwards in short and scattered references. Very useful bibliographical note and annotations.)

————. *The Puritan Mind*. New York: 1930. (Desirous of "sketching the basic theories of Puritanism in America against a background of their social habitat, and [of] describing the effects of events on the lives and deaths of these themes," Schneider makes a valuable con tribution to the study of the relationship of Edwards to the Great Awakening. He gets to the heart of Edwards' position.)

Seldes, Gilbert. "Jonathan Edwards," *Dial,* LXXXIV, pp. 37–46 (Jan., 1928). (Interpretations not always sound, but reveals the appeal Edwards' theories have for the philosophic modern man.)

Silliman, Benjamin. Appendix to N. M. Hentz's article "On North American Spiders," *American Journal of Science and Arts,* XXI, pp. 109–22 (Jan., 1832). (Discusses Edwards' essay on spiders. Says "the subject examined, so sagaciously one hundred and sixteen years ago, by the philosophical child, remains nearly as he left it.")

Simpson, Samuel. "Jonathan Edwards—A Historical Review," *Hartford Seminary Record,* XIV, pp. 3–22 (Nov., 1903). (Good brief biographical sketch.)

Sizes, Theodore. "The Story of the Edwards Portraits," *Yale University Library Gazette,* XXXIV, pp. 82–88 (Oct., 1959). (Notes on family portraits and letters at Yale.)

Slosson, Edwin E. "Jonathan Edwards as a Freudian," *Science,* N. S. LII, p. 609 (Dec. 24, 1920). (Notes Edwards' "use of dream analysis for the discovery of his secret sins.")

Smith, Hilrie Shelton. *Changing Conceptions of Original Sin: A Study in American Theology Since 1750.* New York: 1955. (From Edwards' position to the "rediscovery" of sin by Reinhold Niebuhr and Paul Tillich. Includes an extensive discussion of the Edwards school in American theology. Reiterates the supremacy of biblical authority for Edwards but notes use of empirical data.)

Smyth, Egbert C. "Jonathan Edwards' Idealism," *American Journal of Theology,* I, pp. 950–64 (Oct., 1897). (Analyzes Edwards' idealism as revealed in the early "Notes on Being" and shows how it underlies his whole philosophy and theology. An important article.)

Stephen, Leslie. "Jonathan Edwards," *Fraser's Magazine,* N. S. VIII, pp. 529–51 (Nov., 1873). Reprinted in *Littell's Living Age,* CXX, pp. 219–36 (Jan. 24, 1874), and in *Hours in a Library* (second series), London, 1876, pp. 44–106. (A very influential and brilliant essay. Conclusions often hasty and unjustified, as, for example, the statement that Edwards "in the American forests" was "far away from the main currents of speculation, ignorant of the conclusions reached by his most cultivated contemporaries, and deriving his intellectual substance chiefly from an absolute theology, with some vague knowledge of the English followers of Locke.")

Stokes, Anson Phelps. *Church and State in the United States.* 3 vols. New York: 1950. (Influence of Great Awakening and especially of Edwards' emphasis on piety rather than politics in the role of the church as reinforcing the separation of church and state.)

———. *Memorials of Eminent Yale Men.* New Haven: 1914. (Discusses Edwards and Yale. Interesting letters.)

Stoughton, John A. *Windsor Farmes.* Hartford: 1883. (Invaluable biographical data of Edwards' early years, centering around his father, Timothy.)

Stromberg, Ronald N. *Religious Liberalism in Eighteenth Century England.* New York: 1954. (Good outline of Edwards' English opposition and of the opposed spirit of the age.)

Sullivan, Frank. "Jonathan Edwards, the Contemplative Life, and a Spiritual Stutter," *Los Angeles Tidings,* March 11, 1949, p. 27. (His leaning toward contemplation in an active society resulted in a conflict reflected in Edwards' writings.)

Suter, Rufus. "An American Pascal: Jonathan Edwards," *Scientific Monthly,* LXVIII, pp. 338–42 (May, 1949). ("A precocious early insight into the problems of physical science was sacrificed to the religious passion." Points to the acuity of Edwards' scientific insight, especially as a theoretical physicist.)

————. "The Conception of Morality in the Philosophy of Jonathan Edwards," *Journal of Religion,* XIV, pp. 265–72 (July, 1934). (This presentation of Edwards' "ethical system in as nearly as possible non-theological language" reveals the vitality of Edwards' system.)

————. "A Note on Platonism in the Philosophy of Jonathan Edwards," *Harvard Theological Review,* LII, pp. 283–84 (Oct., 1959). (Presents interpretation of Wm. Wallace Fenn: Edwards failed as a Christian philosopher because of an inability to "reconcile his Platonism with his Calvinism.")

————. "The Strange Universe of Jonathan Edwards," *Harvard Theological Review,* LIV, pp. 125–28 (April, 1961). (The difficulty of understanding Edwards today especially because of the reflection of feudalism in his view of the universe.)

Tarbox, I. N. "Jonathan Edwards as a Man: and the Ministers of the Last Century," *New Englander,* XLIII, pp. 615–31 (Sept., 1884). (More interesting for its description of Edwards' grandfather and predecessor at Northampton, Solomon Stoddard, than for its portrayal of Edwards.)

Taylor, Robert J. *Western Massachusetts in the Revolution.* Providence: 1954. (An excellent monograph with a most interesting description of the politics of Edwards' dismissal from Northampton.)

"The Theology of Edwards as Shown in his Treatise concerning Religious Affections," *American Theological Review,* I, pp. 199–220 (May, 1859). (Good analysis of Edwards' doctrine of supernatural regeneration.)

Thompson, Joseph P. "Jonathan Edwards, his Character, Teaching, and Influence," *Bibliotheca Sacra,* XVIII, pp. 809–39 (Oct., 1861). (Significant as a statement of what New England Congregationalists of the last century felt was Edwards' importance.)

Tomas, Vincent. "The Modernity of Jonathan Edwards," *New England Quarterly*, XXV, pp. 60–84 (March, 1952). (A strong statement against the interpretation of Edwards as a modern. Tomas is especially critical of Perry Miller's use of the Edwards manuscripts, and states that Edwards' argument is that of a medieval not a modern philosopher, based on scriptural revelation not modern "reason" and "experience.")

Townsend, Harvey Gates. "Jonathan Edwards' Later Observations of Nature," *New England Quarterly*, XIII, pp. 510–18 (Sept., 1940). (Compare Perry Miller's introduction to *Images*, above.)

————. *Philosophical Ideas in the United States*. New York: 1934. (An able and valuable sketch of Edwards as a philosopher.)

————. "The Will and the Understanding in the Philosophy of Jonathan Edwards," *Church History*, XVI, pp. 210–20 (Dec., 1940).

Trinterud, Leonard J. *The Forming of an American Tradition, A Re-examination of Colonial Presbyterianism*. Philadelphia: 1949. (Discusses the cross-fertilization of the Edwardean school and the New-Side Presbyterians.)

Tufts, James H. "Edwards and Newton," *Philosophical Review*, XLIX, pp. 609–22 (Nov., 1940). (Influence upon Edwards' conception of the universe and his physical and metaphysical analysis of solidity.)

Turnbull, Ralph G. *Jonathan Edwards, The Preacher*. Grand Rapids, Mich.: 1958. (A detailed analysis of 1185 of Edwards' sermons which concludes that the imprecatory sermons such as "Sinners in the Hands of an Angry God" are more than balanced by sermons on "Charity and its Fruits" and the "Gracious Deliverance" from temptation, and that heaven and hell are balanced in the Calvinism of Edwards. See bibliography for sectarian views of Edwards and for current use of his preaching techniques.)

Upham, William P. "On the Shorthand Notes of Jonathan Edwards," *Massachusetts Historical Society Proceedings* (second series), XV, pp. 514–21 (1902). (A very interesting description, together with facsimiles and a key, of Edwards' shorthand notes.)

Voegelin, Erich. *Ueber die Form des Amerikanischen Geistes*. Tübingen: 1928. (Chapter iv, "Eine Formverwandtschaft mit der puritanischen Mystik," contains an interesting discussion of the combination of Calvinism and mysticism in Edwards and of correspondences between Edwards on the one hand and William James and Santayana on the other.)

Walker, George Leon. "Jonathan Edwards and the Half-Way Covenant," *New Englander*, XLIII, pp. 601–14 (Sept., 1884). (Analyzes change in views regarding the Half-Way Covenant that was a large factor in Edwards' dismissal from the church at Northampton.)

Walker, Williston. *Ten New England Leaders.* New York: 1901. (Includes an excellent account, pp. 217–63, of Edwards' life and work by one thoroughly familiar with the religious background of Edwards' work in New England.)

Warfield, Benjamin B. "Edwards and the New England Theology," in *Encyclopaedia of Religion and Ethics,* ed. by James Hastings. New York: 1912. (Useful.)

Wertenbaker, T. J. *Princeton 1746–1896.* Princeton: 1946. (Describes Edwards' early and continuing involvement in the school's founding and affairs.)

Whedon, D. D. *The Freedom of the Will as a Basis of Human Responsibility and a Divine Government Elucidated and Maintained in its Issue with the Necessitarian Theories of Hobbes, Edwards, the Princeton Essayists, and other Leading Advocates.* New York: 1864. (Highly polemic attack on the necessitarians. Valuable for its detailed analysis of the problems involved in the controversy.)

Winship, Albert E. *Heredity, a History of Jukes-Edwards Families.* Boston: 1925. (Outlines history of Edwards' family to prove importance of heredity.)

Winslow, Ola Elizabeth. *Jonathan Edwards, 1703–1758: A Biography.* New York: 1940. (Well written and solidly researched, this is the standard biography of Edwards the man. In addition to telling the "life story" of Edwards, the writer has not attempted "to do more than indicate the chronology and general import of his ideas, particularly with respect to his changing fortunes." The volume also contains a description of the Edwards manuscript collections.)

Woodbridge, Frederick J. E. "Jonathan Edwards," *Philosophical Review,* XIII, pp. 393–408 (July, 1904). (Thinks Edwards never fulfilled the promises of intellectual power revealed in his youth. Believes that the swaying of his nature "by unanalyzed emotion disrupted him intellectually and robbed him of the opportunity of becoming an important influence in American thought.)

Wright, Conrad. *The Beginnings of Unitarianism in America.* Boston: 1955. (Discusses Edwards versus Arminianism and its chief spokesmen, Charles Chauncey and Jonathan Mayhew. Edwards' "uncomprehending mind" failed to see his essential agreement with the Arminians in their analysis of the mind and the question of human freedom; it was on the question of human depravity that they parted company.)

Zenos, Andrew C. "The Permanent and Passing in the Thought of Edwards," *Interior,* XXXIV, pp. 1274–75 (Oct. 1, 1903). (Presents briefly what he believes will be the significant contributions of Edwards in the development of American theology.)

III. BIBLIOGRAPHY

Johnson, Thomas H. *The Printed Writings of Jonathan Edwards 1703–1758: A Bibliography.* Princeton: 1940. (Gives complete bibliographical data for works of Edwards published up to 1940. For items published since that date, see Section I, above.)

The Cambridge History of American Literature. New York: 1917. (Bibliography of Edwards' works and publications about him by John J. Coss [I, pp. 426–38] is practically exhaustive for the period up to the appearance of the volume.)

It is possible to keep abreast of current additions to knowledge concerning Edwards and his time by reference to the quarterly bibliographies in *American Literature,* to the annual bibliographies in *Publications of the Modern Language Association,* to the bulletins of the Modern Humanities Research Association, and to *Writings on American History* (edited by Grace Griffin, James R. Masterson, *et al.*).

IV. BACKGROUND

The following works are of special value for understanding the background of Edwards' life and work:

Adams, Brooks. *The Emancipation of Massachusetts.* Boston: 1893. (Adams describes what seems to him an important aspect of New England history, the struggles by which "this poor and isolated community freed itself from its gloomy bondage" to the Puritan priests.)

Adams, James Truslow. *The Founding of New England.* Boston: 1921. (Rejects "the old conception of New England history, according to which that section was considered to have been settled by persecuted religious refugees, devoted to liberty of conscience," and interprets this history very largely in terms of "economic and imperial relations."

———. *Provincial Society, 1690–1767.* New York: 1928. (Vol. III of *A History of American Life,* ed. by Arthur M. Schlesinger and Dixon Ryan Fox. An interesting and substantial description of manners, culture, and the economic aspects of life in the colonies. The "Critical Essay on Authorities," pp. 324–56, is of great value.)

Alexander, Archibald. *Theories of the Will in the History of Philosophy.* New York: 1898. (Useful in providing a setting for Edwards' theories.)

Atkins, Gaius Glenn, and Fagley, Frederick L. *History of American Congregationalism.* Boston, Chicago: 1942. (A somewhat superficial general history, useful contextually.)

Bainton, Ronald H. *Yale and the Ministry: A History of Education for the Christian Ministry at Yale from the founding in 1701.* New York: 1957 (Superficial.)

Brynestad, Lawrence E. "The Great Awakening in the New England and Middle Colonies," *Journal of the Presbyterian Historical Society,* XIV, pp. 80–91, 107–41 (1930–31). (Good bibliography.)

Cook, Elizabeth C. *Literary Influences in Colonial Newspapers, 1704–1750.* New York: 1912. (Valuable.)

Crane, R. S. "Suggestions toward a Genealogy of the 'Man of Feeling,'" *Journal of English Literary History,* I, pp. 205–30 (Dec., 1934). (Important for an understanding of the background for Edwards' doctrine of virtue.)

Davis, Arthur Paul. *Issac Watts, his life and works.* New York: 1943. (For a discussion of his influence, especially in regard to *Freedom of the Will,* upon Edwards, see John E. Smith's introduction to that work.)

Dexter, Henry M. *The Congregationalism of the Last Three Hundred Years as Seen in its Literature.* New York: 1880. (A great deal of detailed information and an elaborate bibliography make this a very valuable book.)

Field, Edward. *The Colonial Tavern: A Glimpse of New England Town Life in the Seventeenth and Eighteenth Centuries.* Providence, R. I.: 1897. (The author has searched diaries, letters, colonial newspapers, town histories, and court records for the sake of exposing an aspect of New England life which he thinks is "second only in importance to the colonial meeting house.")

Forbes, Harriette Merrifield. *New England Diaries 1602–1800: A Descriptive Catalogue Of Diaries, Orderly Books And Sea Journals.* n.p., 1923.

Gewehr, W. M. *The Great Awakening in Virginia, 1740–1780.* Durham, N. C.: 1930.

Hall, Thomas Cuming. *The Religious Background of American Culture.* Boston: 1930. (See particularly chapter XII, "The Great Awakening and its Influence upon American Culture." The book contains some loose statements with respect to Edwards' relationship to Luther and to Wyclif.)

Haller, William. *The Rise of Puritanism Or, The Way To The New Jerusalem As Set Forth In Pulpit And Press . . . 1570–1643.* New York: 1938.

Haroutunian, Joseph. *Piety versus Moralism; the Passing of the New England Theology.* New York: 1932. (Believes that the New England theology declined because its theocentric character made it "ill-fitted to give expression to the ideals of the eighteenth century New England and to meet its immediate social needs." The analysis of the development and modification of Edwards' system by his followers is valuable. Useful bibliography.)

Hutchinson, Thomas. *The History of the Colony and Province of Massachusetts-Bay.* Edited by Lawrence Shaw Mayo. 3 vols. Cambridge: 1936. (This administrative and political history by a contemporary of Edwards provides vital background material for the Massachusetts of his time.)

Johnson, E. A. J. *American Economic Thought in the Seventeenth Century.* London: 1932. (Excellent discussion of the economic philosophy of the colonial era. A standard work. Bibliography.)

Jones, Howard Mumford. "American Prose Style: 1700–1770," *Huntington Library Bulletin,* No. 6 (Nov., 1934). (An important study, showing that the pulpit powerfully influenced American literary style in the direction of simplicity and clarity.)

Knappen, M. M. *Tudor Puritanism: A Chapter in the History of Idealism.* Chicago: 1939. (Deals with Puritanism as a transitional movement linking medieval with modern times. Its stress on the medieval aspects of Puritanism is useful in view of recent trends in Edwards scholarship which assert his modernity.)

Koch, Gustav Adolf. *Republican Religion; the American Revolution and the Cult of Reason.* New York: 1933. (Describing the spread of deism "from the intelligentsia to the common man after the American Revolution," its identification with republicanism in politics, and its defeat, this book presents the career of a doctrine against which Edwards fought with all his power.)

Labaree, Leonard W. "The Conservative Attitude Toward the Great Awakening," *William And Mary Quarterly* (third series), I, pp. 331–52 (Oct., 1944). (Noting that the Awakening was part of a general movement in Protestant Christendom, this article deals rather less with New England than elsewhere but includes an interesting interpretation of Edwards' opponent Charles Chauncey as a social conservative and spokesman of the upper class.)

Lee, Umphrey. *The Historical Backgrounds of Early Methodist Enthusiasm.* New York: 1931. (Valuable, well-documented discussion of the philosophical background for the kind of religious emotionalism revealed in the Great Awakening.)

Maxson, Charles Hartshorn. *The Great Awakening in the Middle Colonies.* Chicago: 1920. (Describes the international revival of which that important movement in eighteenth-century America, the Great Awakening, was a part. Good bibliography.)

Mayer, Frederick Emanuel. *The Religious Bodies of America.* St. Louis: 1954. (Good but very general history.)

Meyer, Jacob Conrad. *Church and State in Massachusetts from 1740 to 1833.* Cleveland: 1938. (A monograph with a sociological interpretation and an orientation towards class conflict which finds the importance of Edwards and the Awakening in their divisive effect on the Congregational Church.)

Miller, J. C. "Religion, Finance, and Democracy in Massachusetts," *New England Quarterly,* VI, pp. 28–58 (Jan., 1933). (Recent scholarship has taken issue with Miller's controversial thesis that the emotionalism of the Great Awakening, synchronizing with the prejudice toward the Tories over the Land Bank episode, favored the trend toward democracy. See Gaustad, above, and Taylor, below.)

Miller, Perry. *The New England Mind: From Colony To Province.* Cambridge, Massachusetts: 1953. A continuation of the study begun in *Orthodoxy in Massachusetts.* Dealing with the interrelationship of communal experience and thought in seventeenth-century Massachusetts, the volume deals with the Protestant ethic, the Half-Way Covenant, revivalism, the provincial mentality, the secularization of New England society and the alteration of piety to moralism. Edwards is a thread running through the volume and it serves as a necessary extension of Miller's *Edwards.*)

———. *The New England Mind: The Seventeenth Century.* New York: 1939. (Under the headings of Religion and Learning, Cosmology, Anthropology and Sociology, Miller sets about "defining and classifying the principal concepts of the Puritan mind in New England, . . . accounting for the origins, inter-relations, and significances of the ideas." Miller emphasizes the unity of the first three generations of New England thought which was the backdrop for Edwards' remarkably independent speculation.)

———. *Orthodoxy in Massachusetts, 1630–1650; a Genetic Study.* Cambridge, Mass.: 1933. (A brilliant presentation of the religious objectives of the founders of New England. The discussion of non-separating Congregationalism is of particular value in connection with Edwards.)

———. "Soloman Stoddard," *Harvard Theological Review,* XXXVI, pp. 147–65 (April, 1942). (The article's thesis that the "federal theology" evolved to meet American development is repeated in Miller's *Edwards* but details on "Pope" Stoddard and his relations with the Mathers and the East they represented contribute to an understanding of Edwards.)

Miller, Perry, and Johnson, Thomas H. *The Puritans.* New York: 1938. (A history of Puritan ideas during the first three generations in New England through representative selections with both general and special introductions. Including some fascinating selections by Edwards' grandfather, Soloman Stoddard, the volume also presents a set of splendid bibliographies.)

Mitchell, W. F. *English Pulpit Oratory from Andrewes to Tillotson.* London: 1932. (Extensive and scholarly analysis of literary theory with useful discussion of sermon note-taking and shorthand.)

Selected Bibliography cxli

Morais, Herbert M. *Deism in Eighteenth Century America.* New York: 1934. (A scholarly survey in dissertation form.)

Morgan, Edmund S. *The Puritan Family. Essays on Religion and Domestic Relations in Seventeenth-Century New England.* Boston: 1944.

Morison, Samuel Eliot. *Harvard College In The Seventeenth Century.* 2 vols. Cambridge, Mass.: 1936. (History of Harvard, 1650–1708, stressing liberal and modern aspects.)

Osgood, H. L. *American Colonies in the Eighteenth Century.* 4 vols. New York: 1924. (A standard work.)

Oviatt, Edwin. *Beginnings of Yale, 1701–1726.* New Haven: 1916.

Pratt, Anne Stokely. "The Books Sent From England By Jeremiah Dummer To Yale College," in *Papers In Honor Of Andrew Keogh.* New Haven: 1938. (Rather thin article discribing the gift which Edwards used during his collegiate years. See also, "List of Books Sent By Jeremiah Dummer," prepared by Louise May Bryant and Mary Patterson, *ibid.*)

Richardson, Caroline F. *English Preachers and Preaching, 1640–1670.* New York: 1928. (Valuable for its discussion of models, method, and manner.)

Scott, W. R. *Francis Hutcheson, His Life, Teachings, and Position in the History of Philosophy.* Cambridge, England: 1900. (Best comprehensive treatment. Also treats Shaftesbury.)

Selby-Bigge, L. A. *British Moralists, being Selections from Writers Principally of the Eighteenth Century.* 2 vols. Oxford: 1897. (A valuable collection, with an illuminating introduction and a very useful analytical index.)

Shipton, Clifford K. "The New England Clergy of the 'Glacial Age,'" *Publications of the Colonial Society of Massachusetts,* XXXII, pp. 24–54 (1936). (Vindication.)

———. *Sibley's Harvard Graduates. Biographical Sketches Of Those Who Attended Harvard College In The Classes 1642–1743.* 11 vols. In process, Cambridge, Mass.: 1873 *et seq.* (Vastly useful information on many of Edwards' leading contemporaries. *Cf.* 28 pages on Charles Chauncey in Volume VII or the Great Awakening as it affected the position of ministers in their community, Volume X.)

Stearns, R. R. "Assessing the New England Mind," *Church History,* X, pp. 246–62 (Sept., 1941). (Review of previous decade's scholarship: Miller, Morison, Knappen, Haller.)

Stephen, Leslie. *History of English Thought in the Eighteenth Century.* 2 vols. London: 1876. (The fullest survey of eighteenth-century thought. As a result of Stephen's distillation of eighteenth-century authors, his account must not be accepted uncritically: there are undue emphases and distortions.)

Tracy, Joseph. *The Great Awakening. A History of the Revival of Religion in the Time of Edwards and Whitefield.* Boston: 1841. (Useful because of the numerous extracts from diaries, letters, colonial newspapers, and resolutions of ministerial assemblies which it contains.)

Trinterud, Leonard J. "The Origins Of Puritanism," *Church History,* XX, pp. 37–57 (March, 1951). (Summary stressing the medieval concept of piety and of society as the bases for Puritanism.)

Trumbull, Benjamin. *A Complete History of Connecticut.* 2 vols. New Haven: 1818. (Extensive information on the Connecticut Valley and its Church organization to both of which Northampton was closely tied.)

Trumbull, James Russell. *History of Northampton, from its settlement in 1654.* 2 vols. Northampton: 1898, 1902. (Excellent as long as Trumbull confines himself to Northampton. Depicts scene of Edwards' major ministry in detail.)

Tyler, Moses Coit. *A History of American Literature.* 2 vols. New York: 1877. (These volumes, which carry the account of our literature up to 1765, still provide the best discussion of colonial American literature.)

Walker, Williston. *The Creeds and Platforms of Congregationalism.* New York: 1893. Reprinted with an introduction by Douglas Horton. Boston: 1960. (Essential documents and useful commentary.)

————. *A History of the Congregational Churches in the United States.* New York: 1894. (American Church History series. Authoritative.)

Weeden, William B. *Economic and Social History of New England, 1620–1789.* 2 vols. Boston: 1890. (A mine of information concerning commerce, manufacture, travel, communication, manners, and morals.)

Wilder, Amos N. "The Puritan Heritage in American Culture," *Theology Today,* V, pp. 22–34 (April, 1948). (Surveys the relation of Calvinism and the New England heritage to the intellectual currents of the present. Discloses a source of the modern interest in Edwards although it does not discuss him.)

Winslow, Ola Elizabeth. *Meetinghouse Hill, 1630–1783.* New York: 1952. (For students of Edwards the most important sections of this social picture of religion in colonial New England are those on the learning and sermons of the clergy, and on the government and authority of the congregation.)

Wright, Thomas G. *Literary Culture in Early New England, 1620–1730.* New Haven: 1920. (A brilliant analysis of the reading and literary facilities available to New Englanders during their first century.)

*

Selections from
JONATHAN EDWARDS

*

"OF INSECTS"

Of all Insects no one is more wonderfull than the Spider especially with Respect to their sagacity and admirable way of working. these Spiders for the Present shall be Distinguished into those that keep in houses and those that keep in forests upon trees bushes shrubs &c and those that keep in rotten Logs for I take em to be of very Different kinds and natures; there are also other sorts some of which keep in rotten Logs hollow trees swamps and grass. Of these last every One knows the truth of their marching in the air from tree to tree and these sometimes at five or six rods Distanss sometimes, nor Can any one Go out amongst the trees in a Dewey morning towards the latter end of august or at the beginning of september but that he shall see hundreds of webbs made Conspicuous by the Dew that is lodged upon them reaching from one tree & shrub to another that stand at a Considerable Distance, and they may be seen well enough by an observing eye at noon Day by their Glistening against the sun and what is still more wonderfull: i know I have severall times seen in a very Calm and serene Day at that time of year, standing behind some Opake body that shall Just hide the Disk of the sun and keep of his Dazling rays from my eye and looking close by the side of it, multitudes of little shining webbs and Glistening Strings of a Great Length and at such a height as that one would think they were tack'd to the Sky by one end were it not that they were moving and floating, and there Very Often appears at the end of these Webs a Spider floating and sailing in the air with them, which I have Plainly Discerned in those webs that were nearer to my eye and Once saw a very large spider to my surprise swimming in the air in this manner, and Others have assured me that they Often have seen spiders fly, the appearance is truly very Pretty And Pleasing and it was so pleasing as well as surprising to me that

I Resolved to endeavour to Satisfy my Curiosity about it by
finding Out the way and manner of their Doing of it, being also
Persuaded that If I could find out how the[y] flew I could easily
find out how they made webs from tree to tree, and accordingly
at a time when I was in the Woods I happened to see one of
these spiders on a bush, so I went to the bush and shook it hop-
ing thereby to make him Uneasy upon it and provoke him to
leave it by flying and took Good Care that he should not Get of[f]
from it any other way, So I Continued Constantly to shake it,
which made him severall times let himself fall by his web a little
but he would presently creep up again till at last he was pleased
ho[w]ever to leave that bush and march along in the air to the
next but which way I Did not know nor Could I Concieve but
Resolved to watch him more narrowly next time so I brought
[him] back to the same bush again and to be sure that there was
nothing for him to Go upon the next time I whisked about a
stick I had in my hand on all side[s] of the bush that I might
breake any web Going from it if there were any and leave
nothing else for him to Go on but the Clear air, and then shook
the bush as before but it was not long before he again to my
surprize went to the next bush I took [him] of[f] upon my stick
and holding of him near my eye shook the stick as I had Done
the bush wherupon he let himself Down A little hanging by
his web and [I] Presently Percieved a web Out from his tail a
Good way into the air. I took hold Of it with my hand and
broke it off not knowing but that I might take it out to the
Stick with him from the bush, but then I Plainly Percieved
another such a string to Proceed Out of his tail I now Concieved I had found out the Whole mystery. I Repeated the
triall Over and Over again till I was fully satisfied of his way
of working which I Dont only Conjecture to be on this wise
viz they when they would Go from tree [to] tree or would Sail
in the air let themselves hang Down a little way by their webb
and then put out a web at their tails which being so Exceeding
rare when it first comes from the spider as to be lighter than the
air so as of itself it will ascend in it (which I know by Experience)
the moving air takes it by the End and by the spiders Permis-

sion Pulls it out of his tail to any length and If the further End
Of it happens to catch by a tree or any thing, why there's a web
for him to Go over upon and the Spider immediately percieves
it and feels when it touches, much after the same manner as the
soul in the brain immediately Percieves when any of those little
nervous strings that Proceed from it are in the Least Jarrd by
External things; and this very way I have seen Spiders Go from
one thing to another I believe fifty time[s] at least since I first
Discovered it: but if nothing is in the way of these webs to
hinder their flying out at a sufficient Distance and they Dont
catch by any thing, there will be so much of it Drawn out into
the air as by its ascending force there will be enough to Carry
the spider with it, or which is all one now there is so much of
this web which is rarer than the air as that the web taken with
the spider shall take up as much or more space than the same
quantity of which if it be equall they together will be in a perfect
equilibrium or Poise with the air so as that when they are loose
therein they will neither ascend nor Descend but only as they
are Driven by the wind, but if they together be more will
ascend therein, like as a man at the bottom of the sea if he has
hold on a stick of wood or any thing that is lighter or takes up
more Space for the Quantity of matter than the water, if it be a
little piece it may not be enough to Carry him and Cause him
to swim therin but if there be enough of it it will Carry him up
to the surface of the water, if there be so much as that the
Greater rarity shall more than Counterballance the Greater
Density of the man and if it be Doth but Just Cause to balance,
Put the man any where in the water and there he'll keep without
ascending or Descending; tis Just so with the Spider in the air
as with the man in the water, for what is lighter than the air will
swim Or ascend therin as well as that which is lighter than the
water swims in that, and If a spider has hold on so much of a
web that the Greater Levity of all of it shall more than counter-
poise the Greater Gravity of the spider, so that the ascending
force of the web shall be more than the Descending force of
the spider the web by its ascending will necessarily Carry the
Spider up unto such a height as that the air shall be so much

thinner and lighter as that the lightness of the web with the
Spider shall no longer prevail. Now Perhaps here it will be
asked how the spider knows when he has put out web enough
and when he Does know how Does he Get himself loose from
the web by which he hung to the trees I answer there is no
occasion for the spiders knowing, for their manner is to let out
their web untill the ascending force of their web And the force
the wind has upon it together with the weight of the spider
shall be enough to break the web by which the spider hung to
the tree for the stress of all these Comes upon that and nature
has so provided that Just so much web as is sufficient to break
that shall be sufficient to carry the spider. And this verry way
I very frequently have seen spiders mount away into the air
with a Vast train of Glistening web before them, from a Stick
in my hand and have also shewed it to others and without Doubt
they Do it with a Great Deal of their sort of Pleasure. there
remains only two Difficulties. the One is how should they first
begin to spin out this so fine and even a thread of their bodies
if once there is a web Out it is easy to Concieve how if the end
of it were once out how the Air might take it and so Draw it
out to a greater length but how should they at first let Out of
their tails the End of a fine string when in all Probability the
Web while it is in the Spider is a certain liquour with which
that Great bottle tail of theirs is filld, which immediately upon
its being Exposed to the air turns to a Dry Substance and very
much rarifies, and extends itself now if it be a liquour it is
hardly Concievable how they should let out a fine string except
by Expelling a small Drop at the End of it, but none such Can
be Discovered: to find out this Difficulty I once Got a very
large Spider of the sort, for in lesser ones I Could not Distinctly
Discern how they Did theirs nor Can One Discern their webs
at all except they are held up against the sun or some Dark
Place. I took this Spider and held him up against an open Door
Which being Dark helped me Plainly to Discern and shook
him wherupon he let himself Down by his Web as in the figure
by the web. c. b. and then with his tail fixt with his tail one end
of the Web that he intended to let out into the Air to the web

by which he let himself Down at. a. then pulling away his tail one end of the Web Was thereby Drawn out which being at first exceeding slender the Wind Presently broke it at d. and

Drew it out as in figure the second, and it was immediately spun out to a very Great length. the Other Difficulty is how when they Are Once Carried Up into the air how they Get Down again or whether they are necessitated to Continue till they are beat Down by some shower of Rain without any sustenance which [is] not probable nor Agreeable to Natural Providence. I answer there is a way Whereby they May Come Down again when they Please by only Gathering in their Webs into them

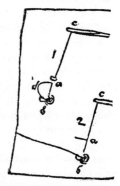

again by Which way they may Come Down Gradually and Gently, but whether that be their Way or no: I Cant say but without scruple that or a better for we Alwaies find things Done by nature as well or better than [we] can imagine beforehand.

Coroll: We hence see the exuberant Goodness of the Creator Who hath not only Provided for all the Necessities but also for the Pleasure and Recreation of all sorts of Creatures And Even the insects and those that are most Despicable

Another thing Particularly Notable and worthy of being Inquired into About these Webs is that they which are so exceeding small and fine as that they Cannot be Discerned except held in a particular Position with Respect to the sun, or against some Dark place when held Close to the eye should Appear at such a Prodigious height in the air when Near betwixt us and the sun so that they must needs some of em appear as big as A Cable would Do if it Appeared Exactly secundum Rationem Distantiae. to solve we ought to Consider that these webs as they are thus Posited very vividly Reflect the Rays of the sun so as to Cause them to be very lightsome bodies and then see if we Can't find and Parallel Phaenomena in other lightsome

bodies and Every body knows that A Candle in the night
appears exceedingly bigger at a Distance than it ought to Do
and we may observe in the moon towards the new When that
Part of it that is not Inlightened by the sun is visible how much
the Inlightened Part thereof is inlarged and extended beyond
the Circumference of the other Part, and astronomers also know
how Exceedingly the fixt stars are beyond their bounds to our
naked eye so that without Doubt they appear many hundreds
of times bigger than the[y] Ought to Do the reason may be
that the multitude and Powerfullness of the Rays affects a
Greater Part of the Retina than their space which they immediately strike Upon, but we find that a light that so Does when
it is alone and when No part of the Retina is affected by any
thing else but that, so that the least impression is felt by it,
wont Do so or att least Not so much in the midst of other Perhaps Greater light, so that other Parts Of the Retina are filled
with impressions of their Own; but these webs are an instance
of the Latter so that this Reason Does not seem fully to Solve
this so great a magnifying though without Doubt that helps,
but the Chief Reason must be Referred [to] that incurvation of
the Rays Passing by the edge of any body which Sir Isaac
Newton has proved

One thing more I shall take notice of before I Dismiss this
Subject Concerning the End of Nature in Giving Spiders this
way Of flying Which though we have found in the Corollary
to be their Pleasure and Recreation, yet we think a Greater end
is at last their Destruction and what makes us think so is because
that is necessarily and Actually brought to Pass by it and we
shall find nothing so brought to Pass by nature but what is the
end of those means by which it is brought to pass. and we shall
further evince it by and by by shew[ing] the Great Usefullness
of it, but we Must shew how their Destruction is brought to
pass by it I say then that by this means almost all the spiders
Upon the Land must necessarily be swept first and last into the
Sea for we have Observed already that they never fly except in
fair Weather and we may now observe that it is never fair
weather neither in this Country nor any other except when the

Wind blows from the Midland Parts and so towards the Sea, so here in newengland I have Observed that they never fly except when the wind is westerly and I Never saw them fly but when they were hastening Directly towards the sea and [the] time of the flying being so long even from the Middle of August to the Middle of October tho their Chief time here in newengland is in the time as was said before towds the Latter End of Aug, And the beginning of Sept, and the[y] keep flying all that while towards the sea must needs almost all of them Get there before they have Done and the same indeed holds true of all other sort of flying insects for at that time of Year the Ground trees and houses the Places of their Residence in summer being Pretty Chill they leave em whenever the sun shines Pretty Warm and mount up into the air and Expand their Wings to the sun and so flying for Nothing but their Ease and Comfort they Suffer themselves to Go that way that they find they Can Go Withe Greatest Ease And so wheresoever the Wind Pleases and besides it being warmth they fly for and it being warmer flying with the wind than against it or sideways to it for thereby the wind has less Power upon them and as was said Of spiders they Never flying but when the winds that blow from the Midland Parts, towards the sea bring fair Weather, they must necessarily flying so long a time all the while towards the sea Get there at last. and I very well Remember that at the same time when I have been viewing the spiders with their webs, In the air I also saw vast Multitudes of flies many of 'em at a Great height all flying the same way with the spiders and webs, Directly seaward and I have many times at that time of Year Looking westward seen Myriads of them towards sunsetting flying Continually towards the sea and this I believe almost every body Specially of my own Country will Call to mind that they have also seen; and as to Other sorts of flying insects such as butterflies, Millers, Moths, &c. I Remember that when I was a boy I have at the same time of year Lien on the Ground upon my Back and beheld Abundance of them busy All Flying southeast which I then thought was Going to a Warm Country so that without any Doubt almost all of all manner of aeriall insects And also spiders which Live upon them and are made up of them are at the end of the year Swept and Wafted in to the sea and buried in the Ocean, and Leave Nothing behind them but their Eggs for a New stock the Next year

Coroll: hence also we may behold and admire at the wisdom Of the Creator and be Convinced from Prvd [Providence] there is exercised about such little things, in this wonderfull Contrivance of Annually Carrying of and burying the Corrupting nauseousness of our Air, of which flying insects are little Collections in the bottom of Ocean where it will Do no harm and Especially the strange way of bringing this About in Spiders (which are Collections of these Collections their food being flying insects) which want wings where by it might be Done; and what Great inconveniences should we labor Under if there were no such way for spiders and flies are so Exceeding Multiplying Creatures that If they Only slept or lay benummed in [Winter?] and were raised again in the Spring which is Commonly supposed it would not be many years before we should be as much Plagued with their vast numbers as Egypt was, and If they Died for good and all in winter they by the Renewed heat of the sun would Presently Again be Dissipated into those nauseous vapours of which they are made up of. and so would be of no use or benefit in that [in] which now they are so verry serviceable

Coroll. 2: Admire also the Creator in so nicely and mathematically adjusting their Multiplying nature that Notwithstanding their Destruction by this means and the Multitudes that are eaten by birds that they Do not Decrease and so by little and little come to nothing, and in so adjusting their Destruction to their multiplication that they Do neither increase but taking one year with another there is alwaies Just an equall number Of them

Another Reason why they will not fly at any other time but when a dry wind blows is because a moist wind moistens the webb and makes it heavier than the air And if they had the sense to fly themselves, we should have hundreds of times more spiders and flies by the sea shore than any where else.

[THE SOUL]

I am informed y^t you have advan[c]ed a notion y^t the Soul is
matereal & keeps wth ye body till ye resur[e]ction as I am a
profes't Lover of Novelty you must alow me to be much entertain'd by this discoverry wch however old in some parts of y^e
world is new in this

I am imformed y^t you have advanced an Notion y^t the Soul is
materiall & attends ye body till ye resurection as I am a profest
Lover of novelty you must immagin I am very much entertained by this discovery (wch however in some parts of ye world
is new to us) but suffer my Curiosity a Littel further I w^d know
ye manner of ye kingdom before I swear alegance 1st I w^d know
whether this materiall Soul keeps wth in ye Coffin and if so
whether it might not be convenient to build a repository for it
in order to wch I w^d know w^t Shape it is of whether round tri-
angular or fore square or whethe is it a number of Long fine
strings reaching from ye head to ye foot and whether it dus not
Live a very discontented Life I am afraid when ye Coffin Gives
way ye earth will fall in and Crush it but if it should Chuse to
Live above Ground and hover about ye Grave how big it is
whether it Covers all ye body or is assined to ye head or breast
or how if it Covers all ye body w^t it dus when another body is
Laid upon y^t whether ye 1st First Gives way and if so where is
ye place of retreat but soppose ye Souls are not so big but y^t 10
or a dozen of you may be about one body whether yy will not
Quarril for ye highest place and as I insist much upon my
honnour and property I w^d know wher I must Quit my dear
head if a Superior Soul Comes in ye way but above all I am
Consearned to know w^t they do where a bureing Place has bin
filled 20 30 or 100 times if they are a top of one another ye uppermost will be so far of y^t it Can take no Care of ye body I strongly
susspect they must march of[f] every time there Comes anew
Set I hope ther is some Good place provided for them but

dupt [d(o)ubt?] yᵉ undergoing so much hard Ship & being deprived of yᵉ body at Last will make them ill temper'd I Live it∧ʷᵗʰ your phisicall Genus to determin whether some medesinall applications might not be proper in such Cases and subscrib your proselite when I can have solution of these maters

[OF THE RAINBOW]

We shall Endeavour to Give a full Account Of the Rainbow and such an One as we think if Well understood will be satisfactory to Any body If they Are fully satisfied Of Sr Isaac Newtons Different Reflexibility and Refrangibility of the Rays of light and If he be not we Refer him to [what] he has said About it and we are Assured if he be A person Of an ordinary logacity and anything Versed in such matters, by that time he has throughly Considered it he [ə]ll be satisfied and after that let him Peruse what we are about to say the first Question then shall be What is that Reflection which we Call a Rainbow from I answer from the falling Drops of Rain for we never see any Rainbow except it be so that the sun Can shine full upon the Drops of Rain except the heavens be so Clear on One side as to let the Uninterrupted Rays Of the sun Come Directly Upon the Rain that [?] falls on the Other side, thus we say it is a sign of fair Weather when there is a Rainbow in the East, because when there is a Rainbow in the east, it is alwaies already fair in the West for If it be Cloudy there the Rays of the sun will be hindered from Coming thence to the Opposite Drops of Rain. It Cannot be the Cloud from whence this Reflection is made, as was once thought, for we almost alwaies see the Ends of Rainbows Come Down Even in amongst the trees below the Hills And to the very Ground where we know there is no part of the Cloud there, but what Descends in Drops of Rain and Can Convince any man by Ocular Demonstration In two Minutes On a fair Day that the Reflection is from Drops by Only taking a little water in my mouth and standing between the sun and something that looks a little Darkish and spirting of it into the Air so as to Disperse all into fine Drops And there will appear as Compleat and plain a Rainbow with all the Colours as ever Was seen in the heavens and there will Appear the same If the sun is near enough to the horizon upon fine Drops of Water

Dashd up by a stick from a puddle, the Reason why the Drops must be fine is because they wont be thick enough but here and there a Drop if they Are Large, And I have frequently heard my Countrymen that are Used to sawmills say that they have seen a Rainbow upon the Drops that are Dispersed in the Air by the Violent Concussion of the Waters in the Mill and what Is Equivalent to A Rainbow, If One take a Drop of water upon the end of a Stick and hold it up On the side that is Opposite to the sun and moving it along towards One side or t'other you will Percieve where the Drop is held just at such a Distance from the Point opposite to the sun that the Rays of the sun are much more vividly Reflected by it to your eye, than at any other Place Nearer Or further of and that in the Colours of the Rainbow too so that If there had been Enough of these Drops there would have appeared a perfect Rainbow. and If you have a mind to see more Distinctly you may fill a Globular Glass bottle with water, the Glass of it must be very thin and Clear, and it will serve your turn as well as so big a Drop of Water and by that means you may also Distinctly see that the Reflection is from the Concave and not from the Convex surface

The Next thing that Wants a solution is what should Cause the Reflection to be Circular, or which is the same thing what should Cause the Reflection to be Just at such a Distance everywhere from the Point that is opposite to the sun, and no reflection at all from the Drops that are within or without that Circle why should not all the Drops that are within the Circle Reflect as many rays as those that are in the Circle or where the Circle is to Resolve this we must Consider this One law of Reflection and Refraction to wit If the Reflecting body be Perfectly Reflexive the Angle of Reflexion will be the same as the Angle of incidence but if the body be not Perfectly so the Angle will be less than the Angle of incidence, by a body Perfectly Reflexive I mean one that is so Solid as Perfectly to Resist the stroke of the incident body and not to Give way to it at all, and by and imperfectly Reflexive a body that Gives way and Does not Obstinately Resist the stroke Of the incident Body so I say that If the body a. b. be Perfectly Reflexive and Does not Give way at

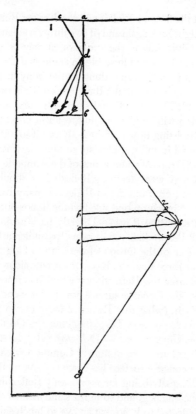

all to the stroke of the incident Ray c. d. It will Reflect by an
angle that shall be equall to that by which it fell upon the body
a. b. from d. to e. but if the body a. b. is not able to Resist the
stroke of the Ray c. d. but Gives way to it it will neither be able
to Reflect by so big an angle büt will Reflect it it may be by the
line d. f. or d. g. according as the Reflexive force of a. b. be
greater or lesser. And the bare Consideration of this will be
enough to Convince any man for we know that there is need of
Greater force by a Great angle than by a little one. if we throw

a ball against the floor or Wall it will much easier Rebound side-
waies than Right back again and [if] we throw it sideways against
a body that Gives way to the stroke of (it may be tried at any
time) it will not Rebound in so big an angle as if the body were
quite hard, so it is the same thing in the body a. b. it might
Give way so much as to let the Ray proceed Right on with very

☞ note
well for
a halo

little Deviation from its old path and if so the Deviation will be greater and greater in proportion to the
Resisting Power of the body and if so if it Gives way
at all it will not Deviate so much as if it Did not at

all Now these Drops of water is one of these imperfectly Reflexive bodies If they were Perfectly Reflexive we should see those
Drops that are right opposite to Reflect as many Rays as those
that are Just so much on one side had the liquor but Resistance
enough to Reflect the Rays so Directly back again, but those
Rays that fall Perpendicularly or near Perpendicularly upon the
Concave surface of the Drop as from a. to b. fig 2 falling with
much Greater force than the Ray, which falls sideways upon it
from e. to b. after the Refraction at e which is made in all pellucid Globes. the Concave surface has not force enough to stop
it and Reflect it, (what that Reflexive force of the [Concav]e*
surface is we are not now Disputing) but lets Go through and
Pass right on Uninterruptedly [N]ow the Ray h. e. b. and the
Rays Which fall about so obliquely Coming with a far [light-]
er stroke the concave surface has force enough to Resist it and
what falls Obliquely being far more easily Reflex[ible] Reflects
it along in the line b. g. and so in the same manner the Ray c. i.
b. will be Reflected to k. so that an eye so much sideways as g.
or k. will take the Rays thus Reflected from the Drops and no
where Else And it being Only those Ray whose Obliquity is ad-
justed [to] the Refractive power that are Reflected by it, and they
being all Reflected Out again with such a Degree of Obliquity
we hence see why the Rays be not Reflected all ways equally, we
hence Also see why the Rays are Only Reflected out at the sides
of the Drop and not Directly back again by that why the Eye
Does not take the Rays from any Drops but those that are so

* Edwards's MS. is defective here.

much sideways of or on one side of the Point that is Right
Oposite to the sun and so why the Parts that are so Opposite
Look Dark and why the Parts that are Just so much on one side
or just At such A Distance all Round from the Opposite Point
Alone Are bright or which is the same thing why there is such a
bright Circle   the next Grand Question is what is it Causes
the Colours Of the Rainbow and this Question indeed is almost
answered already for it is very evident. . .

[OF BEING]

That there should absolutely be nothing at all is utterly impossible, the Mind Can never Let it stretch its Conceptions ever so much bring it self to Concieve of a state of Perfect nothing, it puts the mind into mere Convulsion and Confusion to endeavour to think of such a state, and it Contradicts the very nature of the soul to think that it should be, and it is the Greatest Contradiction and the Aggregate of all Contradictions to say that there should not be, tis true we Cant so Distinctly show the Contradiction by words because we Cannot talk about it without Speaking horrid Nonsense and Contradicting our selve at every word, and because nothing is that whereby we Distinctly show other particular Contradictions, but here we are Run up to Our first principle and have no other to explain the Nothingness or not being of nothing by, indeed we Can mean nothing else by nothing but a state of Absolute Contradiction; and If any man thinks that he Can think well Enough how there should be nothing I'll Engage that what he means by nothing is as much something as any thing that ever He thought of in his Life, and I believe that if he knew what nothing was it would be intuitively Evident to him that it Could not be. So that we see it is necessary some being should Eternally be and tis a more palpable Contradiction still to say that there must be being somewhere and not otherwhere for the words absolute nothing, and where, Contradict each other; and besides it Gives as great a shock to the mind to think of pure nothing being in any one place, as it Does to think of it in all and it is self evident that there Can be nothing in one place as well as in another and so if there Can be in one there Can be in all. So that we see this necessary eternall being must be infinite and Omnipresent*

*Between this paragraph and the next are the words: "Place this as a Lemma where it suits best and Let it be more fully [d]emonstr" [demonstrated]. The last word is very obscurely written. It seems to begin with

This Infinite And omnipresent being Cannot be solid. Let us
see how Contradictory it is to say that an infinite being is solid,
for Solidity surely is nothing but Resistance to other solidities.
Space is this Necessary eternal infinite and Omnipresent being,
we find that we can with ease Concieve how all other beings
should not be, we Can remove them out of our Minds and Place
some Other in the Room of them, but Space is the very thing
that we Can never Remove, and Concieve of its not being, If
a man would imagine space any where to be Divided So as there
should be Nothing between the Divided parts, there Remains
Space between notwithstanding and so the man Contradicts
himself, and it is self evident I believe to every man that space
is necessary, eternal, infinite, & Omnipresent. but I had as Good
speak Plain, I have already said as much as that Space is God,
and it is indeed Clear to me, that all the Space there is not proper
to body, all the space there is without yᵉ Bounds of the Creation,
all the space there was before the Creation, is God himself, and
no body would in the Least stick at it if it were not because of
the Gross Conceptions that we have of space.
A state of Absolute nothing is a state of Absolute Contradiction
absolute nothing is the Aggregate of all the Absurd[?] contradictions in the World, a state wherin there is neither body nor
spirit, nor space neither empty space nor full space neither little
nor Great, narrow nor broad neither infinitely Great space, nor
finite space, nor a mathematical point neither Up nor Down
neither north nor south (I dont mean as it is with Respect to
the body of the earth or some other Great body but no Contrary Point, nor Positions or Directions[)] no such thing as
either here Or there this way or that way or only one way; When
we Go About to form an idea of Perfect nothing we must shut
Out all these things we must shut out of our minds both space
that has something in it and space that has nothing in it we must

not allow our selves to think of the least part of space never so small, nor must we suffer our thoughts to take sanctuary in a mathematical point, when we Go to Expell body out of Our thoughts we must Cease not to leave empty space in the Room of it and when we Go to Expell emptiness from Our thoughts we must not think to squeese it out by any thing Close hard and solid but we must think of the same that the sleeping Rocks Dream of and not till then shall we Get a Compleat idea of nothing

a state of nothing is a state wherin every Proposition in Euclid is not true, nor any of those self evident maxims by which they are Demonstrated & all other Eternal truths are neither true nor false

when we Go to Enquire whether or no there Can be absolutely nothing we speak nonsense in Enquiring the stating of the Question is Nonsense because we make a disjunction where there is none either being or absolute nothing is no Disjunction no more than whether a t[r]iangle is a tiangle or not a tiangle there is no other way but Only for there to be existence there is no such thing as absolute nothing. There is such a thing as nothing with Respect to this Ink & paper there is such a thing as nothing with Respect to you & me there is such a thing as nothing with Respect to this Globe of Earth & with Respect to this Created universe there is another way besides these things having existence but there is no such thing as nothing with Respect to Entity or being absolutely Considered we don't know what we say if we say we think it Possible in it self that there should not be Entity

and how Doth it Grate upon the mind to thin[k] that something should be from all Eternity, and nothing all the while be Conscious of it let us suppose to illustrate it that the world had a being from all Eternity, and had many Great Changes and Wonderfull Revolutions, and all the while nothing knew, there was no knowledge in the Universe of any such thing, how is it possible to bring the mind to imagine, yea it is Really impossible it should be that Any thing should be and nothing know it then you'll say if it be so it is because nothing has

Any existence any where else but in Consciousness no certainly
no where else but either in Created or uncreated Consciousness
Supposing there were Another Universe only of bodies Created
at a Great Distance from this Created in excellent Order and
harmonious motions, and a beautiful variety, and there was
no Created intelligence in it nothing but senseless bodies,
nothing but God knew anything of it I Demand in what Respect
this world has a being but only in the Divine Consciousness
Certainly in no Respect there would be figures and magnitudes,
and motions and Proportions but where where Else but in the
almightie's knowledge how is it possible there should, then you'll
say for the same Reason in a Room Close Shut Up that no body
sees nor hears nothing in it there is nothing any otherway than
in Gods knowledge I answer Created beings are Conscious of
the Effects of what is in the Room, for Perhaps there is not one
leaf of a tree nor Spire of Grass but what has effects All over
the universe and will have to the End of Eternity but any otherwise there is nothing in a Room shut up but only in Gods
Consciousness how Can Any thing be there Any other way this
will appear to be truly so to Any one that thinks of it with the
whole united strength of his mind. Let us suppose for illustration this impossibility that all the Spirits in the Universe to be
for a time to be Deprived of their Consciousness, and Gods
Consciousness at the same time to be intermitted. I say the
Universe for that time would cease to be of it self and not only
as we speak because the almighty Could not attend to Uphold
the world but because God knew nothing of it tis our foolish
imagination that will not suffer us to see we fancy there may be
figures and magnitudes Relations and properties without any
ones knowing of it, but it is our imagination hurts us we Dont
know what figures and Properties Are.

Our imagination makes us fancy we see Shapes an Colours and
magnitudes tho no body is there to behold it but to help our
imagination Let us thus State the Case, Let us suppose the
world Deprived of Every Ray of light so that there should not
be the least Glimering of light in the Universe Now all will own
that in such Case the Universe would be immediately Really

Deprived of all its Colours. one part of the Universe is no More
Red or blue, or Green or Yellow or black or white or light or
dark or transparent or opake there would be no visible Distinction between the world and the Rest of the incomprehensible
Void yea there would be no Difference in these Respect[s] between the world and the infinite void, that is any Part of that
void would really be as light and as Dark, as white and as black
as Red and Green as blue and as brown as transparent and as
opake as Any Part of the universe, or as there would be in such
Case no Difference between the world and nothing in these
Respects so there would be no Difference between one part of
the world and another all in these Respects is alike confounded
with and undistinguishable from infinite emptiness

At the same time also Let us suppose the Universe to be altogether Deprived of motion, and all parts of it to be at perfec[t]
Rest (the same supposition is indeed included in this but we
Distinguish them for better Clearness) then the Universe would
not Differ from the void in this Respect, there will be no more
motion in one than the other then also solidity would cease, all
that we mean or Can be meant by solidity is Resistance Resistance to touch, the Resistance of some parts of Space, this is
all the knowledge we Get of solidity by our senses and I am
sure all that we Can Get any other way, but solidity shall be
shown to be nothing Else more fully hereafter. but there Can be
no Resistance if there is no motion, one body Can [not] Resist
another when there is perfect Rest Amongst them, but you'll say
tho there is not actuall Resistance yet there is potential existence, that is such and such Parts of space would Resist upon
occasion, but this Is all I would have that there is no solidity
now not but that God would Cause there to be on occasion and
if there is no solidity there is no extension for extension is the
extenddness of the solidity, then all figure, and magnitude and
proportion immediately Ceases. put both these suppositions
together that is Deprive the world of light and motion and the
Case would stand thus with the world, there would [be] neither
white nor black neither blew nor brown, bright nor shaded
pellucid nor opake, no noise or sound neither heat nor Cold,

neither fluid nor Wet nor Drie hard nor soft nor solidity nor Extension, nor figure, nor magnitude nor Proportion nor body nor spirit, what then [is] to become of the Universe Certainly it exists no where but in the Divine mind this will be Abundantly Clearer to one after having Read what I have further to say of solidity &c

So that we see that a world without motion Can Exist no where Else but in the mind either infinite or finite

Corollary. it follows from hence that that those beings which have knowledge and Consciousness are the Only Proper and Real And substantial beings, inasmuch as the being of other things is Only by these. from hence we may see the Gross mistake of those who think material things the most substantial beings and spirits more like a shadow, whereas spirits Only Are Properly Substance.

[COLOURS]

COLOURS   we have already supposed that the Different Refrangibility of Rays Arises from their Different bulk, we have
also supposed that they Are very Elastick bodies, from these
suppositions the Colours of natural bodies *may be accounted for**
that is why some Particles of matter Reflect such a sort or sorts
of Rays and no Other the Different Density of Particles whence
Arises a Different attraction and together with their Different
firmness will account for all some bodies have so little of firmness and so Easily Give way that they Are able to Resist the
stroak of no Rays But the Least and weakest, and most Reflexible Rays. all the other Rays that Are bigger and therefore their
force not so Easily Resisted overcome the Resistance of the
Particles that stand in their way such bodies therefore appear
blue as the atmosphere or skies, smoke &c—again tis known
that the most Refrangible Rays are most easily attracted that is
are most easily stay'd or diverted by attraction, for as has been
already shown Refraction & Reflection from Concave surfaces
is by attraction because therefore that the most Refrangible Rays
are most Diverted by Refraction and Easiest Reflected inward
from the surface, and most Diverted by Passing by the edges of
bodies it follows that attraction has most influence on the most
Refrangible Rays

Tis also evident that the Particles of bodies that are the most
Dense have the strongest attraction. the Particles of any body
therefore may be so dense and attract so strongly as to hold
fast all the Lesser and more Refrangible Rays so that they shall
none of them be Reflected but Only the Greater Rays, on Whom
the attraction of these Particles Can have Less influence, hereby
the body will become Red

and as for the intermediate Colours the Particles of a body

---

*The words italicized in print have a line through them in the manu-
script. [Smyth's note.]

24

may be so Dense as to hold all the most Refrangible Rays and may yet not be firm Enough to Resist the stroak of the Least Refrangible hereby the body may become Yellow or Green or of any other intermediate Colour

Or a body may be Coloured by the Reflection of a mixture of Rays the body Particles may be able to Reflect three or four sorts of Rays and have to strong an attraction to Reflect those Rays that are Less and too weak a Resistance to Reflect the Bigger Rays, or the Colour of A body may be Compounded of Reflected Rays of very Distant Degrees of Refrangibility and not Reflect any of the intermediate Colours by Reason of its being Compounded of very heterogeneous Particles [which] have a very Different Degree of Density and firmness. or the Particles of a body may be firm Enough to Reflect all sorts of Rays yet have so little attraction to hold them that the body will be White, or a body may be Compounded of Particles having so little Resistance as to Reflect no Rays, of so Great Density as to hold all or so full of Pores as to Drink in all, then the body is black

Or the Particles of bodies may have Pores and hollows that may be big enough to Let in the Least Rays not the Rest so that the Pores of Particles may have much to Do in the Causing of Colours

The blue of mountains at a Distance is not made by any Rays Reflected from the mountains but from the Air and vapours that is between us and them. the mountain occasions the blueness by intercepting all Rays that would Come from beyond to Disturb the Colour by their mixture

it may therefore seem a Difficulty Why the atmosphere all Round by the horison Dont appear very blue seeing tis Evident that the atmosphere Reflects Chiefly the blue Rays as Appears in the higher Parts of the atmosphere by the blueness of the skie and near the Earth by the blueness of mountains, and the redness or Yellowness of the Rising and setting sun. it would therefore seem that the atmosphere should Appear most blue where no Rays are Intercepted by mountains because the atmos-here beyond the mountain Reflects blue Rays as well as on this

Side. therefore it seems that there would be more blue Rays
Come to Our eyes where none were Intercepted by mountains
And Consequently that the most lively blue would be there. and
so it would be, if blue Rays Came to Our Eyes in the same
Proportion as they are Reflected but most of those blue Rays
that Are Reflected by those Parts of the Atmosphere that Are at
a great Distance are intercepted by the intermediate Air before
they Come to Our eyes (for the Air by supposition intercept
them Easiest) and only those few Yellow Rays and Less Re
flexible Rays that Are Reflected by the Air Come to Our eyes
whence it Comes to Pass that the Atmosphere near the horizon
Dont appear blue but of a Whitish Yellow. And sometimes
when it is filled with more Dense exhalations that Can Reflect
Less Reflexible Rays still, it appears a little Reddish

NOTES ON THE MIND

EXISTENCE. If we had only the sense of Seeing, we should not be as ready to conclude the visible world to have been an existence independent of perception, as we do; because the ideas we have by the sense of Feeling, are as much mere ideas, as those we have by the sense of Seeing. But we know, that the things that are objects of this sense, all that the mind views by Seeing, are merely mental Existences; because all these things, with all their modes, do exist in a looking-glass, where all will acknowledge, they exist only mentally.

It is now agreed upon by every knowing philosopher, that Colours are not really in the things, no more than Pain is in a needle; but strictly no where else but in the mind. But yet I think that Colour may have an existence out of the mind, with equal reason as any thing in Body has any existence out of the mind, beside the very substance of the body itself, which is nothing but the Divine power, or rather the Constant Exertion of it. For what else is that, which we call by the name of Body? I find Colour has the chief share in it. 'Tis nothing but Colour, and Figure, which is the termination of this Colour, together with some powers, such as the power of resisting, and motion, & c. that wholly makes up what we call Body. And if that, which we principally mean by the thing itself, cannot be said to be in the thing itself, I think nothing can be. If Colour exists not out of the mind, then nothing belonging to Body, exists out of the mind but Resistance, which is Solidity, and the termination of this Resistance, with its relations, which is Figure, and the communication of this Resistance, from space to space, which is Motion; though the latter are nothing but modes of the former. Therefore, there is nothing out of the mind but Resistance. And not that neither, when nothing is actually resisted. Then, there is nothing but the Power of Resistance. And as Resistance is nothing else but the actual exertion of God's power, so the Power can be nothing else, but the constant Law or Method of that actual exertion. And how is there any Resistance, except it be in some mind, in idea? What is it that is resisted? It is not Colour. And what else is it? It is ridiculous to say, that Resistance is resisted. That, does not tell us at all what is to be resisted. There must be something resisted before there can be Resistance; but to say Resistance is resisted, is ridiculously to suppose Resistance, before there is anything to be resisted. Let us suppose two globes only existing, and no mind. There is nothing there, ex confesso, but Resistance. That is, there is such a Law, that the space within the limits of a globular figure shall resist. Therefore, there is nothing there but a power, or an establishment. And if there be any Resistance really out of the mind, one power and establishment must resist another establishment and law of Resistance, which is exceedingly ridiculous. But yet it cannot be otherwise, if any way out of the mind. But now it is easy to conceive of Resistance, as a mode of an idea. It is easy to conceive of such a power, or constant manner of stopping or resisting a colour. The idea may be resisted, it may move, and stop and rebound; but how a mere power, which is nothing real, can move and stop, is inconceivable, and it is impossible to say a word about it without contradiction. The world is therefore an ideal one; and the Law of creating, and the succession of these ideas is constant and regular.

Coroll. 1. How impossible is it, that the world should exist from Eternity, without a Mind.

Coroll. 2. Since it is so, and that absolute Nothing is such a dreadful contradiction; hence we learn the necessity of the Eternal Existence of an All-comprehending Mind; and that it is the complication of all contradictions to deny such a mind.

When we say that the World, i.e. the material Universe, exists no where but in the mind, we have got to such a degree of strictness and abstraction, that we must be exceedingly careful, that we do not confound and lose ourselves by misapprehension. That is impossible, that it should be meant, that all the world is contained in the narrow compass of a few inches of space, in little ideas in the place of the brain; for that would be a contradiction; for we are to remember that the human body, and the brain itself, exist only mentally, in the same sense that other things do; and so that, which we call *place*, is an idea too. Therefore things are truly in those places; for what we mean, when we say so, is only, that this mode of our idea of place appertains to such an idea. We would not therefore be understood to deny, that things are where they seem to be. For the principles we lay down, if they are narrowly looked into, do not infer that. Nor will it be found, that they at all make void Natural Philosophy, or the science of the Causes or Reasons of corporeal changes; For to find out the reasons of things, in Natural Philosophy, is only to find out the proportion of God's acting. And the case is the same, as to such proportions, whether we suppose the World, only mental, in our sense, or no.

Though we suppose, that the existence of the whole material Universe is absolutely dependent on Idea, yet we may speak in the old way, and as properly, and truly as ever. God, in the beginning, created such a certain number of Atoms, of such a determinate bulk and figure, which they yet maintain and always will, and gave them such a motion, of such a direction, and of such a degree of velocity; from whence arise all the Natural changes in the Universe, forever, in a continued series. Yet, perhaps all this does not exist any where perfectly, but in the Divine Mind. But then, if it be enquired, What exists in the Divine Mind; and how these things exist there? I answer, There is his determination, his care, and his design, that Ideas shall be united forever, just so, and in such a manner, as is agreeable to such a series. For instance, all the ideas that ever were, or ever shall be to all eternity, in any created mind, are answerable to the existence of such a peculiar Atom in the beginning of the Creation, of such a determinate figure and size, and have such a motion given it: That is, they are all such, as Infinite Wisdom sees would follow, according to the series of nature, from such an Atom, so moved. That is, all ideal changes of creatures are just so, as if just such a particular Atom had actually all along existed even in some finite mind, and never had been out of that mind, and had, in that mind, caused these effects, which are exactly according to nature, that is, according to the nature of other matter, that is actually perceived by the mind. God supposes its existence; that is, he causes all changes to arise, as if all these things had actually existed in such a series, in some created mind, and as if created minds had comprehended all things perfectly. And, although created minds do not; yet, the Divine Mind doth; and he orders all things according to his mind, and his ideas. And these hidden things do not only exist in the Divine idea, but in a sense in created idea; for that exists in created idea, which necessarily supposes it. If a ball of lead were supposed to be let fall from the clouds, and no eye saw it, 'till it got within ten rods of the ground, and then its motion and celerity was perfectly discerned in its exact proportion; if it were not for the imperfection and slowness of our minds, the perfect idea of the rest of the motion would immediately, and of itself arise in the mind, as well as that which is there. So, were our thoughts comprehensive and perfect enough, our view of the present state of the world, would excite in us a perfect idea of all past changes.

And we need not perplex our minds with a thousand questions and doubts that will seem to arise; as, To what purpose is this way of exciting ideas; and, What advantage is there in observing such a series. I answer, It is just all one, as to any benefit or advantage, any end that we can suppose was proposed by the Creator, as if the Material Universe were existent in the same manner as is vulgarly thought. For the corporeal world is to no advantage but to the spiritual; and it is exactly the same advantage this way as the other, for it is all one, as to any thing excited in the mind.

EXCELLENCY. There has nothing been more without a definition, than *Excellency;* although it be what we are more concerned with, than any thing else whatsoever; yea, we are concerned with nothing else. But what is this Excellency? Wherein is one thing excellent, and another evil; one beautiful, and another deformed? Some have said that all Excellency is *Harmony*, *Symmetry*, or *Proportion;* But they have not yet explained it. We would know, Why Proportion is more excellent than Disproportion; that is, why Proportion is pleasant to the mind, and Disproportion unpleasant? Proportion is a thing that may be explained yet further. It is an *Equality*, or *Likeness of Ratios;* so that it is the Equality, that makes the Proportion. Excellency therefore seems to consist in *Equality*. Thus, if there be two perfect *equal* circles, or globes, together, there is something more of beauty than if they were of *unequal*, disproportionate magnitudes. And if two *parallel* lines be drawn, the beauty is greater, than if they were *obliquely* inclined without proportion, because there is equality of distance. And if betwixt two parallel lines, two equal circles be placed, each at the same distance from each parallel line, as in Fig. 1, the beauty is greater, than if they stood at irregular distances from the

parallel lines. If they stand, each in a perpendicular line, going from the parallel lines, (Fig. 2,) it is requisite that they should each stand at an equal distance from the perpendicular line next to them; otherwise there is no beauty. If there be three of these circles between two parallel lines, and near to a perpendicular line run between them, (Fig. 3,) the most beautiful form perhaps, that they could be placed in, is in an equilateral triangle with the cross line, because there are most equalities. The distance of the two next to the cross line is equal from that, and also equal from the parallel lines. The distance of the third from each parallel is equal, and its distance from each of the other two circles is equal, and is also equal to their distance from one another, and likewise equal to their distance from each end of the cross line. There are two equilateral triangles: one made by the three circles, and the other made by the cross line and two of the sides of the first protracted till they meet that line. And if there be another like it, on the opposite side, to correspond with it and it be taken altogether, the beauty is still greater, where the distances from the lines, in the one, are equal to the distances in the other; also the two next to the cross lines are at equal distances from the other two; or, if you go crosswise, from corner to corner. The two cross lines are also parallel, so that all parts are at an equal distance, and innumerable other equalities might be found.

This simple Equality, without Proportion, is the lowest kind of Regularity, and may be called Simple Beauty. All other beauties and excellencies may be resolved into it. Proportion is Complex Beauty. Thus, if we suppose that there are two points, AB, placed at two inches distance, and the next, C, one inch farther; (Fig. 1,)

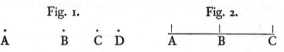

it is requisite, in order to regularity and beauty, if there be another, D, that it should be at half an inch distance; otherwise there is no regularity, and the last, D, would stand out of its proper place; because now the relation that the space C D, bears to B C, is equal to the relation that B C, bears to A B; so that B C D, is exactly similar to A B C. It is evident, this is a more complicated excellency than that which consisted in Equality, because the terms of the relation are here complex, and before were simple. When there are three points set in a right line, it is requisite, in order to regularity, that they should be set at an equal distance, as A B C, (Fig. 2,) where A B, is similar to B C, or the relation of C to B, is the same as of B to A. But in the other are three terms necessary in each of the parts, between which, is the relation, B C D, is as A B C: so that here more simple beauties are omitted, and yet there is a general complex beauty: that is, B C is not as A B, nor is C D as B C, but yet, B C D is as A B C. It is requisite that the consent or regularity of C D to B C, be omitted, for the sake of the harmony of the whole. For although, if C D was perfectly equal to B C, there would be regularity and beauty with respect to them two; yet, if A B be taken into the idea, there is nothing but confusion. And it might be requisite, if these stood with others, even to omit this proposition, for the sake of one more complex still. Thus, if they stood with other points, where B stood at four inches distance from A, C at two from B, and D at six from C: the place where D must stand in, if A, B, C, D, were alone, viz. one inch from C, must be so as to be made proportionate with the other points beneath;

A   B C   D

A   B   C   D

So that although A, B, C, D, are not proportioned, but are confusion among themselves; yet taken with the whole they are proportioned and beautiful.

All beauty consists in similarness or identity of relation. In identity of relation consists all likeness, and all identity between two consists in identity of relation. Thus, when the distance between two is exactly equal, their distance is their relation one to another, the distance is the same, the bodies are two; wherefore this is their correspondency and beauty. So bodies exactly of the same figure, the bodies are two, the relation between the parts of the extremities is the same, and this is their agreement with them. But if there are two bodies of different shapes, having no similarness of relation between the parts of the extremities; this, considered by itself, is a deformity, because being disagrees with being, which must undoubtedly be disagreeable to perceiving being: because what disagrees with Being, must necessarily be disagreeable to Being in general, to every thing that partakes of Entity, and of course to perceiving being; and what agrees with Being, must be agreeable to Being in general, and therefore to perceiving being. But agreeableness of perceiving being is pleasure, and disagreeableness is pain. Disagreement or contrariety to Being, is evidently an approach to Nothing, or a degree of Nothing; which is nothing else but disagreement or contrariety of Being, and the greatest and only evil: And Entity is the greatest and only good. And by how much more perfect Entity is, that is without mixture of Nothing, by so much the more Excellency. Two beings can agree one with another in nothing else but Relation; because otherwise the notion of their twoness (duality,) is destroyed, and they become one.

And so, in every case, what is called Correspondency, Symmetry, Regularity, and the like, may be resolved into Equalities; though the Equalities in a beauty, in any degree complicated, are so numerous, that it would be a most tedious piece of work to enumerate them. There are millions of these Equalities. Of these consist the beautiful shape of flowers, the beauty of the body of man, and of the bodies of other animals. That sort of beauty which is called Natural, as of vines, plants, trees, etc. consists of a very complicated harmony; and all the natural motions, and tendencies, and figures of bodies in the Universe are done according to proportion, and therein is their beauty. Particular disproportions sometimes greatly add to the universal proportion:—So much equality, so much beauty; though it may be noted that the quantity of equality is not to be measured only by the number, but the intenseness, according to the quantity of being. As bodies are shadows of being, so their proportions are shadows of proportion.

The pleasures of the senses, where harmony is not the object of judgment, are the result of equality. Thus in Music, not only in the proportion which the several notes of a tune bear, one among another, but in merely two notes, there is harmony; whereas it is impossible there should be proportion between only two terms. But the proportion is in the particular vibrations of the air, which strike on the ear. And so, in the pleasantness of light, colours, tastes, smells and touch, all arise from proportion of motion. The organs are so contrived that, upon the touch of such and such particles, there shall be a regular and harmonious motion of the animal spirits.

Spiritual harmonies are of vastly larger extent: i.e. the proportions are vastly oftener redoubled, and respect mere beings, and require a vastly larger view to comprehend them; as some simple notes do more affect one, who has not a comprehensive understanding of Music.

The reason, why Equality thus pleases the mind, and Inequality is unpleasing, is because Disproportion, or Inconsistency, is contrary to Being. For Being, if we examine narrowly, is nothing else but Proportion. When one being is inconsistent with another being, then Being is contradicted. But contradiction to Being, is intolerable to perceiving being, and the consent to Being, most pleasing.

Excellency consists in the *Similarness* of one being to another —not merely Equality and Proportion, but any kind of Similarness—thus Similarness of direction. Supposing many globes moving in right lines, it is more beautiful, that they should move all the same way, and according to the same direction, than if they moved disorderly; one, one way, and another, another. This is an universal definition of Excellency:—*The Consent of Being to Being, or Being's Consent to Entity.* The more the Consent is, and the more extensive, the greater is the Excellency.

How exceedingly apt are we, when we are sitting still, and accidentally casting our eye upon some marks or spots in the floor or wall, to be ranging of them into regular parcels and figures: and, if we see a mark out of its place, to be placing of it right, by our imagination; and this even while we are meditating on something else. So we may catch ourselves at observing the rules of harmony and regularity, in the careless motions of our heads or feet, and when playing with our hands, or walking about the room.

EXCELLENCE. 1. When we spake of Excellence in Bodies, we were obliged to borrow the word, *Consent*, from Spiritual things; but Excellence in and among Spirits is in its prime and proper sense, Being's consent to Being. There is no other proper consent but that of *Minds*, even of their Will; which, when it is of Minds towards Minds, it is *Love*, and when of Minds towards other things, it is *Choice*. Wherefore all the Primary and Original beauty or excellence, that is among Minds, is Love; and into this may all be resolved that is found among them.

2. When we spake of External excellency, we said, that *Being's consent to Being*, must needs be agreeable to *Perceiving Being*. But now we are speaking of Spiritual things, we may change the phrase, and say, that *Mind's love to Mind* must needs be lovely to *Beholding Mind;* and Being's love to Being, in general, must needs be agreeable to Being that perceives it, because itself is a participation of Being, in general.

3. As to the proportion of this Love;—to greater Spirits, more, and to less, less;—it is beautiful, as it is a manifestation of love to Spirit or Being in general. And the want of this proportion is a deformity, because it is a manifestation of a defect of such a love. It shows that it is not Being, in general, but something else, that is loved, when love is not in proportion to the Extensiveness and Excellence of Being.

4. Seeing God has so plainly revealed himself to us; and other minds are made in his image, and are emanations from him; we may judge what is the Excellence of other minds, by what is his, which we have shown is Love. His Infinite Beauty, is His Infinite mutual Love of Himself. Now God is the Prime and Original Being, the First and Last, and the Pattern of all, and has the sum of all perfection. We may therefore, doubtless, conclude, that all that is the perfection of Spirits may be resolved into that which is God's perfection, which is Love.

5. There are several degrees of deformity or disagreeableness of dissent from Being. One is, when there is only merely a dissent from Being. This is disagreeable to Being, (for Perceiving Being only is properly Being.) Still more disagreeable is a dissent to very excellent Being, or, as we have explained, to a Being that consents in a high degree to Being, because such a Being by such a consent becomes bigger; and a dissenting from such a Being includes, also, a dissenting from what he consents with, which is other Beings, or Being in general. Another deformity, that is more odious than mere dissent from Being, is, for a Being to dissent from, or not to consent with, a Being who consents with his Being. It is a manifestation of a greater dissent from Being than ordinary; for the Being perceiving, knows that it is natural to Being, to consent with what

consents with it, as we have shown. It therefore manifests an extraordinary dissent, that consent to itself will not draw its consent. The deformity, for the same reason, is greater still, if there be dissent from consenting Being. There are such contrarieties and jars in Being, as must necessarily produce jarring and horror in perceiving Being.

6. Dissent from such Beings, if that be their fixed nature, is a manifestation of Consent to Being in general; for consent to Being is dissent from that, which dissents from Being.

7. Wherefore all Virtue, which is the Excellency of minds, is resolved into *Love to Being;* and nothing is virtuous or beautiful in Spirits, any otherwise than as it is an exercise, or fruit, or manifestation, of this love; and nothing is sinful or deformed in Spirits, but as it is the defect of, or contrary to, these.

RESOLUTIONS

Being sensible that I am unable to do anything without God's help, I do humbly entreat him by his grace, to enable me to keep these Resolutions, so far as they are agreeable to his will, for Christ's sake.

REMEMBER TO READ OVER THESE RESOLUTIONS ONCE A WEEK.

1. *Resolved*, That *I will do whatsoever* I think to be most to the glory of God and my own good, profit and pleasure, in the whole of my duration; without any consideration of the time, whether now, or never so many myriads of ages hence. Resolved to do whatever I think to be my *duty*, and most for the good and advantage of mankind in general. Resolved, so to do, whatever *difficulties* I meet with, how many soever, and how great soever.

2. *Resolved*, To be continually endeavouring to find out some *new contrivance*, and invention, to promote the fore-mentioned things.

3. *Resolved*, If ever I shall fall and grow dull, so as to neglect to keep any part of these Resolutions, to repent of all I can remember, when I come to myself again.

4. *Resolved*, Never *to do* any manner of thing, whether in soul or body, less or more, but what tends to the glory of God, nor *be*, nor *suffer* it, if I can possibly avoid it.

5. *Resolved*, Never to lose one moment of time, but to improve it in the most profitable way I possibly can.

6. *Resolved*, To live with all my might, while I do live.

7. *Resolved*, Never to do any thing, which I should be afraid to do, if it were the last hour of my life.

8. *Resolved*, To act, in all respects, both speaking and doing, as if nobody had been so vile as I, and as if I had committed the same sins, or had the same infirmities or failings as others; and that I will let the knowledge of their failings promote nothing

but shame in myself, and prove only an occasion of my confessing my own sins and misery to God. *Vid. July* 30.

9. *Resolved,* To think much, on all occasions, of my own dying, and of the common circumstances which attend death.

10. *Resolved,* When I feel pain, to think of the pains of Martyrdom, and of Hell.

11. *Resolved,* When I think of any Theorem in divinity to be solved, immediately to do what I can towards solving it, if circumstances do not hinder.

12. *Resolved,* If I take delight in it as a gratification of pride, or vanity, or on any such account, immediately to throw it by.

13. *Resolved,* To be endeavouring to find out fit objects of charity and liberality.

14. *Resolved,* Never to do any thing out of Revenge.

15. *Resolved,* Never to suffer the least motions of anger towards irrational beings.

16. *Resolved,* Never to speak evil of any one, so that it shall tend to his dishonour, more or less, upon no account except for some real good.

17. *Resolved,* That I will live so, as I shall wish I had done when I come to die.

18. *Resolved,* To live so, at all times, as I think is best in my most devout frames, and when I have the clearest notions of the things of the Gospel, and another world.

19. *Resolved,* Never to do any thing, which I should be afraid to do, if I expected it would not be above an hour, before I should hear the last trump.

20. *Resolved,* To maintain the strictest temperance, in eating and drinking.

21. *Resolved,* Never to do any thing, which, if I should see in another, I should count a just occasion to despise him for, or to think any way the more meanly of him.

22. *Resolved,* To endeavour to obtain for myself as much happiness, in the other world, as I possibly can, with all the power, might, vigour, and vehemence, yea violence, I am capable of, or can bring myself to exert, in any way that can be thought of.

23. *Resolved*, Frequently to take some deliberate action, which seems most unlikely to be done, for the glory of God, and trace it back to the original intention, designs and ends of it; and if I find it not to be for God's glory, to repute it as a breach of the fourth Resolution.

24. *Resolved*, Whenever I do any conspicuously evil action, to trace it back, till I come to the original cause; and then, both carefully endeavour to do so no more, and to fight and pray with all my might against the original of it.

25. *Resolved*, To examine carefully, and constantly, what that one thing in me is, which causes me in the least to doubt of the love of God; and to direct all my forces against it.

26. *Resolved*, To cast away such things, as I find do abate my assurance.

27. *Resolved*, Never wilfully to omit any thing, except the omission be for the glory of God; and frequently to examine my omissions.

28. *Resolved*, To study the Scriptures so steadily, constantly and frequently, as that I may find, and plainly perceive myself to grow in the knowledge of the same.

29. *Resolved*, Never to count that a prayer, nor to let that pass as a prayer, nor that as a petition of a prayer, which is so made, that I cannot hope that God will answer it; nor that as a confession, which I cannot hope God will accept.

30. *Resolved*, To strive, every week, to be brought higher in Religion, and to a higher exercise of grace, than I was the week before.

31. *Resolved*, Never to say any thing at all against any body, but when it is perfectly agreeable to the highest degree of christian honour, and of love to mankind, agreeable to the lowest humility, and sense of my own faults and failings, and agreeable to the Golden Rule; often, when I have said any thing against any one, to bring it to, and try it strictly by the test of this Resolution.

32. *Resolved*, To be strictly and firmly faithful to my trust, that that, in Prov. xx, 6, *A faithful man, who can find?* may not be partly fulfilled in me.

33. *Resolved*, To do, always, what I can towards making, maintaining and preserving peace, when it can be done without an over-balancing detriment in other respects. *Dec.* 26, 1722.

34. *Resolved*, In narrations, never to speak any thing but the pure and simple verity.

35. *Resolved*, Whenever I so much question whether I have done my duty, as that my quiet and calm is thereby disturbed, to set it down, and also how the question was resolved. *Dec.* 18, 1722.

36. *Resolved*, Never to speak evil of any, except I have some particular good call to it. *Dec.* 19, 1722.

37. *Resolved*, To enquire every night, as I am going to bed, Wherein I have been negligent,—What sin I have committed,—and wherein I have denied myself;—also, at the end of every week, month and year. *Dec.* 22 *and* 26, 1722.

38. *Resolved*, Never to utter any thing that is sportive, or matter of laughter, on a Lord's day. *Sabbath evening, Dec.* 23, 1722.

39. *Resolved*, Never to do any thing, of which I so much question the lawfulness, as that I intend, at the same time, to consider and examine afterwards, whether it be lawful or not; unless I as much question the lawfulness of the omission.

40. *Resolved*, To enquire every night, before I go to bed, whether I have acted in the best way I possibly could, with respect to eating and drinking. *Jan.* 7, 1723.

41. *Resolved*, To ask myself, at the end of every, day, week, month and year, wherein I could possibly, in any respect, have done better. *Jan.* 11, 1723.

42. *Resolved*, Frequently to renew the dedication of myself to God, which was made at my baptism, which I solemnly renewed, when I was received into the communion of the church, and which I have solemnly re-made this 12th day of January, 1723.

43. *Resolved*, Never, henceforward, till I die, to act as if I were any way my own, but entirely and altogether God's; agreeably to what is to be found in Saturday, Jan. 12th. *Jan.* 12th, 1723.

44. *Resolved*, That no other end but religion, shall have any influence at all on any of my actions; and that no action shall be, in the least circumstance, any otherwise than the religious end will carry it. *Jan.* 12, 1723.

45. *Resolved*, Never to allow any pleasure or grief, joy or sorrow, nor any affection at all, nor any degree of affection, nor any circumstance relating to it, but what helps Religion. *Jan.* 12 *and* 13, 1723.

46. *Resolved*, Never to allow the least measure of any fretting or uneasiness at my father or mother. *Resolved*, To suffer no effects of it, so much as in the least alteration of speech, or motion of my eye; and to be especially careful of it with respect to any of our family.

47. *Resolved*, To endeavour, to my utmost, to deny whatever is not most agreeable to a good and universally sweet and benevolent, quiet, peaceable, contented and easy, compassionate and generous, humble and meek, submissive and obliging, diligent and industrious, charitable and even, patient, moderate, forgiving and sincere, temper; and to do, at all times, what such a temper would lead me to; and to examine strictly, at the end of every week, whether I have so done. *Sabbath Morning, May* 5, 1723.

48. *Resolved*, Constantly, with the utmost niceness and diligence, and the strictest scrutiny, to be looking into the state of my soul, that I may know whether I have truly an interest in Christ or not; that when I come to die, I may not have any negligence respecting this, to repent of. *May* 26, 1723.

49. *Resolved*, That this never shall be, if I can help it.

50. *Resolved*, That I will act so, as I think I shall judge would have been best, and most prudent, when I come into the future world. *July* 5, 1723.

51. *Resolved*, That I will act so, in every respect, as I think I shall wish I had done, if I should at last be damned. *July* 8, 1723.

52. I frequently hear persons in old age, say how they would live, if they were to live their lives over again: *Resolved*, That I will live just so as I can think I shall wish I had done, supposing I live to old age. *July* 8, 1723.

53. *Resolved,* To improve every opportunity, when I am in the best and happiest frame of mind, to cast and venture my soul on the Lord Jesus Christ, to trust and confide in him, and consecrate myself wholly to him; that from this I may have assurance of my safety, knowing that I confide in my Redeemer. *July* 8, 1723.

54. *Resolved,* Whenever I hear any thing spoken in commendation of any person, if I think it would be praiseworthy in me, that I will endeavour to imitate it. *July* 8, 1723.

55. *Resolved,* To endeavour, to my utmost, so to act, as I can think I should do, if I had already seen the happiness of Heaven, and Hell torments. *July* 8, 1723.

56. *Resolved,* Never to give over, nor in the least to slacken, my fight with my corruptions, however unsuccessful I may be.

57. *Resolved,* When I fear misfortunes and adversity, to examine whether I have done my duty, and resolve to do it, and let the event be just as Providence orders it. I will, as far as I can, be concerned about nothing but my duty, and my sin. *June* 9, *and July* 13, 1723.

58. *Resolved,* Not only to refrain from an air of dislike, fretfulness, and anger in conversation, but to exhibit an air of love, cheerfulness and benignity. *May* 27, *and July* 13, 1723.

59. *Resolved,* When I am most conscious of provocations to ill-nature and anger, that I will strive most to feel and act good-naturedly; yea, at such times, to manifest good-nature, though I think that in other respects it would be disadvantageous, and so as would be imprudent at other times. *May* 12, *July* 11, *and July* 13.

60. *Resolved,* Whenever my feelings begin to appear in the least out of order, when I am conscious of the least uneasiness within, or the least irregularity without, I will then subject myself to the strictest examination. *July* 4, *and* 13, 1723.

61. *Resolved,* That I will not give way to that listlessness which I find unbends and relaxes my mind from being fully and fixedly set on religion, whatever excuse I may have for it—that what my listlessness inclines me to do, is best to be done, &c. *May* 21, *and July* 13, 1723.

62. *Resolved*, Never to do any thing but my duty, and then according to Eph. vi, 6—8, to do it willingly and cheerfully, as unto the Lord, and not to man: knowing that whatever good thing any man doth, the same shall he receive of the Lord. *June 25, and July* 13, 1723.

63. On the supposition, that there never was to be but one individual in the world, at any one time, who was properly a complete christian, in all respects of a right stamp, having christianity always shining in its true lustre, and appearing excellent and lovely, from whatever part and under whatever character viewed: *Resolved*, To act just as I would do, if I strove with all my might to be that one, who should live in my time. *Jan.* 14, *and July* 13, 1723.

64. *Resolved*, When I find those "*groanings which cannot be uttered*," of which the Apostle speaks, and those "*breakings of soul* for the longing it hath," of which the Psalmist speaks, Psalm cxix, 20, That I will promote them to the utmost of my power, and that I will not be weary of earnestly endeavouring to vent my desires, nor of the repetitions of such earnestness. *July* 23, *and August* 10, 1723.

65. *Resolved*, Very much to exercise myself in this, all my life long, viz. With the greatest openness, of which I am capable, to declare my ways to God, and lay open my soul to him, all my sins, temptations, difficulties, sorrows, fears, hopes, desires, and every thing, and every circumstance, according to Dr. Manton's Sermon on the 119th Psalm. *July* 26, *and Aug.* 10, 1723.

66. *Resolved*, That I will endeavour always to keep a benign aspect, and air of acting and speaking in all places, and in all companies, except it should so happen that duty requires otherwise.

67. *Resolved*, After afflictions, to enquire, What I am the better for them; What good I have got by them; and, What I might have got by them.

68. *Resolved*, To confess frankly to myself all that which I find in myself, either infirmity or sin; and, if it be what concerns religion, also to confess the whole case to God, and implore needed help. *July* 23, *and August* 10, 1723.

69. *Resolved*, Always to do that, which I shall wish I had done when I see others do it. *Aug.* 11, 1723.

70. Let there be something of benevolence, in all that I speak. *Aug.* 17, 1723.

DIARY

[REMAINDER OF DIARY]

Thursday forenoon, Oct. 4, 1723. Have this day fixed and established it, that Christ Jesus has promised me faithfully, that, if I will do what is my duty, and according to the best of my prudence in the matter, that my condition in this world, shall be better for me than any other condition whatever, and more to my welfare, to all eternity. And, therefore, whatever my condition shall be, I will esteem it to be such; and if I find need of faith in the matter, that I will confess it as impiety before God. *Vid. Resolution* 57, *and June* 9.

Sabbath night, Oct. 7. Have lately erred, in not allowing time enough for conversation.

Friday night, Oct. 12. I see there are some things quite contrary to the soundness and perfection of christianity, in which almost all good men do allow themselves, and where innate corruption has an unrestrained secret vent, which they never take notice of, or think to be no hurt, or cloke under the name of virtue; which things exceedingly darken the brightness, and hide the loveliness, of christianity. Who can understand his errors? O that I might be kept from secret faults!

Sabbath morning, Oct. 14. Narrowly to observe after what manner I act, when I am in a hurry, and to act as much so, at other times, as I can, without prejudice to the business.

Monday morning, Oct. 15. I seem to be afraid, after errors and decays, to give myself the full exercise of spiritual meditation:—Not to give way to such fears.

Thursday, Oct. 18. To follow the example of Mr. B. who, though he meets with great difficulties, yet undertakes them with a smiling countenance, as though he thought them but little; and speaks of them, as if they were very small.

Friday night, Nov. 1. When I am unfit for other business, to perfect myself in writing *characters.*

46

Friday afternoon, Nov. 22. For the time to come, when I am in a lifeless frame in secret prayer, to force myself to expatiate, as if I were praying before others more than I used to do.

Tuesday forenoon, Nov. 26. It is a most evil and pernicious practice, in meditations on afflictions, to sit ruminating on the aggravations of the affliction, and reckoning up the evil, dark circumstances thereof, and dwelling long on the dark side: it doubles and trebles the affliction. And so, when speaking of them to others, to make them as bad as we can, and use our eloquence to set forth our own troubles, is to be all the while making new trouble, and feeding and pampering the old; whereas, the contrary practice, would starve our affliction. If we dwelt on the bright side of things in our thoughts, and extenuated them all that we possibly could, when speaking of them, we should think little of them ourselves, and the affliction would, really, in a great measure, vanish away.

Friday night, Nov. 29. As a help to attention in social prayer, to take special care to make a particular remark, at the beginning of every petition, confession, &c.

Monday morning, Dec. 9. To observe, whether I express any kind of fretting emotion, for the next three weeks.

Thursday night, Dec. 12. If, at any time, I am forced to tell others wherein I think they are somewhat to blame; in order to avoid the important evil that would otherwise ensue, not to tell it to them so, that there shall be a probability of their taking it as the effect of little, fretting, angry emotions of mind.— *Vid. Aug.* 28. When I do want, or am likely to want, good books, to spend time in studying Mathematics, and in reviewing other kinds of old learning; to spend more time in visiting friends, in the more private duties of a pastor, in taking care of worldly business, in going abroad and other things that I may contrive.

Friday morning, Dec. 27. At the end of every month, to examine my behaviour, strictly, by some chapter in the New Testament, more especially made up of rules of life.—At the end of the year, to examine my behaviour by the rules of the New Testament in general, reading many chapters. It would also be convenient, some time at the end of the year, to read, for this purpose, in the book of Proverbs.

Tuesday night, Dec. 31. Concluded never to suffer, nor express, any angry emotions of mind, more or less, except the honour of God calls for it in zeal for him, or to preserve myself from being trampled on.

1724. *Wednesday, Jan.* 1. Not to spend too much time in thinking, even of important and necessary worldly business, and to allow every thing its proportion of thought, according to its urgency and importance.

Thursday night, Jan. 2. These things established—That time gained in things of lesser importance, is as much gained in things of greater; that a minute, gained in times of confusion, conversation, or in a journey, is as good as a minute gained in my study, at my most retired times; and so in general that a minute gained at one time, is as good as at another.

Friday night, Jan. 3. The time and pains laid out in seeking the world, is to be proportioned to the necessity, usefulness, and importance of it, with respect to another world, together with the uncertainty of succeeding, the uncertainty of living, and of retaining; provided, that nothing that our duty enjoins, or that is amiable, be omitted, and nothing sinful or unbecoming be done for the sake of it.

Friday, Jan. 10. [After having written to a considerable extent, in short-hand, which he used, when he wished what he wrote to be effectually concealed from every one but himself, he adds the following.] Remember to act according to Prov. xii. 23, *A prudent man concealeth knowledge.*

Monday, Jan. 20. I have been very much to blame, in that I have not been as full, and plain and downright, in my standing up for virtue and religion, when I have had fair occasion, before those who seemed to take no delight in such things. If such conversation would not be agreeable to them, I have in some degree minced the matter, that I might not displease, and might not speak right against the grain, more than I should have loved to have done with others, to whom it would be agreeable to speak directly for religion. I ought to be exceedingly bold with such persons, not talking in a melancholy strain, but in one confident and fearless, assured of the truth and excellence of the cause.

Monday, Feb. 3. Let every thing have the value now which it will have on a sick bed: and frequently, in my pursuits of whatever kind, let this question come into my mind, "How much shall I value this, on my death-bed?"

Wednesday, Feb. 5. I have not, in times past, in my prayers, enough insisted on the glorifying of God in the world, on the advancement of the kingdom of Christ, the prosperity of the Church and the good of man. Determined, that this objection is without weight, viz. That it is not likely that God will make great alterations in the whole world, and overturnings in kingdoms and nations, only for the prayers of one obscure person, seeing such things used to be done in answer to the united prayers of the whole church; and that if my prayers should have some influence, it would be but imperceptible and small.

Thursday, Feb. 6. More convinced than ever, of the usefulness of free, religious conversation. I find by conversing on Natural Philosophy, that I gain knowledge abundantly faster, and see the reasons of things much more clearly than in private study: wherefore, earnestly to seek, at all times, for religious conversation; for those, with whom I can, at all times, with profit and delight, and with freedom, so converse.

Friday, Feb. 7. *Resolved,* If God will assist me to it, that I will not care about things, when, upon any account, I have prospect of ill-success or adversity; and that I will not think about it, any further than just to do what prudence directs to for prevention, according to Phil. iv. 6, Be careful for nothing; to 1 Pet. v. 7, Cast all your care upon God, for he careth for you; and again, Take no thought for the morrow; and again, Take no thought, saying, What shall *I* eat, and what shall I drink, and wherewithal shall I be clothed: seek ye first the kingdom of God, and all these things shall be added unto you.

Saturday night, Feb. 15. I find that when eating, I cannot be convinced in the time of it, that if I should eat more, I should exceed the bounds of strict temperance, though I have had the experience of two years of the like; and yet, as soon as I have done, in three minutes I am convinced of it. But yet, when I eat again, and remember it, still, while eating, I am fully convinced that I have not eaten what is but for nature, nor can I be convinced that my appetite and feeling is as it was before. It seems to me that I shall be somewhat faint if I leave off then; but when I have finished, I am convinced again, and so it is from time to time.— I have observed that more really seems to be truth, when it makes for my interest, or is, in other respects, according to my inclination, than it seems, if it be otherwise; and it seems to me, that the words in which I express it are more than the thing will properly bear. But if the thing be against my interest, the words of different import seem as much as the thing will properly bear.—Though there is some little seeming, indecorum, as if it looked like affectation, in religious conversation, as there is also in acts of kindness; yet this is to be broke through.

Tuesday, Feb. 18. *Resolved,* To act with sweetness and benevolence, and according to the 47th Resolution, in all bodily dispositions,—sick or well, at ease or in pain, sleepy or watchful, and not to suffer discomposure of body to discompose my mind.

Saturday, Feb. 22. I observe that there are some evil habits which do increase and grow stronger, even in some good people, as they grow older; habits that much obscure the beauty of christianity: some things which are according to their natural tempers, which, in some measure, prevails when they are young in Christ, and the evil disposition, having an unobserved control, the habit at last grows very strong, and commonly regulates the practice until death. By this means, old christians are very commonly, in some respects, more unreasonable than those who are young. I am afraid of contracting such habits, particularly of grudging to give, and to do, and of procrastinating.

Sabbath, Feb. 23. I must be contented, where I have any thing strange or remarkable to tell, not to make it appear so remarkable as it is indeed; lest through the fear of this, and the desire of making a thing appear very remarkable, I should exceed the bounds of simple verity. When I am at a feast, or a meal that very well pleases my appetite, I must not merely take ca to leave off with as much of an appetite as at ordinary meals; for when there is a great variety of dishes, I may do that, after I have eaten twice as much as at other meals, is sufficient. If I act according to my resolution, I shall desire riches no otherwise, than as they are helpful to religion. But this I determine, as what is really evident from many parts of Scripture, that to fallen man, they have a greater tendency to hurt religion.

Monday, March 16. To practice this sort of self-denial, when at sometimes on fair days, I find myself more particularly disposed to regard the glories of the world, than to betake myself to the study of serious religion.

Saturday, May 23. How it comes about I know not, but I have remarked it hitherto, that at those times, when I have read the Scriptures most, I have evermore been most lively and in the best frame.

"AT YALE COLLEGE."

Saturday night, June 6. This week has been a very remarkable week with me, with respect to despondencies, fears, perplexities, multitudes of cares, and distraction of mind: it being the week I came hither to New-Haven, in order to entrance upon the office of Tutor of the College. I have now, abundant reason to be convinced, of the troublesomeness and vexation of the world, and that it never will be another kind of world.

Tuesday, July 7. When I am giving the relation of a thing, remember to abstain from altering either in the matter or manner of speaking, so much, as that, if every one, afterwards, should alter as much, it would at last come to be properly false.

Tuesday, Sept. 2. By a sparingness in diet, and eating as much as may be, what is light and easy of digestion, I shall doubtless be able to think more clearly, and shall gain time; 1. By lengthening out my life; 2. Shall need less time for digestion, after meals; 3. Shall be able to study more closely, without injury to my health; 4. Shall need less time for sleep; 5. Shall more seldom be troubled with the head-ache.

Saturday night, Sept. 12. Crosses of the nature of that, which I met with this week, thrust me quite below all comforts in religion. They appear no more than vanity and stubble, especially when I meet with them so unprepared for them. I shall not be fit to encounter them, except I have a far stronger, and more permanent faith, hope and love.

Wednesday, Sept. 30. It has been a prevailing thought with me, to which I have given place in practice, that it is best, sometimes, to eat or drink, when it will do me no good, because the hurt, that it will do me, will not be equal, to the trouble of denying myself. But I have determined, to suffer that thought to prevail no longer. The hurries of commencement, and diversion of the vacancy, has been the occasion of my sinking so exceedingly, as in the three last weeks.

Monday, Oct. 5. I believe it is a good way, when prone to unprofitable thoughts, to deny myself and break off my thoughts, by keeping diligently to my study, that they may not have time to operate to work me to such a listless frame. I am apt to think it a good way, when I am indisposed to reading and study, to read of my own remarks, the fruit of my study in divinity, &c. to set me agoing again.

Friday, Nov. 6. Felt sensibly, somewhat of that trust and affiance, in Christ, and with delight committing of my soul to him, of which our divines used to speak, and about which, have been somewhat in doubt.

Tuesday, Nov. 10. To mark all that I say in conversation merely to beget in others, a good opinion of myself, and examine it.

Sabbath, Nov. 15. Determined, when I am indisposed to prayer, always to premeditate what to pray for; and that it is better, that the prayer should be of almost any shortness, than that my mind should be almost continually off from what I say.

Sabbath, Nov. 22. Considering that by-standers always copy some faults, which we do not see, ourselves, or of which, at least, we are not so fully sensible; and that there are many secret workings of corruption, which escape our sight, and of which others only are sensible: *Resolved*, therefore, that I will, if I can by any convenient means, learn what faults others find in me, or what things they see in me, that appear any way blame-worthy, unlovely, or unbecoming.

Friday, Feb. 12, 1725. The very thing I now want, to give me a clearer and more immediate view of the perfections and glory of God, is as clear a knowledge of the manner of God's exerting himself, with respect to Spirits and Mind, as I have, of his operations concerning Matter and Bodies.

Tuesday, Feb. 16. A virtue, which I need in a higher degree, to give a beauty and lustre to my behaviour, is gentleness. If I had more of an air of gentleness, I should be much mended.

Friday, May 21. If ever I am inclined to turn to the opinion of any other Sect: *Resolved,* Beside the most deliberate consideration, earnest prayer, &c., privately to desire all the help that can possibly be afforded me, from some of the most judicious men in the country, together with the prayers of wise and holy men, however strongly persuaded I may seem to be, that I am in the right.

Saturday, May 22. When I reprove for faults, whereby I am in any way injured, to defer, till the thing is quite over and done with; for that is the way, both to reprove aright, and without the least mixture of spirit, or passion, and to have reproofs effectual, and not suspected.

Friday, May 28. It seems to me, that whether I am now converted or not, I am so settled in the state I am in, that I shall go on in it all my life. But, however settled I may be, yet I will continue to pray to God, not to suffer me to be deceived about it, nor to sleep in an unsafe condition; and ever and anon, will call all into question and try myself, using for helps, some of our old divines, that God may have opportunities to answer my prayers, and the Spirit of God to show me my error, if I am in one.

Saturday night, June 6. I am sometimes in a frame so listless, that there is no other way of profitably improving time, but conversation, visiting, or recreation, or some bodily exercise. However it may be best in the first place, before resorting to either of these, to try the whole circle of my mental employments.

Nov. 16. When confined at Mr. Stiles'. I think it would be of special advantage to me, with respect to my truer interest, as near as I can in my studies, to observe this rule. To let half a day's, or at most, a day's study in other things, be succeeded, by half a day's, or a day's study in Divinity.

One thing wherein I have erred, as I would be complete in all social duties, is, in neglecting to write letters to friends. And I would be forewarned of the danger of neglecting to visit my friends and relations, when we are parted.

When one suppresses thoughts that tend to divert the run of the mind's operations from Religion, whether they are melancholy, or anxious, or passionate, or any others; there is this good effect of it, that it keeps the mind in its freedom. Those thoughts are stopped in the beginning, that would have set the mind agoing in that stream.

There are a great many exercises, that for the present, seem not to help, but rather impede, Religious meditation and affections, the fruit of which is reaped afterwards, and is of far greater worth than what is lost; for thereby the mind is only for the present diverted; but what is attained is, upon occasion, of use for the whole life-time.

Sept. 26, 1726. 'Tis just about three years, that I have been for the most part in a low, sunk estate and condition, miserably senseless to what I used to be, about spiritual things. 'Twas three years ago, the week before commencement; just about the same time this year, I began to be somewhat as I used to be.

Jan. 1728. I think Christ has recommended rising early in the morning, by his rising from the grave very early.

Jan. 22, 1734. I judge that it is best, when I am in a good frame for divine contemplation, or engaged in reading the Scriptures, or any study of divine subjects, that ordinarily, I will not be interrupted by going to dinner, but will forego my dinner, rather than be broke off.

April 4, 1735. When at any time, I have a sense of any divine thing, then to turn it in my thoughts, to a practical improvement. As for instance, when I am in my mind, on some argument for the Truth of Religion, the Reality of a Future State, and the like, then to think with myself, how safely I may venture to sell all, for a future good. So when, at any time, I have a more than ordinary sense of the Glory of the Saints, in another world; to think how well it is worth my while, to deny myself, and to sell all that I have for this Glory, &c.

May, 18. My mind at present is, never to suffer my thoughts and meditations, at all to ruminate.

June 11. To set apart days of meditation on particular subjects; as sometimes, to set apart a day for the consideration of the Greatness of my Sins; at another, to consider the Dreadfulness and Certainty, of the Future Misery of Ungodly men; at another, the Truth and Certainty of Religion; and so, of the Great Future Things promised and threatened in the Scriptures.

SARAH PIERREPONT

They say there is a young lady in [New Haven] who is beloved of that Great Being, who made and rules the world, and that there are certain seasons in which this Great Being, in some way or other invisible, comes to her and fills her mind with exceeding sweet delight, and that she hardly cares for any thing, except to meditate on him—that she expects after a while to be received up where he is, to be raised up out of the world and caught up into heaven; being assured that he loves her too well to let her remain at a distance from him always. There she is to dwell with him, and to be ravished with his love and delight forever. Therefore, if you present all the world before her, with the richest of its treasures, she disregards it and cares not for it, and is unmindful of any pain or affliction. She has a strange sweetness in her mind, and singular purity in her affections; is most just and conscientious in all her conduct; and you could not persuade her to do any thing wrong or sinful, if you would give her all the world, lest she should offend this Great Being. She is of a wonderful sweetness, calmness and universal benevolence of mind; especially after this Great God has manifested himself to her mind. She will sometimes go about from place to place, singing sweetly; and seems to be always full of joy and pleasure; and no one knows for what. She loves to be alone, walking in the fields and groves, and seems to have some one invisible always conversing with her.

PERSONAL NARRATIVE

I had a variety of concerns and exercises about my soul from my childhood;[1] but had two more remarkable seasons of awakening, before I met with that change by which I was brought to those new dispositions, and that new sense of things, that I have since had. The first time was when I was a boy, some years before I went to college, at a time of remarkable awakening in my father's congregation,[2] I was then very much affected for many months, and concerned about the things of religion, and my soul's salvation; and was abundant in duties. I used to pray five times a day in secret, and to spend much time in religious talk with other boys; and used to meet with them to pray together. I experienced I know not what kind of delight in religion. My mind was much engaged in it, and had much selfrighteous pleasure; and it was my delight to abound in religious duties. I with some of my schoolmates joined together, and built a booth in a swamp, in a very retired spot, for a place of prayer. And besides, I had particular secret places of my own in the woods, where I used to retire by myself; and was from time to time much affected. My affections seemed to be lively and easily moved, and I seemed to be in my element when engaged in religious duties. And I am ready to think, many are deceived with such affections, and such a kind of delight as I then had in religion, and mistake it for grace.

But in process of time, my convictions and affections wore off; and I entirely lost all those affections and delights and left off secret prayer, at least as to any constant performance of it; and returned like a dog to his vomit, and went on in the ways of sin. Indeed I was at times very uneasy, especially towards the latter part of my time at college; when it pleased God, to

[1] Superior figures in the text refer to notes so numbered, to be found under the title of the selection in the section of Notes at the end of this volume.

seize me with a pleurisy; in which he brought me nigh to the grave, and shook me over the pit of hell. And yet, it was not long after my recovery, before I fell again into my old ways of sin. But God would not suffer me to go on with any quietness; I had great and violent inward struggles, till, after many conflicts with wicked inclinations, repeated resolutions, and bonds that I laid myself under by a kind of vows to God, I was brought wholly to break off all former wicked ways, and all ways of known outward sin; and to apply myself to seek salvation, and practise many religious duties; but without that kind of affection and delight which I had formerly experienced. My concern now wrought more by inward struggles and conflicts, and selfreflections. I made seeking my salvation the main business of my life. But yet, it seems to me, I sought after a miserable manner; which has made me sometimes since to question, whether ever it issued in that which was saving; being ready to doubt, whether such miserable seeking ever succeeded. I was indeed brought to seek salvation in a manner that I never was before; I felt a spirit to part with all things in the world, for an interest in Christ. My concern continued and prevailed, with many exercising thoughts and inward struggles; but yet it never seemed to be proper to express that concern by the name of terror.

From my childhood up, my mind had been full of objections against the doctrine of God's sovereignty, in choosing whom he would to eternal life, and rejecting whom he pleased; leaving them eternally to perish, and be everlastingly tormented in hell. It used to appear like a horrible doctrine to me. But I remember the time very well, when I seemed to be convinced, and fully satisfied, as to this sovereignty of God, and his justice in thus eternally disposing of men, according to his sovereign pleasure. But never could give an account, how, or by what means, I was thus convinced, not in the least imagining at the time, nor a long time after, that there was any extraordinary influence of God's Spirit in it; but only that now I saw further, and my reason apprehended the justice and reasonableness of it. However, my mind rested in it; and it put an end to all those cavils and objections. And there has been a wonderful alteration in my mind, in respect to the doctrine of God's sovereignty, from that day to this; so that I scarce ever have found so much as the rising of an objection against it, in the most absolute sense, in God's shewing mercy to whom he will shew mercy, and hardening whom he will. God's absolute sovereignty and justice, with respect to salvation and damnation, is what my mind seems to rest assured of, as much as of any thing that I see with my eyes; at least it is so at times. But I have often, since that first conviction, had quite another kind of sense of God's sovereignty than I had then. I have often since had not only a conviction, but a delightful conviction. The doctrine has very often appeared exceeding pleasant, bright, and sweet. Absolute sovereignty is what I love to ascribe to God. But my first conviction was not so.

The first instance that I remember of that sort of inward, sweet delight in God and divine things that I have lived much in since, was on reading those words, I Tim. **i. 17.** *Now unto the King eternal, immortal, invisible, the only wise God, be honor and glory for ever and ever, Amen.* As I read the words, there came into my soul, and was as it were diffused through it, a sense of the glory of the Divine Being; a new sense, quite different from any thing I ever experienced before. Never any words of scripture seemed to me as these words did. I thought with myself, how excellent a Being that was, and how happy I should be, if I might enjoy that God, and be rapt up to him in heaven, and be as it were swallowed up in him for ever! I kept saying, and as it were singing over these words of scripture to myself; and went to pray to God that I might enjoy him, and prayed in a manner quite different from what I used to do; with a new sort of affection. But it never came into my thought, that there was any thing spiritual, or of a saving nature in this.

From about that time, I began to have a new kind of apprehensions and ideas of Christ, and the work of redemption, and the glorious way of salvation by him. An inward, sweet sense of these things, at times, came into my heart; and my soul was led away in pleasant views and contemplations of them. And my mind was greatly engaged to spend my time in reading and meditating on Christ, on the beauty and excellency of his person, and the lovely way of salvation by free grace in him. I found no books so delightful to me, as those that treated of these subjects. Those words Cant. ii. 1, used to be abundantly with me, *I am the Rose of Sharon, and the Lilly of the valleys.* The words seemed to me, sweetly to represent the loveliness and beauty of Jesus Christ. The whole book of Canticles used to be pleasant to me, and I used to be much in reading it, about that time; and found, from time to time, an inward sweetness, that would carry me away, in my contemplations. This I know not how to express otherwise, than by a calm, sweet abstraction of soul from all the concerns of this world; and sometimes a kind of vision, or fixed ideas and imaginations, of being alone in the mountains, or some solitary wilderness, far from all mankind, sweetly conversing with Christ, and wrapt and swallowed up in God. The sense I had of divine things, would often of a sudden kindle up, as it were, a sweet burning in my heart; an ardor of soul, that I know not how to express.

Not long after I first began to experience these things, I gave an account to my father of some things that had passed in my mind. I was pretty much affected by the discourse we had together; and when the discourse was ended, I walked abroad alone, in a solitary place in my father's pasture, for contemplation. And as I was walking there, and looking up on the sky and clouds, there came into my mind so sweet a sense of the glorious *majesty* and *grace* of God, that I know not how to express. I seemed to see them both in a sweet conjunction; majesty and meekness joined together; it was a sweet, and gentle, and holy majesty; and also a majestic meekness; an awful sweetness; a high, and great, and holy gentleness.

After this my sense of divine things gradually increased, and became more and more lively, and had more of that inward sweetness. The appearance of every thing was altered; there seemed to be, as it were, a calm, sweet cast, or appearance of divine glory, in almost every thing. God's excellency, his wisdom, his purity and love, seemed to appear in every thing; in the sun, moon, and stars; in the clouds, and blue sky; in the grass, flowers, trees; in the water, and all nature; which used greatly to fix my mind. I often used to sit and view the moon for continuance; and in the day, spent much time in viewing the clouds and sky, to behold the sweet glory of God in these things; in the mean time, singing forth, with a low voice my contemplations of the Creator and Redeemer. And scarce any thing, among all the works of nature, was so sweet to me as thunder and lightning; formerly, nothing had been so terrible to me. Before, I used to be uncommonly terrified with thunder, and to be struck with terror when I saw a thunder storm rising; but now, on the contrary, it rejoiced me. I felt God, so to speak, at the first appearance of a thunder storm; and used to take the opportunity, at such times, to fix myself in order to view the clouds, and see the lightnings play, and hear the majestic and awful voice of God's thunder, which oftentimes was exceedingly entertaining, leading me to sweet contemplations of my great and glorious God. While thus engaged, it always seemed natural to me to sing, or chant for my meditations; or, to speak my thoughts in soliloquies with a singing voice.

I felt then great satisfaction, as to my good state; but that did not content me. I had vehement longings of soul after God and Christ, and after more holiness, wherewith my heart seemed to be full, and ready to break; which often brought to my mind the words of the Psalmist, Psal. cxix. 28. *My soul breaketh for the longing it hath*. I often felt a mourning and lamenting in my heart, that I had not turned to God sooner, that I might have had more time to grow in grace. My mind was greatly fixed on divine things; almost perpetually in the contemplation of them. I spent most of my time in thinking of divine things, year after year; often walking alone in the woods, and solitary places, for meditation, soliloquy, and prayer, and converse with God; and it was always my manner, at such times, to sing forth my contemplations. I was almost constantly in ejaculatory prayer, wherever I was. Prayer seemed to be natural to me, as the breath by which the inward burnings of my heart had vent. The delights which I now felt

in the things of religion, were of an exceeding different kind
from those before mentioned, that I had when a boy; and what
I then had no more notion of, than one born blind has of
pleasant and beautiful colors. They were of a more inward,
pure, soul animating and refreshing nature. Those former delights never reached the heart; and did not arise from any sight
of the divine excellency of the things of God; or any taste of the
soul satisfying and life-giving good there is in them.

My sense of divine things seemed gradually to increase, until
I went to preach at Newyork,[3] which was about a year and a
half after they began; and while I was there, I felt them, very
sensibly, in a much higher degree than I had done before. My
longings after God and holiness, were much increased. Pure
and humble, holy and heavenly Christianity, appeared exceeding
amiable to me. I felt a burning desire to be in every thing a
complete Christian; and conformed to the blessed image of
Christ; and that I might live, in all things, according to the
pure, sweet and blessed rules of the gospel. I had an eager
thirsting after progress in these things; which put me upon
pursuing and pressing after them. It was my continual strife
day and night, and constant inquiry, how I should *be* more
holy, and *live* more holily, and more becoming a child of God,
and a disciple of Christ. I now sought an increase of grace and
holiness, and a holy life, with much more earnestness, than ever
I sought grace before I had it. I used to be continually examining myself, and studying and contriving for likely ways and
means, how I should live holily, with far greater diligence and
earnestness, than ever I pursued any thing in my life; but yet
with too great a dependence on my own strength; which afterwards proved a great damage to me. My experience had not
then taught me, as it has done since, my extreme feebleness and
impotence, every manner of way; and the bottomless depths of
secret corruption and deceit there was in my heart. However,
I went on with my eager pursuit after more holiness, and conformity to Christ.

The heaven I desired was a heaven of holiness; to be with
God, and to spend my eternity in divine love, and holy com-

munion with Christ. My mind was very much taken up with contemplations on heaven, and the enjoyments there; and living there in perfect holiness, humility and love: And it used at that time to appear a great part of the happiness of heaven, that there the saints could express their love to Christ. It appeared to me a great clog and burden, that what I felt within, I could not express as I desired. The inward ardor of my soul, seemed to be hindered and pent up, and could not freely flame out as it would. I used often to think, how in heaven this principle should freely and fully vent and express itself. Heaven appeared exceedingly delightful, as a world of love; and that all happiness consisted in living in pure, humble, heavenly, divine love.

I remember the thoughts I used then to have of holiness; and said sometimes to myself, "I do certainly know that I love holiness, such as the gospel prescribes." It appeared to me, that there was nothing in it but what was ravishingly lovely; the highest beauty and amiableness . . . a *divine* beauty; far purer than any thing here upon earth; and that every thing else was like mire and defilement, in comparison of it.

Holiness, as I then wrote down some of my contemplations on it, appeared to me to be of a sweet, pleasant, charming, serene, calm nature; which brought an inexpressible purity, brightness, peacefulness and ravishment to the soul. In other words, that it made the soul like a field or garden of God, with all manner of pleasant flowers; all pleasant, delightful, and undisturbed; enjoying a sweet calm, and the gently vivifying beams of the sun. The soul of a true Christian, as I then wrote my meditations, appeared like such a little white flower as we see in the spring of the year; low and humble on the ground, opening its bosom to receive the pleasant beams of the sun's glory; rejoicing as it were in a calm rapture; diffusing around a sweet fragrancy; standing peacefully and lovingly, in the midst of other flowers round about; all in like manner opening their bosoms, to drink in the light of the sun. There was no part of creature holiness, that I had so great a sense of its loveliness, as humility, brokenness of heart and poverty of spirit; and there was nothing that I so earnestly longed for. My heart panted after this, to lie low before God, as in the dust; that I might be nothing, and that God might be ALL, that I might become as a little child.

While at Newyork, I was sometimes much affected with reflections of my past life, considering how late it was before I began to be truly religious; and how wickedly I had lived till then; and once so as to weep abundantly, and for a considerable time together.

On *January* 12, 1723. I made a solemn dedication of myself to God,[4] and wrote it down; giving up myself, and all that I had to God; to be for the future, in no respect, my own; to act as one that had no right to himself, in any respect. And solemnly vowed, to take God for my whole portion and felicity; looking on nothing else, as any part of my happiness, nor acting as if it were; and his law for the constant rule of my obedience: engaging to fight, with all my might, against the world, the flesh, and the devil, to the end of my life. But I have reason to be infinitely humbled, when I consider, how much I have failed, of answering my obligation.

I had, then, abundance of sweet, religious conversation, in the family where I lived, with Mr. John Smith, and his pious mother. My heart was knit in affection, to those, in whom were appearances of true piety; and I could bear the thoughts of no other companions, but such as were holy, and the disciples of the blessed Jesus. I had great longings, for the advancement of Christ's kingdom in the world; and my secret prayer used to be, in great part, taken up in praying for it. If I heard the least hint, of any thing that happened, in any part of the world, that appeared, in some respect or other, to have a favourable aspect, on the interests of Christ's kingdom, my soul eagerly catched at it; and it would much animate and refresh me. I used to be eager to read public news-letters, mainly for that end; to see if I could not find some news, favourable to the interest of religion in the world.

I very frequently used to retire into a solitary place, on the banks of Hudson's River, at some distance from the city, for contemplation on divine things and secret converse with God:

and had many sweet hours there. Sometimes Mr. Smith and I walked there together, to converse on the things of God; and our conversation used to turn much on the advancement of Christ's kingdom in the world, and the glorious things that God would accomplish for his church in the latter days. I had then, and at other times, the greatest delight in the holy scriptures, of any book whatsoever. Oftentimes in reading it, every word seemed to touch my heart. I felt a harmony between something in my heart, and those sweet and powerful words. I seemed often to see so much light exhibited by every sentence, and such a refreshing food communicated, that I could not get along in reading; often dwelling long on one sentence, to see the wonders contained in it; and yet almost every sentence seemed to be full of wonders.

I came away from Newyork in the month of April, 1723, and had a most bitter parting with Madam Smith and her son. My heart seemed to sink within me, at leaving the family and city, where I had enjoyed so many sweet and pleasant days. I went from New York to Wethersfield, by water; and as I sailed away, I kept sight of the city as long as I could. However, that night after this sorrowful parting, I was greatly comforted in God at Westchester, where we went ashore to lodge: and had a pleasant time of it all the voyage to Saybrook. It was sweet to me to think of meeting dear christians in heaven, where we should never part more. At Saybrook we went ashore to lodge on Saturday, and there kept the Sabbath; where I had a sweet and refreshing season, walking alone in the fields.

After I came home to Windsor, I remained much in a like frame of mind, as when at Newyork; only sometimes I felt my heart ready to sink, with the thoughts of my friends at Newyork. My support was in contemplations on the heavenly state; as I find in my Diary of May 1, 1723. It was a comfort to think of that state, where there is fulness of joy; where reigns heavenly, calm, and delightful love, without alloy; where there are continually the dearest expressions of this love; where is the enjoyment of the persons loved, without ever parting; where those persons who appear so lovely in this world, will really be inexpressibly more lovely, and full of love to us. And how sweetly will the mutual lovers join together, to sing the praises of God and the Lamb! How will it fill us with joy to think, that this enjoyment, these sweet exercises, will never cease, but will last to all eternity. . . . I continued much in the same frame, in the general, as when at Newyork, till I went to Newhaven, as Tutor of the College: particularly, once at Bolton, on a journey from Boston, while walking out alone in the fields. After I went to Newhaven, I sunk in religion; my mind being diverted from my eager pursuits after holiness, by some affairs, that greatly perplexed and distracted my thoughts.

In September, 1725, I was taken ill at Newhaven, and while endeavouring to go home to Windsor, was so ill at the North Village, that I could go no farther; where I lay sick, for about a quarter of a year. In this sickness, God was pleased to visit me again, with the sweet influences of his Spirit. My mind was greatly engaged there, on divine and pleasant contemplations, and longings of soul. I observed, that those who watched with me, would often be looking out wishfully for the morning; which brought to my mind those words of the Psalmist, and which my soul with delight made its own language, *My soul waiteth for the Lord, more than they that watch for the morning; I say, more than they that watch for the morning;* and when the light of day came in at the window, it refreshed my soul, from one morning to another. It seemed to be some image of the light of God's glory.

I remember, about that time, I used greatly to long for the conversion of some, that I was concerned with; I could gladly honour them, and with delight be a servant to them, and lie at their feet, if they were but truly holy. But some time after this, I was again greatly diverted with some temporal concerns, that exceedingly took up my thoughts, greatly to the wounding of my soul; and went on, through various exercises, that it would be tedious to relate, which gave me much more experience of my own heart, than I ever had before.

Since I came to this town,[5] I have often had sweet complacency in God, in views of his glorious perfections and the excellency of Jesus Christ. God has appeared to me a glorious and lovely Being, chiefly on account of his holiness. The holiness of God has always appeared to me the most lovely of all his attributes. The doctrines of God's absolute sovereignty, and free grace, in shewing mercy to whom he would shew mercy; and man's absolute dependence on the operations of God's Holy Spirit, have very often appeared to me as sweet and glorious doctrines. These doctrines have been much my delight. God's sovereignty has ever appeared to me, great part of his glory. It has often been my delight to approach God, and adore him as a sovereign God, and ask sovereign mercy of him.

I have loved the doctrines of the gospel; they have been to my soul like green pastures. The gospel has seemed to me the richest treasure; the treasure that I have most desired, and longed that it might dwell richly in me. The way of salvation by Christ has appeared, in a general way, glorious and excellent, most pleasant and most beautiful. It has often seemed to me, that it would in a great measure spoil heaven, to receive it in any other way. That text has often been affecting and delightful to me, Isa. xxxii. 2. *A man shall be an hiding place from the wind, and a covert from the tempest,&c.*

It has often appeared to me delightful, to be united to Christ; to have him for my head, and to be a member of his body; also to have Christ for my teacher and prophet. I very often think with sweetness, and longings, and pantings of soul, of being a little child, taking hold of Christ, to be led by him through the wilderness of this world. That text, Matth. xviii. 3, has often been sweet to me, *except ye be converted and become as little children, &c.* I love to think of coming to Christ, to receive salvation of him, poor in spirit, and quite empty of self, humbly exalting him alone; cut off entirely from my own root, in order to grow into, and out of Christ; to have God in Christ to be all in all; and to live by faith in the son of God, a life of humble, unfeigned confidence in him. That scripture has often been sweet to me, Psal. cxv. 1. *Not unto us, O Lord, not unto us, but unto thy name give glory, for thy mercy, and for thy truth's sake.* And those words of Christ, Luke x. 21. *In that hour Jesus rejoiced in spirit, and said, I thank thee, O Father, Lord of heaven and earth, that thou hast hid these things from the wise and prudent, and hast revealed them unto babes: Even so, Father, for so it seemed good in thy sight.* That sovereignty of God which Christ rejoiced in, seemed to me worthy of such joy; and that rejoicing seemed to shew the excellency of Christ, and of what spirit he was.

Sometimes, only mentioning a single word caused my heart to burn within me; or only seeing the name of Christ, or the name of some attribute of God. And God has appeared glorious to me, on account of the Trinity. It has made me have exalting thoughts of God, that he subsists in three persons; Father, Son and Holy Ghost. The sweetest joys and delights I have experienced, have not been those that have arisen from a hope of my own good estate; but in a direct view of the glorious things of the gospel. When I enjoy this sweetness, it seems to carry me above the thoughts of my own estate; it seems at such times a loss that I cannot bear, to take off my eye from the glorious pleasant object I behold without me, to turn my eye in upon myself, and my own good estate.

My heart has been much on the advancement of Christ' kingdom in the world. The histories of the past advancement of Christ's kingdom have been sweet to me. When I have read histories of past ages, the pleasantest thing in all my reading has been, to read of the kingdom of Christ being promoted. And when I have expected, in my reading, to come to any such thing I have rejoiced in the prospect, all the way as I read. And my mind has been much entertained and delighted with the scripture promises and prophecies, which relate to the future glorious advancement of Christ's kingdom upon earth.

I have sometimes had a sense of the excellent fulness of Christ, and his meetness and suitableness as a Saviour; whereby he has appeared to me, far above all, the chief of ten thousand. His blood and atonement have appeared sweet, and his righteousness sweet; which was always accompanied with ardency of spirit; and inward strugglings and breathings, and groanings that cannot be uttered, to be emptied of myself, and swallowed up in Christ.

Once, as I rode out into the woods for my health, in 1737, having alighted from my horse in a retired place, as my manner commonly has been, to walk for divine contemplation and prayer, I had a view that for me was extraordinary, of the glory of the Son of God, as Mediator between God and man, and his wonderful, great, full, pure and sweet grace and love, and meek and gentle condescension. This grace that appeared so calm and sweet, appeared also great above the heavens. The person of Christ appeared ineffably excellent with an excellency great enough to swallow up all thought and conception . . . which continued as near as I can judge, about an hour; which kept me the greater part of the time in a flood of tears, and weeping aloud. I felt an ardency of soul to be, what I know not otherwise how to express, emptied and annihilated; to lie in the dust, and to be full of Christ alone; to love him with a holy and pure love; to trust in him; to live upon him; to serve and follow him; and to be perfectly sanctified and made pure, with a divine and heavenly purity. I have, several other times, had views very much of the same nature, and which have had the same effects.

I have many times had a sense of the glory of the third person in the Trinity, in his office of Sanctifier; in his holy operations, communicating divine light and life to the soul. God, in the communications of his Holy Spirit, has appeared as an infinite fountain of divine glory and sweetness; being full, and sufficient to fill and satisfy the soul; pouring forth itself in sweet communications; like the sun in its glory, sweetly and pleasantly diffusing light and life. And I have sometimes had an affecting sense of the exelency of the word of God, as a word of life; as the light of life; a sweet, excellent lifegiving word; accompanied with a thirsting after that word, that it might dwell richly in my heart.

Often, since I lived in this town, I have had very affecting views of my own sinfulness and vileness; very frequently to such a degree as to hold me in a kind of loud weeping, sometimes for a considerable time together; so that I have often been forced to shut myself up. I have had a vastly greater sense of my own wickedness, and the badness of my heart, than ever I had before my conversion. It has often appeared to me, that if God should mark iniquity against me, I should appear the very worst of all mankind; of all that have been, since the beginning of the world to this time; and that I should have by far the lowest place in hell. When others, that have come to talk with me about their soul concerns, have expressed the sense they have had of their own wickedness, by saying that it seemed to them, that they were as bad as the devil himself; I thought their expressions seemed exceeding faint and feeble, to represent my wickedness.

My wickedness, as I am in myself, has long appeared to me perfectly ineffable, and swallowing up all thought and imagination; like an infinite deluge, or mountain over my head. I know not how to express better what my sins appear to me to be, than by heaping infinite upon infinite, and multiplying infinite by infinite. Very often, for these many years, these expressions are in my mind, and in my mouth, "Infinite upon infinite . . . Infinite upon infinite!" When I look into my heart, and take a view of my wickedness, it looks like an abyss infinitely deeper than hell. And it appears to me, that were it not for free grace, exalted and raised up to the infinite height of all the fulness and glory of the great Jehovah, and the arm of his power and grace stretched forth in all the majesty of his power, and in all the glory of his sovereignty, I should appear sunk down in my sins below hell itself; far beyond the sight of every thing, but the eye of sovereign grace, that can pierce even down to such a depth. And yet it seems to me, that my conviction of sin is exceeding small, and faint; it is enough to amaze me, that I have no more sense of my sin. I know certainly, that I have very little sense of my sinfulness. When I have had turns of weeping and crying for my sins I thought I knew at the time, that my repentance was nothing to my sin.

I have greatly longed of late, for a broken heart, and to lie low before God; and, when I ask for humility, I cannot bear the thoughts of being no more humble than other Christians

It seems to me, that though their degrees of humility may be suitable for them, yet it would be a vile selfexaltation in me, not to be the lowest in humility of all mankind. Others speak of their longing to be "humbled to the dust;" that may be a proper expression for them, but I always think of myself, that I ought, and it is an expression that has long been natural for me to use in prayer, "to lie infinitely low before God." And it is affecting to think, how ignorant I was, when a young Christian, of the bottomless, infinite depths of wickedness, pride, hypocrisy and deceit, left in my heart.

I have a much greater sense of my universal, exceeding dependence on God's grace and strength, and mere good pleasure, of late, than I used formerly to have; and have experienced more of an abhorrence of my own righteousness. The very thought of any joy arising in me, on any consideration of my own amiableness, performances, or experiences, or any goodness of heart or life, is nauseous and detestable to me. And yet I am greatly afflicted with a proud and selfrighteous spirit, much more sensibly than I used to be formerly. I see that serpent rising and putting forth its head continually, every where, all around me.

Though it seems to me, that, in some respects, I was a far better Christian, for two or three years after my first conversion, than I am now; and lived in a more constant delight and pleasure; yet, of late years, I have had a more full and constant sense of the absolute sovereignty of God, and a delight in that sovereignty; and have had more of a sense of the glory of Christ, as a Mediator revealed in the gospel. On one Saturday night, in particular, I had such a discovery of the excellency of the gospel above all other doctrines, that I could not but say to myself, "This is my chosen light, my chosen doctrine;" and of Christ, "This is my chosen Prophet." It appeared sweet, beyond all expression, to follow Christ, and to be taught, and enlightened, and instructed by him; to learn of him, and live to him. Another Saturday night, (*January* 1739) I had such a sense, how sweet and blessed a thing it was to walk in the way of duty; to do that which was right and meet to be done, and agreeable to the holy mind of God; that it caused me to break forth into a kind of loud weeping, which held me some time, so that I was forced to shut myself up, and fasten the doors. I could not but, as it were, cry out, "How happy are they which do that which is right in the sight of God! They are blessed indeed, they are the happy ones!" I had, at the same time, a very affecting sense, how meet and suitable it was that God should govern the world, and order all things according to his own pleasure; and I rejoiced in it, that God reigned, and that his will was done.

NARRATIVE OF SURPRISING CONVERSIONS

My Letter to a Brother [the Reverend Benjamin Colman]
May 30. 35.

Dear Sir

In answer to your Desire, I here send you a Particular account of the Present Extraordinary circumstances of this Town, & the neighbouring Towns with Respect to Religion. I have observed that the Town for this several years have gradually been Reforming; There has appeared Less & Less of a party spirit, & a contentious disposition, which before had Prevail'd for many years between two Parties in the Town. The young People also have been Reforming more and more; They by degrees Left off their frolicking, and have been observably more decent in their attendance on the Publick worship. The winter before Last there appeared a strange flexibleness in the young People of the Town, and an unusual disposition to Hearken to Counsel, on this Occasion; It had been their manner of a Long Time, & for Ought I know, alwaies, to make sabbath day nights & Lecture days, to be Especially Times of diversion, & Company Keeping: I then Preach'd a sermon on the Sabbath before the Lecture, to show them the unsuitableness, & Inconvenience of the Practice, & to Perswade them to Reform it; & urged it on Heads of Families that It should be a thing agreed among them to Govern their Families, & keep them in at those times. & There happen'd to be at my house the Evening after, men that belonged to the several parts of the Town, to whom I moved that they should desire the Heads of Families, in my name, to meet together in their several neighbourhoods, that they might Know Each others minds, and agree Every one to restrain his Family; which was done, & my motion Complied with throughout the Town; but the Parents found Little or no occasion for the Exercise of Government in the case; for the young People declared themselves convinced by what they had heard, and willing of themselves to Comply with the Counsel Given them; & I suppose it was almost universally complied with thenceforward. After this there began to be a Remarkeable Religious Concern among some Farm Houses, at a Place Called Pascommuck, & five or six that I hoped were savingly wrought upon there. & in April there was a very sudden and awfull death of a young man in Town, in the very Bloom of his youth, who was violently siezed with a Pleurisy & taken Immediately out of his head, and died in two days; which much affected many young People in the Town. This was followed with another death of a young married woman, who was in Great Distress in the Beginning of her Illness, but was hopefully Converted before her death; so that she died full of Comfort, and in a most Earnest & moving manner, warning & counselling others, which I believe much contributed to the solemnizing of the spirits of the young People in the Town; and there began Evidently to appear more of a Religious concern upon Peoples minds. In the Fall of the year I moved to the young People that they should set up Religious meetings, on Evenings after Lectures, which they complied with; this was followed with the death of an Elderly Person in the Town, which was attended with very unusual Circumstances, which much affected many People. about that Time began the Great noise that there was in this Part of the Countrey about Arminianism, which seemed strangely to be overruled for the Promoting of Religion; People seemed to be Put by it upon Enquiring, with concern & Engagedness of mind, what was the way of salvation, and what were the Terms of our acceptance with God; & what was said Publickly on that occasion; however found fault with by many Elsewhere, & Ridicul'd by some, was most Evidently attended with a very Remarkeable blessing of Heaven, to the souls of the People in this Town, to the Giving of them an universal satisfaction & Engaging their minds with Respect to the thing in Question, the more Earnestly to seek salvation in the way, that had been made Evident to them; & then, a Concern about the Great things of Religion began, about the Latter End of December, & the beginning of January, to Prevail abundantly in the Town, till in a very Little Time it became universal throughout the Town, among old and young, & from the highest to the Lowest; all seemed to be siezed with a deep concern about their Eternal salvation; all the Talk in all companies, & upon occasions was upon the things of Religion, and no other talk was anywhere Relished; & scarcely a single Person in the whole Town was Left unconcerned about the Great things of the Eternal World: Those that were wont to be the vainest, & Loosest Persons in Town seemed in General to be siezed with strong convictions: Those that were most disposed to contemn vital & Experimental Religion, & those that had the Greatest Conceit of their own Reason: the highest Families in the Town, & the oldest Persons in the Town, and many Little Children were affected Remarkeably; no one Family that I know of, & scarcely a Person has been Exempt & the Spirit of God went on in his saving Influences, to the appearance of all Human Reason & Charity, in a truly wonderfull and astonishing manner. The news of it filled the neighbouring Towns with Talk, & there were many in them that scoffed and made a Ridicule of the Religion that appeared in Northampton; But it was observable that it was very frequent & Common that those of other Towns that came into this Town, & observed how it was here, were Greatly affected, and went home with wounded spirits, & were never more able to Shake off the Impression that it made upon them, till at Length there began to appear a General concern in several of the Towns in the County: in the month of march the People in new Hadley seemed to be siezed with a deep concern about their salvation, all as it were at once, which has Continued in a very Great degree Ever since: about the same time there began to appear the Like Concern in the west Part of Suffield, which has since spread into all Parts of the Town. It next began to appear at Sunderland, & soon became universal, & to a very Great Degree. about the same Time it began to appear in Part of Deerfield, Called Green River, & since has filled the Town. It began to appear also at a part of Hatfield, and after that the whole Town in the second week in April seemed to be

siezed at once, & there is a Great & General concern there.
and there Gradually Got in a Considerable degree of the same
Concern into Hadley old society, & Mr Hopkins's Parish in
Springfield, but it is nothing near so Great as in many other
Places. the next Place that we heard of was Northfield, where
the Concern was very Great & General. we have heard that
there is a considerable degree of it at Longmeadow, & there is
something of it in old Springfield in some parts of the society.
about three weeks ago the Town of Enfield were struck down
as it were at once, the worst Persons in the Town seemed to be
suddenly siezed with a Great degree of Concern about their
souls, as I have been informed: & about the same Time, Mr Bull
of Westfield [said] that there began to be a Great alteration
there, & that there had been more done in one week before that
Time that I spoke with him than had been done in seven year
before: the People of Westfield have till now above all other
Places, made a scoff & derision of this concern at Northampton.
There has been a Great Concern of a Like Nature at Windsor,
on the westside of the River, which began about the same
Time that it began to be General here at Northampton; & my
Father has told me that there is an hopefull beginning on the
East side in his society. Mr Noyes writes me word that there
is a Considerable Revival of Religion at New-Haven; & I have
been Credibly Informed that there is something of it at Guil-
ford, and Lime, as there also is at Coventry, Bolton, & a
society in Lebanon called the Crank: I yesterday saw Mr White
of Bolton, and also Last night saw a young man that belongs
to Coventry, who Gave a very Remarkeable account of that
Town, of the manner in which the Rude debauched young People there were suddenly siezed with a concern about their souls.

   as to the nature of Persons Experiences, & the Influences of
that spirit that there is amongst us, Persons when siezed with
concern are brought to forsake their vices, & ill Practices; the
Looser sort are brought to forsake & to dread their former
Extravagances: Persons are soon brought to have done with
their old Quarrels; Contention & Intermeddling with other
mens matters seems to be dead amongst us. I believe there

never was so much done at Confessing of faults to Each other, & making up differences, as there has Lately been: where this concern comes it Immediately Puts an End to differences between ministers & People: there was a considerable uneasiness at New Hadley between some of the People & their minister, but when this Concern came amongst them it Immediately Put an End to it, & the People are now universally united to their minister. There was an Exceeding alienation at Sunderland, between the minister & many of the People; but when this Concern came amongst them it all vanished at once, & the People are universally united, in hearty affection to their minister. There were some men at Deerfield, of Turbulent spirits, that kept up an uneasiness there with Mr ashley; but one of the Chief of them has Lately been Influenced, fully, & freely to confess his fault to him, & is become his hearty Friend.

People are brought off from Inordinate Engagedness after the World, & have been Ready to Run into the other Extreme of too much neglecting their worldly Business & to mind nothing but Religion. Those that are under Convictions are Put upon it Earnestly to Enquire what they shall do to be saved, & diligently to use appointed means of Grace, and apply themselves to all known duty. & those that obtain Hope themselves, & the Charity of others Concerning their Good Estate, Generally seem to be brought to A Great Sense of their own Exceeding misery in a natural Condition, & their utter helplessness, & Insufficiency for themselves, & their Exceeding wickedness & Guiltiness in the sight of God; it seldom fails but that Each one seems to think himself worse than any body Else, & they are brought to see that they deserue no mercy of God, that all their Prayers & Pains are Exceeding worthless & Polluted, & that God, notwithstanding all that they have done, or can do, may Justly Execute his Eternal wrath upon them, & they seem to be brought to a Lively sense of the Excellency of Jesus Christ & his sufficiency & willingness to save sinners, & to be much weaned in their affections from the world, & to have their Hearts filled with Love to God and Christ, and a disposition to Lie in the dust before him. they seem to have Given them a Lively Conviction of the Truth of the Gospel, & the divine authority of the Holy Scriptures; tho they cant have the Excercise of this at all Times alike, nor Indeed of any other Grace. they seem to be brought to abhor themselves for the sins of their Past Life, & to Long to be holy, & to Live holily, & to Gods Glory; but at the same time complain that they can do nothing, they are poor Impotent Creatures, utterly Insufficient to Glorify their Creatour & Redeemer. They Commonly seem to be much more sensible of their own wickedness after their Conversion then before, so that they are often Humbled by it, it seems to them that they are Really become more wicked, when at the same time they are Evidently full of a Gracious Spirit: Their Remaining sin seems to be their very Great Burthen, & many of them seem to Long after Heaven, that there they may be Rid of sin. They Generally seem to be united in dear Love, and affection one to another, & to have a Love to all mankind: I never saw the Christian spirit in Love to Enemies so Exemplified, in all my Life as I have seen it within this Half year. They commonly Express a Great Concern for others salvation; some say that they think they are far more Concern'd for others conversion, after they themselves have been Converted, than Ever they were for their own; several have thought (tho Perhaps they might be deceived in it) that they could freely die for the salvation of any soul, of the meanest of mankind, of any Indian in the woods. This Town never was so full of Love, nor so full of Joy, nor so full of distress as it has Lately been. Some Persons have had those Longing desires after Jesus Christ, that have been to that degree as to take away their strength, and very much to weaken them, & make them faint: many have been Even Overcome with a sense of the dying Love of Christ, so that the home of the body has been Ready to fail under it; there was once three Pious young Persons in this Town talking together of the dying Love of Christ, till they all fainted away; tho tis Probable the fainting of the two Latter was much Promoted by the fainting of the first. many Express a sense of the Glory of the divine Perfections, & of the Excellency & fullness of Jesus Christ, & of their own Littleness &

unworthiness, in a manner Truly wonderfull, & almost vn-paralleld; & so likewise of the Excellency & wonderfullness of the way of Salvation by Jesus Christ. Their Esteem of the Holy Scriptures is Exceedingly Increased. Many of them say the Bible seems to be a new Book to them, as tho they never Read it before: There have been some Instances of Persons that by only an accidental sight of the Bible, have been as much moved, it seem'd to me, as a Lover by the sight of his sweet heart. The Preaching of the Word is Greatly Prized by them, they say they never heard Preaching before; and so are Gods Sabbaths, & ordinances, & opportunities of Publick worship; the Sabbath is Longed for before it comes, some by only hearing the bell Ring on some occasion in the week time, have been Greatly moved, because it has Put them in mind of its Ringing to Call the People together to worship God. But no Part of Publick worship has commonly put an Effect on them as sing-ing Gods Praises. They have a Greater Respect to ministers than they used to have, there is scarcely a minister Preaches here but Gets their Esteem & affection. The Experiences of some Persons Lately amongst [us] have been beyond almost all that Ever I heard or Read of. There is a Pious woman in this Town that is a very modest Bashfull Person, that was moved by what she heard of the Experiences of others Earnestly to seek to God to give her more clear manifestations of himself, and Evidences of her own Good Estate, & God answer'd her Request, and Gradually gave her more & more of a sense of his Glory & Love, which she had with Intermissions for several days, till one morning the week before Last she had it to a more than ordinary degree, and it Prevaild more & more till towards the middle of the day, till her nature began to sink vnder it, as she was alone in the House; but there came sombody into the House, & found her in an unusual, Extraordinary frame She Expressed what she saw & felt to him; it came to that at Last that they Raised the neighbours, they were afraid she would die; I went up to see her & found her Perfectly sober & in the Exer[c]ise of her Reason, but having her nature seem-ingly overborn & sinking, and when she could speak Expressing

in a manner that cant be described the sense she had of the Glory
of God, and Particularly of such & such Perfections, & her
own vnworthiness, her Longing to Lie in the dust, sometimes
her Longing to Go to be with Christ, & crying out of the
Excellency of Christ, & the wonderfullness of his dying Love;
& so she continued for Hours together tho not alwaies in the
same degree; at sometimes she was able to discourse to those
about her; but it seemed to me if God had manifested a Little
more of himself to her she would Immediately have sunk & her
frame dissolved under it. She has since been at my House, &
continues as full as she can hold, but looks on her self not as an
Eminent saint, but as the worst of all, & vnworthy to Go to
speak with a minister; but yet now beyond any Great Doubt
of her Good Estate. There are two Persons that Belong to
other Towns that have had such a sense of Gods Exceeding
Greatness & majesty, that they were as it were swallowed up;
they both of them told me to that Purpose that if they in the Time
of it they had had the Least fear that they were not at Peace with
that Great God, they should Immediately have died. But there
is a very vast variety of degrees of spiritual discoveries, that are
made to those that we hope are Godly. as there is also in the
steps, & method of the spirits operation in convincing & con-
verting sinners, and the Length of Time that Persons are under
conviction before they have comfort. There is an alteration
made in the Town in a few months that strangers can scarcely
[be] conscious of; our Church I believe was the Largest in New
England before, but Persons Lately have thronged in, so that
there are very few adult Persons Left out. There have been a
Great multitude hopefully converted, too many, I find, for me
to declare abroad with Credit to my Judgment. the Town
seems to be full of the Presence of God; our young People when
they Get together instead of frolicking as they used to do are
altogether on Pious subjects; tis so at weddings & on all occasions. The Children in this, & the neighbouring Towns have
been Greatly affected & Influenced by the spirit of God, &
many of them hopefully changed; the youngest in this Town is
between 9. & 10 years of age, some of them seem to be full of

Love to X.* & have Expressed Great Longings after him & willingness to die, & Leave Father & mother & all things in the world to Go to him, together with a Great sense of their unworthiness & admiration at the free Grace of God towards them. & there have been many old People, many above fifty & several near seventy that seem to be wonderfully changed & hopefully new born. the Good People that have been formerly Converted in the Town have many of them been wonderfully enliven'd & Increased. This work seems to be upon Every account an Extraordinary dispensation of Providence. Tis Extraordinary upon the account of [the] universality of it in affecting all sorts high & Low Rich & Poor wise & unwise old & young vicious & moral; tis very Extraordinary as to the numbers that are hopefully savingly wrought upon, & particularly the number of aged Persons & Children & Loose Livers; and also on the account of the Quickness of the work of the Spirit on them, for many seem to have been suddenly taken from a Loose way of Living, & to be so changed as to become truly holy spiritual Heavenly Persons; tis Extraordinary as to the degrees of Gracious Communications, & the abundant measures in which the Spirit of God has been Poured out on many Persons; tis Extraordinary as to the Extent of it, Gods spirit being so Remarkeably Poured out on so many Towns at once, & its making such swift Progress from Place to Place. The Extraordinariness of the thing has been I believe one Principal cause that People abroad have suspected it. There have been as I have heard many odd & strange stories that have been carried about the Countrey of this affair, which it is a wonder some wise men should be so Ready to Believe. Some indeed vnder Great terrours of Conscience have had Impressions on their Imaginations; and also vnder the Power of the spiritual discoveries, they have had Livelily Impressed Ideas of Christ shedding blood for sinners, his blood Running from his veins, & of Christ in his Glory in Heaven & such Like things, but they are alwaies taught, & have been several times taught in Publick not to Lay the weight of their hopes on such things

* Christ

& many have nothing of any such Imaginations. there have been several Persons that have had their natures overborn vnder strong Convictions, have trembled, & han't been able to stand, they have had such a sense of divine wrath; But there are no new doctrines Embraced, but People have been abundantly Established in those that we account orthodox; there is no new way of worship affected. there is no oddity of Behaviour Prevails; People are no more superstitious about their Clothes, or any thing Else than they used to be: Indeed there is a Great deal of talk when they are together of one anothers Experiences, & Indeed no other is to be expected in a Town where the Concern of the soul, is so vniversally the Concern & that to so Great a degree. & doubtless some Persons vnder the strength of Impressions that are made on their minds and vnder the Power of strong affections, are Guilty of Imprudences, their zeal may need to be Regulated by more Prudence, & they may need a Guide to their assistance; as of old when the Church of Corinth had the Extraordinary Gifts of the spirit, they needed to be told by the apostle that the spirit of the Prophets were subject to the Prophets, & that their Gifts were to be exercised with Prudence, because God was not the author of Confusion but of Peace. There is no unlovely oddity in Peoples Temper Prevailing with this work, but on the contrary the face of things is much changed as to the appearance of a meek, humble, amiable behaviour. Indeed the devil has not been Idle, but his hand has Evidently appeared in several Instances Endeavouring to mimick the work of the spirit of God and to cast a slur upon it & no wonder: & there has hereby appeared the need of the watchfull Eye of skillfull Guides, & of wisdom from above to direct them. There Lately Came up hither a Couple of ministers from Connecticut viz. Mr Lord of Preston, & Mr Owen of Groton, who had heard of the Extraordinary circumstances of this & the neighbouring Towns, who had heard the affair well Represented by some, & also had heard many Reports Greatly to its disadvantage, who came on purpose to see & satisfy themselves; & that they might thoroughly Acquaint themselves, went about, & spent Good Part of a day, in hearing the accounts of many of our new Converts, & Examining of them; which was Greatly to their satisfaction & they took Particular notice, among other things of the modesty with which Persons Gave account of themselves, & said that the one half was not told them, & could not be told them; & that if they Renounced these Persons Experiences they must Renounce Christianity it self. and Mr Owen said Particularly as to their Impressions on their Imaginations, they were quite different from what had been Represented, & that they were no more than might naturally be Expected in such cases.

Thus sir I have Given you a Particular account of this affair which satan has so much misrepresented in the Countrey. This is a true account of the matter as far as I have Opportunity to Know, & I suppose I am vnder Greater advantages to Know than any Person Living. Having been thus Long in the account, I forbear to make Reflections, or to Guess what God is about to do; I Leave this to you, and shall only say, as I desire alwaies to say from my Heart *To God be all the Glory whose work alone it is;* & Let him have an Interest in your Prayers, who so much needs divine help at that day, & is your affectionate Brother,

                              & Humble servant,

Northampton May 30. 1735.   Jth Edwards.

Since I wrote the foregoing Letter, there has Happen'd a thing of a very awfull nature in the Town; My Uncle Hawley, the Last Sabbath day morning, Laid violent Hands on himself, & Put an End to his Life, by Cutting his own throat. He had been for a Considerable Time Greatly Concern'd about the Condition of his soul; till, by the ordering of a sovereign Providence he was suffered to fall into deep melancholly, a distemper that the Family are very Prone to; he was much overpowered by it; the devil took the advantage & drove him into despairing thoughts: he was Kept very much awake a nights, so that he had but very Little sleep for two months. till he seemed not to have his Faculties in his own Power: he was in a Great measure Past a Capacity of Receiving advice, or being Reason'd with. the Coroners Inquest Judged him delirious. Satan seems

to be in a Great Rage, at this Extraordinary breaking forth
the work of God. I hope it is because he knows that he has b
a short time: doubtless he had a Great Reach, in this viole
attack of his against the whole affair. We have appointed a da
of Fasting in the Town this week, by Reason of this & oth
appearances of satans Rage amongst us against Poor souls.
yesterday saw a woman that belongs to Durham, who say
there is a Considerable Revival of Religion there.

I am   yours   &c—

J. E.

Northampton June 3. 1735.

NARRATIVE OF SURPRISING CONVERSIONS
(REVISED ACCOUNT)

... But I now proceed to the other instance that I would give an account of, which is of the little child forementioned. Her name is Phebe Bartlet, daughter of William Bartlet. I shall give the account as I took it from the mouths of her parents, whose veracity, none that know them doubt of.

She was born in March, in the year 1731. About the latter end of April, or beginning of May, 1735, she was greatly affected by the talk of her brother, who had been hopefully converted a little before, at about eleven years of age, and then seriously talked to her about the great things of religion. Her parents did not know of it at that time, and were not wont, in the counsels they gave to their children, particularly to direct themselves to her, by reason of her being so young, and, as they supposed not capable of understanding; but after her brother had talked to her, they observed her very earnestly to listen to the advice they gave to the other children, and she was observed very constantly to retire, several times in a day, as was concluded, for secret prayer, and grew more and more engaged in religion, and was more frequent in her closet, till at last she was wont to visit it five or six times in a day, and was so engaged in it, that nothing would, at any time divert her from her stated closet exercises. Her mother often observed and watched her, when such things occurred, as she thought most likely to divert her, either by putting it out of her thoughts, or otherwise engaging her inclinations, but never could observe her to fail. She mentioned some very remarkable instances.

She once, of her own accord, spake of her unsuccessfulness, in that she could not find God, or to that purpose. But on Thursday, the last day of July, about the middle of the day, the child being in the closet, where it used to retire, its mother heard it speaking aloud, which was unusual, and never had been observed before; and her voice seemed to be as of one exceeding importunate and engaged, but her mother could distinctly hear only these words, (spoken in her childish manner, but seemed to be spoken with extraordinary earnestness, and out of distress of soul) Pray BLESSED LORD give me salvation! I PRAY, BEG pardon all my sins! When the child had done prayer, she came out of the closet, and came and sat down by her mother, and cried out aloud. Her mother very earnestly asked her several times, what the matter was, before she would make any answer, but she continued exceedingly crying, and wreathing her body to and fro, like one in anguish of spirit. Her mother then asked her whether she was afraid that God would not give her salvation. She then answered yes, I am afraid I shall go to hell! Her mother then endeavored to quiet her, and told her she would not have her cry . . . she must be a good girl, and pray every day, and she hoped God would give her salvation. But this did not quiet her at all . . . but she continued thus earnestly crying and taking on for some time, till at length she suddenly ceased crying and began to smile, and presently said with a smiling countenance . . . Mother, the kingdom of heaven is come to me! Her mother was surprised at the sudden alteration, and at the speech, and knew not what to make of it, but at first said nothing to her. The child presently spake again, and said, there is another come to me, and there is another. . . . there is three; and being asked what she meant, she answered. . . . One is, thy will be done, and there is another . . . enjoy him forever; by which it seems that when the child said there is three come to me, she meant three passages of its catechism that came to her mind.

After the child had said this, she retired again into her closet; and her mother went over to her brother's, who was next neighbor; and when she came back, the child being come out of the closet, meets her mother with this cheerful speech . . . I can find God now! Referring to what she had before complained of, that she could not find God. Then the child spoke again, and said . . . I love God! Her mother asked her how well she loved God, whether she loved God better than her fathe and mother, she said, yes. Then she asked her whether she loved God better than her little sister Rachel, she answered yes, better than any thing! Then her eldest sister, referring to her saying she could find God now, asked her where she could find God; she answered, in heaven: Why, said she, have you been in heaven? No, said the child. By this it seems not to have been any imagination of any thing seen with bodily eyes that she called God, when she said I can find God now. Her mother asked her whether she was afraid of going to hell, and that had made her cry. She answered, yes, I was; but now I shall not. Her mother asked her whether she thought that God had given her salvation; she answered yes. Her mother asked her, when; she answered, to day. She appeared all that afternoon exceeding cheerful and joyful. One of the neighbors asked her how she felt herself? She answered, I feel better than I did. The neighbor asked her what made her feel better; she answered, God makes me. That evening as she lay a bed, she called one of her little cousins to her, that was present in the room, as having something to say to him; and when he came, she told him that heaven was better than earth. The next day being Friday, her mother asking her her catechism, asked her what God made her for; she answered, to serve him; and added, every body should serve God, and get an interest in Christ.

The same day the elder children, when they came home from school, seemed much affected with the extraordinary change that seemed to be made in Phebe; and her sister Abigail standing by, her mother took occasion to counsel her, now to improve her time, to prepare for another world; on which Phebe burst out in tears, and cried out, poor Nabby! Her mother told her, she would not have her cry, she hoped that God would give Nabby salvation; but that did not quiet her, but she continued earnestly crying for some time; and when she had in a measure ceased, her sister Eunice being by her, she burst out again, and cried, poor Eunice! and cried exceedingly; and when she had almost done, she went into another room, and there looked upon her sister Naomi, and burst out again, crying poor Amy! Her mother was greatly affected at such a behavior in the child, and knew not what to say to her. One of the neighbors coming in a little after, asked her what she had cried for. She seemed, at first backward to tell the reason: Her mother told her she might tell that person, for he had given her an apple; upon which she said, she cried because she was afraid they would go to hell.

At night a certain minister, that was occasionally in the town, was at the house, and talked considerably with her of the things of religion; and after he was gone, she sat leaning on the table, with tears running out of her eyes; and being asked what made her cry, she said it was thinking about God. The next day being Saturday, she seemed great part of the day to be in a very affectionate frame, had four turns of crying, and seemed to endeavor to curb herself, and hide her tears, and was very backward to talk of the occasion of it. On the sabbath day she was asked whether she believed in God; she answered yes: And being told that Christ was the Son of God, she made ready answer, and said, I know it.

From this time there has appeared a very remarkable abiding change in the child: She has been very strict upon the Sabbath, and seems to long for the sabbath day before it comes and will often in the week time be inquiring how long it is to the sabbath day, and must have the days particularly counted over that are between, before she will be contented. And she seems to love God's house . . . is very eager to go thither. Her mother once asked her why she had such a mind to go? Whether it was not to see the fine folks? She said no, it was to hear Mr Edwards preach. When she is in the place of worship, she is very far from spending her time there as children at her age usually do, but appears with an attention that is very extraordinary for such a child. She also appears, very desirous at all opportunities, to go to private religious meetings, and is very still and attentive at home, in prayer time, and has appeared affected in time of family prayer. She seems to delight much in hearing religious conversation. When I once was there with some others that were strangers, and talked to her something of religion, she seemed more than ordinarily attentive; and when

we were gone, she looked out very wistly after us, and said ...
I wish they would come again! Her mother asked her why:
Said she, I love to hear them talk!

She seems to have very much of the fear of God before her
eyes, and an extraordinary dread of sin against him; of which
her mother mentioned the following remarkable instance. Some
time in August, the last year, she went with some bigger children, to get some plumbs, in a neighbor's lot, knowing nothing
of any harm in what she did; but when she brought some of
the plumbs into the house, her mother mildly reproved her,
and told her, that she must not get plumbs without leave, because it was sin: God had commanded her not to steal. The
child seemed greatly surprised, and burst out into tears, and
cried out... I will not have these plumbs! And turning to her
sister Eunice, very earnestly said to her ... why did you ask
me to go to that plumb tree? I should not have gone if you had
not asked me. The other children did not seem to be much
affected or concerned; but there was no pacifying Phebe. Her
mother told her she might go and ask leave, and then it would
not be sin for her to eat them, and sent one of the children to
that end; and when she returned, her mother told her that the
owner had given leave, now she might eat them, and it would
not be stealing. This stilled her a little while, but presently
she broke out again into an exceeding fit of crying: Her mother
asked her what made her cry again? Why she cried now, since
they had asked leave? What it was that troubled her now? And
asked her several times very earnestly, before she made any
answer; but at last, said it was because ... BECAUSE IT WAS SIN.
She continued a considerable time crying; and said she would
not go again if Eunice asked her an hundred times; and she
retained her aversion to that fruit for a considerable time, under the remembrance of her former sin.

She, at some times, appears greatly affected and delighted
with texts of scripture that come to her mind. Particularly,
about the beginning of November, the last year, that text came
to her mind, Rev. iii. 20. *Behold I stand at the door and knock:
If any man hear my voice, and open the door, I will come in, and*

sup with him and he with me. She spoke of it to those of the family, with a great appearance of joy, a smiling countenance, and elevation of voice, and afterwards she went into another room, where her mother overheard her talking very earnestly to the children about it, and particularly heard her say to them, three or four times over, with an air of exceeding joy and admiration . . . Why it is to SUP WITH GOD. At some time about the middle of winter, very late in the night, when all were in bed, her mother perceived that she was awake, and heard her as though she was weeping. She called to her, and asked her what was the matter. She answered with a low voice, so that her mother could not hear what she said; but thinking it might be occasioned by some spiritual affection, said no more to her; but perceived her to lie awake, and to continue in the same frame for a considerable time. The next morning she asked her whether she did not cry the last night: The child answered yes, I did cry a little, for I was thinking about God and Christ, and they loved me. Her mother asked her, whether to think of God and Christ's loving her made her cry: She answered yes, it does sometimes.

She has often manifested a great concern for the good of other souls; and has been wont, many times, affectionately to counsel the other children. Once about the latter end of September, the last year, when she and some others of the children were in a room by themselves a husking Indian corn, the child, after a while, came out and sat by the fire. Her mother took notice that she appeared with a more than ordinary serious and pensive countenance, but at last she broke silence, and said, I have been talking to Nabby and Eunice. Her mother asked her what she had said to them. Why, said she, I told them they must pray and prepare to die, that they had but a little while to live in this world, and they must be always ready. When Nabby came out her mother asked her whether she had said that to them. Yes, said she, she said that and a great deal more. At other times the child took her opportunities to talk to the other children about the great concern of their souls; sometimes so as much to affect them, and set them into tears. She was once exceeding importunate with her mother to go with her sister Naomi to pray: Her mother endeavored to put her off, but she pulled her by the sleeve, and seemed as if she would by no means be denied. At last her mother told her, that Amy must go and pray herself; but, says the child, she will not go, and persisted earnestly to beg of her mother to go with her.

She has discovered an uncommon degree of a spirit of charity, particularly on the following occasion: A poor man that lives in the woods, had lately lost a cow that the family much depended on, and being at the house, he was relating his misfortune, and telling of the straits and difficulties they were reduced to by it. She took much notice of it, and it wrought exceedingly on her compassions; and after she had attentively heard him a while, she went away to her father, who was in the shop, and intreated him to give that man a cow; and told him that the poor man had no cow! That the hunters or something else had killed his cow! And intreated him to give him one of theirs. Her father told her that they could not spare one. Then she intreated him to let him and his family come and live at his house; and had much talk of the same nature, whereby she manifested bowels of compassion to the poor.

She has manifested great love to her minister; particularly when I returned from my long journey for my health, the last fall, when she heard of it, she appeared very joyful at the news, and told the children of it with an elevated voice, as the most joyful tidings, repeating it over and over, Mr. Edwards is come home! Mr. Edwards is come home! She still continues very constant in secret prayer, so far as can be observed, (for she seems to have no desire that others should observe her when she retires, but seems to be a child of a reserved temper) and every night before she goes to bed will say her catechism, and will by no means miss of it: She never forgot it but once, and then after she was a bed, thought of it and cried out in tears . . . I have not said my catechism! And would not be quieted till her mother asked her the catechism as she lay in bed. She sometimes appears to be in doubt about the condition of her soul, and when asked whether she thinks that she is prepared for death, speaks something doubtfully about it: At other times seems to have no doubt, but when asked, replies yes, without hesitation. . . .

THEOLOGICAL AND PHILOSOPHICAL WRITINGS

GOD GLORIFIED IN MAN'S DEPENDENCE

I. There is an absolute and universal dependence of the redeemed on God. The nature and contrivance of our redemption
is such, that the redeemed are in every thing directly, immediately, and entirely dependent on God: They are dependent on
him for all, and are dependent on him every way.

The several ways wherein the dependence of one being may
be upon another for its good, and wherein the redeemed of
Jesus Christ depend on God for all their good, are these, *viz.*
That they have all their good of him, and that they have all
through him, and that they have all in him: That he is the *cause*
and original whence all their good comes, therein it is *of* him;
and that he is the *medium* by which it is obtained and conveyed,
therein they have it *through* him; and that he is the *good itself*
given and conveyed, therein it is *in* him. Now those that are
redeemed by Jesus Christ do, in all these respects, very directly
and entirely depend on God for their all.

First, The redeemed have all their good *of* God. God is the
great *author* of it. He is the *first* cause of it; and not only so, but
he is the *only* proper cause. It is of God that we have our Redeemer. It is God that has provided a Saviour for us. Jesus
Christ is not only of God in his person, as he is the only begotten Son of God, but he is from God, as we are concerned in him,
and in his office of Mediator. He is the gift of God to us: God
chose and anointed him, appointed him his work, and sent him
into the world. And as it is God that *gives*, so it is God that *accepts* the Saviour. He gives the purchaser, and he affords the
thing purchased.

It is of God that Christ becomes ours, that we are brought to
him and are united to him. It is of God that we receive faith to
close with him, that we may have an interest in him. Eph. ii. 8

"For by grace ye are saved, through faith; and that not of yourselves, it is the gift of God." It is of God that we actually receive all the benefits that Christ has purchased. It is God that pardons and justifies, and delivers from going down to hell; and into his favour the redeemed are received, when they are justified. So it is God that delivers from the dominion of sin, cleanses us from our filthiness, and changes us from our deformity. It is of God that the redeemed receive all their true excellency, wisdom, and holiness: and that two ways, *viz.* as the Holy Ghost by whom these things are immediately wrought is from God, proceeds from him, and is sent by him; and also as the Holy Ghost himself is God, by whose operation and indwelling the knowledge of God and divine things, a holy disposition and all grace, are conferred and upheld. And though means are made use of in conferring grace on men's souls, yet it is of God that we have these means of grace, and it is he that makes them effectual. It is of God that we have the holy scriptures: they are his word. It is of God that we have ordinances, and their efficacy depends on the immediate influence of his Spirit. The ministers of the gospel are sent of God, and all their sufficiency is of him.—2 Cor. iv. 7. "We have this treasure in earthen vessels, that the excellency of the power may be of God, and not of us." Their success depends entirely and absolutely on the immediate blessing and influence of God.

1. The redeemed have all from the *grace* of God. It was of mere grace that God gave us his only begotten Son. The grace is great in proportion to the excellency of what is given. The gift was infinitely precious, because it was of a person infinitely worthy, a person of infinite glory; and also because it was of a person infinitely near and dear to God. The grace is great in proportion to the benefit we have given us in him. The benefit is doubly infinite, in that in him we have deliverance from an infinite, because an eternal misery, and do also receive eternal joy and glory. The grace in bestowing this gift is great in proportion to our unworthiness to whom it is given; instead of deserving such a gift, we merited infinitely ill of God's hands. The grace is great according to the manner of giving, or in propor-

tion to the humiliation and expense of the method and means by which a way is made for our having the gift. He gave him to dwell amongst us; he gave him to us incarnate, or in our nature; and in the like though sinless infirmities. He gave him to us in a low and afflicted state; and not only so, but as slain, that he might be a feast for our souls.

The grace of God in bestowing this gift is most free. It was what God was under no obligation to bestow. He might have rejected fallen man, as he did the fallen angels. It was what we never did any thing to merit; it was given while we were yet enemies, and before we had so much as repented. It was from the love of God who saw no excellency in us to attract it; and it was without expectation of ever being requited for it.—And it is from mere grace that the benefits of Christ are applied to such and such particular persons. Those that are called and sanctified are to attribute it alone to the good pleasure of God's goodness by which they are distinguished. He is sovereign, and hath mercy on whom he will have mercy.

Man hath now a greater dependence on the grace of God than he had before the fall. He depends on free goodness of God for much more than he did then. Then he depended on God's goodness for conferring the reward of perfect obedience; for God was not obliged to promise and bestow that reward. But now we are dependent on the grace of God for much more; we stand in need of grace, not only to bestow glory upon us, but to deliver us from hell and eternal wrath. Under the first covenant we depended on God's goodness to give us the reward of righteousness; and so we do now: But we stand in need of God's free and sovereign grace to give us that righteousness; to pardon our sin, and release us from the guilt and infinite demerit of it.

And as we are dependent on the goodness of God for more now than under the first covenant, so we are dependent on a much greater, more free and wonderful goodness. We are now more dependent on God's arbitrary and sovereign good pleasure. We were in our first estate dependent on God for holiness. We had our original righteousness from him; but then holiness was not bestowed in such a way of sovereign good pleasure as it is now. Man was created holy, for it became God to create holy all his reasonable creatures. It would have been a disparagement to the holiness of God's nature, if he had made an intelligent creature unholy. But now when fallen man is made holy, it is from mere and arbitrary grace: God may for ever deny holiness to the fallen creature if he pleases, without any disparagement to any of his perfections.

And we are not only indeed more dependent on the grace of God, but our dependence is much more conspicuous, because our own insufficiency and helplessness in ourselves is much more apparent in our fallen and undone state, than it was before we were either sinful or miserable. We are more apparently dependent on God for holiness, because we are first sinful, and utterly polluted, and afterward holy. So the production of the effect is sensible, and its derivation from God more obvious. If man was ever holy and always was so, it would not be so apparent, that he had not holiness necessarily, as an inseparable qualification of human nature. So we are more apparently dependent on free grace for the favour of God, for we are first justly the objects of his displeasure, and afterward are received into favour. We are more apparently dependent on God for happiness, being first miserable, and afterward happy. It is more apparently free and without merit in us, because we are actually without any kind of excellency to merit, if there could be any such thing as merit in creature-excellency. And we are not only without any true excellency, but are full of, and wholly defiled with, that which is infinitely odious. All our good is more apparently from God, because we are first naked and wholly without any good, and afterward enriched with all good.

2. We receive all from the *power* of God. Man's redemption is often spoken of as a work of wonderful power as well as grace. The great power of God appears in bringing a sinner from his low state from the depths of sin and misery, to such an exalted state of holiness and happiness. Eph. i. 19. "And what is the exceeding greatness of his power to us-ward who believe, according to the working of his mighty power."—

We are dependent on God's power through every step of our

redemption. We are dependent on the power of God to convert us, and give faith in Jesus Christ, and the new nature. It is a work of creation: "If any man be in Christ, he is a new creature," 2 Cor. v. 17. "We are created in Christ Jesus," Eph. ii 10. The fallen creature cannot attain to true holiness, but by being created again, Eph. iv. 24. "And that ye put on the new man, which after God is created in righteousness and true holiness." It is a raising from the dead, Colos. ii. 12, 13. "Wherein also ye are risen with him through the faith of the operation of God, who hath raised him from the dead." Yea, it is a more glorious work of power than mere creation, or raising a dead body to life, in that the effect attained is greater and more excellent. That holy and happy being, and spiritual life which is produced in the work of conversion, is a far greater and more glorious effect, than mere being and life. And the state from whence the change is made—a death in sin, a total corruption of nature, and depth of misery—is far more remote from the state attained, than mere death or non-entity.

It is by God's power also that we are preserved in a state of grace. 1 Pet. i. 5. "Who are kept by the power of God through faith unto salvation." As grace is at first from God, so it is continually from him, and is maintained by him, as much as light in the atmosphere is all day long from the sun, as well as at first dawning, or at sun-rising.—Men are dependent on the power of God for every exercise of grace, and for carrying on that work in the heart, for subduing sin and corruption, increasing holy principles, and enabling to bring forth fruit in good works. Man is dependent on divine power in bringing grace to its perfection, in making the soul completely amiable in Christ's glorious likeness, and filling of it with a satisfying joy and blessedness; and for the raising of the body to life, and to such a perfect state, that it shall be suitable for a habitation and organ for a soul so perfected and blessed. These are the most glorious effects of the power of God, that are seen in the series of God's acts with respect to the creatures.

Man was dependent on the power of God in his first estate, but he is more dependent on his power now; he needs God's power to do more things for him, and depends on a more wonderful exercise of his power. It was an effect of the power of God to make man holy at the first; but more remarkably so now, because there is a great deal of opposition and difficulty in the way. It is a more glorious effect of power to make that holy that was so depraved, and under the dominion of sin, than to confer holiness on that which before had nothing of the contrary. It is a more glorious work of power to rescue a soul out of the hands of the devil, and from the powers of darkness, and to bring it into a state of salvation, than to confer holiness where there was no prepossession or opposition. Luke xi. 21, 22. "When a strong man armed keepeth his palace, his goods are in peace; but when a stronger than he shall come upon him, and overcome him, he taketh from him all his armour wherein he trusted, and divideth his spoils." So it is a more glorious work of power to uphold a soul in a state of grace and holiness, and to carry it on till it is brought to glory, when there is so much sin remaining in the heart resisting, and Satan with all his might opposing, than it would have been to have kept man from falling at first, when Satan had nothing in man.—Thus we have shown how the redeemed are dependent on God for all their good, as they have all of him.

Secondly, They are also dependent on God for all, as they have all *through* him. God is the medium of it, as well as the author and fountain of it. All we have, wisdom, the pardon of sin, deliverance from hell, acceptance into God's favour, grace and holiness, true comfort and happiness, eternal life and glory, is from God by a Mediator; and this Mediator is God; which Mediator we have an absolute dependence upon, as he through whom we receive all. So that here is another way wherein we have our dependence on God for all good. God not only gives us the Mediator, and accepts his mediation, and of his power and grace bestows the things purchased by the Mediator; but he the Mediator is God.

Our blessings are what we have by purchase; and the purchase is made of God, the blessings are purchased of him, and God gives the purchaser; and not only so, but God is the purchaser. Yea, God is both the purchaser and the price; for Christ who is God, purchased these blessings for us, by offering up himself as the price of our salvation. He purchased eternal life by the sacrifice of himself. Heb. vii. 27. "He offered up himself." And chap. ix. 26. "He hath appeared to take away sin by the sacrifice of himself." Indeed it was the human nature that was offered; but it was the same person with the divine, and therefore was an infinite price.

As we thus have our good through God, we have a dependence on him in a respect that man in his first estate had not. Man was to have eternal life then through his own righteousness; so that he had partly a dependence upon what was in himself; for we have a dependence upon that through which we have our good, as well as that from which we have it: and though man's righteousness that he then depended on was indeed from God, yet it was his own, it was inherent in himself; so that his dependence was not so *immediately* on God. But now the righteousness that we are dependent on is not in ourselves, but in God. We are saved through the righteousness of Christ: he *is made unto us righteousness;* and therefore is prophesied of, Jer. xxiii. 6, under that name, "the Lord our righteousness." In that the righteousness we are justified by is the righteousness of Christ, it is the righteousness of God. 2 Cor. v. 21. "That we might be made the righteousness of God in him."—Thus in redemption we have not only all things of God, but by and through him, 1 Cor. viii. 6. "But to us there is but one God, the Father, of whom are all things, and we in him; and one Lord Jesus Christ, by whom are all things, and we by him."

Thirdly, The redeemed have all their good *in God*. We not only have it of him, and through him, but it consists in him; he is all our good.—The good of the redeemed is either objective or inherent. By their objective good, I mean that extrinsic object, in the possession and enjoyment of which they are happy. Their inherent good is that excellency or pleasure which is in the soul itself. With respect to both of which the redeemed have all their good in God, or, which is the same thing, God himself is all their good.

1. The redeemed have all their *objective* good in God. God himself is the great good which they are brought to the possession and enjoyment of by redemption. He is the highest good, and the sum of all that good which Christ purchased. God is the inheritance of the saints; he is the portion of their souls. God is their wealth and treasure, their food, their life, their dwelling-place, their ornament and diadem, and their everlasting honour and glory. They have none in heaven but God; he is the great good which the redeemed are received to at death, and which they are to rise to at the end of the world. The Lord God is the light of the heavenly Jerusalem; and is the "river of the water of life" that runs, and "the tree of life that grows, in the midst of the paradise of God." The glorious excellencies and beauty of God will be what will for ever entertain the minds of the saints, and the love of God will be their everlasting feast. The redeemed will indeed enjoy other things; they will enjoy the angels, and will enjoy one another: but that which they shall enjoy in the angels, or each other, or in any thing else whatsoever, that will yield them delight and happiness, will be what shall be seen of God in them.

2. The redeemed have all their *inherent* good in God. Inherent good is two-fold; it is either excellency or pleasure. These the redeemed not only derive from God, as caused by him, but have them in him. They have spiritual excellency and joy by a kind of participation of God. They are made excellent by a communication of God's excellency. God puts his own beauty, *i. e.* his beautiful likeness, upon their souls. They are made partakers of the divine nature, or moral image of God, 2 Pet. i. 4. They are holy by being made partakers of God's holiness, Heb. xii. 10. The saints are beautiful and blessed by a communication of God's holiness and joy, as the moon and planets are bright by the sun's light. The saint hath spiritual joy and pleasure by a kind of effusion of God on the soul. In these things the redeemed have communion with God; that is, they partake with him and of him.

The saints have both their spiritual excellency and blessedness by the gift of the Holy Ghost, and his dwelling in them.

They are not only caused by the Holy Ghost, but are in him as their principle. The Holy Spirit becoming an inhabitant, is a vital principle in the soul. He, acting in, upon, and with the soul, becomes a fountain of true holiness and joy, as a spring is of water, by the exertion and diffusion of itself. John iv. 14. "But whosoever drinketh of the water that I shall give him, shall never thirst; but the water that I shall give him, shall be in him a well of water springing up into everlasting life." Compared with chap. vii. 38, 39. "He that believeth on me, as the scripture hath said, out of his belly shall flow rivers of living water; but this spake he of the Spirit, which they that believe on him should receive." The sum of what Christ has purchased for us, is that spring of water spoken of in the former of those places, and those rivers of living water spoken of in the latter. And the sum of the blessings, which the redeemed shall receive in heaven, is that river of water of life that proceeds from the throne of God and the Lamb, Rev. xxii. 1. which doubtless signifies the same with those rivers of living water, explained John vii. 38, 39. which is elsewhere called the "river of God's pleasures." Herein consists the fulness of good, which the saints receive of Christ. It is by partaking of the Holy Spirit, that they have communion with Christ in his fulness. God hath given the Spirit, not by measure unto him; and they do receive of his fulness, and grace for grace. This is the sum of the saints' inheritance; and therefore that little of the Holy Ghost which believers have in this world, is said to be the earnest of their inheritance, 2 Cor. i. 22. "Who hath also sealed us, and given us the Spirit in our hearts." And chap. v. 5. "Now he that hath wrought us for the self same thing, is God, who also hath given unto us the earnest of the Spirit." And Eph. i. 13, 14. "Ye were sealed with that Holy Spirit of promise, which is the earnest of our inheritance, until the redemption of the purchased possession."

The Holy Spirit and good things are spoken of in scripture as the same; as if the Spirit of God communicated to the soul comprised all good things. Matt. vii. 11. "How much more shall your heavenly Father give good things to them that ask him?" In Luke it is, chap. xi. 13. "How much more shall your heavenly Father give the Holy Spirit to them that ask him?" This is the sum of the blessings that Christ died to procure, and the subject of gospel-promises. Gal. iii. 13, 14. "He was made a curse for us, that we might receive the promise of the Spirit through faith." The Spirit of God is the great promise of the Father. Luke xxiv. 49. "Behold, I send the promise of my Father upon you." The Spirit of God therefore is called "the Spirit of promise"; Eph. i. 33. This promised thing Christ received, and had given into his hand, as soon as he had finished the work of our redemption, to bestow on all that he had redeemed; Acts ii. 13. "Therefore being by the right hand of God exalted, and having received of the Father the promise of the Holy Ghost, he hath shed forth this, which ye both see and hear." So that all the holiness and happiness of the redeemed is in God. It is in the communications, indwelling, and acting of the Spirit of God. Holiness and happiness are in the fruit, here and hereafter, because God dwells in them, and they in God.

Thus God has given us the Redeemer, and it is by him that our good is purchased. So God is the Redeemer and the price; and he also is the good purchased. So that all that we have is of God, and through him, and in him. Rom. xi. 36. "For of him, and through him, and to him, (or in him,) are all things." The same in the Greek that is here rendered *to him*, is rendered *in him*, 1 Cor. viii. 6.

A DIVINE AND SUPERNATURAL LIGHT

IMMEDIATELY IMPARTED TO THE SOUL BY THE SPIRIT OF GOD, SHOWN TO
BE BOTH A SCRIPTURAL AND RATIONAL DOCTRINE.

MATTHEW XVI. 17.—And Jesus answered and said unto him, Blessed art
thou, Simon Barjona: for flesh and blood hath not revealed it unto thee,
but my Father which is in heaven.

DOCTRINE

That there is such a thing as a Spiritual and Divine Light,
immediately imparted to the soul by God, of a different nature
from any that is obtained by natural means.

In what I say on this subject, at this time, I would,

I. Show what this divine light is.

II. How it is given immediately by God, and not obtained
by natural means.

III. Show the truth of the doctrine.

And then conclude with a brief improvement.

I. I would show what this spiritual and divine light is. And
in order to it, would show,

FIRST, In a few things what it is not. And here,

1. Those convictions that natural men may have of their sin
and misery, is not this spiritual and divine light. Men in a natural condition may have convictions of the guilt that lies upon
them, and of the anger of God, and their danger of divine
vengeance. Such convictions are from light or sensibleness of
truth. That some sinners have a greater conviction of their
guilt and misery than others, is because some have more light,
or more of an apprehension of truth than others. And this light
and conviction may be from the Spirit of God; the Spirit convinces men of sin: but yet nature is much more concerned in it
than in the communication of that spiritual and divine light that
is spoken of in the doctrine; it is from the Spirit of God only as
assisting natural principles, and not as infusing any new principles. Common grace differs from special, in that it influence

only by assisting of nature; and not by imparting grace, or
bestowing any thing above nature. The light that is obtained
is wholly natural, or of no superior kind to what mere nature
attains to, though more of that kind be obtained than would be
obtained if men were left wholly to themselves: or, in other
words, common grace only assists the faculties of the soul to do
that more fully which they do by nature, as natural conscience
or reason will, by mere nature, make a man sensible of guilt,
and will accuse and condemn him when he has done amiss.
Conscience is a principle natural to men; and the work that it
doth naturally, or of itself, is to give an apprehension of right
and wrong, and to suggest to the mind the relation that there is
between right and wrong, and a retribution. The Spirit of God,
in those convictions which unregenerate men sometimes have,
assists conscience to do this work in a further degree than it
would do if they were left to themselves: he helps it against
those things that tend to stupify it, and obstruct its exercise.
But in the renewing and sanctifying work of the Holy Ghost,
those things are wrought in the soul that are above nature, and
of which there is nothing of the like kind in the soul by nature;
and they are caused to exist in the soul habitually, and according
to such a stated constitution or law that lays such a foundation
for exercises in a continued course, as is called a principle of
nature. Not only are remaining principles assisted to do their
work more freely and fully, but those principles are restored
that were utterly destroyed by the fall; and the mind thenceforward habitually exerts those acts that the dominion of sin
had made it as wholly destitute of, as a dead body is of vital
acts.

The Spirit of God acts in a very different manner in the one
case, from what he doth in the other. He may indeed act upon
the mind of a natural man, but he acts in the mind of a saint as
an indwelling vital principle. He acts upon the mind of an unregenerate person as an extrinsic, occasional agent; for in acting
upon them, he doth not unite himself to them; for notwithstanding all his influences that they may be the subjects of, they are
still sensual, having not the Spirit, Jude 19. But he unites him-

self with the mind of a saint, takes him for his temple, actuates and influences him as a new supernatural principle of life and action. There is this difference, that the Spirit of God, in acting in the soul of a godly man, exerts and communicates himself there in his own proper nature. Holiness is the proper nature of the Spirit of God. The Holy Spirit operates in the minds of the godly, by uniting himself to them, and living in them, and exerting his own nature in the exercise of their faculties. The Spirit of God may act upon a creature, and yet not in acting communicate himself. The Spirit of God may act upon inanimate creatures; as, the *Spirit moved upon the face of the waters*, in the beginning of the creation; so the Spirit of God may act upon the minds of men many ways, and communicate himself no more than when he acts upon an inanimate creature. For instance, he may excite thoughts in them, may assist their natural reason and understanding, or may assist other natural principles, and this without any union with the soul, but may act, as it were, as upon an external object. But as he acts in his holy influences and spiritual operations, he acts in a way of peculiar communication of himself; so that the subject is thence denominated spiritual.

2. This spiritual and divine light does not consist in any impression made upon the imagination. It is no impression upon the mind, as though one saw any thing with the bodily eyes: it is no imagination or idea of an outward light or glory, or any beauty of form or countenance, or a visible lustre or brightness of any object. The imagination may be strongly impressed with such things; but this is not spiritual light. Indeed when the mind has a lively discovery of spiritual things, and is greatly affected by the power of divine light, it may, and probably very commonly doth, much affect the imagination; so that impressions of an outward beauty or brightness may accompany those spiritual discoveries. But spiritual light is not that impression upon the imagination, but an exceeding different thing from it. Natural men may have lively impressions on their imaginations; and we cannot determine but the devil, who transforms himself into an angel of light, may cause imaginations of an outward

beauty, or visible glory, and of sounds and speeches, and other such things; but these are things of a vastly inferior nature to spiritual light.

3. This spiritual light is not the suggesting of any new truths or propositions not contained in the word of God. This suggesting of new truths or doctrines to the mind, independent of any antecedent revelation of those propositions, either in word or writing, is inspiration; such as the prophets and apostles had, and such as some enthusiasts pretend to. But this spiritual light that I am speaking of, is quite a different thing from inspiration: it reveals no new doctrine, it suggests no new proposition to the mind, it teaches no new thing of God, or Christ, or another world, not taught in the Bible, but only gives a due apprehension of those things that are taught in the word of God.

4. It is not every affecting view that men have of the things of religion that is this spiritual and divine light. Men by mere principles of nature are capable of being affected with things that have a special relation to religion as well as other things. A person by mere nature, for instance, may be liable to be affected with the story of Jesus Christ, and the sufferings he underwent, as well as by any other tragical story: he may be the more affected with it from the interest he conceives mankind to have in it: yea, he may be affected with it without believing it; as well as a man may be affected with what he reads in a romance, or sees acted in a stage play. He may be affected with a lively and eloquent description of many pleasant things that attend the state of the blessed in heaven, as well as his imagination be entertained by a romantic description of the pleasantness of fairy land, or the like. And that common belief of the truth of the things of religion, that persons may have from education or otherwise, may help forward their affection. We read in Scripture of many that were greatly affected with things of a religious nature, who yet are there represented as wholly graceless, and many of them very ill men. A person therefore may have affecting views of the things of religion, and yet be very destitute of spiritual light. Flesh and blood may be the author of this: one man may give another an affecting view of divine things with

but common assistance: but God alone can give a spiritual discovery of them.

But I proceed to show,

SECONDLY, Positively what this spiritual and divine light is. And it may be thus described: a true sense of the divine excellency of the things revealed in the word of God, and a conviction of the truth and reality of them thence arising.

This spiritual light primarily consists in the former of these, viz., a real sense and apprehension of the divine excellency of things revealed in the word of God. A spiritual and saving conviction of the truth and reality of these things, arises from such a sight of their divine excellency and glory; so that this conviction of their truth is an effect and natural consequence of this sight of their divine glory. There is therefore in this spiritual light,

1. A true sense of the divine and superlative excellency of the things of religion; a real sense of the excellency of God and Jesus Christ, and of the work of redemption, and the ways and works of God revealed in the gospel. There is a divine and superlative glory in these things; an excellency that is of a vastly higher kind, and more sublime nature than in other things; a glory greatly distinguishing them from all that is earthly and temporal. He that is spiritually enlightened truly apprehends and sees it, or has a sense of it. He does not merely rationally believe that God is glorious, but he has a sense of the gloriousness of God in his heart. There is not only a rational belief that God is holy, and that holiness is a good thing, but there is a sense of the loveliness of God's holiness. There is not only a speculatively judging that God is gracious, but a sense how amiable God is upon that account, or a sense of the beauty of this divine attribute.

There is a twofold understanding or knowledge of good that God has made the mind of man capable of. The first, that which is merely speculative and notional; as when a person only speculatively judges that any thing is, which, by the agreement of mankind, is called good or excellent, viz., that which is most to general advantage, and between which and a reward there is a suitableness, and the like. And the other is, that which consists in the sense of the heart: as when there is a sense of the beauty, amiableness, or sweetness of a thing; so that the heart is sensible of pleasure and delight in the presence of the idea of it. In the former is exercised merely the speculative faculty, or the understanding, strictly so called, or as spoken of in distinction from the will or disposition of the soul. In the latter, the will, or inclination, or heart, is mainly concerned.

Thus there is a difference between having an opinion, that God is holy and gracious, and having a sense of the loveliness and beauty of that holiness and grace. There is a difference between having a rational judgment that honey is sweet, and having a sense of its sweetness. A man may have the former, that knows not how honey tastes; but a man cannot have the latter unless he has an idea of the taste of honey in his mind. So there is a difference between believing that a person is beautiful, and having a sense of his beauty. The former may be obtained by hearsay, but the latter only by seeing the countenance. There is a wide difference between mere speculative rational judging any thing to be excellent, and having a sense of its sweetness and beauty. The former rests only in the head, speculation only is concerned in it; but the heart is concerned in the latter. When the heart is sensible of the beauty and amiableness of a thing, it necessarily feels pleasure in the apprehension. It is implied in a person's being heartily sensible of the loveliness of a thing, that the idea of it is sweet and pleasant to his soul; which is a far different thing from having a rational opinion that it is excellent.

2. There arises from this sense of divine excellency of things contained in the word of God, a conviction of the truth and reality of them; and that either directly or indirectly.

First, Indirectly, and that two ways.

1. As the prejudices that are in the heart, against the truth of divine things, are hereby removed; so that the mind becomes susceptive of the due force of rational arguments for their truth. The mind of man is naturally full of prejudices against the truth of divine things: it is full of enmity against the doctrines of the

gospel; which is a disadvantage to those arguments that prove their truth, and causes them to lose their force upon the mind. But when a person has discovered to him the divine excellency of Christian doctrines, this destroys the enmity, removes those prejudices, and sanctifies the reason, and causes it to lie open to the force of arguments for their truth.

Hence was the different effect that Christ's miracles had to convince the disciples from what they had to convince the Scribes and Pharisees. Not that they had a stronger reason, or had their reason more improved; but their reason was sanctified, and those blinding prejudices, that the Scribes and Pharisees were under, were removed by the sense they had of the excellency of Christ and his doctrine.

2. It not only removes the hinderances of reason, but positively helps reason. It makes even the speculative notions the more lively. It engages the attention of the mind, with the more fixedness and intenseness to that kind of objects; which causes it to have a clearer view of them, and enables it more clearly to see their mutual relations, and occasions it to take more notice of them. The ideas themselves that otherwise are dim and obscure, are by this means impressed with the greater strength, and have a light cast upon them; so that the mind can better judge of them. As he that beholds the objects on the face of the earth, when the light of the sun is cast upon them, is under greater advantage to discern them in their true forms and mutual relations, than he that sees them in a dim starlight or twilight.

The mind having a sensibleness of the excellency of divine objects, dwells upon them with delight; and the powers of the soul are more awakened and enlivened to employ themselves in the contemplation of them, and exert themselves more fully and much more to the purpose. The beauty and sweetness of the objects draws on the faculties, and draws forth their exercises: so that reason itself is under far greater advantages for its proper and free exercises, and to attain its proper end, free of darkness and delusion. But,

SECONDLY. A true sense of the divine excellency of the

things of God's word doth more directly and immediately convince of the truth of them; and that because the excellency of these things is so superlative. There is a beauty in them that is so divine and godlike, that is greatly and evidently distinguishing of them from things merely human, or that men are the inventors and authors of; a glory that is so high and great, that when clearly seen, commands assent to their divinity and reality. When there is an actual and lively discovery of this beauty and excellency, it will not allow of any such thought as that it is a human work, or the fruit of men's invention. This evidence that they that are spiritually enlightened have of the truth of the things of religion, is a kind of intuitive and immediate evidence. They believe the doctrines of God's word to be divine, because they see divinity in them; i.e., they see a divine, and transcendent, and most evidently distinguishing glory in them; such a glory as, if clearly seen, does not leave room to doubt of their being of God, and not of men.

Such a conviction of the truth of religion as this, arising, these ways, from a sense of the divine excellency of them, is that true spiritual conviction that there is in saving faith. And this original of it, is that by which it is most essentially distinguished from that common assent, which unregenerate men are capable of.

II. I proceed now to the second thing proposed, viz., to show how this light is immediately given by God, and not obtained by natural means. And here,

1. It is not intended that the natural faculties are not made use of in it. The natural faculties are the subject of this light: and they are the subject in such a manner, that they are not merely passive, but active in it; the acts and exercises of man's understanding are concerned and made use of in it. God, in letting in this light into the soul, deals with man according to his nature, or as a rational creature; and makes use of his human faculties. But yet this light is not the less immediately from God for that; though the faculties are made use of, it is as the subject and not as the cause; and that acting of the faculties in it, is not the cause, but is either implied in the thing itself (in

the light that is imparted) or is the consequence of it. As the use that we make of our eyes in beholding various objects, when the sun arises, is not the cause of the light that discovers those objects to us.

2. It is not intended that outward means have no concern in this affair. As I have observed already, it is not in this affair, as it is in inspiration, where new truths are suggested: for here is by this light only given a due apprehension of the same truths that are revealed in the word of God; and therefore it is not given without the word. The gospel is made use of in this affair: this light is the light of the glorious gospel of Christ, 2 Cor. iv. 4. The gospel is as a glass, by which this light is conveyed to us, 1 Cor. xiii. 12. Now we see through a glass.— But,

3. When it is said that this light is given immediately by God, and not obtained by natural means, hereby is intended, that it is given by God without making use of any means that operate by their own power, or a natural force. God makes use of means; but it is not as mediate causes to produce this effect. There are not truly any second causes of it; but it is produced by God immediately. The word of God is no proper cause of this effect: it does not operate by any natural force in it. The word of God is only made use of to convey to the mind the subject matter of this saving instruction: and this indeed it doth convey to us by natural force or influence. It conveys to our minds these and those doctrines; it is the cause of the notion of them in our heads, but not of the sense of the divine excellency of them in our hearts. Indeed a person cannot have spiritual light without the word. But that does not argue, that the word properly causes that light. The mind cannot see the excellency of any doctrine, unless that doctrine be first in the mind; but the seeing of the excellency of the doctrine may be immediately from the Spirit of God; though the conveying of the doctrine or proposition itself may be by the word. So that the notions that are the subject matter of this light, are conveyed to the mind by the word of God; but that due sense of the heart, wherein this light formally consists, is immediately by the Spirit

of God. As for instance, that notion that there is a Christ, and that Christ is holy and gracious, is conveyed to the mind by the word of God: but the sense of the excellency of Christ by reason of that holiness and grace, is nevertheless immediately the work of the Holy Spirit.

THE JUSTICE OF GOD IN THE DAMNATION
OF SINNERS

ROMANS III. 19.—That every mouth may be stopped.

DOCTRINE

It is just with God eternally to cast off and destroy sinners.

For this is the punishment which the law condemns to; which the things that the law says, may well stop every mouth from all manner of objection against.

The truth of this doctrine may appear by the joint consideration of two things, viz., man's sinfulness, and God's sovereignty.

I. It appears from the consideration of man's sinfulness. And that whether we consider the infinitely evil nature of all sin, or how much sin men are guilty of.

1. If we consider the infinite evil and heinousness of sin in general, it is not unjust in God to inflict what punishment is deserved; because the very notion of deserving punishment is, that it may be justly inflicted: a deserved punishment and a just punishment are the same thing. To say that one deserves such a punishment, and yet to say that he does not justly deserve it, is a contradiction; and if he justly deserves it, then it may be justly inflicted.

Every crime or fault deserves a greater or less punishment, in proportion as the crime itself is greater or less. If any fault deserves punishment, then so much the greater the fault, so much the greater is the punishment deserved. The faulty nature of any thing is the formal ground and reason of its desert of punishment; and therefore the more any thing hath of this nature, the more punishment it deserves. And therefore the terribleness of the degree of punishment, let it be never so terrible, is no argument against the justice of it, if the proportion does but hold between the heinousness of the crime and the dreadfulness of the punishment; so that if there be any such thing as a fault infinitely heinous, it will follow that it is just to inflict a punishment for it that is infinitely dreadful.

A crime is more or less heinous, according as we are under greater or less obligations to the contrary. This is self-evident; because it is herein that the criminalness or faultiness of any thing consists, that it is contrary to what we are obliged or bound to, or what ought to be in us. So the faultiness of one being's hating another, is in proportion to his obligation to love him. The crime of one being's despising and casting contempt on another, is proportionably more or less heinous, as he was under greater or less obligations to honor him. The fault of disobeying another, is greater or less, as any one is under greater or less obligations to obey him. And therefore if there be any being that we are under infinite obligations to love, and honor and obey, the contrary towards him must be infinitely faulty.

Our obligations to love, honor, and obey any being, is in proportion to his loveliness, honorableness, and authority; for that is the very meaning of the words. When we say any one is very lovely, it is the same as to say, that he is one very much to be loved: or if we say such a one is more honorable than another, the meaning of the words is, that he is one that we are more obliged to honor. If we say any one has great authority over us, it is the same as to say, that he has great right to our subjection and obedience.

But God is a being infinitely lovely, because he hath infinite excellency and beauty. To have infinite excellency and beauty, is the same thing as to have infinite loveliness. He is a Being of infinite greatness, majesty, and glory; and therefore is infinitely honorable. He is infinitely exalted above the greatest potentates of the earth, and highest angels in heaven; and therefore is infinitely more honorable than they. His authority over us is infinite; and the ground of his right to our obedience is infinitely strong: for he is infinitely worthy to be obeyed in himself, and we have an absolute, universal, and infinite dependence upon him.

So that sin against God, being a violation of infinite obliga-

tions, must be a crime infinitely heinous, and so deserving of
infinite punishment.—Nothing is more agreeable to the common sense of mankind, than that sins committed against any
one, must be heinous proportionably to the dignity of the being
offended and abused; as it is also agreeable to the word of God:
1 Sam. ii. 25, "If one man sin against another, the judge shall
judge him"; (i.e., shall judge him, and inflict a finite punishment,
such as finite judges can inflict;) "but if a man sin against the
Lord, who shall entreat for him?"   This was the aggravation
of sin that made Joseph afraid of it: Gen. xxxix. 9, "How shall
I commit this great wickedness, and sin against God?" This
was the aggravation of David's sin, in comparison of which he
esteemed all others as nothing, because they were infinitely
exceeded by it.   Psalm li. 4, "Against thee, thee only have I
sinned."—The eternity of the punishment of ungodly men
renders it infinite; and it renders it no more than infinite, and
therefore no more than proportionable to the heinousness of
what they are guilty.

If there be any evil or faultiness in sin against God, there is
certainly infinite evil: for if it be any fault at all, it has an infinite
aggravation, viz., that it is against an infinite object.   If it be
ever so small upon other accounts, yet if it be any thing, it has
one infinite dimension; and so is an infinite evil.   Which may
be illustrated by this: if we suppose a thing to have infinite
length, but no breadth and thickness, but to be only a mere
mathematical line, it is nothing; but if it have any breadth and
thickness at all, though never so small, yet if it have but one
infinite dimension, viz., that of length, the quantity of it is
infinite; it exceeds the quantity of any thing, however broad,
thick and long, wherein these dimensions are all finite.

So that the objections that are made against the infinite punishment of sin, from the necessity, or rather previous certainty
of the futurition of sin, arising from the decree of God, or unavoidable original corruption of nature, if they argue any thing,
do not argue against the infiniteness of the degree of the faultiness of sin directly, and no otherwise than they argue against
any faultiness at all: for if this necessity or certainty leaves any

evil at all in sin, that fault must be infinite by reason of the infinite object.

But every such objector as would argue from hence, that there is no fault at all in sin, confutes himself, and shows his own insincerity in his objection. For at the same time that he objects, that men's acts are necessary, from God's decrees, and original sin, and that this kind of necessity is inconsistent with faultiness in the act, his own practice shows that he does not believe what he objects to be true: otherwise why does he at all blame men? Or why are such persons at all displeased with men, for abusive, injurious, and ungrateful acts towards them? Whatever they pretend, by this they show that indeed they do believe that there is no necessity in men's acts, from divine decrees, or corruption of nature, that is inconsistent with blame. And if their objection be this, that this previous certainty is by God's own ordering, and that where God orders an antecedent certainty of acts, he transfers all the fault from the actor on himself; their practice shows, that at the same time they do not believe this, but fully believe the contrary: for when they are abused by men, they are displeased with men, and not with God only.

The light of nature teaches all mankind, that when an injury is voluntary, it is faulty, without any manner of consideration of what there might be previously to determine the futurition of that evil act of the will. And it really teaches this as much to those that object and cavil most as to others; as their universal practice shows. By which it appears, that such objections are insincere and perverse. Men will mention others' corrupt nature in their own case, or when they are injured, as a thing that aggravates their crime, and that wherein their faultiness partly consists. How common is it for persons, when they look on themselves greatly injured by another, to inveigh against him, and aggravate his baseness, by saying, "He is a man of a most perverse spirit: he is naturally of a selfish, niggardly, or proud and haughty temper: he is one of a base and vile disposition." And yet men's natural, corrupt dispositions are mentioned as an excuse for them, with respect to their sins against God, and as if they rendered them blameless.

2. That it is just with God eternally to cast off wicked men may more abundantly appear, if we consider how much sin they are guilty of. From what has been already said, it appears, that if men were guilty of sin but in one particular, that is sufficient ground of their eternal rejection and condemnation: if they are sinners, that is enough: merely this might be sufficient to keep them from ever lifting up their heads, and cause them to smite on their breasts, with the publican that cried "God be merciful to me a sinner." But sinful men are not only thus, but they are full of sin; full of principles of sin, and full of acts of sin: their guilt is like great mountains, heaped one upon another, till the pile is grown up to heaven. They are totally corrupt, in every part, in all their faculties, and all the principles of their nature, their understandings, and wills; and in all their dispositions and affections, their heads, their hearts, are totally depraved; all the members of their bodies are only instruments of sin; and all their senses, seeing, hearing, tasting, &c., are only inlets and outlets of sin, channels of corruption. There is nothing but sin, no good at all. Rom. vii. 18, "In me, that is, in my flesh, dwells no good thing." There is all manner of wickedness. There are the seeds of the greatest and blackest crimes. There are principles of all sorts of wickedness against men; and there is all wickedness against God. There is pride; there is enmity; there is contempt; there is quarrelling; there is atheism; there is blasphemy. There are these things in exceeding strength; the heart is under the power of them, is sold under sin, and is a perfect slave to it. There is hardheartedness, hardness greater than that of a rock, or an adamant stone. There is obstinacy and perverseness, incorrigibleness and inflexibleness of sin, that will not be overcome by threatenings or promises, by awakenings or encouragements, by judgments or mercies, neither by that which is terrifying, nor that which is winning: the very blood of God will not win the heart of a wicked man.

And there is actual wickedness without number or measure. There are breaches of every command, in thought, word, and deed; a life full of sin; days and nights filled up with sin; mercies abused, and frowns despised; mercy and justice, and all the divine perfections, trampled on; and the honor of each person in the Trinity trod in the dirt. Now if one sinful word or thought has so much evil in it, as to deserve eternal destruction, how do they deserve to be eternally cast off and destroyed, that are guilty of so much sin!

II. If with man's sinfulness, we consider God's sovereignty, it may serve further to clear God's justice in the eternal rejection and condemnation of sinners, from men's cavils and objections. I shall not now pretend to determine precisely, what things are, and what things are not, proper acts and exercises of God's holy sovereignty; but only, that God's sovereignty extends to the following things.

1. That such is God's sovereign power and right, that he is originally under no obligation to keep men from sinning; but may in his providence permit and leave them to sin. He was not obliged to keep either angels or men from falling. It is unreasonable to suppose, that God should be obliged, if he makes a reasonable creature capable of knowing his will, and receiving a law from him, and being subject to his moral government, at the same time to make it impossible for him to sin, or break his law. For if God be obliged to this, it destroys all use of any commands, laws, promises or threatenings, and the very notion of any moral government of God over those reasonable creatures. For to what purpose would it be, for God to give such and such laws, and declare his holy will to a creature, and annex promises and threatenings to move him to his duty, and make him careful to perform it, if the creature at the same time has this to think of, that God is obliged to make it impossible for him to break his laws? How can God's threatenings move to care or watchfulness, when, at the same time, God is obliged to render it impossible that he should be exposed to the threatenings? Or, to what purpose is it for God to give a law at all? For, according to this supposition, it is God, and not the creature, that is under the law. It is the lawgiver's care, and not the subject's, to see that his law is obeyed; and this care is what the lawgiver is absolutely obliged to. If God be obliged never

to permit a creature to fall, there is an end of all divine laws, or government, or authority of God over the creature; there can be no manner of use of these things.

God may permit sin, though the being of sin will certainly ensue on that permission: and so, by permission, he may dispose and order the event. If there were any such thing as chance, or mere contingence, and the very notion of it did not carry a gross absurdity (as might easily be shown that it does), it would have been very unfit, that God should have left it to mere chance, whether man should fall or no. For, chance, if there should be any such thing, is undesigning and blind. And certainly it is more fit that an event of so great importance, and that is attended with such an infinite train of great consequences, should be disposed and ordered by infinite wisdom, than that it should be left to blind chance.

If it be said, that God need not have interposed to render it impossible for man to sin, and yet not leave it to mere contingence, or blind chance neither; but might have left it with man's free will, to determine whether to sin or no; I answer, if God did leave it to man's free will, without any sort of disposal, or ordering in the case, whence it should be previously certain how that free will should determine, then still that first determination of the will must be merely contingent or by chance. It could not have any antecedent act of the will to determine it; for I speak now of the very first act or motion of the will respecting the affair that may be looked upon as the prime ground and highest source of the event. To suppose this to be determined by a foregoing act is a contradiction. God's disposing this determination of the will by his permission, does not at all infringe the liberty of the creature: it is in no respect any more inconsistent with liberty, than mere chance or contingence. For if the determination of the will be from blind undesigning chance, it is no more from the agent himself, or from the will itself, than if we suppose, in the case, a wise divine disposal by permission.

2. It was fit that it should be at the ordering of the divine wisdom and good pleasure, whether every particular man shoul

stand for himself, or whether the first father of mankind should be appointed as the moral and federal head and representative of the rest. If God has not liberty in this matter to determine either of these two as he pleases, it must be because determining that the first father of men should represent the rest, and not that every one should stand for himself, is injurious to mankind. For if it be not injurious to mankind, how is it unjust? But it is not injurious to mankind; for there is nothing in the nature of the case itself, that makes it better for mankind that each man should stand for himself, than that all should be represented by their common father; as the least reflection or consideration will convince any one. And if there be nothing in the nature of the thing that makes the former better for mankind than the latter, then it will follow, that mankind are not hurt in God's choosing and appointing the latter, rather than the former; or, which is the same thing, that it is not injurious to mankind.

3. When men are fallen, and become sinful, God by his sovereignty has a right to determine about their redemption as he pleases. He has a right to determine whether he will redeem any or no. He might, if he had pleased, have left all to perish, or might have redeemed all. Or, he may redeem some, and leave others; and if he doth so, he may take whom he pleases, and leave whom he pleases. To suppose that all have forfeited his favor, and deserved to perish, and to suppose that he may not leave any one individual of them to perish, implies a contradiction; because it supposes that such a one has a claim to God's favor, and is not justly liable to perish; which is contrary to the supposition.

It is meet that God should order all these things according to his own pleasure. By reason of his greatness and glory, by which he is infinitely above all, he is worthy to be sovereign, and that his pleasure should in all things take place: he is worthy that he should make himself his end, and that he should make nothing but his own wisdom his rule in pursuing that end, without asking leave or counsel of any, and without giving any account of any of his matters. It is fit that he that is absolutely perfect, and infinitely wise, and the fountain of all wisdom, should determine every thing by his own will, even things of the greatest importance, such as the eternal salvation or damnation of sinners. It is meet that he should be thus sovereign, because he is the first being, the eternal being, whence all other beings are. He is the Creator of all things; and all are absolutely and universally dependent on him; and therefore it is meet that he should act as the sovereign possessor of heaven and earth.

THE EXCELLENCY OF CHRIST

REVELATION v. 5, 6.—And one of the elders saith unto me, Weep not; behold, the Lion of the tribe of Judah, the Root of David, hath prevailed
to open the book, and to loose the seven seals thereof. And I beheld,
and lo, in the midst of the throne, and of the four beasts, and in the
midst of the elders, stood a Lamb as it had been slain—

I. There is a conjunction of such excellencies in Christ, as,
in our manner of conceiving, are very diverse one from another.
Such are the various divine perfections and excellencies that
Christ is possessed of. Christ is a divine person, or one that
is God; and therefore has all the attributes of God. The difference there is between these is chiefly relative, and in our
manner of conceiving of them. And those that in this sense
are most diverse, do meet in the person of Christ.

I shall mention two instances.

1. There do meet in Jesus Christ infinite highness and infinite
condescension. Christ, as he is God, is infinitely great and high
above all. He is higher than the kings of the earth: for he is
King of kings and Lord of lords. He is higher than the heavens,
and higher than the highest angels of heaven. So great is he,
that all men, all kings and princes, are as worms of the dust
before him; all nations are as the drop of the bucket, and the
light dust of the balance; yea, and angels themselves are as
nothing before him. He is so high, that he is infinitely above
any need of us; above our reach, that we cannot be profitable
to him; and above our conceptions, that we cannot comprehend
him. Prov. xxx. 4, "What is his name, or what is his son's
name, if thou canst tell?" Our understandings, if we stretch
them never so far, cannot reach up to his divine glory. Job xi. 8,
"It is high as heaven, what canst thou do?" Christ is the Creator
and great possessor of heaven and earth: he is sovereign Lord
of all: he rules over the whole universe, and doth whatsoever
pleaseth him: his knowledge is without bound: his wisdom is
perfect, and what none can circumvent: his power is infinite,

and none can resist him: his riches are immense and inexhaustible: his majesty is infinitely awful.

And yet he is one of infinite condescension. None are so low or inferior, but Christ's condescension is sufficient to take a gracious notice of them. He condescends not only to the angels, humbling himself to behold the things that are done in heaven, but he also condescends to such poor creatures as men; and that not only so as to take notice of princes and great men, but of those that are of meanest rank and degree, the "poor of the world," James ii. 5. Such as are commonly despised by their fellow creatures, Christ does not despise. 1 Cor. i. 28, "Base things of the world, and things that are despised, hath God chosen." Christ condescends to take notice of beggars, Luke xvi. 22, and of servants, and people of the most despised nations: in Christ Jesus is neither "Barbarian, Scythian, bond nor free," Col. iii. 11. He that is thus high, condescends to take a gracious notice of little children. Matt. xix. 14, "Suffer little children to come unto me." Yea, which is much more, his condescension is sufficient to take a gracious notice of the most unworthy, sinful creatures, those that have infinite ill deservings.

Yea, so great is his condescension, that it is not only sufficient to take some gracious notice of such as these, but sufficient for every thing that is an act of condescension. His condescension is great enough to become their friend: it is great enough to become their companion, to unite their souls to him in spiritual marriage: it is great enough to take their nature upon him, to become one of them, that he may be one with them: yea, it is great enough to abase himself yet lower for them, even to expose himself to shame and spitting; yea, to yield up himself to an ignominious death for them. And what act of condescension can be conceived of greater? Yet such an act as this, has his condescension yielded to, for those that are so low and mean, despicable and unworthy!

Such a conjunction of such infinite highness and low condescension, in the same person, is admirable. We see, by manifold instances, what a tendency a high station has in men, to make them to be of a quite a contrary disposition. If one worm be a little exalted above another, by having more dust, or a bigger dunghill, how much does he make of himself! What a distance does he keep from those that are below him! And a little condescension is what he expects should be made much of, and greatly acknowledged. Christ condescends to wash our feet; but how would great men (or rather the bigger worms) account themselves debased by acts of far less condescension!

2. There meet in Jesus Christ, infinite justice and infinite grace. As Christ is a divine person he is infinitely holy and just, infinitely hating sin, and disposed to execute condign punishment for sin. He is the Judge of the world, and is the infinitely just judge of it, and will not at all acquit the wicked, or by any means clear the guilty.

And yet he is one that is infinitely gracious and merciful. Though his justice be so strict with respect to all sin, and every breach of the law, yet he has grace sufficient for every sinner, and even the chief of sinners. And it is not only sufficient for the most unworthy to show them mercy, and bestow some good upon them, but to bestow the greatest good; yea, it is sufficient to bestow all good upon them, and to do all things for them. There is no benefit or blessing that they can receive so great, but the grace of Christ is sufficient to bestow it on the greatest sinner that ever lived. And not only so, but so great is his grace, that nothing is too much as the means of this good: it is sufficient not only to do great things, but also to suffer in order to it; and not only to suffer, but to suffer most extremely even unto death, the most terrible of natural evils; and not only death, but the most ignominious and tormenting, and every way the most terrible death that men could inflict; yea, and greater sufferings than men could inflict, who could only torment the body, but also those sufferings in his soul, that were the more immediate fruits of the wrath of God against the sins of those he undertakes for. . . .

Let the consideration of this wonderful meeting of diverse excellencies in Christ induce you to accept him, and close with him as your Saviour. As all manner of excellencies meet in him, so there are concurring in him all manner of arguments and motives, to move you to choose him for your Saviour, and every thing that tends to encourage poor sinners to come and put their trust in him. His fulness and all-sufficiency as a Saviour gloriously appear in that variety of excellencies that has been spoken of.

Fallen man is in a state of exceeding great misery, and is helpless in it, he is a poor weak creature, like an infant, cast out in its blood, in the day that it is born: but Christ is *the Lion of the tribe of Judah;* he is strong, though we are weak; he hath prevailed to do that for us which no creature else could do. Fallen man is a mean, despicable creature, a contemptible worm; but Christ who has undertaken for us, is infinitely honorable and worthy. Fallen man is polluted, but Christ is infinitely holy: fallen man is hateful, but Christ is infinitely lovely: fallen man is the object of God's indignation, but Christ is infinitely dear to him: we have dreadfully provoked God, but Christ has performed that righteousness that is infinitely precious in God's eyes.

And here is not only infinite strength and infinite worthiness, but infinite condescension; and love and mercy, as great as power and dignity: if you are a poor, distressed sinner, whose heart is ready to sink for fear that God never will have mercy on you, you need not be afraid to go to Christ, for fear that he is either unable or unwilling to help you: here is a strong foundation, and an inexhaustible treasure, to answer the necessities of your poor soul; and here is infinite grace and gentleness to invite and embolden a poor, unworthy, fearful soul to come to it. If Christ accepts you, you need not fear but that you will be safe; for he is a strong lion for your defence: and if you come, you need not fear but that you shall be accepted; for he is like a lamb to all that come to him, and receives them with infinite grace and tenderness. It is true he has awful majesty; he is the great God, and is infinitely high above you; but there is this to encourage and embolden the poor sinner, that Christ is a man as well as God; he is a creature as well as the Creator; and he is the most humble and lowly in heart of any creature in heaven or earth. This may well make the poor unworthy creature bold in coming to him. You need not hesitate one moment; but may run to him, and cast yourself upon him; you will certainly be graciously and meekly received by him. Though he be a lion, he will only be a lion to your enemies, but he will be a lamb to you. It could not have been conceived, had it not been so in the person of Christ, that there could have been so much in any Saviour, that is inviting, and tending to encourage sinners to trust in him. Whatever your circumstances are, you need not be afraid to come to such a Saviour as this: be you never so wicked a creature, here is worthiness enough: be you never so poor, and mean, and ignorant a creature, there is no danger of being despised; for though he be so much greater than you, he is also immensely more humble than you. Any one of you that is a father or mother, will not despise one of your own children that comes to you in distress; much less danger is there of Christ despising you, if you in your heart come to him.—Here let me a little expostulate with the poor, burdened, distressed soul.

What are you afraid of, that you dare not venture your soul upon Christ? Are you afraid that he cannot save you; that he is not strong enough to conquer the enemies of your soul? But how can you desire one stronger than the "mighty God"? as Christ is called, Isa. ix. 6. Is there need of greater than infinite strength? Are you afraid that he will not be willing to stoop so low as to take any gracious notice of you? But then, look on him, as he stood in the ring of soldiers, exposing his blessed face to be buffeted and spit upon by them! Behold him bound, with his back uncovered to those that smote him! And behold him hanging on the cross! Do you think that he that had condescension enough to stoop to these things, and that for his crucifiers, will be unwilling to accept you if you come to him? Or, are you afraid, that if he does accept you, that God the Father will not accept him for you? But consider, will God reject his own Son, in whom his infinite delight is and has been, from all eternity, and that is so united to him, that if he should reject him, he would reject himself?

2. What is there that you can desire should be in a Saviour, that is not in Christ? Or, wherein should you desire a Saviour should be otherwise than Christ is? What excellency is there wanting? What is there that is great or good? What is there that is venerable or winning? What is there that is adorable or endearing? Or, what can you think of, that would be encouraging, that is not to be found in the person of Christ? Would you have your Saviour to be great and honorable, because you are not willing to be beholden to a mean person? And is not Christ a person honorable enough to be worthy that you should be dependent on him? Is he not a person high enough to be worthy to be appointed to so honorable a work as your salvation? Would you not only have a Saviour that is of high degree, but would you have him, notwithstanding his exaltation and dignity, to be made also of low degree, that he might have experience of afflictions and trials, that he might learn by the things that he has suffered, to pity them that suffer and are tempted? And has not Christ been made low enough for you? And has he not suffered enough? Would you not only have him have experience of the afflictions you now suffer, but also of that amazing wrath that you fear hereafter, that he may know how to pity those that are in danger of it, and afraid of it? This Christ has had experience of, which experience gave him a greater sense of it, a thousand times, than you have, or any man living has. Would you have your Saviour to be one that is near to God, that so his mediation might be prevalent with him? And can you desire him to be nearer to God than Christ is, who is his only begotten Son, of the same essence with the Father? And would you not only have him near to God, but also near to you, that you may have free access to him? And would you have him nearer to you than to be in the same nature, and not only so, but united to you by a spiritual union, so close as to be fitly represented by the union of the wife to the husband, of the branch to the vine, of the member to the head; yea, so as to be looked upon as one, and called one spirit? For so he will be united to you, if you accept him. Would you have a Saviour that has given some great an

extraordinary testimony of mercy and love to sinners, by something that he has done, as well as by what he says? And can you think or conceive of greater things than Christ has done? Was it not a great thing for him, who was God, to take upon him human nature; to be not only God, but man thenceforward to all eternity? But would you look upon suffering for sinners to be a yet greater testimony of love to sinners, than merely doing, though it be never so extraordinary a thing that he has done? And would you desire that a Saviour should suffer more than Christ has suffered for sinners? What is there wanting, or what would you add if you could, to make him more fit to be your Saviour?

But further, to induce you to accept of Christ as your Saviour, consider two things particularly.

1. How much Christ appears as the Lamb of God in his invitations to you to come to him and trust in him. With what sweet grace and kindness does he from time to time call and invite you; as Prov. viii. 4: "Unto you, O men, I call, and my voice is to the sons of men." And Isa. lv. 1—3, "Ho, every one that thirsteth, come ye to the waters, and he that hath no money; come ye, buy and eat, yea, come, buy wine and milk without money and without price." How graciously is he here inviting every one that thirsts, and in so repeating his invitation over and over, "Come ye to the waters; come, buy and eat, yea, come!" And in declaring the excellency of that entertainment which he invites you to accept of, "Come, buy wine and milk;" and in assuring you that your poverty, and having nothing to pay for it, shall be no objection, "Come, he that hath no money, come without money and without price!" And in the gracious arguments and expostulations that he uses with you! As it follows, "Wherefore do ye spend money for that which is not bread? And your labor for that which satisfieth not? Hearken diligently unto me, and eat ye that which is good, and let your soul delight itself in fatness." As much as to say, "It is altogether needless for you to continue laboring and toiling for that which can never serve your turn, seeking rest in the world, and in your own righteousness: I have made

abundant provision for you, of that which is really good, and will fully satisfy your desires, and answer your end, and stand ready to accept of you: you need not be afraid; if you will come to me, I will engage to see all your wants supplied, and you made a happy creature." As he promises in the third verse, "Incline your ear, and come unto me: hear, and your soul shall live, and I will make an everlasting covenant with you, even the sure mercies of David." And so, Prov. ix. at the beginning. How gracious and sweet is the invitation there! "Whoso is simple, let him turn in hither"; let you be never so poor, ignorant, and blind a creature, you shall be welcome. And in the following words, Christ sets forth the provision that he has made for you: "Come, eat of my bread, and drink of the wine which I have mingled." You are in a poor famishing state, and have nothing wherewith to feed your perishing soul; you have been seeking something, but yet remain destitute: hearken, how Christ calls you to eat of his bread, and to drink of the wine that he hath mingled! And how much like a lamb does Christ appear in Matt. xi. 28—30: "Come unto me, all ye that labor, and are heavy laden, and I will give you rest. Take my yoke upon you, and learn of me, for I am meek and lowly in heart; and ye shall find rest to your souls. For my yoke is easy, and my burden is light." O thou poor distressed soul, whoever thou art, that art afraid that you never shall be saved, consider that this that Christ mentions is your very case, when he calls to them that labor, and are heavy laden! And how he repeatedly promises you rest if you come to him! In the 28th verse he says, "I will give you rest." And in the 29th verse, "Ye shall find rest to your souls." This is what you want. This is the thing you have been so long in vain seeking after. O how sweet would rest be to you, if you could but obtain it! Come to Christ, and you shall obtain it. And hear how Christ, to encourage you, represents himself as a lamb! He tells you, that he is meek and lowly in heart; and are you afraid to come to such a one? And again, Rev. iii. 20, "Behold, I stand at the door and knock: if any man hear my voice, and open the door, I will come in to him, and will sup with him, and he with me."

Christ condescends not only to call you to him, but he comes to you; he comes to your door, and there knocks. He might send an officer and seize you as a rebel and vile malefactor; but instead of that, he comes and knocks at your door, and seeks that you would receive him into your house, as your friend and Saviour. And he not only knocks at your door, but he stands there waiting, while you are backward and unwilling. And not only so, but he makes promises what he will do for you, if you will admit him, what privileges he will admit you to; he will "sup with you and you with him." And again, Rev. xxii. 16, 17, "I am the root and the offspring of David, and the bright and morning star. And the Spirit and the bride say, Come: and let him that heareth, say, Come: and let him that is athirst come: and whosoever will, let him come and take of the water of life freely." How does Christ here graciously set before you his own winning, attractive excellency! And how does he condescend to declare to you not only his own invitation, but the invitation of the Spirit and the bride, if by any means he might encourage you to come! And how does he invite every one that will, that they may "take of the water of life freely," that they may take it a free gift, however precious it be, and though it be the water of life!

2. If you do come to Christ, he will appear as a lion, in his glorious power and dominion, to defend you. All those excellencies of his, in which he appears as a lion, shall be yours, and shall be employed for you in your defence, for your safety, and to promote your glory; he will be as a lion to fight against your enemies: he that touches you, or offends you, will provoke his wrath, as he that stirs up a lion. Unless your enemies can conquer this lion, they shall not be able to destroy or hurt you: unless they are stronger than he, they shall not be able to hinder your happiness. Isa. xxxi. 4, "For thus hath the Lord spoken unto me, Like as the lion and the young lion roaring on his prey, when a multitude of shepherds is called forth against him, he will not be afraid of their voice, nor abase himself for the noise of them; so shall the Lord of hosts come down to fight for mount Zion, and for the hill thereof."

THE CHRISTIAN PILGRIM

SECTION II

Why the Christian's life is a journey or pilgrimage?

1. This world is not our abiding place. Our continuance here is but very short. Man's days on the earth, are as a shadow. It was never designed by God that this world should be our home. Neither did God give us these temporal accommodations for that end. If God has given us ample estates, and children, or other pleasant friends, it is with no such design, that we should be furnished here, as for a settled abode; but with a design that we should use them for the present, and then leave them in a very little time. When we are called to any secular business, or charged with the care of a family, if we improve our lives to any other purpose, than as a journey toward heaven, all our labour will be lost. If we spend our lives in the pursuit of a temporal happiness; as riches, or sensual pleasures; credit and esteem from men; delight in our children, and the prospect of seeing them well brought up, and well settled, &c.—All these things will be of little significancy to us. Death will blow up all our hopes, and will put an end to these enjoyments. "The places that have known us, will know us no more": and "the eye that has seen us, shall see us no more." We must be taken away for ever from all these things; and it is uncertain when: it may be soon after we are put into the possession of them. And then, where will be all our worldly employments and enjoyments, when we are laid in the silent grave! "So man lieth down, and riseth not again, till the heavens be no more." *

2. The future world was designed to be our settled and everlasting abode. There it was intended that we should be fixed; and there alone is a lasting habitation, and a lasting inheritance. The present state is short and transitory; but our state

* Job xiv. 12. [Edwards's note.]

130

in the other world, is everlasting. And as we are there at first, so we must be without change. Our state in the future world, therefore, being eternal, is of so much greater importance than our state here, that all our concerns in this world should be wholly subordinated to it.

3. Heaven is that place alone where our highest end, and highest good is to be obtained. God hath made us for himself. "Of him, and through him, and to him are all things." Therefore, then do we attain to our highest end, when we are brought to God: but that is by being brought to heaven; for that is God's throne, the place of his special presence. There is but a very imperfect union with God to be had in this world, a very imperfect knowledge of him in the midst of much darkness: a very imperfect conformity to God, mingled with abundance of estrangement. Here we can serve and glorify God, but in a very imperfect manner; our service being mingled with sin, which dishonours God.—But when we get to heaven, (if ever that be,) we shall be brought to a perfect union with God, and have more clear views of him. There we shall be fully conformed to God, without any remaining sin: for "we shall see him as he is." There we shall serve God perfectly; and glorify him in an exalted manner, even to the utmost of the powers and capacity of our nature. Then we shall perfectly give up ourselves to God: our hearts will be pure and holy offerings, presented in a flame of divine love.

God is the highest good of the reasonable creature; and the enjoyment of him is the only happiness with which our souls can be satisfied.—To go to heaven fully to enjoy God, is *infinitely* better than the most pleasant accommodations here. Fathers and mothers, husbands, wives, or children, or the company of earthly friends, are but shadows; but the enjoyment of God is the substance. These are but scattered beams; but God is the sun. These are but streams; but God is the fountain. These are but drops; but God is the ocean.—Therefore it becomes us to spend this life only as a journey towards heaven, as it becomes us to make the seeking of our highest end and proper good, the whole work of our lives; to which we should subordinate all other concerns of life. Why should we labour for, or set our hearts on any thing else, but that which is our proper end, and true happiness?

4. Our present state, and all that belongs to it, is designed by him that made all things, to be wholly in order to another world.—This world was made for a place of preparation for another. Man's mortal life was given him, that he might be prepared for his fixed state. And all that God has here given us, is given to this purpose. The sun shines, and the rain falls upon us; and the earth yields her increase to us for this end. Civil, ecclesiastical, and family affairs, and all our personal concerns, are designed and ordered in subordination to a future world, by the maker and disposer of all things. To this therefore they ought to be subordinated by us.

SECTION III

Instruction afforded by the consideration, that life is a journey or pilgrimage, towards heaven.

1. This doctrine may teach us moderation in our mourning for the loss of such dear friends, who, while they lived, improved their lives to right purposes. If they lived a holy life, then their lives were a journey towards heaven. And why should we be immoderate in mourning, when they are got to their journey's end? Death, though it appears to us with a frightful aspect, is to them a great blessing. Their end is happy, and better than their beginning. *"The day of their death, is better than the day of their birth."* * While they lived, they desired heaven, and chose it above this world, or any of its enjoyments. For this they earnestly longed, and why should we grieve that they have obtained it?—Now they have got to their Father's house. They find more comfort a thousand times, now they are got home, than they did in their journey. In this world they underwent much labour and toil; it was a wilderness they passed through. There were many difficulties in the way; mountains and rough places. It was laborious and fatiguing to travel the

*Eccles. vii. 1. [Edwards's note.]

road; and they had many wearisome days and nights: but now they have got to their everlasting rest. "And I heard a voice from heaven, saying unto me, Write, blessed are the dead which die in the Lord from henceforth: yea, saith the Spirit, that they may rest from their labours; and their works do follow them." *
They look back upon the difficulties, and sorrows, and dangers of life, rejoicing that they have surmounted them all.

We are ready to look upon death as their calamity, and to mourn, that those who were so dear to us, should be in the dark grave; that they are there transformed to corruption and worms; taken away from their dear children and enjoyments, &c. as though they were in awful circumstances. But this is owing to our infirmity; they are in a happy condition, inconceivably blessed. They do not mourn, but rejoice with exceeding joy: their mouths are filled with joyful songs, and they drink at rivers of pleasure. They find no mixture of grief that they have changed their earthly enjoyments, and the company of mortals, for heaven. Their life here, though in the best circumstances, was attended with much that was adverse and afflictive: but now there is an end to all adversity. "They shall hunger no more, nor thirst any more; neither shall the sun light on them, nor any heat. For the Lamb which is in the midst of the throne, shall feed them and shall lead them unto living fountains of waters: and God shall wipe away all tears from their eyes." †

It is true, we shall see them no more in this world, yet we ought to consider that we are travelling towards the same place; and why should we break our hearts that they have got there before us? We are following after them, and hope, as soon as we get to our journey's end, to be with them again, in better circumstances. A degree of mourning for near relations when departed is not inconsistent with Christianity, but very agreeable to it; for as long as we are flesh and blood, we have animal propensities and affections. But we have just reason that our mourning should be mingled with joy. "But I would not have you to be ignorant, brethren, concerning them that are asleep,

* Rev. xiv. 13. [Edwards's note.]
† Rev. vii. 16. 17. [Edwards's note.]

that ye sorrow not, even as others that have no hope:"* (*i. e.*)
that they should not sorrow as the Heathen, who had no
knowledge of a future happiness. This appears by the following verse; "*for if we believe that Jesus died and rose again, even
so them also which sleep in Jesus, will God bring with him.*"

2. If our lives ought to be only a journey towards heaven;
how ill do they improve their lives, that spend them in travelling
towards hell?—Some men spend their whole lives, from their
infancy to their dying day, in going down the broad way to
destruction. They not only draw nearer to hell as to time, but
they every day grow more ripe for destruction; they are more
assimilated to the inhabitants of the infernal world. While
others press forward in the straight and narrow way to life, and
laboriously travel up the hill toward Zion, against the inclinations and tendency of the flesh; these run with a swift career
down to eternal death. This is the employment of every day,
with all wicked men; and the whole day is spent in it. As soon
as ever they awake in the morning, they set out anew in the way
to hell, and spend every waking moment in it. They begin in
early days. "The wicked are estranged from the womb, they
go astray as soon as they are born, speaking lies."† They hold
on it with perseverance. Many of them who live to be old, are
never weary in it; though they live to be an hundred years old,
they will not cease travelling in the way to hell, till they arrive
there. And all the concerns of life are subordinated to this employment. A wicked man is a servant of sin; his powers and
faculties are employed in the service of sin; and in fitness for
hell. And all his possessions are so used by him as to be subservient to the same purpose. Men spend their time in treasuring up wrath against the day of wrath. Thus do all unclean
persons, who live in lascivious practices in secret; all malicious
persons; all profane persons, that neglect the duties of religion.
Thus do all unjust persons; and those who are fraudulent and
oppressive in their dealings. Thus do all backbiters and revilers;
all covetous persons, that set their hearts chiefly on the riches of

* I Thess. iv. 13. [Edwards's note.]
† Psalm xlviii. 4. [Edwards's note.]

this world. Thus do tavern-haunters, and frequenters of evil
company; and many other kinds that might be mentioned. Thus
the bulk of mankind are hastening onward in the broad way to
destruction; which is, as it were, filled up with the multitude that
are going in it with one accord. And they are every day going to
hell out of this broad way by thousands. Multitudes are continually flowing down into the great lake of fire and brimstone,
as some mighty river constantly disembogues its water into the
ocean.

3. Hence when persons are converted they do but begin their
work, and set out in the way they have to go.—They never till
then do any thing at that work in which their whole lives ought
to be spent. Persons before conversion never take a step that
way. Then does a man first set out on his journey, when he is
brought home to Christ; and so far is he from having done his
work, that his care and labour in his Christian work and business, is then but begun, in which he must spend the remaining
part of his life.

Those persons do ill, who when they are converted, and have
obtained a hope of their being in a good condition, do not strive
as earnestly as they did before, while they were under awakenings. They ought, henceforward, as long as they live, to be as
earnest and laborious, as watchful and careful as ever; yea, they
should increase more and more. It is no just excuse, that now
they have obtained conversion. Should not we be as diligent
that we may serve and glorify God, as that we ourselves may be
happy? And if we have obtained grace, yet we ought to strive
as much that we may obtain the other degrees that are before, as
we did to obtain that small degree that is behind. The apostle
tells us, that he forgot what was behind, and reached forth towards what was before.*

Yea, those who are converted, have now a further reason to
strive for grace; for they have seen something of its excellency.
A man who has once tasted the blessings of Canaan, has more
reason to press towards it than he had before. And they who are

*Phil. iii. 13. [Edwards's note.]

converted, should strive to "make their calling and election sure." All those who are converted are not sure of it; and those who are sure, do not know that they shall be always so; and still seeking and serving God with the utmost diligence, is the way to have assurance, and to have it maintained.

THE PEACE WHICH CHRIST GIVES
HIS TRUE FOLLOWERS

JOHN XIV. 27.—Peace I leave with you, my peace I give unto you: not as the world giveth, give I unto you.

III. This legacy of Christ to his true disciples is very diverse from all that the men of this world ever leave to their children when they die. The men of this world, many of them, when they come to die, have great estates to bequeath to their children, an abundance of the good things of this world, large tracts of ground, perhaps in a fruitful soil, covered with flocks and herds. They sometimes leave to their children stately mansions, and vast treasures of silver, gold, jewels, and precious things, fetched from both the Indies, and from every side of the globe of the earth. They leave them wherewith to live in much state and magnificence, and make a great show among men, to fare very sumptuously, and swim in worldly pleasures. Some have crowns, sceptres, and palaces, and great monarchies to leave to their heirs. But none of these things are to be compared to that blessed peace of Christ which he has bequeathed to his true followers. These things are such as God commonly, in his providence, gives his worst enemies, those whom he hates and despises most. But Christ's peace is a precious benefit, which he reserves for his peculiar favorites. These worldly things, even the best of them, that the men and princes of the world leave for their children, are things which God in his providence throws out to those whom he looks on as dogs; but Christ's peace is the bread of his children. All these earthly things are but empty shadows, which, however men set their hearts upon them, are not bread, and can never satisfy their souls; but this peace of Christ is a truly substantial, satisfying food, Isai. lv. 2. None of those things, if men have them to the best advantage, and in ever so great abundance, can give true peace and rest to the soul, as is abundantly manifest not only in reason, but experience; it being found in all ages, that those who have the most of them, have commonly the least quietness of mind. It is true, there may be a kind of quietness, a false peace they may have in their enjoyment of worldly things; men may bless their souls, and think themselves the only happy persons, and despise others; may say to their souls, as the rich man did, Luke xii. 19, "Soul, thou hast much goods laid up for many years, take thine ease, eat, drink, and be merry." But Christ's peace, which he gives to his true disciples, vastly differs from this peace that men may have in the enjoyments of the world, in the following respects:

1. Christ's peace is a reasonable peace and rest of soul; it is what has its foundation in light and knowledge, in the proper exercises of reason, and a right view of things; whereas the peace of the world is founded in blindness and delusion. The peace that the people of Christ have, arises from their having their eyes open, and seeing things as they be. The more they consider, and the more they know of the truth and reality of things, the more they know what is true concerning themselves, the state and condition they are in; the more they know of God, and the more certain they are that there is a God, and the more they know what manner of being he is, the more certain they are of another world and future judgment, and of the truth of God's threatenings and promises; the more their consciences are awakened and enlightened, and the brighter and the more searching the light is that they see things in, the more is their peace established: whereas, on the contrary, the peace that the men of the world have in their worldly enjoyments can subsist no otherwise than by their being kept in ignorance. They must be blindfolded and deceived, otherwise they can have no peace: do but let light in upon their consciences, so that they may look about them and see what they are, and what circumstances they are in, and it will at once destroy all their quietness and comfort. Their peace can live nowhere but in the dark. Light turns their ease into torment. The more they know what is true concerning God and concerning themselves, the more they are sensible of the truth concerning those enjoyments which they possess; and the more they are sensible what things now are, and what things are like to be

hereafter, the more will their calm be turned into a storm. The worldly man's peace cannot be maintained but by avoiding consideration and reflection. If he allows himself to think, and properly to exercise his reason, it destroys his quietness and comfort. If he would establish his carnal peace, it concerns him to put out the light of his mind, and turn beast as fast as he can. The faculty of reason, if at liberty, proves a mortal enemy to his peace. It concerns him, if he would keep alive his peace, to contrive all ways that may be, to stupify his mind and deceive himself, and to imagine things to be otherwise than they be. But with respect to the peace which Christ gives, reason is its great friend. The more this faculty is exercised, the more it is established. The more they consider and view things with truth and exactness, the firmer is their comfort, and the higher their joy. How vast a difference is there between the peace of a Christian and the worldling! How miserable are they who cannot enjoy peace any otherwise than by hiding their eyes from the light, and confining themselves to darkness; whose peace is properly stupidity; as the ease that a man has who has taken a dose of stupifying poison, and the ease and pleasure that a drunkard may have in a house on fire over his head, or the joy of a distracted man in thinking that he is a king, though a miserable wretch confined in bedlam: whereas, the peace which Christ gives his true disciples, is the light of life, something of the tranquillity of heaven, the peace of the celestial paradise, that has the glory of God to lighten it.

2. Christ's peace is a virtuous and holy peace. The peace that the men of the world enjoy is vicious; it is a vile stupidity, that depraves and debases the mind, and makes men brutish. But the peace that the saints enjoy in Christ, is not only their comfort, but it is a part of their beauty and dignity. The Christian tranquillity, rest, and joy of real saints, are not only unspeakable privileges, but they are virtues and graces of God's Spirit, wherein the image of God in them does partly consist. This peace has its source in those principles that are in the highest degree virtuous and amiable, such as poverty of spirit, holy resignation, trust in God, divine love, meekness, and charity; the

exercise of such blessed fruits of the Spirit as are spoken of, Gal. 22, 23.

3. This peace greatly differs from that which is enjoyed by the men of the world, with regard to its exquisite sweetness. It is a peace that passes all that natural men enjoy in worldly things so much, that it passes their understanding and conception, Phil. iv. 7. It is exquisitely sweet, because it has so firm a foundation as the everlasting rock that never can be moved. It is sweet, because perfectly agreeable to reason. It is sweet, because it rises from holy and divine principles, that as they are the virtue, so they are the proper happiness of men.

It is exquisitely sweet, because of the greatness of the objective good that the saints enjoy, and have peace and rest in, being no other than the infinite bounty and fulness of that God who is the fountain of all good. It is sweet, on account of the fulness and perfection of that provision that is made for it in Christ and the new covenant, where there is a foundation laid for the saints' perfect peace; and hereafter they shall actually enjoy perfect peace; and though their peace is not now perfect, it is not owing to any defect in the provision made, but in their own imperfection and misery, sin and darkness; and because as yet they do partly cleave to the world and seek peace from thence, and do not perfectly cleave to Christ. But the more they do so, and the more they see of the provision there is made, and accept of it, and cleave to that alone, the nearer are they brought to perfect tranquillity, Isaiah xxvi. 5.

4. The peace of the Christian infinitely differs from that of the worldling, in that it is unfailing and eternal peace. That peace which carnal men have in the things of the world, is, according to the foundation that it is built upon, of short continuance; like the comfort of a dream, 1 John ii. 17, 1 Cor. vii. 31. These things, the best and most durable of them, are like bubbles on the face of the water; they vanish in a moment, Hos. x. 7.

But the foundation of the Christian's peace is everlasting; it is what no time, no change, can destroy. It will remain when the body dies; it will remain when the mountains depart and the hills shall be removed, and when the heavens shall be rolled together as a scroll. The fountain of his comfort shall never be diminished, and the stream shall never be dried. His comfort and joy is a living spring in the soul, a well of water springing up to everlasting life.

APPLICATION

The use that I would make of this doctrine, is to improve it, as an inducement unto all to forsake the world, no longer seeking peace and rest in its vanities, and to cleave to Christ and follow him. Happiness and rest are what all men are in pursuit of. But the things of the world, wherein most men seek it, can never afford it; they are laboring and spending themselves in vain. But Christ invites you to come to him, and offers you this peace which he gives his true followers, that so much excels all that the world can afford, Isa. lv. 2, 3.

You that have hitherto spent your time in the pursuit of satisfaction and peace in the profit and glory of the world, or in the pleasures and vanities of youth, have this day an offer made to you of that excellent and everlasting peace and blessedness, which Christ has purchased with the price of his own blood, and bestows only on those that are his peculiar favorites, his redeemed ones, that are his portion and treasure, the objects of his everlasting love. As long as you continue to reject those offers and invitations of Christ, and continue in a Christless condition, you never will enjoy any true peace or comfort; but in whatever circumstances you are, you will be miserable; you will be like the prodigal, that in vain endeavored to fill his belly with the husks that the swine did eat: the wrath of God will abide upon, and misery will attend you wherever you go, which you never will, by any means, be able to escape. Christ gives peace to the most sinful and miserable that come to him. He heals the broken in heart and bindeth up their wounds. But it is impossible that they should have peace, that continue in their sins, Isa. lvii. 19–21. There is no peace between God and them; as they have the guilt of sin remaining in their souls, and are under the dominion of sin, so God's indignation continually burns against them, and therefore there is reason why they should travail in pain all their days.

While you continue in such a state, you live in a state of dreadful uncertainty what will become of you, and in continual danger. When you are in the enjoyment of things that are the most pleasing to you, where your heart is best suited, and most cheerful, yet you are in a state of condemnation, hanging over the infernal pit, with the sword of divine vengeance hanging over your head, having no security one moment from utter and remediless destruction. What reasonable peace can any one enjoy in such a state as this[?] What does it signify to take such a one and clothe him in gorgeous apparel, or to set him on a throne, or at a prince's table, and feed him with the rarest dainties the earth affords? And how miserable is the ease and cheerfulness that such have! What a poor kind of comfort and joy is it that such take in their wealth and pleasures for a moment, while they are the prisoners of divine justice, and wretched captives of the devil, and have none to befriend them or defend them, being without Christ, aliens from the commonwealth of Israel, strangers from the covenant of promise, having no hope, and without God in the world!

I invite you now to a better portion. There are better things provided for the sinful miserable children of men. There is a surer comfort and more durable peace: comfort that you may enjoy in a state of safety and on a sure foundation: a peace and rest that you may enjoy with reason and with your eyes open; having all your sins forgiven, your greatest and most aggravated transgressions blotted out as a cloud, and buried as in the depths of the sea, that they may never be found more; and being not only forgiven, but accepted to favor; being the objects of God's complacence and delight; being taken into God's family and made his children; and having good evidence that your names were written on the heart of Christ before the world was made, and that you have an interest in that covenant of grace that is well ordered in all things and sure; wherein is promised no less than life and immortality, an inheritance incorruptible and undefiled, a crown of glory that fades not away; being in such circumstances, that nothing shall be able to prevent your being happy to all eternity; having for the foundation of your hope, that love of God which is from eternity unto eternity; and his promise and oath, and his omnipotent power, things infinitely firmer than mountains of brass. The mountains shall depart, and the hills be removed, yea, the heavens shall vanish away like smoke, and the earth shall wax old like a garment, yet these things will never be abolished.

In such a state as this you will have a foundation of peace and rest through all changes, and in times of the greatest uproar and outward calamity be defended from all storms, and dwell above the floods, Psalm xxxii. 6, 7; and you shall be at peace with every thing, and God will make all his creatures throughout all parts of his dominion, to befriend you, Job v. 19, 24. You need not be afraid of any thing that your enemies can do unto you, Psalm iii. 5, 6. Those things that now are most terrible to you, viz., death, judgment, and eternity, will then be most comfortable, the most sweet and pleasant objects of your contemplation, at least there will be reason that they should be so. Hearken therefore to the friendly counsel that is given you this day, turn your feet into the way of peace, forsake the foolish and live; forsake those things which are no other than the devil's baits, and seek after this excellent peace and rest of Jesus Christ, that peace of God which passes all understanding. Taste and see; never was any disappointed that made a trial, Prov. xxiv. 13, 14. You will not only find those spiritual comforts that Christ offers you to be of a surpassing sweetness for the present, but they will be to your soul as the dawning light that shines more and more to the perfect day; and the issue of all will be your arrival in heaven, that land of rest, those regions of everlasting joy, where your peace and happiness will be perfect, without the least mixture of trouble or affliction, and never be interrupted nor have an end.

THE FUTURE PUNISHMENT OF THE WICKED
UNAVOIDABLE AND INTOLERABLE

EZEKIEL XXII. 14.—Can thine heart endure, or can thine hands be strong in the days that I shall deal with thee? I the Lord have spoken it, and will do it.

Thus impenitent sinners will be able neither to shun the punishment threatened, nor to deliver themselves from it, nor to find any relief under it.

I come now,

IV. To show, that neither will they be able to bear it. Neither will their hands be strong to deliver themselves from it, nor will their hearts be able to endure it. It is common with men, when they meet with calamities in this world, in the first place to endeavor to shun them. But if they find, that they cannot shun them, then after they are come, they endeavor to deliver themselves from them as soon as they can; or at least, to order things so, as to deliver themselves in some degree. But if they find that they can by no means deliver themselves, and see that the case is so that they must bear them; then they set themselves to bear them: they fortify their spirits, and take up a resolution, that they will support themselves under them as well as they can. They clothe themselves with all the resolution and courage they are masters of, to keep their spirits from sinking under their calamities.

But it will be utterly in vain for impenitent sinners to think to do thus with respect to the torments of hell. They will not be able to endure them, or at all to support themselves under them: the torment will be immensely beyond their strength. What will it signify for a worm, which is about to be pressed under the weight of some great rock, to be let fall with its whole weight upon it, to collect its strength, to set itself to bear up the weight of the rock, and to preserve itself from being crushed by it? Much more in vain will it be for a poor damned soul, to endeavor to support itself under the weight of the wrath of Almighty God. What is the strength of man, who is but a worm, to support himself against the power of Jehovah, and against the fierceness of his wrath? What is man's strength, when set to bear up against the exertions of infinite power? Matt. xxi. 44, "Whosoever shall fall on this stone shall be broken; but on whomsoever it shall fall, it will grind him to powder."

When sinners hear of hell torments, they sometimes think with themselves: Well, if it shall come to that, that I must go to hell, I will bear it as well as I can: as if by clothing themselves with resolution and firmness of mind, they would be able to support themselves in some measure; when, alas! they will have no resolution, no courage at all. However they shall have prepared themselves, and collected their strength; yet as soon as they shall begin to feel that wrath, their hearts will melt and be as water. However before they may seem to harden their hearts, in order to prepare themselves to bear, yet the first moment they feel it, their hearts will become like wax before the furnace. Their courage and resolution will be all gone in an instant; it will vanish away like a shadow in the twinkling of an eye. The stoutest and most sturdy will have no more courage than the feeblest infant: let a man be an infant, or a giant, it will be all one. They will not be able to keep alive any courage, any strength, any comfort, any hope at all.

I come now as was proposed,

V. To answer an inquiry which may naturally be raised concerning these things.

INQUIRY. Some may be ready to say, If this be the case, if impenitent sinners can neither shun future punishment, nor deliver themselves from it, nor bear it; then what will become of them?

ANSWER. They will wholly sink down into eternal death. There will be that sinking of heart, of which we now cannot conceive. We see how it is with the body when in extreme pain. The nature of the body will support itself for a considerable time under very great pain, so as to keep from wholly sinking. There will be great struggles, lamentable groans and panting, and it may be convulsions. These are the strugglings of nature to support itself under the extremity of the pain. There is, as it were, a great lothness in nature to yield to it; it cannot bear wholly to sink.

But yet sometimes pain of body is so very extreme and exquisite, that the nature of the body cannot support itself under it; however loth it may be to sink, yet it cannot bear the pain; there are a few struggles, and throes, and pantings, and it may be a shriek or two, and then nature yields to the violence of the torments, sinks down, and the body dies. This is the death of the body. So it will be with the soul in hell; it will have no strength or power to deliver itself; and its torment and horror will be so great, so mighty, so vastly disproportioned to its strength, that having no strength in the least to support itself, although it be infinitely contrary to the nature and inclination of the soul utterly to sink; yet it will sink, it will utterly and totally sink, without the least degree of remaining comfort, or strength, or courage, or hope. And though it will never be annihilated, its being and perception will never be abolished, yet such will be the infinite depth of gloominess that it will sink into, that it will be in a state of death, eternal death.

The nature of man desires happiness; it is the nature of the soul to crave and thirst after well-being; and if it be under misery, it eagerly pants after relief; and the greater the misery is, the more eagerly doth it struggle for help. But if all relief be withholden, all strength overborne, all support utterly gone; then it sinks into the darkness of death.

We can conceive but little of the matter; we cannot conceive what that sinking of the soul in such a case is. But to help your conception, imagine yourself to be cast into a fiery oven, all of a glowing heat, or into the midst of a glowing brick-kiln, or of a great furnace, where your pain would be as much greater than that occasioned by accidentally touching a coal of fire, as the heat is greater. Imagine also that your body were to lie there for a quarter of an hour, full of fire, as full within and without as a bright coal of fire, all the while full of quick sense; what horror would you feel at the entrance of such a furnace! And how long would that quarter of an hour seem to you! If it were to be measured by a glass, how long would the glass seem to be running! And after you had endured it for one minute, how overbearing would it be to you to think that you had it to endure the other fourteen!

But what would be the effect on your soul, if you knew you must lie there enduring that torment to the full for twenty-four hours! And how much greater would be the effect, if you knew you must endure it for a whole year; and how vastly greater still, if you knew you must endure it for a thousand years! O then, how would your heart sink, if you thought, if you knew, that you must bear it forever and ever! That there would be no end! That after millions of millions of ages, your torment would be no nearer to an end, than ever it was; and that you never, never should be delivered!

But your torment in hell will be immensely greater than this illustration represents. How then will the heart of a poor creature sink under it! How utterly inexpressible and inconceivable must the sinking of the soul be in such a case!

This is the death threatened in the law. This is dying in the highest sense of the word. This is to die sensibly; to die and know it; to be sensible of the gloom of death. This is to be undone; this is worthy of the name of destruction. This sinking of the soul under an infinite weight, which it cannot bear, is the gloom of hell. We read in Scripture of the blackness of darkness; this is it, this is the very thing. We read in Scripture of sinners being lost, and of their losing their souls: this is the thing intended; this is to lose the soul: they that are the subjects of this are utterly lost.

APPLICATION

This subject may be applied in a use of *awakening* to impenitent sinners. What hath been said under this doctrine is for thee, O impenitent sinner, O poor wretch, who art in the same miserable state in which thou camest into the world, excepting that thou art loaded with vastly greater guilt by thine actual sins. These dreadful things which thou hast heard are for thee, who art yet unconverted, and still remainest an alien and stranger, without Christ and without God in the world. They are for thee, who to this day remainest an enemy to God, and a child of the devil, even in this remarkable season, when others both here and elsewhere, far and near, are flocking to Christ; for thee who hearest the noise, the fame of these things, but knowest nothing of the power of godliness in thine own heart.

Whoever thou art, whether young or old, little or great, if thou art in a Christless, unconverted state, this is the wrath, this is the death to which thou art condemned. This is the wrath that abideth on thee; this is the hell over which thou hangest, and into which thou art ready to drop every day and every night.

If thou shalt remain blind, and hard, and dead in sin a little longer, this destruction will come upon thee: God hath spoken and he will do it. It is vain for thee to flatter thyself with hopes that thou shalt avoid it, or to say in thine heart, perhaps it will not be; perhaps it will not be just so; perhaps things have been represented worse than they are. If thou wilt not be convinced by the word preached to thee by men in the name of God, God himself will undertake to convince thee, Ezek. xiv. 4, 7, 8.

Doth it seem to thee not real that thou shalt suffer such a dreadful destruction, because it seems to thee that thou dost not deserve it? And because thou dost not see any thing so horrid in thyself, as to answer such a dreadful punishment?—Why is it that thy wickedness doth not seem bad enough to deserve this punishment? The reason is, that thou lovest thy wickedness; thy wickedness seems good to thee; it appears lovely to thee; thou dost not see any hatefulness in it, or to be sure, any such hatefulness as to answer such misery.

But know, thou stupid, blind, hardened wretch, that God doth not see, as thou seest with thy polluted eyes: thy sins in his sight are infinitely abominable.—Thou knowest that thou hast a thousand and a thousand times made light of the Majesty of God. And why should not that Majesty, which thou hast thus despised, be manifested in the greatness of thy punishment? Thou hast often heard what a great and dreadful God Jehovah is; but thou hast made so light of it, that thou hast not been afraid of him, thou hast not been afraid to sin against him, nor to go on day after day, by thy sins, to provoke him to wrath, nor to cast his commands under foot, and trample on them. Now why may not God, in the greatness of thy destruction, justly vindicate and manifest the greatness of that Majesty, which thou hast despised?

Thou hast despised the mighty power of God; thou hast not been afraid of it. Now why is it not fit that God should show the greatness of his power in thy ruin? What king is there who will not show his authority in the punishment of those subjects that despise it! And who will not vindicate his royal majesty in executing vengeance on those that rise in rebellion? And art thou such a fool as to think that the great King of heaven and earth, before whom all other kings are so many grasshoppers, will not vindicate his kingly Majesty on such contemptuous rebels as thou art?—Thou art very much mistaken if thou thinkest so. If thou be regardless of God's Majesty, be it known to thee, God is not regardless of his own Majesty; he taketh care of the honor of it, and he will vindicate it.

Think it not strange that God should deal so severely with thee, or that the wrath which thou shalt suffer should be so great. For as great as it is, it is no greater than that love of God which thou hast despised. The love of God, and his grace, condescension, and pity to sinners in sending his Son into the world to die for them, is every whit as great and wonderful as this inexpressible wrath. This mercy hath been held forth to thee, and described in its wonderful greatness hundreds of times, and as often hath it been offered to thee; but thou wouldst not accept Christ; thou wouldst not have this great love of God; thou despisedst God's dying love; thou trampledst the benefits of it under foot. Now why shouldst thou not have wrath as great as that love and mercy which thou despisest and rejectest? Doth it seem incredible to thee, that God should so harden his heart against a poor sinner, as so to destroy him, and to bear him down with infinite power and merciless wrath? And is this a greater thing than it is for thee to harden thy heart, as thou hast done, against infinite mercy, and against the dying love of God?

Doth it seem to thee incredible, that God should be so utterly regardless of the sinner's welfare, as so to sink him into an infinite abyss of misery? Is this shocking to thee? And is it not at all shocking to thee, that thou shouldst be so utterly regardless as thou hast been of the honor and glory of the infinite God?

It arises from thy foolish stupidity and senselessness, and is because thou hast a heart of stone, that thou art so senseless of thine own wickedness as to think thou hast not deserved such a punishment, and that it is to thee incredible that it will be inflicted upon thee.—But if, when all is said and done, thou be not convinced, wait but a little while, and thou wilt be convinced: God will undertake to do the work which ministers cannot do. —Though judgment against thine evil works be not yet executed, and God now let thee alone, yet he will soon come upon thee with his great power, and then thou shalt know what God is, and what thou art.

Flatter not thyself, that if these things shall prove true, and the worst shall come, thou wilt set thyself to bear it as well as thou canst. What will it signify to set thyself to bear, and to collect thy strength to support thyself, when thou shalt fall into the hands of that omnipotent King, Jehovah? He that made thee, can make his sword approach unto thee. His sword is not the sword of man, nor is his wrath the wrath of man. If it were, possibly stoutness might be maintained under it. But it is the fierceness of the wrath of the great God, who is able to baffle and dissipate all thy strength in a moment. He can fill thy poor soul with an ocean of wrath, a deluge of fire and brimstone; or he can make it ten thousand times fuller of torment than ever an oven was full of fire; and at the same time, can fill it with despair of ever seeing any end to its torment, or any rest from its misery: and then where will be thy strength? What will become of thy courage then? What will signify thine attempts to bear?

What art thou in the hands of the great God, who made heaven and earth by speaking a word? What art thou, when dealt with by that strength, which manages all this vast universe, holds the globe of the earth, directs all the motions of the heavenly bodies from age to age, and, when the fixed time shall come, will shake all to pieces?—There are other wicked beings a thousand times stronger than thou: there are the great leviathans, strong and proud spirits, of a gigantic stoutness and hardiness. But how little are they in the hands of the great God! They are less than weak infants; they are nothing, and less than nothing in the hands of an angry God, as will appear at the day of judgment. Their hearts will be broken; they will sink; they will have no strength nor courage left; they will be as weak as water; their souls will sink down into an infinite gloom, an abyss of death and despair.—Then what will become of thee, a poor worm, when thou shalt fall into the hands of that God, when he shall come to show his wrath, and make his power known on thee?

If the strength of all the wicked men on earth, and of all the devils in hell, were united in one, and thou wert possessed of it all; and if the courage, greatness, and stoutness of all their hearts were united in thy single heart, thou wouldst be nothing in the hands of Jehovah. If it were all collected, and thou shouldst set thyself to bear as well as thou couldst, all would sink under his great wrath in an instant, and would be utterly abolished: thine hands would drop down at once and thine heart would melt as wax.—The great mountains, the firm rocks, cannot stand before the power of God; as fast as they stand, they are tossed hither and thither, and skip like lambs, when God appears in his anger. He can tear the earth in pieces in a moment; yea, he can shatter the whole universe, and dash it to pieces at one blow. How then will thine hands be strong, or thine heart endure?

Thou canst not stand before a lion of the forest; an angry wild beast, if stirred up, will easily tear such a one as thou art in pieces. Yea, not only so, but thou art crushed before the moth. A very little thing, a little worm or spider, or some such insect, is able to kill thee. What then canst thou do in the hands of God? It is vain to set the briers and thorns in battle array against glowing flames; the points of thorns, though sharp, do nothing to withstand the fire.

Some of you have seen buildings on fire; imagine therefore with yourselves, what a poor hand you would make at fighting with the flames, if you were in the midst of so great and fierce a

fire. You have often seen a spider, or some other noisome insect, when thrown into the midst of a fierce fire, and have observed how immediately it yields to the force of the flames.
There is no long struggle, no fighting against the fire, no
strength exerted to oppose the heat, or to fly from it; but it
immediately stretches forth itself and yields; and the fire takes
possession of it, and at once it becomes full of fire, and is burned
into a bright coal.——Here is a little image of what you will be
the subjects of in hell, except you repent and fly to Christ.
However you may think that you will fortify yourselves, and
bear as well as you can; the first moment you shall be cast into
hell, all your strength will sink and be utterly abolished. To
encourage yourselves, that you will set yourselves to bear hell
torments as well as you can, is just as if a worm, that is about to
be thrown into a glowing furnace, should swell and fortify
itself, and prepare itself to fight the flames.

What can you do with lightnings? What doth it signify to
fight with them? What an absurd figure would a poor weak
man make, who, in a thunder-storm, should expect a flash of
lightning on his head or his breast, and should go forth sword
in hand to oppose it; when a stream of brimstone would, in
an instant, drink up all his spirits and his life, and melt his
sword!

Consider these things, all you enemies of God, and rejecters
of Christ, whether you be old men or women, Christless heads
of families, or young people and wicked children. Be assured,
that if you do not hearken and repent, God intends to show his
wrath, and make his power known upon you. He intends to
magnify himself exceedingly in sinking you down in hell. He
intends to show his great majesty at the day of judgment, before
a vast assembly, in your misery; before a greater assembly many
thousandfold than ever yet appeared on earth; before a vast
assembly of saints, and a vast assembly of wicked men, a vast
assembly of holy angels, and before all the crew of devils. God
will before all these get himself honor in your destruction; you
shall be tormented in the presence of them all.——Then all will
see that God is a great God indeed; then all will see how dreadful

a thing it is to sin against such a God, and to reject such a Saviour, such love and grace, as you have rejected and despised. All will be filled with awe at the great sight, and all the saints and angels will look upon you, and adore that majesty, and that mighty power, and that holiness and justice of God, which shall appear in your ineffable destruction and misery.

It is probable that here are some, who hear me this day, who at this very moment are unawakened, and are in a great degree careless about their souls. I fear there are some among us who are most fearfully hardened: their hearts are harder than the very rocks. It is easier to make impressions upon an adamant than upon their hearts. I suppose some of you have heard all that I have said with ease and quietness: it appears to you as great big sounding words, but doth not reach your hearts. You have heard such things many times: you are old soldiers, and have been too much used to the roaring of heaven's cannon, to be frighted at it. It will therefore probably be in vain for me to say any thing further to you; I will only put you in mind that erelong God will deal with you. I cannot deal with you, you despise what I say; I have no power to make you sensible of your danger and misery, and of the dreadfulness of the wrath of God. The attempts of men in this way have often proved vain.

However, God hath undertaken to deal with such men as you are. It is his manner commonly first to let men try their utmost strength: particularly to let ministers try, that thus he may show ministers their own weakness and impotency; and when they have done what they can, and all fails, then God takes the matter into his own hands.—So it seems by your obstinacy, as if God intended to undertake to deal with you. He will undertake to subdue you; he will see if he cannot cure you of your senselessness and regardlessness of his threatenings. And you will be convinced; you will be subdued effectually: your hearts will be broken with a witness; your strength will be utterly broken, your courage and hope will sink. God will surely break those who will not bow.—God, having girded himself with his power and wrath, hath heretofore undertaken to deal with many hard, stubborn, senseless, obstinate hearts; and he never failed, he always did his work thoroughly.

It will not be long before you will be wonderfully changed. You who now hear of hell and the wrath of the great God, and sit here in these seats so easy and quiet, and go away so careless; by and by will shake, and tremble, and cry out, and shriek, and gnash your teeth, and will be thoroughly convinced of the vast weight and importance of these great things, which you now despise. You will not then need to hear sermons in order to make you sensible; you will be at a sufficient distance from slighting that wrath and power of God, of which you now hear with so much quietness and indifference.

SINNERS IN THE HANDS OF AN ANGRY GOD

DEUT. XXXII. 35

—Their foot shall slide in due time.—

In this verse is threatened the vengeance of God on the wicked unbelieving Israelites, who were God's visible people, and who lived under the means of grace; but who, notwithstanding all God's wonderful works towards them, remained (as ver. 28.) void of counsel, having no understanding in them. Under all the cultivations of heaven, they brought forth bitter and poisonous fruit; as in the two verses next preceding the text.—The expression I have chosen for my text, *Their foot shall slide in due time*, seems to imply the following things, relating to the punishment and destruction to which these wicked Israelites were exposed.

1. That they were always exposed to *destruction;* as one that stands or walks in slippery places is always exposed to fall. This is implied in the manner of their destruction coming upon them, being represented by their foot sliding. The same is expressed, Psalm lxxiii. 18. "Surely thou didst set them in slippery places; thou castedst them down into destruction."

2. It implies, that they were always exposed to sudden unexpected destruction. As he that walks in slippery places is every moment liable to fall, he cannot foresee one moment whether he shall stand or fall the next; and when he does fall, he falls at once without warning: Which is also expressed in Psalm lxxiii. 18, 19. "Surely thou didst set them in slippery places; thou castedst them down into destruction: How are they brought into desolation as in a moment!"

3. Another thing implied is, that they are liable to fall *of themselves*, without being thrown down by the hand of another; as he that stands or walks on slippery ground needs nothing but his own weight to throw him down.

4. That the reason why they are not fallen already, and do not fall now, is only that God's appointed time is not come. For it is said, that when that due time, or appointed time comes, *their foot shall slide*. Then they shall be left to fall, as they are inclined by their own weight. God will not hold them up in these slippery places any longer, but will let them go; and then, at that very instant, they shall fall into destruction; as he that stands on such slippery declining ground, on the edge of a pit, he cannot stand alone, when he is let go he immediately falls and is lost.

The observation from the words that I would now insist upon is this.—"There is nothing that keeps wicked men at any one moment out of hell, but the mere pleasure of God"—By the *mere* pleasure of God, I mean his *sovereign* pleasure, his arbitrary will, restrained by no obligation, hindered by no manner of difficulty, any more than if nothing else but God's mere will had in the least degree, or in any respect whatsoever, any hand in the preservation of wicked men one moment.— The truth of this observation may appear by the following considerations.

1. There is no want of *power* in God to cast wicked men into hell at any moment. Men's hands cannot be strong when God rises up. The strongest have no power to resist him, nor can any deliver out of his hands.—He is not only able to cast wicked men into hell, but he can most easily do it. Sometimes an earthly prince meets with a great deal of difficulty to subdue a rebel, who has found means to fortify himself, and has made himself strong by the numbers of his followers. But it is not so with God. There is no fortress that is any defence from the power of God. Though hand join in hand, and vast multitudes of God's enemies combine and associate themselves, they are easily broken in pieces. They are as great heaps of light chaff before the whirlwind; or large quantities of dry stubble before devouring flames. We find it easy to tread on and crush a worm that we see crawling on the earth; so it is easy for us to cut or singe a slender thread that any thing hangs by: thus easy is it for God, when he pleases, to cast his enemies down to hell.

What are we, that we should think to stand before him, at whose rebuke the earth trembles, and before whom the rocks are thrown down?

2. They *deserve* to be cast into hell; so that divine justice never stands in the way, it makes no objection against God's using his power at any moment to destroy them. Yea, on the contrary, justice calls aloud for an infinite punishment of their sins. Divine justice says of the tree that brings forth such grapes of Sodom, "Cut it down, why cumbereth it the ground?" Luke xiii. 7. The sword of divine justice is every moment brandished over their heads, and it is nothing but the hand of arbitrary mercy, and God's mere will, that holds it back.

3. They are already under a sentence of *condemnation* to hell. They do not only justly deserve to be cast down thither, but the sentence of the law of God, that eternal and immutable rule of righteousness that God has fixed between him and mankind, is gone out against them, and stands against them; so that they are bound over already to hell. John iii. 18. "He that believeth not is condemned already." So that every unconverted man properly belongs to hell; that is his place; from thence he is, John viii. 23. "Ye are from beneath:" And thither he is bound; it is the place that justice, and God's word, and the sentence of his unchangeable law assign to him.

4. They are now the objects of that very same *anger* and wrath of God, that is expressed in the torments of hell. And the reason why they do not go down to hell at each moment, is not because God, in whose power they are, is not then very angry with them; as he is with many miserable creatures now tormented in hell, who there feel and bear the fierceness of his wrath. Yea, God is a great deal more angry with great numbers that are now on earth: yea, doubtless, with many that are now in this congregation, who it may be are at ease, than he is with many of those who are now in the flames of hell.

So that it is not because God is unmindful of their wickedness, and does not resent it, that he does not let loose his hand and cut them off. God is not altogether such an one as themselves, though they may imagine him to be so. The wrath of

God burns against them, their damnation does not slumber; the pit is prepared, the fire is made ready, the furnace is now hot, ready to receive them; the flames do now rage and glow. The glittering sword is whet, and held over them, and the pit hath opened its mouth under them.

5. The *devil* stands ready to fall upon them, and seize them as his own, at what moment God shall permit him. They belong to him; he has their souls in his possession, and under his dominion. The scripture represents them as his goods, Luke xi. 12. The devils watch them; they are ever by them at their right hand; they stand waiting for them, like greedy hungry lions that see their prey, and expect to have it, but are for the present kept back. If God should withdraw his hand, by which they are restrained, they would in one moment fly upon their poor souls. The old serpent is gaping for them; hell opens its mouth wide to receive them; and if God should permit it, they would be hastily swallowed up and lost.

6. There are in the souls of wicked men those hellish *principles* reigning, that would presently kindle and flame out into hell fire, if it were not for God's restraints. There is laid in the very nature of carnal men, a foundation for the torments of hell. There are those corrupt principles, in reigning power in them, and in full possession of them, that are seeds of hell fire. These principles are active and powerful, exceeding violent in their nature, and if it were not for the restraining hand of God upon them, they would soon break out, they would flame out after the same manner as the same corruptions, the same enmity does in the hearts of damned souls, and would beget the same torments as they do in them. The souls of the wicked are in scripture compared to the troubled sea, Isa. lvii. 20. For the present, God restrains their wickedness by his mighty power, as he does the raging waves of the troubled sea, saying, "Hitherto shalt thou come, but no further;" but if God should withdraw that restraining power, it would soon carry all before it. Sin is the ruin and misery of the soul; it is destructive in its nature; and if God should leave it without restraint, there would need nothing else to make the soul perfectly miserable. The

corruption of the heart of man is immoderate and boundless in its fury; and while wicked men live here, it is like fire pent up by God's restraints, whereas if it were let loose, it would set on fire the course of nature; and as the heart is now a sink of sin, so if sin was not restrained, it would immediately turn the soul into a fiery oven, or a furnace of fire and brimstone.

7. It is no security to wicked men for one moment, that there are no visible means of death at hand. It is no security to a natural man, that he is now in health, and that he does not see which way he should now immediately go out of the world by any accident, and that there is no visible danger in any respect in his circumstances. The manifold and continual experience of the world in all ages, shows this is no evidence, that a man is not on the very brink of eternity, and that the next step will not be into another world. The unseen, unthought-of ways and means of persons going suddenly out of the world are innumerable and inconceivable. Unconverted men walk over the pit of hell on a rotten covering, and there are innumerable places in this covering so weak that they will not bear their weight, and these places are not seen. The arrows of death fly unseen at noon-day; the sharpest sight cannot discern them. God has so many different unsearchable ways of taking wicked men out of the world and sending them to hell, that there is nothing to make it appear, that God had need to be at the expence of a miracle, or go out of the ordinary course of his providence, to destroy any wicked man, at any moment. All the means that there are of sinners going out of the world, are so in God's hands, and so universally and absolutely subject to his power and determination, that it does not depend at all the less on the mere will of God, whether sinners shall at any moment go to hell, than if means were never made use of, or at all concerned in the case.

8. Natural men's prudence and care to preserve their own lives, or the care of others to preserve them, do not secure them a moment. To this, divine providence and universal experience do also bear testimony. There is this clear evidence that men's own wisdom is no security to them from death; that if it were

otherwise we should see some difference between the wise and politic men of the world, and others, with regard to their liableness to early and unexpected death: but how is it in fact? Eccles. ii. 16. "How dieth the wise man? even as the fool."

9. All wicked men's pains and *contrivance* which they use to escape hell, while they continue to reject Christ, and so remain wicked men, do not secure them from hell one moment. Almost every natural man that hears of hell, flatters himself that he shall escape it; he depends upon himself for his own security; he flatters himself in what he has done, in what he is now doing, or what he intends to do. Every one lays out matters in his own mind how he shall avoid damnation, and flatters himself that he contrives well for himself, and that his schemes will not fail. They hear indeed that there are but few saved, and that the greater part of men that have died heretofore are gone to hell; but each one imagines that he lays out matters better for his own escape than others have done. He does not intend to come to that place of torment; he says within himself, that he intends to take effectual care, and to order matters so for himself as not to fail.

But the foolish children of men miserably delude themselves in their own schemes, and in confidence in their own strength and wisdom; they trust to nothing but a shadow. The greater part of those who heretofore have lived under the same means of grace, and are now dead, are undoubtedly gone to hell; and it was not because they were not as wise as those who are now alive: it was not because they did not lay out matters as well for themselves to secure their own escape. If we could speak with them, and inquire of them, one by one, whether they expected, when alive, and when they used to hear about hell, ever to be the subjects of that misery: we doubtless, should hear one and another reply, "No, I never intended to come here: I had laid out matters otherwise in my mind; I thought I should contrive well for myself: I thought my scheme good. I intended to take effectual care; but it came upon me unexpected; I did not look for it at that time, and in that manner; it came as a thief

Death outwitted me: God's wrath was too quick for me. Oh, my cursed foolishness! I was flattering myself, and pleasing myself with vain dreams of what I would do hereafter; and when I was saying, Peace and safety, then suddenly destruction came upon me."

10. God has laid himself under *no obligation*, by any promise to keep any natural man out of hell one moment. God certainly has made no promises either of eternal life, or of any deliverance or preservation from eternal death, but what are contained in the covenant of grace, the promises that are given in Christ, in whom all the promises are yea and amen. But surely they have no interest in the promises of the covenant of grace who are not the children of the covenant, who do not believe in any of the promises, and have no interest in the Mediator of the covenant.

So that, whatever some have imagined and pretended about promises made to natural men's earnest seeking and knocking, it is plain and manifest, that whatever pains a natural man takes in religion, whatever prayers he makes, till he believes in Christ, God is under no manner of obligation to keep him a moment from eternal destruction.

So that, thus it is that natural men are held in the hand of God, over the pit of hell; they have deserved the fiery pit, and are already sentenced to it; and God is dreadfully provoked, his anger is as great towards them as to those that are actually suffering the executions of the fierceness of his wrath in hell, and they have done nothing in the least to appease or abate that anger, neither is God in the least bound by any promise to hold them up one moment; the devil is waiting for them, hell is gaping for them, the flames gather and flash about them, and would fain lay hold on them, and swallow them up; the fire pent up in their own hearts is struggling to break out: and they have no interest in any Mediator, there are no means within reach that can be any security to them. In short, they have no refuge, nothing to take hold of; all that preserves them every moment is the mere arbitrary will, and uncovenanted, unobliged forbearance of an incensed God.

APPLICATION

The use of this awful subject may be for awakening unconverted persons in this congregation. This that you have heard
is the case of every one of you that are out of Christ.—That
world of misery, that lake of burning brimstone, is extended
abroad under you. There is the dreadful pit of the glowing
flames of the wrath of God; there is hell's wide gaping mouth
open; and you have nothing to stand upon, nor any thing to
take hold of; there is nothing between you and hell but the
air; it is only the power and mere pleasure of God that holds
you up.

You probably are not sensible of this; you find you are kept
out of hell, but do not see the hand of God in it; but look at
other things, as the good state of your bodily constitution,
your care of your own life, and the means you use for your own
preservation. But indeed these things are nothing; if God
should withdraw his hand, they would avail no more to keep
you from falling, than the thin air to hold up a person that is
suspended in it.

Your wickedness makes you as it were heavy as lead, and to
tend downwards with great weight and pressure towards hell;
and if God should let you go, you would immediately sink and
swiftly descend and plunge into the bottomless gulf, and your
healthy constitution, and your own care and prudence, and best
contrivance, and all your righteousness, would have no more
influence to uphold you and keep you out of hell, than a spider's
web would have to stop a fallen rock. Were it not for the
sovereign pleasure of God, the earth would not bear you one
moment; for you are a burden to it; the creation groans with
you; the creature is made subject to the bondage of your corruption, not willingly; the sun does not willingly shine upon
you to give you light to serve sin and Satan; the earth does not
willingly yield her increase to satisfy your lusts; nor is it willingly a stage for your wickedness to be acted upon; the air does
not willingly serve you for breath to maintain the flame of life
in your vitals, while you spend your life in the service of God's

enemies. God's creatures are good, and were made for men to serve God with, and do not willingly subserve to any other purpose, and groan when they are abused to purposes so directly contrary to their nature and end. And the world would spew you out, were it not for the sovereign hand of him who hath subjected it in hope. There are black clouds of God's wrath now hanging directly over your heads, full of the dreadful storm, and big with thunder; and were it not for the restraining hand of God, it would immediately burst forth upon you. The sovereign pleasure of God, for the present, stays his rough wind; otherwise it would come with fury, and your destruction would come like a whirlwind, and you would be like the chaff of the summer threshing floor.

The wrath of God is like great waters that are dammed for the present; they increase more and more, and rise higher and higher, till an outlet is given; and the longer the stream is stopped, the more rapid and mighty is its course, when once it is let loose. It is true, that judgment against your evil works has not been executed hitherto; the floods of God's vengeance have been withheld; but your guilt in the mean time is constantly increasing, and you are every day treasuring up more wrath; the waters are constantly rising, and waxing more and more mighty; and there is nothing but the mere pleasure of God, that holds the waters back, that are unwilling to be stopped, and press hard to go forward. If God should only withdraw his hand from the flood-gate, it would immediately fly open, and the fiery floods of the fierceness and wrath of God, would rush forth with inconceivable fury, and would come upon you with omnipotent power; and if your strength were ten thousand times greater than it is, yea, ten thousand times greater than the strength of the stoutest, sturdiest devil in hell, it would be nothing to withstand or endure it.

The bow of God's wrath is bent, and the arrow made ready on the string, and justice bends the arrow at your heart, and strains the bow, and it is nothing but the mere pleasure of God, and that of an angry God, without any promise or obligation at all, that keeps the arrow one moment from being made drunk with your blood. Thus all you that never passed under a great change of heart, by the mighty power of the Spirit of God upon your souls; all you that were never born again, and made new creatures, and raised from being dead in sin, to a state of new, and before altogether unexperienced light and life, are in the hands of an angry God. However you may have reformed your life in many things, and may have had religious affections, and may keep up a form of religion in your families and closets, and in the house of God, it is nothing but his mere pleasure that keeps you from being this moment swallowed up in everlasting destruction. However unconvinced you may now be of the truth of what you hear, by and by you will be fully convinced of it. Those that are gone from being in the like circumstances with you, see that it was so with them; for destruction came suddenly upon most of them; when they expected nothing of it, and while they were saying, Peace and safety: now they see, that those things on which they depended for peace and safety, were nothing but thin air and empty shadows.

The God that holds you over the pit of hell, much as one holds a spider, or some loathsome insect over the fire, abhors you, and is dreadfully provoked: his wrath towards you burns like fire; he looks upon you as worthy of nothing else, but to be cast into the fire; he is of purer eyes than to bear to have you in his sight; you are ten thousand times more abominable in his eyes, than the most hateful venomous serpent is in ours. You have offended him infinitely more than ever a stubborn rebel did his prince; and yet it is nothing but his hand that holds you from falling into the fire every moment. It is to be ascribed to nothing else, that you did not go to hell the last night; that you was suffered to awake again in this world, after you closed your eyes to sleep. And there is no other reason to be given, why you have not dropped into hell since you arose in the morning, but that God's hand has held you up. There is no other reason to be given why you have not gone to hell, since you have sat here in the house of God, provoking his pure eyes by your sinful wicked manner of attending his solemn worship.

Yea, there is nothing else that is to be given as a reason why you do not this very moment drop down into hell.

O sinner! Consider the fearful danger you are in: it is a great furnace of wrath, a wide and bottomless pit, full of the fire of wrath, that you are held over in the hand of that God, whose wrath is provoked and incensed as much against you, as against many of the damned in hell. You hang by a slender thread, with the flames of divine wrath flashing about it, and ready every moment to singe it, and burn it asunder; and you have no interest in any Mediator, and nothing to lay hold of to save yourself, nothing to keep off the flames of wrath, nothing of your own, nothing that you ever have done, nothing that you can do, to induce God to spare you one moment.—And consider here more particularly,

1. *Whose* wrath it is: it is the wrath of the infinite God. If it were only the wrath of man, though it were of the most potent prince, it would be comparatively little to be regarded. The wrath of kings is very much dreaded, especially of absolute monarchs, who have the possessions and lives of their subjects wholly in their power, to be disposed of at their mere will. Prov. xx. 2. "The fear of a king is as the roaring of a lion: Whoso provoketh him to anger, sinneth against his own soul." The subject that very much enrages an arbitrary prince, is liable to suffer the most extreme torments that human art can invent, or human power can inflict. But the greatest earthly potentates in their greatest majesty and strength, and when clothed in their greatest terrors, are but feeble, despicable worms of the dust, in comparison of the great and almighty Creator and King of heaven and earth. It is but little that they can do, when most enraged, and when they have exerted the utmost of their fury. All the kings of the earth, before God, are as grasshoppers; they are nothing, and less than nothing: both their love and their hatred is to be despised. The wrath of the great King of kings, is as much more terrible than theirs, as his majesty is greater. Luke xii. 4, 5. "And I say unto you, my friends, Be not afraid of them that kill the body, and after that, have no more that they can do. But I will forewarn you whom

you shall fear: fear him, which after he hath killed, hath power to cast into hell: yea, I say unto you, Fear him."

2. It is the *fierceness* of his wrath that you are exposed to. We often read of the fury of God; as in Isaiah lix. 18. "According to their deeds, accordingly he will repay fury to his adversaries." So Isaiah lxvi. 15. "For behold, the Lord will come with fire, and with his chariots like a whirlwind, to render his anger with fury, and his rebuke with flames of fire." And in many other places. So, Rev. xix. 15. we read of "the wine press of the fierceness and wrath of Almighty God." The words are exceeding terrible. If it had only been said, "the wrath of God," the words would have implied that which is infinitely dreadful: but it is "the fierceness and wrath of God." The fury of God! the fierceness of Jehovah! Oh, how dreadful must that be! Who can utter or conceive what such expressions carry in them! But it is also "the fierceness and wrath of *Almighty* God." As though there would be a very great manifestation of his almighty power in what the fierceness of his wrath should inflict, as though omnipotence should be as it were enraged, and exerted, as men are wont to exert their strength in the fierceness of their wrath. Oh! then, what will be the consequence! What will become of the poor worms that shall suffer it! Whose hands can be strong? And whose heart can endure? To what a dreadful, inexpressible, inconceivable depth of misery must the poor creature be sunk who shall be the subject of this!

Consider this, you that are here present, that yet remain in an unregenerate state. That God will execute the fierceness of his anger, implies, that he will inflict wrath without any pity. When God beholds the ineffable extremity of your case, and sees your torment to be so vastly disproportioned to your strength, and sees how your poor soul is crushed, and sinks down, as it were, into an infinite gloom; he will have no compassion upon you, he will not forbear the executions of his wrath, or in the least lighten his hand; there shall be no moderation or mercy, nor will God then at all stay his rough wind; he will have no regard to your welfare, nor be at all careful lest you should suffer too much in any other sense, than only that you shall *not suffer beyond what strict justice requires*. Nothing shall be withheld, because it is so hard for you to bear. Ezek. viii. 18. "Therefore will I also deal in fury: mine eye shall not spare, neither will I have pity; and though they cry in mine ears with a loud voice, yet I will not hear them." Now God stands ready to pity you; this is a day of mercy; you may cry now with some encouragement of obtaining mercy. But when once the day of mercy is past, your most lamentable and dolorous cries and shrieks will be in vain; you will be wholly lost and thrown away of God, as to any regard to your welfare. God will have no other use to put you to, but to suffer misery; you shall be continued in being to no other end; for you will be a vessel of wrath fitted to destruction; and there will be no other use of this vessel, but to be filled full of wrath. God will be so far from pitying you when you cry to him, that it is said he will only "laugh and mock," Prov. i. 25, 26, &c.

How awful are those words, Isa. lxiii. 3, which are the words of the great God. "I will tread them in mine anger, and will trample them in my fury, and their blood shall be sprinkled upon my garments, and I will stain all my raiment." It is perhaps impossible to conceive of words that carry in them greater manifestations of these three things, *viz.* contempt, and hatred, and fierceness of indignation. If you cry to God to pity you, he will be so far from pitying you in your doleful case, or showing you the least regard or favour, that instead of that, he will only tread you under foot. And though he will know that you cannot bear the weight of omnipotence treading upon you, yet he will not regard that, but he will crush you under his feet without mercy; he will crush out your blood, and make it fly, and it shall be sprinkled on his garments, so as to stain all his raiment. He will not only hate you, but he will have you, in the utmost contempt: no place shall be thought fit for you, but under his feet to be trodden down as the mire of the streets.

3. The *misery* you are exposed to is that which God will inflict to that end, that he might show what that wrath of Jehovah is. God hath had it on his heart to show to angels and

men, both how excellent his love is, and also how terrible his wrath is. Sometimes earthly kings have a mind to show how terrible their wrath is, by the extreme punishments they would execute on those that would provoke them. Nebuchadnezzar, that mighty and haughty monarch of the Chaldean empire, was willing to show his wrath when enraged with Shadrach, Meshech, and Abednego; and accordingly gave orders that the burning fiery furnace should be heated seven times hotter than it was before; doubtless, it was raised to the utmost degree of fierceness that human art could raise it. But the great God is also willing to show his wrath, and magnify his awful majesty and mighty power in the extreme sufferings of his enemies. Rom. ix. 22. "What if God, willing to show his wrath, and to make his power known, endure with much long-suffering the vessels of wrath fitted to destruction?" And seeing this is his design, and what he has determined, even to show how terrible the unrestrained wrath, the fury and fierceness of Jehovah is, he will do it to effect. There will be something accomplished and brought to pass that will be dreadful with a witness. When the great and angry God hath risen up and executed his awful vengeance on the poor sinner, and the wretch is actually suffering the infinite weight and power of his indignation, then will God call upon the whole universe to behold that awful majesty and mighty power that is to be seen in it. Isa. xxxiii. 12–14. "And the people shall be as the burnings of lime, as thorns cut up shall they be burnt in the fire. Hear ye that are far off, what I have done; and ye that are near, acknowledge my might. The sinners in Zion are afraid; fearfulness hath surprised the hypocrites," &c.

Thus it will be with you that are in an unconverted state, if you continue in it; the infinite might, and majesty, and terribleness of the omnipotent God shall be magnified upon you, in the ineffable strength of your torments. You shall be tormented in the presence of the holy angels, and in the presence of the Lamb; and when you shall be in this state of suffering, the glorious inhabitants of heaven shall go forth and look on the awful spectacle, that they may see what the wrath and fierceness of the Almighty is; and when they have seen it, they will fall down and adore that great power and majesty. Isa. lxvi. 23, 24. "And it shall come to pass, that from one new moon to another, and from one sabbath to another, shall all flesh come to worship before me, saith the Lord. And they shall go forth and look upon the carcasses of the men that have transgressed against me; for their worm shall not die, neither shall their fire be quenched, and they shall be an abhorring unto all flesh."

4. It is *everlasting* wrath. It would be dreadful to suffer this fierceness and wrath of Almighty God one moment; but you must suffer it to all eternity. There will be no end to this exquisite horrible misery. When you look forward, you shall see a long for ever, a boundless duration before you, which will swallow up your thoughts, and amaze your soul; and you will absolutely despair of ever having any deliverance, any end, any mitigation, any rest at all. You will know certainly that you must wear out long ages, millions of millions of ages, in wrestling and conflicting with this almighty merciless vengeance; and then when you have so done, when so many ages have actually been spent by you in this manner, you will know that all is but a point to what remains. So that your punishment will indeed be infinite. Oh, who can express what the state of a soul in such circumstances is! All that we can possibly say about it, gives but a very feeble, faint representation of it; it is inexpressible and inconceivable: For "who knows the power of God's anger?"

How dreadful is the state of those that are daily and hourly in the danger of this great wrath and infinite misery! But this is the dismal case of every soul in this congregation that has not been born again, however moral and strict, sober and religious, they may otherwise be. Oh that you would consider it, whether you be young or old! There is reason to think, that there are many in this congregation now hearing this discourse, that will actually be the subjects of this very misery to all eternity. We know not who they are, or in what seats they sit, or what thoughts they now have. It may be they are now at ease, and hear all these things without much disturbance, and

are now flattering themselves that they are not the persons,
promising themselves that they shall escape. If we knew that
there was one person, and but one, in the whole congregation,
that was to be the subject of this misery, what an awful thing
would it be to think of! If we knew who it was, what an awful
sight would it be to see such a person! How might all the rest
of the congregation lift up a lamentable and bitter cry over him!
But, alas! instead of one, how many is it likely will remember
this discourse in hell? And it would be a wonder, if some that
are now present should not be in hell in a very short time, even
before this year is out. And it would be no wonder if some
persons, that now sit here, in some seats of this meeting-house,
in health, quiet and secure, should be there before to-morrow
morning. Those of you that finally continue in a natural condition, that shall keep out of hell longest will be there in a little
time! your damnation does not slumber; it will come swiftly,
and, in all probability, very suddenly upon many of you. You
have reason to wonder that you are not already in hell. It is
doubtless the case of some whom you have seen and known,
that never deserved hell more than you, and that heretofore
appeared as likely to have been now alive as you. Their case
is past all hope; they are crying in extreme misery and perfect
despair; but here you are in the land of the living and in the
house of God, and have an opportunity to obtain salvation.
What would not those poor damned hopeless souls give for
one day's opportunity such as you now enjoy!

And now you have an extraordinary opportunity, a day
wherein Christ has thrown the door of mercy wide open, and
stands in calling and crying with a loud voice to poor sinners
a day wherein many are flocking to him, and pressing into the
kingdom of God. Many are daily coming from the east, west
north and south; many that were very lately in the same miserable condition that you are in, are now in a happy state
with their hearts filled with love to him who has loved them
and washed them from their sins in his own blood, and rejoicing in hope of the glory of God. How awful is it to be left
behind at such a day! To see so many others feasting, while yo

are pining and perishing! To see so many rejoicing and singing for joy of heart, while you have cause to mourn for sorrow of heart, and howl for vexation of spirit! How can you rest one moment in such a condition? Are not your souls as precious as the souls of the people at Suffield,* where they are flocking from day to day to Christ?

Are there not many here who have lived long in the world, and are not to this day born again? and so are aliens from the commonwealth of Israel, and have done nothing ever since they have lived, but treasure up wrath against the day of wrath? Oh, sirs, your case, in an especial manner, is extremely dangerous. Your guilt and hardness of heart is extremely great. Do you not see how generally persons of your years are passed over and left, in the present remarkable and wonderful dispensation of God's mercy? You had need to consider yourselves, and awake thoroughly out of sleep. You cannot bear the fierceness and wrath of the infinite God.—And you, young men, and young women, will you neglect this precious season which you now enjoy, when so many others of your age are renouncing all youthful vanities, and flocking to Christ? You especially have now an extraordinary opportunity; but if you neglect it, it will soon be with you as with those persons who spent all the precious days of youth in sin, and are now come to such a dreadful pass in blindness and hardness.—And you, children, who are unconverted, do not you know that you are going down to hell, to bear the dreadful wrath of that God, who is now angry with you every day and every night? Will you be content to be the children of the devil, when so many other children in the land are converted, and are become the holy and happy children of the King of kings?

And let every one that is yet of Christ, and hanging over the pit of hell, whether they be old men and women, or middle aged, or young people, or little children, now hearken to the loud calls of God's word and providence. This acceptable year of the Lord, a day of such great favours to some, will doubtless be a day of as remarkable vengeance to others. Men's hearts

*A town in the neighbourhood. [Edwards's note.]

harden, and their guilt increases apace at such a day as this, if they neglect their souls; and never was there so great danger of such persons being given up to hardness of heart and blindness of mind. God seems now to be hastily gathering in his elect in all parts of the land; and probably the greater part of adult persons that ever shall be saved, will be brought in now in a little time, and that it will be as it was on the great out-pouring of the Spirit upon the Jews in the apostles' days; the election will obtain, and the rest will be blinded. If this should be the case with you, you will eternally curse this day, and will curse the day that ever you was born, to see such a season of the pouring out of God's Spirit, and will wish that you had died and gone to hell before you had seen it. Now undoubtedly it is, as it was in the days of John the Baptist, the axe is in an extraordinary manner laid at the root of the trees, that every tree which brings not forth good fruit, may be hewn down and cast into the fire.

Therefore, let every one that is out of Christ, now awake and fly from the wrath to come. The wrath of Almighty God is now undoubtedly hanging over a great part of this congregation: Let every one fly out of Sodom: "Haste and escape for your lives, look not behind you, escape to the mountain, lest you be consumed."

FUNERAL SERMON FOR DAVID BRAINERD

APPLICATION

The subject which we have been considering, may be usefully applied in the way of *exhortation*. Let us all be exhorted hence earnestly to seek after that great privilege which has been spoken of; that when "*we* are absent from the body, we may be present with the Lord." We cannot continue always in these earthly tabernacles. They are very frail, and will soon decay and fall; and are continually liable to be overthrown by innumerable means. Our souls must soon leave them, and go into the eternal world. O, how infinitely great will be the privilege and happiness of those, who, at that time shall go to be with Christ in his glory, in the manner that has been represented! The privilege of the twelve disciples was great, in being so constantly with Christ as his family, in his state of humiliation. The privilege of those three disciples was great who were with him in the mount of his Transfiguration; where was exhibited to them a faint semblance of his future glory in heaven, such as they might safely behold in the present frail, feeble and sinful state. They were greatly delighted with what they saw; and were desirous of making tabernacles to dwell there, and return no more down the mount. Great, also, was the privilege of Moses when he was with Christ in Mount Sinai, and besought him to show him his glory, and he saw his backparts as he passed by, and heard him proclaim his name. But is not that privilege infinitely greater which has now been spoken of: the privilege of being with Christ in heaven, where he sits on the throne, as the King of angels, and the God of the universe; shining forth as the Sun of that world of glory;—there to dwell in the full, constant, and everlasting view of his beauty and brightness;—there most freely and intimately to converse with him, and fully to enjoy his love, as his friends and brethren; there to share with him in the infinite pleasure and joy which he has in the enjoyment of his Father;—there to sit with him on his throne, to reign with him in the possession of all things, to partake with him in the glory of his victory over his enemies, and the advancement of his kingdom in the world, and to join with him in joyful songs of praise to his Father and our Father, to his God and our God, for ever and ever? Is not this a privilege worth the seeking after?

Here, as a powerful enforcement of this exhortation, I would improve that afflictive dispensation of God's holy Providence, which is the occasion of our coming together at this time: the death of that eminent servant of Jesus Christ, whose funeral is this day to be attended; together with what was observable in him, living and dying.

In this dispensation of Providence, God puts us in mind of our mortality, and forewarns us that the time is approaching when we must be "absent from the body"; and "must appear," as the Apostle observes in the next verse but one to the text, "before the judgment-seat of Christ, that every one of us may receive the things done in the body, according to what we have done, whether it be good or bad."

In him, whose death we are now called to consider and improve, we have not only an instance of mortality; but, as we have all imaginable reason to conclude, an instance of one, who being absent from the body, is present with the Lord. Of this we shall be convinced, whether we consider the nature of his experience at the time whence he dates his conversion; or the nature and course of his inward exercises from that time forward; or his outward conversation and practice in life; or his frame and behaviour during the whole of that long space wherein he looked death in the face.

His convictions of sin, preceding his first consolations in Christ, as appears by a written account which he has left of his inward exercises and experiences, were exceedingly deep and thorough. His trouble and sorrow arising from a sense of guilt and misery, were very great and long continued, but yet sound and rational; consisting in no unsteady, violent, and unaccountable frights, and perturbations of mind; but arising from the most serious considerations, and a clear illumination of the conscience to discern and consider the true state of things. The light let into his mind at conversion, and the influences and exercises to which his mind was subject at that time, appear very agreeable to reason and the gospel of Jesus Christ. The change was very great and remarkable; yet without any appearance of strong impressions on the imagination, of sudden flights of the affections, or of vehement emotions of the animal nature. It was attended with just views of the supreme glory of the divine Being; consisting in the infinite dignity and beauty of the perfections of his nature, and of the transcendent excellency of the way of salvation by Christ.—This was about eight years ago, when he was twenty-one years of age.

Thus God sanctified, and made meet for his use, that vessel, which he intended to make eminently a vessel of honour in his house, and which he had made of large capacity, having endowed him with very uncommon abilities and gifts of nature. He was a singular instance of a ready invention, natural eloquence, easy flowing expression, sprightly apprehension, quick discernment, and very strong memory, and yet of a very penetrating genius, close and clear thought, and piercing judgment. He had an exact taste: his understanding was, if I may so express it, of a quick, strong, and distinguishing scent.

His learning was very considerable. He had a great taste for learning; and applied himself to his studies in so close a manner when he was at college, that he much injured his health; and was obliged on that account for a while to leave college, throw by his studies, and return home. He was esteemed one who excelled in learning in that society.

He had extraordinary knowledge of men, as well as of things; and an uncommon insight into human nature. He excelled most whom I ever knew in the power of communicating his thoughts; and had a peculiar talent at accommodating himself to the capacities, tempers, and circumstances, of those whom he would instruct or counsel.

He had extraordinary gifts for the pulpit. I never had an opportunity to hear him preach; but have often heard him pray.

I think that his manner of addressing himself to God, and expressing himself before him, in that duty, almost inimitable; such as I have very rarely known equalled. He expressed himself with such exact propriety and pertinency; in such significant, weighty, pungent expressions; with such an appearance of sincerity, reverence, and solemnity, and so great a distance from all affectation, as forgetting the presence of men, and as being in the immediate presence of a great and holy God; as I have scarcely ever known paralleled. His manner of preaching, by what I have often heard of it from good judges, was no less excellent; being clear and instructive, natural, nervous and moving, and very searching and convincing. He nauseated an affected noisiness, and violent boisterousness in the pulpit; and yet much disrelished a flat, cold delivery, when the subject required affection and earnestness.

Not only had he excellent talents for the study and the pulpit, but also for conversation. He was of a social disposition; was remarkably free, entertaining, and profitable in his ordinary discourse: and discovered uncommon ability in disputing; in defending truth and confuting error.

He excelled in his knowledge of Theology, and was truly, for one of his standing, an extraordinary divine; but above all in matters relating to experimental religion. In this, I know that I have the concurring opinion of some, who are generally regarded as persons of the best judgment. According to what ability I have to judge of things of this nature, and according to my opportunities, which of late have been very great, never knew his equal, of his age and standing, for clear, accurate notions of the nature and essence of true religion, and its distinctness from its various false appearances. This I suppose to be owing to the strength of his understanding; to the great opportunities which he had of observing others, both white and Indians; and to his own great experience.

His experiences of the holy influences of God's Spirit were not only great at his first conversion; but they were so *in a continued course*, from that time forward. This appears from diary, which he kept of his daily inward exercises, from th time of his conversion, until he was disabled by the failing of his strength, a few days before his death. The change, which he looked upon as his conversion, was not only a great change of the present views, affections, and frame of his mind; but was evidently the beginning of that work of God in his heart, which God carried on, in a very wonderful manner, from that time to his dying day. He abhorred the course pursued by those, who live on their first evidences of piety, as though they had now finished their work; and thenceforward gradually settle into a cold, lifeless, negligent, worldly frame.

His experiences were very different from many things, which have lately been regarded by multitudes, as the very height of Christian experience. When that false religion, which arises chiefly from impressions on the imaginations, began first to gain a very great prevalence in the land, he was for a little while deceived with it, so as to think highly of it. Though he knew that he never had such experiences as others told of, yet he thought it was because their attainments were superior to his; and so coveted them, and sought after them, but could never obtain them. He told me that he never had what is called *an impulse, or a strong impression on his imagination*, in things of religion, in his life; yet owned, that during the short time in which he thought well of these things, he was tinged with that spirit of false zeal, which was wont to attend them; but added, that, even at this time, he was not in his element, but as a fish out of water. When, after a little while, he came clearly to see the vanity and perniciousness of such things, it cost him abundance of sorrow and distress of mind, and to my knowledge he afterwards freely and openly confessed the errors in conduct into which he had run, and humbled himself before those whom he had offended. Since his conviction of his error in those respects, he has ever had a peculiar abhorrence of that kind of bitter zeal, and those delusive experiences which have been the principal source of it. He detested enthusiasm in all its forms and operations; and condemned whatever in opinion or experience seemed to verge towards Antinomianism. He regarded with abhorrence the experiences of those, whose first faith consists in believing that Christ died for them in particular; whose first love consists in loving God, because they suppose themselves the objects of his love; and whose assurance of their good estate arises from some immediate testimony, or suggestion, either with or without texts of Scripture, that their sins are forgiven, and that God loves them; as well as the joys of those who rejoice more in their own supposed distinction above others, in honour, privileges, and high experiences, than in God's excellence and Christ's beauty; and the spiritual pride of those laymen, who set themselves up as *public* teachers, and decry human learning, and a learned ministry. He greatly nauseated every thing like noise and ostentation in religion, and the disposition which many possess to publish and proclaim their own experiences; though he did not condemn, but approved of Christians speaking of their experiences, on some occasions, and to some persons, with modesty, discretion and reserve. He abominated the spirit and practice of the generality of the Separatists in this land. I heard him say once and again, that he had had much intercourse with this class of people, and was acquainted with many of them in various parts of the country; and that by this acquaintance he knew, that what was chiefly and most generally in repute among them, as the power of godliness, was entirely a different thing from that vital piety recommended in the Scriptures, and had nothing in it of that nature. He never was more full in condemning these things than in his last illness and after he ceased to have any expectations of life: particularly when he had the greatest and nearest views of approaching eternity; and several times, when he thought himself actually dying, and expected in a few minutes to be in the eternal world as he himself told me.

As his inward appearances appear to have been of the right kind, and were very remarkable as to their degree, so were his outward behaviour and practice agreeable. In his whole course he acted as one who had indeed sold all for Christ, had entirely devoted himself to God, had made *his* glory his highest end and was fully determined to spend his whole time and strength in *his* service. He was animated in religion, in the right way animated not merely, nor chiefly, with his tongue, in professing and talking; but animated in the *work* and *business* of religion. He was not one of those who contrive to shun the cross, and get to heaven in the indulgence of ease and sloth. His life of labour and self-denial, the sacrifices which he made, and the readiness and constancy with which he spent his strength and substance to promote the glory of his Redeemer, are probably without a parallel in this age in these parts of the world. Much of this may be perceived by any one who reads his printed Journal; but much more has been learned by long and intimate acquaintance with him, and by looking into his Diary since his death, which he purposely concealed in what he published.

As his desires and labours for the advancement of Christ's kingdom were great, so was his *success*. God was pleased to make him the instrument of bringing to pass the most remarkable alteration among the poor savages, in enlightening, awakening, reforming and changing their disposition and manners, and wonderfully transforming them, of which perhaps any instance can be produced in these latter ages of the world. An account of this has been given the public in his Journal, drawn up by order of the Honourable Society in Scotland, which employed him. This I would recommend to the perusal of all who take pleasure in the wonderful works of God's grace, and who wish to read that which will peculiarly tend both to entertain and profit a Christian mind.

Not less extraordinary were his constant calmness, peace, assurance and joy in God, during the long time he looked death in the face, without the least hope of recovery; continuing without interruption to the last; while his distemper very sensibly preyed upon his vitals, from day to day, and often brought him to that state in which he looked upon himself, and was thought by others, to be dying. The thoughts of approaching death never seemed in the least to damp him, but rather to encourage him, and exhilarate his mind. The nearer death approached, the more desirous he seemed to be to die. He said, not long before his death, that "the consideration of the day of death and the day of judgment, had a long time been peculiarly sweet to him." At another time he observed, that he could not but think of the propriety there was in throwing such a rotten carcass as his into the grave: ["]It seemed to him to be the right way of disposing of it." He often used the epithet *glorious*, when speaking of the day of his death, calling it *that glorious day.* On Sabbath morning, Sep. 27, feeling an unusually violent appetite for food, and looking on it as a sign of approaching death, he said "he should look on it as a favour, if this might be his dying day, and that he longed for the time." He had before expressed himself desirous of seeing his brother again, whose return had been expected from New-Jersey; but then, [speaking of him] he said, "I am willing to go, and never see him again; I care not what I part with, to be for ever with the Lord." Being asked that morning, how he did? he answered, "I am almost in eternity; God knows, I long to be there. My work is done: I have done with all my friends: All the world is nothing to me." On the evening of the next day, when he thought himself dying, and was apprehended to be so by others, and he could utter himself only by broken whispers, he often repeated the word *Eternity;* and said, "I shall soon be with the holy angels. Jesus will come, he will not tarry." He told me one night, as he went to bed, that "he expected to die that night"; and added "I am not at all afraid, I am willing to go this night, if it be the will of God. Death is what I long for." He sometimes expressed himself as "having nothing to do but to die: and being willing to go that minute, if it was the will of God." He sometimes used that expression, "O why is his chariot so long in coming!"

He seemed to have remarkable exercises of resignation to the will of God. He once told me that "he had longed for the outpouring of the Holy Spirit of God, and the glorious times of the church, and hoped they were coming: and should have been willing to have lived to promote religion at that time, if that had been the will of God." "But," said he, "I am willing it should be as it is: I would not have the choice to make for myself for ten thousand worlds."

He several times spoke of the different kinds of willingness to die: and mentioned it as an ignoble, mean kind of willing-ness to die, *to be willing only to get rid of pain; or to go to heaven only to get honour and advancement there.* His own longings for death seemed to be quite of a different kind, and for nobler ends. When he was first taken with one of the last and most fatal symptoms in a consumption, he said, "O now the glorious time is coming! I have longed to serve God perfectly; and God will gratify these desires." At one time and another, in the latter part of his illness, he uttered these expressions. "My heaven is, to please God, to glorify him, to give all to him, and to be wholly devoted to his glory: That is the heaven I long for; that is my religion; that is my happiness; and always was, ever since I supposed I had any true religion. All those who are of that religion, shall meet me in heaven."—"I do not go to heaven to be advanced; but to give honour to God. It is no matter where I shall be stationed in heaven; whether I have a high or low seat there; but I go to love, and please, and glorify God. If I had a thousand souls, if they were worth any thing, I would give them all to God: But I have nothing to give, when all is done. It is impossible for any rational creature to be happy without acting all for God; God himself could not make me happy in any other way."—"I long to be in heaven, praising and glorifying God with the holy angels; all my desire is to glorify God."—"My heart goes out to the burying place, it seems to me a desirable place: But O to glorify God! That is it! That is above all!"—"It is a great comfort to me to think that I have done a little for God in the world: It is but a very small matter; yet I have done a little; and I lament it that I have not done more for him."—"There is nothing in the world worth living for, but doing good, and finishing God's work; doing the work that Christ did. I see nothing else in the world that can yield any satisfaction, beside living to God, pleasing him, and doing his whole will. My greatest joy and comfort has been to do something for promoting the interest of religion, and the souls of particular persons."

After he came to be in so low a state that he ceased to have the least expectation of recovery, his mind was peculiarly carried

forth with earnest concern for the prosperity of the church of
God on earth: this seemed very manifestly to arise from a pure
disinterested love to Christ, and a desire of his glory. The
prosperity of Zion was a theme on which he dwelt much, and
of which he spake much; and more and more, the nearer death
approached. He told me when near his end, that "he never, in
all his life, had his mind so led forth in desires and earnest
prayers for the flourishing of Christ's kingdom on the earth,
as since he was brought so exceedingly low at Boston." He
seemed much to wonder, that there appeared no more of a
disposition in ministers and people, to pray for the flourishing
of religion through the world. Particularly, he several times
expressed his wonder that there appeared no more forwardness
to comply with the proposal lately made from Scotland, for
united extraordinary prayer among God's people, and for the
coming of Christ's kingdom; and sent it as his dying advice
to his own congregation, that they should practice agreeably
to that proposal.

But a little before his death, he said to me, as I came into the
room, "My thoughts have been employed on the old dear
theme, the prosperity of God's church on earth. As I waked
out of sleep, I was led to cry for the pouring out of God's Spirit,
and the advancement of Christ's kingdom, for which the dear
Redeemer did and suffered so much. It is that, especially, which
makes me long for it."

But a few days before his death, he desired us to sing a psalm,
which related to the prosperity of Zion, which he signified
engaged his thoughts and desires above all things. At his desire
we sung part of the 102d psalm. When we had done, though
he was then so low that he could scarcely speak; he so exerted
himself, that he made a prayer, very audibly, in which, beside praying for those present, and for his own congregation, he earnestly
prayed for the reviving and flourishing of religion in the world.

His own congregation especially, lay much on his heart. He
often spoke of them; and commonly when he did so, it was with
peculiar tenderness; so that his speech was interrupted and
drowned with weeping.

Thus I have endeavoured to represent something of the character and behaviour of that excellent servant of Christ, whose funeral is now to be attended.—Though I have done it very imperfectly; yet I have endeavoured to do it faithfully, and as in the presence and fear of God, without flattery; which surely is to be abhorred in ministers of the Gospel, when speaking "as messengers of the Lord of hosts."

Such reason have we to be satisfied that the person of whom I have been speaking, now he is "absent from the body," is "present with the Lord"; not only so, but also with him, now wears a crown of glory, of distinguished brightness.

How much is there in the consideration of such an example, and so blessed an end, to excite us, who are yet alive, with the greatest diligence and earnestness, to improve the time of life, that we also may go to be with Christ, when we forsake the body? The time is coming, and will soon come, we know not how soon, when we must eternally take leave of all things here below, to enter on a fixed unalterable state in the eternal world. O, how well it is worth the while to labour and suffer, and deny ourselves, to lay up in store a good foundation of support and supply, against that time! How much is such a peace as we have heard of, worth at such a time? How dismal would it be, to be in such circumstances, under the outward distresses of a consuming, dissolving frame, and looking death in the face from day to day, with hearts uncleansed, and sin unpardoned, under a dreadful load of guilt and divine wrath, having much sorrow and wrath in our sickness, and nothing to comfort and support our minds, nothing before us but a speedy appearance before the judgment seat of an almighty, infinitely holy, and angry God, and an endless eternity in suffering his wrath without pity or mercy! The person of whom we have been speaking, had a great sense of this. He said, not long before his death, "It is sweet to me to think of eternity: The endlessness of it makes it sweet. But, Oh, what shall I say to the eternity of the wicked!—I cannot mention it, nor think of it!—The thought is too dreadful!" At another time, speaking of an heart devoted to God and his glory, he said, "O, of what importance is it, to have such a frame of mind, such an heart as this, when we come to die! It is this now that gives me peace."

How much is there, in particular, in the things which have been observed of this eminent minister of Christ, to excite us who are called to the same great work of the Gospel-Ministry, to earnest care and endeavours, that we may be in like manner faithful in our work; that we may be filled with the same spirit, animated with the same pure and fervent flame of love to God, and the same earnest concern to advance the kingdom and glory of our Lord and Master, and the prosperity of Zion? How lovely did these principles render him in his life; and how blessed in his end!—The time will soon come, when we also must leave our earthly tabernacles, and go to our Lord, who sent us to labour in his harvest, to render an account of ourselves to him. O how does it concern us so to run as not uncertainly; so to fight, not as those that beat the air! Should not what we have heard excite us to a careful dependence on God for his help and assistance in our great work, and to be much in seeking the influences of his Spirit, and success in our labours, by fasting and prayer; in which the person of whom I have been speaking abounded? This practice he earnestly recommended on his death-bed, from his own experience of its great benefits to some candidates for the ministry who stood by his bedside. He was often speaking of the great need which ministers have of much of the Spirit of Christ in their work, and how little good they are like to do without it; and how "when ministers were under the special influences of the Spirit of God, it assisted them to come at the consciences of men, and, as he expressed it, to handle them with *hands:* whereas, without the Spirit of God, said he, whatever reason and oratory we employ, we do but make use of *stumps*, instead of hands."

Oh that the things which were seen and heard in this extra-ordinary person; his holiness, heavenliness, labour and self-denial in life; his so remarkably devoting himself and his all, in heart and practice, to the glory of God; and the wonderful frame of mind manifested, in so steadfast a manner, under the expectation of death, and under the pains and agonies which brought it on; may excite in us all, both ministers and people, a due sense of the greatness of the work which we have to do in the world, of the excellency and amiableness of thorough religion in experience and practice, of the blessedness of the end of those whose death finishes such a life, and of the infinite value of their eternal reward, when "absent from the body and present with the Lord"; and effectually stir us up to constant and effectual endeavours that, in the way of such an holy life, we may at last come to so blessed an end! Amen.

FAREWELL SERMON

APPLICATION

The improvement I would make of the things which have been observed, is to lead the people here present, who have been under my pastoral care, to some reflections, and to give them some advice, suitable to our present circumstances; relating to what has been lately done, in order to our being separated, as to the relation we have heretofore stood in one to another; but expecting to meet each other before the great tribunal at the day of judgment.

The deep and serious consideration of that our future most solemn meeting, is certainly most suitable at such a time as this; there having so lately been that done, which, in all probability, will (as to the relation we have heretofore stood in) be followed with an everlasting separation.

How often have we met together in the house of God, in this relation? How often have I spoken to you, instructed, counselled, warned, directed and fed you, and administered ordinances among you, as the people which were committed to my care, and whose precious souls I had the charge of? But in all probability, this never will be again.

The prophet Jeremiah, (chap. xxv. 3.) puts the people in mind how long he had laboured among them in the work of the ministry; *From the thirteenth year of Josiah, the son of Amon, king of Judah, even unto this day, (that is, the three and twentieth year), the word of the Lord came unto me, and I have spoken unto you, rising early and speaking.* I am not about to compare myself with the prophet Jeremiah; but in this respect I can say as he did, that *I have spoken the word of God to you, unto the three and twentieth year, rising early and speaking.* It was three and twenty years, the 15th day of last February, since I have laboured in the work of the ministry, in the relation of a pastor to this church and congregation. And though my strength has been weakness, having always laboured under great infirmity of body, beside my insufficiency for so great a charge, in other respects, yet I have not spared my feeble strength, but have exerted it for the good of your souls. I can appeal to you, as the apostle does to his hearers, Gal. iv. 13. *Ye know how through infirmity of the flesh, I preached the Gospel unto you.* I have spent the prime of my life and strength, in labours for your eternal welfare. You are my witnesses, that what strength I have had I have not neglected in idleness, nor laid out in prosecuting worldly schemes, and managing temporal affairs, for the advancement of my outward estate, and aggrandizing myself and family; but have given myself to the work of the ministry, labouring in it night and day, rising early and applying myself to this great business to which Christ appointed me. I have found the work of the ministry among you to be a great work indeed, a work of exceeding care, labour and difficulty: many have been the heavy burdens that I have borne in it, which my strength has been very unequal to. GOD called me to bear these burdens, and I bless his name, that he has so supported me as to keep me from sinking under them, and that his power herein has been manifested in my weakness; so that although I have often been troubled on every side, yet I have not been distressed; perplexed, but not in despair; cast down, but not destroyed.

But now I have reason to think, my work is finished which I had to do as your minister: you have publicly rejected me, and my opportunities cease.

How highly therefore does it now become us, to consider of that time when we must meet one another before the chief Shepherd? When I must give an account of my stewardship, of the service I have done *for*, and the reception and treatment I have had *among*, the people he sent me to: and you must give an account of your own conduct towards me, and the improvement you have made of these *three and twenty years* of my ministry. For then both you and I must appear together, and we both must give an account, in order to an infallible, righteous and eternal, sentence to be passed upon us, by him who will judge us, with respect to all that we have said or done in our

meetings here, all our conduct one towards another, in the house
of God and elsewhere, on sabbath-days and on other days; who
will try our hearts, and manifest our thoughts, and the principles and frames of our minds, will judge us with respect to
all the controversies which have subsisted between us, with the
strictest impartiality, and will examine our treatment of each
other in those controversies: there is nothing covered, that shall
not be revealed, nor hid, which shall not be known; all will be
examined in the searching, penetrating light of God's omniscience and glory, and by him whose eyes are as a flame of fire;
and truth and right shall be made plainly to appear, being
stripped of every veil; and all error, falsehood, unrighteousness
and injury, shall be laid open, stripped of every disguise; every
specious pretence, every cavil, and all false reasoning, shall
vanish in a moment, as not being able to bear the light of that
day. And then our hearts will be turned inside out, and the
secrets of them will be made more plainly to appear than our
outward actions do now. Then it shall appear what the ends
are, which we have aimed at, what have been the governing
principles which we have acted from, and what have been the
dispositions, we have exercised in our ecclesiastical disputes and
contests. Then it will appear, whether I acted uprightly, and
from a truly conscientious, careful regard to my duty to my
great Lord and master, in some former ecclesiastical controversies, which have been attended with exceeding unhappy circumstances, and consequences: it will appear, whether there
was any just cause for the resentment which was manifested
on those occasions. And then our late grand controversy, concerning the Qualifications necessary for admission to the privileges of members, in complete standing, in the Visible Church
of Christ, will be examined and judged, in all its parts and circumstances, and the whole set forth in a clear, certain and perfect light. Then it will appear, whether the doctrine, which I
have preached and published, concerning this matter, be Christ's
own doctrine, whether he will not own it as one of the precious
truths which have proceeded from his own mouth, and vindicate
and honour, as such, before the whole universe. Then it will

appear, what was meant by *the man that comes without the wedding garment;* for that is the day spoken of, Matt. xxii. 13. wherein such an one *shall be bound hand and foot, and cast into outer darkness, where shall be weeping and gnashing of teeth.* And then it will appear, whether, in declaring this doctrine, and acting agreeably to it, and in my general conduct in this affair, I have been influenced from any regard to my own temporal interest, or honour, or any desire to appear wiser than others; or have acted from any sinister, secular views whatsoever; and whether what I have done has not been from a careful, strict and tender regard to the will of my Lord and Master, and because I dare not offend him, being satisfied what his will was, after a long, diligent, impartial and prayerful, enquiry; having this constantly in view and prospect, to engage me to great solicitude, not rashly to determine truth to be on this side of the question, where I am now persuaded it is, that such a determination would not be for my temporal interest, but every way against it, bringing a long series of extreme difficulties, and plunging me into an abyss of trouble and sorrow. And then it will appear, whether my people have done their duty to their pastor, with respect to this matter; whether they have shown a right temper and spirit on this occasion; whether they have done me justice in hearing, attending to, and considering, what I had to say in evidence of what I believed and taught, as part of the counsel of God; whether I have been treated with that impartiality, candour and regard, which the just Judge esteemed due; and whether, in the many steps which have been taken, and the many things that have been said and done, in the course of this controversy, righteousness and charity and christian decorum have been maintained: or, if otherwise, to how great a degree these things have been violated. Then every step of the conduct of each of us, in this affair, from first to last, and the spirit we have exercised in all, shall be examined and manifested, and our own consciences will speak plain and loud, and each of us shall be convinced, and the world shall know; and never shall there be any more mistake, misrepresentation or misapprehension of the affair, to eternity.

This controversy is now probably brought to an issue, between you and me, as to this world; it has issued in the event of the week before last; but it must have another decision at that great day, which certainly will come, when you and I shall meet together before the great judgment seat: and therefore I leave it to that time, and shall say no more about it at present.

But I would now proceed to address myself particularly to several sorts of persons.

I. To those who are professors of godliness among us.

I would now call you to a serious consideration of that great day, wherein you must meet him, who has heretofore been your pastor, before the Judge, whose eyes are as a flame of fire.

I have endeavoured, according to my best ability, to search the word of God, with regard to the distinguishing notes of true piety, those by which persons might best discover their state, and most surely and clearly judge of themselves. And those rules and marks, I have from time to time, applied to you, in the preaching of the word, to the utmost of my skill, and in the most plain and searching manner, that I have been able; in order to the detecting the deceived hypocrite, and establishing the hopes and comforts of the sincere. And yet it is to be feared, that after all that I have done, I now leave some of you in a deceived deluded state; for it is not to be supposed, that among several hundred professors, none are deceived.

Henceforward, I am like to have no more opportunity to take the care and charge of your souls, to examine and search them. But still I intreat you to remember and consider the rules which I have often laid down to you, during my ministry, with a solemn regard to the future day, when you and I must meet together before our Judge; when the uses of examination you have heard from me, must be rehearsed again before you, and those rules of trial must be tried, and it will appear, whether they have been good or not, and it will also appear, whether you have impartially heard them, and tried yourselves by them; and the Judge himself, who is infallible, will try both you and me: and after this, none will be deceived concerning the state of their souls.

I have often put you in mind, that whatever your pretences to experiences, discoveries, comforts, and joys, have been; at that day, every one will be judged according to his works: and then you will find it so.

May you have a minister of greater knowledge of the word of God, and better acquaintance with soul cases, and of greater skill in applying himself to souls, whose discourses may be more searching and convincing; that such of you as have held fast deceit under my preaching, may have your eyes opened by his; that you may be undeceived before that great day.

What means and helps for instruction and self-examination, you may hereafter have, is uncertain; but one thing is certain, that the time is short; your opportunity for rectifying mistakes in so important a concern, will soon come to an end. We live in a world of great changes. There is now a great change come to pass; you have withdrawn yourselves from my ministry, under which you have continued for so many years: but the time is coming, and will soon come, when you will pass out of time into eternity; and so will pass from under all means of grace whatsoever.

The greater part of you who are professors of godliness, have, (to use the phrase of the apostle,) *acknowledged me in part.* You have heretofore acknowledged me to be your spiritual father, the instrument of the greatest good to you, that ever is, or can be, obtained, by any of the children of men. Consider of that day, when you and I shall meet before our Judge, when it shall be examined, whether you have had from me the treatment which is due to spiritual children, and whether you have treated me, as you ought to have treated a spiritual father.—As the relation of a natural parent brings great obligations on children, in the sight of God; so much more, in many respects, does the relation of a spiritual father, bring great obligations on such, whose conversion and eternal salvation they suppose God has made them the instruments of; 1 Cor. iv. 15. *For though you have ten thousand instructors in Christ, yet have ye not many fathers; for in Christ Jesus, I have begotten you through the gospel.*

II. Now I am taking my leave of this people, I would apply myself to such among them as I leave in a christless, graceless condition; and would call on such, seriously to consider of that solemn day, when they and I must meet before the Judge of the world.

My parting with you, is in some respects, in a peculiar manner, a melancholy parting; in as much as I leave you in the most melancholy circumstances, because I leave you in the gall of bitterness, and bond of iniquity, having the wrath of God abiding on you, and remaining under condemnation to everlasting misery and destruction. Seeing I must leave you, it would have been a comfortable and happy circumstance of our parting, if I had left you in Christ, safe and blessed in that sure refuge and glorious rest of the saints.—But it is otherwise, I leave you far off, aliens and strangers, wretched subjects and captives of sin and satan, and prisoners of vindictive justice; without Christ, and without God in the world.

Your consciences bear me witness, that while I had opportunity, I have not ceased to warn you, and set before you your danger. I have studied to represent the misery and necessity of your circumstances, in the clearest manner possible. I have tried all ways, that I could think of, tending to awaken your consciences, and make you sensible of the necessity of your improving your time, and being speedy in fleeing from the wrath to come, and thorough in the use of means for your escape and safety. I have diligently endeavoured to find out, and use, the most powerful motives, to persuade you to take care for your own welfare and salvation. I have not only endeavoured to awaken you, that you might be moved with fear, but I have used my utmost endeavours to win you: I have sought out acceptable words, that if possible, I might prevail upon you to forsake sin, and turn to God, and accept of Christ as your Saviour and Lord. I have spent my strength very much, in these things. But yet, with regard to you whom I am now speaking to, I have not been successful: but have this day reason to complain in those words, Jer. vi. 29. *The bellows are burnt, the lead is consumed of the fire, the founder melteth in vain, for the wicked are not plucked away.* It is to be feared, that all my labours, as to many of you, have served to no other purpose but to harden you; and that the word which I have preached, instead of being a savour of life unto life, has been a savour of death unto death. Though I shall not have any account to give for the future, of such as have openly and resolutely renounced my ministry, as of a betrustment committed to me: yet remember you must give account for yourselves, of your care of your own souls, and your improvement of all means past and future, through your whole lives. God only knows what will become of your poor perishing souls, what means you may hereafter enjoy, or what disadvantages and temptations you may be under. May God in mercy grant, that however all past means have been unsuccessful, you may have future means, which may have a new effect; and that the word of God, as it shall be hereafter dispensed to you, may prove as the fire and the hammer that breaketh the rock in pieces. However, let me now at parting, exhort and beseech you, not wholly to forget the warnings you have had while under my ministry. When you and I shall meet at the day of judgment, then you will remember them: the sight of me your former minister, on that occasion, will soon revive them in your memory; and that in a very affecting manner. O do not let that be the first time that they are so revived.

You and I are now parting one from another as to this world; let us labour that we may not be parted, after our meeting at the last day. If I have been your faithful pastor, (which will that day appear, whether I have or no,) then I shall be acquitted, and shall ascend with Christ. O do your part, that in such a case, it may not be so, that you should be forced eternally to part from me, and all that have been faithful in Christ Jesus. This is a sorrowful parting, that now is between you and me; but that would be a more sorrowful parting to you than this. This you may perhaps bear without being much affected with it, if you are not glad of it; but such a parting, in that day, will most deeply, sensibly and dreadfully, affect you.

III. I would address myself to those who are under some awakenings.

Blessed be God, that there are some such, and that (although I have reason to fear I leave multitudes, in this large congregation, in a christless state,) yet I do not leave them all in total stupidity and carelessness, about their souls. Some of you, that I have reason to hope are under some awakenings, have acquainted me with your circumstances; which has a tendency to cause me, now I am leaving you, to take my leave of you with peculiar concern for you. What will be the issue of your present exercise of mind, I know not: but it will be known at that day when you and I shall meet before the judgment seat of Christ. Therefore now be much in consideration of that day.

Now I am parting with this flock, I would once more press upon you the counsels I have heretofore given, to take heed of being slighty in so great a concern, to be thorough and in good earnest in the affair, and to beware of backsliding, to hold on and hold out to the end. And cry mightily to God, that these great changes, that pass over this church and congregation, do not prove your overthrow. There is great temptation in them; and the devil will undoubtedly seek to make his advantage of them, if possible, to cause your present convictions and endeavours to be abortive. You had need to double your diligence, and watch and pray, lest you be overcome by temptation.

Whoever may hereafter stand related to you, as your spiritual guide, my desire and prayer is, that the great Shepherd of the sheep would have a special respect to you, and be your guide, (for there is none teacheth like him,) and that he who is the infinite Fountain of light, would *open your eyes, and turn you from darkness unto light, and from the power of Satan unto God; that you may receive forgiveness of sins, and inheritance among them that are sanctified, through faith that is in Christ;* that so, in that great day, when I shall meet you again, before your Judge and mine, we may meet in joyful and glorious circumstances, never to be separated any more.

IV. I would apply myself to the young people of the congregation.

Since I have been settled in the work of the ministry, in this place, I have ever had a peculiar concern for the souls of the young people, and a desire that religion might flourish among them; and have especially exerted myself in order to it; because I knew the special opportunity they had beyond others, and that ordinarily those, whom God intended mercy for, were brought to fear and love him in their youth. And it has ever appeared to me a peculiarly amiable thing to see young people walking in the ways of virtue and christian piety, having their hearts purified and sweetened with a principle of divine love. And it has appeared a thing exceeding beautiful, and what would be much to the adorning and happiness of the town, if the young people could be persuaded, when they meet together, to converse as christians, and as the children of God; avoiding impurity, levity, and extravagance; keeping strictly to the rules of virtue, and conversing together of the things of God, and Christ and heaven. This is what I have longed for: and it has been exceedingly grievous to me, when I have heard of vice, vanity and disorder, among our youth. And so far as I know my heart, it was from hence that I formerly led this church to some measures, for the suppressing of vice among our young people, which gave so great offence, and by which I became so obnoxious. I have sought the good and not the hurt of our young people. I have desired their truest honour and happiness, and not their reproach; knowing that true virtue and religion tended, not only to the glory and felicity of young people in another world, but their greatest peace and prosperity, and highest dignity and honour in this world, and above all things to sweeten and render pleasant and delightful even the days of youth.

But whether I have loved you and sought your good more or less, yet God in his providence, now calling me to part with you, committing your souls to him who once committed the pastoral care of them to me, nothing remains, but only (as I am now taking my leave of you) earnestly to beseech you, from love to yourselves, if you have none to me, not to despise and forget the warnings and counsels I have so often given you; remembering the day when you and I must meet again before the great Judge of quick and dead; when it will appear whether the things I have taught you were true, whether the counsels I have given you were good, and whether I truly sought your good, and whether you have well improved my endeavours.

I have, from time to time, earnestly warned you against frolicking (as it is called,) and some other liberties commonly taken by young people in the land. And whatever some may say, in justification of such liberties and customs, and may laugh at warnings against them, I now leave you my parting testimony against such things; not doubting but God will approve and confirm it, in that day when we shall meet before Him.

V. I would apply myself to the children of the congregation, the lambs of this flock, who have been so long under my care.

I have just now said, that I have had a peculiar concern for the young people: and in so saying, I did not intend to exclude you. You are in youth, and in the most early youth: and therefore I have been sensible, that if those that were young had a precious opportunity for their souls' good, you who are very young had, in many respects, a peculiarly precious opportunity. And accordingly I have not neglected you: I have endeavoured to do the part of a faithful shepherd, in feeding the lambs as well as the sheep. Christ did once commit the care of your souls to me as your minister; and you know, dear children, how I have instructed you, and warned you from time to time: you know how I have often called you together for that end: and some of you, sometimes, have seemed to be affected with what I have said to you. But I am afraid it has had no saving effect, as to many of you; but that you remain still in an unconverted condition, without any real saving work wrought in your souls, convincing you thoroughly of your sin and misery, causing you to see the great evil of sin, and to mourn for it, and hate it above all things; and giving you a sense of the excellency of the Lord Jesus Christ, bringing you, with all your hearts, to cleave to Him as your Saviour; weaning your hearts from the world; and causing you to love God above all, and to delight in holiness more than in all the pleasant things of this earth: and so that I now leave you in a miserable condition, having no interest in Christ, and so under the awful displeasure and anger of God, and in danger of going down to the pit of eternal misery.

But now I must bid you farewell: I must leave you in the hands of God. I can do no more for you than to pray for you. Only I desire you not to forget, but often think of the counsels and warnings I have given you, and the endeavours I have used, that your souls might be saved from everlasting destruction.

Dear children, I leave you in an evil world, that is full of snares and temptations. God only knows what will become of you. This the Scripture has told us, that there are but few saved: and we have abundant confirmation of it from what we see. This we see, that children die as well as others: multitudes die before they grow up; and of those that grow up, comparatively few ever give good evidence of saving conversion to God. I pray God to pity you, and take care of you, and provide for you the best means for the good of your souls; and that God himself would undertake for you, to be your heavenly Father, and the mighty Redeemer of your immortal souls. Do not neglect to pray for yourselves: take heed you be not of the number of those, who cast off fear, and restrain prayer before God. Constantly pray to God in secret; and often remember that great day, when you must appear before the judgment-seat of Christ, and meet your minister there, who has so often counselled and warned you.

I conclude with a few words of advice to all in general, in some particulars, which are of great importance in order to the future welfare and prosperity of this church and congregation.

1. One thing that greatly concerns you, as you would be an happy people, is the maintaining of *family order*.

We have had great disputes how the church ought to be regulated; and indeed the subject of these disputes was of great importance: but the due regulation of your families is of no less, and in some respects, of much greater importance. Every christian family ought to be, as it were, a little church, consecrated to Christ, and wholly influenced and governed by his rules. And family education and order are some of the chief of the means of grace. If these fail, all other means are like to prove ineffectual. If these are duly maintained, all the means of grace will be like to prosper and be successful.

Let me now, therefore, once more, before I finally cease to speak to this congregation, repeat and earnestly press the counsel, which I have often urged on heads of families here, while I was their pastor, to great painfulness, in teaching, warning and directing their children; bringing them up in the nurture and admonition of the Lord; beginning early, where there is yet opportunity; and maintaining a constant diligence in labours of this kind: remembering that, as you would not have all your instructions and counsels ineffectual, there must be government as well as instructions, which must be maintained with an even hand, and steady resolution; as a guard to the religion and morals of the family, and the support of its good order. Take heed that it be not with any of you, as it was with Eli of old, who reproved his children, but restrained them not; and that by this means you do not bring the like curse on your families, as he did on his.

And let children obey their parents, and yield to their instructions, and submit to their orders, as they would inherit a blessing, and not a curse. For we have reason to think, from many things in the word of God, that nothing has a greater tendency to bring a curse on persons, in this world, and on all their temporal concerns, than an undutiful, unsubmissive, disorderly behaviour in children towards their parents.

2. As you would seek the future prosperity of this society, it is of vast importance that you should avoid *contention*.

A contentious people will be a miserable people. The contentions, which have been among you, since I first became your pastor, have been one of the greatest burdens I have laboured under, in the course of my ministry: not only the contentions you have had with me, but those you have had one with another, about your lands, and other concerns: because I knew that contention, heat of spirit, evil speaking, and things of the like nature, were directly contrary to the spirit of christianity, and did, in a peculiar manner, tend to drive away God's spirit from a people, and to render all means of grace ineffectual, as well as to destroy a people's outward comfort and welfare.

Let me, therefore, earnestly exhort you, as you would seek

your own future good, hereafter to watch against a contentious spirit. *If you would see good days, seek peace and ensue it*, 1 Pet. iii. 10, 11. Let the contention, which has lately been about the terms of christian communion, as it has been the greatest of your contentions, so be the last of them. I would, now I am preaching my Farewell Sermon, say to you, as the apostle to the Corinthians, 2 Cor. xiii. 11, *Finally, brethren, farewell. Be perfect: be of one mind: live in peace: and the God of love and peace shall be with you.*

And here I would particularly advise those, that have adhered to me in the late controversy, to watch over their spirits, and avoid all bitterness towards others. Your temptations are, in some respects, the greatest: because what has been lately done is grievous to you. But, however wrong you may think others have done, maintain, with great diligence and watchfulness, a christian meekness and sedateness of spirit: and labour, in this respect, to excel others who are of the contrary part: and this will be the best victory: for *he that rules his spirit, is better than he that takes a city*. Therefore let nothing be done through strife or vainglory: indulge no revengeful spirit in any wise; but watch and pray against it: and by all means in your power, seek the prosperity of this town: and never think you behave yourselves as becomes christians, but when you sincerely, sensibly and fervently, love all men, of whatever party or opinion, and whether friendly or unkind, just or injurious, to you, or your friends, or to the cause and kingdom of Christ.

3. Another thing, that vastly concerns the future prosperity of the town, is, that you should watch against the encroachments of Error; and particularly *Arminianism*, and doctrines of like tendency.

You were many of you, as I well remember, much alarmed, with the apprehension of the danger of the prevailing of these corrupt principles, near sixteen years ago. But the danger then was small, in comparison of what appears now: these doctrines, at this day, are much more prevalent, than they were then: the progress they have made in the land, within this seven years, seems to have been vastly greater, than at any time in the like space before: and they are still prevailing, and creeping into almost all parts of the land, threatening the utter ruin of the credit of those doctrines, which are the peculiar glory of the gospel, and the interests of vital piety. And I have of late perceived some things among yourselves, that show that you are far from being out of danger, but on the contrary remarkably exposed. The elder people may perhaps think themselves sufficiently fortified against infection: but it is fit that all should beware of self-confidence and carnal security, and should remember those needful warnings of sacred writ, *Be not high minded but fear*, and *let him that stands, take heed lest he fall*. But let the case of the elder people be as it will, the rising generations are doubtless greatly exposed. These principles are exceedingly taking with corrupt nature, and are what young people, at least such as have not their hearts established with grace, are easily led away with.

And if these principles should greatly prevail in this town, as they very lately have done in another large town I could name, formerly greatly noted for religion, and so for a long time, it will threaten the spiritual and eternal ruin of this people, in the present and future generations. Therefore you have need of the greatest and most diligent care and watchfulness with respect to this matter.

4. Another thing which I would advise to, that you may hereafter be a prosperous people, is, that you would give yourselves much to prayer.

God is the fountain of all blessing and prosperity, and he will be sought to for his blessing. I would therefore advise you, not only to be constant in secret and family prayer, and in the public worship of God in his house, but also often to assemble yourselves in private praying societies. I would advise all such, as are grieved for the afflictions of Joseph, and sensibly affected with the calamities of this town, of whatever opinion they be, with relation to the subject of our late controversy, often to meet together for prayer, and cry to God for his mercy to themselves, and mercy to this town, and mercy to Zion, and to the people of God in general through the world.

5. The last article of advice, I would give, (which doubtless does greatly concern your prosperity,) is, that you would take great care with regard to the settlement of a minister, to see to it who or what manner of person he is, whom you settle: and particularly in these two respects.

(1.) That he be a man of thoroughly sound principles, in the scheme of doctrine which he maintains.

This you will stand in the greatest need of, especially at such a day of corruption as this is. And, in order to obtain such an one, you had need to exercise extraordinary care and prudence. I know the danger. I know the manner of many young gentlemen of corrupt principles, their ways of concealing themselves, the fair specious disguises they are wont to put on, by which they deceive others, to maintain their own credit, and get themselves into others' confidence and improvement, and secure and establish their own interest, until they see a convenient opportunity to begin, more openly, to broach and propagate their corrupt tenets.

(2.) Labour to obtain a man, who has an established character, as a person of serious religion and fervent piety.

It is of vast importance that those, who are settled in this work, should be men of true piety, at all times, and in all places; but more especially at some times and in some towns and churches. And this present time, which is a time wherein religion is in danger, by so many corruptions in doctrine and practice, is in a peculiar manner, a day wherein such ministers are necessary. Nothing else but sincere piety of heart is at all to be depended on, at such a time as this, as a security to a young man, just coming into the world, from the prevailing infection, to thoroughly engage him, in proper and successful endeavours, to withstand and oppose the torrent of error and prejudice, against the high, mysterious, evangelical doctrines of the religion of Jesus Christ, and their genuine effects in true experimental religion. And this place is a place, that does peculiarly need such a minister, for reasons obvious to all.

If you should happen to settle a minister, who knows nothing, truly, of Christ, and the way of salvation by him, nothing experimentally of the nature of vital religion; alas, how will you be exposed as sheep without a shepherd. Here is need of one in this place, who shall be eminently fit to stand in the gap, and make up the hedge, and who shall be as the chariots of Israel and the horsemen thereof. You need one, that shall stand as a champion, in the cause of truth and godliness.

Having briefly mentioned these important articles of advice, nothing remains, but that I take my leave of you, and bid you all farewell, wishing and praying for your prosperity. I would now commend your immortal souls to HIM, who formerly committed them to me; expecting the day, when I must meet you again before him, who is the Judge of quick and dead. I desire that I may never forget this people, who have been so long my special charge, and that I may never cease fervently to pray for your prosperity. May God bless you with a faithful pastor, one that is well acquainted with his mind and will, thoroughly warning sinners, wisely and skilfully searching professors, and conducting you in the way to eternal blessedness. May you have truly a burning and shining light set up in this candlestick; and may you not only for a season, but during his life, and that a long life, be willing to rejoice in his light.

And let me be remembered, in the prayers of all God's people, that are of a calm spirit, and are peaceable and faithful in Israel, of whatever opinion they may be, with respect to terms of Church Communion.

And let us all remember, and never forget, our future, solemn meeting, on that Great day of the Lord: the day of infallible and of the unalterable sentence. AMEN.

SERMON NOTES

MATT. VII. 14—"Few there be that find it."

Doc[trine.] 'Tis a hard thing to find the right way to Heaven.

I. There is a way to Heaven.

God has opened a door.

II. There is but one right way.

III. 'Tis a hard thing to find this one right way.

Appears: In that there are so few that find the way.

Tho[ugh] all have so much need to find.

Tho[ugh] so many desire to find and seek after it.

Tho[ugh] so many think they have found.

...... so many are mistaken.

That many of those that do find it, first take a great deal of pains.

Some for a long time.

Many prayers.

Many difficulties.

Reason: Negatively, not that [God] han't [has not] called us.

       "   "   very plain in itself.

Reasons:

Many wrong ways.

Like travelling through a great wilderness.

Full of difficulties ... dangers. ...

But one right way.

[A] narrow way.

Many wrong ways.

Mention some of the wrong ways.

Do right in some things only.

Outward Religion only.

Affections that go away.

Religious out of regard to men.

Religious only out of fear of hell.

.... from self-love.

Don't love God for Himself.

Trust in their own righteousness.

Depend on the good opinion of others.

Apt to think themselves convicted when they are not.

High pride: apt to think well of themselves.

A little good looks great.

Don't see what is bad.

How many things men often think are CONVERSION.

2. Men's own lust blind[s] 'em.

The way is good and plain.

Right way is what men don't like.

Up-hill.

Contrary to all their lusts.

. . . . . to their pride.

. . . . . to their worldliness.

. . . . sensuality.

. . . . slothfulness.

Enmity against God.

Wrong ways are

Easy.

Broad.

Down-hill.

3. Devils.

Blind them and deceive them.

4. Things of this world blind 'em.

5. Wicked men implead [?] 'em.

APPLICA[TION]

What a great mercy to have the Word of God.

Mercy that God has appointed ministers.

Great need of Prayer—

Never without God's help.

Dont trust . . . v. 22 . . .

What need of God's power and striving.

DIRECTIONS.

Pray earnestly.

Not trust . . . [As above, v. 22].

Take advice.
Begin soon.
Hold on and hold out.
Don't take hope *too soon*.
In every thing follow the Word of God.
You need be much concerned.

RELIGIOUS AFFECTIONS

PART I

CONCERNING THE NATURE OF THE AFFECTIONS, AND THEIR IMPORTANCE IN RELIGION

1 PETER i. 8.—Whom having not seen, ye love; in whom, though now ye see him not, yet believing, ye rejoice with joy unspeakable, and full of glory.

In these words, the apostle represents the state of the minds of the Christians he wrote to, under the persecutions they were then the subjects of. These persecutions are what he has respect to, in the two preceding verses, when he speaks of *the trial of their faith*, and of *their being in heaviness through manifold temptations*.

Such trials are of threefold benefit to true religion. Hereby the truth of it is manifested, and it appears to be indeed true religion; they, above all other things, have a tendency to distinguish between true religion and false, and to cause the difference between them evidently to appear. Hence they are called by the name of *trials*, in the verse nextly preceding the text, and in innumerable other places; they try the faith and religion of professors, of what sort it is, as apparent gold is tried in the fire, and manifested, whether it be true gold or no. And the faith of true Christians being thus tried and proved to be true, is "found to praise, and honor, and glory," as in that preceding verse.

And then, these trials are of further benefit to true religion; they not only manifest the truth of it, but they make its genuine beauty and amiableness remarkably to appear. True virtue never appears so lovely, as when it is most oppressed; and the divine excellency of real Christianity, is never exhibited with such advantage, as when under the greatest trials: then it is that true faith appears much more precious than gold! And upon this account is "found to praise, and honor, and glory."

And again, another benefit that such trials are of to true religion, is, that they purify and increase it. They not only manifest it to be true, but also tend to refine it, and deliver it from those mixtures of that which is false, which encumber and impede it; that nothing may be left but that which is true. They tend to cause the amiableness of true religion to appear to the best advantage, as was before observed; and not only so, but they tend to increase its beauty, by establishing and confirming it, and making it more lively and vigorous, and purifying it from those things that obscured its lustre and glory. As gold that is tried in the fire, is purged from its alloy, and all remainders of dross, and comes forth more solid and beautiful; so true faith being tried as gold is tried in the fire, becomes more precious, and thus also is "found unto praise, and honor, and glory." The apostle seems to have respect to each of these benefits, that persecutions are of to true religion, in the verse preceding the text.

And in the text, the apostle observes how true religion operated in the Christians he wrote to, under their persecutions, whereby these benefits of persecution appeared in them; or what manner of operation of true religion, in them, it was, whereby their religion, under persecution, was manifested to be true religion, and eminently appeared in the genuine beauty and amiableness of true religion, and also appeared to be increased and purified, and so was like to be "found unto praise, and honor, and glory, at the appearing of Jesus Christ." And there were two kinds of operation, or exercise of true religion, in them, under their sufferings, that the apostle takes notice of in the text, wherein these benefits appeared.

1. *Love to Christ:* "Whom having not yet seen, ye love." The world was ready to wonder, what strange principle it was, that influenced them to expose themselves to so great sufferings, to forsake the things that were seen, and renounce all that was dear and pleasant, which was the object of sense. They seemed to the men of the world about them, as though they were beside themselves, and to act as though they hated themselves; there was nothing in their view, that could induce them thus to suffer, and support them under, and carry them through such

trials. But although there was nothing that was seen, nothing that the world saw, or that the Christians themselves ever saw with their bodily eyes, that thus influenced and supported them, yet they had a supernatural principle of love to something unseen; they loved Jesus Christ, for they saw him spiritually whom the world saw not, and whom they themselves had never seen with bodily eyes.

2. *Joy in Christ.* Though their outward sufferings were very grievous, yet their inward spiritual joys were greater than their sufferings; and these supported them, and enabled them to suffer with cheerfulness.

There are two things which the apostle takes notice of in the text concerning this joy. 1. The manner in which it rises, the way in which Christ, though unseen, is the foundation of it, viz., by faith; which is the evidence of things not seen: "In whom, though now ye see him not, yet believing, ye rejoice." 2. The nature of this joy; "unspeakable and full of glory." Unspeakable in the kind of it; very different from worldly joys, and carnal delights; of a vastly more pure, sublime, and heavenly nature, being something supernatural, and truly divine, and so ineffably excellent; the sublimity and exquisite sweetness of which, there were no words to set forth. Unspeakable also in degree; it pleasing God to give them this holy joy, with a liberal hand, and in large measure, in their state of persecution.

Their joy was full of glory. Although the joy was unspeakable, and no words were sufficient to describe it, yet something might be said of it, and no words more fit to represent its excellency than these, that it was *full of glory;* or, as it is in the original, *glorified joy*. In rejoicing with this joy, their minds were filled, as it were, with a glorious brightness, and their nature exalted and perfected. It was a most worthy, noble rejoicing that did not corrupt and debase the mind, as many carnal joy do; but did greatly beautify and dignify it; it was a prelibation of the joy of heaven, that raised their minds to a degree of heavenly blessedness; it filled their minds with the light of God's glory, and made themselves to shine with some communication of that glory.

Hence the proposition or doctrine, that I would raise from these words, is this:

DOCTRINE. *True religion, in great part, consists in holy affections.*

We see that the apostle, in observing and remarking the operations and exercises of religion in the Christians he wrote to, wherein their religion appeared to be true and of the right kind, when it had its greatest trial of what sort it was, being tried by persecution as gold is tried in the fire, and when their religion not only proved true, but was most pure, and cleansed from its dross and mixtures of that which was not true, and when religion appeared in them most in its genuine excellency and native beauty, and was found to praise, and honor, and glory; he singles out the religious affections of *love* and *joy*, that were then in exercise in them: these are the exercises of religion he takes notice of, wherein their religion did thus appear true and pure, and in its proper glory. Here I would,

1. Show what is intended by the affections.

2. Observe some things which make it evident, that a great part of true religion lies in the affections.

I. It may be inquired, what the affections of the mind are?

I answer: The affections are no other than the more vigorous and sensible exercises of the inclination and will of the soul.

God has endued the soul with two faculties: one is that by which it is capable of perception and speculation, or by which it discerns, and views, and judges of things; which is called the understanding. The other faculty is that by which the soul does not merely perceive and view things, but is some way inclined with respect to the things it views or considers; either is inclined *to* them, or is disinclined and averse *from* them; or is the faculty by which the soul does not behold things, as an indifferent unaffected spectator, but either as liking or disliking, pleased or displeased, approving or rejecting. This faculty is called by various names; it is sometimes called the *inclination:* and, as it has respect to the actions that are determined and governed by it, is called the *will:* and the mind, with regard to the exercises of this faculty, is often called the *heart.*

The exercise[s] of this faculty are of two sorts; either those by which the soul is carried out towards the things that are in view, in approving of them, being pleased with them, and inclined to them; or those in which the soul opposes the things that are in view, in disapproving of them, and in being displeased with them, averse from them, and rejecting them.

And as the exercises of the inclination and will of the soul are various in their kinds, so they are much more various in their degrees. There are some exercises of pleasedness or displeasedness, inclination or disinclination, wherein the soul is carried but a little beyond a state of perfect indifference.—And there are other degrees above this, wherein the approbation or dislike, pleasedness or aversion, are stronger, wherein we may rise higher and higher, till the soul comes to act vigorously and sensibly, and the actings of the soul are with that strength, that (through the laws of the union which the Creator has fixed between the soul and the body) the motion of the blood and animal spirits begins to be sensibly altered; whence oftentimes arises some bodily sensation, especially about the heart and vitals, that are the fountain of the fluids of the body: from whence it comes to pass, that the mind, with regard to the exercises of this faculty, perhaps in all nations and ages, is called the *heart*. And, it is to be noted, that they are these more vigorous and sensible exercises of this faculty that are called the *affections*.

The will, and the affections of the soul, are not two faculties the affections are not essentially distinct from the will, nor do they differ from the mere actings of the will, and inclination of the soul, but only in the liveliness and sensibleness of exercise

It must be confessed, that language is here somewhat imperfect, and the meaning of words in a considerable measure loose and unfixed, and not precisely limited by custom, which governs the use of language. In some sense, the affection of the soul differs nothing at all from the will and inclination, and the will never is in any exercise any further than it is affected; it not moved out of a state of perfect indifference, any otherwise than as it is affected one way or other, and acts nothing an further. But yet there are many actings of the will and inclination, that are not so commonly called *affections:* in every thing we do, wherein we act voluntarily, there is an exercise of the will and inclination; it is our inclination that governs us in our actions; but all the actings of the inclination and will, in all our common actions of life, are not ordinarily called affections. Yet, what are commonly called affections are not essentially different from them, but only in the degree and manner of exercise. In every act of the will whatsoever, the soul either likes or dislikes, is either inclined or disinclined to what is in view: these are not essentially different from those affections of love and hatred: that liking or inclination of the soul to a thing, if it be in a high degree, and be vigorous and lively, is the very same thing with the affection of love; and that disliking and disinclining, if in a greater degree, is the very same with hatred. In every act of the will for, or towards something not present, the soul is in some degree inclined to that thing; and that inclination, if in a considerable degree, is the very same with the affection of desire. And in every degree of the act of the will, wherein the soul approves of something present, there is a degree of pleasedness; and that pleasedness, if it be in a considerable degree, is the very same with the affections of joy or delight. And if the will disapproves of what is present, the soul is in some degree displeased, and if that displeasedness be great, it is the very same with the affection of grief or sorrow.

Such seems to be our nature, and such the laws of the union of soul and body, that there never is in any case whatsoever, any lively and vigorous exercise of the will or inclination of the soul, without some effect upon the body, in some alteration of the motion of its fluids, and especially of the animal spirits. And, on the other hand, from the same laws of the union of the soul and body, the constitution of the body, and the motion of its fluids, may promote the exercise of the affections. But yet it is not the body, but the mind only, that is the proper seat of the affections. The body of man is no more capable of being really the subject of love or hatred, joy or sorrow, fear or hope, than the body of a tree, or than the same body of man is capable of thinking and understanding. As it is the soul only that has ideas, so it is the soul only that is pleased or displeased with its ideas. As it is the soul only that thinks, so it is the soul only that loves or hates, rejoices or is grieved at what it thinks of. Nor are these motions of the animal spirits, and fluids of the body, any thing properly belonging to the nature of the affections, though they always accompany them, in the present state; but are only effects or concomitants of the affections that are entirely distinct from the affections themselves, and no way essential to them; so that an unbodied spirit may be as capable of love and hatred, joy or sorrow, hope or fear, or other affections, as one that is united to a body.

The affections and passions are frequently spoken of as the same; and yet in the more common use of speech, there is in some respect a difference; and affection is a word that in its ordinary signification, seems to be something more extensive than passion, being used for all vigorous lively actings of the will or inclination; but passion for those that are more sudden, and whose effects on the animal spirits are more violent, and the mind more overpowered, and less in its own command.

As all the exercises of the inclination and will, are either in approving and liking, or disapproving and rejecting; so the affections are of two sorts; they are those by which the soul is carried out to what is in view, cleaving to it, or seeking it; or those by which it is averse from it, and opposes it.

Of the former sort are love, desire, hope, joy, gratitude, complacence. Of the latter kind are hatred, fear, anger, grief, and such like; which it is needless now to stand particularly to define.

And there are some affections wherein there is a composition of each of the aforementioned kinds of actings of the will; as in the affection of *pity*, there is something of the former kind, towards the person suffering, and something of the latter towards what he suffers. And so in zeal, there is in it high approbation of some person or thing, together with vigorous opposition to what is conceived to be contrary to it.

There are other mixed affections that might be also mentioned, but I hasten to,

II. The second thing proposed, which was to observe some things that render it evident, that true religion, in great part consists in the affections. And here,

1. What has been said of the nature of the affections makes this evident, and may be sufficient, without adding any thing further, to put this matter out of doubt; for who will deny that true religion consists in a great measure, in vigorous and lively actings of the inclination and will of the soul, or the fervent exercises of the heart?

That religion which God requires, and will accept, does not consist in weak, dull, and lifeless wishes, raising us but a little above a state of indifference: God, in his word, greatly insists upon it, that we be good in earnest, "fervent in spirit," and our hearts vigorously engaged in religion: Rom. xii. 11, "Be ye fervent in spirit, serving the Lord." Deut. x. 12, "And now, Israel, what doth the Lord thy God require of thee, but to fear the Lord thy God, to walk in all his ways, and to love him, and to serve the Lord thy God with all thy heart, and with all thy soul?" and chap. vi. 4, 6, "Hear, O Israel, the Lord our God is one Lord: And thou shalt love the Lord thy God with all thy heart, and with all thy might." It is such a fervent vigorous engagedness of the heart in religion, that is the fruit of a real circumcision of the heart, or true regeneration, and that has the promises of life; Deut. xxx. 6, "And the Lord thy God will circumcise thine heart, and the heart of thy seed, to love the Lord thy God with all thy heart, and with all thy soul, that thou mayest live."

If we be not in good earnest in religion, and our wills and inclinations be not strongly exercised, we are nothing. The things of religion are so great, that there can be no suitableness in the exercises of our hearts, to their nature and importance, unless they be lively and powerful. In nothing is vigor in the actings of our inclinations so requisite, as in religion; and in nothing is lukewarmness so odious. True religion is evermore a powerful thing; and the power of it appears, in the first place in the inward exercises of it in the heart, where is the principal and original seat of it. Hence true religion is called the *power of godliness*, in distinction from the external appearances of it, that are the *form* of it, 2 Tim. iii. 5: "Having a form of godliness, but denying the power of it." The Spirit of God, in those that have sound and solid religion, is a spirit of powerful holy affection; and therefore, God is said "to have given the Spirit of power, and of love, and of a sound mind," 2 Tim. i. 7. And such, when they receive the Spirit of God, in his sanctifying and saving influences, are said to be "baptized with the Holy Ghost, and with fire;" by reason of the power and fervor of those exercises the Spirit of God excites in their hearts, whereby their hearts, when grace is in exercise, may be said to "burn within them;" as is said of the disciples, Luke xxiv. 32.

The business of religion is from time to time compared to those exercises, wherein men are wont to have their hearts and strength greatly exercised and engaged, such as running, wrestling or agonizing for a great prize or crown, and fighting with strong enemies that seek our lives, and warring as those, that by violence take a city or kingdom.

And though true grace has various degrees, and there are some that are but babes in Christ, in whom the exercise of the inclination and will, towards divine and heavenly things, is comparatively weak; yet every one that has the power of godliness in his heart, has his inclinations and heart exercised towards God and divine things, with such strength and vigor that these holy exercises do prevail in him above all carnal or natural affections, and are effectual to overcome them: for every true disciple of Christ "loves him above father or mother, wife and children, brethren and sisters, houses and lands: yea, than his own life." From hence it follows, that wherever true religion is, there are vigorous exercises of the inclination and will towards divine objects: but by what was said before, the vigorous, lively, and sensible exercises of the will, are no other than the affections of the soul.

2. The Author of the human nature has not only given affections to men, but has made them very much the spring of

men's actions. As the affections do not only necessarily belong to the human nature, but are a very great part of it; so (inasmuch as by regeneration persons are renewed in the whole man, and sanctified throughout) holy affections do not only necessarily belong to true religion, but are a very great part of it. And as true religion is of a practical nature, and God hath so constituted the human nature, that the affections are very much the spring of men's actions, this also shows, that true religion must consist very much in the affections.

Such is man's nature, that he is very inactive, any otherwise than he is influenced by some affection, either love or hatred, desire, hope, fear, or some other. These affections we see to be the springs that set men agoing, in all the affairs of life, and engage them in all their pursuits: these are the things that put men forward, and carry them along, in all their worldly business; and especially are men excited and animated by these, in all affairs wherein they are earnestly engaged, and which they pursue with vigor. We see the world of mankind to be exceeding busy and active; and the affections of men are the springs of the motion: take away all love and hatred, all hope and fear, all anger, zeal, and affectionate desire, and the world would be, in a great measure motionless and dead; there would be no such thing as activity amongst mankind, or any earnest pursuit whatsoever. It is affection that engages the covetous man, and him that is greedy of worldly profits, in his pursuits; and it is by the affections, that the ambitious man is put forward in his pursuit of worldly glory; and it is the affections also that actuate the voluptuous man, in his pursuit of pleasure and sensual delights: the world continues, from age to age, in a continual commotion and agitation, in a pursuit of these things; but take away all affection, and the spring of all this motion would be gone, and the motion itself would cease. And as in worldly things, worldly affections are very much the spring of men's motion and action; so in religious matters, the spring of their actions is very much religious affection: he that has doctrinal knowledge and speculation only, without affection, never is engaged in the business of religion.

3. Nothing is more manifest in fact, than that the things of religion take hold of men's souls, no further than they affect them. There are multitudes that often hear the word of God, and therein hear of those things that are infinitely great and important, and that most nearly concern them, and all that is heard seems to be wholly ineffectual upon them, and to make no alteration in their disposition or behavior; and the reason is, they are not affected with what they hear. There are many that often hear of the glorious perfections of God, his almighty power and boundless wisdom, his infinite majesty, and that holiness of God, by which he is of purer eyes than to behold evil, and cannot look on iniquity, and the heavens are not pure in his sight, and of God's infinite goodness and mercy, and hear of the great works of God's wisdom, power and goodness, wherein there appear the admirable manifestations of these perfections; they hear particularly of the unspeakable love of God and Christ, and of the great things that Christ has done and suffered, and of the great things of another world, of eternal misery in bearing the fierceness and wrath of Almighty God, and of endless blessedness and glory in the presence of God, and the enjoyment of his dear love; they also hear the peremptory commands of God, and his gracious counsels and warnings, and the sweet invitations of the gospel; I say, they often hear these things and yet remain as they were before, with no sensible alteration in them, either in heart or practice, because they are not affected with what they hear; and ever will be so till they are affected.—I am bold to assert, that there never was any considerable change wrought in the mind or conversation of any person, by any thing of a religious nature, that ever he read, heard or saw, that had not his affections moved. Never was a natural man engaged earnestly to seek his salvation; never were any such brought to cry after wisdom, and lift up their voice for understanding, and to wrestle with God in prayer for mercy; and never was one humbled, and brought to the foot of God, from any thing that ever he heard or imagined of his own unworthiness and deserving of God's displeasure; nor was ever one induced to fly for refuge unto Christ, while his heart

remained unaffected. Nor was there ever a saint awakened out of a cold, lifeless frame, or recovered from a declining state in religion, and brought back from a lamentable departure from God, without having his heart affected. And in a word, there never was any thing considerable brought to pass in the heart or life of any man living, by the things of religion, that had not his heart deeply affected by those things.

4. The holy Scriptures do everywhere place religion very much in the affection; such as fear, hope, love, hatred, desire, joy, sorrow, gratitude, compassion, and zeal.

The Scriptures place much of religion in godly fear; insomuch, that it is often spoken of as the character of those that are truly religious persons, that they tremble at God's word, that they fear before him, that their flesh trembles for fear of him, and that they are afraid of his judgments, that his excellency makes them afraid, and his dread falls upon them, and the like: and a compellation commonly given the saints in Scripture, is "fearers of God," or, "they that fear the Lord." And because the fear of God is a great part of true godliness, hence true godliness in general, is very commonly called by the name of *the fear of God;* as every one knows, that knows any thing of the Bible.

So hope in God and in the promises of his word, is often spoken of in the Scripture, as a very considerable part of true religion. It is mentioned as one of the three great things of which religion consists, 1 Cor. xiii. 13. Hope in the Lord is also frequently mentioned as the character of the saints: Psal. cxlvi. 5, "Happy is he that hath the God of Jacob for his help, whose hope is in the Lord his God." Jer. xvii. 7, "Blessed is the man that trusteth in the Lord, and whose hope the Lord is." Psal. xxxi. 24, "Be of good courage, and he shall strengthen your heart, all ye that hope in the Lord." And the like in many other places. Religious fear and hope are, once and again, joined together, as jointly constituting the character of the true saints; Psal. xxxiii. 18, "Behold, the eye of the Lord is upon them that fear him, upon them that hope in his mercy." Psal. cxlvii. 11, "The Lord taketh pleasure in them that fear him, in those that hope in his mercy." Hope is so great a part of true religion, that the apostle says, "we are saved by hope," Rom. viii. 24. And this is spoken of as the helmet of the Christian soldier. 1 Thess. v. 8, "And for a helmet, the *hope* of salvation;" and the sure and steadfast anchor of the soul, which preserves it from being cast away by the storms of this evil world. Heb. vi. 19, "Which hope we have as an anchor of the soul, both sure and steadfast, and which entereth into that within the vail." It is spoken of as a great fruit and benefit which true saints receive by Christ's resurrection: 1 Pet. i. 3, "Blessed be the God and Father of our Lord Jesus Christ, which, according to his abundant mercy, hath begotten us again unto a lively hope, by the resurrection of Jesus Christ from the dead."

The Scriptures place religion very much in the affection of *love*, in love to God, and the Lord Jesus Christ, and love to the people of God, and to mankind. The texts in which this is manifest, both in the Old Testament and New, are innumerable. But of this more afterwards.

The contrary affection of *hatred* also, as having sin for its object, is spoken of in Scripture as no inconsiderable part of true religion. It is spoken of as that by which true religion may be known and distinguished; Prov. viii. 13, "The fear of the Lord is to hate evil." And accordingly the saints are called upon to give evidence of their sincerity by this; Psal. xcvii. 10, "Ye that love the Lord hate evil." And the Psalmist often mentions it as an evidence of his sincerity; Psal. 2, 3, "I will walk within my house with a perfect heart. I will set no wicked thing before mine eyes; I hate the work of them that turn aside." Psal. cxix. 104, "I hate every false way." So ver. 127. Again, Psal. cxxxix. 21, "Do I not hate them, O Lord, that hate thee?"

·   ·   ·   ·   ·   ·   ·   ·   ·   ·   ·   ·   ·   ·

5. The Scriptures do represent true religion, as being summarily comprehended in love, the chief of the affections, and fountain of all other affections.

So our blessed Saviour represents the matter, in answer to the lawyer, who asked him, which was the great commandment of the law—Matt. xxii. 37-40: "Jesus said unto him, Thou shalt love the Lord thy God with all thy heart, and with all thy soul, and with all thy mind. This is the first and great commandment. And the second is like unto it, Thou shalt love thy neighbor as thyself. On these two commandments hang all the law and the prophets." Which last words signify as much, as that these two commandments comprehend all the duty prescribed, and the religion taught in the law and the prophets. And the apostle Paul does from time to time make the same representation of the matter; as in Rom. xiii. 8, "He that loveth another, hath fulfilled the law." And ver. 10, "Love is the fulfilling of the law." And Gal. v. 14, "For all the law is fulfilled in one word, even in this, Thou shalt love thy neighbor as thyself." So likewise in 1 Tim. i. 5, "Now the end of the commandment is charity, out of a pure heart," &c. So the same apostle speaks of love, as the greatest thing in religion, and as the vitals, essence and soul of it; without which, the greatest knowledge and gifts, and the most glaring profession, and every thing else which appertains to religion, are vain and worthless; and represents it as the fountain from whence proceeds all that is good, in 1 Cor. xiii. throughout; for that which is there rendered *charity*, in the original is αγαπη, the proper English of which is *love*.

Now, although it be true, that the love thus spoken of includes the whole of a sincerely benevolent propensity of the soul towards God and man; yet it may be considered, that it is evident from what has been before observed, that this propensity or inclination of the soul, when in sensible and vigorous exercise, becomes affection, and is no other than affectionate love. And surely it is such vigorous and fervent love which Christ speaks of, as the sum of all religion, when he speaks of loving God with all our hearts, with all our souls, and with all our minds, and our neighbor as ourselves, as the sum of all that was taught and prescribed in the law and the prophets.

Indeed it cannot be supposed, when this affection of love is here, and in other Scriptures, spoken of as the sum of all religion, that hereby is meant the act, exclusive of the habit, or that the exercise of the understanding is excluded, which is

implied in all reasonable affection. But it is doubtless true, and
evident from these Scriptures, that the essence of all true religion
lies in holy love; and that in this divine affection, and an habitual
disposition to it, and that light which is the foundation of it,
and those things which are the fruits of it, consists the whole of
religion.

From hence it clearly and certainly appears, that great part
of true religion consists in the affections. For love is not only
one of the affections, but it is the first and chief of the affections,
and the fountain of all the affections. From love arises hatred of
those things which are contrary to what we love, or which
oppose and thwart us in those things that we delight in: and
from the various exercises of love and hatred, according to the
circumstances of the objects of these affections, as present or
absent, certain or uncertain, probable or improbable, arise all
those other affections of desire, hope, fear, joy, grief, gratitude,
anger, &c. From a vigorous, affectionate, and fervent love to
God, will necessarily arise other religious affections; hence will
arise an intense hatred and abhorrence of sin, fear of sin, and a
dread of God's displeasure, gratitude to God for his goodness,
complacence and joy in God, when God is graciously and
sensibly present, and grief when he is absent, and a joyful hope
when a future enjoyment of God is expected, and fervent zeal
for the glory of God. And in like manner, from a fervent love
to men, will arise all other virtuous affections towards men.

. . . .

Upon the whole, I think it clearly and abundantly evident,
that true religion lies very much in the affections. Not that I
think these arguments prove, that religion in the hearts of the
truly godly, is ever in exact proportion to the degree of affection, and present emotion of the mind: for undoubtedly, there
is much affection in the true saints which is not spiritual; their
religious affections are often mixed; all is not from grace, but
much from nature. And though the affections have not their
seat in the body; yet the constitution of the body may very
much contribute to the present emotion of the mind. And the
degree of religion is rather to be judged of by the fixedness and

strength of the habit that is exercised in affection, whereby holy affection is habitual, than by the degree of the present exercise; and the strength of that habit is not always in proportion to outward effects and manifestations, or inward effects, in the hurry and vehemence, and sudden changes of the course of the thoughts of the mind. But yet it is evident, that religion consists so much in affection, as that without holy affection there is no true religion; and no light in the understanding is good, which does not produce holy affection in the heart: no habit or principle in the heart is good, which has no such exercise; and no external fruit is good, which does not proceed from such exercises.

Having thus considered the evidence of the proposition laid down, I proceed to some inferences.

1. We may hence learn how great their error is, who are for discarding all religious affections, as having nothing solid or substantial in them.

There seems to be too much of a disposition this way, prevailing in this land at this time. Because many who, in the late extraordinary season, appeared to have great religious affections, did not manifest a right temper of mind, and run into many errors, in the time of their affections, and the heat of their zeal; and because the high affections of many seem to be so soon come to nothing, and some who seemed to be mightily raised and swallowed up with joy and zeal, for a while, seem to have returned like the dog to his vomit; hence religious affections in general are grown out of credit with great numbers, as though true religion did not at all consist in them. Thus we easily and naturally run from one extreme to another. A little while ago we were in the other extreme; there was a prevalent disposition to look upon all high religious affections as eminent exercises of true grace, without much inquiring into the nature and source of those affections, and the manner in which they arose: if persons did but appear to be indeed very much moved and raised, so as to be full of religious talk, and express themselves with great warmth and earnestness, and to be filled, or to be very full, as the phrases were; it was too much the manner, without further examination, to conclude such persons were full of the Spirit of God, and had eminent experience of his gracious influences. This was the extreme which was prevailing three or four years ago. But of late, instead of esteeming and admiring all religious affections without distinction, it is a thing much more prevalent, to reject and discard all without distinction. Herein appears the subtilty of Satan. While he saw that affections were much in vogue, knowing the greater part of the land were not versed in such things, and had not had much experience of great religious affections to enable them to judge well of them, and distinguish between true and false; then he knew he could best play his game, by sowing tares amongst the wheat, and mingling false affections with the works of God's Spirit: he knew this to be a likely way to delude and eternally ruin many souls, and greatly to wound religion in the saints, and entangle them in a dreadful wilderness, and by and by, to bring all religion into disrepute.

But now, when the ill consequences of these false affections appear, and it is become very apparent, that some of those emotions which made a glaring show, and were by many greatly admired, were in reality nothing; the devil sees it to be for his interest to go another way to work, and to endeavor to his utmost to propagate and establish a persuasion, that all affections and sensible emotions of the mind, in things of religion, are nothing at all to be regarded, but are rather to be avoided, and carefully guarded against, as things of a pernicious tendency. This he knows is the way to bring all religion to a mere lifeless formality, and effectually shut out the power of godliness, and every thing which is spiritual, and to have all true Christianity turned out of doors. For although to true religion there must indeed be something else besides affection; yet true religion consists so much in the affections, that there can be no true religion without them. He who has no religious affection, is in a state of spiritual death, and is wholly destitute of the powerful, quickening, saving influences of the Spirit of God upon his heart. As there is no true religion where there is nothing else but affection, so there is no true religion where there is no religious affection.

As on the one hand, there must be light in the understanding, as well as an affected fervent heart; where there is heat without light, there can be nothing divine or heavenly in that heart; so on the other hand, where there is a kind of light without heat, a head stored with notions and speculations, with a cold and unaffected heart, there can be nothing divine in that light, that knowledge is no true spiritual knowledge of divine things. If the great things of religion are rightly understood, they will affect the heart. The reason why men are not affected by such infinitely great, important, glorious, and wonderful things, as they often hear and read of, in the word of God, is undoubtedly because they are blind; if they were not so, it would be impossible, and utterly inconsistent with human nature, that their hearts should be otherwise than strongly impressed, and greatly moved by such things.

This manner of slighting all religious affections, is the way exceedingly to harden the hearts of men, and to encourage them in their stupidity and senselessness, and to keep them in a state of spiritual death as long as they live, and bring them at last to death eternal. The prevailing prejudice against religious affections at this day, in the land, is apparently of awful effect to harden the hearts of sinners, and damp the graces of many of the saints, and stun the life and power of religion, and preclude the effect of ordinances, and hold us down in a state of dulness and apathy, and undoubtedly causes many persons greatly to offend God, in entertaining mean and low thoughts of the extraordinary work he has lately wrought in this land.

And for persons to despise and cry down all religious affections, is the way to shut all religion out of their own hearts, and to make thorough work in ruining their souls.

They who condemn high affections in others, are certainly not likely to have high affections themselves. And let it be considered, that they who have but little religious affection, have certainly but little religion. And they who condemn others for their religious affections, and have none themselves, have no religion.

There are false affections, and there are true. A man's having much affection, does not prove that he has any true religion: but if he has no affection, it proves that he has no true religion. The right way, is not to reject all affections, nor to approve all; but to distinguish between affections, approving some, and rejecting others; separating between the wheat and the chaff, the gold and the dross, the precious and the vile.

2. If it be so, that true religion lies much in the affections, hence we may infer, that such means are to be desired, as have much of a tendency to move the affections. Such books, and such a way of preaching the word, and administration of ordinances, and such a way of worshipping God in prayer, and singing praises, is much to be desired, as has a tendency deeply to affect the hearts of those who attend these means.

Such a kind of means would formerly have been highly approved of, and applauded by the generality of the people of the land, as the most excellent and profitable, and having the greatest tendency to promote the ends of the means of grace. But the prevailing taste seems of late strangely to be altered: that pathetical manner of praying and preaching, which would formerly have been admired and extolled, and that for this reason, because it had such a tendency to move the affections, now, in great multitudes, immediately excites disgust, and moves no other affections, that those of displeasure and contempt.

Perhaps, formerly the generality (at least of the common people) were in the extreme, of looking too much to an affectionate address, in public performances: but now, a very great part of the people seem to have gone far into a contrary extreme. Indeed there may be such means, as may have a great tendency to stir up the passions of weak and ignorant persons, and yet have no great tendency to benefit their souls: for though they may have a tendency to excite affections, they may have little or none to excite gracious affections, or any affections tending to grace. But undoubtedly, if the things of religion, in the means used, are treated according to their nature, and exhibited truly, so as tends to convey just apprehensions, and a right judgment of them; the more they have a tendency to move the affections the better.

3. If true religion lies much in the affections, hence we may learn, what great cause we have to be ashamed and confounded before God, that we are no more affected with the great things of religion. It appears from what has been said, that this arises from our having so little true religion.

God has given to mankind affections, for the same purpose which he has given all the faculties and principles of the human soul for, viz., that they might be subservient to man's chief end, and the great business for which God has created him, that is, the business of religion. And yet how common is it among mankind, that their affections are much more exercised and engaged in other matters, than in religion! In things which concern men's worldly interest, their outward delights, their honor and reputation, and their natural relations, they have their desires eager, their appetites vehement, their love warm and affectionate, their zeal ardent; in these things their hearts are tender and sensible, easily moved, deeply impressed, much concerned, very sensibly affected, and greatly engaged; much depressed with grief at worldly losses, and highly raised with joy at worldly successes and prosperity. But how insensible and unmoved are most men, about the great things of another world! How dull are their affections! How heavy and hard their hearts in these matters! Here their love is cold, their desires languid, their zeal low, and their gratitude small. How they can sit and hear of the infinite height, and depth, and length, and breadth of the love of God in Christ Jesus, of his giving his infinitely dear Son, to be offered up a sacrifice for the sins of men, and of the unparalleled love of the innocent, and holy, and tender Lamb of God, manifested in his dying agonies, his bloody sweat, his loud and bitter cries, and bleeding heart, and all this for enemies, to redeem them from deserved, eternal burnings, and to bring to unspeakable and everlasting joy and glory; and yet be cold, and heavy, insensible, and regardless! Where are the exercises of our affections proper, if not here? What is it that does more require them? And what can be a fit occasion of their lively and vigorous exercise, if not such a one as this? Can any thing be set in our view, greater and more important? Any thing more wonder-

ful and surprising? Or more nearly concerning our interest?
Can we suppose the wise Creator implanted such principles in
the human nature as the affections, to be of use to us, and to be
exercised on certain proper occasions, but to lie still on such an
occasion as this? Can any Christian who believes the truth of
these things, entertain such thoughts?

If we ought ever to exercise our affections at all, and if the
Creator has not unwisely constituted the human nature in
making these principles a part of it, when they are vain and useless; then they ought to be exercised about those objects which
are most worthy of them. But is there any thing which Christians can find in heaven or earth, so worthy to be the objects of
their admiration and love, their earnest and longing desires,
their hope, and their rejoicing, and their fervent zeal, as those
things that are held forth to us in the gospel of Jesus Christ?
In which not only are things declared most worthy to affect us,
but they are exhibited in the most affecting manner. The glory
and beauty of the blessed Jehovah, which is most worthy in itself, to be the object of our admiration and love, is there exhibited in the most affecting manner that can be conceived of, as
it appears, shining in all its lustre, in the face of an incarnate,
infinitely loving, meek, compassionate, dying Redeemer. All
the virtues of the Lamb of God, his humility, patience, meekness, submission, obedience, love and compassion, are exhibited
to our view, in a manner the most tending to move our affections, of any that can be imagined; as they all had their greatest
trial, and their highest exercise, and so their brightest manifestation, when he was in the most affecting circumstances; even
when he was under his last sufferings, those unutterable and unparalleled sufferings he endured, from his tender love and pity
to us. There also the hateful nature of our sins is manifested in
the most affecting manner possible: as we see the dreadful effects
of them, in what our Redeemer, who undertook to answer for us,
suffered for them. And there we have the most affecting manifestation of God's hatred of sin, and his wrath and justice in
punishing it; as we see his justice in the strictness and inflexibleness of it; and his wrath in its terribleness, in so dreadfully

punishing our sins, in one who was infinitely dear to him, and loving to us. So has God disposed things, in the affair of our redemption, and in his glorious dispensations, revealed to us in the gospel, as though every thing were purposely contrived in such a manner, as to have the greatest possible tendency to reach our hearts in the most tender part, and move our affections most sensibly and strongly. How great cause have we therefore to be humbled to the dust, that we are no more affected!

PART II

SHOWING WHAT ARE NO CERTAIN SIGNS THAT RELIGIOUS AFFECTIONS ARE TRULY GRACIOUS, OR THAT THEY ARE NOT

IF any one, on the reading of what has been just now said, is ready to acquit himself, and say, "I am not one of those who have no religious affections; I am often greatly moved with the consideration of the great things of religon": let him not content himself with this, that he has religious affections: for as we observed before, as we ought not to reject and condemn all affections, as though true religion did not at all consist in affection; so on the other hand, we ought not to approve of all, as though every one that was religiously affected had true grace, and was therein the subject of the saving influences of the Spirit of God; and that therefore the right way is to distinguish among religious affections, between one sort and another. Therefore let us now endeavor to do this; and in order to do it, I would do two things.

I. I would mention some things, which are no signs one way or the other, either that affections are such as true religion consists in, or that they are otherwise; that we may be guarded against judging of affections by false signs.

II. I would observe some things, wherein those affections which are spiritual and gracious, differ from those which are not so, and may be distinguished and known.

FIRST, I would take notice of some things, which are no signs that affections are gracious, or that they are not.

I. It is no sign one way or the other, that religious affections are very great, or raised very high.

Some are ready to condemn all high affections: if persons appear to have their religious affections raised to an extraordinary pitch, they are prejudiced against them, and determine that they are delusions, without further inquiry. But if it be, as has been proved, that true religion lies very much in religious affections, then it follows, that if there be a great deal of true religion, there will be great religious affections; if true religion in the hearts of men be raised to a great height, divine and holy affections will be raised to a great height.

Love is an affection, but will any Christian say, men ought not to love God and Jesus Christ in a high degree? And will any say, we ought not to have a very great hatred of sin, and a very deep sorrow for it? Or that we ought not to exercise a high degree of gratitude to God for the mercies we receive of him, and the great things he has done for the salvation of fallen men? Or that we should not have very great and strong desires after God and holiness? Is there any who will profess, that his affections in religion are great enough; and will say, "I have no cause to be humbled, that I am no more affected with the things of religion than I am; I have no reason to be ashamed, that I have no greater exercises of love to God and sorrow for sin, and gratitude for the mercies which I have received"? Who is there that will bless God that he is affected enough with what he has read and heard of the wonderful love of God to worms and rebels, in giving his only begotten Son to die for them, and of the dying love of Christ; and will pray that he may not be affected with them in any higher degree, because high affections are improper, and very unlovely in Christians, being enthusiastical, and ruinous to true religion?

. . . .

II. It is no sign that affections have the nature of true religion, or that they have not, that they have great effects on the body.

All affections whatsoever, have in some respect or degree, an effect on the body. As was observed before, such is our nature, and such are the laws of union of soul and body, that the mind can have no lively or vigorous exercise, without some effect upon the body. So subject is the body to the mind, and so much do its fluids, especially the animal spirits, attend the motions and exercises of the mind, that there cannot be so much as an intense thought, without an effect upon them. Yea, it is questionable whether an imbodied soul ever so much as thinks one thought, or has any exercise at all, but that there is some corresponding motion or alteration of motion, in some degree, of the fluids, in some part of the body. But universal experience shows, that the exercise of the affections have in a special manner a tendency to some sensible effect upon the body. And if this be so, that all affections have some effect upon the body, we may then well suppose, the greater those affections be, and the more vigorous their exercise (other circumstances being equal) the greater will be the effect on the body. Hence it is not to be wondered at, that very great and strong exercises of the affections should have great effects on the body. And therefore, seeing there are very great affections, both common and spiritual; hence it is not to be wondered at, that great effects on the body should arise from both these kinds of affections. And consequently these effects are no signs, that the affections they arise from, are of one kind or the other.

Great effects on the body certainly are no sure evidences that affections are spiritual; for we see that such effects oftentimes arise from great affections about temporal things, and when religion is no way concerned in them. And if great affections about secular things, that are purely natural, may have these effects, I know not by what rule we should determine that high affections about religious things, which arise in like manner from nature, cannot have the like effect.

Nor, on the other hand, do I know of any rule any have to determine, that gracious and holy affections, when raised as high as any natural affections, and have equally strong and vigorous exercises, cannot have a great effect on the body. No such rule can be drawn from reason: I know of no reason, why a being affected with a view of God's glory should not cause the body to faint, as well as being affected with a view of Solomon's glory. And no such rule has as yet been produced from the Scripture;

none has ever been found in all the late controversies which have
been about things of this nature. There is a great power in
spiritual affections: we read of the power which worketh in
Christians,* and of the Spirit of God being in them as the Spirit
of power,† and of the effectual working of his power in them.‡
But man's nature is weak: flesh and blood are represented in
Scripture as exceeding weak; and particularly with respect to its
unfitness for great spiritual and heavenly operations and exercises, Matt. xxvi. 41, 1 Cor. xv. 43, and 50. The text we are
upon speaks of "joy unspeakable, and full of glory." And who
that considers what man's nature is, and what the nature of the
affections is, can reasonably doubt but that such unutterable and
glorious joys, may be too great and mighty for weak dust and
ashes, so as to be considerably overbearing to it? It is evident by
the Scripture, that true divine discoveries, or ideas of God's
glory, when given in a great degree, have a tendency, by affecting the mind, to overbear the body; because the Scripture teaches us often, that if these ideas or views should be given to such a
degree, as they are given in heaven, the weak frame of the body
could not subsist under it, and that no man can, in that manner,
see God and live. The knowledge which the saints have of God's
beauty and glory in this world, and those holy affections that
arise from it, are of the same nature and kind with what the
saints are the subjects of in heaven, differing only in degree and
circumstances: what God gives them here, is a foretaste of
heavenly happiness, and an earnest of their future inheritance.
And who shall limit God in his giving this earnest, or say he
shall give so much of the inheritance, such a part of the future
reward, as an earnest of the whole, and no more? And seeing
God has taught us in his word, that the whole reward is such,
that it would at once destroy the body, is it not too bold a thing
for us, so to set bounds to the sovereign God, as to say, that in
giving the earnest of this reward in this world, he shall never
give so much of it, as in the least to diminish the strength of the
body, when God has nowhere thus limited himself?

. . . .

*Eph. iii. 7. †Tim. i. 7. ‡Eph. iii. 7, 20. [Edwards's notes.]

PART III

I COME now to the second thing appertaining to the trial of religious affections, which was proposed, viz., To take notice of some things, wherein those affections that are spiritual and gracious, do differ from those that are not so.

.   .   .   .

I. Affections that are truly spiritual and gracious, do arise from those influences and operations on the heart, which are spiritual, supernatural and divine.

I will explain what I mean by these terms, whence will appear their use to distinguish between those affections which are spiritual, and those which are not so.

We find that true saints, or those persons who are sanctified by the Spirit of God, are in the New Testament called spiritual persons. And their being spiritual is spoken of as their peculiar character, and that wherein they are distinguished from those who are not sanctified. This is evident, because those who are spiritual are set in opposition to natural men, and carnal men. Thus the spiritual man and the natural man are set in opposition one to another, 1 Cor. ii. 14, 15: "The natural man receiveth not the things of the Spirit of God; for they are foolishness unto him; neither can he know them, because they are spiritually discerned. But he that is spiritual judgeth all things." The Scripture explains itself to mean an ungodly man, or one that has no grace, by a natural man: thus the Apostle Jude, speaking of certain ungodly men, that had crept in unawares among the saints, ver. 4, of his epistle, says, v. 19, "These are sensual, having not the Spirit." This the apostle gives as a reason why they behaved themselves in such a wicked manner as he had described. Here the word translated *sensual*, in the original is ψυχικοι, which is the very same, which in those verses in 1 Cor. chap. ii. is translated *natural*. In the like manner, in the continuation of the same discourse, in the next verse but one, spiritual men are opposed to carnal men; which the connection plainly shows mean the same, as spiritual men and natural men, in the foregoing verses; "And I, brethren, could not speak unto you, as unto spiritual, but as unto carnal;" i. e., as in a great measure unsanctified. That by carnal the apostle means corrupt and unsanctified, is abundantly evident, by Rom. vii. 25, and viii. 1, 4, 5, 6, 7, 8, 9, 12, 13, Gal. v. 16, to the end, Col. ii. 18. Now therefore, if by natural and carnal in these texts, be intended unsanctified, then doubtless by spiritual, which is opposed thereto, is meant sanctified and gracious.

. . . .

1. The Spirit of God is given to the true saints to dwell in them, as his proper lasting abode; and to influence their hearts, as a principle of new nature, or as a divine supernatural spring of life and action. The Scriptures represent the Holy Spirit not only as moving, and occasionally influencing the saints, but as dwelling in them as his temple, his proper abode, and everlasting dwelling place, 1 Cor. iii. 16, 2 Cor. vi. 16, John xiv. 16, 17. And he is represented as being there so united to the faculties of the soul, that he becomes there a principle or spring of new nature and life.

So the saints are said to live by Christ living in them, Gal. ii. 20. Christ by his Spirit not only *is* in them, but *lives* in them; and so that they live by his life; so is his Spirit united to them, as a principle of life in them; they do not only drink living water, but this "living water becomes a well or fountain of water," in the soul, "springing up into spiritual and everlasting life," John iv. 14, and thus becomes a principle of life in them. This living water, this evangelist himself explains to intend the Spirit of God, chap. vii. 38, 39. The light of the Sun of righteousness does not only shine upon them, but is so communicated to them that they shine also, and become little images of that Sun which shines upon them; the sap of the true vine is not only conveyed into them, as the sap of a tree may be conveyed into a vessel, but is conveyed as sap is from a tree into one of its living branches, where it becomes a principle of life. The Spirit of God being thus communicated and united to the saints, they are from thence properly denominated from it, and are called *spiritual*.

On the other hand, though the Spirit of God may many ways influence natural men; yet because it is not thus communicated to them, as an indwelling principle, they do not derive any denomination or character from it: for, there being no union, it is not their own. The light may shine upon a body that is very dark or black; and though that body be the subject of the light, yet, because the light becomes no principle of light in it, so as to cause the body to shine, hence that body does not properly receive its denomination from it, so as to be called a lightsome body. So the Spirit of God acting upon the soul only, without communicating itself to be an active principle in it, cannot denominate it spiritual. A body that continues black, may be said not to have light, though the light shines upon it: so natural men are said "not to have the Spirit," Jude 19, sensual or natural (as the word is elsewhere rendered), having not the Spirit.

2. Another reason why the saints and their virtues are called spiritual (which is the principal thing) is, that the Spirit of God, dwelling as a vital principle in their souls, there produces those effects wherein he exerts and communicates himself in his own proper nature. Holiness is the nature of the Spirit of God, therefore he is called in Scripture the Holy Ghost. Holiness, which is as it were the beauty and sweetness of the divine nature, is as much the proper nature of the Holy Spirit, as heat is the nature of fire, or sweetness was the nature of that holy anointing oil, which was the principal type of the Holy Ghost in the Mosaic dispensation; yea, I may rather say, that holiness is as much the proper nature of the Holy Ghost, as sweetness was the nature of the sweet odor of that ointment. The Spirit of God so dwells in the hearts of the saints, that he there, as a seed or spring of life, exerts and communicates himself, in this his sweet and divine nature, making the soul a partaker of God's beauty and Christ's joy, so that the saint has truly fellowship with the Father, and with his Son Jesus Christ, in thus having the communion or participation of the Holy Ghost. The grace which is in the hearts of the saints, is of the same nature with the divine holiness, as much as it is possible for that holiness to be, which is infinitely less in degree; as the brightness that is in a diamond

which the sun shines upon, is of the same nature with the brightness of the sun, but only that it is as nothing to it in degree.
Therefore Christ says, John iii. 6, "That which is born of the
Spirit, is spirit"; i. e., the grace that is begotten in the hearts of
the saints, is something of the same nature with that Spirit, and
so is properly called a spiritual nature; after the same manner as
that which is born of the flesh is flesh, or that which is born of
corrupt nature is corrupt nature.

But the Spirit of God never influences the minds of natural
men after this manner. Though he may influence them many
ways, yet he never, in any of his influences, communicates himself to them in his own proper nature. Indeed he never acts dis-
agreeably to his nature, either on the minds of saints or sinners:
but the Spirit of God may act upon men agreeably to his own
nature, and not exert his proper nature in the acts and exercises
of their minds: the Spirit of God may act so, that his actions may
be agreeable to his nature, and yet may not at all communicate
himself in his proper nature, in the effect of that action. Thus, for
instance, the Spirit of God moved upon the face of the waters,
and there was nothing disagreeable to his nature in that action;
but yet he did not at all communicate himself in that action,
there was nothing of the proper nature of the Holy Spirit in that
motion of the waters. And so he may act upon the minds of
men many ways, and not communicate himself any more than
when he acts on inanimate things.

Thus not only the manner of the relation of the Spirit, who is
the operator, to the subject of his operations, is different; as the
Spirit operates in the saints, as dwelling in them, as an abiding
principle of action, whereas he doth not so operate upon sinners; but the influence and operation itself is different, and the
effect wrought exceeding different. So that not only the persons
are called *spiritual*, as having the Spirit of God dwelling in them;
but those qualifications, affections, and experiences, that are
wrought in them by the Spirit, are also *spiritual*, and therein
differ vastly in their nature and kind from all that a natural man
is or can be the subject of, while he remains in a natural state;
and also from all that men or devils can be the authors of. It is a

spiritual work in this high sense; and therefore above all other works is peculiar to the Spirit of God.

. . . .

From these things it is evident, that those gracious influences which the saints are subjects of, and the effects of God's Spirit which they experience, are entirely above nature, altogether of a different kind from any thing that men find within themselves by nature, or only in the exercise of natural principles; and are things which no improvement of those qualifications, or principles that are natural, no advancing or exalting them to higher degrees, and no kind of composition of them, will ever bring men to; because they not only differ from what is natural, and from every thing that natural men experience, in degree and circumstances, but also in kind; and are of a nature vastly more excellent. And this is what I mean, by supernatural, when I say that gracious affections are from those influences that are supernatural.

From hence it follows, that in those gracious exercises and affections which are wrought in the minds of the saints, through the saving influences of the Spirit of God, there is a new inward perception or sensation of their minds, entirely different in its nature and kind, from any thing that ever their minds were the subjects of before they were sanctified. For doubtless if God by his mighty power produces something that is new, not only in degree and circumstances, but in its whole nature, and that which could be produced by no exalting, varying, or compounding of what was there before, or by adding any thing of the like kind; I say, if God produces something thus new in a mind, that is a perceiving, thinking, conscious thing; then doubtless something entirely new is felt, or perceived, or thought; or, which is the same thing, there is some new sensation or perception of the mind, which is entirely of a new sort, and which could be produced by no exalting, varying, or compounding of that kind of perceptions or sensations which the mind had before; or there is what some metaphysicians call a new simple idea. If grace be, in the sense above described, an entirely new kind of principle, then the exercises of it are also entirely a new kind of exercises.

And if there be in the soul a new sort of exercises which it is conscious of, which the soul knew nothing of before, and which no improvement, composition, or management of what it was before conscious or sensible of, could produce, or any thing like it; then it follows that the mind has an entirely new kind of perception or sensation; and here is, as it were, a new spiritual sense that the mind has, or a principle of a new kind of perception or spiritual sensation, which is in its whole nature different from any former kinds of sensation of the mind, as tasting is diverse from any of the other senses; and something is perceived by a true saint, in the exercise of this new sense of mind, in spiritual and divine things, as entirely diverse from any thing that is perceived in them, by natural men, as the sweet taste of honey is diverse from the ideas men have of honey by only looking on it, and feeling of it. So that the spiritual perceptions which a sanctified and spiritual person has, are not only diverse from all that natural men have after the manner that the ideas or perceptions of the same sense may differ one from another, but rather as the ideas and sensations of different senses do differ. Hence the work of the Spirit of God in regeneration is often in Scripture compared to the giving a new sense, giving eyes to see, and ears to hear, unstopping the ears of the deaf, and opening the eyes of them that were born blind, and turning from darkness unto light. And because this spiritual sense is immensely the most noble and excellent, and that without which all other principles of perception, and all our faculties are useless and vain, therefore the giving this new sense, with the blessed fruits and effects of it in the soul, is compared to a raising the dead, and to a new creation.

This new spiritual sense, and the new dispositions that attend it, are no new faculties, but are new principles of nature. I use the word principles for want of a word of a more determinate signification. By a principle of nature in this place, I mean that foundation which is laid in nature, either old or new, for any particular manner or kind of exercise of the faculties of the soul, or a natural habit or foundation for action, giving a person ability and disposition to exert the faculties in exercises of such certain kind; so that to exert the faculties in that kind of exercises may be said to be his nature. So this new spiritual sense is not a new faculty of understanding, but it is a new foundation laid in the nature of the soul, for a new kind of exercises of the same faculty of understanding. So that new holy disposition of heart that attends this new sense is not a new faculty of will, but a foundation laid in the nature of the soul, for a new kind of exercises of the same faculty of will.

The Spirit of God, in all his operations upon the minds of natural men, only moves, impresses, assists, improves, or some way acts upon natural principles; but gives no new spiritual principle. Thus when the Spirit of God gives a natural man visions, as he did Balaam, he only impresses a natural principle, viz., the sense of seeing, immediately exciting ideas of that sense; but he gives no new sense; neither is there any thing supernatural, spiritual, or divine in it. So if the Spirit of God impresses on a man's imagination, either in a dream, or when he is wake, any outward ideas of any of the senses, either voices, or shapes and colors, it is only exciting ideas of the same kind that he has by natural principles and senses. So if God reveals to any natural man any secret fact: as, for instance, something that he shall hereafter see or hear; this is not infusing or exercising any new spiritual principle, or giving the ideas of any new spiritual sense; it is only impressing, in an extraordinary manner, the ideas that will hereafter be received by sight and hearing.—So in the more ordinary influences of the Spirit of God on the hearts of sinners, he only assists natural principles to do the same work in a greater degree, which they do of themselves by nature. Thus the Spirit of God by his common influences may assist men's natural ingenuity, as he assisted Bezaleel and Aholiab in the curious works of the tabernacle: so he may assist men's natural abilities in political affairs, and improve their courage and other natural qualifications, as he is said to have put his Spirit on the seventy elders, and on Saul, so as to give him another heart: so God may greatly assist natural men's reason, in their reasoning about secular things, or about the doctrines of religion, and may greatly advance the clearness of their apprehensions and notions of things of religion in many respects, without giving any spiritual sense. So in those awakenings and convictions that natural men may have, God only assists conscience, which is a natural principle, to do that work in a further degree, which it naturally does. Conscience naturally gives men an apprehension of right and wrong, and suggests the relation there is between right and wrong, and a retribution: the Spirit of God assists men's consciences to do this in a greater degree, helps conscience against the stupifying influence of worldly objects and their lusts. And so many other ways might be mentioned wherein the Spirit acts upon, assists, and moves natural principles; but after all it is no more than nature moved, acted and improved; here is nothing supernatural and divine. But the Spirit of God in his spiritual influences on the hearts of his saints, operates by infusing or exercising new, divine, and supernatural principles; principles which are indeed a new and spiritual nature, and principles vastly more noble and excellent than all that is in natural men.

From what has been said it follows, that all spiritual and gracious affections are attended with and do arise from some apprehension, idea, or sensation of mind, which is in its whole nature different, yea, exceeding different, from all that is, or can be in the mind of a natural man; and which the natural man discerns nothing of, and has no manner of idea of (agreeable to Cor. ii. 14), and conceives of no more than a man without the sense of tasting can conceive of the sweet taste of honey, or a man without the sense of hearing can conceive of the melody of a tune, or a man born blind can have a notion of the beauty of the rainbow.

But here two things must be observed, in order to the right understanding of this.

1. On the one hand it must be observed, that not every thing which in any respect appertains to spiritual affections, is new and entirely different from what natural men can conceive of, and do experience; some things are common to gracious affections with other affections; many circumstances, appendages and effects are common. Thus a saint's love to God has a great many

things appertaining to it, which are common with a man's natural love to a near relation; love to God makes a man have desires of the honor of God, and a desire to please him; so does a natural man's love to his friend make him desire his honor, and desire to please him; love to God causes a man to delight in the thoughts of God, and to delight in the presence of God, and to desire conformity to God, and the enjoyment of God; and so it is with a man's love to his friend; and many other things might be mentioned which are common to both. But yet that idea which the saint has of the loveliness of God, and that sensation, and that kind of delight he has in that view, which is as it were the marrow and quintessence of his love, is peculiar, and entirely diverse from any thing that a natural man has, or can have any notion of. And even in those things that seem to be common, there is something peculiar; both spiritual and natural love cause desires after the object beloved; but they be not the same sort of desires: there is a sensation of soul in the spiritual desires of one that loves God, which is entirely different from all natural desires: both spiritual love and natural love are attended with delight in the object beloved; but the sensations of delight are not the same, but entirely and exceedingly diverse. Natural men may have conceptions of many things about spiritual affections; but there is something in them which is as it were the nucleus, or kernel of them, that they have no more conception of, than one born blind, has of colors.

It may be clearly illustrated by this: we will suppose two men; one is born without the sense of tasting, the other has it; the latter loves honey, and is greatly delighted in it, because he knows the sweet taste of it; the other loves certain sounds and colors; the love of each has many things that appertain to it, which is common; it causes both to desire and delight in the object beloved, and causes grief when it is absent, &c., but yet that idea or sensation which he who knows the taste of honey has of its excellency and sweetness, that is the foundation of his love, is entirely different from any thing the other has or can have; and that delight which he has in honey is wholly diverse from any thing that the other can conceive of, though they both delight in their beloved objects. So both these persons may in some respects love the same object: the one may love a delicious kind of fruit, which is beautiful to the eye, and of a delicious taste; not only because he has seen its pleasant colors, but knows its sweet taste; the other, perfectly ignorant of this, loves it only for its beautiful colors: there are many things seen, in some respect, to be common to both; both love, both desire, and both delight; but the love and desire, and delight of the one, is altogether diverse from that of the other. The difference between the love of a natural man and a spiritual man is like to this; but only it must be observed, that in one respect it is vastly greater, viz., that the kinds of excellency which are perceived in spiritual objects, by these different kinds of persons, are in themselves vastly more diverse than the different kinds of excellency perceived in delicious fruit, by a tasting and a tasteless man; and in another respect it may not be so great, viz., as the spiritual man may have a spiritual sense or taste, to perceive that divine and most peculiar excellency but in small beginnings, and in a very imperfect degree.

2. On the other hand, it must be observed that a natural man may have those religious apprehensions and affections, which may be in many respects very new and surprising to him, and what before he did not conceive of; and yet what he experiences be nothing like the exercises of a principle of new nature, or the sensations of a new spiritual sense; his affections may be very new, by extraordinarily moving natural principles in a very new degree, and with a great many new circumstances, and a new co-operation of natural affections, and a new composition of ideas; this may be from some extraordinary powerful influence of Satan, and some great delusion; but there is nothing but nature extraordinarily acted. As if a poor man that had always dwelt in a cottage, and had never looked beyond the obscure village where he was born, should in a jest be taken to a magnificent city and prince's court, and there arrayed in princely robes, and set on the throne, with the crown royal on his head, peers and nobles bowing before him, and should be made to believe that he was now a glorious monarch; the ideas he would have, and the affections he would experience, would in many respects be

very new, and such as he had no imagination of before; but all this is no more than extraordinarily raising and exciting natural principles, and newly exalting, varying, and compounding such sort of ideas, as he has by nature; here is nothing like giving him a new sense.

Upon the whole, I think it is clearly manifest, that all truly gracious affections do arise from special and peculiar influences of the Spirit, working that sensible effect or sensation in the souls of the saints, which are entirely different from all that is possible a natural man should experience, not only different in degree and circumstances, but different in its whole nature; so that a natural man not only cannot experience that which is individually the same, but cannot experience any thing but what is exceeding diverse, and immensely below it, in its kind; and that which the power of men or devils is not sufficient to produce the like of, or any thing of the same nature.

I have insisted largely on this matter, because it is of great importance and use evidently to discover and demonstrate the delusions of Satan, in many kinds of false religious affections, which multitudes are deluded by, and probably have been in all ages of the Christian church; and to settle and determine many articles of doctrine, concerning the operations of the Spirit of God, and the nature of true grace.

Now, therefore, to apply these things to the purpose of this discourse.

From hence it appears, that impressions which some have made on their imagination, or the imaginary ideas which they have of God or Christ, or heaven, or any thing appertaining to religion, have nothing in them that is spiritual, or of the nature of true grace. Though such things may attend what is spiritual, and be mixed with it, yet in themselves they have nothing that is spiritual, nor are they any part of gracious experience.

Here, for the sake of common people, I will explain what is intended by impressions on the imagination and imaginary ideas. The imagination is that power of the mind whereby it can have a conception, or idea of things of an external or outward nature (that is, of such sort of things as are the objects of the outward senses) when those things are not present, and be not perceived by the senses. It is called imagination from the word *image;* because thereby a person can have an image of some external thing in his mind, when that thing is not present in reality, nor any thing like it. All such things as we perceive by our five external senses, seeing, hearing, smelling, tasting, and feeling, are external things: and when a person has an idea or image of any of these sorts of things in his mind, when they are not there, and when he does not really see, hear, smell, taste, nor feel them; that is to have an imagination of them, and these ideas are imaginary ideas: and when such kinds of ideas are strongly impressed upon the mind, and the image of them in the mind is very lively, almost as if one saw them, or heard them, &c., that is called an impression on the imagination. Thus colors and shapes, and a form of countenance, they are outward things; because they are that sort of things which are the objects of the outward sense of seeing; and therefore when any person has in his mind a lively idea of any shape, or color, or form of countenance; that is to have an imagination of those things. So if he has an idea, of such sort of light or darkness, as he perceives by the sense of seeing; that is to have an idea of outward light, and so is an imagination. So if he has an idea of any marks made on paper, suppose letters and words written in a book; that is to have an external and imaginary idea of such kind of things as we sometimes perceive by our bodily eyes. And when we have the ideas of that kind of things which we perceive by any of the other senses, as of any sounds or voices, or words spoken; this is only to have ideas of outward things, viz., of such kind of things as are perceived by the external sense of hearing, and so that also is imagination: and when these ideas are livelily impressed, almost as if they were really heard with the ears, this is to have an impression on the imagination. And so I might go on, and instance in the ideas of things appertaining to the other three senses of smelling, tasting, and feeling.

Many who have had such things have very ignorantly supposed them to be of the nature of spiritual discoveries. They have had lively ideas of some external shape, and beautiful form of countenance; and this they call spiritually seeing Christ. Some have had impressed upon them ideas of a great outward light; and this they call a spiritual discovery of God's or Christ's glory. Some have had ideas of Christ's hanging on the cross, and his blood running from his wounds; and this they call a spiritual sight of Christ crucified, and the way of salvation by his blood. Some have seen him with his arms open ready to embrace them; and this they call a discovery of the sufficiency of Christ's grace and love. Some have had lively ideas of heaven, and of Christ on his throne there, and shining ranks of saints and angels; and this they call seeing heaven opened to them. Some from time to time have had a lively idea of a person of a beautiful countenance smiling upon them; and this they call a spiritual discovery of the love of Christ to their souls, and tasting the love of Christ. And they look upon it as sufficient evidence that these things are spiritual discoveries, and that they see them spiritually, because they say they do not see these things with their bodily eyes, but in their hearts; for they can see them when their eyes are shut. And in like manner, the imaginations of some have been impressed with ideas of the sense of hearing; they have had ideas of words, as if they were spoken to them, sometimes they are the words of Scripture, and sometimes other words: they have had ideas of Christ's speaking comfortable words to them. These things they have called having the inward call of Christ, hearing the voice of Christ spiritually in their hearts, having the witness of the Spirit, and the inward testimony of the love of Christ, &c.

The common and less considerate and understanding sort of people, are the more easily led into apprehensions that these things are spiritual things, because spiritual things being invisible, and not things that can be pointed forth with the finger, we are forced to use figurative expressions in speaking of them, and to borrow names from external and sensible objects to signify them by. Thus we call a clear apprehension of things spiritual by the name of *light;* and a having such an apprehension of such or such things, by the name of *seeing* such things; and the conviction of the judgment, and the persuasion of the will, by the word of Christ in the gospel, we signify by spiritually hearing the call of Christ: and the Scripture itself abounds with such like figurative expressions. Persons hearing these often used, and having pressed upon them the necessity of having their eyes opened, and having a discovery of spiritual things, and seeing Christ in his glory, and having the inward call, and the like, they ignorantly look and wait for some such external discoveries, and imaginary views as have been spoken of; and when they have them are confident, that now their eyes are opened, now Christ has discovered himself to them, and they are his children; and hence are exceedingly affected and elevated with their deliverance and happiness, and many kinds of affections are at once set in a violent motion in them.

But it is exceedingly apparent that such ideas have nothing in them which is spiritual and divine, in the sense wherein it has been demonstrated that all gracious experiences are spiritual and divine. These external ideas are in no wise of such a sort, that they are entirely, and in their whole nature diverse from all that men have by nature, perfectly different from, and vastly above any sensation which it is possible a man should have by any natural sense or principle, so that in order to have them, a man must have a new spiritual and divine sense given him, in order to have any sensations of that sort: so far from this, that they are ideas of the same sort which we have by the external senses, that are some of the inferior powers of the human nature; they are merely ideas of external objects, or ideas of that nature, of the same outward, sensitive kind; the same sort of sensations of mind (differing not in degree, but only in circumstances) that we have by those natural principles which are common to us with the beasts, viz., the five external senses. This is a low, miserable notion of spiritual sense, to suppose that it is only a conceiving or imagining that sort of ideas which we have by our animal senses, which senses the beasts have in as great perfection as we; it is, as it were, a turning Christ, or the divine nature in the soul, into a mere animal

There is nothing wanting in the soul, as it is by nature, to render it capable of being the subject of all these external ideas, without any new principles. A natural man is capable of having an idea, and a lively idea of shapes, and colors, and sounds, when they are absent, and as capable as a regenerate man is: so there is nothing supernatural in them. And it is known by abundant experience, that it is not the advancing or perfecting human nature, which makes persons more capable of having such lively and strong imaginary ideas, but that on the contrary, the weakness of body and mind, and distempers of body, make persons abundantly more susceptive of such impressions.*

As to a truly spiritual sensation, not only is the manner of its coming into the mind extraordinary, but the sensation itself is totally diverse from all that men have, or can have, in a state of nature, as has been shown. But as to these external ideas, though the way of their coming into the mind is sometimes unusual, yet the ideas in themselves are not the better for that; they are still of no different sort from what men have by their senses; they are of no higher kind, nor a whit better. For instance, the external idea a man has now of Christ hanging on the cross, and shedding his blood, is no better in itself, than the external idea that the Jews his enemies had, who stood round his cross, and saw this with their bodily eyes. The imaginary idea which men have now of an external brightness and glory of God, is no better than the idea the wicked congregation in the wilderness had of the external glory of the Lord at Mount Sinai, when they saw it with their bodily eyes; or any better than that idea which millions of cursed reprobates will have of the external glory of Christ at the day of judgment, who shall see, and have a very lively idea of ten thousand times greater external glory of Christ, than ever yet was con-

* "Conceits and whimsies abound most in men of weak reason; children, and such as are cracked in their understanding, have most of them; strength of reason banishes them, as the sun does mists and vapors. But now the more rational any gracious person is, by so much more is he fixed and settled, and satisfied in the grounds of religion; yea, there is the highest and purest reason in religion; and when this change is wrought upon men, it is carried on in a rational way. Isa. i. 18, John xix. 9." *Flavel's Preparation for Sufferings*, Chap. vi. [Edwards's note.]

ceived in any man's imagination:* yea, the image of Christ, which men conceive in their imaginations, is not in its own nature of any superior kind to the idea the Papists conceive of Christ, by the beautiful and affecting images of him which they see in their churches (though the way of their receiving the idea may not be so bad); nor are the affections they have, if built primarily on such imaginations, any better than the affections raised in the ignorant people, by the sight of those images, which oftentimes are very great; especially when these images, through the craft of the priests, are made to move, and speak, and weep, and the like.† Merely the way of persons receiving these imaginary ideas, does not alter the nature of the ideas themselves that are received; let them be received in what way they will, they are still but external ideas, or ideas of outward appearances, and so are not spiritual. Yea, if men should actually receive such external ideas by the immediate power of the most high God upon their minds, they would not be spiritual, they would be no more than a common work of the Spirit of God; as is evident in fact, in the instance of Balaam,

* "If any man should see, and behold Christ really and immediately, this is not the saving knowledge of him. I know the saints do know Christ as if immediately present; they are not strangers by their distance: if others have seen him more immediately, I will not dispute it. But if they have seen the Lord Jesus as immediately as if here on earth, yet Capernaum saw him so; nay, some of them were disciples for a time, and followed him, John vi. And yet the Lord was hid from their eyes. Nay, all the world shall see him in his glory, which shall amaze them; and yet this is far short of having the saving knowledge of him, which the Lord doth communicate to the elect. So that though you see the Lord so really, as that you become familiar with him, yet, Luke xiii, 26: 'Lord have we not eat and drank,' &c.—and so perish." *Shepard's Par. of the Ten Virgins*, Part I, p. 197, 198. [Edwards's note.]

† "Satan is transformed into an angel of light: and hence we have heard that some have heard voices; some have seen the very blood of Christ dropping on them, and his wounds in his side: some have seen a great light shining in the chamber; some have been wonderfully affected with their dreams; some in great distress have had inward witness, 'Thy sins are forgiven'; and hence such liberty and joy, that they are ready to leap up and down the chamber. O adulterous generation! this is natural and usual with men, they would fain see Jesus, and have him present to give them peace; and hence Papists have his images. Wo to them that have no other manifested Christ, but such a one." *Shepard's Parable of the Ten Virgins*, Part I, p. 198. [Edwards's note.]

who had impressed on his mind, by God himself, a clear and lively outward representation or idea of Jesus Christ, as "the Star rising out of Jacob, when he heard the words of God, and knew the knowledge of the Most High, and saw the vision of the Almighty, falling into a trance," Numb. xxiv. 16, 17, but yet had no manner of spiritual discovery of Christ; that Day Star never spiritually rose in his heart, he being but a natural man.

And as these external ideas have nothing divine or spiritual in their nature and nothing but what natural men, without any new principles, are capable of; so there is nothing in their nature which requires that peculiar, inimitable and unparalleled exercise of the glorious power of God, in order to their production, which it has been shown there is in the production of true grace. There appears to be nothing in their nature above the power of the devil. It is certainly not above the power of Satan to suggest thoughts to men; because otherwise he could not tempt them to sin. And if he can suggest any thoughts or ideas at all, doubtless imaginary ones, or ideas of things external, are not above his power;* for the external ideas men have are the lowest sort of ideas. These ideas may be raised only by impressions made on the body, by moving the animal spirits, and impressing the brain.—Abundant experience does certainly show, that alterations in the body will excite imaginary or external ideas in the mind; as often, in the case of a high fever, melancholy, &c. These external ideas are as much below the more intellectual exercises of the soul, as the body is a less noble part of man than the soul.

And there is not only nothing in the nature of these external ideas or imaginations of outward appearances, from whence we can infer that they are above the power of the devil; but it is certain also that the devil can excite, and often hath excited such ideas. They were external ideas which he excited in the

---

* "Consider how difficult, yea and impossible it is to determine that such a voice, vision, or revelation is of God, and that Satan cannot feign or counterfeit it: seeing he hath left no certain marks by which we may distinguish one spirit from another." *Flavel's Causes and Cures of Mental Terrors*, clause 14. [Edwards's note.]

dreams and visions of the false prophets of old, who were under the influence of lying spirits, that we often read of in Scripture, as Deut. xiii. 1, 1 Kings xxii. 22, Isa. xxviii. 7, Ezek. xiii. 7. And they were external ideas that he often excited in the minds of the heathen priests, magicians and sorcerers, in their visions and ecstasies, and they were external ideas that he excited in the mind of the man Christ Jesus, when he showed him all the kingdoms of the world, with the glory of them, when those kingdoms were not really in sight.

And if Satan or any created being, has power to impress the mind with outward representations, then no particular sort of outward representations can be any evidence of a divine power. Almighty power is no more requisite to represent the shape of man to the imagination, than the shape of anything else: there is no higher kind of power necessary to form in the brain one bodily shape or color than another: it needs a no more glorious power to represent the form of the body of a man, than the form of a chip or block; though it be of a very beautiful human body, with a sweet smile in his countenance, or arms open, or blood running from the hands, feet and side: that sort of power which can represent black or darkness to the imagination, can also represent white and shining brightness: the power and skill which can well and exactly paint a straw, or a stick of wood, on a piece of paper or canvass; the same in kind, only perhaps further improved, will be sufficient to paint the body of a man, with great beauty and in royal majesty, or a magnificent city, paved with gold, full of brightness, and a glorious throne, &c. So it is no more than the same sort of power that is requisite to paint one as the other of these on the brain. The same sort of power that can put ink upon paper, can put on leaf gold. So that it is evident to a demonstration, if we suppose it to be in the devil's power to make any sort of external representation at all on the fancy (as without doubt it is, and never any one questioned it who believed there was a devil, that had any agency with mankind): I say, if so, it is demonstrably evident, that a created power may extend to all kinds of external appearances and ideas in the mind. From hence it again clearly appears, that no such things have any thing in them that is spiritual, supernatural, and divine, in the sense in which it has been proved that all truly gracious experiences have. And though external ideas, through man's make and frame, do ordinarily in some degree attend spiritual experiences, yet these ideas are no part of their spiritual experience, any more than the motion of the blood, and beating of the pulse, that attend experiences, are a part of spiritual experience. And though undoubtedly, through men's infirmity in the present state, and especially through the weak constitution of some persons, gracious affections which are very strong, do excite lively ideas in the imagination; yet it is also undoubted, that when persons' affections are founded on imaginations, which is often the case, those affections are merely natural and common, because they are built on a foundation that is not spiritual; and so are entirely different from gracious affections, which, as has been proved, do evermore arise from those operations that are spiritual and divine.

These imaginations do oftentimes raise the carnal affections of men to an exceeding great height: and no wonder, when the subjects of them have an ignorant, but undoubting persuasion, that they are divine manifestations, which the great Jehovah immediately makes to their souls, therein giving them testimonies in an extraordinary manner, of his high and peculiar favor.

Again, it is evident from what has been observed and proved of the manner in which gracious operations and effects in the heart are spiritual, supernatural and divine, that the immediate suggesting of the words of Scripture to the mind has nothing in it which is spiritual.

.   .   .   .

But I am come now to the last distinguishing mark of holy affections that I shall mention.

XII. Gracious and holy affections have their exercise and fruit in Christian practice.—I mean, they have that influence and power upon him who is the subject of them, that they cause that a practice, which is universally conformed to and directed by Christian rules, should be the practice and business of his life.

This implies three things: 1. That his behavior or practice in the world, be universally conformed to, and directed by Christian rules. 2. That he makes a business of such a holy practice above all things; that it be a business which he is chiefly engaged in, and devoted to, and pursues with highest earnestness and diligence: so that he may be said to make this practice of religion eminently his work and business. And 3. That he persists in it to the end of life: so that it may be said, not only to be his business at certain seasons, the business of Sabbath days, or certain extraordinary times, or the business of a month, or a year, or of seven years, or his business under certain circumstances; but the business of his life; it being that business which he perseveres in through all changes, and under all trials, as long as he lives.

. . . .

The reason why gracious affections have such a tendency and effect appears from many things that have already been observed, in the preceding parts of this discourse.

The reason of it appears from this, that gracious affections do arise from those operations and influences which are spiritual, and that the inward principle from whence they flow, is something divine, a communication of God, a participation of the divine nature, Christ living in the heart, the Holy Spirit dwelling there, in union with the faculties of the soul, as an internal vital principle, exerting his own proper nature, in the exercise of those faculties. This is sufficient to show us why true grace should have such activity, power, and efficacy. No wonder that which is divine, is powerful and effectual; for it has omnipotence on its side. If God dwells in the heart, and be vitally united to it, he will show that he is a God, by the efficacy of his operation. Christ is not in the heart of a saint, as in a sepulchre, or as a dead saviour, that does nothing; but as in his temple, and as one that is alive from the dead. For in the heart where Christ savingly is, there he lives, and exerts himself after the power of that endless life that he received at his resurrection. Thus every saint that is a subject of the benefit of Christ's sufferings, is made to know and experience the power of his resurrection. The Spirit of Christ, which is the immediate spring of grace in the heart, is all life, all power, all act: 1 Cor. ii. 4, "In demonstration of the Spirit, and of power." 1 Thess. i. 5, "Our gospel came not unto you in word only, but also in power, and in the Holy Ghost." 1 Cor. iv. 20, "The kingdom of God is not in word, but in power." Hence saving affections, though oftentimes they do not make so great a noise and show as others, yet have in them a secret solidity, life, and strength, whereby they take hold of, and carry away the heart, leading it into a kind of captivity, 2 Cor. x. 5, gaining a full and steadfast determination of the will for God and holiness. Psal. cx. 3, "Thy people shall be willing in the day of thy power." And thus it is that holy affections have a governing power in the course of a man's life. A statue may look very much like a real man, and a beautiful man; yea, it may have, in its appearance to the eye, the resemblance of a very lively, strong, and active man; but yet an inward principle of life and strength is wanting; and therefore it does nothing, it brings nothing to pass, there is no action or operation to answer the show. False discoveries and affections do not go deep enough to reach and govern the spring of men's actions and practice. The seed in stony ground had not deepness of earth, and the root did not go deep enough to bring forth fruit. But gracious affections go to the very bottom of the heart, and take hold of the very inmost springs of life and activity.

Herein chiefly appears the power of true godliness, viz., in its being effectual in practice. And the efficacy of godliness in this respect, is what the apostle has respect to, when he speaks of the power of godliness, 2 Tim. iii. 5, as is very plain; for he there is particularly declaring, how some professors of religion would notoriously fail in the practice of it, and then in the 5th verse observes, that in being thus of an unholy practice, they deny the power of godliness, though they have the form of it. Indeed the power of godliness is exerted in the first place within the soul, in the sensible, lively exercise of gracious affections there. Yet the principal evidence of this power of godliness, is in those exercises of holy affections that are practical, and in their being practical; in conquering the will, and conquering the lusts and corruptions of men, and carrying men on in the way of holiness, through all temptations, difficulty, and opposition.

Again, the reason why gracious affections have their exercise and effect in Christian practice, appears from this (which has also been before observed), that "the first objective ground of gracious affections, is the transcendently excellent and amiable nature of divine things, as they are in themselves, and not any conceived relation they bear to self, or self-interest." This shows why holy affections will cause men to be holy in their practice universally. What makes men partial in religion is, that they seek themselves, and not God, in their religion; and close with religion, not for its own excellent nature, but only to serve a turn. He that closes with religion only to serve a turn, will close with no more of it than he imagines serves that turn; but he that closes with religion for its own excellent and lovely nature, closes with all that has that nature: he that embraces religion for its own sake, embraces the whole of religion. This also shows why gracious affections will cause men to practise religion perseveringly, and at all times. Religion may alter greatly in process of time, as to its consistence with men's private interest, in many respects; and therefore he that complies with it only for selfish views, is liable, in change of times, to forsake it; but the excellent nature of religion, as it is in itself, is invariable; it is always the same, at all times, and through all changes; it never alters in any respect.

The reason why gracious affections issue in holy practice, also further appears from the kind of excellency of divine things, that it has been observed is the foundation of all holy affections, viz., "their moral excellency, or the beauty of their holiness." No wonder that a love to holiness, for holiness' sake, inclines persons to practise holiness, and to practise every thing that is holy. Seeing holiness is the main thing that excites, draws, and governs all gracious affections, no wonder that all such affections tend to holiness. That which men love, they desire to have and to be united to, and possessed of. That beauty which men delight in, they desire to be adorned with. Those acts which men delight in, they necessarily incline to do.

And what has been observed of that divine teaching and leading of the Spirit of God, which there is in gracious affections, shows the reason of this tendency of such affections to a universally holy practice. For, as has been observed, the Spirit of God in this his divine teaching and leading, gives the soul a natural relish of the sweetness of that which is holy, and of every thing that is holy, so far as it comes in view and excites a disrelish and disgust of every thing that is unholy.

The same also appears from what has been observed of the nature of that spiritual knowledge, which is the foundation of all holy affection, as consisting in a sense and view of that excellency in divine things, which is supreme and transcendent. For hereby these things appear above all others, worthy to be chosen and adhered to. By the sight of the transcendent glory of Christ, true Christians see him worthy to be followed; and so are powerfully drawn after him; they see him worthy that they should forsake all for him: by the sight of that superlative amiableness, they are thoroughly disposed to be subject to him, and engaged to labor with earnestness and activity in his service, and made willing to go through all difficulties for his sake. And it is the discovery of this divine excellency of Christ, that makes them constant to him: for it makes a deep impression upon their minds, that they cannot forget him; and they will follow him whithersoever he goes, and it is in vain for any to endeavor to draw them away from him.

The reason of this practical tendency and issue of gracious affections, further appears from what has been observed of such affections being "attended with a thorough conviction of the judgment of the reality and certainty of divine things." No wonder that they who were never thoroughly convinced that there is any reality in the things of religion, will never be at the labor and trouble of such an earnest, universal, and persevering practice of religion, through all difficulties, self-denials, and sufferings in a dependence on that, which they are not convinced of. But on the other hand, they who are thoroughly convinced of the certain truth of those things, must needs be governed by them in their practice, for the things revealed in the word of God are so great, and so infinitely more important than all other things, that it is inconsistent with the human nature, that a man should fully believe the truth of them, and not be influenced by them above all things in his practice.

Again, the reason of this expression and effect of holy affections in the practice, appears from what has been observed of "a change of nature, accompanying such affections." Without a change of nature, men's practice will not be thoroughly changed. Until the tree be made good, the fruit will not be good. Men do not gather grapes of thorns, nor figs of thistles. The swine may be washed, and appear clean for a little while, but yet, without a change of nature he will still wallow in the mire. Nature is a more powerful principle of action, than any thing that opposes it: though it may be violently restrained for a while, it will finally overcome that which restrains it: it is like the stream of a river, it may be stopped a while with a dam, but if nothing be done to dry the fountain, it will not be stopped always; it will have a course, either in its old channel, or a new one. Nature is a thing more constant and permanent, than any of those things that are the foundation of carnal men's reformation and righteousness. When a natural man denies his lust, and lives a strict, religious life, and seems humble, painful, and earnest in religion, it is not natural; it is all a force against nature; as when a stone is violently thrown upwards; but that force will be gradually spent; yet nature will remain in its full strength, and so prevails again, and the stone returns downwards. As long as corrupt nature is not mortified, but the principle left whole in a man, it is a vain thing to expect that it should not govern. But if the old nature be indeed mortified, and a new and heavenly nature infused, then may it will be expected, that men will walk in newness of life, and continue to do so to the end of their days.

.   .   .   .

REFLECTION VIII

One thing more may not be unprofitably observed in the preceding account of Brainerd; and that is the *special* and *remarkable disposal* of divine providence, with regard to the *circumstances* of his last *sickness and death.*

Though he had been long infirm, his constitution being much broken by his fatigues and hardships; and though he was often brought very low by illness before he left *Kaunaumeek,* and also while he lived at the *Forks of Delaware;* yet his life was preserved, till he had seen that which he had so long and greatly desired and sought, a glorious work of grace among the Indians, and had received the wished for blessing of God on his labours. Though as it were "in deaths oft," yet he lived to behold the happy fruits of the long continued travail of his soul and labour of his body, in the wonderful conversion of many of the heathen, and the happy effects of it in the great change of their conversation, with many circumstances which afforded a fair prospect of the continuance of God's blessing upon them; as may appear by what I shall presently further observe.—Thus he did not "depart till his eyes had seen God's salvation."

Though it was the pleasure of God, that he should be taken off from his labours among that people to whom God had made him a spiritual father, who were so dear to him, and for whose spiritual welfare he was so greatly concerned; yet this was not before they were well initiated and instructed in the Christian religion, thoroughly weaned from their old heathenish and brutish notions and practices, and all their prejudices and jealousies, which tended to keep their minds unsettled, were fully removed. They were confirmed and fixed in the Christian faith and manners; were formed into a church; had ecclesiastical ordinances and discipline introduced and settled; were brought into a good way with respect to the education of children; had a schoolmaster excellently qualified for the business; and had a school set up and established, in good order, among them. They had been well brought off from their former idle, strolling, sottish way of living; had removed from their former scattered uncertain habitations, were collected in a town by themselves, on a good piece of land of their own; were introduced into the way of living by husbandry; and had begun to experience the benefits of it. These things were but just brought to pass by his indefatigable application and care; and then he was taken off from his work by illness. If this had been but a little sooner, they would by no means have been so well prepared for such a dispensation; and it probably would have been unspeakably more to the hurt of their spiritual interest, and of the cause of Christianity among them.

The time and circumstances of his illness were so ordered, that he had just opportunity to finish his JOURNAL, and prepare it for press; giving an account of the marvellous display of divine power and grace among the Indians in *New-Jersey*, and at the *Forks of Delaware*. His doing this was of great consequence and therefore urged upon him by the *correspondents* who have honoured his Journal with a preface. The world being particularly and justly informed of that affa[i]r by BRAINERD before his death, a foundation was hereby laid for a concern in *others* for that cause, and proper care and measures to be taken for maintaining it after his death. It has actually proved to be of great influence and benefit in this respect; for it has excited and engaged many in those parts, and also more distant parts of America, to exert themselves for upholding and promoting the good and glorious work, remarkably opening their hearts and hands to that end: and not only in America, but in Great Britain, that Journal, which I have earnestly recommended to my readers, has been an occasion of some large benefactions, made for promoting the interest of Christianity among the Indians.—If BRAINERD had been taken ill but a little sooner, he had not been able to complete his Journal, and prepare a copy for the press.

He was not taken off from the work of the ministry among his people, till his *brother* was in a capacity and circumstances to *succeed* him in his care of them; who succeeds him in the like spirit, and under whose prudent and faithful care his congregation has flourished, and been very happy, since he left them; and probably could not have been so well provided for otherwise. If BRAINERD had been disabled sooner, his *brother* would by no means have been ready to stand up in his place; having taken his first degree at college but about that very time that he was seized with his fatal consumption.

Though in that winter in which he lay sick at Mr. Dickinson's, in Elizabeth-Town, he continued for a long time in an extremely low state, so that his life was almost despaired of, and his state was sometimes such that it was hardly expected that he would live a day; yet his life was spared a while longer; he lived to see his *brother* arrived in New-Jersey, being come to succeed him in the care of his Indians; and he himself had opportunity to assist in his examination and introduction into his business: and to commit the conduct of his dear people to one whom he well knew, and could put confidence in, and use freedom with, in giving him particular instructions and charges, and under whose care he could leave his congregation with great cheerfulness.

The providence of God was remarkable in so ordering it, that before his death he should take a journey in New-England, and go to Boston; which was, in many respects, of very great and happy consequence to the interest of religion, and especially among his own people. By this means, as before observed, he was brought in acquaintance with many persons of note and influence, ministers and others, belonging both to the town and various parts of the country; and had opportunity, under the best advantages, to bear a testimony for God and true religion, and against those false appearances of it which have proved most pernicious to the interest of Christ's kingdom in the land. The providence of God is particularly observable in this circumstance of the testimony which he there bore for true religion, *viz.* that he there was brought so near the *grave*, and continued for so long a time on the very brink of eternity; and from time to time, looked on himself, and was looked on by others, as just leaving the world; and that in these circumstances he should be so particularly directed and assisted in his thoughts and views of religion, to distinguish between the true and the false, with such clearness and evidence; and that after this he should be unexpectedly and surprisingly restored and strengthened, so far as to be able to converse freely. Then he had an opportunity, and special occasions to declare the sentiments he had in these, which to human apprehension, were his dying circumstances; and to bear his testimony concerning the nature of true religion, and concerning the mischievous tendency of its most prevalent counterfeits and false appearances; as things he had a special, clear, distinct view of at that time, when he expected in a few minutes to be in eternity; and the certainty and importance of which were then, in a peculiar manner, impressed on his mind.

Among the happy consequences of his going to Boston, were those liberal benefactions that have been mentioned, which were made by piously disposed persons, for maintaining and promoting the interest of religion among his people; and also the meeting of a number of gentlemen in Boston, of note and ability to consult upon measures for that purpose; who were excited by their acquaintance and conversation with BRAINERD, and by the account of the great things which God had wrought by his ministry, to unite themselves, that by their joint endeavours and contributions they might promote the kingdom of Christ, and the spiritual good of their fellow-creatures, among the Indians in New-Jersey; and elsewhere.

. . . .

The providence of God was observable in his going to Boston at a time when not only the honourable commissioners were seeking missionaries to the Six Nations, but also just after his Journal, which gives an account of his labours and success among the Indians had been received and spread in Boston. His name was thus known, and the minds of serious people were well prepared to receive his person, and the testimony he there gave for God; to exert themselves for the upholding and promoting the interest of religion in his congregation, and among the Indians elsewhere; and to regard his judgment concerning the qualifications of missionaries. If he had gone there the fall before, (when he had intended to make his journey into New-England, but was prevented by a sudden great increase of his illness;) or if he had not been unexpectedly detained in Boston; (for when he went from my house, he intended to make but a very short stay there,) it would not probably have been in any measure to so good effect; but divine providence, by his being brought so low there, detained him long; thereby to make way for the fulfilling his own gracious designs.

The providence of God was remarkable in so ordering, that although he was brought so very near the grave in Boston, that it was not in the least expected he would ever come alive out of his chamber; yet he was wonderfully revived, and preserved several months longer; so that he had opportunity to see, and fully to converse with both his younger brothers before he died. This he greatly desired; especially to see his brother John, with whom was left the care of his congregation; that he might by him be fully informed of their state, and leave with him such instructions and directions as were requisite in order to their spiritual welfare; and send to them his dying charge, and counsels. He had also opportunity, by means of this suspension of his death, to find and recommend two persons fit to be employed as missionaries to the Six Nations, as had been desired of him.

Thus, although it was the pleasure of a sovereign God, that he should be taken away from his congregation, the people, whom he had begotten through the gospel, who were so dear to him; yet it was granted him, that before he died he should see them well provided for, every way. He saw them provided for, with one to instruct them, and to take care of their souls; his own brother, in whom he could confide. He saw a good foundation laid for the support of the school among them; those things, which before were wanting in order to it, being supplied. He had the prospect of a charitable society being established, of able and well-disposed persons, who seem to make the spiritual interest of his congregation their own; whereby he had a comfortable view of their being well provided for, for the future. He had also opportunity to leave all his dying charges with his successor in the pastoral care of his people, and by him to send his dying counsels to them. Thus God granted him to see all things happily settled, or in a hopeful way of being so, before his death, with respect to his dear people. —And whereas not only his own congregation, but the souls of the Indians in North-America in general, were very dear to him, and he had greatly set his heart on propagating and extending the kingdom of Christ among them; God was pleased to grant him—though not to be the immediate instrument of their instruction and conversion—yet, that before his death, he should see unexpected extraordinary provisions made for this also. It is remarkable, that God not only allowed him to *see* such provision made for maintaining the interest of religion among his own people, and the propagation of it elsewhere; but honoured him by making *him* the means or occasion of it. So that it is very probable, although BRAINERD during the last four months of his life, was ordinarily in an extremely weak and low state, very often scarcely able to speak; yet that he was made the instrument or means of much more good in that space of time, than he would have been if well, and in full strength of body. Thus *God's power* was manifested in *his weakness*, and the *life of Christ* was manifested in *his mortal flesh*.

Another thing, wherein appears the merciful disposal of providence with respect to his death, was, that he did not die in the wilderness, among the savages, at *Kaunaumeek*, or the *Forks of Delaware*, or on the *Susquehannah;* but in a place where his dying behaviour and speeches might be observed and remembered, and some account given of them for the benefit of survivors; and where care might be taken of him in his sickness, and proper honours done him at his death.

The providence of God is also worthy of remark, in so overruling and ordering the matter, that he did not finally leave absolute orders for the entire suppressing of his *private papers;* as he had intended and fully resolved, insomuch that all the importunity of his friends could scarce restrain him from doing it, when sick at *Boston*. One thing relating to this is peculiarly remarkable, that his brother, a little before his death, should come unexpectedly from New-Jersey, and bring his *Diary* to him, though he had received no such order. Thus he had opportunity of access to these his reserved papers, and of reviewing the same; without which, it appears, he would at last have ordered them to be wholly suppressed; but after this, he the more readily yielded to the desires of his friends, and was willing to leave them in their hands to be disposed of as they thought might be most for God's glory. By this means, "he, being dead, yet speaketh," in these memoirs of his life, taken from those private writings; whereby it is to be hoped that he may still be as it were the instrument of promoting the interest of religion in this world; the advancement of which he so much desired, and hoped would be accomplished after his death.

If these circumstances of BRAINERD's death be duly considered, I doubt not but they will be acknowledged as a notable instance of God's fatherly care, and covenant-faithfulness towards them who are devoted to him, and faithfully serve him while they live; whereby "he never fails nor forsakes them, but *is with them* living and dying; so that whether they live, they live to the Lord; or whether they die, they die to the Lord;" and both in life and death they are owned and taken care of as *his*—BRAINERD himself, as was before observed, was much in taking notice when near his end, of the merciful circumstances of his death; and said, from time to time, that "God had granted him all his desire."

I would not conclude my observations on the merciful circumstances of BRAINERD's death, without acknowledging with thankfulness, the gracious dispensation of providence to me and my family, in so ordering, that he, though the ordinary place of his abode was more than two hundred miles distant, should be brought to my house, in his last sickness, and should die here. Thus we had opportunity for much acquaintance and conversation with him, to show him kindness in such circumstances, to see his dying *behaviour*, to hear his dying *speeches*, to receive his dying *counsels*, and to have the benefit of his dying *prayers*. May God in infinite mercy grant, that we may ever retain a proper remembrance of these things, and make a due improvement of the advantages we have had, in these respects! The Lord grant also, that the foregoing account of BRAINERD's life and death may be for the great spiritual benefit of all who shall read it, and prove a happy means of promoting the revival of true religion! *Amen.*

FREEDOM OF THE WILL

PART I

WHEREIN ARE EXPLAINED AND STATED VARIOUS TERMS AND THINGS
BELONGING TO THE SUBJECT OF THE ENSUING DISCOURSE

Section I

Concerning the Nature of the Will

It may possibly be thought, that there is no great need of going about to define or describe the Will; this word being generally as well understood as any other words we can use to explain it: and so perhaps it would be, had not philosophers, metaphysicians and polemic divines brought the matter into obscurity by the things they have said of it. But since it is so, I think it may be of some use, and will tend to the greater clearness in the following discourse to say a few things concerning it.

And therefore I observe, that the Will (without any metaphysical refining) is plainly, that by which the mind chooses any thing. The faculty of the Will is that faculty or power or principle of mind by which it is capable of choosing; an act of the Will is the same as an act of choosing or choice.

If any think it is a more perfect definition of the Will, to say, that it is that by which the soul either chooses or refuses; I am content with it: though I think that it is enough to say, it is that by which the soul chooses: for in every act of Will whatsoever, the mind chooses one thing rather than another; it chooses something rather than the contrary, or rather than the want or non-existence of that thing. So in every act of refusal, the mind chooses the absence of the thing refused; the positive and the negative are set before the mind for its choice, and it chooses the negative; and the mind's making its choice in that case is properly the act of the Will; the Will's determining between the two is a voluntary determining; but that is the

same thing as making a choice. So that whatever names we
call the act of the Will by, choosing, refusing, approving,
disapproving, liking, disliking, embracing, rejecting, determining, directing, commanding, forbidding, inclining or being
averse, a being pleased or displeased with; all may be reduced
to this of choosing. For the soul to act voluntarily, is evermore
to act electively.

Mr. Locke says,* "the Will signifies nothing but a power or
ability to prefer or choose." And in the foregoing page says,
"the word preferring seems best to express the act of volition;"
but adds, that "it does it not precisely; for (says he) though a
man would prefer flying to walking, yet who can say he ever
wills it?" But the instance he mentions does not prove that
there is any thing else in willing, but merely preferring: for it
should be considered what is the next and immediate object of
the Will, with respect to a man's walking, or any other external
action; which is not being removed from one place to another;
on the earth, or through the air; these are remoter objects of
preference; but such or such an immediate exertion of himself.
The thing nextly chosen or preferred when a man wills to
walk, is not his being removed to such a place where he would
be, but such an exertion and motion of his legs and feet, &c. in
order to it. And his willing such an alteration in his body in
the present moment, is nothing else but his choosing or preferring such an alteration in his body at such a moment, or his
liking it better than the forbearance of it. And God has so
made and established the human nature, the soul being united
to a body in proper state, that the soul preferring or choosing
such an immediate exertion or alteration of the body, such an
alteration instantaneously follows. There is nothing else in the
actions of my mind, that I am conscious of while I walk, but
only my preferring or choosing, through successive moments
that there should be such alterations of my external sensation
and motions; together with a concurring habitual expectation
that it will be so; having ever found by experience, that on
such an immediate preference, such sensations and motions do

* *Human Understanding.* Edit. 7. vol. i. p. 197. [Edwards's note.]

actually, instantaneously, and constantly arise. But it is not so in the case of flying: though a man may be said remotely to choose or prefer flying; yet he does not choose or prefer, incline to or desire, under circumstances in view, any immediate exertion of the members of his body in order to it; because he has no expectation that he should obtain the desired end by any such exertion; and he does not prefer or incline to any bodily exertion or effort under this apprehended circumstance, of its being wholly in vain. So that if we carefully distinguish the proper objects of the several acts of the Will, it will not appear by this, and such like instances, that there is any difference between volition and preference; or that a man's choosing, liking best, or being best pleased with a thing, are not the same with his willing that thing; as they seem to be according to those general and more natural notions of men, according to which language is formed. Thus an act of the Will is commonly expressed by its pleasing a man to do thus or thus; and a man's doing as he wills, and doing as he pleases, are the same thing in common speech.

Mr. Locke says,* "the Will is perfectly distinguished from Desire; which in the very same action may have a quite contrary tendency from that which our Wills set us upon. A man (says he) whom I cannot deny, may oblige me to use persuasions to another, which, at the same time I am speaking, I may wish may not prevail on him. In this case it is plain the Will and Desire run counter." I do not suppose, that Will and Desire are words of precisely the same signification: Will seems to be a word of a more general signification, extending to things present and absent. Desire respects something absent. I may prefer my present situation and posture, suppose, sitting still, or having my eyes open, and so may will it. But yet I cannot think they are so entirely distinct, that they can ever be properly said to run counter. A man never, in any instance, wills any thing contrary to his desires, or desires any thing contrary to his Will. The forementioned instance, which Mr. Locke produces, does not prove that he ever does. He may, on some

Human Understanding, vol i. p. 203, 204. [Edwards's note.]

consideration or other, will to utter speeches which have a
tendency to persuade another, and still may desire that they
may not persuade him; but yet his Will and Desire do not run
counter. The thing which he wills, the very same he desires;
and he does not will a thing, and desire the contrary in any
particular. In this instance, it is not carefully observed, what
is the thing willed, and what is the thing desired: if it were, it
would be found that Will and Desire do not clash in the least.
The thing willed on some consideration, is to utter such words;
and certainly, the same consideration, so influences him, that
he does not desire the contrary: all things considered, he
chooses to utter such words, and does not desire not to utter
them. And so as to the thing which Mr. Locke speaks of as
desired, viz., that the words, though they tend to persuade,
should not be effectual to that end; his Will is not contrary to
this; he does not will that they should be effectual, but rather
wills that they should not, as he desires. In order to prove that
the Will and Desire may run counter, it should be shown that
they may be contrary one to the other in the same thing, or
with respect to the very same object of Will or Desire: but here
the objects are two; and in each, taken by themselves, the Will
and Desire agree. And it is no wonder that they should not
agree in different things, however little distinguished they are
in their nature. The Will may not agree with the Will, nor
Desire agree with Desire, in different things. As in this very
instance which Mr. Locke mentions, a person may, on some
consideration, desire to use persuasions, and at the same time
may desire they may not prevail; but yet nobody will say, that
Desire runs counter to Desire; or that this proves that Desire
is perfectly a distinct thing from Desire.—The like might be
observed of the other instance Mr. Locke produces, of a man's
desiring to be eased of pain, &c.

But not to dwell any longer on this, whether *Desire* and *Will*
and whether *Preference* and *Volition* be precisely the same
things or no; yet, I trust it will be allowed by all, that in every
act of Will there is an act of choice; that in every volition there
is a preference, or a prevailing inclination of the soul, whereby

the soul, at that instant, is out of a state of perfect indifference, with respect to the direct object of the volition. So that in every act, or going forth of the Will, there is some preponderation of the mind or inclination, one way rather than another; and the soul had rather *have* or *do* one thing than another, or than not have or do that thing; and that there, where there is absolutely no preferring or choosing, but a perfect continuing equilibrium, there is no volition.

Section II

Concerning the Determination of the Will

By *determining the Will*, if the phrase be used with any meaning, must be intended, causing that the act of the Will or choice should be thus, and not otherwise: and the Will is said to be determined, when, in consequence of some action or influence, its choice is directed to, and fixed upon a particular object. As when we speak of the determination of motion, we mean causing the motion of the body to be such a way, or in such a direction, rather than another.

To talk of the determination of the Will, supposes an effect, which must have a cause. If the Will be determined, there is a determiner. This must be supposed to be intended even by them that say, the Will determines itself. If it be so, the Will is both determiner and determined; it is a cause that acts and produces effects upon itself, and is the object of its own influence and action.

With respect to that grand inquiry, What determines the Will? it would be very tedious and unnecessary at present to enumerate and examine all the various opinions which have been advanced concerning this matter; nor is it needful that I should enter into a particular disquisition of all points debated in disputes on that question, whether the Will always follows the last dictate of the understanding. It is sufficient to my present purpose to say, it is that motive, which, as it stands in the view of the mind, is the strongest, that determines the Will. But it may be necessary that I should a little explain my meaning in this.

By *motive*, I mean the whole of that which moves, excites or invites the mind to volition, whether that be one thing singly, or many things conjunctly. Many particular things may concur and unite their strength to induce the mind; and, when it is so, all together are as it were one complex motive. And when I speak of the *strongest motive*, I have respect to the strength of the whole that operates to induce to a particular act of volition, whether that be the strength of one thing alone, or of many together.

Whatever is a motive, in this sense, must be something that is extant in the view or apprehension of the understanding, or perceiving faculty. Nothing can induce or invite the mind to will or act any thing, any further than it is perceived, or in some way or other in the mind's view; for what is wholly unperceived, and perfectly out of the mind's view, cannot affect the mind at all. It is most evident, that nothing is in the mind, or reaches it, or takes any hold of it, any otherwise than as it is perceived or thought of.

And I think it must also be allowed by all, that every thing that is properly called a motive, excitement or inducement to a perceiving, willing agent, has some sort and degree of *tendency* or *advantage* to move or excite the Will, previous to the effect, or to the act of the Will excited. This previous tendency of the motive is what I call the strength of the motive. That motive which has a less degree of previous advantage or tendency to move the Will, or that appears less inviting, as it stands in the view of the mind, is what I call a *weaker motive*. On the contrary, that which appears most inviting, and has by what appears concerning it to the understanding or apprehension, the greatest degree of previous tendency to excite and induce the choice, is what I call the *strongest motive*. And in this sense, I suppose the Will is always determined by the strongest motive.

Things that exist in the view of the mind have their strength, tendency or advantage to move or excite its Will, from many things appertaining to the nature and circumstances of the thing viewed, the nature and circumstances of the mind that views, and the degree and manner of its view; of which it would perhaps be hard to make a perfect enumeration. But so much I think may be determined in general, without room for controversy, that whatever is perceived or apprehended by an intelligent and voluntary agent, which has the nature and influence of a motive to volition or choice, is considered or viewed as good; nor has it any tendency to invite or engage the election of the soul in any further degree than it appears such. For to say otherwise, would be to say, that things that appear have a tendency by the appearance they make, to engage the mind to elect them, some other way than by their appearing eligible to it; which is absurd. And therefore it must be true, in some sense, that the Will always is as the greatest apparent good is. For the right understanding of this, two things must be well and distinctly observed.

. . . .

It appears from these things, that in some sense, the Will always follows the last dictate of the understanding. But then the understanding must be taken in a large sense, as including the whole faculty of perception or apprehension, and not merely what is called reason or judgment. If by the dictate of the understanding is meant what reason declares to be best or most for the person's happiness, taking in the whole of his duration, it is not true, that the Will always follows the last dictate of the understanding. Such a dictate of reason is quite a different matter from things appearing now most agreeable; all things being put together which pertain to the mind's present perceptions, apprehensions or ideas, in any respect. Although that dictate of reason, when it takes place, is one thing that is put into the scales, and is to be considered as a thing that has concern in the compound influence which moves and induces the Will; and is one thing that is to be considered in estimating the degree of that appearance of good which the Will always follows; either as having its influence added to other things, or subducted from them. When it concurs with other things, then its weight is added to them, as put into the same scale; but when it is against them, it is as a weight in the opposite scale, where it resists the influence of other things: yet its resistance is often overcome by their greater weight, and so the act of the Will is determined in opposition to it.

The things which I have said, may, I hope, serve in some measure, to illustrate and confirm the position I laid down in the beginning of this section, viz., that the will is always determined by the strongest motive, or by that view of the mind which has the greatest degree of previous tendency to excite volition. But whether I have been so happy as rightly to explain the thing wherein consists the strength of motives, or not, yet my failing in this will not overthrow the position itself; which carries much of its own evidence with it, and is the thing of chief importance to the purpose of the ensuing discourse: and the truth of it, I hope, will appear with great clearness, before I have finished what I have to say on the subject of human liberty.

Section III

Concerning the meaning of the terms Necessity, Impossibility Inability, &c., and of Contingence

The words necessary, impossible, &c., are abundantly used in controversies about Free Will and moral agency; and therefore the sense in which they are used, should be clearly understood.

Here I might say, that a thing is then said to be necessary when it must be and cannot be otherwise. But this would not properly be a definition of Necessity, or an explanation of the word, any more than if I explained the word *must*, by there being a necessity. The words *must*, *can*, and *cannot*, need explication, as much as the words *necessary* and *impossible* excepting that the former are words that children commonly use, and know something of the meaning of earlier than the latter.

The word *necessary*, as used in common speech, is a relative term; and relates to some supposed opposition made to the existence of the thing spoken of, which is overcome, or proves in vain to hinder or alter it. That is necessary, in the origin and proper sense of the word, which is, or will be, notwithstanding all supposable opposition. To say, that a thing is necessary, is the same thing as to say, that it is impossible it should not be: but the word *impossible* is manifestly a relative term, and has reference to supposed power exerted to bring a thing to pass, which is insufficient for the effect; as the word *unable* is relative, and has relation to ability or endeavor which is insufficient; and as the word *irresistible* is relative, and has always reference to resistance which is made, or may be made to some force or power tending to an effect, and is insufficient to withstand the power or hinder the effect. The common notion of necessity and impossibility implies something that frustrates endeavor or desire.

Here several things are to be noted.

1. Things are said to be necessary in general, which are or will be notwithstanding any supposable opposition from us or others, or from whatever quarter. But things are said to be necessary to us, which are or will be notwithstanding all opposition supposable in the case from us. The same may be observed of the word *impossible*, and other such like terms.

2. These terms *necessary*, *impossible*, *irresistible*, &c., do especially belong to the controversy about liberty and moral agency, as used in the latter of the two senses now mentioned, viz., as necessary or impossible to us, and with relation to any supposable opposition or endeavor of ours.

3. As the word *Necessity* in its vulgar and common use, is relative, and has always reference to some supposable insufficient opposition; so when we speak of any thing as necessary to us, it is with relation to some supposable opposition of our Wills, or some voluntary exertion or effort of ours to the contrary; for we do not properly make opposition to an event, any otherwise than as we voluntarily oppose it. Things are said to be what must be, or necessarily are, as to us, when they are, or will be, though we desire or endeavor the contrary, or try to prevent or remove their existence: but such opposition of ours always either consists in, or implies, opposition of our Wills.

It is manifest that all such like words and phrases, as vulgarly used, are used and accepted in this manner. A thing is said to be necessary, when we cannot help it, let us do what we will. So any thing is said to be impossible to us, when we would do it, or would have it brought to pass, and endeavor it; or at least may be supposed to desire and seek it; but all our desires and endeavors are, or would be vain. And that is said to be irresistible, which overcomes all our opposition, resistance, and endeavors to the contrary. And we are said to be unable to do a thing, when our supposable desires and endeavors to do it are insufficient.

We are accustomed, in the common use of language, to apply and understand these phrases in this sense; we grow up with such a habit; which by the daily use of these terms, in such a sense, from our childhood, becomes fixed and settled; so that the idea of a relation to a supposed will, desire and endeavor of ours, is strongly connected with these terms, and naturally excited in our minds, whenever we hear the words used. Such ideas, and these words, are so united and associated, that they unavoidably go together; one suggests the other, and carries the other with it, and never can be separated as long as we live. And if we use the words, as terms of art, in another sense, yet, unless we are exceeding circumspect and wary, we shall insensibly slide into the vulgar use of them, and so apply the words in a very inconsistent manner: this habitual connection of ideas will deceive and confound us in our reasonings and discourses, wherein we pretend to use these terms in that manner, as terms of art.

4. It follows from what has been observed, that when these terms *necessary*, *impossible*, *irresistible*, *unable*, &c., are used in cases wherein no opposition, or insufficient will or endeavor, is supposed, or can be supposed, but the very nature of the supposed case itself excludes and denies any such opposition, will or endeavor, these terms are then not used in their proper signification, but quite beside their use in common speech. The reason is manifest; namely, that in such cases we cannot use the words with reference to a supposable opposition, will or endeavor. And therefore, if any man uses these terms in such

cases, he either uses them nonsensically, or in some new sense, diverse from their original and proper meaning. As for instance; if a man should affirm after this manner, that it is necessary for a man, and what must be, that a man should choose virtue rather than vice, during the time that he prefers virtue to vice; and that it is a thing impossible and irresistible, that it should be otherwise than that he should have this choice, so long as this choice continues; such a man would use the terms *must*, *irresistible*, &c., with perfect insignificance and nonsense; or in some new sense, diverse from their common use; which is with reference, as has been observed, to supposable opposition, unwillingness and resistance; whereas, here, the very supposition excludes and denies any such thing: for the case supposed is that of being willing and choosing.

5. It appears from what has been said, that these terms *necessary, impossible*, &c., are often used by philosophers and metaphysicians in a sense quite diverse from their common use and original signification: for they apply them to many cases in which no opposition is supposed or supposable. Thus they use them with respect to God's existence before the creation of the world, when there was no other being but He: so with regard to many of the dispositions and acts of the Divine Being, such as his loving himself, his loving righteousness, hating sin, &c. So they apply these terms to many cases of the inclinations and actions of created intelligent beings, angels and men; wherein all opposition of the Will is shut out and denied, in the very supposition of the case.

Metaphysical or Philosophical Necessity is nothing different from their certainty. I speak not now of the certainty of knowledge, but the certainty that is in things themselves, which is the foundation of the certainty of the knowledge of them; or that wherein lies the ground of the infallibility of the proposition which affirms them.

What is sometimes given as the definition of philosophical Necessity, namely, that by which a thing cannot but be, or whereby it cannot be otherwise, fails of being a proper explanation of it, on two accounts: first, the words *can*, or *cannot*, need explanation as much as the word *Necessity;* and the former may as well be explained by the latter, as the latter by the former. Thus, if any one asked us what we mean, when we say, a thing cannot but be, we might explain ourselves by saying, we mean, it must necessarily be so; as well as explain Necessity, by saying, it is that by which a thing cannot but be. And secondly, this definition is liable to the forementioned great inconvenience: the words *cannot*, or *unable*, are properly relative, and have relation to power exerted, or that may be exerted, in order to the thing spoken of; to which, as I have now observed, the word *Necessity*, as used by philosophers, has no reference.

Philosophical Necessity is really nothing else than the full and fixed connection between the things signified by the subject and predicate of a proposition, which affirms something to be true. When there is such a connection, then the thing affirmed in the proposition is necessary, in a philosophical sense; whether any opposition, or contrary effort be supposed, or supposable in the case, or no. When the subject and predicate of the proposition, which affirms the existence of any thing, either substance, quality, act or circumstance, have a full and certain connection, then the existence or being of that thing is said to be necessary in a metaphysical sense. And in this sense I use the word *Necessity*, in the following discourse, when I endeavor to prove that Necessity is not inconsistent with liberty.

·   ·   ·   ·   ·   ·   ·   ·   ·   ·   ·   ·   ·   ·   ·

Section IV

Of the Distinction of Natural and Moral Necessity, and Inability

That Necessity which has been explained, consisting in an infallible connection of the things signified by the subject and predicate of a proposition, as intelligent beings are the subjects of it, is distinguished into *moral* and *natural* Necessity.

I shall not now stand to inquire whether this distinction be a proper and perfect distinction; but shall only explain how these two sorts of Necessity are understood, as the terms are sometimes used, and as they are used in the following discourse.

The phrase, *moral* Necessity, is used variously; sometimes it is used for a Necessity of moral obligation. So we say, a man is under Necessity, when he is under bonds of duty and conscience, which he cannot be discharged from. So the word Necessity is often used for great obligation in point of interest. Sometimes by moral Necessity is meant that apparent connection of things, which is the ground of moral evidence; and so is distinguished from absolute Necessity, or that sure connection of things, that is a foundation for infallible certainty. In this sense, moral Necessity signifies much the same as that high degree of probability, which is ordinarily sufficient to satisfy, and be relied upon by mankind, in their conduct and behavior in the world, as they would consult their own safety and interest, and treat others properly as members of society. And sometimes by moral Necessity is meant that Necessity of connection and consequence, which arises from such moral causes, as the strength of inclination, or motives, and the connection which there is in many cases between these, and such certain volitions and actions. And it is in this sense, that I use the phrase, *moral Necessity*, in the following discourse.

By natural Necessity, as applied to men, I mean such Necessity as men are under through the force of natural causes; as distinguished from what are called moral causes, such as habits and dispositions of the heart, and moral motives and inducements. Thus men placed in certain circumstances, are the subjects of particular sensations by Necessity; they feel pain when their bodies are wounded; they see the objects presented before them in a clear light, when their eyes are opened; so they assent to the truth of certain propositions, as soon as the terms are understood; as that two and two make four, that black is not white, that two parallel lines can never cross one another; so by a natural Necessity men's bodies move downwards, when there is nothing to support them.

But here several things may be noted concerning these two kinds of Necessity.

1. Moral Necessity may be as absolute, as natural Necessity. That is, the effect may be as perfectly connected with its moral

cause, as a natural necessary effect is with its natural cause. Whether the Will in every case is necessarily determined by the strongest motive, or whether the Will ever makes any resistance to such a motive, or can ever oppose the strongest present inclination, or not; if that matter should be controverted, yet I suppose none will deny, but that, in some cases, a previous bias and inclination, or the motive presented, may be so powerful, that the act of the Will may be certainly and indissolubly connected therewith. When motives or previous biases are very strong, all will allow that there is some *difficulty* in going against them. And if they were yet stronger, the difficulty would be still greater. And therefore, if more were still added to their strength, to a certain degree, it would make the difficulty so great, that it would be wholly *impossible* to surmount it; for this plain reason, because whatever power men may be supposed to have to surmount difficulties, yet that power is not infinite; and so goes not beyond certain limits. If a man can surmount ten degrees of difficulty of this kind with twenty degrees of strength, because the degrees of strength are beyond the degrees of difficulty; yet if the difficulty be increased to thirty, or a hundred, or a thousand degrees, and his strength not also increased, his strength will be wholly insufficient to surmount the difficulty. As therefore it must be allowed, that there may be such a thing as a sure and perfect connection between moral causes and effects; so this only is what I call by the name of moral Necessity.

2. When I use this distinction of moral and natural Necessity I would not be understood to suppose, that if any thing comes to pass by the former kind of Necessity, the nature of things is not concerned in it, as well as in the latter. I do not mean to determine, that when a moral habit or motive is so strong, that the act of the Will infallibly follows, this is not owing to the nature of things. But these are the names that these two kind of Necessity have usually been called by; and they must be distinguished by some names or other; for there is a distinction or difference between them, that is very important in its consequences; which difference does not lie so much in the nature of the connection, as in the two terms connected. The cause with

which the effect is connected, is of a particular kind, viz., that which is of moral nature; either some previous habitual disposition, or some motive exhibited to the understanding. And the effect is also of a particular kind; being likewise of a moral nature; consisting in some inclination or volition of the soul or voluntary action.

I suppose, that Necessity which is called natural, in distinction from moral necessity, is so called, because *mere nature*, as the word is vulgarly used, is concerned, without any thing of *choice*. The word nature is often used in opposition to choice; not because nature has indeed never any hand in our choice; but this probably comes to pass by means that we first get our notion of nature from that discernible and obvious course of events, which we observe in many things that our choice has no concern in; and especially in the material world; which, in very many parts of it, we easily perceive to be in a settled course; the stated order and manner of succession being very apparent. But where we do not readily discern the rule and connection, (though there be a connection, according to an established law, truly taking place,) we signify the manner of event by some other name. Even in many things which are seen in the material and inanimate world, which do not discernibly and obviously come to pass according to any settled course, men do not call the manner of the event by the name of *nature*, but by such names as *accident, chance, contingence,* &c. So men make a distinction between nature and choice; as though they were completely and universally distinct. Whereas, I suppose none will deny but that choice, in many cases, arises from nature, as truly as other events. But the dependence and connection between acts of volition or choice, and their causes, according to established laws, is not so sensible and obvious. And we observe that choice is as it were a new principle of motion and action, different from that established law and order of things which is most obvious, that is seen especially in corporeal and sensible things; and also the choice often interposes, interrupts and alters the chain of events in these external objects, and causes them to proceed otherwise than they would do, if let alone, and left to go on according to the laws of motion among themselves. Hence it is spoken of as if it were a principle of motion entirely distinct from nature, and properly set in opposition to it. Names being commonly given to things, according to what is most obvious, and is suggested by what appears to the senses without reflection and research.

3. It must be observed, that in what has been explained, as signified by the name of moral Necessity, the word Necessity is not used according to the original design and meaning of the word; for, as was observed before, such terms, *necessary, impossible, irresistible,* &c., in common speech, and their most proper sense, are always relative; having reference to some supposable voluntary opposition or endeavor, that is insufficient. But no such opposition, or contrary will and endeavor, is supposable in the case of moral Necessity; which is a certainty of the inclination and will itself; which does not admit of the supposition of a will to oppose and resist it. For it is absurd to suppose the same individual will to oppose itself, in its present act; or the present choice to be opposite to, and resisting present choice; as absurd as it is to talk of two contrary motions, in the same moving body, at the same time. And therefore the very case supposed never admits of any trial whether an opposing or resisting will can overcome this Necessity.

What has been said of natural and moral Necessity, may serve to explain what is intended by natural and moral *Inability*. We are said to be *naturally* unable to do a thing, when we cannot do it if we will, because what is most commonly called *nature* does not allow of it, or because of some impeding defect or obstacle that is extrinsic to the will, either in the faculty of understanding, constitution of body, or external objects. *Moral* Inability consists not in any of these things; but either in the want of inclination, or the strength of a contrary inclination, or the want of sufficient motives in view, to induce and excite the act of the will, or the strength of apparent motives to the contrary. Or both these may be resolved into one; and it may be said in one word, that moral Inability consists in the opposition or want of inclination. For when a person is unable to will or choose such a thing, through a defect of motives, or prevalence of contrary motives, it is the same thing as his being unable through the want of an inclination, or the prevalence of a contrary inclination, in such circumstances, and under the influence of such views.

To give some instances of this moral Inability. A woman of great honor and chastity may have a moral Inability to prostitute herself to her slave. A child of great love and duty to his parents, may be unable to be willing to kill his father. A very lascivious man, in case of certain opportunities and temptations, and in the absence of such and such restraints, may be unable to forbear gratifying his lust. A drunkard, under such and such circumstances, may be unable to forbear taking of strong drink. A very malicious man may be unable to exert benevolent acts to an enemy, or to desire his prosperity; yea, some may be so under the power of a vile disposition, that they may be unable to love those who are most worthy of their esteem and affection. A strong habit of virtue, and a great degree of holiness may cause a moral Inability to love wickedness in general, may render a man unable to take complacence in wicked persons or things; or to choose a wicked life, and prefer it to a virtuous life. And on the other hand, a great degree of habitual wickedness may lay a man under an inability to love and choose holiness; and render him utterly unable to love an infinitely holy being, or to choose and cleave to him as his chief good.

Section V

Concerning the Notion of Liberty, and of Moral Agency

The plain and obvious meaning of the words *Freedom* and *Liberty*, in common speech, is *power, opportunity or advantage, that any one has, to do as he pleases.* Or in other words, his being free from hinderance or impediment in the way of doing, or conducting in any respect, as he wills.* And the contrary to

*I say not only doing, but conducting; because a voluntary forbearing to do, sitting still, keeping silence, &c., are instances of persons' conduct, about which Liberty is exercised; though they are not so properly called doing. [Edwards's note.]

Liberty, whatever name we call that by, is a person's being hindered or unable to conduct as he will, or being necessitated to do otherwise.

If this which I have mentioned be the meaning of the word Liberty, in the ordinary use of language; as I trust that none that has ever learned to talk, and is unprejudiced, will deny; then it will follow, that in propriety of speech, neither Liberty, nor its contrary, can properly be ascribed to any being or thing, but that which has such a faculty, power or property, as is called will. For that which is possessed of no such thing as will, cannot have any power or opportunity of doing according to its will, nor be necessitated to act contrary to its will, nor be restrained from acting agreeably to it. And therefore to talk of Liberty, or the contrary, as belonging to the very will itself, is not to speak good sense; if we judge of sense, and nonsense, by the original and proper signification of words. For the will itself is not an agent that has a will: the power of choosing itself, has not a power of choosing. That which has the power of volition or choice is the man or the soul, and not the power of volition itself. And he that has the Liberty of doing according to his will, is the agent or doer who is possessed of the will; and not the will which he is possessed of. We say with propriety, that a bird let loose has power and Liberty to fly; but not that the bird's power of flying has a power and Liberty of flying. To be free is the property of an agent, who is possessed of powers and faculties, as much as to be cunning, valiant, bountiful, or zealous. But these qualities are the properties of men or persons and not the properties of properties.

There are two things that are contrary to this which is called Liberty in common speech. One is constraint; the same is otherwise called force, compulsion, and coaction; which is a person's being necessitated to do a thing contrary to his will. The other is restraint; which is his being hindered, and not having power to do according to his will. But that which has no will, cannot be the subject of these things. I need say the less on this head, Mr. Locke having set the same thing forth, with so great clearness, in his *Essay on the Human Understanding*.

But one thing more I would observe concerning what is vulgarly called Liberty; namely, that power and opportunity for one to do and conduct as he will, or according to his choice, is all that is meant by it; without taking into the meaning of the word any thing of the cause or original of that choice; or at all considering how the person came to have such a volition; whether it was caused by some external motive or internal habitual bias; whether it was determined by some internal antecedent volition, or whether it happened without a cause; whether it was necessarily connected with something foregoing, or not connected. Let the person come by his volition or choice how he will, yet, if he is able, and there is nothing in the way to hinder his pursuing and executing his will, the man is fully and perfectly free, according to the primary and common notion of freedom.

What has been said may be sufficient to show what is meant by Liberty, according to the common notions of mankind, and in the usual and primary acceptation of the word: but the word, as used by Arminians, Pelagians and others, who oppose the Calvinists, has an entirely different signification. These several things belong to their notion of Liberty. 1. That it consists in a self-determining power in the will, or a certain sovereignty the will has over itself, and its own acts, whereby it determines its own volitions; so as not to be dependent in its determinations, on any cause without itself, nor determined by any thing prior to its own acts. 2. Indifference belongs to Liberty in their notion of it, or that the mind, previous to the act of volition, be in equilibrio. 3. Contingence is another thing that belongs and is essential to it; not in the common acceptation of the word, as that has been already explained, but as opposed to all necessity, or any fixed and certain connection with some previous ground or reason of its existence. They suppose the essence of Liberty so much to consist in these things, that unless the will of man be free in this sense, he has no real freedom, how much soever he may be at Liberty to act according to his will.

A moral Agent is a being that is capable of those actions that have a moral quality, and which can properly be denominated good or evil in a moral sense, virtuous or vicious, commendable or faulty. To moral Agency belongs a moral faculty, or sense of moral good and evil, or of such a thing as desert or worthiness, of praise or blame, reward or punishment; and a capacity which an agent has of being influenced in his actions by moral inducements or motives, exhibited to the view of understanding and reason, to engage to a conduct agreeable to the moral faculty.

The sun is very excellent and beneficial in its action and influence on the earth, in warming it, and causing it to bring forth its fruits; but it is not a moral Agent. Its action, though good, is not virtuous or meritorious. Fire that breaks out in a city, and consumes great part of it, is very mischievous in its operation; but is not a moral Agent. What it does is not faulty or sinful, or deserving of any punishment. The brute creatures are not moral Agents. The actions of some of them are very profitable and pleasant; others are very hurtful; yet, seeing they have no moral faculty, or sense of desert, and do not act from choice guided by understanding, or with a capacity of reasoning and reflecting, but only from instinct, and are not capable of being influenced by moral inducements, their actions are not properly sinful or virtuous; nor are they properly the subjects of any such moral treatment for what they do, as moral Agents are for their faults or good deeds.

· · · · · · · · · · · · · ·

PART II

WHEREIN IT IS CONSIDERED WHETHER THERE IS OR CAN BE ANY SUCH SORT OF FREEDOM OF WILL, AS THAT WHEREIN ARMINIANS PLACE THE ESSENCE OF THE LIBERTY OF ALL MORAL AGENTS; AND WHETHER ANY SUCH THING EVER WAS OR CAN BE CONCEIVED OF

SECTION I

Showing the Manifest Inconsistence of the Arminian Notion of Liberty of Will, Consisting in the Will's Self-determining Power

HAVING taken notice of those things which may be necessary to be observed, concerning the meaning of the principal terms and phrases made use of in controversies, concerning human Liberty, and particularly observed what Liberty is, according to the common language and general apprehension of mankind, and what it is as understood and maintained by Arminians; I proceed to consider the Arminian notion of the Freedom of the Will, and the supposed necessity of it in order to moral agency, or in order to any one's being capable of virtue or vice, and properly the subject of command or counsel, praise or blame, promises or threatenings, rewards or punishments; or whether that which has been described, as the thing meant by Liberty in common speech, be not sufficient, and the only Liberty which makes or can make any one a moral agent, and so properly the subject of these things. In this Part, I shall consider whether any such thing be possible or conceivable, as that Freedom of Will which Arminians insist on; and shall inquire, whether any such sort of Liberty be necessary to moral agency, &c., in the next Part.

And first of all, I shall consider the notion of a self-determining Power in the Will; wherein, according to the Arminians, does most essentially consist the Will's Freedom; and shall particularly inquire, whether it be not plainly absurd, and a manifest inconsistence, to suppose that the Will itself determines all the free acts of the Will.

Here I shall not insist on the great impropriety of such phrases and ways of speaking as the Will's determining itself; because actions are to be ascribed to agents, and not properly to the powers of agents; which improper way of speaking leads to many mistakes, and much confusion, as Mr. Locke observes. But I shall suppose that the Arminians, when they speak of the Will's determining itself, do by the Will mean the soul willing. I shall take it for granted, that when they speak of the Will, as the determiner, they mean the soul in the exercise of a power of willing, or acting voluntarily. I shall suppose this to be their meaning, because nothing else can be meant, without the grossest and plainest absurdity. In all cases when we speak of the powers or principles of acting, as doing such things, we mean that the agents which have these Powers of acting, do them in the exercise of those Powers. So when we say, valor fights courageously, we mean, the man who is under the influence of valor fights courageously. When we say, love seeks the object loved, we mean, the person loving seeks that object. When we say, the understanding discerns, we mean the soul in the exercise of that faculty. So when it is said, the Will decides or determines, the meaning must be, that the person in the exercise of a Power of willing and choosing, or the soul acting voluntarily, determines.

Therefore, if the Will determines all its own free acts, the soul determines all the free acts of the Will in the exercise of a Power of willing and choosing; or which is the same thing, it determines them of choice; it determines its own acts by choosing its own acts. If the Will determines the Will, then choice orders and determines the choice; and acts of choice are subject to the decision, and follow the conduct of other acts of choice. And therefore if the Will determines all its own free acts, then every free act of choice is determined by a preceding act of choice, choosing that act. And if that preceding act of the Will or choice be also a free act, then by these principles, in this act too, the Will is self-determined; that is, this, in like manner, is an act that the soul voluntarily chooses; or, which is the same thing, it is an act determined still by a preceding act of the Will, choosing that. And the like may again be observed of the last mentioned act, which brings us directly to a contradiction; for it supposes an act of the Will preceding the first act in the whole train, directing and determining the rest; or a free act of the Will, before the first free act of the Will. Or else we must come at last to an act of the Will, determining the consequent acts, wherein the Will is not self-determined, and so is not a free act, in this notion of freedom; but if the first act in the train, determining and fixing the rest, be not free, none of them all can be free; as is manifest at first view, but shall be demonstrated presently.

If the Will, which we find governs the members of the body and determines and commands their motions and actions, does also govern itself, and determine its own motions and actions, it doubtless determines them the same way, even by antecedent volitions. The Will determines which way the hands and feet shall move, by an act of volition or choice; and there is no other way of the Will's determining, directing or commanding any thing at all. Whatsoever the Will commands, it commands by an act of the Will. And if it has itself under its command, and determines itself in its own actions, it doubtless does it the same way that it determines other things which are under its command. So that if the freedom of the Will consists in this, that it has itself and its own actions under its command and direction, and its own volitions are determined by itself, it will follow, that every free volition arises from another antecedent volition, directing and commanding that; and if that directing volition be also free, in that also the Will is determined; that is to say, that directing volition is determined by another going before that, and so on, until we come to the first volition in the whole series; and if that first volition be free, and the Will self-determined in it, then that is determined by another volition preceding that, which is a contradiction; because by the supposition, it can have none before it to direct or determine it, being the first in the train. But if that first volition is not determined by any preceding act of the Will, then that act is not determined by the Will, and so is not free in the *Arminian* notion of freedom, which consists in the Will's self-determination. And if that first act of the Will, which determines and fixes the subsequent acts, be not free, none of the following acts, which are determined by it, can be free. If we suppose there are five acts in the train, the fifth and last determined by the fourth, and the fourth by the third, the third by the second, and the second by the first; if the first is not determined by the Will, and so not free, then none of them are truly determined by the Will; that is, that each of them is as it is, and not otherwise, is not first owing to the Will, but to the determination of the first in the series, which is not dependent on the Will, and is that which the Will has no hand in the determination of. And this being that which decides what the rest shall be, and determines their existence; therefore the first determination of their existence is not from the Will. The case is just the same, if instead of a chain of five acts of the Will, we should suppose a succession of ten, or a hundred, or ten thousand. If the first act be not free, being determined by something out of the Will, and this determines the next to be agreeable to itself, and that the next, and so on; they are none of them free, but all originally depend on, and are determined by some cause out of the Will; and so all freedom in the case is excluded, and no act of the Will can be free, according to this notion of freedom. If we should suppose a long chain of ten thousand links, so connected, that if the first link moves, it will move the next, and that the next, and so the whole chain must be determined to motion, and in the direction of its motion, by the motion of the first link, and that is moved by something else. In this case, though all the links but one, are moved by other parts of the same chain; yet it appears that the motion of no one, nor the direction of its motion, is from any self-moving or self-determining power in the chain, any more than if every link were immediately moved by something that did not belong to the chain. If the Will be not free in the first act, which causes the next, then neither is it free in the next, which is caused by that first act; for though indeed the Will caused it, yet it did not cause it freely, because the preceding act, by which it was caused, was not free. And again, if the Will be not free in the second act, so neither can it be in the third, which is caused by that; because in like manner, that third was determined by an act of the Will that was not free. And so we may go on to the next act, and from that to the next; and how long soever the succession of acts is, it is all one. If the first on which the whole chain depends, and which determines all the rest, be not a free act, the Will is not free in causing or determining any one of those acts, because the act by which it determines them all, is not a free act, and therefore the Will is no more free in determining them, than if it did not cause them at all. Thus, this *Arminian* notion of Liberty of the Will, consisting in the Will's *self-determination*, is repugnant to itself, and shuts itself wholly out of the world.

    .   .   .   .

Section III

Whether any Event whatsoever, and Volition in particular,
can come to pass without a Cause of its existence

Before I enter on any argument on this subject, I would
explain how I would be understood, when I use the word *Cause*
in this discourse: since, for want of a better word, I shall have
occasion to use it in a sense which is more extensive, than that
in which it is sometimes used. The word is often used in so
restrained a sense as to signify only that which has a positive
efficiency or influence to produce a thing, or bring it to pass.
But there are many things which have no such positive pro-
ductive influence; which yet are Causes in that respect, that
they have truly the nature of a ground or reason why some
things are, rather than others; or why they are as they are,
rather than otherwise. Thus the absence of the sun in the night,
is not the Cause of the falling of the dew at that time, in the
same manner as its beams are the Cause of the ascending of the
vapors in the day time; and its withdrawment in the winter, is
not in the same manner the Cause of the freezing of the waters,
as its approach in the spring is the Cause of their thawing. But
yet the withdrawment or absence of the sun is an antecedent,
with which these effects in the night and winter are connected,
and on which they depend; and is one thing that belongs to the
ground and reason why they come to pass at that time, rather
than at other times; though the absence of the sun is nothing
positive, nor has any positive influence.

It may be further observed, that when I speak of connection
of Causes and Effects, I have respect to moral Causes, as well as
those that are called natural in distinction from them. Moral
Causes may be Causes in as proper a sense, as any causes whatsoever; may have as real an influence, and may as truly be the
ground and reason of an Event's coming to pass.

Therefore I sometimes use the word *Cause*, in this inquiry,
to signify any antecedent, either natural or moral, positive or
negative, on which an Event, either a thing, or the manner and
circumstance of a thing, so depends, that it is the ground and

reason, either in whole, or in part, why it is, rather than not; or why it is as it is, rather than otherwise; or, in other words, any antecedent with which a consequent Event is so connected, that it truly belongs to the reason why the proposition which affirms that Event, is true; whether it has any positive influence or not. And in agreeableness to this, I sometimes use the word Effect for the consequence of another thing, which is perhaps rather an occasion than a Cause, most properly speaking.

I am the more careful thus to explain my meaning, that I may cut off occasion, from any that might seek occasion to cavil and object against some things which I may say concerning the dependence of all things which come to pass, on some Cause, and their connection with their Cause.

Having thus explained what I mean by Cause, I assert that nothing ever comes to pass without a Cause. What is self-existent must be from eternity, and must be unchangeable; but as to all things that begin to be, they are not self-existent, and therefore must have some foundation of their existence without themselves; that whatsoever begins to be which before was not, must have a Cause why it then begins to exist, seems to be the first dictate of the common and natural sense which God hath implanted in the minds of all mankind, and the main foundation of all our reasonings about the existence of things, past, present, or to come.

And this dictate of common sense equally respects substances and modes, or things and the manner and circumstances of things. Thus, if we see a body which has hitherto been at rest, start out of a state of rest, and begin to move, we do as naturally and necessarily suppose there is some Cause or reason of this new mode of existence, as of the existence of a body itself which had hitherto not existed. And so if a body, which had hitherto moved in a certain direction, should suddenly change the direction of its motion; or if it should put off its old figure, and take a new one; or change its color: the beginning of these new modes is a new Event, and the mind of mankind necessarily supposes that there is some Cause or reason of them.

If this grand principle of common sense be taken away, all

arguing from effects to Causes ceaseth, and so all knowledge of any existence, besides what we have by the most direct and immediate intuition. Particularly all our proof of the being of God ceases: we argue His being from our own being and the being of other things, which we are sensible once were not, but have begun to be; and from the being of the world, with all its constituent parts, and the manner of their existence; all which we see plainly are not necessary in their own nature, and so not self-existent, and therefore must have a Cause. But if things, not in themselves necessary, may begin to be without a Cause, all this arguing is vain.

Indeed, I will not affirm, that there is in the nature of things no foundation for the knowledge of the Being of God without any evidence of it from His works. I do suppose there is a great absurdity in the nature of things simply considered, in supposing that there should be no God, or in denying Being in general, and supposing an eternal, absolute, universal nothing; and therefore that here would be foundation of intuitive evidence that it cannot be; and that eternal, infinite, most perfect Being must be; if we had strength and comprehension of mind sufficient, to have a clear idea of general and universal Being, or, which is the same thing, of the infinite, eternal, most perfect Divine Nature and Essence. But then we should not properly come to the knowledge of the Being of God by arguing; but our evidence would be intuitive: we should see it, as we see other things that are necessary in themselves, the contraries of which are in their own nature absurd and contradictory; as we see that twice two is four; and as we see that a circle has no angles. If we had as clear an idea of universal infinite entity, as we have of these other things, I suppose we should most intuitively see the absurdity of supposing such Being not to be; should immediately see there is no room for the question, whether it is possible that Being, in the most general abstracted notion of it, should not be. But we have not that strength and extent of mind, to know this certainly in this intuitive independent manner; but the way that mankind come to the knowledge of the Being of God, is that which the apostle speaks of, Rom.

i. 20. "The invisible things of Him, from the creation of the world, are clearly seen; being understood by the things that are made; even his eternal power and Godhead." We first ascend, and prove *a posteriori*, or from effects, that there must be an eternal Cause; and then secondly, prove by argumentation, not intuition, that this Being must be necessarily existent; and then thirdly, from the proved necessity of his existence, we may descend, and prove many of his perfections *a priori*.

But if once this grand principle of common sense be given up, that what is not necessary in itself, must have a Cause; and we begin to maintain, that things may come into existence, and begin to be, which heretofore have not been, of themselves without any Cause; all our means of ascending in our arguing from the creature to the Creator, and all our evidence of the Being of God, is cut off at one blow. In this case, we cannot prove that there is a God, either from the Being of the world, and the creatures in it, or from the manner of their being, their order, beauty and use. For if things may come into existence without any Cause at all, then they doubtless may without any Cause answerable to the effect. Our minds do alike naturally suppose and determine both these things; namely, that what begins to be has a Cause, and also that it has a Cause proportionable and agreeable to the effect. The same principle which leads us to determine, that there cannot be any thing coming to pass without a Cause, leads us to determine that there cannot be more in the effect than in the Cause.

Yea, if once it should be allowed, that things may come to pass without a Cause, we should not only have no proof of the Being of God, but we should be without evidence of the existence of any thing whatsoever, but our own immediately present ideas and consciousness. For we have no way to prove any thing else, but by arguing from effects to causes: from the ideas now immediately in view, we argue other things not immediately in view: from sensations now excited in us, we infer the existence of things without us, as the Causes of these sensations; and from the existence of these things, we argue other things, which they depend on, as effects on Causes. We infer the past existence of ourselves, or any thing else, by memory; only as we argue, that the ideas, which are now in our minds, are the consequences of past ideas and sensations.—We immediately perceive nothing else but the ideas which are this moment extant in our minds. We perceive or know other things only by means of these, as necessarily connected with others, and dependent on them. But if things may be without Causes, all this necessary connection and dependence is dissolved, and so all means of our knowledge is gone. If there be no absurdity nor difficulty in supposing one thing to start out of non-existence into being, of itself without a Cause; then there is no absurdity nor difficulty in supposing the same of millions of millions. For nothing, or no difficulty multiplied, still is nothing, or no difficulty, nothing multiplied by nothing, does not increase the sum.

. . . .

If any should imagine, there is something in the sort of Event that renders possible for it to come into existence without a Cause, and should say, that the free acts of the Will are existences of an exceeding different nature from other things; by reason of which they may come into existence without any previous ground or reason of it, though other things cannot; if they make this objection in good earnest, it would be an evidence of their strangely forgetting themselves; for they would be giving an account of some ground of the existence of a thing, when at the same time they would maintain there is no ground of its existence. Therefore I would observe, that the particular nature of existence, be it ever so diverse from others, can lay no foundation for that thing's coming into existence without a Cause; because to suppose this, would be to suppose the particular nature of existence to be a thing prior to the existence; and so a thing which makes way for existence, with such a circumstance, namely, without a cause or reason of existence. But that which in any respect makes way for a thing's coming into being, or for any manner or circumstance of its first existence, must be prior to the existence. The distinguished nature of the effect, which is something belonging to the effect, cannot have influence backward, to act before it is. The peculiar nature of that thing called volition, can do nothing, can have no influence, while it is not. And afterwards it is too late for its influence; for then the thing has made sure of existence already, without its help.

So that it is indeed as repugnant to reason, to suppose that an act of the Will should come into existence without a Cause, as to suppose the human soul, or an angel, or the globe of the earth, or the whole universe, should come into existence without a Cause. And if once we allow, that such a sort of effect as a Volition may come to pass without a Cause, how do we know but that many other sorts of effects may do so too? It is not the particular kind of effect that makes the absurdity of supposing it has been without a Cause, but something which is common to all things that ever begin to be, viz., that they are not self-existent, or necessary in the nature of things.

. . . .

PART III

WHEREIN IS INQUIRED, WHETHER ANY SUCH LIBERTY OF WILL AS ARMIN-IANS HOLD, BE NECESSARY TO MORAL AGENCY, VIRTUE AND VICE, PRAISE AND DISPRAISE, ETC.

SECTION I

God's Moral Excellency necessary, yet virtuous and praiseworthy

Having considered the *first* thing that was proposed to be inquired into, relating to that freedom of Will which *Arminians* maintain; namely, Whether any such thing does, ever did, or ever can exist, or be conceived of; I come now to the *second* thing proposed to be the subject of inquiry, viz., Whether any such kind of liberty be requisite to moral agency, virtue and vice, praise and blame, reward and punishment, &c.

I shall begin with some consideration of the virtue and agency of the Supreme moral agent, and fountain of all agency and virtue.

Dr. Whitby, in his discourses on the Five Points, p. 14, says,

"If all human actions are necessary, virtue and vice must be empty names; we being capable of nothing that is blameworthy, or deserveth praise; for who can blame a person for doing only what he could not help, or judge that he deserveth praise only for what he could not avoid?" To the like purpose he speaks in places innumerable; especially in his discourse on the *Freedom of the Will;* constantly maintaining, that a *freedom not only from coaction, but necessity,* is absolutely requisite, in order to actions being either worthy of blame, or deserving of praise. And to this agrees, as is well known, the current doctrine of *Arminian* writers, who, in general, hold, that there is no virtue or vice, reward or punishment, nothing to be commended or blamed, without this freedom. And yet Dr. Whitby, p. 300, allows, that God is without this freedom; and *Arminians,* so far as I have had opportunity to observe, generally acknowledge that God is necessarily holy, and his Will necessarily determined to that which is good.

So that putting these things together, the infinitely holy God, who used always to be esteemed by God's people not only virtuous, but a Being in whom is all possible virtue, and every virtue in the most absolute purity and perfection, and in infinitely greater brightness and amiableness than in any creature; the most perfect pattern of virtue, and the fountain from whom all others' virtue is as beams from the sun; and who has been supposed to be, on the account of his virtue and holiness, infinitely more worthy to be esteemed, loved, honored, admired, commended, extolled and praised, than any creature: and He, who is thus everywhere represented in Scripture; I say, this Being, according to this notion of Dr. Whitby, and other *Arminians,* has no virtue at all: virtue, when ascribed to him, is but *an empty name;* and he is deserving of no commendation or praise: because he is under necessity. He cannot avoid being holy and good as he is; therefore no thanks to him for it. It seems, the holiness, justice, faithfulness, &c., of the Most High, must not be accounted to be of the nature of that which is virtuous and praiseworthy. They will not deny, that these things in God are good; but then we must understand them, that they

are no more virtuous, or of the nature of any thing commendable, than the good that is in any other being that is not a moral
agent; as the brightness of the sun, and the fertility of the earth,
are good, but not virtuous, because these properties are necessary to these bodies, and not the fruit of self-determining power.

There needs no other confutation of this notion of God's not
being virtuous or praiseworthy, to Christians acquainted with
the Bible, but only stating and particularly representing it. To
bring texts of Scripture, wherein God is represented as in every
respect, in the highest manner virtuous, and supremely praiseworthy, would be endless, and is altogether needless to such as
have been brought up in the light of the gospel.

. . . .

PART IV

WHEREIN THE CHIEF GROUNDS OF THE REASONINGS OF ARMINIANS, IN
SUPPORT AND DEFENCE OF THE FOREMENTIONED NOTIONS OF LIBERTY,
MORAL AGENCY, ETC., AND AGAINST THE OPPOSITE DOCTRINE, ARE CON-
SIDERED

Section II

The Falseness and Inconsistence of that metaphysical Notion
    of Action and Agency, which seems to be generally enter-
    tained by the Defenders of the Arminian Doctrine concerning
    Liberty, moral Agency, &c.

One thing that is made very much a ground of argument
and supposed demonstration by *Arminians*, in defence of the
forementioned principles, concerning moral agency, virtue,
vice, &c., is their metaphysical notion of agency and action.
They say, unless the soul has a self-determining power, it has
no power of action; if its volitions be not caused by itself, but
are excited and determined by some extrinsic cause, they cannot be the soul's own acts; and that the soul cannot be active,
but must be wholly passive, in those effects which it is the subject of necessarily, and not from its own free determination.

Mr. Chubb lays the foundation of his scheme of liberty, and
of his arguments to support it, very much in this position, that

man is an agent, and capable of action. Which doubtless is true; but self-determination belongs to his notion of action, and is the very essence of it. Whence he infers, that it is impossible for a man to act and be acted upon, in the same thing, at the same time; and that nothing, that is an action, can be the effect of the action of another; and he insists, that a necessary agent, or an agent that is necessarily determined to act, is a plain contradiction.

But those are a precarious sort of demonstrations, which men build on the meaning that they arbitrarily affix to a word; especially when that meaning is abstruse, inconsistent, and entirely diverse from the original sense of the word in common speech.

That the meaning of the word *action*, as Mr. Chubb and many others use it, is utterly unintelligible and inconsistent, is manifest, because it belongs to their notion of an action, that it is something wherein is no passion or passiveness; that is (according to their sense of passiveness), it is under the power, influence or action of no cause. And this implies, that action has no cause, and is no effect; for to be an effect implies passiveness, or the being subject to the power and action of its cause. And yet they hold, that the mind's action is the effect of its own determination, yea, the mind's free and voluntary determination; which is the same with free choice. So that action is the effect of something preceding, even a preceding act of choice; and consequently, in this effect the mind is passive, subject to the power and action of the preceding cause, which is the foregoing choice, and therefore cannot be active. So that here we have this contradiction, that action is always the effect of foregoing choice; and therefore cannot be action; because it is passive to the power of that preceding causal choice; and the mind cannot be active and passive in the same thing, at the same time. Again, they say, necessity is utterly inconsistent with action, and a necessary action is a contradiction; and so their notion of action implies contingence, and excludes all necessity. And therefore, their notion of action implies, that it has no necessary dependence or connection with any thing foregoing; for such a dependence or connection excludes contingence, and implies necessity. And yet their notion of action implies necessity, and supposes that it is necessary, and cannot be contingent. For they suppose, that whatever is properly called action, must be determined by the Will and free choice; and this is as much as to say, that it must be necessary, being dependent upon, and determined by something foregoing; namely, a foregoing act of choice. Again, it belongs to their notion of action, of that which is a proper and mere act, that it is the beginning of motion, or of exertion of power; but yet it is implied in their notion of action, that it is not the beginning of motion or exertion of power, but is consequent and dependent on a preceding exertion of power, viz., the power of Will and choice; for they say there is no proper action but what is freely chosen; or, which is the same thing, determined by a foregoing act of free choice. But if any of them shall see cause to deny this, and say they hold no such thing as that every action is chosen or determined by a foregoing choice; but that the very first exertion of Will only, undetermined by any preceding act, is properly called action; then I say, such a man's notion of action implies necessity; for what the mind is the subject of, without the determination of its own previous choice, it is the subject of necessarily, as to any hand that free choice has in the affair, and without any ability the mind has to prevent it, by any Will or election of its own; because by the supposition it precludes all previous acts of the Will or choice in the case, which might prevent it. So that it is again, in this other way, implied in their notion of act, that it is both necessary and not necessary. Again, it belongs to their notion of an act, that it is no effect of a predetermining bias or preponderation, but springs immediately out of indifference; and this implies, that it cannot be from foregoing choice, which is foregoing preponderation: if it be not habitual, but occasional, yet if it causes the act, it is truly previous, efficacious and determining. And yet, at the same time, it is essential to their notion of an act, that it is what the agent is the author of freely and voluntarily, and that is, by previous choice and design.

So that, according to their notion of an act, considered with regard to its consequences, these following things are all essential to it, viz., that it should be necessary, and not necessary; that it should be from a cause, and no cause; that it should be the fruit of choice and design, and not the fruit of choice and design; that it should be the beginning of motion or exertion, and yet consequent on previous exertion; that it should be before it is; that it should spring immediately out of indifference and equilibrium, and yet be the effect of preponderation; that it should be self-originated, and also have its original from something else; that it is what the mind causes itself, of its own Will, and can produce or prevent, according to its choice or pleasure, and yet what the mind has no power to prevent, it precluding all previous choice in the affair.

So that an act, according to their metaphysical notion of it, is something of which there is no idea: it is nothing but a confusion of the mind, excited by words without any distinct meaning, and is an absolute nonentity; and that in two respects: (1,) there is nothing in the world that ever was, is, or can be, to answer the things which must belong to its description, according to what they suppose to be essential to it; and (2,) there neither is, nor ever was, nor can be, any notion or idea to answer the word, as they use and explain it. For if we should suppose any such notion, it would many ways destroy itself. But it is impossible any idea or notion should subsist in the mind, whose very nature and essence, which constitutes it, destroys it. If some learned philosopher, who had been abroad, in giving an account of the curious observations he had made in his travels, should say, "He had been in *Terra del Fuego*, and there had seen an animal, which he calls by a certain name, that begat and brought forth itself, and yet had a sire and dam distinct from itself; that it had an appetite, and was hungry before it had a being; that his master, who led him, and governed him at his pleasure, was always governed by him, and driven by him where he pleased; that when he moved, he always took a step before the first step; that he went with his head first, and yet always went tail foremost; and this, though he had neither head nor tail:" it would be no imprudence at all, to tell such a

traveller, though a learned man, that he himself had no notion
or idea of such an animal, as he gave an account of, and never
had, nor ever would have.

Section IV

It is agreeable to Common Sense, and the Natural Notions of Mankind, to suppose moral Necessity to be consistent with Praise and Blame, Reward and Punishment

Whether the reasons that have been given, why it appears
difficult to some persons, to reconcile with common sense the
praising or blaming, rewarding or punishing, those things
which are morally necessary, are thought satisfactory or not;
yet it most evidently appears, by the following things, that if
this matter be rightly understood, setting aside all delusion
arising from the impropriety and ambiguity of terms, this is not
at all inconsistent with the natural apprehensions of mankind,
and that sense of things which is found everywhere in the
common people; who are furthest from having their thoughts
perverted from their natural channel, by metaphysical and
philosophical subtilties; but, on the contrary, altogether agreeable to, and the very voice and dictate of, this natural and
vulgar sense.

I. This will appear, if we consider what the vulgar notion of
blameworthiness is. The idea which the common people,
through all ages and nations, have of faultiness, I suppose to be
plainly this; a person's being or doing wrong, with his own will
and pleasure; containing these two things: 1. His doing wrong
when he does as he pleases. 2. His pleasure being wrong. Or,
in other words, perhaps more intelligibly expressing their notion; a person's having his heart wrong, and doing wrong from
his heart. And this is the sum total of the matter.

The common people do not ascend up in their reflections
and abstractions to the metaphysical sources, relations and de-
pendencies of things, in order to form their notion of faultiness
or blameworthiness. They do not wait till they have decided

y their refinings, what first determines the Will; whether it be determined by something extrinsic, or intrinsic; whether volition determines volition, or whether the understanding determines the Will; whether there be any such thing as metaphysicians mean by contingence (if they have any meaning); whether here be a sort of a strange, unaccountable sovereignty in the Will, in the exercise of which, by its own sovereign acts, it rings to pass all its own sovereign acts. They do not take any part of their notion of fault or blame from the resolution of any such questions. If this were the case, there are multitudes, yea, the far greater part of mankind, nine hundred and ninety-nine out of a thousand, would live and die, without having any such notion, as that of fault, ever entering into their heads, or without so much as once having any conception that any body was to be either blamed or commended for any thing. To be sure, would be a long time before men came to have such notions. Whereas it is manifest, they are some of the first notions that appear in children; who discover, as soon as they can think, or speak, or act at all as rational creatures, a sense of desert. And, certainly, in forming their notion of it, they make no use of metaphysics. All the ground they go upon, consists in these two things; experience, and a natural sensation of a certain fitness or agreeableness, which there is in uniting such moral evil is above described, viz., a being or doing wrong with the Will, and resentment in others, and pain inflicted on the person whom this moral evil is. Which natural sense is what we all by the name of conscience.

It is true, the common people and children, in their notion a faulty act or deed, of any person, do suppose that it is the person's own act and deed. But this is all that belongs to what they understand by a thing's being a person's own deed or action; even that it is something done by him of choice. That some exercise or motion should begin of itself, does not belong their notion of an action, or doing. If so, it would belong to their notion of it, that it is something, which is the cause of its own beginning; and that is as much as to say, that it is before begins to be. Nor is their notion of an action some motion or exercise, that begins accidentally, without any cause or reason; for that is contrary to one of the prime dictates of common sense, namely, that every thing that begins to be, has some cause or reason why it is.

The common people, in their notion of a faulty or praiseworthy deed or work done by any one, do suppose, that the man does it in the exercise of liberty. But then their notion of liberty is only a person's having opportunity of doing as he pleases. They have no notion of liberty consisting in the Will's first acting, and so causing its own acts; and determining, and so causing its own determinations; or choosing, and so causing its own choice. Such a notion of liberty is what none have, but those that have darkened their own minds with confused metaphysical speculation, and abstruse and ambiguous terms. If a man is not restrained from acting as his Will determines, or constrained to act otherwise; then he has liberty, according to common notions of liberty, without taking into the idea that grand contradiction of all, the determinations of a man's free Will being the effects of the determinations of his free Will. Nor have men commonly any notion of freedom consisting in indifference. For if so, then it would be agreeable to their notion, that the greater indifference men act with, the more freedom they act with; whereas, the reverse is true. He that in acting, proceeds with the fullest inclination, does what he does with the greatest freedom, according to common sense. And so far is it from being agreeable to common sense, that such liberty as consists in indifference is requisite to praise or blame, that on the contrary, the dictate of every man's natural sense through the world is, that the further he is from being indifferent in his acting good or evil, and the more he does either with or without full and strong inclination, the more is he to be esteemed or abhorred, commended or condemned.

II. If it were inconsistent with the common sense of mankind, that men should be either to be blamed or commended for any volitions, they have, or fail of, in case of moral necessity or impossibility; then it would surely also be agreeable to the same sense and reason of mankind, that the nearer the case a proaches to such a moral necessity or impossibility, either through a strong antecedent moral propensity, on the one hand,* or a great antecedent opposition and difficulty on the other, the nearer does it approach to a being neither blamable nor commendable; so that acts exerted with such preceding propensity, would be worthy of proportionably less praise; and when omitted, the act being attended with such difficulty, the omission would be worthy of the less blame. . . .

But it is apparent, that the reverse of these things is true. If there be an approach to a moral necessity in a man's exertion of good acts of Will, they being the exercise of a strong propensity to good, and a very powerful love to virtue; it is so far from being the dictate of common sense, that he is less virtuous, and the less to be esteemed, loved and praised; that it is agreeable to the natural notions of all mankind, that he is so much the better man, worthy of greater respect, and higher commendation. And the stronger the inclination is, and the nearer it approaches to necessity in that respect; or to impossibility of neglecting the virtuous act, or of doing a vicious one, still the more virtuous, and worthy of higher commendation. And, on the other hand, if a man exerts evil acts of mind; as, for instance, acts of pride or malice from a rooted and strong habit, or principle of haughtiness and maliciousness, and a violent propensity of heart to such acts; according to the natural sense of all men, he is so far from being the less hateful and blamable on that account, that he is so much the more worthy to be detested and condemned, by all that observe him.

Moreover, it is manifest that it is no part of the notion, which mankind commonly have of a blamable or praiseworthy act of the Will, that it is an act which is not determined by an antecedent bias or motive, but by the sovereign power of the Will itself; because, if so, the greater hand such causes have in determining any acts of the Will, so much the less virtuous or vicious would they be accounted; and the less hand, the more

*It is here argued, on supposition that not all propensity implies moral necessity, but only some very high degree; which none will deny. [Edwards's note.]

virtuous or vicious. Whereas, the reverse is true: men do not think a good act to be the less praiseworthy, for the agent's being much determined in it by a good inclination or a good motive, but the more. And if good inclination or motive, has but little influence in determining the agent, they do not think his act so much the more virtuous, but the less. And so concerning evil acts, which are determined by evil motives or inclinations.

Yea, if it be supposed that good or evil dispositions are implanted in the hearts of men, by nature itself (which, it is certain is vulgarly supposed in innumerable cases), yet it is not commonly supposed, that men are worthy of no praise or dispraise for such dispositions; although what is natural, is undoubtedly necessary, nature being prior to all acts of the Will whatsoever. Thus, for instance, if a man appears to be of a very haughty or malicious disposition, and is supposed to be so by his natural temper, it is no vulgar notion, no dictate of the common sense and apprehension of men, that such dispositions are no vices or moral evils, or that such persons are not worthy of disesteem odium and dishonor; or that the proud or malicious acts which flow from such natural dispositions, are worthy of no resentment. Yea, such vile natural dispositions, and the strength of them, will commonly be mentioned rather as an aggravation of the wicked acts, that come from such a fountain, than an extenuation of them. Its being natural for men to act thus, is often observed by men in the height of their indignation: they will say, "It is his very nature: he is of a vile natural temper: it is as natural to him to act so as it is to breathe; he cannot help serving the devil," &c. But it is not thus with regard to hurtful, mischievous things, that any are the subjects or occasion of, by a natural necessity, against their inclinations. In such case, the necessity, by the common voice of mankind, will be spoken of as a full excuse. Thus it is very plain, that common sense makes a vast difference between these two kinds of necessity, as to the judgment it makes of their influence on the moral quality and desert of men's actions.

.   .   .   .

Upon the whole, I presume there is no person of good understanding, who impartially considers the things which have been observed, but will allow, that it is not evident, from the dictates of the common sense, or natural notions of mankind, that moral necessity is inconsistent with praise and blame. And therefore, if the Arminians would prove any such inconsistency, it must be by some philosophical and metaphysical arguments, and not common sense.

. . . .

CONCLUSION

Whether the things which have been alleged, are liable to any tolerable answer in the way of calm, intelligible and strict reasoning, I must leave others to judge; but I am sensible they are liable to one sort of answer. It is not unlikely that some, who value themselves on the supposed rational and generous principles of the modern, fashionable divinity, will have their indignation and disdain raised at the sight of this discourse, and on perceiving what things are pretended to be proved in it. And if they think it worthy of being read, or of so much notice as to say much about it, they may probably renew the usual exclamations, with additional vehemence and contempt, about the *fate of the heathen*, Hobbes' *necessity*, and *making men mere machines;* accumulating the terrible epithets of *fatal, unfrustrable, inevitable, irresistible*, &c., and it may be, with the addition of *horrid* and *blasphemous;* and perhaps much skill may be used to set forth things, which have been said, in colors which shall be shocking to the imaginations, and moving to the passions of those, who have either too little capacity, or too much confidence of the opinions they have imbibed, and contempt of the contrary, to try the matter by any serious and circumspect examination.* Or difficulties may be started and insisted on,

---

*A writer of the present age, whom I have several times had occasion to mention, speaks once and again of those who hold the doctrine of *necessity*, as scarcely worthy of the name of *philosophers*.—I do not know, whether he has respect to any particular notion of necessity, that some may have maintained; and, if so, what doctrine of necessity it is that he

which do not belong to the controversy; because, let them be more or less real, and hard to be resolved, they are not what are owing to any thing distinguishing of this scheme from that of the Arminians, and would not be removed nor diminished by renouncing the former, and adhering to the latter. Or some particular things may be picked out, which they may think will sound harshest in the ears of the generality; and these may be glossed and descanted on, with tart and contemptuous words; and from thence, the whole treated with triumph and insult.

It is easy to see, how the decision of most of the points in controversy, between *Calvinists* and *Arminians*, depends on the determination of this grand article concerning *the freedom of the Will, requisite to moral agency;* and that by clearing and establishing the *Calvinistic* doctrine in this point, the chief arguments are obviated, by which *Arminian* doctrines in general are supported, and the contrary doctrines demonstratively confirmed. Hereby it becomes manifest, that God's moral government over mankind, his treating them as moral agents, making them the objects of his commands, counsels, calls, warnings, expostulations, promises, threatenings, rewards and punishments, is not inconsistent with a *determining disposal* of all events, of every kind, throughout the universe, in his *providence;* either by positive efficiency, or permission. Indeed, such an *universal, determining Providence* infers some kind of necessity of all events, such a necessity as implies an infallible, previous fixedness of the futurity of the event; but no other necessity of moral events, or volitions of intelligent agents, is needful in order to this, than *moral necessity;* which does as much ascertain

---

means.—Whether I am worthy of the name of a philosopher, or not, would be a question little to the present purpose. If any, and ever so many, should deny it, I should not think it worth the while to enter into a dispute on that question. Though at the same time I might expect some better answer should be given to the arguments brought for the truth of the doctrine I maintain; and I might further reasonably desire, that it might be considered, whether it does not become those, who are truly worthy of the name of philosophers, to be sensible, that there is a difference between *argument* and *contempt;* yea, and a difference between the contemptibleness of the *person* that argues, and the inconclusiveness of the *arguments* he offers. [Edwards's note.]

the futurity of the event, as any other necessity. But, as has been demonstrated, such a necessity is not at all repugnant to moral agency, and a reasonable use of commands, calls, rewards, punishments, &c. Yea, not only are objections of this kind against the doctrine of an universal *determining Providence*, removed by what has been said, but the truth of such a doctrine is demonstrated.

As it has been demonstrated, that the futurity of all future events is established by previous necessity, either natural or moral; so it is manifest that the Sovereign Creator and Disposer of the world has ordered this necessity, by ordering his own conduct, either in designedly acting or forbearing to act. For, as the being of the world is from God, so the circumstances in which it had its being at first, both negative and positive, must be ordered by him, in one of these ways; and all the necessary consequences of these circumstances, must be ordered by him. And God's active and positive interpositions, after the world was created, and the consequence of these interpositions; also every instance of his forbearing to interpose, and the sure consequences of this forbearance, must all be determined according to his pleasure. And therefore every event, which is the consequence of any thing whatsoever, or that is connected with any foregoing thing or circumstance, either positive or negative, as the ground or reason of its existence, must be ordered of God; either by a designed efficiency and interposition, or a designed forbearing to operate or interpose. But, as has been proved, all events whatsoever are necessarily connected with something foregoing, either positive or negative, which is the ground of their existence: it follows, therefore, that the whole series of events is thus connected with something in the state of things, either positive or negative, which is original in the series; i.e. something which is connected with nothing preceding that, but God's own immediate conduct, either his acting or forbearing to act. From whence it follows, that as God designedly orders his own conduct, and its connected consequences, it must necessarily be, that he designedly orders all things.

. . . .

But I must leave all these things to the consideration of the fair and impartial reader; and when he has maturely weighed them, I would propose it to his consideration, whether many of the first reformers, and others that succeeded them, whom God in their day made the chief pillars of his church, and greatest instruments of their deliverance from error and darkness, and of the support of the cause of piety among them, have not been injured in the contempt with which they have been treated by many late writers, for their teaching and maintaining such doctrines as are commonly called *Calvinistic*. Indeed, some of these new writers, at the same time that they have represented the doctrines of these ancient and eminent divines as in the highest degree ridiculous, and contrary to common sense, in an ostentation of a very generous charity, have allowed that they were honest, well-meaning men; yea, it may be, some of them, as though it were in great condescension and compassion to them, have allowed that they did pretty well for the day in which they lived, and considering the great disadvantages they labored under; when at the same time, their manner of speaking has naturally and plainly suggested to the minds of their readers, that they were persons, who, through the lowness of their genius, and greatness of the bigotry with which their minds were shackled and thoughts confined, living in the gloomy caves of superstition, fondly embraced, and demurely and zealously taught the most absurd, silly, and monstrous opinions, worthy of the greatest contempt of gentlemen possessed of that noble and generous freedom of thought, which happily prevails in this age of light and inquiry. When, indeed, such is the case, that we might, if so disposed, speak as big words as they, and on far better grounds. And really all the *Arminians* on earth might be challenged, without arrogance or vanity, to make these principles of theirs, wherein they mainly differ from their fathers, whom they so much despise, consistent with common sense; yea, and perhaps to produce any doctrine ever embraced by the blindest bigot of the church of Rome, or the most ignorant Mussulman or extravagant enthusiast, that might be reduced to more demonstrable inconsistencies, and repugnancies to common sense, and to themselves; though their inconsistencies indeed may not lie so deep, or be so artfully veiled by a deceitful ambiguity of words, and an indeterminate signification of phrases. I will not deny, that these gentlemen, many of them, are men of great abilities, and have been helped to higher attainments in philosophy, than those ancient divines, and have done great service to the church of God in some respects; but I humbly conceive that their differing from their fathers with such magisterial assurance, in these points in divinity, must be owing to some other cause than superior wisdom.

It may also be worthy of consideration, whether the great alteration, which has been made in the state of things in our nation, and some other parts of the Protestant world, in this and the past age, by the exploding so generally Calvinistic doctrines, that is so often spoken of as worthy to be greatly rejoiced in by the friends of truth, learning and virtue, as an instance of the great increase of light in the Christian church; I say, it may be worthy to be considered, whether this be indeed a happy change, owing to any such cause as an increase of true knowledge and understanding in things of religion; or whether there is not reason to fear, that it may be owing to some worse cause.

And I desire it may be considered, whether the boldness of some writers may not be worthy to be reflected on, who have not scrupled to say, that if these and those things are true (which yet appear to be the demonstrable dictates of reason, as well as the certain dictates of the mouth of the Most High) then God is unjust and cruel, and guilty of manifest deceit and double dealing, and the like. Yea, some have gone so far, as confidently to assert, that if any book which pretends to be Scripture, teaches such doctrines, that alone is sufficient warrant for mankind to reject it, as what cannot be the word of God.—Some, who have not gone so far, have said, that if the Scripture seems to teach any such doctrines, so contrary to reason, we are obliged to find out some other interpretation of those texts, where such doctrines seem to be exhibited. Others express themselves yet more modestly: they express a tenderness and religious fear, lest they should receive and teach any thing that should seem to reflect on God's moral character, or be a disparagement to his methods of administration, in his moral government; and therefore express themselves as not daring to embrace some doctrines, though they seem to be delivered in Scripture, according to the more obvious and natural construction of the words. But indeed it would show a truer modesty and humility, if they would more entirely rely on God's wisdom and discerning, who knows infinitely better than we, what is agreeable to his own perfections, and never intended to leave these matters to the decision of the wisdom and discerning of men; but by his own unerring instruction, to determine for us what the truth is; knowing how little our judgment is to be depended on, and how extremely prone vain and blind men are to err in such matters.

The truth of the case is, that if the Scripture plainly taught the opposite doctrines, to those that are so much stumbled at, viz., the *Arminian* doctrine of free Will, and others depending thereon, it would be the greatest of all difficulties that attend the Scriptures, incomparably greater than its containing any, even the most mysterious of those doctrines of the first reformers, which our late free-thinkers have so superciliously exploded.—Indeed, it is a glorious argument of the divinity of the holy Scriptures, that they teach such doctrines, which in one age and another, through the blindness of men's minds, and strong prejudices of their hearts, are rejected, as most absurd and unreasonable, by the wise and great men of the world; which yet, when they are most carefully and strictly examined, appear to be exactly agreeable to the most demonstrable, certain and natural dictates of reason. By such things it appears, that the *foolishness of God is wiser than men*, and God does as is said in 1 Cor. i. 19, 20: "For it is written, I will destroy the wisdom of the wise; I will bring to nothing the understanding of the prudent. Where is the wise? Where is the scribe? Where is the disputer of this world? Hath not God made foolish the wisdom of this world?" And as it used to be in time past, so it is probable it will be in time to come, as it is there written, in verses 27, 28, 29: "But God hath chosen the foolish things of the world, to confound the wise; and God hath chosen the weak things of the world, to confound the things that are mighty; and base things of the world, the things which are despised, hath God chosen: yea, and things which are not, to bring to nought things that are; that no flesh should glory in his presence." AMEN.

REMARKS[1]

ON THE ESSAYS ON THE PRINCIPLES OF MORALITY AND NATURAL RELIGION, IN A LETTER TO A MINISTER OF THE CHURCH OF SCOTLAND

Reverend Sir:

The intimations you have given me of the use which has, by some, been made of what I have written on the *Freedom of the Will*, &c., to vindicate what is said on the subject of liberty and necessity, by the author of the *Essays on the Principles of Morality and Natural Religion*, has occasioned my reading this author's essay on that subject, with particular care and attention. And I think it must be evident to every one, that has read both his *Essay* and my *Inquiry*, that our schemes are exceeding reverse from each other. The wide difference appears particularly in the following things.

This author supposes, that such a necessity takes place with respect to all men's actions, as is inconsistent with liberty, and plainly denies that men have any liberty in acting. Thus in p. 168, after he had been speaking of the necessity of our determinations, as connected with motives, he concludes with saying, "In short, if motives are not under our power or direction, which is confessedly the fact, we can at bottom have—— NO LIBERTY." Whereas, I have abundantly expressed it as my mind, that man, in his moral actions, has true liberty; and that the moral necessity, which universally takes place, is not in the least inconsistent with any thing that is properly called liberty, and with the utmost liberty that can be desired, or that can possibly exist or be conceived of.

I find that some are apt to think, that in that kind of moral necessity of men's volitions, which I suppose to be universal, at least some degree of liberty is denied; that though it be true I allow a sort of liberty, yet those who maintain a self-determining power in the Will, and a liberty of contingence and indifference, hold a higher sort of freedom than I do; but I think this is certainly a great mistake.

Liberty, as I have explained it, in p. 17, and other places, is *the power, opportunity, or advantage, that any one has to do as he pleases, or conducting* in any respect, *according to his pleasure;* without considering how his pleasure comes to be as it is. It is demonstrable, and, I think, has been demonstrated, that no necessity of men's volitions that I maintain, is inconsistent with this liberty; and I think it is impossible for any one to rise higher in his conceptions of liberty than this: if any imagine they desire higher, and that they conceive of a higher and greater liberty than this, they are deceived, and delude themselves with confused ambiguous words, instead of ideas. If any one should here say, "Yes, I conceive of a freedom above and beyond the liberty a man has of conducting in any respect as he pleases, viz., a liberty of *choosing* as he pleases." Such a one, if he reflected, would either blush or laugh at his own instance. For, is not choosing as he pleases, conducting, *in some respect*, according to his pleasure, and still without determining how he came by that pleasure? If he says, "Yes, I came by that pleasure by my own choice." If he be a man of common sense, by this time he will see his own absurdity; for he must needs see that his notion or conception, even of this liberty, does not contain any judgment or conception, how he comes by that choice, which first determines his pleasure, or which originally fixed his own will respecting the affair. Or, if any shall say, "That a man exercises liberty in this, even in determining his own choice, but not as he pleases, or not in consequence of any choice, preference, or inclination of his own, but by a determination arising contingently out of a state of absolute indifference;" this is not rising higher in his conception of liberty; as such a determination of the Will would not be a voluntary determination of it. Surely he that places liberty in a power of doing something not according to his own choice, or from his choice, has not a higher notion of it, than he that places it in doing as he pleases, or acting from his own election. If there were a power in the mind to determine itself, but not by its choice or according to its pleasure, what advantage would it give? And what liberty, worth contending for, would be exercised in it?

Therefore no *Arminian, Pelagian,* or *Epicurean,* can rise higher in his conceptions of liberty, than the notion of it which I have explained: which notion is apparently, perfectly consistent with the whole of that necessity of men's actions, which I suppose takes place. And I scruple not to say, it is beyond all their wits to invent a higher notion, or form a higher imagination of liberty; let them talk of *sovereignty of the Will, self-determining power, self-motion, self-direction, arbitrary decision, liberty* ad utrumvis, *power of choosing differently in given cases,* &c. &c., as long as they will. It is apparent that these men, in their strenuous affirmation and dispute about these things, aim at they know not what, fighting for something they have no conception of, substituting a number of confused, unmeaning words, instead of things, and instead of thoughts. They may be challenged clearly to explain what they would have: they never can answer the challenge.

. . . .

The author of the *Essays* most manifestly supposes that if men had the truth concerning the real necessity of all their actions clearly in view, they would not appear to themselves, or one another, as at all praiseworthy or culpable, or under any moral obligation, or accountable for their actions; which supposes, that men are not to be blamed or praised for any of their actions, and are not under any obligations, nor are truly accountable for any thing they do, by reason of this necessity; which is very contrary to what I have endeavored to prove, throughout the *third part* of my *Inquiry.* I humbly conceive it is there shown, that this is so far from the truth, that the moral necessity of men's actions, which truly take place, is requisite to the being of virtue and vice, or any thing praiseworthy or culpable: that the liberty of indifference and contingence, which is advanced in opposition to that necessity, is inconsistent with the being of these; as it would suppose that men are not determined in what they do, by any virtuous or vicious principles, nor act from any motives, intentions or aims whatsoever; or have any end, either good or bad, in acting. And is it not remarkable, that this author should suppose, that, in order to men's actions truly having any desert, they must be performed *without any view, purpose, design, or desire, or any principle of action,* or any thing *agreeable to a rational nature?* As it will appear that he does, if we compare p. 206, 207, with p. 175.

The author of the *Essays* supposes, that God has deeply implanted in man's nature, a strong and invincible apprehension or feeling, as he calls it, of a liberty and contingence, of his own actions, opposite to that necessity which truly attends them; and which in truth does not agree with real fact, is not agreeable to strict, philosophic truth, is contradictory to the truth of things, and which truth contradicts, not tallying with the real plan; and that therefore such feelings are deceitful, are in reality of the delusive kind. He speaks of them as a wise delusion, as nice, artificial feelings, merely that conscience may have a commanding power; meaning plainly, that these feelings are a cunning artifice of the Author of Nature, to make men believe they are free, when they are not. He supposes that, by these feelings, the moral world has a disguised appearance. And other things of this kind he says. He supposes that all self-approbation, and all remorse of conscience, all commendation or condemnation of ourselves or others, all sense of desert, and all that is connected with this way of thinking, all the ideas which at present are suggested by the words *ought, should,* arise from this delusion, and would entirely vanish without it.

All which is very contrary to what I have abundantly insisted on and endeavored to demonstrate in my *Inquiry,* where I have largely shown that it is agreeable to the natural sense of mankind, that the moral necessity or certainty that attends men's actions, is consistent with praise and blame, reward and punishment; and that it is agreeable to our natural notions, that moral evil, with its desert of dislike and abhorrence, and all its other ill-deservings, consists in a certain deformity in the nature of the dispositions and acts of the heart, and not in the evil of something else, diverse from these, supposed to be their cause or occasion.

I might well ask here, whether any one is to be found in the world of mankind, who is conscious to a sense or feeling, naturally and deeply rooted in his mind, that in order to a man's performing any action that is praise or blame-worthy, he must exercise a liberty that implies and signifies a power of acting without any motive, view, design, desire or principle of action? For such a liberty, this author supposes that must be which is opposed to moral necessity, as I have already observed once and again. Supposing a man should actually do good, independent of desire, aim, inducement, principle, or end, is it a dictate of invincible, natural sense, that his act is more meritorious or praiseworthy, than if he had performed it for some *good end*, and had been governed in it by *good principles* and *motives?* And so I might ask on the contrary, with respect to evil actions.

.   .   .   .

On the whole, I humbly conceive, that whosoever will give himself the trouble of weighing what I have offered to consideration in my *Inquiry*, must be sensible, that such a moral necessity of men's actions as I maintain, is not at all inconsistent with any liberty that any creature has, or can have, as a free, accountable, moral agent, and subject of moral government; and that this moral necessity is so far from being inconsistent with praise and blame, and the benefit and use of men's own care and labor, that, on the contrary, it implies the very ground and reason, why men's actions are to be ascribed to them as their own, in that manner as to infer desert, praise and blame, approbation and remorse of conscience, reward and punishment; and that it establishes the moral system of the universe, and God's moral government, in every respect, with the proper use of motives, exhortations, commands, counsels, promises, and threatenings; and the use and benefit of endeavors, care and industry; and that therefore there is no need that the strict philosophic truth should be at all concealed from men; no danger in *contemplation* and *profound discovery* in these things. So far from this that the truth in this matter is of vast importance, and extremely needful to be known; and that the more clearly and perfectly the real fact is known, and the more constantly it is in view, the better; and particularly, that the clear and full knowledge of that, which is the true system of the universe, in these respects, would greatly establish the doctrines which teach the true Christian scheme of Divine Administration in the city of God, and the gospel of Jesus Christ, in its most important articles; and that these things never can be well established, and the opposite errors, so subversive of the whole gospel, which at this day so greatly and generally prevail, be well confuted, or the arguments by which they are maintained, answered, till these points are settled. While this is not done, it is, to me, beyond doubt, that the friends of those great gospel truths will but poorly maintain their controversy with the adversaries of those truths. They will be obliged often to dodge, shuffle, hide, and turn their backs: and the latter will have a strong fort, from whence they never can be driven, and weapons to use, which those whom they oppose will find no shield to screen themselves from; and they will always puzzle, confound, and keep under the friends of sound doctrine, and glory and vaunt themselves in their advantage over them; and carry their affairs with a high hand, as they have done already for a long time past.

I conclude, sir, with asking your pardon for troubling you with so much said in vindication of myself from the imputation of advancing a scheme of necessity, of a like nature with that of the author of the *Essays on the Principles of Morality and Natural Religion.* Considering that what I have said is not only in vindication of myself, but, as I think, of the most important articles of moral philosophy and religion; I trust in what I know of your candor, that you will excuse,

Your obliged friend and brother,
JONATHAN EDWARDS.

STOCKBRIDGE, *July* 25, 1757.

DOCTRINE OF ORIGINAL SIN DEFENDED

PART I

WHEREIN ARE CONSIDERED SOME EVIDENCES OF ORIGINAL SIN FROM FACTS
AND EVENTS, AS FOUND BY OBSERVATION AND EXPERIENCE, TOGETHER
WITH REPRESENTATIONS AND TESTIMONIES OF HOLY SCRIPTURE, AND
THE CONFESSION AND ASSERTIONS OF OPPOSERS

CHAPTER I

THE EVIDENCE OF ORIGINAL SIN FROM WHAT APPEARS IN FACT OF THE
SINFULNESS OF MANKIND

SECTION I

All Mankind do constantly, in all Ages, without Fail in any one
Instance, run into that moral Evil, which is, in Effect, their
own utter and eternal Perdition, in a total Privation of GOD's
Favor, and Suffering of his Vengeance and Wrath.

By *Original Sin*, as the phrase has been most commonly
used by divines, is meant *the innate, sinful depravity of the heart*.
But yet, when the doctrine of Original Sin is spoken of, it is
vulgarly understood in that latitude, as to include not only the
depravity of nature, but the *imputation of Adam's* first Sin; or
in other words, the liableness or exposedness of *Adam's* posterity, in the divine judgment, to partake of the punishment of
that Sin. So far as I know, most of those who have held one of
these, have maintained the other; and most of those who have
opposed one have opposed the other; both are opposed by the
author chiefly attended to in the following discourse, in his book
against Original Sin: and it may perhaps appear in our future
consideration of the subject, that they are closely connected,
and that the arguments which prove the one, establish the
other, and that there are no more difficulties attending the allowing of one than the other.

I shall, in the first place, consider this doctrine more especially
with regard to the corruption of nature; and as we treat of this,

the other will naturally come into consideration, in the prosecution of the discourse, as connected with it.

As all moral qualities, all principles either of virtue or vice, lie in the disposition of the heart, I shall consider whether we have any evidence, that the heart of man is naturally of a corrupt and evil disposition. This is strenuously denied by many late writers, who are enemies to the doctrine of Original Sin; and particularly by Dr. *Taylor*.[1]

The way we come by the idea of any such thing as disposition or tendency is by observing what is constant or general in event; especially under a great variety of circumstances; and above all, when the effect or event continues the same through great and various opposition, much and manifold force and means used to the contrary not prevailing to hinder the effect. I do not know, that such a prevalence of effects is denied to be an evidence of prevailing tendency in causes and agents; or that it is expressly denied by the opposers of the doctrine of Original Sin, that if, in the course of events, it universally or generally proves that mankind are actually corrupt, this would be an evidence of a prior, corrupt propensity in the world of mankind; whatever may be said by some which, if taken with its plain consequences, may seem to imply a denial of this; which may be considered afterwards.—But by many the fact is denied; that is, it is denied, that corruption and moral evil are commonly prevalent in the world: on the contrary, it is insisted on that good preponderates, and that virtue has the ascendant.

To this purpose Dr. *Turnbull*[2] says, "With regard to the prevalence of vice in the world, men are apt to let their imagination run out upon all the robberies, piracies, murders, perjuries, frauds, massacres, assassinations they have either heard of, or read in history; thence concluding all mankind to be very wicked. As if a court of justice was a proper place to make an estimate of the morals of mankind, or a hospital of the healthfulness of a climate. But ought they not to consider, that the number of honest citizens and farmers far surpasses that of all sorts of criminals in any state, and that the innocent and kind actions of even criminals themselves surpass their crimes in

numbers; that it is the rarity of crimes, in comparison of innocent or good actions, which engages our attention to them, and
makes them to be recorded in history; while honest, generous,
domestic actions are overlooked, only because they are so common? As one great danger, or one month's sickness shall become a frequently repeated story during a long life of health and
safety.—Let not the vices of mankind be multiplied or magnified. Let us make a fair estimate of human life, and set over
against the shocking, the astonishing instances of barbarity
and wickedness that have been perpetrated in any age, not only
the exceeding generous and brave actions with which history
shines, but the prevailing innocency, good nature, industry,
felicity, and cheerfulness of the greater part of mankind at all
times; and we shall not find reason to cry out, as objectors
against Providence do on this occasion, that all men are vastly
corrupt, and that there is hardly any such thing as virtue in the
world. Upon a fair computation, the fact does indeed come
out, that very great villanies have been very uncommon in all
ages, and looked upon as monstrous; so general is the sense and
esteem of virtue." It seems to be with a like view that Dr.
Taylor says, "We must not take the measure of our health and
enjoyments from a lazar house, nor of our understanding from
bedlam, nor of our morals from a gaol."

With respect to the propriety and pertinence of such a representation of things, and its force as to the consequence designed, I hope we shall be better able to judge, and in some
measure to determine, whether the natural disposition of the
hearts of mankind be corrupt or not, when the things which
follow have been considered.

But for the greater clearness, it may be proper here to pre-
mise one consideration, that is of great importance in this controversy, and is very much overlooked by the opposers of the
doctrine of Original Sin in their disputing against it; which is
this:

That is to be looked upon as the true tendency of the natural
or innate disposition of man's heart, which appears to be its
tendency, when we consider things as they are in themselves,

or in their own nature, without the *interposition of divine grace*. Thus, that state of man's nature, that disposition of the mind, is to be looked upon as evil and pernicious, which, as it is in itself, tends to extremely pernicious consequences, and would certainly end therein, were it not that the free mercy and kindness of God interposes to prevent that issue. It would be very strange if any should argue, that there is no evil tendency in the case, because the mere favor and compassion of the Most High may step in and oppose the tendency, and prevent the sad effect tended to. Particularly, if there be any thing in the nature of man, whereby he has a universal, unfailing tendency to that moral evil, which, according to the real nature and true demerit of things, as they are in themselves, implies his utter ruin, that must be looked upon as an evil tendency or propensity; however divine grace may interpose, to save him from deserved ruin, and to overrule things to an issue contrary to that which they tend to of themselves. Grace is a sovereign thing, exercised according to the good pleasure of God, bringing good out of evil. The effect of it belongs not to the nature of things themselves, that otherwise have an ill tendency, any more than the remedy belongs to the disease; but is something altogether independent on it, introduced to oppose the natural tendency, and reverse the course of things. But the event that things tend to, according to their own demerit, and according to divine justice, that is the event which they tend to in their own nature, as Dr. Taylor's own words fully imply. "God alone (says he) can declare whether he will pardon or punish the ungodliness and unrighteousness of mankind, which is in *its own nature* punishable." Nothing is more precisely according to the truth of things, than divine justice: it weighs things in an even balance: it views and estimates things no otherwise than they are truly in their own nature. Therefore undoubtedly that which implies a tendency to ruin, according to the estimate of divine *justice*, does indeed imply such a tendency in its *own nature*.

And then it must be remembered that it is a *moral depravity* we are speaking of; and therefore when we are considering whether such depravity do not appear by a tendency to a bad effect or issue, it is a *moral tendency* to such an issue, that is the thing to be taken into the account. A moral tendency or influence is by *desert*. Then may it be said, man's nature or state is attended with a pernicious or destructive tendency, in a *moral* sense, when it tends to that which *deserves* misery and destruction. And therefore it equally shows the moral depravity of the nature of mankind in their present state, whether that nature be universally attended with an effectual tendency to destructive vengeance actually *executed*, or to their deserving misery and ruin, or their just exposedness to destruction, however that fatal consequence may be prevented by grace, or whatever the actual event be.

One thing more is to be observed here, viz., that the topic mainly insisted on by the opposers of the doctrine of Original Sin, is the justice of God; both in their objections against the imputation of Adam's sin, and also against its being so ordered, that men should come into the world with a corrupt and ruined nature, without having merited the displeasure of their Creator by any personal fault. But the latter is not repugnant to God's justice, if men can be, and actually are, born into the world with a tendency to sin, and to misery and ruin for their sin, which actually will be the consequence, unless *mere grace* steps in and prevents it. If this be allowed, the argument from *justice* is given up; for it is to suppose that their liableness to misery and ruin comes in a way of justice; otherwise there would be no need of the interposition of divine grace to save them. Justice alone would be sufficient security, if exercised, without grace. It is all one in this dispute about what is just and righteous, whether men are born in a miserable state, by a tendency to ruin, which *actually follows*, and that *justly;* or whether they are born in such a state as tends to a desert of ruin, which *might justly* follow, and *would actually follow*, did not grace prevent. For the controversy is not, what grace will do, but what justice might do.

.   .   .   .

Having premised these things, I now proceed to say,

That mankind are all naturally in such a state, as is attended, without fail, with this consequence or issue: that they universally run themselves into that which is, in effect, their own utter, eternal perdition, as being finally accursed of God, and the subjects of his remediless wrath through sin.

From which I infer that the natural state of the mind of man, is attended with a propensity of nature, which is prevalent and effectual, to such an issue; and that therefore their nature is corrupt and depraved with a moral depravity, that amounts to and implies their utter undoing.

Here I would first consider the truth of the proposition; and then would show the certainty of the consequences which I infer from it. If both can be clearly and certainly proved, then, I trust, none will deny but that the doctrine of original depravity is evident, and so the falseness of Dr. Taylor's scheme demonstrated; the greatest part of whose book, called "*The Scripture Doctrine of Original Sin*," &c., is against the doctrine of *innate depravity*. In page 107, *S*., he speaks of the conveyance of a corrupt and sinful nature to Adam's posterity as *the grand point* to be proved by the maintainers of the Doctrine of Original Sin.

In order to demonstrate what is asserted in the proposition laid down, there is need only that these two things should be made manifest: *one* is this fact, that all mankind come into the world in such a state, as without fail comes to this issue, namely, the universal commission of sin; or that every one who comes to act in the world as a moral agent, is, in a greater or less degree, guilty of sin. The *other* is, that all sin deserves and exposes to utter and eternal destruction, under God's wrath and curse; and would end in it, were it not for the interposition of divine grace to prevent the effect. Both which can be abundantly demonstrated to be agreeable to the word of God, and to Dr. Taylor's own doctrine.

That every one of mankind, at least of them that are capable of acting as moral agents, are guilty of sin (not now taking it for granted that they come guilty into the world) is a thing most clearly and abundantly evident from the holy Scriptures. 1 Kings viii. 46, "If any man sin against thee; for there is no man that sinneth not." Eccl. vii. 20, "There is not a just man upon earth that doeth good, and sinneth not." Job ix. 2, 3, "I know it is so of a truth (i.e., as Bildad had just before said, that *God would not cast away a perfect man*, &c.), but how should man be just with God? If he will contend with him, he cannot answer him one of a thousand." To the like purpose, Psalm cxliii. 2, "Enter not into judgment with thy servant; for in thy sight shall no man living be justified." So the words of the apostle (in which he has apparent reference to those of the Psalmist), Rom. iii. 19, 20, "That every mouth may be stopped, and all the world become guilty before God. Therefore by the deeds of the law there shall no flesh be justified in his sight; for by the law is the knowledge of sin." So Gal. ii. 16, and 1 John i. 7–10, "If we walk in the light, the blood of Christ cleanseth us from all sin. If we say that we have no sin, we deceive ourselves, and the truth is not in us. If we confess our sins, he is faithful and just to forgive us our sins, and to cleanse us from all unrighteousness. If we say that we have not sinned, we make him a liar, and his word is not in us." As in this place, so in innumerable other places, confession and repentance of sin are spoken of, as duties proper for all; as also prayer to God for pardon of sin; and forgiveness of those that injure us, from that motive, that we hope to be forgiven of God. Universal guilt of sin might also be demonstrated from the appointment, and the declared use and end of the ancient sacrifices; and also from the ransom, which every one that was numbered in Israel, was directed to pay, to make atonement for his soul, Exod. xxx. 11–16. All are represented, not only as being sinful, but as having great and manifold iniquity, Job ix. 2, 3, James iii. 1, 2.

There are many scriptures which both declare the universal sinfulness of mankind, and also that all sin deserves and justly exposes to everlasting destruction, under the wrath and curse of God; and so demonstrate both parts of the proposition I have laid down. To which purpose that in Gal. iii. 10, is exceeding full: "For as many as are of the works of the law are under the curse; for it is written, Cursed is every one that continueth not in all things which are written in the book of the law, to do them." How manifestly is it implied in the apostle's meaning here, that there is no man but what fails in some instances of doing all things that are written in the book of the law, and therefore as many as have their dependence on their fulfilling the law, are under that curse which is pronounced on them that do fail of it? And here the apostle infers in the next verse, *that no man is justified by the law in the sight of God*, as he had said before in the preceding chapter, verse 16, "*By the works of the law shall no flesh be justified*." The apostle shows us that he understands, that by this place which he cites from Deuteronomy, the Scripture hath concluded, or shut up, all under sin, as in chap. iii. 22. So that here we are plainly taught, both that every one of mankind is a sinner, and that every sinner is under the curse of God.

. . . .

PART IV

CONTAINING ANSWERS TO OBJECTIONS

CHAPTER II

CONCERNING THAT OBJECTION AGAINST THE DOCTRINE OF NATIVE CORRUPTION, THAT TO SUPPOSE MEN RECEIVE THEIR FIRST EXISTENCE IN SIN, IS TO MAKE HIM WHO IS THE AUTHOR OF THEIR BEING, THE AUTHOR OF THEIR DEPRAVITY.

One argument against men's being supposed to be born with sinful depravity, which Dr. Taylor greatly insists upon is, "That this does in effect charge him, who is *the author of our nature, who formed us in the womb*, with being the *author of a sinful corruption of nature;* and that it is *highly injurious* to the God of our nature, *whose hands have formed and fashioned us*, to believe *our nature* to be *originally corrupted*, and *that in the* worst *sense of corruption*."[3]

With respect to this, I would observe in the first place, that this writer, in his handling this grand objection, supposes something to *belong* to the doctrine objected against, as maintained by the divines whom he is opposing, which does *not* belong to it, nor does follow from it: as particularly, he supposes the

doctrine of Original Sin to imply, that nature must be corrupted
by some *positive influence;* "something, by some means or other,
infused into the human nature; some *quality* or other, not from
the *choice* of our minds, but like a *taint, tincture,* or *infection,*
altering the natural constitution, faculties, and dispositions of
our souls.[4] That sin and evil dispositions are *implanted* in the
fœtus in the womb."[5] Whereas truly our doctrine neither implies
nor infers any such thing. In order to account for a sinful corruption of nature, yea, a total native depravity of the heart of
man, there is not the least need of supposing any evil quality,
infused, implanted, or *wrought* into the nature of man, by any
positive cause, or influence whatsoever, either from God, or the
creature; or of supposing, that man is conceived and born with
a *fountain of evil* in his heart, such as is any thing properly
positive. I think, a little attention to the nature of things will
be sufficient to satisfy any impartial, considerate inquirer, that
the absence of positive good principles, and so the withholding
of a special divine influence to impart and maintain those good
principles, leaving the common natural principles of self-love,
natural appetite, &c. (which were in man in innocence), leaving
these, I say to themselves, without the government of superior
divine principles, will certainly be followed with the corruption, yea, the total corruption of the heart, without occasion for
any positive influence at all: and, that it was thus indeed that
corruption of nature came on Adam, immediately on his fall,
and comes on all his posterity, as sinning in him, and falling
with him.

The case with man was plainly this: when God made man
at first, he implanted in him two kinds of principles. There was
an *inferior* kind, which may be called *natural,* being the principles
of mere human nature; such as self-love, with those natural
appetites and passions, which belong to the *nature of man,* in
which his love to his own liberty, honor, and pleasure, were
exercised: these, when alone, and left to themselves, are what
the Scriptures sometimes call *flesh.* Besides these, there were
superior principles, that were spiritual, holy, and divine, summarily comprehended in divine love; wherein consisted the

spiritual image of God, and man's righteousness and true holiness; which are called in Scripture the *divine nature*. These principles may, in some sense, be called *supernatural*,* being (however concreated or connate, yet) such as are above those principles that are essentially implied in, or necessarily resulting from, and inseparably connected with, *mere human nature;* and being such as immediately depend on man's union and communion with God, or divine communications and influences of God's Spirit: which, though withdrawn, and man's nature forsaken of these principles, human nature would be human nature still: man's nature, as such, being entire, without these divine *principles*, which the Scripture sometimes calls *spirit*, in contradistinction to *flesh*. These superior principles were given to possess the throne, and maintain an absolute dominion in the heart: the other to be wholly subordinate and subservient. And while things continued thus, all things were in excellent order, peace, and beautiful harmony, and in their proper and perfect state.

These divine principles thus reigning, were the dignity, life, happiness, and glory of man's nature. When man sinned, and broke God's covenant, and fell under his curse, these superior principles left his heart: for indeed God then left him; that communion with God, on which these principles depended, entirely ceased; the Holy Spirit, that divine inhabitant, forsook the house. Because it would have been utterly improper in itself,

* To prevent all cavils, the reader is desired particularly to observe, in what sense I here use the words *natural* and *supernatural:* not as epithets of distinction between that which is concreated or connate, and that which is extraordinarily introduced afterwards, besides the first state of things, or the order established originally, beginning when man's nature began; but as distinguishing between what belongs to, or flows from, that nature which man has, merely as man, and those things which are above this, by which one is denominated, not only a man, but a truly virtuous, holy, and spiritual man; which, though they began in Adam, as soon as humanity began, and are necessary to the perfection and well being of the human nature, yet are not essential to the constitution of it, or necessary to its being: inasmuch as one may have every thing needful to his being man, exclusively of them. If in thus using the words, *natural* and *supernatural*, I use them in an uncommon sense, it is not from any affectation of singularity, but for want of other terms more aptly to express my meaning. [Edwards's note.]

and inconsistent with the covenant and constitution God had established, that God should still maintain communion with man, and continue, by his friendly, gracious, vital influences, to dwell with him and in him, after he was become a rebel, and had incurred God's wrath and curse. Therefore immediately the superior divine principles wholly ceased; so light ceases in a room when the candle is withdrawn; and thus man was left in a state of darkness, woful corruption and ruin; nothing but flesh without spirit. The inferior principles of self-love, and natural appetite, which were given only to serve, being alone, and left to themselves, *of course* became reigning principles; having no superior principles to regulate or control them, they became absolute masters of the heart. The immediate consequence of which was a *fatal catastrophe*, a turning of all things upside down, and the succession of a state of the most odious and dreadful confusion. Man did immediately set up *himself*, and the objects of his private affections and appetites, as supreme; and so they took the place of *God*. These inferior principles are like *fire* in a house; which we say is a good servant, but a bad master; very useful while kept in its place, but if left to take possession of the whole house, soon brings all to destruction. Man's love to his own honor, separate interest, and private pleasure, which before was wholly subordinate unto love to God, and regard to his authority and glory, now disposes and impels him to pursue those objects, without regard to God's honor or law; because there is no true regard to these divine things left in him. In consequence of which, he seeks those objects as much when against God's honor and law, as when agreeable to them. And God, still continuing strictly to require supreme regard to himself, and forbidding all gratifications of these inferior passions, but only in perfect subordination to the ends, and agreeableness to the rules and limits, which his holiness, honor, and law prescribe, hence immediately arises *enmity* in the heart, now wholly under the power of self-love; and nothing but *war* ensues, in a constant course, against God. As, when a subject has once renounced his lawful sovereign, and set up a pretender in his stead, a state of enmity and war against his rightful king necessarily ensues. It were easy to show, how every lust, and depraved disposition of man's heart would naturally arise from this *privative* original, if here were room for it. Thus it is easy to give an account, how total corruption of heart should follow on man's eating the forbidden fruit, though that was but one act of sin, *without God's putting* any evil into his heart, or *implanting* any bad principle, or *infusing* any corrupt taint, and so becoming the *author* of depravity. Only God's *withdrawing*, as it was highly proper and necessary that he should, from rebel man, being as it were driven away by his abominable wickedness, and men's *natural* principles being *left to themselves*, this is sufficient to account for his becoming entirely corrupt, and bent on sinning against God.

And as Adam's nature became corrupt without God's implanting or infusing any evil thing into his nature; so does the nature of his posterity. God dealing with Adam as the head of his posterity (as has been shown) and treating them as one, he deals with his posterity as having *all sinned in him.* And therefore, as God withdrew spiritual communion, and his vital, gracious influence from the common head, so he withholds the same from all the members, as they come into existence; whereby they come into the world mere *flesh*, and entirely under the government of natural and inferior principles; and so become wholly corrupt, as Adam did.

. . . .

But now the grand objection is against the *reasonableness* of such a *constitution*, by which Adam and his posterity should be looked upon as *one*, and dealt with accordingly, in an affair of such infinite consequence; so that if Adam sinned, they must necessarily be made *sinners* by his disobedience, and come into existence with the same *depravity* of disposition, and be looked upon and treated as though they were partakers with Adam in his act of sin. I have not room here to rehearse all Dr. Taylor's vehement exclamations against the reasonableness and justice of this. The reader may at his leisure consult his book and see them in the places referred to below. Whatever black colors and frightful representations are employed on this occasion, all may be summed up in this, That Adam and his posterity are *not one*, but entirely *distinct agents*. But with respect to this mighty outcry made against the *reasonableness* of any such *constitution*, by which God is supposed to treat Adam and his posterity as *one*, I would make the following observations.

I. It signifies nothing to exclaim against plain *fact*. Such is the *fact*, most evident and acknowledged *fact*, with respect to the state of all mankind, without exception of one individual among all the natural descendants of Adam, as makes it apparent, that God actually deals with Adam and his posterity as *one*, in the affair of his apostasy, and its infinitely terrible consequences. It has been demonstrated, and shown to be in effect plainly acknowledged, that every individual of mankind comes into the world in such circumstances, as that there is no hope or possibility of any other than their violating God's holy law (if they ever live to act at all as moral agents), and being thereby justly exposed to eternal ruin. And it is thus by God's ordering and disposing of things. And God either thus deals with mankind, because he looks upon them as *one* with their first father, and so treats them as *sinful* and *guilty* by his apostasy; or (which will not mend the matter) he, *without* viewing them as at all concerned in that affair, but as in every respect perfectly *innocent*, does nevertheless subject them to this infinitely dreadful calamity. Adam, by his sin, was exposed to the *calamities and sorrows of this life*, to *temporal death and eternal ruin;* as is confessed. And it is also in effect confessed, that all his posterity come into the world in such a state, as that the certain consequence is their being *exposed*, and *justly* so, to the *sorrows of this life*, to *temporal death and eternal ruin*, unless saved by grace. So that we see, God in fact deals with them together, or as *one*. If God orders the consequences of Adam's sin, with regard to his posterity's welfare, even in those things which are most important, and which do in the highest degree concern their eternal interest, to be the *same* with the consequences to Adam himself, then he treats Adam and his posterity as *one* in that affair. Hence, however the matter be attended with difficulty, *fact* obliges us to *get over* the difficulty, either by finding out some solution, or by shutting our mouths, and acknowledging the weakness and scantiness of our understandings; as we must in innumerable other cases, where apparent and undeniable *fact*, in God's works of creation and providence, is attended with events and circumstances, the *manner* and *reason* of which are difficult to our understandings. But to proceed:

II. We will consider the *difficulties* themselves, insisted on in the objections of our opposers. They may be reduced to these two: *First*, That such a constitution is *injurious* to Adam's posterity. *Secondly*, That it is altogether *improper*, as it implies *falsehood*, viewing and treating those as one which indeed are not one, but entirely *distinct*.

FIRST DIFFICULTY. That the appointing Adam to stand, in this great affair, as the moral *head* of his posterity, and so treating them as one with him, as standing or falling with him, is *injurious* to them, and tends to their hurt. To which I answer, it is demonstrably *otherwise;* that such a constitution was so far from being *injurious* and hurtful to Adam's posterity, or tending to their calamity, any more than if every one had been appointed to stand for himself personally, that it was, in itself considered, very much of a *contrary* tendency, and was attended with a more eligible *probability* of a *happy* issue than the latter would have been: and so is a constitution truly expressing the *goodness* of its author.

. . . .

SECOND DIFFICULTY. It being thus manifest that this constitution, by which Adam and his posterity are dealt with as *one*, is not unreasonable upon account of its being *injurious* and *hurtful* to the interest of mankind, the only thing remaining in the objection against such a constitution, is the *impropriety* of it, as implying *falsehood*, and contradiction to the true nature of things; as hereby they are viewed and treated *as one*, who are *not* one, but wholly distinct; and no arbitrary constitution can ever make that to be true, which in itself considered is not true.

This objection, however specious, is really founded on a false hypothesis, and wrong notion of what we call *sameness* or *oneness*, among created things; and the seeming force of the objection arises from ignorance or inconsideration of the *degree*, in which created identity or oneness with past existence, in general, depends on the sovereign constitution and law of the Supreme Author and Disposer of the Universe.

Some things, being most simply considered, are *entirely distinct*, and *very diverse*, which yet are so united by the established law of the Creator, in some respects, and with regard to some purposes and effects, that by virtue of that establishment it is with them as if they were *one*. Thus a *tree*, grown great, and a hundred years old, is *one* plant with the little *sprout*, that first came out of the ground, from whence it grew, and has been continued in constant succession, though it is now so exceeding *diverse*, many thousand times bigger, and of a very different form, and perhaps not one atom the very same; yet God, according to an established law of nature, has in a constant succession communicated to it many of the same qualities and most important properties, as if it were *one*. It has been his pleasure to constitute a union in these respects, and for these purposes, naturally leading us to look upon all as *one*. So the *body* of *man* at forty years of age, is *one* with the *infant body* which first came into the world from whence it grew; though now constituted of different substance, and the greater part of the substance probably changed scores (if not hundreds) of times; and though it be now in so many respects exceeding diverse, yet God, according to the course of nature, which he has been pleased to establish, has caused that in a certain method it should communicate with that *infantile* body, in the same life, the same senses, the same features, and many of the same qualities, and in union with the same soul, and so, with regard to these purposes, it is dealt with by him as *one* body. Again, the *body* and *soul* of a man are *one*, in a very different manner, and for different purposes. Considered in themselves, they are exceeding different beings, of a nature as diverse as can be conceived; and yet by a very peculiar divine constitution or law of nature, which God has been pleased to establish, they are strongly united, and become *one*, in most important respects; a wonderful mutual communication is established; so that both become different parts of the *same man*. Bu the union and mutual communication they have, has existence, and is entirely regulated and limited, according to the sovereign pleasure of God, and the constitution he has been pleased to establish.

And if we come even to the *personal identity* of created intelligent beings, though this be not allowed to consist wholly in that which Mr. Locke places it in, i. e. *same consciousness;* yet I think it cannot be denied, that this is one thing essential to it. But it is evident that the communication or continuance of the same consciousness and memory to any subject, through successive parts of duration, depends wholly on a divine establishment. There would be no necessity that the remembrance and ideas of what is past should continue to exist, but by an arbitrary constitution of the Creator. If any should here insist that there is no need of having recourse to such a *constitution,* in order to account for the continuance of the *same consciousness,* and should say, that the very *nature* of the soul is such as will sufficiently account for it; and that the soul will retain the ideas and consciousness it once had, according to the *course of nature;* then let it be remembered, who it is gives the soul this nature; and let that be remembered which Dr. Taylor says of the course of nature, before observed; denying, that "the course of nature is a proper active cause, which will work and go on by itself without God, if he lets and permits it;" saying that "the course of nature, separate from the agency of God, is no cause, or nothing;" and affirming that "it is absolutely impossible the course of nature should continue itself, or go on to operate by itself, any more than produce itself;"[6] and that "God, the Original of all Being, is the *Only Cause* of all natural effects."[7] Here is worthy also to be observed, what Dr. Turnbull says of the *laws of nature,* in words which he cites from Sir Isaac Newton.[8] "It is the will of the mind that is the *first cause,* that gives subsistence and efficacy to all those *laws,* who is the *efficient cause* that produces the *phenomena* which appear in analogy, harmony and agreement, according to these *laws.*" And he says, "the same principles must take place in things pertaining to *moral* as well as natural philosophy."[9]

From these things it will clearly follow, that identity of

consciousness depends wholly on a law of *nature*, and so, on the sovereign *will* and *agency* of GOD; and therefore, that personal identity, and so the derivation of the pollution and guilt of past sins in the same person, depends on an arbitrary divine *constitution;* and this, even though we should allow the same consciousness not to be the only thing which constitutes oneness of person, but should, besides that, suppose sameness of substance requisite. For if same consciousness be *one thing* necessary to personal identity, and this depends on God's sovereign *constitution*, it will still follow that personal identity depends on God's sovereign *constitution*.

And with respect to the identity of created substance itself, in the different moments of its duration, I think we shall greatly mistake, if we imagine it to be like that absolute, independent identity of the FIRST BEING, whereby he is *the same, yesterday, to-day, and forever*. Nay, on the contrary, it may be demonstrated that even this oneness of created substance, existing at different times, is a merely *dependent* identity, dependent on the pleasure and sovereign constitution of Him who *worketh all in all*. This will follow from what is generally allowed, and is certainly true, that God not only created all things, and gave them being at first, but continually preserves them, and upholds them in being. This being a matter of considerable importance, it may be worthy here to be considered with a little attention. Let us inquire, therefore, in the first place, whether it be not evident that God does continually, by his immediate power *uphold* every created substance in being; and then let us see the *consequence*.

That God does, by his immediate power, *uphold* every created substance in being, will be manifest, if we consider that their present existence is a *dependent* existence, and therefore is an *effect*, and must have some *cause;* and the cause must be one of these two: either the *antecedent existence* of the same substance, or the *power* of the Creator. But it cannot be the *antecedent existence* of the same substance. For instance, the existence of the body of the *moon* at this present moment, cannot be the *effect* of its existence at the last foregoing moment. For not only was what existed the last moment no active cause, but wholly a passive thing; but this is also to be considered, that no cause can produce effects in a *time* and *place* in which itself is *not*. It is plain, nothing can exert itself, or operate, when and where it is not existing. But the moon's past existence was neither *where* nor *when* its present existence is. In point of time, what is *past*, entirely ceases, when *present* existence begins; otherwise it would not be *past*. The past moment is ceased and gone, when the present moment takes place; and does no more *coexist* with it, than does any other moment that had ceased twenty years ago. Nor could the past existence of the particles of this *moving body* produce effects in any *other place* than where it then was. But its existence at the present moment, in every point of it, is in a different *place* from where its existence was at the last preceding moment. From these things I suppose it will certainly follow that the present existence, either of this, or any other created substance, cannot be an effect of its past existence. The existences (so to speak) of an effect, or thing dependent, in different parts of space or duration, though ever so *near* one to another, do not at all *coexist* one with the other; and therefore are as truly different effects, as if those parts of space and duration were ever so far asunder; and the prior existence can no more be the proper cause of the new existence, in the next moment, or next part of space, than if it had been in an age before, or at a thousand miles distance, without any existence to fill up the intermediate time or space. Therefore the existence of created substances, in each successive moment, must be the effect of the *immediate* agency, will, and power of God.

If any shall say this reasoning is not good, and shall insist upon it, that there is no *need* of any immediate *divine* power to produce the present existence of created substances, but that their present existence is the effect or consequence of past existence, according to the *nature* of things; that the established *course of nature* is sufficient to *continue* existence, where existence is once given; I allow it: but then it should be remembered *what* nature is in created things; and *what* the established *course* of nature is; that, as has been observed already, *it is nothing separate from the agency of God;* and that, as Dr. Taylor says, GOD, *the Original* of all being, is the ONLY *cause of all natural effects*. A father, according to the course of nature, begets a child; an oak, according to the course of nature, produces an acorn, or a bud; so, according to the course of nature, the former existence of the trunk of the tree is followed by its new or present existence. In the one case and the other, the new effect is consequent on the former, only by the *established laws* and *settled course* of nature, which is allowed to be nothing but the continued immediate efficiency of God, according to a *constitution* that he has been pleased to establish. Therefore, according to what our author urges, as the child and the acorn, which come into existence according to the *course of nature*, in consequence of the prior existence and state of the parent and the oak, are truly, *immediately* created or made by God, so must the existence of each created person and thing, at each moment of it, be from the immediate *continued* creation of God. It will certainly follow from these things, that God's *preserving* created things in being is perfectly equivalent to a *continued creation*, or to his creating those things out of nothing at *each moment* of their existence. If the continued existence of created things be wholly dependent on God's preservation, then those things would drop into nothing, upon the ceasing of the present moment, without a new exertion of the divine power to cause them to exist in the following moment. If there be any who own that God preserves things in being, and yet hold that they would continue in being without any further help from him, after they once have existence; I think it is hard to know what they mean. To what purpose can it be to talk of God's *preserving* things in being, when there is no *need* of his preserving them? Or to talk of their being *dependent* on God for continued existence, when they would of themselves continue to exist without his help; nay, though he should wholly withdraw his sustaining power and influence?

It will follow from what has been observed, that God's upholding created substance, or causing its existence in each successive moment, is altogether equivalent to an *immediate production out of nothing*, at each moment. Because its existence at this moment is not merely in part from *God*, but wholly from him, and not in any part or degree, from its *antecedent existence*. For the supposing that its antecedent existence *concurs* with God in *efficiency*, to produce some *part* of the effect, is attended with all the very same absurdities, which have been shown to attend the supposition of its producing it *wholly*. Therefore the antecedent existence is nothing, as to any proper influence or assistance in the affair; and consequently *God* produces the effect as much from *nothing*, as if there had been nothing *before*. So that this effect differs not at all from the first creation, but only *circumstantially;* as in *first* creation there had been no such act and effect of God's power *before;* whereas, his giving existence afterwards, *follows* preceding acts and effects of the same kind, in an established order.

Now, in the next place, let us see how the *consequence* of these things is to my present purpose. If the existence of created *substance*, in each successive moment, be wholly the effect of God's immediate power, in *that* moment, without any dependence on prior existence, as much as the first creation out of *nothing*, then what exists at this moment, by this power, is a *new effect*, and simply and absolutely considered, not the same with any past existence, though it be like it, and follows it according to a certain established method.* And there is no identity or oneness in

* When I suppose that an effect which is produced every moment, by a new action or exertion of power, must be a *new* effect in each moment, and not absolutely and numerically the same with that which existed in preceding moments, the thing that I intend, may be illustrated by this example. The lucid color or brightness of the *moon*, as we look steadfastly upon it, seems to be a *permanent* thing, as though it were perfectly the same brightness continued. But indeed it is an effect produced every moment. It ceases, and is renewed, in each successive point of time; and so becomes altogether a *new* effect at each instant; and no one thing that belongs to it is numerically the same that existed in the preceding moment. The rays of the sun, impressed on that body, and reflected from it, which cause the effect, are none of them the same. The impression, made in each moment on our sensory, is by the stroke of *new* rays; and the sensation, excited by the stroke, is a new effect, an effect of a *new* impulse. Therefore the brightness or lucid whiteness of this body is no more numerically the same thing with that which existed in the preceding moment, than the *sound* of the wind that blows now, is individually the same with the sound of the wind that blew just before, which, though it be like it, is not the same, any more than the agitated *air*, that makes the sound, is the same; or than the *water*, flowing in a river, that now passes by, is individually

the case, but what depends on the *arbitrary* constitution of the Creator; who by his wise sovereign establishment so unites these successive new effects, that he *treats them as one*, by communicating to them like properties, relations and circumstances; and so leads *us* to regard and treat them as *one*. When I call this an *arbitrary constitution*, I mean, it is a constitution which depends on nothing but the *divine will;* which divine will depends on nothing but the *divine wisdom*. In this sense, the whole *course of nature*, with all that belongs to it, all its laws and methods, and constancy and regularity, continuance and proceeding, is an *arbitrary constitution*. In this sense, the continuance of the very being of the world and all its parts, as well as the manner of con-

---

the same with that which passed a little before. And if it be thus with the brightness or color of the moon, so it must be with its *solidity*, and every thing else belonging to its substance, if all be, each moment, as much the immediate effect of a *new* exertion or application of power.

The matter may perhaps be in some respects still more clearly illustrated by this. The *images* of things in a *glass*, as we keep our eye upon them, seem to remain precisely the same, with a continuing, perfect identity. But it is known to be otherwise. Philosophers well know that these images are constantly *renewed*, by the impression and reflection of *new* rays of light; so that the image impressed by the former rays is constantly vanishing, and a *new* image impressed by *new* rays every moment, both on the glass and on the eye. The image constantly renewed, by new successive rays, is no more numerically the same, than if it were by some artist put on anew with a pencil, and the colors constantly vanishing as fast as put on. And the new images being put on *immediately* or *instantly*, do not make them the same, any more than if it were done with the intermission of an *hour* or a *day*. The image that exists this moment, is not at all *derived* from the image which existed the last preceding moment; as may be seen, because if the succession of new *rays* be intercepted, by something interposed between the object and the glass, the image immediately ceases; the *past existence* of the image has no influence to uphold it, so much as for one moment. Which shows that the image is altogether new made every moment; and strictly speaking, is in no part numerically the same with that which existed the moment preceding. And truly so the matter must be with the *bodies* themselves, as well as their images. They also cannot be the same, with an absolute identity, but must be wholly renewed every moment, if the case be as has been proved, that their present existence is not, strictly speaking, at all the effect of their past existence; but is wholly, every instant, the effect of a new agency, or exertion of the power, of the cause of their existence. If so, the existence caused is every instant a new effect, whether the cause be *light*, or immediate *divine power*, or whatever it be. [Edwards's note.]

tinued being, depends entirely on an *arbitrary constitution*. For it does not at all necessarily follow, that because there was sound, or light, or color, or resistance, or gravity, or thought, or consciousness, or any other dependent thing the last moment, that therefore there shall be the like at the next. All dependent existence whatsoever is in a constant flux, ever passing and returning; renewed every moment, as the colors of bodies are every moment renewed by the light that shines upon them; and all is constantly proceeding from *God*, as light from the sun. *In him we live, and move, and have our being.*

Thus it appears, if we consider matters strictly, there is no such thing as any identity or oneness in created objects, existing at different times, but what depends on *God's sovereign constitution.* And so it appears that the *objection* we are upon, made against a supposed divine constitution, whereby Adam and his posterity are viewed and treated as *one*, in the manner and for the purposes supposed, as if it were *not consistent with truth*, because no constitution can make those to be *one*, which are *not* one: I say, it appears that this objection is built on a false hypothesis: for it appears, that a *divine constitution* is the thing which *makes truth*, in affairs of this nature. The objection supposes, there is a oneness in created beings, whence qualities and relations are derived down from past existence, *distinct* from, and *prior* to any oneness that can be supposed to be founded on divine *constitution*. Which is demonstrably false, and sufficiently appears so from things conceded by the adversaries themselves: and therefore the objection wholly falls to the ground.

There are *various kinds* of identity and oneness, found among created things, by which they become one in *different manners*, *respects*, and *degrees*, and to *various purposes;* several of which differences have been observed; and every kind is ordered, regulated, and limited, in every respect, by *divine constitution*. Some things, existing in different times and places, are treated by their Creator as one in *one respect*, and others in *another;* some are united for *this communication*, and others for *that;* but all according to the *sovereign pleasure* of the fountain of all being and operation.

It appears particularly, from what has been said, that all one ness, by virtue whereof *pollution* and *guilt* from *past* wickednes are derived, depends entirely on a *divine establishment*. It is this and this only, that must account for guilt and an evil taint on an individual soul, in consequence of a crime committed twenty o forty years ago, remaining still, and even to the end of the worl and forever. It is this that must account for the continuance o any such thing, anywhere, as *consciousness* of acts that are pas and for the continuance of all *habits*, either good or bad: and o this depends every thing that can belong to *personal identity* And all communications, derivations, or continuation of quali ties, properties or relations, natural or moral, from what is *pas* as if the subject were *one*, depends on no other foundation.

And I am persuaded, no solid reason can be given, why God who constitutes all other created union or oneness, according t his pleasure, and for what purposes, communications, and effect he pleases, may not establish a constitution whereby the natura posterity of Adam, proceeding from him, much as the buds an branches from the stock or root of a tree, should be treated a *one* with him, for the derivation, either of righteousness, an communion in rewards, or of the loss of righteousness, and con sequent corruption and guilt.*

. . . .

*I appeal to such as are not wont to content themselves with judgin by a superficial appearance and view of things, but are habituated to ex amine things strictly and closely, that they may judge righteous judgmen whether on supposition that all mankind had *coexisted*, in the mann mentioned before, any good reason can be given, why their Creator migl not, if he had pleased, have established such a *union* between Adam an the rest of mankind, as was in the case supposed. Particularly, if it had bee the case, that Adam's posterity had actually, according to a law of natur somehow *grown out of him*, and yet remained *contiguous* and literally *unite to him*, as the branches to a tree, or the members of the body to the hea and had all, before the fall, existed together at the *same time*, though i *different places*, as the head and members are in different places: in this cas who can determine, that the author of nature might not, if it had please him, have established such a *union* between the root and branches of th complex being, as that all should constitute *one* moral whole; so that b the law of union, there should be a communion in each *moral alteratio* and that the heart of every *branch* should at the same moment participa with the heart of the *root*, be conformed to it, and concurring with it in a its affections and acts, and so jointly partaking in its state, as a *part* of th *same thing?* Why might not God, if he had pleased, have fixed such a kind of union as this, a union of the various parts of such a *moral whole*, as well as many other unions, which he has actually fixed, according to his sovereign pleasure? And if he might, by his sovereign constitution, have established such a union of the various branches of mankind, when existing in different *places*, I do not see why he might not also do the same, though they exist in different times. I know not why succession, or diversity of *time*, should make any such constituted union more unreasonable, than diversity of *place*. The only reason, why diversity of *time* can seem to make it unreasonable, is, that difference of time shows, there is no absolute identity of the things existing in those different times: but it shows this, I think, not at all more than the difference of the *place* of existence. [Edwards's note.]

DISSERTATION CONCERNING THE END FOR WHICH GOD CREATED THE WORLD

Section VII

Showing that the Ultimate End of the Creation of the World, is but one, and what that one End is

From what has been observed in the last section, it appears, that however the last end of the creation is spoken of in Scripture under various denominations; yet if the whole of what is said relating to this affair, be duly weighed, and one part compared with another, we shall have reason to think, that the design of the Spirit of God does not seem to be to represent God's ultimate end as manifold, but as one. For though it be signified by various names, yet they appear not to be names of different things, but various names involving each other in their meaning; either different names of the same thing, or names of several parts of one whole, or of the same whole viewed in various lights, or in its different respects and relations. For it appears that all that is ever spoken of in the Scripture as an ultimate end of God's works, is included in that one phrase, *the glory of God;* which is the name by which the last end of God's works is most commonly called in Scripture; and seems to be the name which most aptly signifies the thing.

The thing signified by that name, *the glory of God*, when spoken of as the supreme and ultimate end of the work of creation, and of all God's works, is the emanation and true external expression of God's internal glory and fulness; meaning by his fulness, what has already been explained. Or, in other words, God's internal glory extant, in a true and just exhibition, or external existence of it. It is confessed that there is a degree of obscurity in these definitions; but perhaps an obscurity which is unavoidable, through the imperfection of language, and words being less fitted to express things of so sublime a nature. And therefore the thing may possibly be better understood, by using many words and a variety of expressions, by a particular consideration of it, as it were by parts, than by any short definition.

There is included in this, the exercise of God's perfections to produce a proper effect, in opposition to their lying eternally dormant and ineffectual; as his power being eternally without any act or fruit of that power; his wisdom eternally ineffectual in any wise production, or prudent disposal of any thing, &c. The manifestation of his internal glory to created understandings. The communication of the infinite fulness of God to the creature. The creature's high esteem of God, love to God, and complacence and joy in God, and the proper exercises and expressions of these.

These at first view may appear to be entirely distinct things: but if we more closely consider the matter, they will all appear to be one thing, in a variety of views and relations. They are all but the emanation of God's glory; or the excellent brightness and fulness of the Divinity diffused, overflowing, and as it were, enlarged; or, in one word, existing *ad extra*. God's exercising his perfection to produce a proper effect, is not distinct from the emanation or communication of his fulness; for this is the effect, viz., his fulness communicated, and the producing this effect is the communication of his fulness; and there is nothing in this effectual exerting of God's perfection, but the emanation of God's internal glory. The emanation or communication is of the internal glory or fulness of God as it is. Now God's internal glory, as it is in God, is either in his understanding or will. The glory or fulness of his understanding, is his knowledge. The internal glory and fulness of God, which we must conceive of as having its special seat in his will, is his holiness and happiness. The whole of God's internal good or glory, is in these three things, viz., his infinite knowledge; his infinite virtue or holiness, and his infinite joy and happiness. Indeed there are a great many attributes in God, according to our way of conceiving or talking of them, but all may be reduced to these, or to the degree, circumstances and relations of these. We have no conception of God's power, different from the degree of these things, with a certain relation of them to effects. God's infinity is not so properly a distinct kind of good in God, but only expresses the *degree* of the good there is in him. So God's eternity is not a distinct good; but is the duration of good. His immutability is still the same good, with a negation of change. So that, as I said, the fulness of the Godhead is the fulness of his understanding, consisting in his knowledge, and the fulness of his will, consisting in his virtue and happiness. And therefore the eternal glory of God consists in the communication of these. The communication of his knowledge is chiefly in giving the knowledge of himself; for this is the knowledge in which the fulness of God's understanding chiefly consists. And thus we see how the manifestation of God's glory to created understandings, and their seeing and knowing it, is not distinct from an emanation or communication of God's fulness, but clearly implied in it. Again, the communication of God's virtue or holiness is principally in communicating the love of himself, (which appears by what has before been observed). And thus we see how, not only the creature's seeing and knowing God's excellence, but also supremely esteeming and loving him, belongs to the communication of God's fulness. And the communication of God's joy and happiness, consists chiefly in communicating to the creature, that happiness and joy, which consists in rejoicing in God, and in his glorious excellency; for in such joy God's own happiness does principally consist. And in these things, viz., in knowing God's excellency, loving God for it, and rejoicing in it; and in the exercise and expression of these, consists God's honor and praise; so that these are clearly implied in that glory of God, which consists in the emanation of his internal glory. And though we suppose all these things, which seem to be so various, are signified by that *glory*, which the Scripture speaks of as the last end of all God's works; yet it is manifest there is no greater, and no other variety in it, than in the internal and essential glory of God itself. God's internal glory is partly in his understanding, and partly in his will. And this internal glory, as seated in the will of God, implies both his holiness and his happiness; both are evidently God's glory, according to the use of the phrase. So that as God's external glory is only the emanation of his internal glory, this variety necessarily follows. And again, it hence appears that here there is no other variety or distinction, but what necessarily arises from the distinct faculties of the creature, to which the communication is made, as created in the image of God; even as having these two faculties of under-standing and will. God communicates himself to the under-standing of the creature, in giving him the knowledge of his glory; and to the will of the creature, in giving him holiness, consisting primarily in the love of God; and in giving the crea-ture happiness, chiefly consisting in joy in God. These are the sum of that emanation of divine fulness, called in Scripture *the glory of God*. The first part of this glory is called *truth*, the latter, *grace*. John i. 14, "We beheld his *glory*, the glory as of the only begotten of the Father, full of *grace* and *truth*."

Thus we see that the great and last end of God's works which is so variously expressed in Scripture, is indeed but *one;* and this *one* end is most properly and comprehensively called, THE GLORY OF GOD; by which name it is most commonly called in Scripture: and is fitly compared to an effulgence or emanation of light from a luminary, by which this glory of God is abundantly repre-sented in Scripture. Light is the external expression, exhibition and manifestation of the excellency of the luminary, of the sun for instance: it is the abundant, extensive emanation and com-munication of the fulness of the sun to innumerable beings that partake of it. It is by this that the sun itself is seen, and his glory beheld, and all other things are discovered; it is by a participa-tion of this communication from the sun, that surrounding ob-jects receive all their lustre, beauty and brightness. It is by this that all nature is quickened and receives life, comfort and joy. Light is abundantly used in Scripture to represent and signify these three things, knowledge, holiness and happiness. It is used to signify knowledge, or that manifestation and evidence by which knowledge is received, Psalm xix. 8, and cxix. 105, 130. Prov. vi. 23. Isaiah viii. 20, and ix. 2, and xxix. 18. Dan. v. 11. Eph. v. 13, "But all things that are reproved are made manifest by the light; for whatsoever doth make manifest, is light." And in other places of the New Testament innumerable.

It is used to signify virtue or moral good, Job xxv. 5, and other places. And it is abundantly used to signify comfort, joy and happiness, Esth. viii. 16, Job xviii. 18, and many other places.

What has been said may be sufficient to show how those things which are spoken of in Scripture as ultimate ends of God's works, though they may seem at first view to be distinct, are all plainly to be reduced to this one thing, viz., God's internal glory or fulness extant externally, or existing in its emanation. And though God in seeking this end, seeks the creature's good; yet therein appears his supreme regard to himself.

The emanation or communication of the divine fulness, consisting in the knowledge of God, love to God, and joy in God, has relation indeed both to God, and the creature; but it has relation to God as its fountain, as it is an emanation from God; and as the communication itself, or thing communicated, is something divine, something of God, something of his internal fulness, as the water in the stream is something of the fountain, and as the beams of the sun, are something of the sun. And again, they have relation to God, as they have respect to him as their object; for the knowledge communicated is the knowledge of God; and so God is the object of the knowledge, and the love communicated is the love of God; so God is the object of that love, and the happiness communicated is joy in God; and so he is the object of the joy communicated. In the creature's knowing, esteeming, loving, rejoicing in, and praising God, the glory of God is both exhibited and acknowledged; his fulness is received and returned. Here is both an *emanation* and *remanation*. The refulgence shines upon and into the creature, and is reflected back to the luminary. The beams of glory come from God, and are something of God, and are refunded back again to their original. So that the whole is *of* God, and *in* God, and *to* God, and God is the beginning, middle and end in this affair.

And though it be true that God has respect to the creature in these things; yet his respect to himself and to the creature in this matter, are not properly to be looked upon, as a double and divided respect of God's heart. What has been said in Chap. I.

Sect. 3, 4, may be sufficient to show this. Nevertheless, it may not be amiss here briefly to say a few things; though they are mostly implied in what has been said already.

When God was about to create the world, he had respect to that emanation of his glory, which is actually the consequence of the creation, just as it is with regard to all that belongs to it, both with regard to its relation to himself, and the creature. He had regard to it, as an emanation from himself, and a communication of himself, and as the thing communicated, in its nature returned to himself, as its final term. And he had regard to it also, as the emanation was to the creature, and as the thing communicated was in the creature, as its subject. And God had regard to it in this manner, as he had a supreme regard to himself, and value for his own infinite, internal glory. It was this value for himself that caused him to value and seek that his internal glory should flow forth from himself. It was from his value for his glorious perfections of wisdom and righteousness, &c., that he valued the proper exercise and effect of these perfections, in wise and righteous acts and effects. It was from his infinite value for his internal glory and fulness, that he valued the thing itself, which is communicated, which is something of the same, extant in the creature. Thus, because he infinitely values his own glory, consisting in the knowledge of himself, love to himself, and complacence and joy in himself; he therefore valued the image, communication or participation of these, in the creature. And it is because he values himself, that he delights in the knowledge, and love, and joy of the creature; as being himself the object of this knowledge, love and complacence. For it is the necessary consequence of the true esteem and love of any person or being (suppose a son or friend) that we should approve and value others' esteem of the same object, and disapprove and dislike the contrary. For the same reason is it the consequence of a being's esteem and love of himself, that he should approve of others' esteem and love of himself.

Thus it is easy to conceive, how God should seek the good of the creature, consisting in the creature's knowledge and holiness, and even his happiness, from a supreme regard to himself; as his

happiness arises from that which is an image and participation of
God's own beauty; and consists in the creature's exercising a
supreme regard to God, and complacence in him; in beholding
God's glory, in esteeming and loving it, and rejoicing in it, and
in his exercising and testifying love and supreme respect to God;
which is the same thing with the creature's exalting God as his
chief good, and making him his supreme end.

And though the emanation of God's fulness which God intended in the creation, and which actually is the consequence of
it, is to the creature as its object, and the creature is the subject
of the fulness communicated, and is the creature's good; and
was also regarded as such, when God sought it as the end of his
works; yet it does not necessarily follow, that even in so doing,
he did not make himself his end. It comes to the same thing.
God's respect to the creature's good, and his respect to himself,
is not a divided respect; but both are united in one, as the happiness of the creature aimed at, is happiness in union with himself.
The creature is no further happy with this happiness which God
makes his ultimate end, than he becomes one with God. The
more happiness the greater the union: when the happiness is perfect, the union is perfect. And as the happiness will be increasing to eternity, the union will become more and more strict and
perfect; nearer and more like to that between God the Father,
and the Son; who are so united, that their interest is perfectly
one. If the happiness of the creature be considered as it will be,
in the whole of the creature's eternal duration, with all the infinity of its progress, and infinite increase of nearness and union
to God; in this view the creature must be looked upon as united
to God in an infinite strictness.

If God has respect to something in the creature, which he
views as of everlasting duration, and as rising higher and higher
through that infinite duration, and that not with constantly
diminishing (but perhaps an increasing) celerity; then he has
respect to it, as in the whole, of infinite height, though there
never will be any particular time, when it can be said already to
have come to such a height.

Let the most perfect union with God be represented by something at an infinite height above us; and the eternally increasing union of the saints with God, by something that is ascending constantly towards that infinite height, moving upwards with a given velocity, and that is to continue thus to move to all eternity. God, who views the whole of this eternally increasing height, views it as an infinite height. And if he has respect to it, and makes it his end, as in the whole of it, he has respect to it as an infinite height, though the time will never come when it can be said it has already arrived at this infinite height.

God aims at that which the motion or progression which he causes, aims at, or tends to. If there be many things supposed to be so made and appointed, that by a constant and eternal motion, they all tend to a certain centre; then it appears that he who made them, and is the cause of their motion, aimed at that centre, that term of their motion, to which they eternally tend, and are eternally, as it were, striving after. And if God be this centre, then God aimed at himself. And herein it appears, that as he is the first author of their being and motion, so he is the last end, the final term, to which is their ultimate tendency and aim.

We may judge of the end that the Creator aimed at, in the being, nature and tendency he gives the creature, by the mark or term which they constantly aim at in their tendency and eternal progress; though the time will never come, when it can be said it is attained to, in the most absolutely perfect manner.

But if strictness of union to God be viewed as thus infinitely exalted, then the creature must be regarded as infinitely, nearly, and closely united to God. And viewed thus, their interest must be viewed as one with God's interest, and so is not regarded properly with a disjunct and separate, but an undivided respect. And as to any difficulty of reconciling God's not making the creature his ultimate end, with a respect properly distinct from a respect to himself, with his benevolence and free grace, and the creature's obligation to gratitude, the reader must be referred to Chap. I. Sec. 4, Object. 4, where this objection has been considered and answered at large.

If by reason of the strictness of the union of a man and his family, their interest may be looked upon as one, how much more one is the interest of Christ and his church (whose first union in heaven is unspeakably more perfect and exalted than that of an earthly father and his family), if they be considered with regard to their eternal and increasing union! Doubtless it may justly be esteemed as so much one, that it may be supposed to be aimed at and sought, not with a distinct and separate, but an undivided respect.

It is certain that what God aimed at in the creation of the world, was the good that would be the consequence of the creation, in the whole continuance of the thing created.

It is no solid objection against God's aiming at an infinitely perfect union of the creature with himself, that the particular time will never come when it can be said, the union is now infinitely perfect. God aims at satisfying justice in the eternal damnation of sinners; which will be satisfied by their damnation, considered no otherwise than with regard to its eternal duration. But yet there never will come that particular moment, when it can be said, that now justice is satisfied. But if this does not satisfy our modern freethinkers, who do not like the talk about satisfying justice with an infinite punishment; I suppose it will not be denied by any, that God, in glorifying the saints in heaven with eternal felicity, aims to satisfy his infinite grace or benevolence, by the bestowment of a good infinitely valuable because eternal; and yet there never will come the moment, when it can be said, that now this infinitely valuable good has been actually bestowed.

THE NATURE OF TRUE VIRTUE

CHAPTER I

Whatever controversies and variety of opinions there are about the nature of virtue, yet all (excepting some skeptics, who deny any real difference between virtue and vice) mean by it, something *beautiful*, or rather some kind of *beauty*, or excellency. —It is not *all* beauty, that is called virtue; for instance, not the beauty of a building, of a flower, or of the rainbow: but some beauty belonging to Beings that have *perception* and *will*.—It is not all beauty of *mankind*, that is called virtue; for instance, not the external beauty of the countenance, or shape, gracefulness of motion, or harmony of voice: but it is a beauty that has its original seat in the mind.—But yet perhaps not *every* thing that may be called a beauty of mind, is properly called virtue. There is a beauty of understanding and speculation. There is something in the ideas and conceptions of great philosophers and statesmen, that may be called beautiful; which is a different thing from what is most commonly meant by virtue. But virtue is the beauty of those qualities and acts of the mind, that are of a *moral* nature, i. e., such as are attended with desert or worthiness of *praise*, or *blame*. Things of this sort, it is generally agreed, so far as I know, are not any thing belonging merely to speculation; but to the *disposition* and *will*, or (to use a general word, I suppose commonly well understood) the *heart*. Therefore I suppose, I shall not depart from the common opinion, when I say, that virtue is the beauty of the qualities and exercises of the heart, or those actions which proceed from them. So that when it is inquired, What is the nature of true *virtue?*—this is the same as to inquire, what that is which renders any habit, disposition, or exercise of the heart truly *beautiful*. I use the phrase *true* virtue, and speak of things *truly* beautiful, because I suppose it will generally be allowed, that there is a distinction to be made between some things which are truly virtuous, and others which only seem to be virtuous, through a partial and imperfect view of things: that some actions and dispositions appear beautiful, if considered partially and superficially, or with regard to some things belonging to them, and in some of their circumstances and tendencies, which would appear otherwise in a more extensive and comprehensive view, wherein they are seen clearly in their whole nature and the extent of their connections in the universality of things.—There is a general and a particular beauty. By a *particular* beauty, I mean that by which a thing appears beautiful when considered only with regard to its connection with, and tendency to some particular things within a limited, and, as it were, a private sphere. And a *general* beauty is that by which a thing appears beautiful when viewed most perfectly, comprehensively and universally, with regard to all its tendencies, and its connections with every thing it stands related to. The former may be without and against the latter. As, a few notes in a tune, taken only by themselves, and in their relation to one another, may be harmonious; which when considered with respect to all the notes in the tune, or the entire series of sounds they are connected with, may be very discordant and disagreeable.—(Of which more afterwards.)—*That only*, therefore, is what I mean by true virtue, which is *that*, belonging to the *heart* of an intelligent Being, that is beautiful by a *general* beauty, or beautiful in a comprehensive view as it is in itself, and as related to every thing that it stands in connection with. And therefore when we are inquiring concerning the nature of true virtue, viz., wherein this true and general beauty of the heart does most essentially consist—this is my answer to the inquiry:

True virtue most essentially consists in benevolence to Being in general. Or perhaps to speak more accurately, it is that consent, propensity and union of heart to Being in general, that is immediately exercised in a general good will.

The things which were before observed of the nature of true virtue, naturally lead us to such a notion of it. If it has its seat in the heart, and is the general goodness and beauty of the disposition and exercise of that, in the most comprehensive view, considered with regard to its universal tendency, and as related to every thing that it stands in connection with; what can it consist in, but a consent and good will to Being in general?—Beauty does not consist in discord and dissent, but in consent and agreement. And if every intelligent Being is some way related to Being in general, and is a part of the universal system of existence; and so stands in connection with the whole; what can its general and true beauty be, but its union and consent with the great whole?

If any such thing can be supposed as a union of heart to some particular Being, or number of Beings, disposing it to benevolence to a private circle or system of Beings, which are but a small part of the whole; not implying a tendency to a union with the great system, and not at all inconsistent with enmity towards Being in general; this I suppose not to be of the nature of true virtue: although it may in some respects be good, and may appear beautiful in a confined and contracted view of things.—But of this more afterwards.

It is abundantly plain by the holy Scriptures, and generally allowed, not only by Christian divines, but by the more considerable deists, that virtue most essentially consists in love. And I suppose, it is owned by the most considerable writers, to consist in general love of benevolence, or kind affection: though it seems to me, the meaning of some in this affair is not sufficiently explained, which perhaps occasions some error or confusion in discourses on this subject.

When I say, true virtue consists in love to Being in general, I shall not be likely to be understood, that no one act of the mind or exercise of love is of the nature of true virtue, but what has Being in general, or the great system of universal existence, for its direct and immediate object: so that no exercise of love or kind affection to any one particular Being, that is but a small part of this whole, has any thing of the nature of true virtue. But, that the nature of true virtue consists in a disposition to benevolence towards Being in general. Though, from such a disposition may arise exercises of love to particular Beings, as objects are presented and occasions arise. No wonder, that he who is of a generally benevolent disposition, should be more disposed than another to have his heart moved with benevolent affection to particular persons, whom he is acquainted and conversant with, and from whom arise the greatest and most frequent occasions for exciting his benevolent temper. But my meaning is, that no affections towards particular persons or Beings are of the nature of true virtue, but such as arise from a generally benevolent temper, or from that habit or frame of mind, wherein consists a disposition to love Being in general.

And perhaps it is needless for me to give notice to my readers, that when I speak of an intelligent Being's having a heart united and benevolently disposed to Being in general, I thereby mean *intelligent* Being in general. Not inanimate things, or Beings that have no perception or will, which are not properly capable objects of benevolence.

Love is commonly distinguished into love of benevolence and love of complacence. Love of *benevolence* is that affection or propensity of the heart to any Being, which causes it to incline to its well being, or disposes it to desire and take pleasure in its happiness. And if I mistake not, it is agreeable to the common opinion, that beauty in the object is not always the ground of this propensity: but that there may be such a thing as benevolence, or a disposition to the welfare of those that are not considered as beautiful; unless mere existence be accounted a beauty. And benevolence or goodness in the Divine Being is generally supposed, not only to be prior to the beauty of many of its objects, but to their existence: so as to be the ground both of their existence and their beauty, rather than they the foundation of God's benevolence; as it is supposed that it is God's goodness which moved him to give them both Being and beauty. So that if all virtue primarily consists in that affection of heart to Being, which is exercised in benevolence, or an inclination to its good, then God's virtue is so extended as to include a propensity, not only to Being actually existing, and actually beautiful, but to possible Being, so as to incline him to give Being, beauty and happiness. But not now to insist particularly on this. What I would have observed at present, is, that it must be allowed, benevolence doth not necessarily presuppose beauty in its object.

What is commonly called love of *complacence*, presupposes beauty. For it is no other than delight in beauty; or complacence in the person or Being beloved for his beauty.

If virtue be the beauty of an intelligent Being, and virtue consists in love, then it is a plain inconsistence, to suppose that virtue primarily consists in any love to its object *for its beauty;* either in a love of complacence, which is delight in a Being for his beauty, or in a love of benevolence, that has the beauty of its object for its foundation. For that would be to suppose, that the beauty of intelligent beings primarily consists in love to beauty; or, that their virtue first of all consists in their love to virtue. Which is an inconsistence, and going in a circle. Because it makes virtue, or beauty of mind, the foundation or first motive of that love wherein virtue originally consists, or wherein the very first virtue consists; or, it supposes the first virtue to be the consequence and effect of virtue. So that virtue is originally the foundation and exciting cause of the very beginning or first Being of virtue. Which makes the first virtue, both the ground, and the consequence, both cause and effect of itself. Doubtless virtue primarily consists in something else besides any effect or consequence of virtue. If virtue consists primarily in love to virtue, then virtue, the thing loved, is the love of virtue: so that virtue must consist in the love of the love of virtue. And if it be inquired, what that virtue is, which virtue consists in the love of the love of, it must be answered, it is the love of virtue. So that there must be the love of the love of the love of virtue, and so on *in infinitum*. For there is no end of going back in a circle. We never come to any beginning, or foundation. For it is without beginning and hangs on nothing.

Therefore if the essence of virtue or beauty of mind lies in love, or a disposition to love, it must primarily consist in something *different* both from complacence, which is a delight in beauty, and also from any benevolence that has the beauty of its object for its foundation. Because it is absurd, to say that virtue is primarily and first of all the consequence of itself. For this makes virtue primarily prior to itself.

Nor can virtue primarily consist in *gratitude;* or one Being's benevolence to another for his benevolence to him. Because this implies the same inconsistence. For it supposes a benevolence prior to gratitude, that is the cause of gratitude. Therefore the first benevolence, or that benevolence which has none prior to it, cannot be gratitude.

Therefore there is room left for no other conclusion than that the primary object of virtuous love is Being, simply considered; or, that true virtue primarily consists, not in love to any particular Beings, because of their virtue or beauty, nor in gratitude, because they love us; but in a propensity and union of heart to Being simply considered; exciting absolute benevolence (if I may so call it) to Being in general.—I say, true virtue *primarily* consists in this. For I am far from asserting that there is no true virtue in any other love than this absolute benevolence. But I would express what appears to me to be the truth on this subject, in the following particulars.

The *first* object of a virtuous benevolence is *Being*, simply considered: and if Being, *simply* considered, be its object, then Being *in general* is its object; and the thing it has an ultimate propensity to, is the *highest good* of Being in general. And it will seek the good of every *individual* Being unless it be conceived as not consistent with the highest good of Being in general. In which case the good of a particular Being, or some Beings, may be given up for the sake of the highest good of Being in general. And particularly if there be any Being that is looked upon as statedly and irreclaimably opposite and an enemy to Being in general, then consent and adherence to Being in general will induce the truly virtuous heart to forsake that Being, and to oppose it.

And further, if Being, simply considered, be the first object of a truly virtuous benevolence, then that Being who has *most* of Being, or has the greatest share of existence, other things being equal, so far as such a Being is exhibited to our faculties or set in our view, will have the *greatest* share of the propensity and benevolent affection of the heart. I say, *other things being equal*, especially because there is a *secondary* object of virtuous benevolence, that I shall take notice of presently. Which is one thing that must be considered as the ground or motive to a purely virtuous benevolence. Pure benevolence in its first exercise is nothing else but Being's uniting consent, or propensity to Being; appearing true and pure by its extending to Being in general, and inclining to the general highest good, and to each Being, whose welfare is consistent with the highest general good, in proportion to the degree of *existence** understood, other things being equal.

The *second* object of a virtuous propensity of heart is *benevolent* Being. A secondary ground of pure benevolence is virtuous benevolence itself in its object. When any one under the influence of general benevolence, sees another Being possessed of the like general benevolence, this attaches his heart to him, and draws forth greater love to him, than merely his having existence: because so far as the Being beloved has love to Being in general, so far his own Being is, as it were, enlarged, extends to, and in some sort comprehends, Being in general: and therefore he that is governed by love to Being in general must of necessity have complacence in him, and the greater degree of benevolence to him, as it were out of gratitude to him for his love to general existence, that his own heart is extended and united to, and so looks on its interest as its own. It is because his heart is thus united to Being in general, that he looks on a benevolent propensity to Being in general, wherever he sees it, as the beauty of the Being in whom it is; an excellency, that renders him worthy of esteem, complacence, and the greater good will.

* I say, in proportion to the degree of *existence*, because one Being may have more *existence* than another, as he may be *greater* than another. That which is *great*, has more existence, and is further from nothing, than that which is *little*. One Being may have every thing positive belonging to it, or every thing which goes to its positive existence (in opposition to defect) in a higher degree than another; or a greater capacity and power, greater understanding, every faculty and every positive quality in a higher degree. An *archangel* must be supposed to have more existence, and to be every way further removed from *nonenity*, than a *worm*, or a *flea*. [Edwards's note.]

But several things may be noted more particularly concerning this secondary ground of a truly virtuous love.

1. That loving a Being on *this ground* necessarily arises from pure benevolence to Being *in general*, and comes to the same thing. For he that has a simple and pure good will to general entity or existence, must love that temper in others, that agrees and conspires with itself. A spirit of consent to Being must agree with consent to Being. That which truly and sincerely seeks the good of others, must approve of, and love, that which joins with him in seeking the good of others.

2. This which has been now mentioned as a secondary ground of virtuous love, is the thing wherein true moral or spiritual *beauty* primarily consists. Yea, spiritual beauty consists wholly in this, and the various qualities and exercises of mind which proceed from it, and the external actions which proceed from these internal qualities and exercises. And in these things consists all true *virtue*, viz., in this love of Being, and the qualities and acts which arise from it.

3. As all spiritual beauty lies in these virtuous principles and acts, so it is primarily *on this account* they are beautiful, *viz.*, that they imply *consent* and *union* with Being *in general*. This is the primary and most essential Beauty of every thing that can justly be called by the name of virtue, or is any moral excellency in the eye of one that has a perfect view of things. I say, the *primary* and *most essential* beauty—because there is a secondary and inferior sort of beauty; which I shall take notice of afterwards.

4. This spiritual beauty, that is but a *secondary* ground of a virtuous benevolence, is the ground, not only of benevolence, but *complacence*, and is the *primary* ground of the latter; that is, when the complacence is truly virtuous. Love to us in particular, and kindness received, may be a secondary ground. But this is the primary objective foundation of it.

5. It must be noted, that the *degree* of the *amiableness* or *valuableness* of true virtue, primarily consisting in consent and a benevolent propensity of heart to Being in general, in the eyes of one that is influenced by such a spirit, is not in the *simple* proportion of the degree of benevolent affection seen, but in a propor-

tion *compounded* of the greatness of the benevolent Being or the degree of *Being* and the degree of *benevolence*. One that loves Being in general, will necessarily value good will to Being in general, wherever he sees it. But if he sees the same benevolence in *two* Beings, he will value it *more* in two, than in one only. Because it is a greater thing, more favorable to Being in general, to have two Beings to favor it, than only one of them. For there is more Being that favors Being: both together having more Being than one alone. So, if one Being be as great as two, has as much existence as both together, and has the same degree of general benevolence, it is more favorable to Being in general than if there were general benevolence in a Being that had but half that share of existence. As a large quantity of gold, with the same degree of preciousness, i. e. with the same excellent quality of matter, is more valuable than a small quantity of the same metal.

6. It is impossible that any one should truly *relish* this beauty, consisting in general benevolence, who has *not* that temper himself. I have observed, that if any Being is possessed of such a temper, he will unavoidably be pleased with the same temper in another. And it may in like manner be demonstrated, that it is such a spirit, and nothing else, which will relish such a spirit. For if a Being, destitute of benevolence, should love benevolence to Being in general, it would prize and seek that which it had no value for. Because to love an inclination to the good of Being in general, would imply a loving and prizing the good of Being in general. For how should one love and value a *disposition* to a thing, or a *tendency to promote* a thing, and for that very reason, because it tends to promote it—when the *thing* itself is what he is regardless of, and has no value for, nor desires to have promoted.

. . . .

CHAPTER IV

OF SELF-LOVE, AND ITS VARIOUS INFLUENCE, TO CAUSE LOVE TO
OTHERS, OR THE CONTRARY

Many assert, that all love arises from self-love. In order to
determine this point, it should be clearly ascertained what is
meant by self-love.

Self-love, I think, is generally defined—a man's love of his
own happiness. Which is short, and may be thought very plain:
but indeed is an ambiguous definition, as the pronoun *his own*, is
equivocal, and liable to be taken in two very different senses.
For a man's *own happiness* may either be taken universally, for
all the happiness and pleasure which the mind is in any regard
the subject of, or whatever is grateful and pleasing to men; or it
may be taken for the pleasure a man takes in his own proper,
private, and separate good.—And so, *self-love* may be taken two
ways.

1. Self-love may be taken for the same as his loving whatsoever is grateful or pleasing to him. Which comes only to this,
that self-love is a man's liking, and being suited and pleased in
that which he likes, and which pleases him; or, that it is a man's
loving what he loves. For whatever a man loves, that thing is
grateful and pleasing to him, whether that be his own peculiar
happiness, or the happiness of others. And if this be all that they
mean by self-love, no wonder they suppose that all love may be
resolved into self-love. For it is undoubtedly true, that whatever a man loves, his love may be resolved into his loving what
he loves—if that be proper speaking. If by self-love is meant
nothing else but a man's loving what is grateful or pleasing to
him, and being averse to what is disagreeable, this is calling *that*
self-love, which is only a general capacity of loving, or hating;
or a capacity of being either pleased or displeased; which is the
same thing as a man's having a faculty of will. For if nothing
could be either pleasing or displeasing, agreeable or disagreeable
to a man, then he could incline to nothing, and will nothing.
But if he is capable of having inclination, will and choice, then
what he inclines to, and chooses, is grateful to him; whatever

that be, whether it be his own private good, the good of his neighbors, or the glory of God. And so far as it is grateful or pleasing to him, so far it is a part of his pleasure, good, or happiness.

But if this be what is meant by self-love, there is an impropriety and absurdity even in the putting of the question, Whether all our love, or our love to each particular object of our love, does not arise from self-love? For that would be the same as to inquire, Whether the reason why our love is fixed on such and such particular objects, is not, that we have a capacity of loving some things? This may be a general reason why men love or hate any thing at all; and therein differ from stones and trees, which love nothing, and hate nothing. But it can never be a reason why men's love is placed on such and such objects. That a man, in general, loves and is pleased with happiness, or (which is the same thing) has a capacity of enjoying happiness, cannot be the reason why such and such things become his happiness: as for instance, why the good of his neighbor, or the happiness and glory of God, is grateful and pleasing to him, and so becomes a part of his happiness.

Or if what they mean, who say that all love comes from self-love, be not, that our loving such and such particular persons and things, arises from our love to happiness in general, but from a love to love our own happiness, which consists in these objects; so the reason why we love benevolence to our friends, or neighbors, is, because we love our happiness, consisting in their happiness, which we take pleasure in;—still the notion is absurd. For here the effect is made the cause of that, of which it is the effect: our happiness, consisting in the happiness of the person beloved, is made the cause of our love to that person. Whereas, the truth plainly is, that our love to the person is the cause of our delighting, or being happy in his happiness. How comes our happiness to consist in the happiness of such as we love, but by our hearts being first united to them in affection, so that we, as it were, look on them as ourselves, and so on their happiness as our own?

Men who have benevolence to others, have pleasure when

they see others' happiness, because seeing their happiness grati-
fies some inclination that was in their hearts before.—They before inclined to their happiness; which was by benevolence or
good will; and therefore when they see their happiness, their
inclination is suited, and they are pleased. But the Being of
inclinations and appetites is prior to any pleasure in gratifying
these appetites.

2. Self-love, as the phrase is used in common speech, most
commonly signifies a man's regard to his confined *private self*,
or love to himself with respect to his *private interest*.

By *private* interest I mean that which most immediately consists in those pleasures, or pains, that are *personal*. For there is
a comfort, and a grief, that some have in others' pleasures or
pains; which are in others originally, but are derived to them,
or in some measure become theirs, by virtue of a benevolent
union of heart with others. And there are other pleasures and
pains that are originally our own, and not what we have by
such a participation with others. Which consist in preceptions
agreeable, or contrary, to certain personal inclinations implanted
in our nature; such as the sensitive appetites and aversions.
Such also is the disposition or the determination of the mind to
be pleased with external beauty, and with all inferior secondary
beauty, consisting in uniformity, proportion, &c., whether in
things external or internal, and to dislike the contrary deformity.
Such also is the natural disposition in men to be pleased in a
perception of their being the objects of the honor and love of
others, and displeased with others' hatred and contempt. For
pleasures and uneasinesses of this kind are doubtless as much
owing to an immediate determination of the mind by a fixed
law of our nature, as any of the pleasures or pains of external
sense. And these pleasures are properly of the private and personal kind; being not by any participation of the happiness or
sorrow of others, through benevolence. It is evidently mere
self-love, that appears in this disposition. It is easy to see, that
a man's love to himself will make him love love to himself,
and hate hatred to himself. And as God has constituted our
nature, self-love is exercised in no one disposition more than in

this. Men, probably, are capable of much more pleasure and pain through this determination of the mind, than by any other personal inclination, or aversion, whatsoever. Though perhaps we do not so very often see instances of extreme suffering by this means, as by some others, yet we often see evidences of men's dreading the contempt of others more than death; and by such instances many conceive something what men would suffer, if universally hated and despised; and many reasonably infer something of the greatness of the misery, that would arise under a sense of universal abhorrence, in a great view of intelligent Being in general, or in a clear view of the Deity, as incomprehensibly and immensely great, so that all other Beings are as nothing and vanity—together with a sense of his immediate continual presence, and an infinite concern with him and dependence upon him—and living constantly in the midst of most clear and strong evidences and manifestations of his hatred and contempt and wrath.

But to return.—These things may be sufficient to explain what I mean by private interest; in regard to which, self-love, most properly so called, is immediately exercised.

And here I would observe, that if we take self-love in this sense, so love to some others may truly be the effect of self-love; i. e., according to the common method and order, which is maintained in the laws of nature. For no created thing has power to produce an effect any otherwise than by virtue of the laws of nature. Thus that a man should love those that are of his party, when there are different parties contending one with another; and that are warmly engaged on his side, and promote his interest—this is the natural consequence of a private self-love. Indeed there is no metaphysical necessity, in the nature of things, that because a man loves himself, and regards his own interest, he therefore should love those that love him, and promote his interest, i. e., to suppose it to be otherwise, implies no contradiction. It will not follow from any absolute metaphysical necessity, that because bodies have solidity, cohesion, and gravitation towards the centre of the earth, therefore a weight suspended on the beam of a balance should have greater power to counterbalance a weight on the other side, when at a distance from the fulcrum, than when it is near. It implies no contradiction, that it should be otherwise: but only as it contradicts that beautiful proportion and harmony, which the author of nature observes in the laws of nature he has established. Neither is there any absolute necessity, the contrary implying a contradiction, that because there is an internal mutual attraction of the parts of the earth, or any other sphere, whereby the whole becomes one solid coherent body, therefore other bodies that are around it, should also be attracted by it, and those that are nearest, be attracted most. But according to the order and proportion generally observed in the laws of nature, one of these effects is connected with the other, so that it is justly looked upon as the same power of attraction in the globe of the earth, which draws bodies about the earth towards its centre, with that which attracts the parts of the earth themselves one to another; only exerted under different circumstances. By a like order of nature, a man's love to those that love him, is no more than a certain expression or effect of self-love. No other principle is needful in order to the effect, if nothing intervenes to countervail the natural tendency of self-love. Therefore there is no more true virtue in a man's thus loving his friends merely from self-love, than there is in self-love itself, the principle from whence it proceeds. So, a man's being disposed to hate those that hate him, or to resent injuries done him, arises from self-love in like manner as the loving those that love us, and being thankful for kindness shown us.

But it is said by some, that it is apparent, there is some other principle concerned in exciting the passions of gratitude and anger, besides self-love, viz., a moral sense, or sense of moral beauty and deformity, determining the minds of all mankind to approve of, and be pleased with virtue, and to disapprove of vice, and behold it with displicence; and that their seeing or supposing this moral beauty or deformity, in the kindness of a benefactor, or opposition of an adversary, is the occasion of these affections of gratitude or anger. Otherwise, why are not these affections excited in us towards inanimate things, that do us good, or hurt? Why do we not experience gratitude to a garden, or fruitful field? And why are we not angry with a tempest, or blasting mildew, or an overflowing stream? We are very differently affected towards those that do us good from the virtue of generosity, or hurt us from the vice of envy and malice, than towards things that hurt or help us, which are destitute of reason and will. Now concerning this, I would make several remarks.

1. Those who thus argue, that gratitude and anger cannot proceed from self-love, might argue in the same way, and with equal reason, that neither can these affections arise from love to others; which is contrary to their own scheme.

They say that the reason why we are affected with gratitude and anger towards men, rather than things without life, is moral sense; which they say, is the effect of that principle of benevolence or love to others, or love to the public, which is naturally in the hearts of all mankind. But now I might say, according to their own way of arguing, gratitude and anger cannot arise from love to others, or love to the public, or any sense of mind that is the fruit of public affection. For how differently are we affected towards those that do good or hurt to the public from understanding and will, and from a general public spirit, or public motive.—I say, how differently affected are we towards these, from what we are towards such inanimate things as the sun and the clouds, that do good to the public by enlightening and enlivening beams and refreshing showers; or mildew, and an overflowing stream, that does hurt to the public, by destroying the fruits of the earth? Yea, if such a kind of argument be good, it will prove that gratitude and anger cannot arise from the united influence of self-love, and public love, or moral sense arising from the public affection. For, if so, why are we not affected towards inanimate things, that are beneficial or injurious both to us and the public, in the same manner as to them that are profitable or hurtful to both on choice and design, and from benevolence, or malice?

2. On the supposition of its being indeed so, that men love those who love them, and are angry with those who hate them,

from the natural influence of self-love; it is not at all strange that the author of nature, who observes order, uniformity and harmony in establishing its laws, should so order that it should be natural for self-love to cause the mind to be affected differently towards exceedingly different objects; and that it should cause our heart to extend itself in one manner towards inanimate things, which gratify self-love, without sense or will, and in another manner towards Beings which we look upon as having understanding and will, like ourselves, and exerting these faculties in our favor, and promoting our interest from love to us. No wonder, seeing we love ourselves, that it should be natural to us to extend something of that same kind of love which we have for ourselves, to them who are the same kind of Beings as ourselves, and comply with the inclinations of our self-love, by expressing the same sort of love towards us.

3. If we should allow that to be universal, that in gratitude and anger there is the exercise of some kind of moral sense (as it is granted, there is something that may be so called). All the moral sense, that is essential to those affections, is a sense of DESERT; which is to be referred to that sense of *justice*, before spoken of, consisting in an apprehension of that secondary kind of beauty, that lies in uniformity and proportion: which solves all the difficulty in the objection.—This, or some appearance of it to a narrow private view, indeed attends all anger and gratitude. Others' love and kindness to us, or their ill will and injuriousness, appears to us to *deserve* our love, or our resentment. Or, in other words, it seems to us no other than *just*, that as they love us, and do us good, we also should love them, and do them good. And so it seems *just*, that when others' hearts oppose us, and they from their hearts do us hurt, our hearts should oppose them, and that we should desire they themselves may suffer in like manner as we have suffered; i. e. there appears to us to be a natural agreement, proportion, and adjustment between these things. Which is indeed a kind of moral sense or sense of a beauty in moral things. But as was before shown, it is a moral sense of a *secondary* kind, and is entirely different from a sense or relish of the original essential

beauty of true virtue; and may be without any principle of true virtue in the heart. Therefore doubtless it is a great *mistake* in any to suppose, all that moral sense which appears and is exercised in a sense of *desert*, is the same thing as a love of virtue, or a disposition and determination of mind to be pleased with true virtuous beauty, consisting in public benevolence. Which may be further confirmed, if it be considered that even with respect to a sense of *justice* or *desert*, consisting in uniformity [and agreement between others' actions towards us, and our actions towards them, in a way of well doing, or of ill doing] it is not absolutely necessary to the being of these passions of gratitude and anger, that there should be any notion of justice in them, in any public or general view of things;—as will appear by what shall be next observed.

4. Those authors who hold that that moral sense which is natural to all mankind, consists in a natural relish of the beauty of virtue, and so arises from a principle of true virtue implanted by nature in the hearts of all—they hold that true virtue consists in *public benevolence*. Therefore, if the affections of gratitude and anger necessarily imply such a moral sense as they suppose, then these affections imply some delight in the public good, and an aversion of the mind to public evil. And if this were so, then every time any man feels anger for opposition he meets with, or gratitude for any favor, there must be at least a supposition of a tendency to public injury in that opposition, and a tendency to public benefit in the favor that excites his gratitude. But how far is this from being true? As, in such instances as these, which, I presume, none will deny to be possible, or unlike to any thing that happens among mankind. A ship's crew enter into a conspiracy against the master, to murder him, and run away with the ship and turn pirates; but before they bring their matters to a ripeness for execution, one of them repents and opens the whole design; whereupon the rest are apprehended and brought to justice. The crew are enraged with him that has betrayed them, and earnestly seek opportunity to revenge themselves upon him.—And for an instance of gratitude, a gang of robbers that have long infested the

neighboring country, have a particular house whither they resort, and where they meet from time to time, to divide their booty or prey, and hold their consultations for carrying on their pernicious designs. The magistrates and officers of the country, after many fruitless endeavors to discover their secret haunt and place of resort, at length by some means are well informed where it is, and are prepared with sufficient force to surprise them, and seize them all, at the place of rendezvous, at an hour appointed when they understand they will all be there. A little before the arrival of the appointed hour, while the officers with their bands are approaching, some person is so kind to these robbers as to give them notice of their danger, so as just to give them opportunity to escape. They are thankful to him, and give him a handful of money for his kindness.—Now in such instances, I think it is plain, that there is no supposition of a public injury in that which is the occasion of their *anger;* yea, they know the contrary. Nor is there any supposition of public good in that which excites their gratitude; neither has public benevolence, or moral sense, consisting in a determination to approve of what is for the public good, any influence at all in the affair. And though there be some affection, besides a sense of uniformity and proportion, that has influence in such anger and gratitude, it is not public affection or benevolence, but private affection; yea, that affection which is to the highest degree private, consisting in a man's love of his own person.

5. The passion of *anger*, in particular, seems to have been unluckily chosen as a medium to prove a sense and determination to delight in virtue, consisting in benevolence, natural to all mankind.

For, if that moral sense which is exercised in anger, were that which arose from a benevolent temper of heart, being no other than a sense or relish of the beauty of benevolence, one would think a disposition to anger should increase, at least in some proportion, as a man had more of a sweet, benign, and benevolent temper; which seems something disagreeable to reason, as well as contrary to experience, which shows that the less men have of benevolence, and the more they have of a contrary temper, the more are they disposed to anger and deep resentment of injuries.

And though *gratitude* be that which many speak of as a certain noble principle of virtue, which God has implanted in the hearts of all mankind; and though it be true, there is a gratitude, that is truly virtuous, and the want of gratitude or an ungrateful temper, is truly vicious, and argues an abominable depravity of heart (as I may have particular occasion to show afterwards) yet, I think what has been observed, may serve to convince such as impartially consider it, not only that not all anger, or hating those who hate us, but also that not all gratitude, or loving those who love us, arises from a truly virtuous benevolence of heart.

Another sort of affections, which may be properly referred to self-love, as their source, and which might be expected to be the fruit of it, according to the general analogy of nature's laws, are affections to such as are near to us by the ties of nature; that we look upon as those whose Beings we have been the occasions of, and that we have a very peculiar propriety in, and whose circumstances, even from the first beginning of their existence, do many ways lead them, as it were, necessarily, to a high esteem of us, and to treat us with great dependence, submission and compliance; and whom the constitution of the world makes to be united in interest, and accordingly to act as one in innumerable affairs, with a communion in each other's affections, desires, cares, friendships, enmities, and pursuits. Which is the cause of men's affection to their children. And in like manner self-love will also beget in a man some degree of affections, towards others, with whom he has connection in any degree parallel. As to the opinion of those that ascribe the natural affection there is between parents and children, to a particular *instinct* of nature, I shall take notice of it afterwards.

And as men may love persons and things from self-love, so may love to qualities and characters arise from the same source. Some represent as though there were need of a great degree of metaphysical refining to make it out, that men approve of others from self-love, whom they hear of at a distance, or read of in history, or see represented on the stage, from whom they expect no profit or advantage. But perhaps it is not considered, that what we approve of in the first place is the character, and from the character we approve the person; and is it a strange thing, that men should, from self-love, like a temper or character which in its nature and tendency falls in with the nature and tendency of self-love; and which, we know by experience and self-evidence, without metaphysical refining, in the general, tends to men's pleasure and benefit? And on the contrary, should dislike what they see tends to men's pain and misery? Is there need of a great degree of subtilty and abstraction, to make it out, that a child, which has heard and seen much, strongly to fix an idea of the pernicious deadly nature of the rattlesnake, should have aversion to that species or form, from self-love; so as to have a degree of this aversion and disgust excited by seeing even the picture of that animal? And that from the same self-love it should be pleased and entertained with a lively figure and representation of some pleasant fruit which it has often tasted the sweetness of? Or, with the image of some bird, which it has always been told, is innocent, and whose pleasant singing it has often been entertained with? Though the child neither fears being bitten by the picture of the snake, nor expects to eat of the painted fruit, or to hear the figure of the bird sing. I suppose none will think it difficult to allow, that such an approbation or disgust of a child may be accounted for from its natural delight in the pleasures of taste and hearing, and its aversion to pain and death, through self-love, together with the habitual connection of these agreeable or terrible ideas with the form and qualities of these objects, the ideas of which are impressed on the mind of the child by their images.

And where is the difficulty of allowing, that a child or man may hate the general character of a spiteful and malicious man, for the like reason, as he hates the general nature of a serpent; knowing, from reason, instruction and experience, that malice in men is pernicious to mankind, as well as spite or poison in a serpent? And if a man may, from self-love, disapprove the vices of malice, envy, and others of that sort, which naturally tend to the hurt of mankind, why may he not from the same principle approve the contrary virtues of meekness, peaceableness, benevolence, charity, generosity, justice, and the social virtues in general; which he as easily and clearly knows, naturally tend to the good of mankind?

It is undoubtedly true that some have a love to these virtues from a higher principle. But yet I think it as certainly true that there is generally in mankind a sort of approbation of them, which arises from self-love.

Besides what has been already said, the same thing further appears from this; that men commonly are most affected towards, and do most highly approve, those virtues which agree with their interest most, according to their various conditions in life. We see that persons of low condition are especially enamored with a condescending, accessible, affable temper in the great; not only in those whose condescension has been exercised towards themselves; but they will be peculiarly taken with such a character when they have accounts of it from others, or when they meet with it in history or even in romance. The poor will most highly approve and commend liberality. The weaker sex, who especially need assistance and protection, will peculiarly esteem and applaud fortitude and generosity in those of the other sex, they read or hear of, or have represented to them on a stage.

As I think it plain from what has been observed, that men may approve and be disposed to commend a benevolent temper, from self-love, so the higher the degree of benevolence is, the more may they approve of it. Which will account for some kind of approbation, from this principle, even of love to enemies, viz., as a man's loving his enemies is an evidence of a high degree of benevolence of temper;—the degree of it appearing from the obstacles it overcomes.

And it may be here observed, that the consideration of the tendency and influence of self-love may show, how men in general may approve of *justice* from another ground, besides that approbation of the secondary beauty there is in uniformity and proportion, which is natural to all. Men from their infancy see the necessity of it, not only that it is necessary for others, or for human society; but they find the necessity of it for themselves, in instances that continually occur; which tends to prejudice them in its favor, and to fix an habitual approbation of it from self-love.

And again, that forementioned approbation of justice and desert arising from a sense of the beauty of natural agreement and proportion, will have a kind of reflex, and indirect influence to cause men to approve benevolence, and disapprove malice; as men see that he who hates and injures others, deserves to be hated and punished, and that he who is benevolent, and loves others, and does them good, deserves himself also to be loved and rewarded by others, as they see the natural congruity or agreement and mutual adaptedness of these things. And having always seen this, malevolence becomes habitually connected in the mind with the idea of being hated and punished, which is disagreeable to self-love; and the idea of benevolence is habitually connected and associated with the idea of being loved and rewarded by others, which is grateful to self-love. And by virtue of this association of ideas, benevolence itself becomes grateful, and the contrary displeasing.

Some vices may become in a degree odious by the influence of self-love, through an habitual connection of ideas of contempt with it; contempt being what self-love abhors. So it may often be with drunkenness, gluttony, sottishness, cowardice, sloth, niggardliness. The idea of contempt becomes associated with the idea of such vices, both because we are used to observe that those things are commonly objects of contempt, and also find that they excite contempt, in ourselves.—Some of them appear marks of littleness, i. e., of small abilities, and weakness of mind, and insufficiency for any considerable effects among mankind.—By others, men's influence is contracted into a narrow sphere, and by such means persons become of less importance, and more insignificant among mankind. And things of little importance are naturally little accounted of.—And some of these ill qualities are such as mankind find it their interest to treat with contempt, as they are very hurtful to human society.

There are no particular moral virtues whatsoever, but what in some or other of these ways, and most of them in several of these ways, come to have some kind of approbation from self-love, without the influence of a truly virtuous principle; nor any particular vices, but what by the same means meet with some disapprobation.

This kind of approbation and dislike, through the joint influence of self-love and association of ideas, is in very many vastly heightened by education; as this is the means of a strong, close, and almost irrefragable association, in innumerable instances, of ideas which have no connection any other way than by education; and of greatly strengthening that association, or connection, which persons are led into by other means; as any one would be convinced, perhaps more effectually than in most other ways, if they had opportunity of any considerable acquaintance with *American* savages and their children.

COVENANT OF REDEMPTION:
"EXCELLENCY OF CHRIST"

When we behold a beautiful body, a lovely proportion and beautiful harmony of features, delightful airs of countenance and voice, and sweet motions and gestures, we are charmed with it, not under the notion of a corporeal but a mental beauty. For if there could be a statue that should have exactly the same, that could be made to have the same sounds and the same motions precisely, we should not be so delighted with it, we should not fall entirely in love with the image, if we knew certainly that it had no perception or understanding. The reason is, we are apt to look upon this agreeableness, those airs, to be emanations of perfections of the mind, and immediate effects of internal purity and sweetness. Especially it is so, when we love the person for the airs of voice, countenance, and gesture, which have much greater power upon us than barely colours and proportion of dimensions. And it is certainly because there is an analogy between such a countenance and such airs and those excellencies of the mind,—a sort of I know not what in them that is agreeable, and does consent with such mental perfections; so that we cannot think of such habitudes of mind without having an idea of them at the same time. Nor can it be only from custom, for the same dispositions and actings of mind naturally beget such kind of airs of countenance and gesture; otherwise they never would have come into custom. I speak not here of the ceremonies of conversation and behavior, but of those simple and natural motions and airs. So it appears, because the same habitudes and actings of mind do beget (airs and movements) in general the same amongst all nations, in all ages.

And there is really likewise an analogy or consent between the beauty of the skies, trees, fields, flowers, etc., and spiritual excellencies, though the agreement be more hid, and require a more discerning, feeling mind to perceive it, than the other. Those have their airs, too, as well as the body and countenance of man, which have a strange kind of agreement with such mental beauties. This makes it natural in such frames of mind to think of them and fancy ourselves in the midst of them. Thus there seem to be love and complacency in flowers and be-spangled meadows; this makes lovers so much delight in them. So there is a rejoicing in the green trees and fields, and majesty in thunder beyond all other noises whatever.

Now we have shown that the Son of God created the world for this very end, to communicate Himself in an image of His own excellency. He communicates Himself, properly, only to spirits, and they only are capable of being proper images of His excellency, for they only are properly *beings*, as we have shown. Yet He communicates a sort of a shadow, or glimpse, of His excellencies to bodies, which, as we have shown, are but the shadows of beings, and not real beings. He, who, by His im-mediate influence, gives being every moment, and, by His Spirit, actuates the world, because He inclines to communicate Himself and His excellencies, doth doubtless communicate His excellency to bodies, as far as there is any consent or analogy. And the beauty of face and sweet airs in men are not always the effect of the corresponding excellencies of mind; yet the beauties of nature are really emanations or shadows of the excellencies of the Son of God.

So that, when we are delighted with flowery meadows, and gentle breezes of wind, we may consider that we see only the emanations of the sweet benevolence of Jesus Christ. When we behold the fragrant rose and lily, we see His love and purity. So the green trees, and fields, and singing of birds are the em-anations of His infinite joy and benignity. The easiness and naturalness of trees and vines are shadows of His beauty and loveliness. The crystal rivers and murmuring streams are the footsteps of His favor, grace, and beauty. When we behold the light and brightness of the sun, the golden edges of an evening cloud, or the beauteous bow, we behold the adumbra-tions of His glory and goodness; and, in the blue sky, of His mildness and gentleness. There are also many things wherein we may behold His awful majesty, in the sun in his strength, in comets, in thunder, in the hovering thunder-clouds, in ragged rocks, and the brows of mountains. That beauteous light with which the world is filled in a clear day, is a lively shadow of His spotless holiness, and happiness and delight in communicating Himself; and doubtless this is a reason that Christ is compared so often to those things, and called by their names, as the sun of Righteousness, the morning star, the rose of Sharon, and lily of the valley, the apple tree amongst the trees of the wood, a bundle of myrrh, a roe, or a young hart. By this we may discover the beauty of many of those metaphors and similes, which to an unphilosophical person do seem so uncouth.

In like manner, when we behold the beauty of man's body, in its perfection, we still see like emanations of Christ's divine perfections: although they do not always flow from the mental excellencies of the person that has them. But we see far the most proper image of the beauty of Christ when we see beauty in the human soul.

COROL. I. From hence it is evident that man is in a fallen state; and that he has naturally scarcely anything of those sweet graces, which are an image of those which are in Christ. For no doubt seeing that other creatures have an image of them according to their capacity: so all the rational and intelligent part of the world once had according to theirs.

COROL. II. There will be a future state wherein man will have them according to his capacity. How great a happiness will it be in Heaven for the saints to enjoy the society of each other, since one may see so much of the loveliness of Christ in those things which are only shadows of being. With what joy are philosophers filled in beholding the aspectable world. How sweet will it be to behold the proper image and communications of Christ's excellency in intelligent beings, having so much of the beauty of Christ upon them as Christians shall have in heaven. What beautiful and fragrant flowers will those be, reflecting all the sweetnesses of the Son of God! How will Christ delight to walk in this garden among those beds of spices, to feed in the gardens, and to gather lilies!

AN ESSAY ON THE TRINITY*

Tis common when speaking of the Divine happiness to say that God is Infinitely Happy in the Enjoyment of himself, in Perfectly beholding & Infinitely loving, & Rejoicing in, his own Essence & Perfections, and accordingly it must be supposed that God Perpetually and Eternally has a most Perfect Idea of himself, as it were an exact Image and Representation of himself ever before him and in actual view, & from hence arises a most pure and Perfect act or energy in the Godhead, which is the divine Love, Complacence and Joy.

Tho we cannot concieve of the manner of the divine understanding, yet if it be understanding or any thing that can be any way signified by that word of ours, it is by Idea. Tho the divine nature be vastly different from that of created spirits, yet our souls are made in the Image of God, we have understanding & will, Idea & Love as God hath, and the difference is only in the Perfection of degree and manner. The Perfection of the manner will Indeed Infer this that there is no distinction to be made in God between Power or habit and act, & with Respect to Gods understanding that there are no such distinctions to be admitted as in ours between Perception or Idea, and Reasoning & Judgment, (excepting what the will has to do in Judgment), but that the whole of the divine understanding or wisdom consists in the meer Perception or unvaried Presence of his Infinitely Perfect Idea., & with Respect to the other faculty as it is

* The Essay is printed from a careful transcription of the original. It is given in the unrevised form in which it was left by the author, with no attempt to mend the orthography or the structure of the sentences. The alterations are few and trifling in their nature, being designed exclusively to remove obscurities as to the meaning which might perplex the reader. I have thought it better to err by too slight changes than in the opposite direction. The following is a list of the Author's abbreviations: Chh. = church, or churches; F. = Father; G. = God; G. H. = Ghost; Gosp. = Gospel; H. G. = Holy Ghost; L. = Lord; L. J. X. = Lord Jesus Christ; So. = Son; Sp. = Spirit, or Spirits; SS. = Scriptures (or Scripture); X. = Christ; Xtians. = Christians. [Fisher's note.]

in God there are no distinctions to be admitted of faculty, habit, and act, between will, Inclination, & love, But that it is all one simple act. But the divine Perfection will not Infer [*i.e.*, imply] that his understanding is not by Idea and that there is not Indeed such a thing as Inclination & Love in God.*

[That in John   God is Love shews that there are more persons than one in the deity, for it shews Love to be essential & necessary to the deity so that his nature consists in it, & this supposes that there is an Eternal & necessary object, because all Love respects another that is the beloved. By Love here the Apostle certainly means something beside that which is commonly called self-love: that is very improperly called Love & is a thing of an exceeding diverse nature from the affection or virtue of Love the Apostle is speaking of.]

The sum of the divine understanding and wisdom consists in his having a Perfect Idea of himself, he being Indeed the all: the all-comprehending being,—he that is, and there is none else. So the sum of his Inclination, Love, & Joy is his love to & delight in himself. Gods Love to himself, & complacency & delight in himself,—they are not to be distinguished, they are the very same thing in God; which will easily be allowed, Love in man being scarcely distinguishable from the Complacence he has in any Idea: if there be any difference it is meerly modal, & circumstantial.

The knowledge or view which God has of himself must necessarily be concieved to be some thing distinct from his meer direct existence. There must be something that answers to our Reflection. The Reflection as we Reflect on our own minds carries some thing of Imperfection in it. However, if God beholds himself so as thence to have delight & Joy in himself he must become his own Object. There must be a duplicity. There is God and the Idea of God, if it be Proper to call a conception of that that is Purely spiritual an Idea.

And I do suppose the deity to be truly & Properly Repeated by Gods thus having an Idea of himself & that this Idea of God

* The next paragraph is inserted at a later date. [Fisher's note.]

is truly God, to all Intents and Purposes, & that by this means the Godhead is Really Generated and Repeated.

. . . .

Therefore as G. with Perfect Clearness, fullness & strength, understands himself, views his own essence (in which there is no Distinction of substance & act but which is wholly substance & wholly act), that Idea which G. hath of himself is absolutely himself. This Representation of the divine nature & essence is the divine nature & essence again: so that by Gods thinking of the Deity must certainly be generated. Hereby there is another Person begotten, there is another Infinite Eternal Almighty & most holy & the same G., the very same divine nature.

And this Person is the second Person in the Trinity, the Only begotten & dearly beloved Son of G.; he is the Eternal, necessary, Perfect, substantial & Personal Idea which G. hath of himself; & that it is so seems to me to be abundantly confirmed by the word of G.

. . . .

The Godhead being thus begotten by Gods loving an Idea of himself & shewing forth in a distinct subsistence or Person in that Idea, there Proceeds a most Pure act, & an Infinitely holy & sacred energy arises between the F. & Son in mutually Loving & delighting in each other, for their love & Joy is mutual, Prov. 8, 30, I was daily his delight Rejoicing alwaies before him. This is the eternal & most Perfect & essential act of the divine nature, wherin the Godhead acts to an Infinite degree and in the most Perfect manner Possible. The deity becomes all act, the divine essence it self flows out & is as it were breathed forth in Love & Joy. So that the Godhead therin stands forth in yet another manner of subsistence, & there Proceeds the 3d Person in the Trinity, the holy spirit, viz. the Deity in act, for there is no other act but the act of the will.

. . . .

3. This is very consonant to the office of the holy Ghost or his work with Respect to Creatures, which is threefold, viz. to quicken, enliven & beautify all things, to sanctify Intelligent

[beings] & to comfort & delight them. 1. he quickens & beautifies all things. So we Read that the Sp. of G. moved upon the face of the waters or of the Chaos to bring it out of its Confusion into harmony & beauty. So we read, Job 26 13, That G. by his Spirit garnished the heavens. Now whose office can it be so Properly to actuate & enliven all things as his who is the Eternal & essential act & energy of G. & whose office can it be so Properly to give all things their sweetness & beauty as he who is himself the beauty & Joy of the Creator. 2. Tis he that sanctifies created Sp., that is, he gives them divine Love, for the SS. teaches us that all holiness & true Grace & virtue is Resolvable into that as its universal spring & Principle. As it is the office of the Person that is Gods Idea & understanding to be the light of the world, to communicate understanding, so tis the office of the Person that is Gods Love to communicate divine love to the Creature. In so doing, Gods spirit or love doth but communicate of it self. Tis the same love so far as a Creature is capable of being made partaker of it. Gods Sp. or his love doth but, as it were, come and dwell in our hearts and act there as a vital Principle, and we become the living temples of the holy Gh., & when men are Regenerated & sanctified, G. Pours forth of his Sp. upon them and they have fellowship or, which is the same thing, are made partakers with the F. & Son of their love, i.e. of their Joy & beauty. Thus the matter is Represented in the Gospel—and this agreable to what was taken notice of before—of the Apostle John, his making love dwelling in us & Gods Spirit dwelling in us the same thing, and the explaining of them one by another, 1 Joh. 4, 12, 13.

When X says to his F., Joh. 17, 26, and I have declared unto them thy name & will declare it, that the Love wherewith thou hast loved me may be in them and I in them, I cant think of any way that this will appear so Easy and Intelligible as upon this hypothesis, viz. that the love with which the F. loveth the Son is the H. Sp., that X here concludeth & sums up his Prayer for his disciples with the Request that the holy Sp. might be in his disciples & so he might be in them thereby, for X dwells in his disciples by his Sp., as X teaches in Joh. 14, 16, 17, 18, I will give you another Comforter—even the Spirit of truth—he shall be in you.

.   .   .   .

& This I suppose to be that Blessed Trinity that we Read of In the Holy SS. The F. is the Deity subsisting in the Prime, unoriginated & most absolute manner, or the deity in its direct existence. The Son is the deity generated by Gods understanding, or having an Idea of himself & subsisting in that Idea. The Holy Gh. is the Deity subsisting in act, or the divine essence flowing out and Breathed forth in Gods Infinite love to & delight in himself. & I believe the whole divine Essence does Truly & distinctly subsist both in the divine Idea & divine Love, and that each of them are Properly distinct Persons.

& It confirms me in it that this is the True Trinity because Reason is sufficient to tell us that there must be these distinctions In the deity, viz., of G. (absolutely considered), & the Idea of G., & Love & delight, & there are no other Real distinctions in G. that can be thought. There are but these three distinct Real things in G. Whatsoever else can be mentioned in G. are nothing but meer modes or Relations of Existence. There are his attributes of Infinity, Eternity and Immortality; they are meer modes of existence. There is Gods understanding, his wisdom & omniscience that we Have shewn to be the same with his Idea. There is Gods will, But this is not Really distinguished from his love, But is the same but only with a different Relation. As the sum of Gods understanding consists in his having an Idea of himself, so the sum of his will or Inclination consists in his loving himself, as we have already observed. There is Gods Power or Ability to bring things to Pass. But this is not Really distinct from his understanding & will; it is the same but only with the Relation they have to those effects that are, or are to be Produced. There is Gods holiness, but this is the same, as we have shewn in what we have said of the nature of excellency, with his love to himself. There is Gods Justice, which is not Really distinct from his holiness. There are the attributes of Goodness, mercy and Grace, but these are but the overflowing of Gods Infinite love. The sum of all Gods Love is his Love to himself. These three, G., and the Idea of G., & the Inclination, affection & love of G., must be conceived as Really distinct. But as for all these other things of extent, duration, being with or without change, ability to do, they are not distinct Real things even in created spirits but only meer modes and Relations. So that our natural Reason is sufficient to tell us that there are these three in G., and we can think of no more.

It is a maxim amongst divines that everything that is in G. is G. which must be understood of Real attributes and not of meer modalities. If a man should tell me that the Immutability of G. is G. or that the omnipresence of G. & authority of G., is God, I should not be able to think of any Rational meaning of what he said. It hardly sounds to me Proper to say that Gods being without change is G., or that Gods being Every where is God, or that Gods having a Right of Government over Creatures is G. But if it be meant that the Real attributes of G., viz. his understanding & love are G., then what we have said may in some measure explain how it is so, for deity subsists in them distinctly; so they are distinct divine persons.

.   .   .   .

One of the Principal Objections that I can think of against what has been supposed is concerning the Personality of the holy Gh.—that this scheme of things dont seem well to consist with [the fact] that a person is that which hath understanding & will. If the three in the Godhead are Persons they doubtless each of them have understanding, but this makes the understanding one distinct person & Love another. How therefore can this Love be said to have understanding? (Here I would observe that divines have not been wont to suppose that these three had three distinct understandings, but all one and the same understanding.) In order to clear up this matter Let it be considered that the whole divine office is supposed truly & Properly to subsist in Each of these three, viz., G. & his understanding & love, & that there is such a wonderfull union between them that they are, after an Ineffable & Inconcievable manner, one in another, so that one hath another & they have communion in one another & are as it were Predicable one of another.

. . . .

But I dont Pretend fully to explain how these things are & I am sensible a hundred other objections may be made & puzzling doubts & questions Raised that I cant solve. I am far from Pretending to explaining the Trinity so as to Render it no Longer a mystery. I think it to be the highest & deepest of all divine mysteries still, notwithstanding anything that I have said or conceived about it. I dont Intend to explain the Trinity. But Scripture with Reason may Lead to say something further of it than has been wont to be said, tho there are still Left many things Pertaining to it Incomprehensible. It seems to me that what I have here supposed concerning the Trinity is exceeding analogous to the Gospel scheme and agreeable to the Tenour of the whole N. T. & abundantly Illustrative of Gospel doctrines, as might be Particularly shewn, would it not exceedingly Lengthen out this discourse.

[TO THE REV. MR. TIMOTHY EDWARDS,
WINDSOR, CONNECTICUT]

Yale Coll: March 1st 1721

HONOURED SIR:

It was not with a little Joy; and satisfaction that I Reciev'd your Letter of yᵉ 21st of Feb by Mr Grant,[1] And with a Great Deal Of thankfulness from the Bottom of My Heart for your Wholsom advice, and counsel, and the Abundance of Father-like tenderness therin expressed. As concerning the complaint of the scholars about their Commons; the Manner of it I Believe was no less surprizing to me than to you: It was on this wise, Every Undergraduate, one, and all, that had any thing to Do with Colledge Commons, all on a sudden, Before Mʳ Cutler,[2] or (I Believe) any Body Knew yᵗ they were Discontented, entered into a Bond of 15ˢ never to have any More Commons of the steward, wherupon they all forewarn'd him never to Provide more for them, telling him If he did they would not pay him for it. Mr Brown Notwithstanding Ordered commons to be provided, and set upon the table as it used to be, and Accordingly it was, But there was no body to eat it: Mr Cutler as soon as he was apprized of this Cabal sent on the same Day for Mr Andrew,[3] and Mr Russel,[4] who came on the next, and with the Rector ordered all to appear Before them; Where the Rector manifested himself exceedingly vex'd, and Displeased at the Act, which so affrighted the scholars that they unanimously agreed to come into commons again. I believe the scholars that were in this Agreement have so lost Mr Cutler's favour that they scarce ever will Regain it. Stiles[5] (to my Grief and I Believe much more to his) was one that set his hand to this Bond; He Did it By the strong instigation of Others who Perswaded him to it; neither had he a minutes time to consider before his hand was Down: as soon as I Understood him to be One of them, I told him y^t I thought he had Done exceeding unadvisedly, and I told him also what I thought the Ill consequences of it would be, and quickly made him sorry that he did not take advice in the matter. I am apt to think that this thing will be the greatest Obstacle of any to Stiles's being Butler. I must needs say for my own part, that although the commons at sometimes have not been sufficient as to quality, yet I think there has been very little Occasion for such an Insurrection as this. Although these Disturbances were so speedyly Quash'd, yet they are succeeded By Much Worse, and Greater; and I Believe Greater than Ever were in the Colledge before, they Are Occasion'd By the Discovery Of some Monstrous impieties, And Acts of Immorality Lately Committed In the Colledge, Particularly stealing of Hens, Geese, turkies, piggs, meat, wood &c—, unseasonable nightwalking, Breaking People's windows, playing at Cards, cursing, swearing, and Damning, and Using all manner of Ill Language, which never were at such a pitch in the Colledge as they now are; The Rector has Called a meeting of the trustees On this Occasion, they are expected here to Day, tis thought the upshot will be the Expulsion of some, and the Publick Admonition of Others: Through the goodness of God I am perfectly free of all their janglings. My condition att the Colledge at present is every way comfortable: I Live in very Good Amity And Agreement with my Chambermate.[6] there has no new quarrels Broke Out betwixt me and any of the scholars, though they still Persist in their former Combination, But I Am not Without Hopes that it will be abolish'd by this meeting Of the Trustees. I Have Not as yet wrote to Uncle Mix,[7] Because I Heard he was Coming Down, But he Delaying His Coming I Shall Do it Speedily. I Am at present in perfect health and it is a time of health throughout the Colledge and Town. I am about taking the remainder of my lignum vitae.[8] I am much Reformed with Respect to visiting of Friends, and Intend to do more att it for the future than in time past. I think I shall not have Occasion for the Coat you mentioned in your letter till I Come home. I Recieved a Letter from my sister Mary[9] the week before last and have heard of her welfare this week By a Man that Came

Directly from thence. I Pray you in your Next letter Please to Give My humble Duty to my Mother, hearty love to sisters, and Mercy.[10] and still to be mindfull before the throne of Grace of [*sic*] me, who am,

	Honoured sir
Stiles presents his Duty to	your
your self with my mother	most Dutyfull
and service to my sisters	son
	Jonathan E:

[TO MRS. SARAH EDWARDS IN BOSTON]

[MY] DEAR COMPANION.

I wrote you a few lines the last Sabbath [da]y by Ens[n] Dwight,[1] which I hope you [w]ill receive.—By this I would inform [y]ou that Betty[2] seems really to be on the [m]ending Hand; I cant but think she [is] truly better, both as to her Health & [he]r sores, since she has been at Mrs Phelps's.[3] [Th]e first two or three days, before she [wa]s well acquainted, she was very un[qu]iet; but now more quiet than she [us]ed to be at Home.—This is Lecture [da]y Morning, and your two eldest daugh[ter]s[4] went to Bed last night, both [si]ck; and *Rose* beat out, & having the [he]ad-ach. we got Hannah Root to [h]elp them yesterday in the afternoon, [we] expect her again to day. How Sarah [&] Esther do to day I can't tell, for they [ar]e not up. We have been without [yo]u almost as long as we know how to [be]; but yet are willing you should obey [th]e calls of Providence with [re]gard to Col. Stoddard.[5]

If you have money to spare, & it [is]n't too late, I should be glad if [yo]u would buy us some cheese in Boston, & [bring it] with other things if it can [be sa]fely:—give my humble service to Mr. Bromfield[6] & Madam & proper salutation to other Friends.

I am your most affectionate
Companion

Northampton June 22   Jonathan Edwards
1748

[TO THE REV. MR. JOHN ERSKINE,
KIRKINTILLOCH, SCOTLAND]

Northampton Aug. 31. 1748.

REV & DEAR SIR,

I this summer received your Kind Letter of Feb. 9. 1748. with your most acceptable present of Taylor on original sin,' and his Key to the Apostolic Writings, with his Paraphrase on the Epistle to the Romans;[2] together with your sermons & answer to Dr Campbel, I had your sermons before, sent, either by you, or Mr. McLaurin.[3] I am exceeding glad of these two Books of Taylor's. I had before borrowed and read Taylor on original sin; But am very glad to have one of my own: If you had not sent it, I intended to have sought opportunity to buy it. The other Book his Paraphrase &c. I had not heard of; If I had, I should not have been easy till I had seen it, and been possessed of it. These Books, If I should live may probably be of great use to me.—such kindness from you was unexpected: I hoped to receive a Letter from you, which alone I should have received as a special Favour.

I have for the present, been diverted from the design I hinted to you, of publishing something against some of the Arminian Tenets,[4] by something else that divine Providence unexpectedly laid in my way, and seem'd to render unavoidable, viz. publishing Mr. Brainerd's Life.[5] of which the inclosed Paper of Proposals gives some account.

It might be of particular advantage to me here in this remote part of the world, to be better informed what Books there are that are published on the other side of the Atlantick, and especially if there be any thing that comes out that is very remarkable. I have seen many notable things that have been written in this century against the Truth, But nothing very notable on our side of the Controversies of the present day, at least of the Arminian Controversy: You would much oblige me, if you would inform me what are the best Books that have lately been written in defence of Calvinism.

I have herewith sent the two Books of Mr. Stoddards[6] you desired. The lesser of the two was my own; and tho' I have no other, yet you laid me under such obligations, that I am glad I have it to send to you. The other I procured of one of my neighbours.

I have lately heard some things that have excited Hope in me that God was about to cause there to be a Turn in England, with Regard to the state of Religion there for the better; particularly what we have heard that one Mr. West, a Clerk of the Privy Council, has written in defence of Christianity, tho' once a notorious deist: & also what Mr Littleton, a member of the House of Commons has written. I should be glad if you would inform me more particularly in your next, concerning this affair, and what the present state of Infidelity in great Britain is.

It has pleased God, since I wrote my last to you, sorely to afflict this Family, by taking away by death, the last February, my second daughter, in the 18 year of her age, a very pleasant & useful member of this Family, & that was generally esteem'd the Flower of the Family. Herein we have a great Loss; But the Remembrance of the remarkable appearances of Piety in her, from her childhood, in Life, and also at her death, are very comfortable to us, & give us great Reason to mingle Thanksgiving with our mourning. I desire your Prayers, dear sir, that God would make up our great Loss to us in Himself.

Please to accept of one of my sermons on Mr. Brainerds death,[7] & also my sermon on Mr. Buel's Instalment.[8]—I desire that for the future your Letters to me may be directed to be left with Mr Edward Bromfield[9] Merch^t in Boston, & not with Mr. Prince,[10] who is so forgetful, that his care is not to be depended on.—My wife joins with me in respectful & affectionate salutations to you, & Mrs Erskine.—Desiring that we may meet often at the Throne of Grace in supplications for each other, I am dear Brother,

> your obliged Friend,
> Fellow-Labourer & humble serv^t
> Jonath. Edwards.

P.S. I desired Mr Prince to send to you one of my Books on the subject of the Concert for Prayer,[11] for a general Revival of Religion, this last year; and He engaged to do it; but I perceive he forgot it. & it was long neglected. But I have since taken some further care to have the Book conveyed, so that I hope that e're this Time you have received it.

In the conclusion of your Letter of Feb. 9. you mention a design of writing to me again, by a ship that was to sail the next month for Boston.—That Letter I have not received.

[TO THE REV. MR. JOSEPH BELLAMY,
BETHLEHEM, CONNECTICUT]

Northampton
Decem. 6. 1749

MY DEAR FRIEND,

The expected opportunity of sending your MSS to N. Haven has failed, and having now an opportunity by Simeon Lyman of Salsbury of sending them directly to his Brother at Goshen, I now embrace it and here send with your MSS the Notes I have made.

As for the present state of things here with Regard to our Controversy, 'tis not very easy for me to give you an Idea of it, without writing a sheet or two of Paper. But in brief, things are in great Confusion: the Tumult is vastly greater than when you was here, and is rising higher & higher continually. The People have got their Resentments up to a great Height towards you since you have been gone; and you are spoken of by 'em with great Indignation & Contempt. And I have been informed that Col. Williams[1] of Weathersfield has written a Letter to one of the principal men of that Church, where in He speaks contemptibly & with Resentment of your & Mr. Searl's last visit here.—There have been abundance of meetings about our affairs since you was here, society meetings, & church meetings, & meetings—of Committees, of Committees of the Parish & Committees of the Church, Conferences, Debates, Reports, &

Proposals drawn up, & Replies & Remonstrances. The People have a Resolution to get me out of Town speedily, that disdains all Controul or Check. To make the matter strong, there is a Precinct meeting kept alive by adjournment, They have already had three or four conventions and have a standing Committee of nineteen men (chiefly of such as are strongly engaged), to oversee and manage the affair affectually. And we have another committee of the church of 15 men (in the Choice of which they picked out those that are most violent) and these appointed for the same End. But not withstanding such great doings nothing is yet done or concluded, the true grand difficulties that the People stick at about calling a Council, are *first*, that they would have a Council all on their own side in the controversy; and are contriving & struggling to their utmost to cut me off from liberty of chusing any Part of the council of such as are of my opinion & *secondly*, they are utterly against a Council having Liberty to look into the whole state of our Case, and giving advice in General; but would tie them up to some Particulars, in Judging of which they think they can have no Power to look into & Condemn any thing in their conduct, or to thwart their designs. I have been openly reproached in Church meetings, as apparently regarding my own Temporal Interest more than the Honour of Christ & the good of the Church. As to the affair of a publick dispute, it was quickly at an End after you went from hence, The People at their next Parish meeting rejected it, as what would tend to make Parties among us. They seem to be determined that the arguments for my opinion shall never be publickly heard, if it be possible to prevent it   the Church Committee have voted expressly that no Council shall have Power to give Advice in that matter i.e. whether I shall preach on the subject or no: & have drawn up a writing, containing 9 or 10 votes or conclusions of theirs, manifesting what They would have as to the measure that shall be taken relating to a Council to be called: and in the same writing have added at the End a Threatening, that If they & I don't agree, They will report it to the Church as their Opinion that the Church should vote that my opinion is so & so pernicious, & declare their desire of a speedy separation, & immediate Call a Council themselves to dismiss me.—

I might have observed before, that I have been informed that Rector Williams wrote 'em up advice, not to have a publick dispute; because it would tend to Parties.

You may easily be sensible dear sir, that 'tis a Time of great Trial with me, and that I stand in Continual need of the divine Presence & merciful Conduct in such a state of things as this. I need Gods Counsel in every step I take & every word I speak; so all that I do & say is watched by the multitude around me with the utmost strictness & with eyes of the greatest uncharitableness & severity and let me do or say what I will, my words & actions are represented in dark colours, and the state of Things is come to that, that they seem to think it greatly concerns 'em to blacken me, & represent me in Odious Colours to the world, to justify their own Conduct—They seem to be sensible that now their Character can't stand unless it be on the Ruin of mine. They have publickly voted that they will have no more sacraments; & they have no way to justify themselves in that, but to represent me as very bad. I therefore desire dear sir, your fervent Prayers to God. If He be for me, who can be against me? If He be with me, I need not fear ten thousands of the People. But I know myself unworthy of his Presence & help, yet would humbly trust in his infinite Grace & all sufficience.

My Love to your spouse.

I am your Brother
& near Friend
Jonathan Edwards.

[TO THE REV. MR. JOSEPH BELLAMY, BETHLEHEM, CONNECTICUT]

Northampton, Jan. 15. 1749/50.

MY DEAR FRIEND—

I thank you for your two Letters by Mr. Lyman. As to your Questions in your last Letter: I would say, that the difficulty that is in Them seems to arise from the ambiguity, or want of a fixed meaning to some Phrases. Your second Question is *Are we to blame for that wherein we are not voluntary.* I say, yes, as the word *voluntary* is often used, *viz* to signifie that which *arises from* a bad or good will, or things that are *the Fruits* of the will. for we are to Blame for something else besides the fruits of a Bad will, or a Bad disposition or Temper & we are to Blame for the Bad will it self. Blame or Faultiness consists primarily in the Being of a bad will or disposition & not only in the Spirit of it. and therefore we may be to blame for that which don't arise from a Bad Temper: viz. the Bad Temper it self: for if the Bad temper it self was not blame-worthy, I think the Effects of it, or those things that arise from it could not be blame-worthy But as the word *voluntary* may be understood, we are to blame for nothing but what is voluntary, as if by voluntary we understand both that which consists in the will, & also that which arises from it. we are to blame for that which consists in the will or which the will consists in, & so we are to blame for a bad Temper or bad disposition, not because a bad temper is the fruit of a Bad will, but because a bad will consists in it. A Bad Temper of mind is nothing else but the Habit of a bad will. You enquire whether it is not Inconsistent to say that a sense of the divine Beauty arises from a good Temper, & a good Temper arises from a sense of the divine Beauty. I answer yes, as the Expressions may be understood. If by a sense of the d. Beauty, you mean an habitual sensibility of moral Beauty. I say in this sense a sense of the d. B— don't arise from a good Temper for an habitual sensibility of moral Beauty (or an habitual good Taste of mind) and a good Temper of mind are the very same thing: 'Tis what goodness of Temper does primarily consist in. and therefore a good Temper in that primary notion of it don't arise from a sense of the d. B. For a good Taste or habitual Taste of moral good dont arise from a Taste of moral Good. But in another sense, a good Temper does arise from a sense of the d. B. viz every thing else that belongs to what we call a good Temper, excepting the good Taste & relish of the mind, as good desires, Inclinations to good Resolutions, a disposition to good choice and to good actions & Behaviour, a disposition to proper meditation, and proper & suitable affections, to a right Fear, sorrow, Joy, Hope, dependance &c. all These things arise from a sense of the d. B.

I thank you for your Care in dispersing my Books. as to the present state of things in this Town.—We have had a great Deal of struggle & difficulty about calling a Council, whether I should be allowed in my choice of half the Council to go out of the county, in order to having my half on my side in the main controversy. Finally we agreed to call a Council of five out of the seven next neighbouring churches which five Churches should be mutually chosen, and to Leave it to Them whether in the Choice of the decisive Council that is to determine whether I shall be dismissed from my Pastoral office, I may go out of the County, & whether the state of Things be now ripe for such a Council The Council met the 26. of last month, & sat two days. as to the latter Question they determined that the state of things was not ripe for a decisive Council, for two Reasons 1. That the People were not in a proper Temper for such a Proceeding. & 2. thorough means had not yet been used to convince me of my supposed Errour. with Regard to this latter they signified that they expected an answer to my Book speedily from the Press, which They hoped might [be the] means of reconciling minister & People

The Person they expect this Answer from as I understand is Mr. Clark[1] of Salem-village. But whether He is truly writing an Answer or no I cannot certainly Learn. as to the first Question viz I might go out of the County in choosing my part of the Council. This Council did not determine but refer'd it for further consideration, and to that End adjourned Themselves to the 1st Wednesday in February when they are to meet again to determine this Point. The Churches of which this Council consists are the Chh of Hatfield the 1st Chh in Hadley, the Chh in Sunderland, the Chh of Cold-springs, & the Chh in New-Hampton What this Council will determine on this removing Point I know not. But let their determination be what it will I don't suppose it will make any alteration as to my continuing

here. I expect to leave my Pastoral office here when this year is
out, which Ends in the last of April, as the People have reckoned
from the Beginning for the Payment of my salary. I desire your
fervent & constant Prayer   give my Love to Mrs. Bellamy
I am your very affectionate

                     & obliged Friend & Brother
                             Jonathan Edwards.

P.S. I hope t[o see you] here in the sp[rin]g

[TO MAJOR JOSEPH HAWLEY, NORTHAMPTON]

Stockbridge Nov. 18. 1754.

DEAR SIR,

I now, as soon as I am able, set my self about answering your
Letter of Aug. 11: tho' I am still so weak that I can write but
with a trembling Hand, as you may easily perceive. I was taken
ill about the middle of July, and my Fits have now left me a little
more than a Fortnight: but I have been greatly reduced by so
long continued an Illness, and gain strength very slowly and
cannot be so particular in my answer to your Letter as I might
be if I had more strength.

I rejoyce in the good Temper & disposition of mind which
seems to be manifested in your Letter; and hope that whatever I
may have suffered, and however greatly I m[a]y think my self
injured in that affair which is the subject of your Letter, wherein
you was so much of a Leader, I have a disposition, in my consideration of the affair, and what I shall write upon it, to treat
you with true Candour and Christian Charity. Nevertheless, I
confess that the thing you desire of me is disagreeable to me, *viz*
very particularly giving my Judgment concerning your Conduct in that affair; and it is with no small Reluctance that I go
about answering such a Request, upon two accounts; 1. As it
obliges me renewedly to revolve in my mind, and particularly
to look over, that most disagreeable and dreadful scene, the
Particulars of which I have long since very much dismiss'd from
my mind, as having no Pleasure in the Thoughts of them. &

edly as 'tis (& will be looked upon by you, however serious & Conscientious you may be in your desires & Endeavours to know the Truth) a giving a Judgment in my own Case, a Case wherein I was concerned to a very high degree; and therefore will be much more likely to be a giving of it in vain.

Notwithstanding   seeing you desire it, and seem to desire it in so Christian a manner, I will give you my Judgment plainly, such as it is, and as impartially as I am able, leaving the Consequence to God.

You know very well that I looked on my self, in the Time of the affair, as very greatly injured by the People in general, in the general Conduct Managem[en]t & Progress of it from the Beginning to the End. That this was then my Judgm[en]t was plain enough to be seen; and I suppose no man in the Town was insensible of it. And what were the main things wherein I looked on my self injured, and what I supposed to be the Aggravation of the Injury was also manifest. as particularly that the Ch[urc]h & Precinct had all Imaginable Reason to think that in my receiving that Opinion which was the subject of the Controversy, and in the steps I took upon it, the declaration I made of it &c. I acted altogether Conscientiously, & from Tenderness of spirit, and because I greatly feared to offend God; without, yea to the highest degree against all Influence of worldly interest, and all private and sinister views. I think it was hardly possible for the affair to be attended with Circumstances exhibiting greater Evidence of this. I think if my People therefore, when the affair was first divulged, had been act[uat]ed by a Christian spirit or indeed by Humanity (tho' they might have been very sorry & full of Concern about the affair) would, especially considering how long I had been their Pastor, and they had alwaies from the Beginning, & from so long Experience, acknowledged me to be their faithful Pastor, & most of them esteemed [me] to be the chief Instrument in the Hand of God of the eternal salvation of their souls; I say they would have treated me, if influenced by Christianity & humanity, with the utmost Tenderness, Calmness & moderation, not to say Honour & Reverence; and would have thought themselves obliged to have gone far in the Exercise of Patience. But instead of this, the Town and Ch[urc]h were at once put into the greatest Flame: the Town was soon filld with Talk of dismissing & expelling me, and with Contrivances how to do it speedily & effectually. and a most Jealous Eye, from that day forward, was kept upon me, least I should do that slyly & craftily that should tend to hinder such a design. and almost every step that I took in the affair, was by their suspicious Eyes, looked upon in such a view; & therefore every thing served to renew and heighten the flame of their Indignation. Even when I addressed my self to em in the Language of Moderation and Intreaty, it was interpreted as a design to flatter the People, especially the more ignorant, to work upon their affections, and so to gain a Party, & prevent a vote for my dismission, or at least to prevent the Peoples being united in any such vote. And there was no way that I could turn my self, nothing that I could do or say but it would have some such uncharitable construction put upon it.— As I began the affair in the Fear of God, after much & long continued Prayer to Him, so I was very careful in the whole Progress of it, & in every step to act uprightly and to avoid every unrighteous & underhanded Measure: nor had I ever once formed a design forever to establish my self at Northampton, & impose my self on the People, whether we should remain differing in our opinion in the Point in controversy, or not; nor did I ever take one step with any such view. The things I aimed at were these two 1. that the People should be brought to a Calm Temper before Extremes were Proceeded to, & 2. that they should, in such a Temper, hear What I had to say for my self, & my opinion.—But nothing could be done: The People most manifestly continued in a constant flame of high Resentment, & vehement opposition, for more than two years together; & this spirit, instead of subsiding, grew higher & higher, 'till they had obtained their End in my Expulsion. Nor indeed did it cease then, but still they maintain'd their Jealousy of me, as if I was secretly doing the Part of an Enemy to 'em, so long as I had a being in the Town; yea 'till they saw the Town well cleared of all my Family. So deep were their Prejudices, that their Heat was maintained, nothing would quiet 'em till they could see the Town clear of Root & Branch, Name and Remnant.

I could mention many things that were said & done in a publick manner, in meetings of the Precinct, Ch[urc]h & their Committees, from time to time, from the Beginning, fully to justify & support what I have said & supposed till my dismission, (besides the continual Talk in all parts of the Town, in private Houses, & occasional Companies) But I think this can't be expected; as it would be writing a History that would take up no less than a quire of Paper. I would only observe that I was from Time to Time reprehended by one that commonly was chosen moderator of Precinct & Ch[urc]h meetings, & Chairman of their Com[mi]ttees, in a very dogmatical & magisterial manner, for making so much mischief, putting the Ch[urc]h to so much Trouble. and once he told me he did it by the desire & vote of the whole Committee; which was very large, consisting of all or most of the Chief men of the Town. I was often charged with acting only from sinister views, from stiffness of spirit, & from Pride, & an arbitrary & Tyrannical spirit, and a design, & vain Expectation of forcing all to Comply with my opinion. The above mention'd Person chiefly improved by the Town & Ch[urc]h, & set at their Head, in these affairs, once said expressly, in a Ch[urc]h meeting in the meeting House, "That it was apparent that I regarded my own temporal Interest "more than the good of the Good of the Ch[urc]h; that the "Ch[urc]h. had Reason to think I designedly laid a snare to en- "snare the Ch[urc]h; & that they had best by all means to be- "ware and see to it that they were not ensnared." & said much more to the same Purpose. and he was never frowned upon but smiled upon by the Ch[urc]h; continuing in such a way of Treatment of me, was still made much of, and set foremost in the management of the affair.—There were multitudes of Precinct and Church meetings, many meetings of Committees, & conferences with me about this affair. I am perswaded there was not one meeting, but that this unreasonable violent spirit was apparent, and as governing & prevalent. It seemed from the very Beginning to govern in all Proceedings, & almost every step that was taken. The People were so far from seeking any composition, that it was often declared in the meetings that If I should retain my opinion, tho' I should be convinced that continuing in it, I might go on in Mr. Stoddards way, they would by no means have me for their minister; and their committee declared against any Endeavours to bring me to this before the last council; yea, they seemed to have a dread of my conforming to this. It being thus, I think the whole management of the affair was exceeding provoking and abominable to God; as most contrary to what ought to be in all publick affairs, especially affairs of Religion and the Worship of Christian societies; & so contrary to the Treatment due to me from that People; and especially in an affair so circumstanced, wherein they had such glaring Evidences of my acting only from Tenderness of Conscience, & with Regard to the account I had to give to my great Master, and wherein I so carefully avoided every thing irritating, & never offered the People any Provocation, unless yielding and condescending, as I did to them (in things which I supposed they insisted on meerly from Humour and Prejudice) in many Instances for Peace sake near a Provocation; an affair wherein I with great constancy maintain'd a diligent watch over my own spirit; an affair wherein I sought Peace and pursued it, and strove to my utmost to avoid occasions of strife, and to treat every one in a Christian manner.

Such an affair being so managed, I think no one should have put their hand to it, unless it were to check and restrain, and if possible to bring the People to an exceeding different Temper & Manner of Conduct, and convince & shew 'em how far they were out of the way of their Duty, and 'till this could be done, I think not a step should have been taken by any means, to promote and forward their designs. Instead of this, I am perswaded a Judicious Christian, in a right temper of mind, being a by stander, would have beheld the Scene with Horrour. especially considering the dreadful work that [it] was making with the Credit & Interest of Religion, by such a Town & Church as that of N[orthampto]n, of such a Profession and Fame.

And therefore sir, I think you made your self greatly guilty in the light of God, in the Part you acted in this affair; becoming, especially towards the latter Part of it, very much their Leader in it; & much from your own Forwardness, putting your self forward as it were, as tho' fond of intermeddling & Helping. which was the less becoming, considering your Youth, and considering your Relation to me. Your Forwardness especially appeared on this Occasion, that after you was chosen as one of a committee to plead their Cause before a Council, you came to me, and desired me to stay the Ch[urc]h. on Purpose that you might have opportunity to excuse your self from the Business; which was accordingly done, and you did excuse your self, and was excused. but yet when the matter came to be pleaded before the Council, you, (I think very inconsistently) thrust your self forward, and pleaded the Cause with much Earnestness notwithstanding. 'Tis manifest that what you did in the affair from Time to Time, not only helped the People to gain their End in dismissing me, but much encouraged and promoted the spirit with which it was done; your confident, magisterial, vehement manner had a natural & direct Tendency to it.

As to your Remonstrance to the last Council, it not only contained things that were uncharitable and censorious, by which Facts were misinterpreted and overstrain'd, but it was full of direct, bold slanders asserted in strong Terms, & delivered in very severe opprobrious Language, meerly on suspicion & surmise. as particularly therein if I mistake not was asserted that I had said after my dismission, that "I was *de jure & de facto* still the Pastor of that Church," which was a false charge. again I was charged with "having a desire to be settled over a few of the members of the Church to the destruction of the whole; & that I set out on a Journey with a certain Gentleman to procure a council to instal me at N[or]th[ampto]n, & that I contrived to do it at such a Time, because I knew the Church was at that Time about to send for a Candidate &c. that I might prevent their success therein, and that I was ready to settle in that Place, and for the sake of it had refused an Invitation to Stockbridge, that I had neglected this opportunity for the sake of setting over an handful, That I had a great Inclination to continue at N[or]th-

[ampto]n as a minister, at the Expence of the Peace and Prosperity of the greater Part of the Town, yea that I was greatly engaged for it.["] Here is a Heap of direct slanders, positively
asserted, all contrary to the Truth of Fact. I had not refused the
Invitation to St[ockbrid]ge, or neglected that opportunity. I
had no Inclination or desire to settle over these few at Northampton, but a very great opposition in my mind to it, abundantly manifested in what I continually said to them on occasion
of their great & constant urgency. It was much more agreeable
to my Inclination to settle at St[ockbrid]ge, and tho' I complied
to the calling of a Council to advise in the affair, it was on these
Terms, that it should not be thought hard that I should fully &
strongly lay before 'em all my objections against it. My discourse with particular ministers applied to in their own Houses,
was chiefly in opposition to Col. D[wigh]t; & so was my discourse before the Council when met. I earnestly argued before
them against their advising me to settle there, with hopes that
what I said would prevail against it, & very much with that conclusion; and what I said against it was the thing that did prevail
against it, & that only. I complied to the calling of the Council
with a view to these two things   1. To quiet the minds of those,
who in so trying a Time had appeared my steadfast friends, that
they might not alwaies think exceeding hardly of me. & 2. The
Country having been filled with gross misrepresentations of
[the] controversy between me & my People, & the affair of my
dismission, & the grounds of it, to the great wounding of my
character at a distance, I was willing some ministers of chief
Note should come from different Parts of the Countrey, & be
upon the spot, & see the true state of Things with their own
Eyes. It was very contrary to Truth that I contrived to set out
at that particular Time, because just then the Church were about
to apply to a Candidate &c–, that I might prevent their success;
For I knew not of any such Thing: I had then no Notice of that
design or determination of the Church. Nor was that true that
is suggested, that the procuring a Council was the Thing
that occasion'd our setting out on that Journey. Each of us had
other Business, & should have gone had no such Thing as a

Council been projected; & therefore we went far beyond all Parts where any of those ministers dwelt, & spent much more Time there than with any of them—as to my seeking to disappoint & Ruin the Town & destroy its Peace &c—I did not in all this affair take one step with any view at all to a disappointment of the Town & Church in any of these measures for the settling another minister.—I might mention other things in the Remonstrance but I am weary.

These things, being so, I cannot think the Ch[urc]h's Reflections do in any wise answer their Faults in this Paper, & the Injuries therein done to me. In their Reflections they grant that they used too strong Terms, & Language too harsh, that in some Things they were too censorious, & had not sufficient Grounds to go so far in their charges, that they should not have expressed themselves thus & thus; but had better have used other specified Terms, which yet would have been for the hurt of my Reputation. I confess dear sir, I have no Imagination that such sort of Reflections and Retractations as these, will be accepted in the sight of God as sufficient, & all that is proper in such a Case; and that it will be found that they that think so do greatly deceive themselves. The Church in their Remonstrance seem'd to contrive for the strongest, most severe & opprobrious aggravating kind of Terms, to blacken my Character, & wound my Reputation in the most publick manner Possible. In their Reflections on themselves a contrary course is taken. there, instead of aggravating their own Fault (which is the manner of true Penitents) They most manifestly contrive for the softest, mildest Terms, to touch their own Faults in the most gentle manner possible, by the softest Language.

On the whole sir (as you have asked my opinion) I think that That Town & Church lies under great Guilt in the sight of God. and they never more can reasonably expect God's Favour & Blessing 'till they have their Eyes opened to be convinced of their Great Provocation of the most high, & injuriousness to man, and have their Temper greatly altered, 'till they are deeply humbled, and till they openly & in full Terms confess themselves guilty, in the manner in which they are guilty indeed (and

what my opinion of that is, I have in some measure declared)
and openly humble, & take shame to themselves before the
world, and particularly confess their Faults & seek forgiveness
where they have been peculiarly injurious. Such Terms, I am
perswaded, the righteous God will hold that People to; & that it
will forever be in vain for 'em to think to go free and escape
with impunity in any other way. Palliating & extenuating matters, and dawbing themselves over with untempered mortar, &
sowing Figleaves will be in vain before him whose pure & om-
niscient Eye is as a Flame of Fire.—It has often been observed
what a Curse Persons have lived under, & been pursued by, for
their ill Treatment of their natural Parents: but especially may
this be expected to follow such abuses offered by a People to one
which in their own esteem is their spiritual Father. Expositours
& divines often observe, that abuse of God's messengers has
commonly been the last sin of an offending backsliding People
which has filled up the measure of their sin, put an End to God's
Patience with them, & brought on them Ruin. And 'tis also
commonly observed that the Heads & Leaders of such a People
have been remarkeably distinguished in the Fruits of God's
vengeance in such cases. And as you sir, distinguished your
self as a Head and Leader to that People in these affairs, at leas
the main of them; so I think the Guilt that lies on you in the
sight of God is distinguishing, and that you may expect to be
distinguished by God's Frowns, unless there be true Repentance, and properly express'd & manifested, with Endeavours to
be a Leader of the People in the affair of Repentance, as in their
Transgression. One thing which I think aggravated your Fault
was that you your self thought me in the Right in that opinion
wherein I differed from my People. As to the Nature & Essence
of true Religion, my People & I in general were agreed. The
strong point wherein we differed was that supposing that our
Common opinion of the nature of true Godliness to be right, a
Profession of it, or of those Things wherein we supposed the
Essence of it consisted, was necessary to Ch[urc]h Communion
In this you agreed with me & not with the People. So that in
Effect you own'd my Cause (in the Thing which was the main

Foundation of Controversy) to be good. & yet, in the manner before observed, set your self at their Head in their violent opposition to me.—You say that in all your disputes, you ever had a full Perswasion of my sincerity and true sanctity. If so, then doubtless what Christ said to his disciples takes hold of you. *He that receiveth you receiveth me, & he that despiseth you despiseth me, & He that despiseth me despiseth Him that sent me.* And *Take heed ye despise not one of these little ones.*—*He that offendeth one of them it were better for Him that a milstone were hanged about his neck & He drowned in the Depths of the Sea.*

Thus sir, I have done the Thing you requested of me. I wish you may accept it in as Christian a manner as you asked it. You may possibly think that the plain way in which I have given my Judgm[en]t shews that I am far from being impartial, & that I shew a disposition to aggravate & enhanse Things, & set 'em forth in the blackest colours; and that I plainly manifest ill will to you. All that I shall say to this is, that if you think so, I think you are mistaken. And having performed the disagreeable Task you desired of me, I must leave you to judge for your self concerning what I say. I have spoken my Judgment with as great a degree of Impartiality as I am master of, and that which is my steady & constant Judgm[en]t of this awful affair; and I doubt not will be my Judgment as long as I live.—One thing I must desire of you, & that is, that If you dislike what I have written, you would not expect that I should carry on any Paper or Letter Controversy with you on the subject. I have had enough of this Controversy, and desire to have done with it. I have spent enough of the precious Time of my Life in it heretofore. I desire and pray that God may enable you to view things truly, & as he views them; and so to act in the affair as shall be best for you, & most for your Peace living & dying.

with respectful salutations to your spouse, I am Sir, your Kinsman & Friend, that sincerely wishes your truest & greatest wellfare & happiness, in this world & the world to come,   Jonath. Edwards.

To Maj^r Joseph Hawley
in Northampton

[TO THE REV. MR. JOHN ERSKINE,[1]
CULROSS, SCOTLAND]

Stockbridge, April 15, 1755.

REV. AND DEAR SIR,

The last year, in the spring, I received, without a letter, a
pacquet, containing the following books: Casaubon on Enthusiasm; Warburton's Principles of Natural and Revealed Religion;
Merrick on Christ the True Vine; Campbell's Apostles no Enthusiasts; Discourse on the Prevailing evils of the present time;
Remarks on Apostles no Enthusiasts; Moncrief's Review and
Examination of some principles in Campbell's Apostles no Enthusiasts; Gilbert on the Guilt and Pardon of Sin; Hervey on the
Cross of Christ; An account of the Orphan School, etc. at Edinburgh; Memorial concerning the Surgeon's Hospital; Gairdner's
Account of the Old People's Hospital; State of the Society in
Scotland for propagating Christian Knowledge; Abridgement
of the Rules of said Society; Regulations of the Town's Hospital
at Glasgow; and Annals of the Persecution of the Protestants in
France.

In the beginning of last December, I received another pac-
quet, without a letter: the wrapper superscribed with your hand.
In this, were the following pamphlets: A Sermon by a Lay Elder,
before the Commission; A Letter to a gentleman at Edinburgh;
Resolutions of the General Assembly, of May 22d, 1736;
Rutherford's Power of Faith and Prayer; Enquiry into the
method of settling Parishes; The nature of the Covenant and
Constitution of the Church of Scotland; Essay on Gospel and
Legal Preaching; Necessity of Zeal for the Truth; A Vindication
of the Protestant Doctrine of Justification, against the charge of
Antinomianism. The last week, I received a letter from you,
dated 11th July, '54; which was found at Mr. Prince's, by one
that went to Boston from hence, and had lain there, Mr. Prince
could not tell how long. In this letter, you make mention of
these last mentioned pamphlets, received last December. I now
return you my hearty thanks for this letter, and these generous

presents. I should have written to you long ago, had I not been prevented, by the longest and most tedious sickness, that ever I had in my life: I being followed with fits of ague, which came upon me about the middle of last July, and were, for a long time, very severe, and exceedingly wasted my flesh and strength, so that I became like a skeleton. I had several intermissions of the fits, by the use of the Peruvian bark; but they never wholly left me, till the middle of last January. In the mean time, I several times attempted to write letters to some of my friends, about affairs of importance, but found that I could bear but little of such writing. Once, in attempting to write a letter to Mr. Burr, a fit of the ague came upon me, while I was writing, so that I was obliged to lay by my pen. When my fits left me, they left me in a poor, weak state, so that I feared whether I was not going into a dropsy. Nevertheless, I have, of late, gradually gained strength.

I lately received a letter from Mr. M'Laurin,[2] dated Aug. 13, '54; which Mr. Prince sent me, with a letter from himself, wherein he informed me, that a Captain of a ship from Glasgow, then lately arrived, brought an account of Mr. M'Laurin's death, that he died very suddenly, with an apoplexy, a little before he left Glasgow. Since I received that letter, I sent to Mr. Prince, desiring to know more of the certainty of the account. This is an affecting piece of news. It is an instance of death, which I have much cause to lament. He has long shown himself to be a very worthy, kind and obliging, friend and correspondent of mine. And doubtless, the Church of Scotland has much cause to lament his death. There is reason to think, that he was one of them that stood in the gap, to make up the hedge, in these evil times. He was a wise, steady and most faithful, friend of Gospel truth, and vital piety, in these days of great corruption. I wish that I may take warning by it, as well as by my own late sickness, to prepare for my own departure hence.

I have nothing very comfortable to write, respecting my own success in this place. The business of the Indian mission, since I have been here, has been attended with strange embarrassments, such as I never could have expected, or so much as once dreamed of: of such a nature, and coming from such a quarter.

that I take no delight in being very particular and explicit upon it. But, beside what I especially refer to, some things have lately happened, that have occasioned great disturbance among the Indians, and have tended to alienate them from the English. As particularly, the killing of one of them in the woods, by a couple of travellers white men, who met him, and contended with him. And though the men were apprehended and imprisoned; yet, on their trial they escaped the sentence of death: one of them only receiving a lighter punishment, as guilty of manslaughter: by which these Indians, and also the Indians of some other tribes, were greatly displeased, and disaffected towards the English. Since the last fall, some Indians from Canada, doubtless instigated by the French, broke in upon us, on the Sabbath, between meetings, and fell upon an English family, and killed three of them; and about an hour after, killed another man, coming into the town from some distant houses; which occasioned a great alarm in the town, and in the country. Multitudes came from various parts, for our defence, that night, and the next day; and many of these conducted very foolishly towards our Indians, on this occasion, suspecting them to be guilty of doing the mischief, charging them with it, and threatening to kill them, and the like. After this, a reward being offered by some private gentlemen, to some that came this way as soldiers, if they would bring them the scalp of a Canada Indian; two men were so extremely foolish and wicked, that they, in the night, dug up one of our Indians, that had then lately died, out of his grave, to take off his scalp; that, by pretending that to be a scalp of a Canada Indian, whom they had met and killed in the woods, they might get the promised reward. When this was discovered, the men were punished. But this did not hinder, but that such an act greatly increased the jealousy and disaffection of the Indians, towards the English. Added to these things, we have many white people, that will, at all times, without any restraint, give them ardent spirits, which is a constant temptation to their most predominant lust.

Though I have but little success, and many discouragements, here at Stockbridge, yet Mr. Hawley, now a missionary among the Six Nations, who went from New-England to Onohquauga, a place more than 200 miles distant from hence, has, of late, had much encouragement. Religion seems to be a growing, spreading thing, among the savages in that part of America, by his means. And there is a hopeful prospect, of way being made for another missionary in those parts, which may have happy consequences, unless the Six Nations should go over to the French; which there is the greatest reason to expect, unless the English should exert themselves, vigorously and successfully, against the French, in America, this year. They seem to be waiting, to see whether this will be so or no, in order to determine, whether they will entirely desert the English, and cleave to the French. And if the Six Nations should forsake the English, it may be expected, that the Stockbridge Indians, and almost all the nations of Indians in North America, will follow them. It seems to be the most critical season, with the British dominions in America, that ever was seen, since the first settlement of these colonies; and all, probably, will depend on the warlike transactions of the present year. What will be done, I cannot tell. We are all in commotion, from one end of British America, to the other; and various expeditions are projected, and preparing for; one to Ohio, another to the French Forts in Nova Scotia, another to Crown Point. But these affairs are not free from embarrassments: great difficulties arise, in our present most important affairs, through the dispirited state of the several governments. It is hard for them to agree upon means and measures. And we have no reason to think, that the French are behind us, in their activity and preparations. A dark cloud seems to hang over us: we need the prayers of all our friends, and all friends to the Protestant interest. Stockbridge is a place much exposed; and what will become of us, in the struggles that are coming on, God only knows. I have heard that Messrs. Tennent [3] and Davies [4] are arrived in America, having had good success, in the errand they went upon. Mr. Bellamy is not likely to go to New-York, principally by reason of the opposition of some of the congregation, and also of some of the neighbouring ministers. I have heard, they have lately unanimously agreed to apply themselves to Mr. M'Gregor, of New-Londonderry, alias Nutfield, in New-England, to be their minister; who is a gentleman, that, I think, if they can obtain him, will be likely to suit them, and competent to fill the place. And I have heard, that there has been some difference in his own congregation, that has lately made his situation there uneasy. If so, he will be more likely to consent to the motion from New-York.

My wife joins with me, in respectful and affectionate salutations, to you and Mrs. Erskine.

I am, dear Sir, your affectionate and obliged brother,

JONATHAN EDWARDS.

P. S. In a journey I went to Northampton, the last April, I carried the foregoing letter, with others for Scotland, so far, seeking an opportunity to send them from thence to Boston; and there I met another letter from Mr. Prince, with a joyful contradiction of his former account of Mr. M'Laurin's death; which occasioned my bringing my pacquet home again. Nevertheless, after I had broken open, and perused this letter, I thought best to send it along, enclosed in a wrapper to Mr. M'Laurin; who, I hope, is yet living, and will convey it to you.   J. E.

Stockbridge, June 2, 1755.

[TO THE REV. MR. AARON BURR,
PRINCETON, NEW JERSEY]

[February 12, 1756
Stockbridge]

Rev. & dear Sir,

I received your Letter of Feb. 10. the day before yesterday: for which I thank you. We rejoyce in the smiles of Heaven on you & your Family, & particularly on the late addition[1] to your Family. & the comfortable circumstances of both mother and child. For these Favours we would bless God. I had before heard of the Birth of your son two ways, one by a Letter from Dr. Burr before your return from Philadelphia, another by Doctor Reynold, whom I saw at Windsor with Mr. Henry Dwight (the Brigadier's son) in their Return from their long

Journey for Mr. Dwight's Health. They came thro' Newark a few days after your wife's Delivery. This Mr. Dwight is since dead. He died a Fortnight ago last Saturday morning, at Springfield, the same week that I met him at Windsor, at Mr. Perry's, on Monday. I was then at Windsor on a visit to my Father and was gone two Sabbaths: one of which I spent at Windsor, the other at West Springfield. I found my Father more broken than ever I saw him, but yet he knew me, and was capable of some degree of conversation, & was able to walk a little my mother infirm, but holds the Powers of the mind unbroken. Sister Hopkins[2] was very sorrowful, & in a low state of Health. She hoped for a letter from you in her affliction Her son at Hadley was married about a month ago to Mrs. Williams, the former minister's widdow. They have as yet no man on Probation at Springfield. We in this Place have of late been free from alarms, thro' supposed appearances of Canada Indians, as I think have the People on all our Frontiers in N. England. Brig. D[wigh]t & his wife have talked much about moving away, & seemed determined upon it, the winter past: but he has been long absent at Boston; possibly soliciting for a post in Gov. Sherley's army: If he obtains one, He will probably leave his family here.

We are all thro' mercy in a tolerable state of Health. I saw Daughter Dwight[3] at Springfield She gave an account that her Family were well. I don't know but Mr. Dwight, your Brother, may go into the war this year, tho' I have nothing to certify of it.

I desire you would send word when you would have Timmy[4] come down. If the vacancy is like to be early this year, perhaps it will be needless for him to come till that is past.—Please to convey the Inclosed to Gov. Belcher[5]—Give our Love to your wife, & to little Sally[6]—& remember us in your Prayers.

I am, Dear sir,
Your affectionate Friend & Father,
Jonath. Edwards.

[TO THE REV. MR. JOSEPH BELLAMY,
BETHLEHEM, CONNECTICUT]

Stockbridge
[June, 1756]

Rev. & dear Sir.

I should be glad that you would use thorough Endeavours
with the Boys to teach 'em arithmetick; let there be a thorough
trial with them whether they can learn. If they can't I shall
think it is hardly worth the while to send 'em abroad under the
Notion of giving them an extraordinary Education. I would
also propose the following things viz that pains be taken with
'em to teach 'em the English Tongue to learn 'em the meaning
of English words & what the name of every thing is in English;
and as far as may be, teach 'em the meaning of the English that
they read, & make 'em turn it into Indian. and that they be
taught to pray, that you write out for them various forms of
Prayer, and make 'em understand them, & turn them after into
Indian. and to teach 'em the assemblies Catechism, & endeavour
as far as may be to make 'em to understand it. To ask 'em Questions of the scripture History, not only the lessons they read,
but of the main Things in the general History of the Bible in
their order. I wish you would send to york to Mr. Smith, or
some body that understands & get some plain maps of the Land
of Canaan, & places adjacent, & if you don't chuse to have 'em
for your own for the use of your Children, I will be at the Cost
of 'em for the use of Mr. Hollis's school, & shew them where the
places are they read of in the Bible, or that you tell 'em of from
the scripture History. And also teach 'em a little of the Chronology of the scripture, How long the Flood was after the creation, How long the Calling of Abraham was after the Flood &c
—Mr. Hollis expects that I should give Him an account very
particularly of the progress of his Boys, and as I have given him
an account of my putting These Boys—under your care as giving them great advantage for Learning, so I am concerned—
that I may be able to give Him a good account, that shall be

encouraging to Him I find there are some good Folks here, that can enquire how much the Boys have learned at your House in arithmetick &c—and can make observations & Reflections on the Profit the[y] obtain by going to you, & can put the Question whether there these [*sic*] be anything to answer extraordinary Expence and Trouble, and ask whether they might not have profited as much here.—But you must give no Hints that I have told you of it.

'Tis with a vast deal of difficulty that I have at last got the Boys away, after manifold objecting hiding & skulking, to avoid going I have sent one of my Books to the Library at N'-Haven: I would pray you to take care to convey it.—My Love & Service to Mrs. Bellamy I am sir,

your cordial Friend & Brother

J. Edwards.

P. S. I suppose Isaac will bring down two Coats, & that there will be no need to get him a new one this winter; & therefore I would not have a new one made for him, unless you see it absolutely necessary; as I suppo[s]e it will not be.

Mr. Bellamy

To the Rev.
Mr. Joseph Bellamy
at Bethlehem

[TO THE TRUSTEES OF THE COLLEGE OF NEW JERSEY AT PRINCETON]

Stockbridge, Oct. 19, 1757.

REV. AND HON. GENTLEMEN,

I was not a little surprised, on receiving the unexpected notice, of your having made choice of me, to succeed the late President Burr, as the Head of Nassau Hall.—I am much in doubt, whether I am called to undertake the business, which you have done me the unmerited honour to choose me for.—If some regard may be had to my outward comfort, I might mention the many inconveniences, and great detriment, which may be sustained, by my removing, with my numerous family, so far from all the estate I have in the world, (without any prospect of disposing of it, under present circumstances, but with great loss,) now when we have scarcely got over the trouble and damage, sustained by our removal from Northampton, and have but just begun to have our affairs in a comfortable situation, for a subsistence in this place; and the expense I must immediately be at, to put myself into circumstances, tolerably comporting with the needful support of the honours of the office I am invited to; which will not well consist with my ability.

But this is not my main objection. The chief difficulties in my mind, in the way of accepting this important and arduous office, are these two: First, my own defects, unfitting me for such an undertaking, many of which are generally known; beside others, of which my own heart is conscious.—I have a constitution, in many respects peculiarly unhappy, attended with flaccid solids, vapid, sizy and scarce fluids, and a low tide of spirits; often occasioning a kind of childish weakness and contemptibleness of speech, presence, and demeanor, with a disagreeable dulness and stiffness, much unfitting me for conversation, but more especially for the government of a college.—This makes me shrink at the thoughts of taking upon me, in the decline of life, such a new and great business, attended with such a multiplicity of cares, and requiring such a degree of activity, alertness, and spirit of government; especially as succeeding one so remarkably well qualified in these respects, giving occasion to every one to remark the wide difference. I am also deficient in some parts of learning, particularly in Algebra, and the higher parts of Mathematics, and in the Greek Classics; my Greek learning having been chiefly in the New Testament.—The other thing is this; that my engaging in this business will not well consist with those views, and that course of employ in my study, which have long engaged and swallowed up my mind, and been the chief entertainment and delight of my life.

And here, honoured Sirs, (emboldened, by the testimony I have now received of your unmerited esteem, to rely on your candour,) I will with freedom open myself to you.

My method of study, from my first beginning the work of the ministry, has been very much by writing; applying myself, in this way, to improve every important hint; pursuing the clue to my utmost, when any thing in reading, meditation, or conversation, has been suggested to my mind, that seemed to promise light, in any weighty point; thus penning what appeared to me my best thoughts, on innumerable subjects, for my own benefit.—The longer I prosecuted my studies, in this method, the more habitual it became, and the more pleasant and profitable I found it.—The farther I travelled in this way, the more and wider the field opened, which has occasioned my laying out many things in my mind, to do in this manner, if God should spare my life, which my heart hath been much upon; particularly many things against most of the prevailing errors of the present day, which I cannot with any patience see maintained, (to the utter subverting of the gospel of Christ,) with so high a hand, and so long continued a triumph, with so little control, when it appears so evident to me, that there is truly no foundation for any of this glorying and insult. I have already published something on one of the main points in dispute between the Arminians and Calvinists: and have it in view, God willing, (as I have already signified to the public,) in like manner to consider all the other controverted points, and have done much towards a preparation for it.—But beside these, I have had on my mind and heart, (which I long ago began, not with any view to publication,) a great work, which I call a *History of the Work of Redemption*, a body of divinity in an entire new method, being thrown into the form of a history; considering the affair of Christian Theology, as the whole of it, in each part, stands in reference to the great work of redemption by Jesus Christ; which I suppose to be, of all others, the grand design of God, and the *summum* and *ultimum* of all the divine operations and decrees; particularly considering all parts of the grand scheme, in their historical order.—The order of their existence, or their being brought forth to view, in the course of divine dispensations, or the wonderful series of successive acts and events; beginning from eternity, and descending from thence to the great work and successive dispensations of the infinitely wise God, in time, considering the chief events coming to pass in the church of God, and revolutions in the world of mankind, affecting the state of the church and the affair of redemption, which we have an account of in history or prophecy; till at last, we come to the general resurrection, last judgment, and consummation of all things; when it shall be said, *It is done. I am Alpha and Omega, the Beginning and the End.*—Concluding my work, with the consideration of that perfect state of things, which shall be finally settled, to last for eternity.—This history will be carried on with regard to all three worlds, heaven, earth and hell; considering the connected, successive events and alterations in each, so far as the scriptures give any light; introducing all parts of divinity in that order which is most scriptural and most natural; a method which appears to me the most beautiful and entertaining, wherein every divine doctrine will appear to the greatest advantage, in the brightest light, in the most striking manner, shewing the admirable contexture and harmony of the whole.

I have also, for my own profit and entertainment, done much towards another great work, which I call the *Harmony of the Old and New Testament*, in three parts. The first, considering the Prophecies of the Messiah, his redemption and kingdom; the evidences of their references to the Messiah, etc. comparing them all one with another, demonstrating their agreement, true scope, and sense; also considering all the various particulars wherein those prophecies have their exact fulfilment; showing the universal, precise, and admirable correspondence between predictions and events. The second part, considering the Types of the Old Testament, shewing the evidence of their being intended as representations of the great things of the gospel of Christ; and the agreement of the type with the antitype. The third and great part, considering the Harmony of the Old and New Testament, as to doctrine and precept. In the course of this work, I find there will be occasion for an explanation of a very great part of the holy Scriptures; which may, in such a view, be explained in a method, which to me seems the most entertaining and profitable, best tending to lead the mind to a view of the true spirit, design, life and soul of the scriptures, as well as their proper use and improvement.—I have also many other things in hand, in some of which I have made great progress, which I will not trouble you with an account of. Some of these things, if divine providence favour, I should be willing to attempt a publication of. So far as I myself am able to judge of what talents I have, for benefitting my fellow creatures by word, I think I can write better than I can speak.

My heart is so much in these studies, that I cannot find it in my heart to be willing to put myself into an incapacity to pursue them any more in the future part of my life, to such a degree as I must, if I undertake to go through the same course of employ, in the office of president, that Mr. Burr did, instructing in all the languages, and taking the whole care of the instruction of one of the classes, in all parts of learning, besides his other labours. If I should see light to determine me to accept the place offered me, I should be willing to take upon me the work of a president, so far as it consists in the general inspection of the whole society; and to be subservient to the school, as to their order and methods of study and instruction, assisting, myself, in the immediate instruction in the arts and sciences, (as discretion should direct, and occasion serve, and the state of things require,) especially of the senior class; and added to all, should be willing to do the whole work of a professor of divinity, in public and private lectures, proposing questions to be answered, and some to be discussed in writing and free conversation, in meetings of graduates, and others, appointed in proper seasons, for these ends. It would be now out of my way, to spend time, in a constant teaching of the languages; unless it be the Hebrew tongue; which I should be willing to improve myself in, by instructing others.

On the whole, I am much at a loss, with respect to the way of duty, in this important affair: I am in doubt, whether, if I should engage in it, I should not do what both you and I would be sorry for afterwards. Nevertheless, I think the greatness of the affair, and the regard due to so worthy and venerable a body, as that of the trustees of Nassau Hall, requires my taking the matter into serious consideration. And unless you should appear to be discouraged, by the things which I have now represented, as to any farther expectation from me, I shall proceed to ask advice, of such as I esteem most wise, friendly and faithful: if, after the mind of the Commissioners in Boston is known, it appears that they consent to leave me at liberty, with respect to the business they have employed me in here.

[TO MRS. ESTHER BURR, PRINCETON, NEW JERSEY]

Stockbridge Novem. 20. 1757

DEAR DAUGHTER,

I thank you for your most comfortable Letter; but more especially would I thank God that has granted you such things to write. How good & kind is your heavenly Father! how do the Bowels of his tender Love and compassion appear. While he is correcting you by so great a shake of his Head! Indeed, he is a faithful God; he will remember his covenant forever; and never will fail them that trust in him. But don't be surprised, or think some strange thing has happened to you, if after this Light, clouds of Darkness should return. Perpetual sunshine is not usual in this world, even to Gods true saints. But I hope, if God should hide his Face in some respect, even this will be in Faithfulness to you, to purify you, & fit you for yet further & better Light.

As to removing to Princeton, to take on me the office of President I have agreed with the Church here to refer it to a council of ministers, to sit here Decem. 21, to determine whether It be my Duty.—Mr. Tennent can inform you more of the matter. I with this, inclose a Letter to him which I desire may be delivered to him as soon as possible. I have wrote more particularly about the Council in my Letter to the Trustees. directed to Mr Stockton; which Mr. Tennent will see.—I know I can't live at Princeton, as a President must, on the salary they offer:—Yet I have left that matter to their Generosity—I shall have no money wherewith to furnish the House. I hope Mr. Tennent will exert himself to get a full Trustees meeting, to settle college affairs. I shall not be willing to come thither 'till that is well done. If the

Trustees don't send me an account of their doings immediately by the Post to Claverack I wish you would do it & direct your Letter to be left with Capt. Jeremiah Hoghoboom. I should be glad on some account, to have the letter before the Council. What the Council will do, I cannot tell. I shall endeavour as fairly & justly as possible to lay the matter before 'em with every material circumstance. Dea[con] W[oodbrid]ge is a coming man, & an eloquent speaker; he will strive to his utmost to influence the Council by his Representations, & perhaps by influencing the Indians to make such Representations before the Council as will tend to perswade them that its best for me to stay. And their Judgment must determine the matter. Not only has Mr. W[oodbrid]ge & others a Friendship for me, & liking to my ministry, but it is greatly against their temporal Interest for me to leave them.

As to Lucy's[1] coming Home, her mother will greatly need her, especially if we remove in the spring. But yet, whether your circumstances dont much more loudly call for her continuance there, must be left with you & her. She must judge whether she can come consistently with her Health & comfort at such a season of the year. If she comes, let her buy me a staff, & after advice, & get a good one, or none. Mr. Effelsteen has promised her a good Horse and side saddle, & his son to wait on her to St[ockbrid]ge. And I presume Mr Fonda can let her have a Horse & side saddle to Mr Effelsteen's.

If you think of selling Harry[2] your mother desires you not to sell him, without letting her know it.

Timmy[3] is considerably better, tho' yet very weak. We all unite in Love to you Lucy & your children. Your Mother is very willing to leave Lucy's coming away wholly to you & her.

I am / Your most tender & affectionate Father

JONATHAN EDWARDS.

NOTES

"OF INSECTS"

Of insects, the widely known account of the Balloon, or Flying, Spider, is a remarkable monograph. Edwards wrote it in the summer of 1715, when he was but eleven years old. At least that was the opinion of Professor E. C. Smyth when he edited the MS in the *Andover Review* for January, 1890, and later examination confirms Smyth's view. This three thousand word essay was prepared by Edwards evidently at the behest of his father to be sent to an English correspondent of his father's. No one who has concerned himself with Edwards's writings has failed to marvel at this precocious exhibition of detailed and accurate observation, with its startling mixture of childlike naïveté and mature analysis. Professor H. C. McCook believed himself to be the first who had made certain of the observations, until he discovered that Edwards had anticipated him by one hundred and sixty years (H. C. McCook, *American Spiders and their Spinning-Work*, Philadelphia, 1889–1893, I, 68). For further discussions of Edwards's interest in science, see H. C. McCook, "Jonathan Edwards as a Naturalist," *Presbyterian and Reformed Review*, I, 395 (1890); C. H. Faust, "Jonathan Edwards as a Scientist," *American Literature*, I, 393–404 (1930).

The text is from the *Andover Review*, XIII, 5–13 (1890), and is the earlier of two accounts which Edwards wrote. The latter account, a reworking of this, was the letter written to his father's correspondent a few months later.

THE SOUL, OF THE RAINBOW, OF BEING, COLOURS

Among the very earliest extant writings of Edwards is this group, first printed by Dwight in the appendix to *The Life of President Edwards* (1829), but properly edited only by Professor E. C. Smyth, "Some Early Writings of Jonathan Edwards, A.D. 1714–1726," *Proceedings of the American Antiquarian Society* (1895), N. S. X, 237–247, from which this text is transcribed.

Of the Rainbow looks as if it had been written not much later than *Of insects*, and is generally thought to belong to the same very early period. The remaining two supposedly were undertaken while he was in college —thoughts suggested by his studies in natural science. These essays give powerful evidence of Edwards's capacity for thinking directly in terms of whatever subject he undertook to study.

NOTES ON THE MIND

The selections on "Excellency" and "Existence," chosen from Edwards, *Works* (ed. Dwight, 1829), I, 668–670; 693–696; 699–700, were undertaken by Edwards during his college years (1716–1720). The *Notes* were written on nine sheets of foolscap, transcripts of which are deposited in Andover Theological Seminary, Cambridge, Mass., and are arranged under such headings as Space, Substance, Matter, Thought, Motion, Union, Seeing, Perception, Memory, Reason, Power, Judgment, Ideas, Love, Appetite, Truth, and Certainty. For a discussion of Edwards's sources and the use to which he put them, see Introduction, pp. xxv ff.

RESOLUTIONS

Of the seventy *Resolutions*, the first thirty-four were written before December 18, 1722 (see Dwight, *Life*, p. 76), and the last, dated August 17, 1723, was therefore completed before Edwards's twenty-first year. They must have been written during the very last of his study for the ministry in New Haven, the eight months that he was preaching in New York, and the summer he spent in East Windsor before returning to Yale as a tutor. The MS of the *Resolutions* is not extant, but according to Dwight (*Life*, p. 67, note), "the first twenty-one were written at once, with the same pen; as were the next ten, at a subsequent sitting. The rest were written occasionally . . . all on two detached pieces of paper."

Resolution 8. Vid. July 30. This refers to Edwards's *Diary* entry, July 30, 1723 (Dwight, *Life*, p. 91): "Have concluded to endeavour to work myself into duties by searching and tracing back all the real reasons why I do them not, and narrowly searching out all the subtle subterfuges of my thoughts. . . . "

Resolution 65. Dr. Manton's Sermon. Thomas Manton, *Sermons* (1678). The text is from Edwards, *Works* (ed. Dwight, 1829), I, 68–73.

DIARY

Shortly after Edwards began his *Resolutions*, he commenced a *Diary;* it extends from December 18, 1722, to June 11, 1735. The entries from the beginning through 1724—while he was a tutor at Yale—are made with some regularity; during the next eleven years they are spasmodic and brief. The MS is lost, and the text survives only in Dwight, *Life*, pp. 76–94, 99–106, from which this text is taken.

On the whole it is a colorless document, largely a supplement to his *Resolutions*, introspective and self-condemnatory. He does not record his readings, interest in affairs or people, or his doings from day to day. Such things, no doubt, seemed to him of small moment. The *Diary* was a check and a prod whereby he could register his achievements in carrying out his resolutions. Two things appear, however: a will, goading him to constant religious meditation, and a sense of shame if any moment of the day were frittered—even by the interruption of meals. But compared with other colonial diaries—those of Samuel Sewall, John Winthrop, John Endicott, Cotton Mather, Nathaniel Ames, for instance—it is insignificant as a document of the times. For a discussion of colonial diaries, see Evan Evans, *New England Diaries, 1700–1730*, MS of Ph.D. thesis in Harvard College Library.

Thursday forenoon, Oct. 4, 1723. For Resolution 57 see p. 43, Selections preceding. The *Diary* entry of June 9, 1723, reads: "When I fear misfortunes, to examine whether I have done my duty; and at the same time, to resolve to do it, and let it go, and be concerned about nothing, but my duty and my sin." (Dwight, *Life*, p. 87.)

Thursday, Oct. 18. Mr. B. Not identified.

Friday night, Nov. 1. Characters. The reference is probably to shorthand characters. For a discussion of the use of shorthand by seventeenth century ministers for speed and concealment, see C. F. Richardson, *English Preachers and Preaching, 1640–1670* (New York, 1928), pp. 76, 77. See also W. F. Mitchell, *English Pulpit Oratory from Andrewes to Tillotson* (London, 1932). For an account of and key to Edwards's shorthand, with ample evidence that Edwards did not employ it for concealment, see W. P. Upham, *Massachusetts Historical Society Proceedings* (second series), XV, 514 ff.; and *idem*, *Massachusetts Historical Society Collections*, VI, 481.

Thursday night, Dec. 12.—Vid. Aug. 28. See Dwight, *Life*, p. 94, where he resolves to spend more time reading Scripture types and Resolutions, and "in studying the languages."

Friday, Jan. 10. Dwight, who first published the *Diary*, did not know the key to Edwards's shorthand, and the MS is now lost.

SARAH PIERREPONT

This apostrophe, as widely known as any of Edwards's writings by its frequent quotation, was written, according to Dwight (*Life*, pp. 114–115 —from which this text was taken), in 1723, upon a blank leaf in a book. No record of the holograph is preserved, though it was known to J. A. Stoughton. See his *Windsor Farmes* (Hartford, Conn., 1883), p. 82.

Sarah Pierrepont was but thirteen and Edwards, twenty, when he wrote this tribute. Four years later they were married.

PERSONAL NARRATIVE

The *Personal Narrative* or *Narrative of His Conversion* is one of the most charming of all Edwards's writings. His conversion took place when he was but twenty years old, though he did not record it until twenty years later. (See note 5 below).

The text is from Edwards, *Works* (ed. Austin, 1808), I, 31–48.

For a general discussion of Edwards's early religious awakening, see Introduction, *passim*.

1. Edwards was born in East Windsor, Connecticut, the parish on the bank of the Connecticut River of which his father was minister; and lived there until, just before his thirteenth birthday, he entered Yale College in 1715.

2. The exact year to which Edwards refers cannot be determined, for revivals throughout the valley repeated themselves with almost tiresome regularity.

3. Edwards was pastor from August, 1722, till May, 1723, of a newly formed Presbyterian church in New York.

4. See Resolution for this date, p. 42, Selections preceding.

5. *Northampton*. The *Personal Narrative* must have been written some time after January, 1739, for Edwards mentions that month and year in the concluding paragraph of this essay as a time during which his conversion seemed to be fully established.

Students should compare this conversion and the attitude of Edwards toward it with passages from Emerson's *Nature* (1836), with Wordsworth's *Tintern Abbey*, and with Thoreau's *Journals*.

NARRATIVE OF SURPRISING CONVERSIONS

The Reverend Dr. Benjamin Colman (1673–1747) graduated from Harvard in 1692, and preached in England till 1699, in which year he returned to Boston where he served as pastor of the Brattle Street Church till his death. He refused the presidency of Harvard in 1724, was given a Doctor of Divinity degree by the University of Glasgow in 1731, and throughout his life published sermons and poems.

Colman, hearing of the religious revivals in western Massachusetts, wrote Edwards to ask for an account from him. To Colman's request, Edwards replied by this letter dated May 30, 1735. So impressed was Colman with the phenomenon that he published Edwards's letter in 1736. So far as has been reported, this eighteen-page printed pamphlet is unique, deposited in the Boston Public Library. The text used here is taken from Edwards's MS in the Andover Theological Library—a copy evidently made by Edwards for his own use at the time he wrote Colman.

The published letter was forwarded to certain London divines, and became so popular in England that Edwards was induced to rewrite his letter in expanded form, signed under date of November 6, 1736. The revision, similar in content, but with additional examples of conversions, was published in London late in 1737 under the title *A Faithful Narrative of the Surprising Work of God . . .* It went through three editions and twenty printings between 1737 and 1739, and is, of course, the text most widely known. It is from this text (Edwards, *Works*, ed. Austin, 1808, III, 70–77) that the continuation, telling of Phebe Bartlet's conversion, has been chosen. The earlier account does not incorporate the extraordinary story. For a discussion of Edwards and the Great Awakening, see Introduction, pp. xvi–xxiv.

GOD GLORIFIED

On July 8, 1731, when he was but twenty-seven, Edwards was invited to preach in Boston "on the Publick Lecture." He chose a text from Judges

7:2, and preached a sermon which was shortly thereafter published "at the desire of several Ministers and others in Boston, who heard it" (Preface). This was called *God Glorified in the Work of Redemption, by the Greatness of Man's Dependence upon Him, in the Whole of It*, and was Edwards's first published work. As the occasion was representative, so also was the character of the sermon, and it is said to have made a profound impression—probably because the subject was little known in America. It began Edwards's fame as a theologian.

The text is from Edwards, *Works* (ed. Dwight, 1829), VII, 151–158. For a discussion of its theological importance, see A. V. G. Allen, *Jonathan Edwards* (1889), pp. 57 ff.

SUPERNATURAL LIGHT

In the same category of doctrinal sermons with *God Glorified* is *A Divine and Supernatural Light, Immediately Imparted to the Soul by the Spirit of God, Shown to be both a Scriptural and Rational Doctrine*. It was preached at Northampton, and published at the desire of some of the hearers in 1734.

The text is from Edwards, *Works* (1858), IV, 439–444. For a discussion of its importance as an example of early transcendental thought, see Introduction, pp. cxi, *et passim*.

JUSTICE OF GOD and EXCELLENCY OF CHRIST

While Edwards was laboring to prepare sermons for the daily or occasional needs of his people, he was also writing sermons which were closely allied to some single text or event, and so formed a series. Such were the [*Five*] *Discourses on Various Important Subjects, nearly concerning the Great Affair of the Soul's Eternal Salvation* delivered in 1734, and published on the earnest desire of those to whom they were preached in 1738. Two of the five are chosen for this text: *The Justice of God in the Damnation of Sinners* and *The Excellency of Christ*—the first from Edwards, *Works* (1858), IV, 227–232; the second, *ibid.*, 180–197, with omissions indicated.

For a discussion of the development of Edwards's thought relative to these sermons, see Introduction, pp. ci ff.

THE CHRISTIAN PILGRIM

Selections from this sermon and that following are included in the text as examples of Edwards's pastoral style. For comment upon the types of Edwards's sermons, see Introduction, pp. cx–cxi.

The text is from Edwards, *Works* (ed. Dwight, 1829), VII, 139–144.

THE PEACE WHICH CHRIST GIVES HIS TRUE FOLLOWERS

See note above. The text is from Edwards, *Works* (1858), IV, 434–437.

FUTURE PUNISHMENT

This imprecatory sermon, in which Edwards first compares man to a spider held over the bottomless pit, was preached in April, 1741, three months before the delivery of the more famous Enfield sermon.

The text is from Edwards, *Works* (1858), IV, 259–265.

SINNERS IN THE HANDS OF AN ANGRY GOD

Sermons were as much in request during the eighteenth century as novels are today, and no gentleman's library but held in tooled calf many dozen volumes of sermons written by men whose names today have disappeared into a literary limbo. Yet one sermon of Edwards has survived: *Sinners in the Hands of an Angry God.* It is a curious anomaly that the reputation of one of the quietest, least spectacular preachers should derive chiefly from his delivery of this imprecatory sermon, preached at Enfield, Connecticut, on that day in 1741. Published in Boston during the same year as a twenty-five page pamphlet, it went through at least four editions and six reprintings before the nineteenth century. Since then it has been reprinted in whole or in part countless times. Undoubtedly Edwards gives more vividness and rapid variety to the wrath of God here than he does elsewhere, and for that reason the sermon is presented entire in the text. In fact, this sermon exhibits the only extended metaphor to be found in any of his writings. (See p. 163 above, the sentence beginning, "The bow of God's wrath . . .") There is dramatic effect of suspense and climax and figure which is suggestive of moments in the climax of Webster's *Duchess of Malfi.* No wonder that the audience became hysterical. And yet Edwards preached in an exemplary manner. It was Sunday, July 8, 1741. He stood calmly in the pulpit with his small sermon-book held in his left hand, turning the pages with his right, and he read in a level, clearly modulated voice; yet, said one listener, the Reverend Eleazar Wheelock, future founder of Dartmouth College: "There was such a breathing of distress, and weeping, that the preacher was obliged to speak to the people and desire silence, that he might be heard." (Benjamin Trumbull, *A Complete History of Connecticut* [1797, 1818], II, 145.) For a discussion of Edwards's attitude toward the preaching of hell-fire, see Introduction above, p. xxii.

The text is from Edwards, *Works* (ed. Dwight, 1829), VII, 163–177.

FUNERAL SERMON

Among the sermons preached for special occasions is that delivered by Edwards at the funeral of his young friend David Brainerd: *True Saints, when Absent from the Body, are Present with the Lord.* The sermon is long, and the first part—the longest—is devoted to a thorough exposition of the future state of the soul of a true saint; the latter part is given over to a summary of the "character and behavior" of Brainerd. So completely had Edwards sublimated his dependence upon human love that one would never realize from the sermon that the bond of fellowship between Edwards and Brainerd had been especially strong. The complete restraint of feeling is not compensated by any unusual beauty of diction or phrasing.

The text is from Edwards, *Works* (ed. Dwight, 1829), X, 471–483.

FAREWELL SERMON

The *Farewell Sermon*, preached on July 1, 1750, after his dismissal from the Northampton pastorate, has throughout a quality of pathos not elsewhere found in Edwards's sermons. Its text is poignant: "As also ye have acknowledged us in part, that we are your rejoicing, even as ye also are ours, in the day of the Lord Jesus." (II Cor. 1:14.) In no other published sermon is the personal reference so noticeable. Yet it is free from recrimination, for Edwards's spirit was not petty. In all honesty, he tells them, it is their tragedy more than his, for God's vicars cannot be cast aside without retributive justice following.

Read in the light of its time, and with the knowledge that Edwards's conviction of his own rightness—stern, yet truly humble—was as an armor of invincibility, the sermon becomes profoundly moving. He stood for a dogma that the people were rejecting; he stood incorruptible in a moral world where compromise with lax tenets foreboded spiritual death; and he, not the laity, was qualified to judge the tenets of faith. Its spell lies in our knowledge of Edwards's absolute certainty of his ideas which he held to be unquestionable, delivered before an audience that he knew repudiated them.

One cannot fail, after pondering its sad beauty, to compare it with two other notable farewell sermons of the next century: John Henry Newman's, preached on September 25, 1843, in his parish at Littelmore (see J. H. Newman, *Sermons bearing on Subjects of the Day*, London, 1918, pp. 395–409), and Ralph Waldo Emerson's, preached September 9, 1832, in Boston (see R. W. Emerson, *Complete Works*, Boston, 1904, XI, 3–25). The nineteenth-century pastors were leaving their parishes voluntarily, and both were younger men than Edwards: Newman was forty-two, Emerson, twenty-nine. For them there was no bitterness in separation. The poetry of Newman's spirit, and the geniality of Emerson's, together with their rare talent for expression, gives to their sermons a finish lacking in Edwards's. His fervid, more touching, more mystical earnestness gives his an eloquence that cannot be found in theirs.

The text is from Edwards, *Works* (ed. Dwight, 1829), I, 640–651.

SERMON NOTES

In 1865 appeared privately from an Edinburgh press new Edwards material: a few sermons and four miscellanies edited by the indefatigable antiquary, the Reverend Mr. Alexander Grosart. Grosart had come to

America shortly before to gather material for an edition of Edwards's works, and claimed to have "priceless" letters, sermons, and treatises in his possession. His volume, *Selections from the Unpublished Writings of Jonathan Edwards*, was more notable for its rarity than for its choice of remarkable "finds." A controversy ensued between Grosart and the American executors of Edwards's estate, the latter claiming that Grosart had no right to take material from the country, but querying what he had taken. At the turn of this century a search was undertaken in Scotland to discover the missing MSS, but none was turned up. It is now thought probable that Grosart did not really possess documents of great interest.

These sermon notes (Grosart, *Selections*, pp. 189–190) from the leaf of a letter scrap are not significant in any way, but they are included in the text as typical of Edwards's later manner of sermon preparation when he had become thoroughly familiar with his own pulpit ability and was not intending a sermon for publication.

RELIGIOUS AFFECTIONS

This treatise in three parts was first prepared as a series of sermons, written and preached probably in 1742–1743. It was so successful that Edwards developed it into treatise form and published it in Boston in 1746. Immediately it was republished in England and Scotland. Its purpose was to state clearly his stand on communion after the Great Awakening, and to show his change of heart about Stoddardeanism—the belief of his grandfather, Solomon Stoddard, that the fact a man believed himself regenerate was sufficient evidence to accept him into church fellowship. For a detailed discussion of the importance of the treatise as a contribution to philosophical problems of the time, see Introduction, pp. xxv–xxxix, *passim*.

The text is from Edwards, *Works* (1858), III, 1 ff., with omissions indicated.

MEMOIRS OF BRAINERD

In October, 1747, David Brainerd died at Edwards's house in Northampton of consumption after a long and torturing illness, at the age of thirty. Edwards immediately undertook his biography, and two years later appeared *An Account of the Life of the Late Reverend Mr. David Brainerd, minister of the gospel; missionary to the Indians from the honorable society, in Scotland, for the propagation of Christian knowledge; and pastor of a Church of Christian Indians in New Jersey.* Though above three hundred pages long in its first edition and still longer in subsequent ones, it mostly consisted of Brainerd's Journal and Diary, to which Edwards added observations and reflections of his own. It is a curious document. Edwards's interest in Brainerd had begun in 1743 when Brainerd was dismissed from Yale in his junior year for thoughtlessly remarking of one of his teachers: "He has no more grace than this chair." Even though powerful friends interceded in his behalf, Brainerd found that the college could not pardon such blasphemy. Impetuous, enthusiastic, zealous, he became a martyr to the cause of revivals—for which the college had scant sympathy; and his illness and early death gave him the glamorous notoriety that surrounds a martyr. Thus Edwards undertook his biography, impelled by a desire to furnish evidence against the deists, who denied validity to emotional experience; it is therefore only incidentally a biography. (On Edwards's views of deism, see Introduction, *passim*.) The Journal is brooding and introspective, and Edwards's interest in it is scarcely less so. But Edwards had reason to feel deeply moved. His second daughter, Jerusha—"the flower of the family"—was betrothed to Brainerd, and for nineteen weeks before his death had attended him constantly, only to die herself four months later of the same disease at the age of seventeen.

The biographical sketch is, like so many written by puritan ministers (e.g., Increase Mather, *The Life and Death of . . . Richard Mather*, 1670; Cotton Mather, *Parentator*, 1724), a spiritual history concluding with morbid realism upon a deathbed scene. But the work itself, though interesting only as *curiosa*, is historically important as the first biography written in America that achieved wide notice abroad as well as at home. It was soon translated into Dutch and published in Utrecht (1756), and went through four editions and was printed at least fourteen times between 1749 and 1883.

The text is from the conclusion of the *Memoirs* (Reflection VIII), Edwards, *Works* (ed. Dwight, 1829), X, 442–448, and shows Edwards characteristically finding in Brainerd's death, as in his life, the shaping hand of divine providence.

FREEDOM OF THE WILL

The most famous treatise of Edwards, and one of the greatest philosophical essays ever written in this country was *A Careful and Strict Enquiry into the Modern Prevailing Notion, of that Freedom of Will which is supposed to be Essential to Moral Agency, Vertue and Vice, Reward and Punishment, Praise and Blame*, published in Boston in 1754, translated into Dutch in the same year, and reprinted a dozen times here and in England and Scotland during the next hundred years. To Calvinists the work was the firm rock on which they could meet deistic opponents and demolish them. The work must give Edwards a high place in letters if only because it is one of the few great books in English theology: it discussed the neglected subject of the human will. Naturally opinion upon it has been violent, both for and against. President Stiles of Yale records in his diary on June 24, 1779: "Yesterday I put the Senior Class into President Claps Ethics... Afterwards President Edw^{ds} on the Will was recited: this giving Offence was dropped." (Ezra Stiles, *Diary*, ed. Dexter, 1901, II, 349.) Today Dean C. R. Brown probably expresses the prevailing opinion of it when he says in his article on Edwards in the 14th edition of the *Encyclopædia Britannica* that it is a "tedious discussion . . . a solemn bit of special pleading, rather than a disinterested effort to reach the truth." But in the main Edwards's thought was in the tradition of great humanists: to show that man was free even though his actions were necessary or certain; and if free then responsible for his actions, and deserving of the consequences when the choice, even though unintentionally so, was wrong.

For a discussion of the treatise, its sources, and its contributions to the thought of Edwards's time, see Introduction, pp. xxxix–lxxiv.

The text is from Edwards, *Works* (1858), II, 1–189, with omissions indicated.

1. On this letter, see Introduction, p. xlviii. Edwards's footnote references in this letter to the main body of his treatise have been omitted.

ORIGINAL SIN

The last work of Edwards to reach the press before his death was *The Great Christian Doctrine of Original Sin Defended*. The preface is dated Stockbridge, May 26, 1757, and the work was finished early in August before he left for Princeton. It appeared in the following year.

The work is polemical in character—a continuation of the Arminian controversy, and its purpose was to condemn Dr. John Taylor's humanitarian theory that corruption and moral evil are not universally present, that good predominates, and that virtue is latent in natural man and in the ascendant. In a century where deism was the gentleman's religion this treatise was out of the main stream. For a discussion of its intellectual and literary character, see Introduction, pp. lxix–lxxiv.

The text is from Edwards, *Works* (1858), II, 309–491, with omissions indicated.

1. John Taylor, *The Scripture-Doctrine of Original Sin* (1738).

2. George Turnbull, *Principles of Moral Philosophy* (1740), pp. 289, 290.

3. Taylor, *op. cit.* Though Edwards appears to be quoting directly from Taylor, he is actually abstracting thoughts that appear on pages 137, 187–189, and elsewhere.

4. *Ibid.*, pp. 146, 148, 149, 187.

5. *Idem.*

6. Taylor, *op. cit.*, p. 134.

7. *Ibid.*, p. 140.

8. Turnbull, *op. cit.*, p. 7.

9. *Ibid.*, p. 9.

CONCERNING THE END FOR WHICH GOD CREATED THE WORLD and THE NATURE OF TRUE VIRTUE

After Edwards's death some of his writings that had been roughly drafted were shaped enough by editors to whip through the press. In

1765 a volume of one hundred and ninety pages appeared in Boston entitled *Two Dissertations*. I. *Concerning the End for which God Created the World*. II. *The Nature of True Virtue*. They were probably written during the last five years of his life.

The Nature of True Virtue stands isolated among the treatises by its comparative freedom from polemic. Edwards's wrath against Arminianism was nearly spent, and he gives himself over to discussing the essence of moral beauty.

Edwards's attack on Arminianism came to a close with *Concerning the End for which God Created the World*. He sublimates the Deity, and separates him from humanity to a degree he had not before expressed. No treatises of Edwards deserve more lasting praise than these. For a discussion of them, see Introduction, pp. lxxv ff.

The text is from Edwards, *Works* (1858), II, 252-257, 261-266, and 277-285.

COVENANT OF REDEMPTION

In 1880 Professor E. C. Smyth published from the yet unprinted miscellanies of Edwards *Observations concerning the Scripture Œconomy of the Trinity and Covenant of Redemption*—some thirty-five pages in which Edwards deals with the mutual relation of the persons of the Trinity and their relation to the supposed covenant of redemption. One such *Observation* is "Excellency of Christ." It is perhaps the most exquisite idyl from its author's pen. It is impossible to determine at what period of his life or under what circumstances he wrote it. Among the Miscellanies it is numbered 152, and logically, therefore, may have been written when, not far from the time of his marriage and the happiness of undertaking a pastorate of his own, he was looking upon the world with fresh and exciting vigor. For a further discussion of it, see Introduction, p. cv.

The text is from *Observations*, pp. 92-97.

ESSAY ON THE TRINITY

In 1903 Professor G. P. Fisher published in fifty-five pages *An Unpublished Essay of Edwards on the Trinity*, recovered some years before, which Fisher thought must be the famous lost essay that caused the controversy whether Edwards was swinging away from Trinitarianism. (Fisher, *An Unpublished Essay*, Introd., p. xv.) But it proved to be orthodox enough, and of its kind it is considered one of the ablest arguments which the history of doctrine affords—certainly the best on the subject by Edwards. As it was never prepared for the press by its author, and seems to have been written at intervals, its form is unpolished, though always lucid. He attempts to deal with the important mysteries of the Scripture in a manner as intelligent as it is bold, for he believed the human mind capable of grasping numinous concepts if it can be made to understand them, and he had faith in his own ability to prepare heart and mind for the understanding.

The text is from Fisher, *An Unpublished Essay of Edwards on the Trinity* (New York, 1903), pp. 77–117, with omissions indicated.

LETTERS

To the Rev. Mr. Timothy Edwards, March 1st, 1721.

Edwards had graduated from Yale in September, 1720, with first honors as Salutatorian in a class of ten, but he remained in college for two years to prepare for the ministry. In June, 1723, the belated degree of Master of Arts was conferred upon him. The letter touches upon one of the many troubles that beset the young college in its early days.

1. *Mr Grant.* Thomas Grant, one of the trustees of a newly formed Presbyterian church in New York, who invited Edwards, aged eighteen, to come to preach to them. Edwards accepted, and remained in New York from August, 1722, until May, 1723.

2. *Mr Cutler.* Rector Timothy Cutler (1684–1765); Harvard, 1701; minister in Stratford, Connecticut, 1709–1719; President of Yale, 1719–1722. To the great shock of the college, Cutler renounced Congregationalism, gave up his position at the head of the college, and went to England where he took orders in the Established Church. He later returned to New England.

3. *Mr Andrew.* The Reverend Mr. Samuel Andrews, pastor in Milford, Connecticut; a founder, trustee, and acting president of Yale from 1707 to 1719—during the years of the schism, when part of the college resided in Milford.

4. *Mr Russel.* The Reverend Mr. Samuel Russell of Branford, Connecticut, a founder and trustee of the college. The earliest library of the college—some forty folio volumes—was housed by him.

5. *Stiles.* Isaac Stiles of Windsor, Connecticut. He was prepared for college by Edwards's father, Timothy Edwards, and was a junior when this letter was written. He was minister at New Haven for thirty-five years. His more noted son, Ezra Stiles, was president of Yale, 1777–1795. The undergraduate office of butler—i.e., collecting board bills, overseeing the kitchen and dormitory rooms—was appointive by vote of the trustees, and something of an honor. Edwards had been so appointed in 1719.

6. *Chambermate.* Elisha Mix of Wethersfield, Connecticut, a cousin of Edwards, and a sophomore in the college. He later became a physician.

7. *Uncle Mix.* The Reverend Mr. Stephen Mix of Wethersfield, Connecticut, father of Elisha, Edwards's roommate. His wife, Mary (Stoddard) Mix, was a sister of Edwards's mother.

8. *lignum vitae.* The wood of a tropical American tree of the genus *Guaiacum*, once considered to have medicinal properties, especially useful in the treatment of rheumatism.

9. *sister Mary.* Mary Edwards, born February 11, 1701, the next in age above Jonathan of the eleven children. Jonathan was the only son.

10. *Mercy*. Perhaps the "help."

The letter is now first printed from the holograph in Andover Theological Library, Cambridge, Massachusetts, by kind permission.

To Mrs. Sarah Edwards, June 22, 1748.

The letter was written on a scrap of paper when Mrs. Edwards was in attendance on Mr. Edwards's uncle, Colonel John Stoddard of Northampton, while he was in Boston. Stoddard died of apoplexy in Boston, June 15, and the letter was probably never sent. On Sunday, June 26, Edwards preached Stoddard's funeral sermon at Northampton: *A Strong Rod Broken and Withered* . . .

Sarah Edwards was a daugher of the Reverend Mr. James Pierrepont of New Haven, trustee of Yale and Professor of Moral Philosophy. Her mother was a granddaughter of the Reverend Mr. Thomas Hooker, first minister in Hartford. She died in Philadelphia, October 25, 1758, aged forty-eight years, seven months after her husband's death. She was the mother of eleven children.

1. *Ensn Dwight*. Ensign Timothy Dwight, junior (later Major); a son of Colonel Timothy Dwight, both of Northampton, where the son, born in 1726, resided as a merchant. He died in Natchez, Mississippi, in 1777. In 1750, he married Mary, Edwards's fourth daughter. Their eldest child, Timothy, became president of Yale, and their youngest daughter was the mother of President Woolsey of Yale. All the Dwights remained firm supporters of Edwards during the trying days of his trouble with the Northampton church.

2. *Betty*. Their daughter Elizabeth, born May 6, 1747; died January 1, 1762.

3. *Mrs Phelps*. A neighbor who evidently took the baby while Mrs. Edwards was away.

4. *two eldest daughters*. Sarah, born August 25, 1728; and Esther, born February 13, 1732. Jerusha, born April 26, 1730, had died February 14, 1748, four months before the letter was written.

5. *Col. Stoddard*. (1682–1748.) Harvard, 1701. A very wealthy and influential citizen in western Massachusetts. He died while attending a session of the General Court, and was buried in Boston. Referred to above in first paragraph of notes on this letter.

6. *Bromfield*. Edwards Bromfield, second generation of a line of distinguished Boston merchants, through whom Edwards often passed letters and books to correspondents abroad.

The text is from a sermon scrap in the Edwards Collection, Yale University, and used by kind permission.

To the Rev. Mr. John Erskine, August 31, 1748.

John Erskine (1721?–1803) was born in Edinburgh. His grandfather was the first Baron Cardross, and his father was a professor of law at the

University of Edinburgh. He entered the ministry and occupied small pulpits near Edinburgh until in 1758 he was called to a large church in Edinburgh where he remained for the rest of his life. He was a close friend of the noted evangelist, George Whitefield, and is described by Scott in *Guy Mannering* in the pulpit at White Friars, the church where Scott's own parents worshipped.

1. *Taylor on original sin.* John Taylor, *The Scripture-Doctrine of Original Sin* (1738).

2. *Key to the Apostolic Writings* and *Paraphrase.* *Paraphrase on the Epistle to the Romans* (1745).

3. *McLaurin.* The Reverend Mr. John McLaurin of Glasgow, a minister in the Church of Scotland. No Edwards-McLaurin correspondence exists, though Edwards frequently refers to him in letters to other correspondents.

4. *Arminian Tenets.* This when finished was *Freedom of the Will*, published in Boston in 1754.

5. *Brainerd's Life.* *An Account of the Life of . . . Brainerd* (Boston, 1749).

6. *Books of Mr. Stoddards.* Twenty-three books by Stoddard were published between 1687 and 1729.

7. *Brainerds death.* *True Saints . . .* (Boston, 1747).

8. *Buel's Instalment.* *The Church's Marriage . . .* (Boston, 1746).

9. *Edwards Bromfield.* See note 6, p. 429 above.

10. *Mr. Prince.* The Reverend Dr. Thomas Prince (1687–1758). Harvard, 1707. He traveled abroad and preached in England for a time. In 1717 he returned to Boston, and remained pastor of the Old South Church until his death. He was a collector of books and MSS on New England, all of which are now in the Boston Public Library.

11. *Concert for Prayer.* *An Humble Attempt to Promote Explicit Agreement . . .* (Boston, 1747).

The letter was published in Dwight, *Life*, pp. 251, 252, but the text is taken from the holograph in the Andover Theological Library, Cambridge, Massachusetts, by kind permission.

To the Rev. Mr. Joseph Bellamy, December 6, 1749.

This letter, with its affecting conclusion, gives a very personal view of events toward the close of the year 1749, which culminated in Edwards's dismissal from Northampton.

Joseph Bellamy (1719–1790; Yale, 1735) went to Northampton to study theology with Edwards in 1738. He was pastor in Bethlehem, Connecticut (1740–1742), and went about extensively preaching revival sermons till 1745. He then returned to Bethlehem where he resided till his death. Many of his sermons were published (1750–1762).

1. *Col. Williams.* The Reverend Elisha Williams, rector of Yale (1726–1739), was known by the title of colonel after the attempted expedition against Canada in 1748.

The letter, deposited in the Edwards Collection at Yale University, is transcribed from the *New England Quarterly*, I, 237–240 (1928).

To the Rev. Mr. Joseph Bellamy, January 15, 1749/50.

The letter, not elsewhere transcribed in print, is important in giving Edwards's views on the question of Free Will at the time he was writing his chief work. It also gives Edwards's account of the state of affairs in Northampton during the period previous to his dismissal.

1. *Mr. Clark.* The Reverend Mr. Peter Clark of Danvers, Massachusetts, had been asked by the council to reply to Edwards's *Qualifications for Communion*, which had appeared in August, 1749, and no answer coming from Clark, the citizens of Northampton, on June 22, 1750, voted Edwards's dismissal.

The text is from the holograph in the Library of Congress, used by kind permission.

To Major Joseph Hawley, November 18, 1754.

On August 11, Hawley had written a letter (now lost) to ask Edwards's frank opinion of his (Hawley's) part in the affair of Edwards's dismissal from the Northampton pastorate five years before. This is Edwards's reply. No letter of Edwards better manifests compelling logic and embracing memory for details. Here the event of his dismissal is dispassionately reviewed after a lapse of time, but the sting of the injustice done him still rankles painfully, though there is not now—as there never had been— any complaint. Hawley received what he asked for straight from the shoulder, even though he must have quailed before the quiet invective of the concluding paragraphs; and it is well to know that in the following January Hawley replied, in a letter preserved with this among the Hawley Papers in the New York Public Library, saying that he received the strictures "kindly and thankfully." In 1760, his conscience still bothering him, he made a further confession by letter to the Reverend Mr. Hall of Sutton, published at that time in a Boston newspaper and incorporated in Dwight's *Life*, pp. 421–427.

Major Joseph Hawley was born in Northampton in 1724, graduated from Yale in 1742, and was, with Edwards and Colonel Stoddard, a distinguished figure in provincial Massachusetts. His mother was a sister of Edwards's mother, hence the weight of his judgment against Edwards was the more telling, even though Hawley was but twenty-six years old at the time of the affair. After graduating from college he studied theology with Edwards, and, though never ordained, preached for several years. He was a chaplain in the provincial army, and was present at the siege of Louisbourg. In 1748 he was studying law in Suffield in the office of General Phineas Lyman, whose daughter he married, and in 1749 took up practice in Northampton. He became a very able political figure, was a member of the Legislature in 1764, was repeatedly elected a member of the Council, but consistently refused to sit in the House of Representatives. Though he lacked polish, he was a most able and influential magistrate; grave, austere, and vigilant for the rights of the colonists. In later life the hereditary affliction of insanity overtook him—his father had been a suicide—and he died March 10, 1788.

This letter was somewhat inaccurately published in *Bibliotheca Sacra*, I, 579–591 (1844), and it is now transcribed from the holograph in the Hawley Papers through the kind permission of the New York Public Library.

To the Rev. Mr. John Erskine, April 15, 1755.

Here Edwards gives much detail about his reading, and discusses the Stockbridge mission, Indian raids, and the difficulties of living in a wilderness.

For a discussion of the many titles enumerated, see T. H. Johnson, "Jonathan Edwards' Background of Reading," *Publications of the Colonial Society of Massachusetts*, XXVIII, 207–209 (1933).

1. For Erskine, see note, p. 429.

2. For McLaurin, see note 3, p. 430.

3. *Tennent*. Gilbert Tennent (1703–1764) came to America in 1718 from Ireland. He entered the ministry, received his M.A. from Yale in 1725, and became pastor of a Presbyterian church in New Brunswick, New Jersey. At Whitefield's request he undertook a preaching tour through New England in 1740–1741. In 1743 he was called to Philadelphia, where he remained. In 1753 he went to England in company with Davies to gather contributions for the College of New Jersey (Princeton). His three brothers, John, William, and Charles, were all eminent New Jersey ministers.

4. *Samuel Davies* (1723–1761) was a Presbyterian minister in Hanover County, Virginia, and a warm admirer of Edwards. He succeeded Edwards as president of Princeton.

The letter is transcribed from Dwight, *Life* (1829), I, 545–548.

To the Rev. Mr. Aaron Burr, February 12, 1756.

Aaron Burr (1716–1757; Yale, 1735) was ordained pastor of a Presbyterian church in Newark, New Jersey. In 1748 he was unanimously elected president of the College of New Jersey (then at Newark), as Dickinson's successor, and married Esther Edwards in June, 1752. He died September 24, 1757.

1. *late addition*. Aaron Burr, who later became the brilliant and erratic vice-president of the United States.

2. *sister Hopkins*. Mrs. Esther Hopkins of Springfield, sister to Edwards, therefore aunt by marriage to Burr. Burr's wife was her namesake. Her husband, pastor of the church in Springfield, had just died.

3. *Daughter Dwight*. Née Mary Edwards, born in 1734—the fourth child. She married Major Timothy Dwight of Northampton.

4. *Timmy*. Timothy Edwards (1738–1813) was the eldest son, and a

junior at Princeton when this letter was written. He was a merchant in Elizabethtown (Elizabeth), New Jersey, and later moved to Stockbridge, Massachusetts, in 1770, where he died. He was a member of the state council (1775–1780), and Judge of the Probate Court (1778–1782). He declined a nomination for Congress in 1779.

5. *Gov. Belcher* (1681–1757). Harvard, 1699. He was Governor of Massachusetts, 1730–1741; Governor of New Jersey, 1747–1757.

6. *little Sally.* Sarah Burr, the elder of the two Burr children.

The text is from a facsimile of the holograph, here used by the kind permission of Princeton University Library. A somewhat inaccurate transcript appeared in the *Independent* for 1895, p. 1185.

To the Rev. Mr. Joseph Bellamy, June, 1756.

The Indian Mission at Stockbridge, in existence since 1735, was benefited by gifts of money and books sent by a clergyman near London, England, the Reverend Mr. Isaac Hollis. Some of the funds were misappropriated by Col. Ephraim Williams, a frontier soldier whose son, Col. Ephraim Williams, founded Williams College. Edwards, as guardian of the mission, had considerable trouble protecting the school's disbursements. Bellamy evidently was one of the school's correspondents, and Edwards's ideas on education, typical of ideas expressed in other letters, were therefore in the nature of a report.

The letter, edited by Professor S. T. Williams, was published in the *New England Quarterly*, I, 240–242 (1928), and is transcribed by kind permission.

To the Princeton Trustees, October 19, 1757.

President Burr had died, aged forty-two years, on September 24, 1757, two days before Commencement. On the 29th of the month the Corporation of the college met and chose Edwards as Burr's successor. During Edwards's Stockbridge years he had been constantly in touch with the leading ministers of the day, and after publication of *Freedom of the Will* was ranked first among the apologists of Calvinism. Gov. Belcher, who had known and admired Edwards for many years, was, until his death in the summer of 1757, president of the corporation of the college, and had hoped to secure Edwards for the college from the beginning. The council that Edwards speaks of calling met in Stockbridge in the following January and decided that he should accept the trustees' offer. He was inducted into office February 16, 1758.

As Edwards lived but a scant five weeks after he went to Princeton, his project for *A History of the Work of Redemption* remains one of the vast unwritten works of literature.

The letter is transcribed from Dwight, *Life* (1829), pp. 568–571.

To Mrs. Esther Burr, November 20, 1757.

This letter of sympathy to his daughter after the death of her husband —one of the last from his pen—was written after the offer of the presidency, but before his acceptance. The council, called for December 21, really did not sit till the following month.

1. *Lucy.* Esther's younger sister, aged 21.
2. *Harry.* Probably the negro slave.
3. *Timmy.* Timothy had just been graduated from Princeton.

This letter is transcribed from a MS copy of the holograph in the Princeton University Library, by kind permission. It is to be found, with minor inaccuracies, in the *Independent* for August 22, 1895, p. 1121.